Teacher Edition

Strategies for Writers

Level H

Authors

Leslie W. Crawford, Ed.D.
Georgia College & State University

Rebecca Bowers Sipe, Ed.D.
Eastern Michigan University

Consulting Authors

Julie Coiro, Ph.D.
University of Connecticut

Ken Stewart
Master Teacher
Bexley Middle School
Bexley, Ohio

Zaner-Bloser

Strategies for Writers

A proven-effective, research-based program that powers the writing process and provides students with the tools for developing lifelong skills and success in all areas of writing. Strategies from the program can be immediately applied throughout all of a student's classwork.

Correlates to Your State Standards

► *Strategies for Writers* is correlated to your state standards to make lesson planning easy.

► The *Strategies for Writers* online lesson planner integrates the state standards into your daily plans automatically.

Integrates Six Traits of Effective Writing

► The Six Traits of Writing are incorporated into every unit.

► Detailed guidelines assist students in revising, editing, and effectively assessing their work.

Rubric-Based Instruction

► Assessment is rubric-based, so students know exactly what they need to do to succeed.

► Rubrics provide clear guidelines for students to assess their own and other students' writing.

Flexible Units

► Units can be taught in any order.

► The Teacher Edition contains a variety of activities to reinforce **writing across the curriculum**.

► **Grammar** is introduced early in each unit with multiple opportunities provided for instruction and practice.

Test-Writing Practice

► Each unit contains a chapter designed specifically to help improve high-stakes test results.

Research Report Rubric

The traits of a good research report from page 226 have been used to make the rubric below. By using 1, 2, 3, or 4 check marks to judge each trait, you can decide how well any research report was written.

	Excelling ✓✓✓✓	Achieving ✓✓✓	Developing ✓✓	Beginning ✓
Information/ Organization	The report focuses on one topic; it is well organized.	Most of the report focuses on one topic; it is mostly organized.	Some of the report focuses on one topic; it is organized in some places.	The report should focus on one topic; it should be well organized.
Voice/ Audience	The introduction is attention grabbing.	The introduction is interesting.	The introduction is mildly interesting.	The introduction should be attention grabbing.
Content/ Ideas	Quotes and paraphrased information are included throughout.	Quotes and paraphrased information are included in some places.	Quotes and paraphrased information are included in a few places.	Quotes and paraphrased information should be included throughout.
Word Choice/ Clarity	Citations and the Works Consulted are correct.	Citations and the Works Consulted are mostly correct.	There are some errors in citations and in the Works Consulted.	Citations and the Works Consulted need to be correct.
Sentence Fluency	Introductory verbal phrases provide sentence variety throughout.	Introductory verbal phrases provide some sentence variety.	Introductory verbal phrases provide little sentence variety.	More introductory verbal phrases are needed for sentence variety.
Grammar/ Mechanics	Spelling, grammar, and compound/ complex sentences are correct.	There are a few errors in spelling, grammar, and compound/ complex sentences.	There are several errors in spelling, grammar, and compound/ complex sentences.	There are many errors in spelling, grammar, and compound/ complex sentences.

230 Expository Writing ■ Research Report

Level H Student Edition shown

Independent Study
Research Proven
by Marzano and Associates, Inc.

Students who used *Strategies for Writers* outperformed students who used other programs. See page 16 for more details.

YOUR ENERGY SOURCE FOR POWERFUL WRITING

Strategies for Writers **is a complete writing source that provides students with the tools for developing lifelong skills and success in all areas of writing—including test-taking situations!**

Student Edition provides a powerful source for learning to write within the four modes of writing—narrative, descriptive, expository, and persuasive.

► **Student-friendly** format.

► **Level appropriate student guides** clearly define expectations and model good writing strategies to motivate students, step-by-step, through the writing process.

► **Test-writing practice** is integrated into every unit to build student confidence and boost test scores.

► **Integrated Grammar/Mechanics activities** help students develop essential skills, foundational to writing.

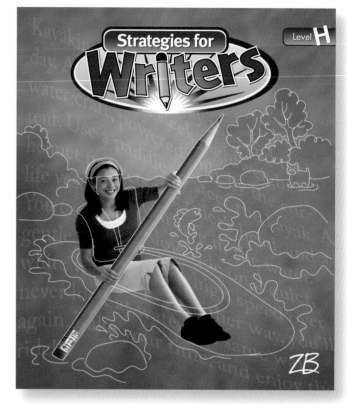

Level H Student Edition

Teacher Edition presents each unit in a clear, easy-to-follow format for flexible instruction.

► **Time Management charts** assist busy teachers with daily planning.

► **Differentiated instruction** is emphasized through helpful suggestions and tips to meet the needs of all students.

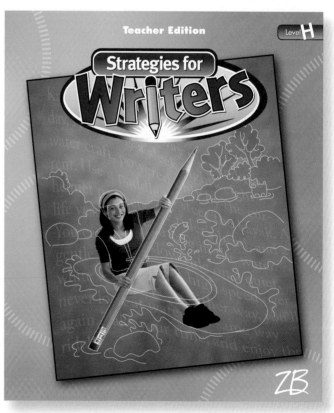

Level H Teacher Edition

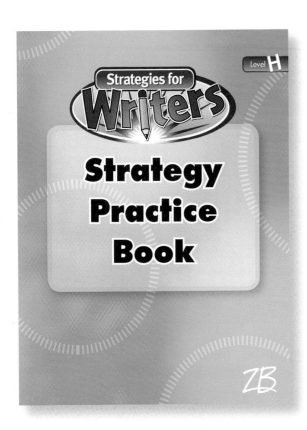

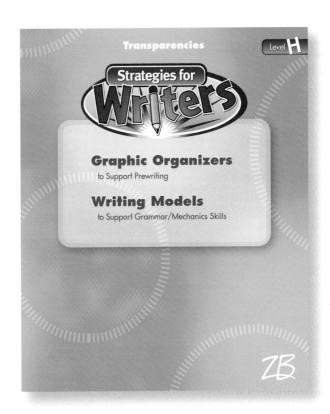

Strategy Practice Book provides guided practice for the strategies taught in each unit.

Transparencies include blank graphic organizers and writing models for proofreading practice and additional grammar instruction and practice.

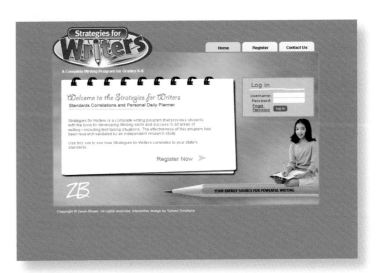

Kidspiration™ & Inspiration™ Graphic Organizer CD-ROM offers students additional practice using graphic organizer templates for building writing success.

Online Lesson Planner correlates daily lesson plans to **your state standards** online at **www.zaner-bloser.com/sfw**.

The Six Traits of Effective Writing

Strategies for Writers integrates the six traits of effective writing in instruction and assessment.

Writing Traits are explained throughout each unit and applied to each genre of writing.

Guides topic focus and text construction ▬▬▬▶

Supports writer's voice and awareness of audience ▬▬▬▶

Promotes richness and interest of content ▬▬▬▶

Develops clarity and appropriateness of language ▬▬▬▶

Supports text fluency and flow ▬▬▬▶

Integrates the conventions of writing ▬▬▬▶

Research Report
Writing Traits

I know that there are six traits of good writing. Here's a list of what makes a good research report. I'll use this list to help me write.

Information/Organization	The report focuses on one topic. The report is well organized.
Voice/Audience	The introduction is attention grabbing.
Content/Ideas	Quotes and paraphrased information are included throughout.
Word Choice/Clarity	Citations and the Works Consulted are correct.
Sentence Fluency	The report contains introductory verbal phrases, which provide sentence variety.
Grammar/Mechanics	Spelling, punctuation, and capitalization are correct. Compound and complex sentences are formed correctly.

I can use Julie Fleming's research report on the next three pages as a model for my own writing. Later, we'll check out how Julie used the traits to help her write.

226 Expository Writing ■ Research Report

Level H Student Edition *shown*

Research Report Rubric

The traits of a good research report from page 226 have been used to make the rubric below. By using 1, 2, 3, or 4 check marks to judge each trait, you can decide how well any research report was written.

	Excelling ✓✓✓✓	Achieving ✓✓✓	Developing ✓✓	Beginning ✓
Information/ Organization	The report focuses on one topic; it is well organized.	Most of the report focuses on one topic; it is mostly organized.	Some of the report focuses on one topic; it is organized in some places.	The report should focus on one topic; it should be well organized.
Voice/ Audience	The introduction is attention grabbing.	The introduction is interesting.	The introduction is mildly interesting.	The introduction should be attention grabbing.
Content/ Ideas	Quotes and paraphrased information are included throughout.	Quotes and paraphrased information are included in some places.	Quotes and paraphrased information are included in a few places.	Quotes and paraphrased information should be included throughout.
Word Choice/ Clarity	Citations and the Works Consulted are correct.	Citations and the Works Consulted are mostly correct.	There are some errors in citations and in the Works Consulted.	Citations and the Works Consulted need to be correct.
Sentence Fluency	Introductory verbal phrases provide sentence variety throughout.	Introductory verbal phrases provide some sentence variety.	Introductory verbal phrases provide little sentence variety.	More introductory verbal phrases are needed for sentence variety.
Grammar/ Mechanics	Spelling, grammar, and compound/ complex sentences are correct.	There are a few errors in spelling, grammar, and compound/ complex sentences.	There are several errors in spelling, grammar, and compound/ complex sentences.	There are many errors in spelling, grammar, and compound/ complex sentences.

Level H Student Edition shown

Clearly Organized Rubrics

Rubrics are clearly organized, mode- and genre-specific guides that let students know exactly what is expected and help them evaluate their progress.

► Rubrics help students clearly understand writing terminology and assessment criteria.

► The rubric in each chapter is specific to the mode and genre being taught.

► Students learn to use the rubric by applying it to deconstruct an exemplary model.

► Throughout the chapter, the writing strategies being taught support the points of the rubric.

A flexible instructional plan guides the students through the four modes of writing.

1. Narrative
2. Descriptive
3. Expository
4. Persuasive

A student guide walks students, step-by-step, through the writing process.

NARRATiVE
writing tells a story to the audience.

Hi, I'm Ashley. I'm studying narrative writing in school, and I think it's going to be one of my favorite types of writing. I love telling stories, so I'm looking forward to sharing them in print, too!

IN THIS UNIT

1. Memoir
2. Historical Episode
3. Biography
4. Writing for a Test

6 Narrative Writing

Level H Student Edition shown

Strategies for Writers

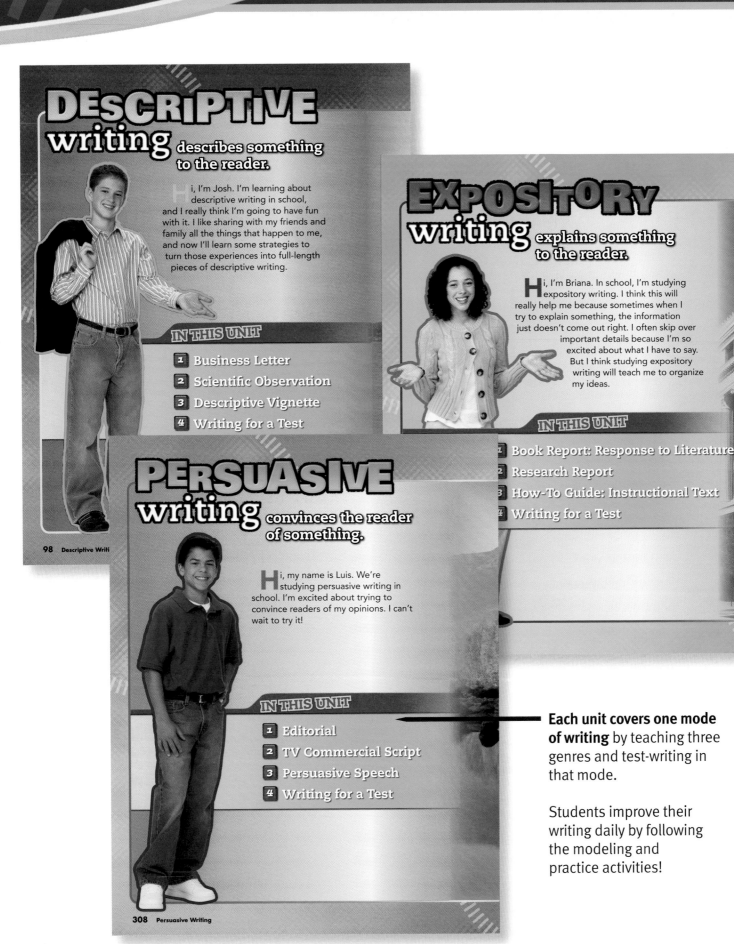

DESCRIPTIVE
writing describes something to the reader.

Hi, I'm Josh. I'm learning about descriptive writing in school, and I really think I'm going to have fun with it. I like sharing with my friends and family all the things that happen to me, and now I'll learn some strategies to turn those experiences into full-length pieces of descriptive writing.

IN THIS UNIT

1. Business Letter
2. Scientific Observation
3. Descriptive Vignette
4. Writing for a Test

98 Descriptive Writi

EXPOSITORY
writing explains something to the reader.

Hi, I'm Briana. In school, I'm studying expository writing. I think this will really help me because sometimes when I try to explain something, the information just doesn't come out right. I often skip over important details because I'm so excited about what I have to say. But I think studying expository writing will teach me to organize my ideas.

IN THIS UNIT

1. Book Report: Response to Literature
2. Research Report
3. How-To Guide: Instructional Text
4. Writing for a Test

PERSUASIVE
writing convinces the reader of something.

Hi, my name is Luis. We're studying persuasive writing in school. I'm excited about trying to convince readers of my opinions. I can't wait to try it!

IN THIS UNIT

1. Editorial
2. TV Commercial Script
3. Persuasive Speech
4. Writing for a Test

308 Persuasive Writing

Each unit covers one mode of writing by teaching three genres and test-writing in that mode.

Students improve their writing daily by following the modeling and practice activities!

Level H Student Edition shown

Independent Study
Research Proven
by Marzano and Associates, Inc.

In *Strategies for Writers*, each step of the process is explicitly taught and clearly modeled.

Writing Strategies are presented to help students meet each point of the rubric.

Writer's Terms are defined to make the language of writing easy to understand.

Writing a Research Report

Prewriting **Gather Information**

Information/Organization

The report focuses on one topic.

Writing Strategy Choose a topic, survey some sources, and make a 3 W's Chart. Then, make note cards.

My teacher told us that we'd be writing research reports. I really like watching the night sky with my telescope, so I decided to choose a topic related to astronomy. I just read an article about deadly asteroid threats, so I chose asteroids as my topic. My first step was to look at books and magazine articles, so I went to the library and searched for information about asteroids. Here's a list of some of the information I read for my report.

Source	Why I Chose It
"Deadly Space Threats Get More Attention." The Columbus Dispatch	Newspaper article about asteroids and comets that could hit Earth
"Danger from the Sky." Cricket	Magazine article about asteroids and meteors
The Search for the Killer Asteroid	Book about the times that asteroids have hit Earth

Practice!

Now it's your turn. Choose a topic and gather information from sources.

Writer's Term

3 W's Chart

A **3 W's Chart** organizes your ideas about a topic. It lists **what** your questions are, **what** information you already know, and **where** you might find answers to your questions.

After I chose my topic and began my research, I decided to make a 3 W's Chart to organize the information that I found. Notice on my chart how some of the information can be found in more than one place. This is good because if I find the same information in different sources, it's probably correct.

3 W's Chart

What are some of my questions?	What do I already know?	Where can I find answers/explanations?
What are asteroids, and where are they found?	They're pieces of rock that move through space.	The Search for the Killer Asteroid
What are the differences among asteroids, meteoroids, meteors, and meteorites?	I'm not sure—will need to find out.	article in Cricket magazine, The Search for the Killer Asteroid
What important meteorites have hit Earth? What were their effects?	One hit Arizona around 50,000 years ago. It left a huge crater.	Web site on Barringer Meteorite Crater, Cricket article
Why are scientists so concerned about asteroids, and why do they study them so closely?	They're afraid one could slam into Earth and cause mass destruction—and possible extinction.	Internet article from Space.com, newspaper article on space threats, MIT Web site, Cricket article
Is there any way to stop asteroids from slamming into Earth?	I don't know—will need to find out.	The Search for the Killer Asteroid, newspaper article on space threats, Cricket article

Practice!

Now it's your turn. Make a 3 W's Chart to decide what you want to know, what you already know, and where you can find the answers.

Level H Student Edition shown

Strategies for **Writers**

Practice! is provided for each writing trait and strategy.

Grammar/Mechanics practice is seamlessly integrated throughout each chapter for streamlined instruction.

Seamless Integration

Grammar/Mechanics Practice! provides additional activities to support grammar instruction.

Editing Proofread Writing

Grammar/Mechanics
Spelling, punctuation, and capitalization are correct. Compound and complex sentences are formed correctly.

Writing Strategy
Make sure I've formed compound and complex sentences correctly.

Writer's Term

Compound Sentences/Complex Sentences
A **compound sentence** consists of two closely related independent clauses joined by a comma and a coordinating conjunction (*and, but, or*) or by a semicolon. A **complex sentence** consists of an independent clause and a dependent clause that begins with a subordinating conjunction (*although, because, if, as,* or *when*).

Now I need to check for errors in spelling and punctuation. The rubric also says that I should pay special attention to compound and complex sentences. Here's how I edited two complex sentences.

[DRAFT]

[correctly formed complex sentences]

What are meteoroids, meteors, and meteorites? When

asteroic

Compound and Complex Sentences

KNOW the RULE

A **compound sentence** consists of two closely related independent clauses. An independent clause can stand alone as a sentence, but two independent clauses should be joined by a comma and a coordinating conjunction (*and, but, or*) or by a semicolon.
Example: An NEO passes Earth, **but** a meteorite hits it.
Example: An NEO passes Earth; a meteorite hits it.

Practice the Rule

Number a separate sheet of paper 1–5. Read the sentences below. Write *CX* if the sentence is complex. Write *CD* if the sentence is compound. Then, copy each dependent clause onto the paper.

a Torino rating of 0.

Practice the Rule

Number a separate sheet of paper 1–5. Read the sentences below. Write *CX* if the sentence is complex. Write *CD* if the sentence is compound. Then, copy each dependent clause onto the paper.

1. The Torino Impact Hazard Scale is relatively new; it was adopted in 1999.
2. It was developed by Richard Binzel; he worked on it for several years.
3. Because so many new asteroids were being discovered, Binzel felt the need to help the public understand them.
4. When a new asteroid is discovered, scientists gather information about it.
5. They calculate where the asteroid will be in the future, and they assign a rating to it.

Apply the Rule

Read the research report, looking for errors in the use of compound/complex sentences. Then, rewrite the passage correctly on a separate sheet of paper.

A meteor is the streak of light that appears when a meteorite, an actual piece of falling rock, enters Earth's atmosphere. Meteorites are genuine bits of our solar system. Most of them have broken off of asteroids, which are space rocks that are too small to be classified as planets. Some meteorites come from comets, which are balls of ice and frozen gas.

When a meteor shower occurs the sky lights up with thousands of meteor trails. Scientists use the path of Earth's rotation to predict these spectacular light shows, which repeat each year as the planet crosses the path of a comet.

Regular meteor showers have names that come from the

for schedules on Web sites such as www.nasa.com.

Apply the Rule

Read the research report, looking for errors in the use of compound/complex sentences. Then, rewrite the passage correctly on a separate sheet of paper.

Level H Student Edition shown

Every unit contains a *Writing for a Test* chapter to provide practice for high-stakes testing.

Planning My Time

When our teacher gives us a writing prompt, she always tells us how much time we'll have to complete the test. I'm already familiar with the writing process, so I'll think about how much time I need for each step. Then, I'll add it all up to see if it meets the amount of time my teacher has given us. She has allowed us an hour for this test, so here's how I plan to organize my time. Remember, planning your time will help you, too!

Step 4:
Editing
10 minutes

Step 1:
Prewriting
25 minutes

Step 3:
Revising
10 minutes

Student guides model the application of writing strategies to test-writing situations for better results on high-stakes tests.

Plan for Success

► **Time planning** is taught to help students manage their time for test writing success.

Using the Writing Prompt

Stages of the **Writing Process** are used in a test-taking scenario.

Student guides examine a **test-writing prompt** and model how to respond to the task.

Writing an Expository Test

Prewriting Study the Writing Prompt

Writing Strategy   Study the writing prompt to be sure I know what to do.

I always study my writing prompt so that I know exactly what I'm supposed to do. I know that it usually has three parts, and that it will help to first find and then label the setup, task, and scoring guide. You should also circle key words in the setup and the task that show what kind of writing you need to do and who your audience will be. I used orange to circle my topic and red to circle my task. The writing prompt doesn't say who the audience is, but my purpose is to teach someone to do something, so I'll keep that in mind as I write.

My Writing Test Prompt

Setup — Think about something you know how to do really well. Is there anything about this activity that others would find useful?

Task — Write a how-to guide that "teaches" others how to do something beneficial.

Be sure your writing

- is sequentially ordered.
- contains a lot of explanatory details that help the reader understand the process.
- is supported with factual information.
- has been checked for proper use of homophones.

Scoring Guide
- flows smoothly.
- contains correct grammar, punctuation, capitalization, and spelling.

294 Expository Writing ■ Expository Test

Level H Student Edition shown

Writing a Research Report

Prewriting Gather Information

Information/Organization The report focuses on one topic.

Writing Strategy Choose a topic, survey some sources, and make a 3 W's Chart. Then, make note cards.

Practice the Strategy Survey sources and make a 3 W's Chart for the topic you've chosen. Then, make note cards by writing one or more questions from your 3 W's Chart near the top of each card. Use each card to help gather information that answers the question(s) at the top.

My 3 W's Question(s): _____

My 3 W's Question(s): _____

Apply the ____ ____king note cards until y____
to each ____ ____ W's Chart.

Additional activities provide further practice for learning essential writing skills.

After each writing process step is modeled, students may use their *Strategy Practice Book* for additional guided practice.

Writing a Research Report

Prewriting Organize Ideas

Information/Organization The report is well organized.

Writing Strategy Make an Outline to organize my information.

Practice the Strategy Organize the information on your note cards by including it on an Outline. 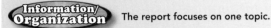 OUTLINE

I. _____
  A. _____
    1. _____
    2. _____
  B. _____
    1. _____
    2. _____
II. _____
  A. _____
    1. _____
    2. _____
  B. _____
    1. _____
    2. _____
III. _____
  A. _____
    1. _____
    2. _____
  B. _____
    1. _____
    2. _____
IV. _____
  A. _____
    1. _____
    2. _____
  B. _____
    1. _____
    2. _____

36 Expository Writing ■ Research Report

Level H Strategy Practice Book shown

Make lesson planning easy!

► **Time Management charts** assist with flexible planning.

► **Online Lesson Planner** provides seamless integration of **your state standards** at:

www.zaner-bloser.com/sfw

Learning Objectives and Daily Activities are clearly stated.

Research Report Time Management

WEEK 1

	Day 1	Day 2	Day 3	Day 4	Day 5
Learning Objectives					
	Students will: • learn the components of a research report.	Students will: • learn how to gather information for a research report.	Students will: • practice gathering information for their own research reports.	Students will: • learn how to organize their information into an Outline.	Students will: • practice organizing their notes into an Outline.
Activities					
	• Discuss the elements and traits of a research report (Student pages 224–226). • Use the rubric to study the model (Student pages 227–233).	• Read and discuss **Prewriting: Gather Information** (Student pages 234–236).	• Choose a topic, survey sources, and make a 3 W's Chart. • Make note cards.	• Read and discuss **Prewriting: Organize Ideas** (Student pages 237–239).	• Review note cards. • Make an Outline to organize information.

WEEK 2

	Day 1	Day 2	Day 3	Day 4	Day 5
Learning Objectives					
	Students will: • learn how to include an attention-grabbing introduction in their drafts.	Students will: • practice writing their own drafts.	Students will: • learn how to add quotes and paraphrased information from experts.	Students will: • practice adding quotes and paraphrased information from experts.	Students will: • learn how to cite quotes correctly. • learn how to make a list of Works Consulted.
Activities					
	• Read and discuss **Drafting: Write a Draft** (Student pages 240–243).	• Use an Outline to write a draft. • Include an introduction that grabs the reader's attention.	• Read and discuss **Revising: Extend Writing** (Student pages 244–245).	• Add quotes and paraphrased information from experts.	• Read and discuss **Revising: Clarify Writing** (Student pages 246–247).

WEEK 3

	Day 1	Day 2	Day 3	Day 4	Day 5
Learning Objectives					
	Students will: • practice citing quotes correctly. • practice making a list of Works Consulted.	Students will: • learn how to use introductory verbal phrases to vary sentences.	Students will: • learn how to form compound and complex sentences correctly.	Students will: • practice editing their drafts for spelling, capitalization, and punctuation.	Students will: • learn different ways to publish their research reports.
Activities					
	• Reread drafts, making sure quotes are cited correctly. • Make a list of Works Consulted.	• Read and discuss **Editing: Check Sentences** (Student page 248). • Use introductory verbal phrases to vary sentences.	• Read and discuss **Editing: Proofread Writing** (Student page 249).	• Fix any spelling, capitalization, or punctuation errors. • Use compound and complex sentences correctly.	• Read and discuss **Publishing: Share Writing** (Student page 252).

* To complete the chapter in fewer days, teach the learning objectives and activities for two days in one day.

This planning chart, correlated to your state's writing standards, is available on-line at http://www.zaner-bloser.com/sfw.

Expository Writing ■ Research Report **171**

Level H Teacher Edition shown

Strategies for Writers

Writing Across the Curriculum offers ideas that connect writing with other content areas. ◄━━━

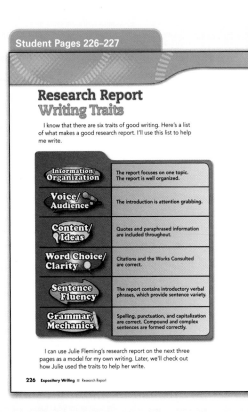

Writing Across the Curriculum

Science/Social Studies Encourage students who are writing science or social-studies related reports to note questions raised by their research. Explain that keeping track of these questions can help them get more out of their research as well as provide possible topics for future research assignments. Remind students that these further research topics should be ones that go beyond the scope of their current reports. To illustrate this concept, ask students to identify the information in Briana's research report that could prompt further research. **Possible responses:** the Spacewatch center in Arizona; careers in astronomy; a day in the life of a scientist at a space observatory

Teaching tips provide useful ideas. ━━━►

Writing Traits
(Student pages 226–229)

Research Report

Share with students a time when you were motivated to find answers to an important question. Note that people often do not need class deadlines to conduct research. Sometimes our own personal interests drive us to seek out answers.

Ask students to share examples of subjects they have researched on their own. Acknowledge that an assigned [topic may se]em more demanding than independent [research. Howe]ver, any kind of research report can proceed [more smoothly] if writers first learn specific skills and traits.

[Call students' att]ention to the traits of a good research [report listed on] Student page 226. Have one or more vol[unteers read alo]ud the traits and their descriptions. Then, [ask your stu]dents why someone might use these traits [to present t]heir findings in writing.

[Tell students th]at they are going to study and use [traits while w]riting research reports, and that a good [report] has the traits listed on Student page 226.

School-Home Connection

Differentiating Instruction ◄━━━ provides options and activities to meet the needs of all learners, including English-Language Learners.

Differentiating Instruction

English-Language Learners **Preteach** key words and concepts that may prevent students from focusing on the writing traits modeled in "Understanding Phobias." Begin by telling students that this report describes types of exaggerated, or overstated, fears called phobias. Point out the quoted definition of *phobia* near the end of the second paragraph. Then, explain that the author organizes her report into three types of phobias:

- Simple, or specific phobias involve the fear of a specific thing or place. For example, some people fear spiders or elevators.
- Social phobias involve peoples' anxiety, or mental distress, about certain social situations, such as giving a speech or going to a party.
- Agoraphobia, in which peoples' fears keep them from leaving home, is the most extreme phobia.

Point out that after describing these phobias, the author discusses their causes, noting that one may be hereditary, or passed from parent to child through genes.

Expository Writing ■ Research Report **173**

Level H Teacher Edition shown

◄━━━ **School-Home Connection Letters** provide a quick and easy way to communicate with families.

Research

Evidence-Based Research

Students who used *Strategies for Writers* outperformed students who used other programs.

An independent study, conducted by Marzano and Associates, Inc., measured the impact of *Strategies for Writers* (SFW) on the improvement of students' writing performance. Below is a brief synopsis from the first year's investigation, conducted in 2003–2004.*

- Given any group of 100 students, when 50 are taught using *Strategies for Writers* and 50 are taught using OTHER† materials and/or methodologies, students using SFW outperform students using OTHER materials 49 out of 50 times on writing tests.

- There are no differences in student performance among grade levels. *Strategies for Writers* consistently produces a 49 to 1 ratio result.

- It doesn't matter whether a school is urban or suburban. *Strategies for Writers* students score higher on holistic writing tests than students taught with OTHER materials or methodologies.

- In general, this independent first-year (2003–2004) evidence-based research study found that using *Strategies for Writers* produces superior writing scores (on standardized or state tests) compared to those scores produced by students using other writing materials and methodologies.

* The above data has been excerpted from the complete final report of the first-year evaluation (2003–2004) of the *Strategies for Writers* program. The complete report, conducted by **Marzano and Associates, Inc.,** can be found on the Zaner-Bloser Web site **www.zaner-bloser.com**.

† OTHER represents a variety of methods and materials.

Foundational Research

Strategies for Writers Research-Based Program for Writing Success
By Leslie W. Crawford, Ed.D.

In the last decade of the twentieth century, concerted effort in the field of literacy began to achieve an approach that would balance instruction between skills and process. With this in mind, *Strategies for Writers* was designed to embed strategies within a process approach to writing (Collins, 1998; Collins & Collins, 1996; Englert, 1990; and Harris & Graham, 1992).

Strategy instruction
- makes students aware of when, how, and why strategies work (Harris & Pressley, 1991; and Poindexter & Oliver, 1999).
- teaches students to think carefully and strategically about writing instruction (Christenson, 2002).
- focuses on developing writers who are able to write independently using the processes of writing (Englert, 1990).
- gives students the support needed to overcome difficulties in writing (Danoff, Harris, & Graham, 1993).

Rubrics include elements and criteria that provide students the scaffolds needed for judging and revising their work (Hillocks, 1986; James, Abbott, & Greenwood, 2001). Experience using rubrics leads students to become effective evaluators of their compositions.

Strategies for Writers Research Base for the Use of Rubrics
By Rebecca B. Sipe, Ed.D.

When used as instructional tools, rubrics
- help students become more thoughtful about their work as they engage in ongoing peer and self-assessments (Goodrich, 1996; Andrade, 1997, 2000).
- provide a platform of technical vocabulary to help students think about important aspects of their writing regardless of the genre. Terms like *purpose*, *audience*, and *organization* become part of the class vocabulary because teachers frequently start with established rubrics and then modify or expand these rubrics as the class discusses the important aspects of writing (DeLisle-Walker, 1996; Wolf & Wolf, 2002; Wolf & Gearhart, 1994; Wyngaard & Gehrke, 1996; Marzano, 2000; Skillings & Ferrell, 2000; Allington, Johnston, & Day, 2002). Used in this way, rubrics provide excellent tools for:
  1. engaging the students in a class discussion of writing elements (which are also sometimes called *domains* or *traits*).
  2. building student understanding of the qualities of good writing.
  3. supporting student writing.
  4. guiding students as they evaluate their own writing (Wyngaard & Gehrke, 1996; Strickland & Strickland, 1998).

Table of Contents

NARRATIVE writing

DESCRIPTIVE writing

(Continued on page 18)

DESCRIPTIVE writing
(Continued)

EXPOSITORY writing

EXPOSITORY writing (Continued)

PERSUASIVE writing

NARRATIVE
writing strategies

IN THIS UNIT

1 Memoir

- Jot down notes about a major life experience.
- Use a Story Frame to sequence events.
- Use a reflective tone to convey meaning and insight to the reader.
- Add details to bring the story to life.
- Use a thesaurus to help me vary my word choice.
- Use questions to build suspense.
- Make sure that simple and perfect tense are used correctly.

2 Historical Episode

- Choose a historical event and gather information from several resources, including the Internet and primary sources.
- Make a Story Map to organize story elements.
- Clearly describe the setting and theme for the reader.
- Add historical details.
- Make sure dialogue reflects the time and place in which the characters live.
- Vary sentence length.
- Make sure that I have punctuated dialogue correctly.

3 Biography

- Choose a person as the focus of my biography. Then, write interview questions and conduct an interview.
- Plot important events on a Timeline.
- Grab the reader's attention with an interesting event in the introduction.
- Add direct quotations to bring the biography to life.
- Use a dictionary to make sure I have used words correctly.
- Reorder awkwardly placed sentences and paragraphs.
- Correct sentence fragments and run-ons.

4 Writing for a Test

- Study the writing prompt to be sure I know what to do.
- Respond to the task.
- Choose a graphic organizer.
- Check my graphic organizer against the scoring guide.
- Engage the reader with interesting details.
- Add dialogue to strengthen characterization.
- Use clear, concrete words.
- Use prepositional phrases to add sentence variety.
- Check my grammar, punctuation, capitalization, and spelling.

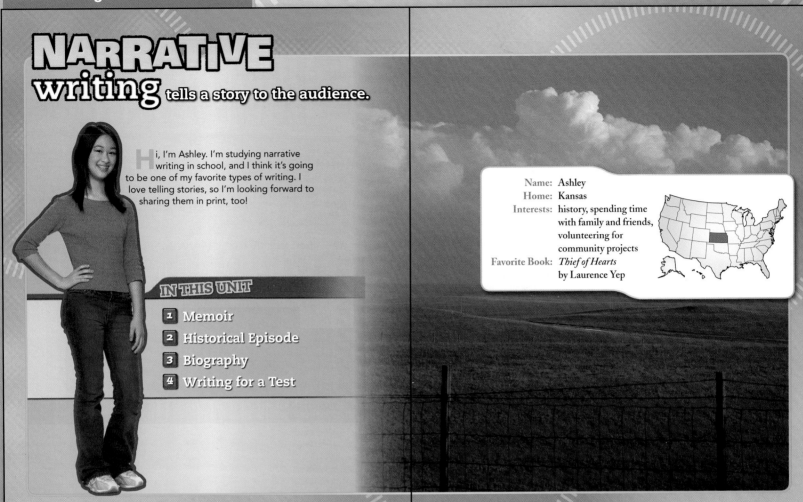

NARRATIVE
writing tells a story to the audience.

Hi, I'm Ashley. I'm studying narrative writing in school, and I think it's going to be one of my favorite types of writing. I love telling stories, so I'm looking forward to sharing them in print, too!

IN THIS UNIT

1. Memoir
2. Historical Episode
3. Biography
4. Writing for a Test

Name:	Ashley
Home:	Kansas
Interests:	history, spending time with family and friends, volunteering for community projects
Favorite Book:	*Thief of Hearts* by Laurence Yep

6 Narrative Writing

Narrative Writing 7

IN THIS UNIT

Memoir This genre gives students the opportunity to tell a true story about a meaningful life experience.

Historical Episode This genre introduces students to important skills that will help them combine factual information about a specific era with fictional story elements.

Biography This genre gives students a chance to use interview skills to gather background details so they can write about a person of interest.

Narrative Test Students learn and practice how to read a narrative test prompt and how to plan their time. They also learn and practice writing strategies for successful test writing in the narrative mode.

Meet Ashley

The student guide for this chapter is Ashley, a girl from Kansas. You may wish to explore with students how Ashley's background, hobbies, interests, and personality connect with her choices of writing topics. Explain to students that Ashley will use what she knows to make decisions about her topics—a process that will make her writing special and real. Encourage students to follow Ashley's lead by using their own background knowledge, interests, and personality as they write. Narrative writing tells the reader a story, and your students will have many interesting, unique, and authentic stories to tell.

by Julie Coiro, Ph.D.
University of Connecticut

Locating Resources: Search Engines for Adults and Students

For adults looking for specific information quickly, one search engine to try first is **Google** at **http://www.google.com**. It has a huge database that very quickly scans sites and returns a list of relevant Web sites with short annotations and links. The list is ranked in order, with the most popular and relevant annotations at the top. Your students may also wish to use **Google**, but you will want to select the "Google Safe Search" option from the preferences menu to block inappropriate Web sites.

Other popular search engines for adults include **Yahoo** at **http://www.yahoo.com**, **Alta Vista** at **http://www.altavista.com**, **MSN** at **http://www.msn.com**, and **Dogpile** at **http://www.dogpile.com**.

A number of search engines and Web portals have been designed with the needs and interests of a younger audience in mind. Here are a few of the most popular.

- **KidsClick!** at **http://www.kidsclick.org** was created by librarians. It organizes around 5,000 Web sites into more than 600 categories.

- **AOL@School** at **http://www.aolatschool.com** searches a database of educator-reviewed classroom materials for students in grades K–12.

- **Kids.Net.Au** at **http://www.kids.net.au** is designed for children, parents, and teachers. It links to reference materials, including a thesaurus, a dictionary, and an encyclopedia.

- **Fact Monster** at **http://www.factmonster.com** is a Web site for kids that combines the contents of reference materials with other educational resources.

- **Enchanted Learning** at **http://www.enchantedlearning.com/Home.html** provides access to a huge database guaranteed to spark writing ideas.

- **TekMom Search Tools for Students** at **http://tekmom.com/search/index.html** links readers to research tools designed with young learners in mind.

Critical Evaluation: Evaluating Reliability

As children begin using the Internet as a source for information, it is important that they realize Web sites do not go through the same editing process as books. Students need to expect that they may find information on the Internet that has mistakes or that has been created as a joke. One strategy you may wish to discuss with your students involves evaluating the reliability of on-line information.

For educational purposes, a reliable Web site is one created by a person or people with a reputation for publishing high quality, truthful information for children. It is critical that students be prepared to investigate who created a Web site, why it was created, and what authority the creators have to publish the information.

All quality Web sites should have a page that tells more about the authors, their qualifications, their contact information, and their purpose for creating the site. You can usually find this information at a "Who We Are" or "About Us" link on the starting page of a Web site. All of the biography Web sites listed on page 23 include such links. You may wish to explore a few of these Web sites as a class activity.

To begin, select two or three Web sites, using a digital projector to view each site with your students. Scroll up and down the site's homepage to look for the "About Us" link. Once you have found the link, discuss the answers to these questions:

- *Who created the information?*
- *What is the purpose of this Web site?*
- *When was the information updated?*
- *What qualifications does the author have?*
- *Is the information at this Web site worthy of being used in your own biography? Why or why not?*

Encourage students to consider these questions each time they visit a Web site. Answers will often provide the insights needed to critically evaluate whether the information is reliable and worthy of use.

Communicating Globally: Publishing Biographies

The Internet provides wonderful models for publishing for a public audience. You can create your own class project Web site to display your students' writing in a format that fits their interests. Here are three Web sites to get you thinking about the possibilities.

- *The Children's Encyclopedia of Women* at **http://www2. lhric.org/pocantico/womenenc/womenenc.htm** was first published in 1998 by Terry Hongell's third and fourth graders from Sleepy Hollow, New York. It is published as part of the Pocantico Hills Central School Web site. Each year, students add new content to the collection. It is truly an example of the power of on-line publishing.

- *Different People, Different Countries, Same Dream* at **http://gvctemp01.virtualclassroom.org** was published as a telecollaboration among elementary school students in India, Israel, and the United States. The students helped design this interactive Web site, and they continue to exchange their biographies of leaders of different cultures. This Web site was created for a contest sponsored by the **Global Virtual Classroom** at **http:// www.virtualclassroom.org**, an initiative designed to empower, enable, and connect students around the world using Internet technology.

- *Images of Greatness: The Lives of Twelve Enduringly Famous Individuals* at **http://www.kyrene.k12. az.us/schools/brisas/sunda/great/great.htm** was created by a group of fourth and fifth graders from Kyrene de las Brisas Elementary School in Chandler, Arizona. The students organized their twelve short biographies in an amazing table that charts the similarities and differences among the contributions of famous individuals. The Web site also contains a "Quotations Quiz" about these great achievers.

Supporting and Extending Writing: Sparking Writing Ideas

There are many Web sites that may spark students' ideas about a historical episode. Here are some examples:

- **EASE History** at **http://www.easehistory.org/ index2.html** provides access to hundreds of historical videos and photographs searchable by theme, keyword, or classroom topic in an Experience Accelerated Support Environment (EASE) created by professors at Michigan State University.

- **American Memory** at **http://memory.loc.gov/ ammem/index.html** is made available by the American Library of Congress to provide free and open on-line access to written and spoken words, sound recordings, still and moving images, prints, maps, and sheet music that document the American experience. Students can browse the archive by topic, time period, or geographical location.

- **CNN Millennium: A Thousand Years of History** at **http://www.cnn.com/SPECIALS/1999/millennium** offers a panoramic sweep over the last 1,000 years of the people, events, and achievements that shaped the world. Students may wish to start by exploring **Timelines** at **http://www.cnn.com/SPECIALS/1999/millennium/ learning/timelines**.

- **An Outline of American History** at **http://odur. let.rug.nl/~usa/H/1994** is primarily in text form, but it provides readable and reliable historical details for students who may need to check the accuracy of historical information they find elsewhere.

- Students can also use Web sites that focus on one period in history such as the **Civil Rights Documentation Project** at **http://www.usm.edu/crdp**, **Berlin Wall Online** at **http://www.dailysoft.com/berlinwall/ index.html**, and **Holocaust Survivors** at **http://www. holocaustsurvivors.org**.

- For current events, students may wish to use *The New York Times* **Learning Network** at **http://www. nytimes.com/learning/index.html** or current news releases from news Web sites such as the **Online Newshour** at **http://www.pbs.org/newshour**, **BBC News** at **http://news.bbc.co.uk**, or **CNN World News** at **http://www.cnn.com/WORLD**.

Memoir Overview

In this chapter, students will learn how to write a memoir. They will learn the different elements of a memoir—first-person narrator, voice, reflective tone, and sequence—and some reasons why they might choose to write one. Students will then use a memoir rubric to study a model writing sample.

Students will follow the student guide as she goes through the writing stages—prewriting, drafting, revising, editing, and publishing. As the student guide learns new writing strategies in each step, students will be directed to practice the strategies in their own writing.

During prewriting and drafting, students will
- focus on one major life experience.
- jot down notes about this experience.
- use a Story Frame to sequence events.
- use a reflective tone to convey meaning and insight to the reader.

During revising and editing, students will
- add details to bring the story to life.
- use a thesaurus to help vary their word choice.
- use questions to build suspense.
- edit their drafts for spelling, capitalization, punctuation, and simple and perfect tense errors.

Finally, students will publish a final draft.

You may wish to send to families the School-Home Connection Letter for this chapter, located at the end of this unit in the Teacher Edition.

Memoir Writing Traits

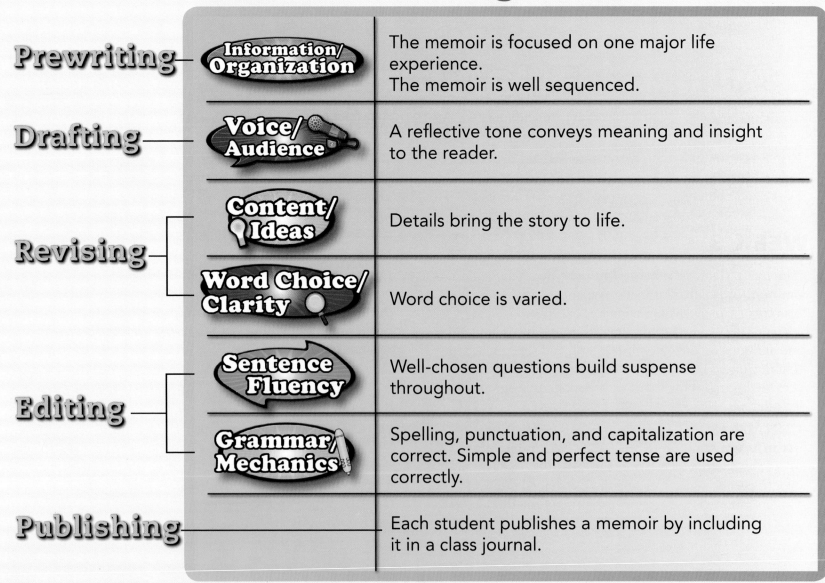

Prewriting — **Information/Organization**: The memoir is focused on one major life experience. The memoir is well sequenced.

Drafting — **Voice/Audience**: A reflective tone conveys meaning and insight to the reader.

Revising — **Content/Ideas**: Details bring the story to life.

Word Choice/Clarity: Word choice is varied.

Editing — **Sentence Fluency**: Well-chosen questions build suspense throughout.

Grammar/Mechanics: Spelling, punctuation, and capitalization are correct. Simple and perfect tense are used correctly.

Publishing: Each student publishes a memoir by including it in a class journal.

Memoir Time Management

WEEK 1

	Day 1	Day 2	Day 3	Day 4	Day 5
Learning Objectives					
	Students will: • learn the components of a memoir.	Students will: • learn how to gather information for a memoir.	Students will: • practice gathering information for their own memoirs.	Students will: • learn how to make a Story Frame to sequence events.	Students will: • practice organizing their story events into a Story Frame.
Activities					
	• Discuss the elements and traits of a memoir (Student pages 8–10). • Use the rubric to study the model (Student pages 11–15).	• Read and discuss **Prewriting: Gather Information** (Student page 16).	• Brainstorm ideas and choose one major life experience. • Gather information by jotting down notes.	• Read and discuss **Prewriting: Organize Ideas** (Student page 17).	• Review notes taken while gathering information. • Make a Story Frame to sequence story events.

WEEK 2

	Day 1	Day 2	Day 3	Day 4	Day 5
Learning Objectives					
	Students will: • learn how to use a reflective tone to convey meaning and insight to the reader.	Students will: • practice writing their drafts.	Students will: • learn how adding details can bring their stories to life.	Students will: • practice adding details to their drafts.	Students will: • learn how to use a thesaurus to help vary their word choice.
Activities					
	• Read and discuss **Drafting: Write a Draft** (Student pages 18–19).	• Use a Story Frame to write a draft. • Use a reflective tone.	• Read and discuss **Revising: Extend Writing** (Student page 20).	• Choose details to add.	• Read and discuss **Revising: Clarify Writing** (Student page 21).

WEEK 3

	Day 1	Day 2	Day 3	Day 4	Day 5
Learning Objectives					
	Students will: • practice varying their word choice.	Students will: • learn how to use questions to build suspense.	Students will: • learn how to use simple and perfect verb tenses correctly.	Students will: • practice editing their drafts for spelling, capitalization, and punctuation.	Students will: • learn different ways to publish their memoirs.
Activities					
	• Reread drafts, looking for places to vary word choice.	• Read and discuss **Editing: Check Sentences** (Student page 22). • Make sure to use questions to build suspense.	• Read and discuss **Editing: Proofread Writing** (Student page 23).	• Fix any spelling, capitalization, or punctuation errors. • Fix any simple and perfect verb tenses that are not used correctly.	• Read and discuss **Publishing: Share Writing** (Student page 26).

To complete the chapter in fewer days, teach the learning objectives and activities for two days in one day.

This planning chart, correlated to your state's writing standards, is available on-line at http://www.zaner-bloser.com/sfw.

What's a Memoir?

It's a description of an important experience in the author's life. I'll need to figure out which of my experiences will make an interesting memoir.

What's in a Memoir?

Narrator
Because the narrator is the person writing the memoir, the story is told in the first-person point of view, using the word *I*.

Reflective Tone
This is how I want my memoir to sound. I'll use a reflective, or thoughtful, tone so the reader will understand how I feel. I can create a reflective tone by asking questions and/or drawing conclusions.

Voice? I totally thought voice was just used for talking.

Voice
The writer uses voice to express his or her unique style. In other words, my writing should sound like me. To create voice in my writing, I can include phrases and words that I often use.

Sequence
This is the order in which I'll describe my story events. I can include flashbacks that interrupt the chronological order, and I can use transition words to help readers follow the sequence of my story.

Why write a Memoir?

There are tons of reasons for writing a memoir. I jotted some down to help me think about why I want to write.

Entertainment
I've done some interesting stuff, and even if I didn't see the humor at the time, things have happened to me that could make readers laugh. Entertaining the reader is one reason to write a memoir.

Personal Reflection
Writing about an experience can help me reflect on why it was important or what I learned. The reader might be able to connect to my experience and learn from it as well.

Education
Some events or experiences can be educational. If I describe what I've learned from my experiences, maybe my readers will learn something, too.

Relay a Message
The experiences I remember best are ones that have affected me in serious ways. They have taught me something about myself or about life in general. Relaying these messages to the reader is another reason to write a memoir.

Define the Genre

(Student page 8)

Memoir

Discuss with students the definition of a memoir. Ask whether students have ever written about something that happened to them. **Possible response: yes** Point out that any time they reflectively write about a personal experience, they are using the memoir genre.

Elements of the Genre

Memoir

Read and discuss with students the various elements of a memoir. Ask volunteers which elements are also common to other forms of writing. **Possible responses: Narrator— fiction, autobiography; Reflective Tone—essay, opinions; Voice—editorial, stories; Sequence—instructions, historical writing** Discuss why each element may be important to writing a memoir.

Authentic Writing

(Student page 9)

Memoir

Read and discuss with students the reasons for writing a memoir listed on Student page 9. Point out that all writing has a purpose and is aimed at a specific audience. These authentic purposes help authors shape their writing. Ask a volunteer to read aloud the Entertainment box. Then, have students discuss other reasons why someone might write a memoir for entertainment. Repeat this process for the Personal Reflection, Education, and Relay a Message boxes. Then, have students brainstorm other purposes for writing a memoir that are not listed on Student page 9. Encourage students to think about their own reasons for writing a memoir, and how these reasons will affect the tone and focus of their writing.

Memoir Writing Traits

I know that there are six traits of good writing, so I'll use them to help me as I write. Here are the traits of a good memoir.

Information/ Organization	The memoir is focused on one major life experience. The memoir is well sequenced.
Voice/ Audience	A reflective tone conveys meaning and insight to the reader.
Content/ Ideas	Details bring the story to life.
Word Choice/ Clarity	Word choice is varied.
Sentence Fluency	Well-chosen questions build suspense throughout.
Grammar/ Mechanics	Spelling, punctuation, and capitalization are correct. Simple and perfect tense are used correctly.

I can use Manny's memoir on the next page as a model for my own writing. Later, we'll check out how he used the traits to help him write.

Memoir Model

Summer Surprise
by Manny Reyes

Narrator

If someone had told me in June that the most surprising event of the summer wouldn't happen until the beginning of September, I would have laughed.

But right before school began, my best friend, Kenny, invited me to spend Labor Day weekend with his family. I thought it was going to be awesome. But when Kenny told me this year's destination, my jaw dropped. "Camping?" I asked. "You're kidding—right?"

Voice

Sequence "Nope," said Kenny. "Mom and Dad want to try something totally new."

I really wasn't sure whether to accept the invitation. Me? Camping? I am a city kid through and through. Then, I thought about how Kenny and I always have a great time no matter what we do. So reluctantly, I said yes.

But when that fateful Friday afternoon arrived, all I wanted to do was hole myself up under my bedcovers and disappear. My heart was filled with dread, and my backpack was stuffed with city comforts. If the bathroom sink had fit, I totally would've crammed it in!

Eventually, the Millers pulled up in their SUV. Gear was tied on top and piled in the seats, along with Kenny and his annoying sister, Grace. Everyone was so chirpy that I really hoped they wouldn't notice my gloomy mood.

We cruised for about two hours, the signs of civilization disappearing as we approached the campsite. Finally, Mr. Miller parked the car, and we unpacked all the stuff. Twilight was descending. "Better start setting up these tents," said Kenny's dad.

A question popped into my head: "Could I make it back to the city on foot?" But I was quickly distracted as Mrs. Miller called out directions while we fumbled around with poles and pegs. It was pitch black by the time we finished. Mr. Miller built a campfire, and Kenny and I checked out our tent. It was pretty big inside. I thought, "Maybe this won't be so bad after all!"

Reflective Tone

As we sat by the fire, we toasted marshmallows and sang campfire songs. It was then that I noticed the knot in my stomach had loosened. I was actually beginning to enjoy this! Bug spray kept away the mosquitoes, and there were bathrooms right down the hill. There was even a lake on the way in, which we were planning on swimming in the next day. "Check it out," said Kenny, pointing up. The sight took my breath away. A sea of stars lit up the sky.

The next day, I woke early. I was excited about eating an outdoor breakfast, and I was a little amazed, too, at how life can surprise you!

Writing Traits
(Student pages 10–11)

Memoir

Some students might believe that only famous people write memoirs. Make sure students understand that a memoir describes a personal experience and can be written by anyone. Then, ask students what might prompt them to read a memoir. **Possible responses: because it's written by a celebrity or other interesting person; because it tells a good story** Remind students that a good memoir does not have to tell a wild or an extraordinary story. Rather, it can tell an everyday story about an experience with which people can identify.

Tell students that they are going to study and use strategies for writing memoirs, and that a good memoir has the traits listed on Student page 10. Then, ask students to listen for these traits as you read aloud "Summer Surprise" on Student page 11.

Differentiating Instruction

English-Language Learners **Preteach** idioms and other forms of figurative language that might cause difficulty for these students. Read "Summer Surprise" aloud, stopping at each of the following expressions. Have students use context to explain the phrases' meanings. Make sure students understand each expression, reminding them that the meaning of an idiom is different from the separate meanings of its component words.

my jaw dropped	I was surprised
through and through	totally or entirely
hole myself up	hide away alone
chirpy	happily chatty
pitch black	very dark
knot in my stomach	nerves
took my breath away	rendered awestruck
a sea of stars	many stars

Memoir
Rubric

The traits of a good memoir from page 10 have been used to make the rubric below. By using 1, 2, 3, or 4 check marks to judge each trait, you can decide how well any memoir was written.

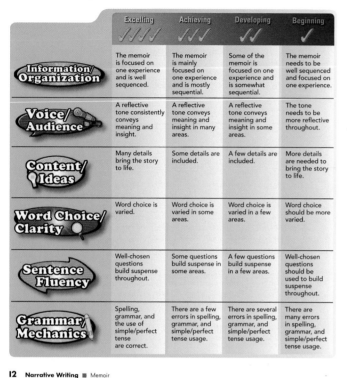

	Excelling ✓✓✓✓	Achieving ✓✓✓	Developing ✓✓	Beginning ✓
Information/Organization	The memoir is focused on one experience and is well sequenced.	The memoir is mainly focused on one experience and is mostly sequential.	Some of the memoir is focused on one experience and is somewhat sequential.	The memoir needs to be well sequenced and focused on one experience.
Voice/Audience	A reflective tone consistently conveys meaning and insight.	A reflective tone conveys meaning and insight in many areas.	A reflective tone conveys meaning and insight in some areas.	The tone needs to be more reflective throughout.
Content/Ideas	Many details bring the story to life.	Some details are included.	A few details are included.	More details are needed to bring the story to life.
Word Choice/Clarity	Word choice is varied.	Word choice is varied in some areas.	Word choice is varied in a few areas.	Word choice should be more varied.
Sentence Fluency	Well-chosen questions build suspense throughout.	Some questions build suspense in some areas.	A few questions build suspense in a few areas.	Well-chosen questions should be used to build suspense throughout.
Grammar/Mechanics	Spelling, grammar, and the use of simple/perfect tense are correct.	There are a few errors in spelling, grammar, and simple/perfect tense usage.	There are several errors in spelling, grammar, and simple/perfect tense usage.	There are many errors in spelling, grammar, and simple/perfect tense usage.

Using the Rubric (Memoir) to Study the Model

Let's use the rubric to check Manny Reyes's memoir, "Summer Surprise." How many check marks would you give Manny for each trait?

Information/Organization
- The memoir is focused on one major life experience.
- The memoir is well sequenced.

Manny focuses his memoir on a specific experience—his first time camping. I like the way he introduces his topic, while also explaining how he feels. His writing is also easy for the reader to understand.

[from the writing model]

> But right before school began, my best friend, Kenny, invited me to spend Labor Day weekend with his family. I thought it was going to be awesome. But when Kenny told me this year's destination, my jaw dropped. "Camping?" I asked. "You're kidding—right?"

Voice/Audience
- A reflective tone conveys meaning and insight to the reader.

Manny uses a reflective tone to express his current views on a past experience. In the passage below, notice how he uses an "if" clause to reflect on the views he had at the beginning of the summer.

[from the writing model]

> If someone had told me in June that the most surprising event of the summer wouldn't happen until the beginning of September, I would have laughed.

Using the Rubric
(Student page 12)

Explain that a rubric is a tool that can be used to evaluate a piece of writing. The rubric on Student page 12 can be used to evaluate a memoir. It is based on the same traits listed on Student page 10.

Now point out the terms above each rubric column: *Excelling, Achieving, Developing,* and *Beginning*. Explain that each column symbolizes a degree of writing skill, and that each rubric row focuses on a specific writing trait. When students use the rubric to evaluate their own work at each step of the writing process, they increase the likelihood of producing polished, well-written memoirs.

Study the Model
(Student pages 13–15)

Explain that Student pages 13–15 show how the writing model on Student page 11 meets all six traits of the rubric. Read each section with the students. Then, have them look for other examples of each trait in the writing model.

Ask students how many check marks they would assign the writing model for each trait. Then, as a class, decide how the writing model should be rated overall.

Remind students to use the rubric as they write their own memoir, to be sure they are meeting all six writing traits.

Memoir

• Details bring the story to life.

Manny makes his story interesting by using specific details to describe his experience. In this paragraph, he not only tells his readers that he was waiting for the Millers, he also shows them. He uses specific images and details to express his fear and nervousness.

> [from the writing model]
>
> But when that fateful Friday afternoon arrived, all I wanted to do was hole myself up under my bedcovers and disappear. My heart was filled with dread, and my backpack was stuffed with city comforts. If the bathroom sink had fit, I totally would've crammed it in!

Word Choice/ Clarity

• Word choice is varied.

Manny uses a wide variety of words so that he doesn't bore his reader with repetitive language. In this passage, he could have written *It was getting dark*. But I like what he chose much better.

> [from the writing model]
>
> Finally, Mr. Miller parked the car, and we unpacked all the stuff. Twilight was descending.

Sentence Fluency

• Well-chosen questions build suspense throughout.

There are plenty of ways to keep the action moving and build suspense in a story. Sometimes it helps to use a question, which can act as a cliff-hanger. This leaves the reader wondering what will happen next. In the passage below, Manny uses a question to make the reader wonder if he will really try and walk back to the city.

> [from the writing model]
>
> A question popped into my head: "Could I make it back to the city on foot?"

Grammar/ Mechanics

• Spelling, punctuation, and capitalization are correct. Simple and perfect tense are used correctly.

When describing a series of events, it's important to use the correct verb tense so that readers can tell when things really happened. Manny begins this paragraph in the simple past tense, but then he uses the past perfect tense *had loosened* to show how his stomach settled before he began enjoying himself.

> [from the writing model]
>
> As we sat by the fire, we toasted marshmallows and sang campfire songs. It was then that I noticed the knot in my stomach had loosened. I was actually beginning to enjoy this!

My Turn! I'm going to write a memoir about an important experience in my own life. I'll make sure to follow the rubric and use good writing strategies. Keep reading to see how I do it!

Differentiating Instruction

Support Discuss with students how two traits from the rubric—sequencing and using well-chosen questions to build suspense—can work together in crafting a good memoir. First, ask students to describe some of the ways they might sequence a memoir. Make sure they understand the following organizational forms:

• chronological, or time order
• chronology with flashbacks
• compare and contrast
• order of importance

Note that sequencing events in chronological order—with or without flashbacks—is probably the most common way to structure a narrative.

Next, write the following questions on the board:

What would Dad say when I told him?
What was I going to do next?

Ask students how the questions might work in building a narrative sequence. **Possible response: The questions might act as cliffhangers, making readers want to find out what will happen next.** Remind students to use well-chosen questions to build sequence and suspense in their own memoirs.

Writing a Memoir

Prewriting Gather Information

Information/Organization The memoir is focused on one major life experience.

Writing Strategy Jot down notes about a major life experience.

When I found out I'd be writing a memoir, I realized there are a bunch of ideas to choose from. I could write about the first time I saw a major league baseball game or about the time I helped build houses for the homeless. But those are memories from a while ago. I think I'll write about a recent rainy weekend at my family's lake house instead. At the time, I had no idea the experience would turn out to be so memorable. And since my classmates are my audience, I think they'll appreciate the unexpected message of my memoir. I'll begin by brainstorming some notes.

My Notes About the Lake House
- ✔ family goes there on weekends and vacations
- ✔ usually swim, canoe, relax on beach, barbecue
- ✔ disappointing rainy weather—boredom and bickering
- ✔ did puzzles, read, wrote
- ✔ found an old photo album
- ✔ pictures included woman in red dress, grandparents' wedding, lake house

Practice!

Now it's your turn. Choose an experience to write about. Jot down notes about the things you remember the most.

Prewriting Organize Ideas

Information/Organization The memoir is well sequenced.

Writing Strategy Use a Story Frame to sequence events.

Writer's Term
Story Frame
Use a **Story Frame** to sequence important story elements such as setting, introduction, rising/falling action, climax, and resolution.

The rubric says my memoir should be well sequenced. I'll use a Story Frame to help me organize ideas. As I write, it will serve as an outline of events.

Story Frame	
Setting:	My family's lake house
Introduction:	My family needed a getaway; we went to the lake house to relax.
Rising Action (Event 1):	It rains.
Rising Action (Event 2):	I'm disappointed, but I keep busy by writing in my journal, doing a puzzle, and reading.
Rising Action (Event 3):	The next day brings more rain.
Climax:	I find an old photo album.
Falling Action (Event 1):	My family enjoys viewing photos together.
Resolution:	I realize that the rain has caused us to reconnect and enjoy each other's company.

Practice!

Now it's your turn. Use a Story Frame to sequence the events of your memoir.

Reflect
Is my topic interesting? Will my Story Frame help me sequence events as I write?

Prewriting
(Student pages 16–17)

Ask volunteers to describe a memorable experience, and to explain why it's memorable. Point out that a good memoir fulfills two purposes: it tells an interesting story and it reflects upon something meaningful.

Now, point out Ashley's notes on Student page 16. Remind students that writers are not limited to their notes, and that Ashley may think of more details—or delete a few—as she drafts her memoir. Tell students that they will structure their memoir notes into a Story Frame after they have reviewed Ashley's Story Frame on Student page 17.

More Practice!

For more practice with these writing strategies, you may wish to have students use the Strategy Practice Book. See the appendix for annotated Strategy Practice Book pages.

Differentiating Instruction

English-Language Learners Have these students brainstorm memoir ideas by working in pairs or small groups with English-proficient classmates. Suggest that they use the following category prompts to help jog their memories: family, friends, school, interests/hobbies.

Have students jot down notes related to each category. Then, suggest that they add other categories if they wish. Finally, have them pick one idea to explore by freewriting, or by discussing it with partners or the group.

WORK with a PARTNER
Have students work in pairs to brainstorm memoir topics. Then, have them share stories and brainstorm details, choosing the best ones for their drafts.

Writing a Memoir

Drafting Write a Draft

Voice/Audience A reflective tone conveys meaning and insight to the reader.

Writing Strategy Use a reflective tone to convey meaning and insight to the reader.

Writer's Term

Tone

Tone reflects the author's attitude or manner of expression. It's how the writing sounds. Tone can be funny, sarcastic, or even sad, but it should match the writer's purpose. A writer can use a **reflective tone** to express meaning and insight.

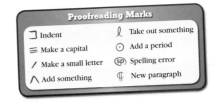

Now I'll use my Story Frame to help me write. The rubric says I should use a reflective tone to express meaning, so I'll try to be thoughtful about the experience I'm describing.

I'll do my best with spelling and grammar. However, I plan to concentrate more on the big picture and worry about mistakes later. I can always fix those when I revise. Read the beginning of my draft on the next page.

Proofreading Marks

⏋ Indent	ℓ Take out something
≡ Make a capital	⊙ Add a period
/ Make a small letter	(SP) Spelling error
∧ Add something	¶ New paragraph

[DRAFT]

Rained In

by Ashley

It had been a long, hectic September, so I was thrilled when I heard we would be spending the weekend at our lake house. I couldn't wait to relax on the beach, go canoeing, and eat barbeque. But when we arrived it was raining.

This was a big drag. But I tried not to let it get me down. I spent the day writing in my journal and putting together a 300-piece dinosaur puzzle. When I snapped at my little brother, Steve, Mom asked me what was wrong.

"Hello! It's raining!"   [used a reflective tone]

"Don't worry, Ashley. There's always tomorrow," said Mom.

Practice!

Now it's your turn. Use a reflective tone so that your readers understand how you feel.

Reflect

Is my tone thoughtful enough? Will it help my readers understand how I feel?

18 Narrative Writing ■ Memoir

Narrative Writing ■ Memoir 19

Drafting
(Student pages 18–19)

Remind students that drafting is a chance to get ideas on paper without having to worry about making mistakes.

Read aloud Ashley's words on Student page 18. Then, read the section of her draft on Student page 19. Refer to the Practice and the Reflect boxes on Student page 19, which remind students to use a reflective tone as they write. Ask whether Ashley used a reflective tone on Student page 19. **yes** Have students find more words in her draft (other than those already highlighted) that illustrate her tone. Also discuss whether Ashley's draft includes details from her Story Frame. Then, have students use the events in their Story Frames to draft their memoirs.

Point out that Ashley repeatedly refers to the rubric as she writes. Encourage students to get into the habit of using the rubric to help guide their own writing.

Writing Across the Curriculum

Literature Students may benefit from reading sample memoirs. Look through your own class library, or search the Internet for a variety of appropriate titles. After students have read a few different samples, discuss possible memoir styles, formats, and themes that they could use in their own drafts.

Include in the discussion students' opinions about the memoirs they have read, including which style they enjoyed best, which story was the most interesting, and which author's work they would like to read more of.

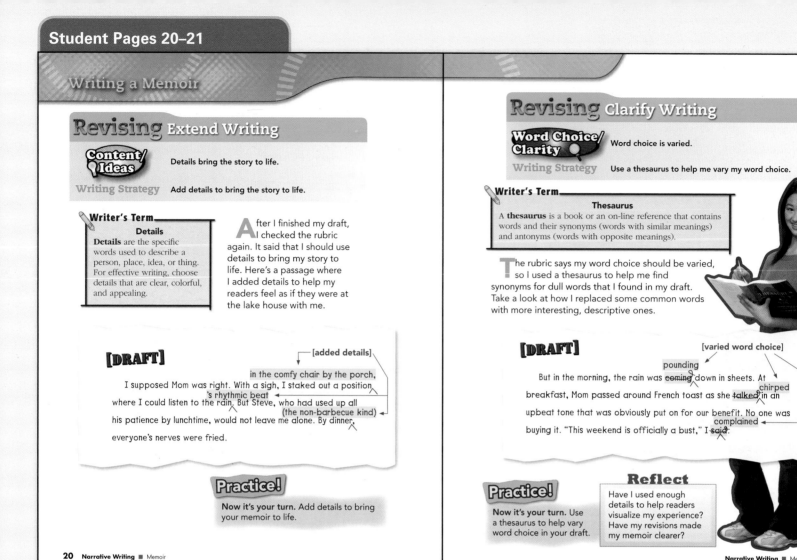

Writing a Memoir

Revising Extend Writing

Content/Ideas Details bring the story to life.

Writing Strategy Add details to bring the story to life.

Writer's Term

Details
Details are the specific words used to describe a person, place, idea, or thing. For effective writing, choose details that are clear, colorful, and appealing.

After I finished my draft, I checked the rubric again. It said that I should use details to bring my story to life. Here's a passage where I added details to help my readers feel as if they were at the lake house with me.

[DRAFT]

[added details]

I supposed Mom was right. With a sigh, I staked out a position in the comfy chair by the porch, where I could listen to the rain's rhythmic beat. But Steve, who had used up all his patience by lunchtime, would not leave me alone (the non-barbecue kind). By dinner, everyone's nerves were fried.

Practice!
Now it's your turn. Add details to bring your memoir to life.

20 **Narrative Writing** ■ Memoir

Revising Clarify Writing

Word Choice/Clarity Word choice is varied.

Writing Strategy Use a thesaurus to help me vary my word choice.

Writer's Term

Thesaurus
A **thesaurus** is a book or an on-line reference that contains words and their synonyms (words with similar meanings) and antonyms (words with opposite meanings).

The rubric says my word choice should be varied, so I used a thesaurus to help me find synonyms for dull words that I found in my draft. Take a look at how I replaced some common words with more interesting, descriptive ones.

[DRAFT]

[varied word choice]

But in the morning, the rain was ~~coming~~ pounding down in sheets. At breakfast, Mom passed around French toast as she ~~talked~~ chirped in an upbeat tone that was obviously put on for our benefit. No one was buying it. "This weekend is officially a bust," I ~~said~~ complained.

Practice!
Now it's your turn. Use a thesaurus to help vary word choice in your draft.

Reflect
Have I used enough details to help readers visualize my experience? Have my revisions made my memoir clearer?

Narrative Writing ■ Memoir 21

Revising

(Student pages 20–21)

Write the word *detail* on the board and ask students to offer synonyms for it. **Possible responses: feature, component, element, fact, aspect, point, item, specification** Explain that details help writers bring stories to life because they enable readers to visualize. Highlight this point by writing the following sentence on the board: *Dad pulled into the driveway in our new car.* Ask students if this sentence helps them visualize anything specific about the scene. Then, invite them to suggest details that could help bring this scene to life. **Possible responses: green SUV; blue Mustang; red convertible; black luxury sedan** Tell students to note how Ashley added details to her draft on Student page 20. Then, have them add details to their memoirs to help bring their writing to life.

Now, turn students' attention to the revisions Ashley made to her draft on Student page 21. Ask why she replaced the deleted words with the highlighted words. **Possible response: because the new words are more specific** Challenge students to come up with other words

Ashley might have used to replace each deleted word. Have them use a thesaurus if necessary. Then, have them replace common words with specific words to add variety and interest to their own drafts.

Differentiating Instruction

English-Language Learners When using a thesaurus, some students may be confused by the number of synonym categories listed under each keyword. To make sure students select appropriate synonyms, write the following on the board.

Main Entry: pass
Part of Speech: noun

Main Entry: pass
Part of Speech: verb

Point out the word *passed* in Ashley's draft on Student page 21. Then, have students choose the correct entry listed on the board and use it to find a synonym for *passed*. To choose correctly, they should look up the verb form of the word, choose from the synonyms listed, and then form the past tense of the chosen synonym.

Writing a Memoir

Editing Check Sentences

Sentence Fluency

Well-chosen questions build suspense throughout.

Writing Strategy Use questions to build suspense.

Now I have to edit my writing. The rubric says I should use well-chosen questions to build suspense. At first, I was confused about how to do this, but then I remembered a mystery novel I once read. Each time the author used a question at the end of a paragraph or a chapter, it made me want to read on to find out the answer. Now that I think about it, I can use a question to help build suspense right before the climax of my memoir.

[DRAFT]
[used a question to build suspense]

How was I going to get through another soggy day? ~~I couldn't make it through another day.~~ I plopped on the floor next to the bookcase and looked for something to read.

Practice!
Now it's your turn. Use questions to make your reader wonder what will happen next.

Editing Proofread Writing

Grammar/Mechanics

Spelling, punctuation, and capitalization are correct. Simple and perfect tense are used correctly.

Writing Strategy Make sure that simple and perfect tense are used correctly.

✎ Writer's Term___
Simple Tense/Perfect Tense
The **simple tense** tells what happens in the present, what happened in the past, and what will happen in the future. The **perfect tense** tells what started in the past and is still happening, what began in the past and was completed, and what will begin and end in the future.

Now I'll check for errors in grammar and mechanics. Also, the rubric says I should make sure that simple and perfect tense are used correctly. When I reviewed my draft, I found some errors, so I think I'll fix them now.

[DRAFT]
photo
[corrected past perfect tense]
└─► had

"I see you found the ~~foto~~ album," said Mom. She seen me take out a thick, leather-bound book.
[changed past perfect to simple past tense] ─► fell
As I leafed through the pictures, my eyes ~~had fallen~~ on a striking girl in a red dress. "Who's this, Mom? She's beautiful."

Practice!
Now it's your turn. Edit for errors in grammar and mechanics, making sure that simple and perfect tense are also used correctly.

Grammar/Mechanics
For more practice with simple and perfect tense, use the exercises on the next two pages.

Reflect
I added a question to build suspense. Did it work? Do my edits make sense?

Editing
(Student pages 22–23)

Call students' attention to the edits Ashley made to her draft on Student page 22. Ask a volunteer to describe how she edited the deleted sentence. **Possible response: She formed a question to build suspense.** Then, have students check their memoirs for places where they could add or form questions to help build suspense.

Now, point out the Writer's Term box on Student page 23, and ask a volunteer to read it aloud. Then, have students note how Ashley edited two sentences for correct use of the simple and perfect tense on the same page. Ask students what Ashley corrected in the first verb-tense edit. **Possible response: She added the helping verb** *had.* Then, have them point out how she made the second verb-tense edit. **She deleted the past perfect** *had fallen* **and added the simple past** *fell.* Have students check their drafts to make sure they have used simple and perfect tense verbs correctly. Remind them that they should also check for proper spelling, capitalization, and punctuation.

If any of your students are having trouble understanding the simple and perfect verb tense, you may wish to teach the Mini-Lesson on pages 34–35 of this Teacher Edition. Then, have students complete the exercises on pages 24–25 of their books. Review the answers and possible rewrites with them.

WORK with a PARTNER Have pairs of students read one another's drafts, using sticky notes to mark errors in spelling, punctuation, and grammar. Then, tell students to perform a second read that focuses on the editing strategies they learned in this chapter.

Simple and Perfect Tense

KNOW the RULE

- The **simple present tense** tells what happens now.
  Example: Beth and her dog **walk** to the river.
- The **simple past tense** tells what happened in the past. In most cases, add *–ed* to the end of a simple present tense verb.
  Example: Beth **walked** to the river yesterday.
- The **simple future tense** tells what will happen in the future. Add the helping verb *will* to a simple present tense verb.
  Example: Beth **will walk** to the river tomorrow.
- The **present perfect tense** tells what began in the past and may still be happening. Add the helping verb *has or have* to a simple past tense verb.
  Example: Beth **has walked** to the river many times.
- The **past perfect tense** tells what began in the past and was completed. Add the helping verb *had* to a simple past tense verb.
  Example: Beth **had walked** to the river many times.
- The **future perfect tense** tells what will begin in the future and end in the future. Add the helping verb *will* to a present perfect tense verb.
  Example: Beth **will have walked** many times by the week's end.

Practice the Rule

On a separate sheet of paper, write the verb in parentheses that correctly completes each sentence.

1. Yesterday, Mom (need/needed) almost a dozen eggs to make breakfast.
2. If the rain (stopped/had stopped), we could have gone swimming.
3. Viewing photos (has made/will have made) my family closer.
4. We (have vacationed/vacation) at the lake house many times.
5. By the week's end, we (have learned/had learned) the value of family.

Apply the Rule

Read the following memoir, looking for simple/perfect tense errors. Then, rewrite the story correctly on another sheet of paper.

Dog Business

My mom suggested that I start my own dog-walking business, so I posted over a hundred flyers around town and waited for a call.

Then, Mrs. Gould call and ask me to walk her little dog, Lucy. By the time we hung up, Mrs. Gould and I agree on a fee. We also have discussed where I should walk Lucy.

I was really happy with my job, so it was great to hear from Joey Danes. He will have owned two 100-pound golden retrievers. I would have to walk three dogs at once, but I knew I could do it.

The next day, Lucy and I pick up Rover and Arnold, and I immediately realized what I have gotten myself into. Each dog wanted to go a different route. As we were entering the park, a family of ducks came by, stealing the attention of both Rover and Arnold. Holding on for dear life, I had picked up Lucy and tried desperately to keep up with the retrievers, but they sprint after the ducks. Unfortunately, we were headed straight for the pond. Before I could control the situation, we were all soak!

Now, I know they say you can't teach an old dog new tricks, but by the time I get this business up and running, I'm sure I will learn all kinds of old tricks from new dogs!

(Student pages 24–25)

Simple and Perfect Tense

Write the following sentences on the board:

My sister plays the flute in the school band.
My sister has played the flute since the third grade.

Ask students to describe what is different about the two sentences. **Possible response: The first sentence tells what is happening in the present; the second sentence tells about something that began in the past and is still happening.** Explain that the first sentence is written in the simple present tense and the second is written in the present perfect tense.

Review the simple and perfect tense by repeating the above process with the following sentences. (For your reference, the correct verb tense has been included in parentheses following each sentence.)

My sister played the flute in yesterday's concert. (simple past)
My sister had played the flute in two previous concerts. (past perfect)
My sister will play the flute at the Spring Fair. (simple future)
My sister will have played the flute for five years next week. (future perfect)

Remind students that when checking their writing for proper use of simple and perfect tense, they should think about when the action happens over time to help them decide whether they have used verbs correctly.

Answers for Practice the Rule

1. needed
2. had stopped
3. has made
4. have vacationed
5. had learned

(Answers continue on page 35.)

 For more practice with grammar/mechanics skills, see Zaner-Bloser's *G.U.M.* materials.

Writing a Memoir

Publishing Share Writing

Publish my memoir in a class journal.

Now that I've finished my memoir, I need to think about how to publish it. I could post my story on a Web page or read it to a classmate, but I'd really like to publish it in our class journal. That way, all of my classmates can read it. First, I'll read through it one last time to make sure it includes all of the items on my checklist.

My Checklist

✓ The memoir focuses on one experience.
✓ It has a clear sequence of events.
✓ A reflective tone adds meaning.
✓ Details make the memoir lively.
✓ Word choice is varied.
✓ Spelling, capitalization, and punctuation are correct. Simple and perfect tense verbs are used correctly.

Practice!

Now it's your turn. Make a checklist to check your memoir. Then, make a final draft to publish.

Rained In
by Ashley

It had been a long, hectic September, so I was thrilled when I heard we would be spending the weekend at our lake house. I couldn't wait to relax on the beach, go canoeing, and eat barbecue. But when we arrived, it was raining.

This was a big drag. But I tried not to let it get me down. I spent the day writing in my journal and putting together a 300-piece dinosaur puzzle. When I snapped at my little brother, Steve, Mom asked me what was wrong.

"Hello! It's raining!"

"Don't worry, Ashley. There's always tomorrow," said Mom.

I supposed Mom was right. With a sigh, I staked out a position in the comfy chair by the porch, where I could listen to the rain's rhythmic beat. But Steve, who had used up all his patience by lunchtime, would not leave me alone. By dinner (the non-barbecue kind), everyone's nerves were fried. As I tucked myself into bed, I hoped for clear skies the next day.

But in the morning, the rain was pounding down in sheets. At breakfast, Mom passed around French toast as she chirped in an upbeat tone that was obviously put on for our benefit. No one was buying it. "This weekend is officially a bust," I complained. How was I going to get through another soggy day? I plopped on the floor next to the bookcase and looked for something to read.

"I see you found the photo album," said Mom. She had seen me take out a thick, leather-bound book.

As I leafed through the pictures, my eyes fell on a striking girl in a red dress. "Who's this, Mom? She's beautiful."

My mother laughed, "Well thank you, dear. That's me."

"Get out of town!" I said in disbelief. But it was Mom, posing in her prom dress. She told me she had shopped for weeks without finding anything she liked. Then, my grandmother brought down the red dress from the attic—and it was perfect.

We settled on the couch, and soon, we were joined by Dad and Steve. Slowly, we flipped through the album, savoring each page. Each photograph held a story, a piece of our family's past. Finally, peace settled over us, and we were able to enjoy the rest of the day inside, in each other's company.

As we drove home that night, I realized we not only went to the lake house to discover the open space of the outdoors, we also went to discover each other.

Reflect

Did I use all of the traits of a good memoir? Check it against the rubric, and don't forget to use the rubric to check your own memoir, too.

(Answers continued from page 34.)

Answers for Apply the Rule
Dog Business

My mom suggested that I start my own dog-walking business, so I posted over a hundred flyers around town and waited for a call.

Then, Mrs. Gould called and asked me to walk her little dog, Lucy. By the time we hung up, Mrs. Gould and I had agreed on a fee. We also had discussed where I should walk Lucy.

I was really happy with my job, so it was great to hear from Joey Danes. He owns two 100-pound golden retrievers. I would have to walk three dogs at once, but I knew I could do it.

The next day, Lucy and I picked up Rover and Arnold, and I immediately realized what I had gotten myself into. Each dog wanted to go a different route. As we were entering the park, a family of ducks came by, stealing the attention of both Rover and Arnold. Holding on for dear life, I picked up Lucy and tried desperately to keep up with the retrievers, but they sprinted after the ducks.

Unfortunately, we were headed straight for the pond. Before I could control the situation, we were all soaked!

Now, I know they say you can't teach an old dog new tricks, but by the time I get this business up and running, I'm sure I will have learned all kinds of old tricks from new dogs!

Publishing
(Student pages 26–27)

Ask students if they like Ashley's choice for sharing her memoir. Tell the class that her choice is not the only option for publishing her work. Invite students to name other ways they could publish their own memoirs.

Have each student make a checklist and perform a final evaluation of his or her memoir before publishing it. Encourage students to share copies of their memoirs with friends and relatives who might be interested in reading about what they wrote.

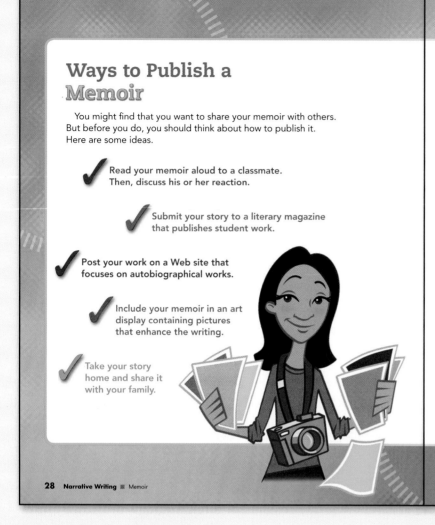

Ways to Publish a Memoir

You might find that you want to share your memoir with others. But before you do, you should think about how to publish it. Here are some ideas.

✓ Read your memoir aloud to a classmate. Then, discuss his or her reaction.

✓ Submit your story to a literary magazine that publishes student work.

✓ Post your work on a Web site that focuses on autobiographical works.

✓ Include your memoir in an art display containing pictures that enhance the writing.

✓ Take your story home and share it with your family.

Writing Across the Content Areas Memoir

Your school subjects can be a great source of writing ideas. Choose a subject and see what topics you can come up with. Here are some examples.

Science
• Write about a memorable nature hike or other outdoor activity.
• Describe a time when violent weather affected you in some way.

Art and/or Music
• Have you ever attended a live music concert? Share your experience.
• Write about a time when you created a piece of art or wrote a piece of music.

Math
• Describe what you would do if you received a gift of money.
• Write about a time when you studied particularly hard for a math test and it paid off.

Ways to Publish
(Student page 28)

Read and discuss with students the different publishing options listed on Student page 28. Encourage students to consider some of these options when publishing their own writing. Remind students that Ashley chose to publish her memoir by including it in a class journal, but they can choose their own way of publishing. Perhaps one student will want to submit his or her memoir to a literary magazine that publishes student work, while another will want to include it in an art display.

Writing Across the Content Areas
(Student page 29)

Explain to students that writing is not just for English or language arts class. Many other school subjects contain ideas, issues, and events that students may want to write about. Encourage students to consider using one of the content areas listed on Student page 29 as a springboard for more writing options. Students may also wish to consult with other teachers for more ideas on writing in the content areas.

Books for Professional Development

Behrman, Carol H. *Ready-to-Use Writing Proficiency Lessons and Activities: 8th Grade Level.* **San Francisco: Jossey-Bass, 2003.**

This book gives classroom teachers and language arts specialists a powerful and effective tool for addressing curriculum standards and competencies at the eighth-grade level and preparing their students for comprehensive assessment testing.

Mooney, Margaret E., and Terrell A. Young, eds. *Caught in the Spell of Writing and Reading: Grade 3 and Beyond.* **Katonah: Richard C. Owens, 2006.**

Based on their classroom and leadership experiences, seven experienced educators from the United States, New Zealand, and Australia share new perspective on what it means to write in the intermediate and middle school realm. The authors' practical insights about effective techniques for assessing and instructing bring clarity to what it means to engage, inspire, and instruct writers and readers in today's and tomorrow's classrooms.

Brusko, Mike. *Writing Rules! Teaching Kids to Write for Life, Grades 4–8.* **Beeline Ser. Portsmouth: Heinemann, 1999.**

The author focuses on the writing skills that students need in everyday life. He pays special attention to clarifying the purpose for writing and getting the reader's attention.

Portalupi, JoAnn, and Ralph Fletcher. *Nonfiction Craft Lessons: Teaching Information Writing K–8.* **Portland: Stenhouse, 2001.**

Portalupi and Fletcher present a series of one-page descriptions of strategies that address all aspects of the writing process. Focusing on informative writing in general, the book includes some lessons specific to persuasion, comparison, and how-to writing.

Historical Episode Overview

In this chapter, students will learn how to write a historical episode. They will learn the different elements of a historical episode—setting, characters, dialogue, and theme—and some reasons why they might choose to write one. Students will then use a historical episode rubric to study a model writing sample.

Students will follow the student guide as she goes through the writing stages—prewriting, drafting, revising, editing, and publishing. As the student guide learns new writing strategies in each step, students will be directed to practice the strategies in their own writing.

During prewriting and drafting, students will
- choose a historical event.
- gather information from several resources.
- organize story elements on a Story Map.
- clearly describe the setting and theme.

During revising and editing, students will
- add historical details.
- make sure dialogue reflects the time and place in which their characters live.
- vary sentence length.
- edit their drafts for spelling, capitalization, and correct use of dialogue punctuation.

Finally, students will publish a final draft.

You may wish to send to families the School-Home Connection Letter for this chapter, located at the end of this unit in the Teacher Edition.

Historical Episode Writing Traits

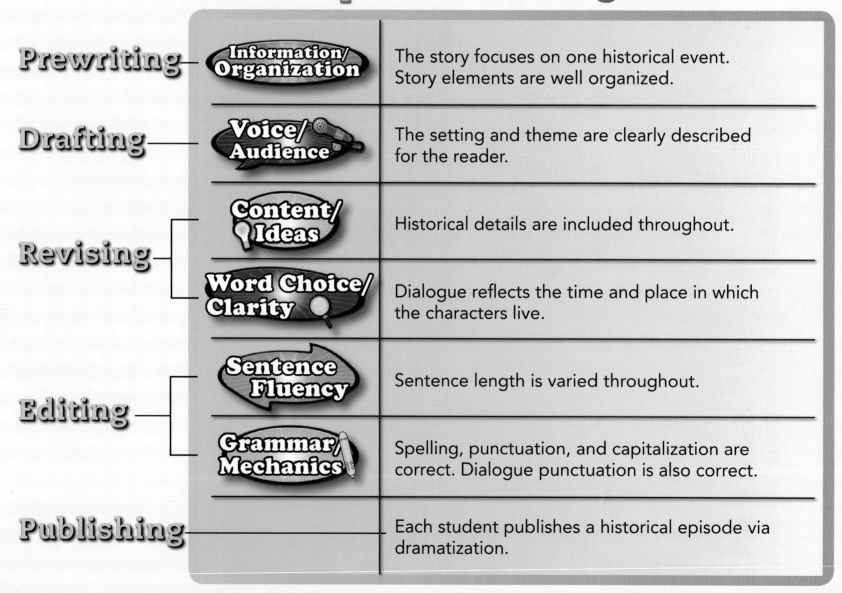

Stage	Trait	Description
Prewriting	Information/Organization	The story focuses on one historical event. Story elements are well organized.
Drafting	Voice/Audience	The setting and theme are clearly described for the reader.
Revising	Content/Ideas	Historical details are included throughout.
	Word Choice/Clarity	Dialogue reflects the time and place in which the characters live.
Editing	Sentence Fluency	Sentence length is varied throughout.
	Grammar/Mechanics	Spelling, punctuation, and capitalization are correct. Dialogue punctuation is also correct.
Publishing		Each student publishes a historical episode via dramatization.

Historical Episode Time Management

WEEK 1

Day 1	Day 2	Day 3	Day 4	Day 5
Learning Objectives				
Students will: • learn the components of a historical episode.	Students will: • learn how to gather information for a historical episode.	Students will: • practice gathering information for their own historical episodes.	Students will: • learn how to make a Story Map to organize story elements.	Students will: • practice organizing story elements into a Story Map.
Activities				
• Discuss the elements and traits of a historical episode (Student pages 30–32). • Use the rubric to study the model (Student pages 33–37).	• Read and discuss **Prewriting: Gather Information** (Student page 38).	• Brainstorm ideas and choose one historical event. • Gather information from several resources, including the Internet and primary sources.	• Read and discuss **Prewriting: Organize Ideas** (Student page 39).	• Review the notes taken while gathering information. • Make a Story Map to organize story elements.

WEEK 2

Day 1	Day 2	Day 3	Day 4	Day 5
Learning Objectives				
Students will: • learn how to clearly describe the setting and theme for the reader.	Students will: • practice writing their drafts.	Students will: • learn how to add historical details.	Students will: • practice adding historical details to their drafts.	Students will: • learn how to write dialogue that reflects a specific time and place.
Activities				
• Read and discuss **Drafting: Write a Draft** (Student pages 40–41).	• Use a Story Map to write a draft. • Describe the setting and theme for the reader.	• Read and discuss **Revising: Extend Writing** (Student page 42).	• Add historical details.	• Read and discuss **Revising: Clarify Writing** (Student page 43).

WEEK 3

Day 1	Day 2	Day 3	Day 4	Day 5
Learning Objectives				
Students will: • practice writing dialogue that reflects a specific time and place.	Students will: • learn how to vary sentence length.	Students will: • learn how to punctuate dialogue correctly.	Students will: • practice editing their drafts for spelling, capitalization, and dialogue punctuation.	Students will: • learn different ways to publish their historical episodes.
Activities				
• Reread drafts, making sure dialogue reflects a specific time and place.	• Read and discuss **Editing: Check Sentences** (Student page 44). • Make sure to vary sentence length.	• Read and discuss **Editing: Proofread Writing** (Student page 45).	• Fix any spelling, capitalization, or punctuation errors. • Fix any dialogue that is not punctuated correctly.	• Read and discuss **Publishing: Share Writing** (Student page 48).

* To complete the chapter in fewer days, teach the learning objectives and activities for two days in one day.
This planning chart, correlated to your state's writing standards, is available on-line at http://www.zaner-bloser.com/sfw.

Define the Genre

(Student page 30)

Historical Episode

Discuss with students the definition of a historical episode. Ask students whether any of them have ever written about something that happened in another historical era. **Possible response: yes** Point out that any time they base stories on historical events that actually happened, they are using the historical episode genre.

Elements of the Genre

Historical Episode

Read and discuss with students the various elements of a historical episode. Ask volunteers which elements are also common to other forms of writing. **Possible responses: Setting—fiction, memoir; Characters—essay, biography; Dialogue—short story, fantasy; Theme—poetry, essay** Discuss why each element may be important to writing a historical episode.

Authentic Writing

(Student page 31)

Historical Episode

Read and discuss with students the reasons for writing a historical episode listed on Student page 31. Point out that all writing has a purpose and is aimed at a specific audience. These authentic purposes help authors shape their writing. Ask a volunteer to read aloud the Entertainment box. Then, have students discuss other reasons why someone might write a historical episode for entertainment. Repeat this process for the Information and Make Connections boxes. Then, have students brainstorm other purposes for writing a historical episode that are not listed on Student page 31. Encourage students to think about their own reasons for writing a historical episode, and how these reasons will affect the tone and focus of their writing.

Historical Episode Writing Traits

I know that there are six traits of good writing. But what makes a good historical episode? I'll use this list to help me write.

Information/ Organization	The story focuses on one historical event. Story elements are well organized.
Voice/ Audience	The setting and theme are clearly described for the reader.
Content/ Ideas	Historical details are included throughout.
Word Choice/ Clarity	Dialogue reflects the time and place in which the characters live.
Sentence Fluency	Sentence length is varied throughout.
Grammar/ Mechanics	Spelling, punctuation, and capitalization are correct. Dialogue punctuation is also correct.

I can use Carrie Taylor's historical episode on the next page as a model for my own writing. Later, we'll check out how Carrie used the traits to help her write.

Historical Episode Model

Edie's Other Engagement
by Carrie Taylor

Characters — *Setting*

Theme

"Edie, you must be dreaming!" cried Hank. "This is America in 1943! No matter what you want, they'll never let women fly planes in this war. No, Edie, I won't allow it. No fiancée of mine is going to be a World War II Fly Girl."

"Well, Hank," said Edie, "I agree with you on two things. First, I *am* dreaming. I'm dreaming of the day that I graduate from Women Airforce Service Pilot training and get my pilot's wings. And second, you're right: No fiancée of yours is going to be a pilot in the war. If you're not going to support me in this, I'll just have to do it alone."

Dialogue

"Then I guess this is it, Edie," Hank said slowly. "I'm very sorry. But I want my wife at home, not on a plane!"

"Then this is good-bye," sighed Edie. "I leave tomorrow for flight school. I'll always remember you, Hank. I hope you'll understand someday."

It's hard to believe that was almost six months ago. Poor Hank. I miss him sometimes. But I wasn't about to let him tell me that I couldn't follow my dream. And now, can you believe it? I've finished my WASP training, and I'm graduating. Today—December 17, 1943—I will finally get my wings.

I always dreamed I would fly someday. And now I'll have the chance. My mission now is to join other women in ferrying planes to bases across the United States so that our male pilots, who are badly needed at the front, will be released from ferrying duties. Just imagine my excitement!

When I applied to be a Woman Airforce Service Pilot, I thought I didn't stand a chance. Thank goodness my parents didn't feel the same way as Hank. No, Mother and Dad were right there behind me, cheering me on. And now it is graduation day. If only Hank were here to see me now. But wait a minute—there he is!

"Edie, I'm so proud of you," cried Hank. "Now, how about putting this engagement ring back on? It goes perfectly with your new wings."

"No, Hank," said Edie. "I'm afraid that my only engagement right now is with the U.S. Air Force. It's too bad you couldn't be with me when I really needed your support. I think I'll fly solo for a while."

Writing Traits

(Student pages 32–33)

Historical Episode

Explain to students that a historical episode focuses on the past, contains a mix of fact and fiction, features a mix of real and imagined people and events, and contains dialogue.

Make sure students understand that unless they are familiar with certain historical people and events, they may need to ask questions or conduct research to figure out what is fact and what is fiction. Also note that because it tells a narrative story, a historical episode may be an interesting and effective way to learn about history.

Tell students that they are going to study and use strategies for writing historical episodes, and that a good historical episode has the traits listed on Student page 32. Then, ask students to listen for these traits as you read aloud "Edie's Other Engagement" on Student page 33.

Differentiating Instruction

English-Language Learners **Preteach** examples of wordplay that might cause difficulty for these students. Read the model aloud, stopping at each of the following phrases. Have students use context to try figuring out what each one means.

- " . . . *you must be dreaming!"*
  "I'm dreaming of the day that I graduate . . ."

The first phrase is an idiom meaning "That's impossible!" The second phrase uses the literal meaning of *dreaming*, "imagining."

- *"Now, how about putting this engagement ring back on?"*
  "I'm afraid that my only engagement right now is with the U.S. Air Force."

These two sentences play on two different meanings of *engagement*: "an agreement for marriage" and "an appointment or arrangement."

- *"I think I'll fly solo for a while."*

Here the phrase *fly solo* expresses two things at the same time: the literal meaning "pilot alone" and the figurative meaning "be independent."

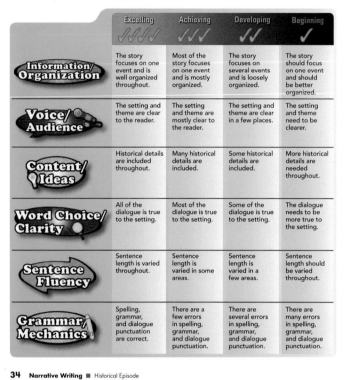

Using the Rubric
(Student page 34)

Explain that a rubric is a tool that can be used to evaluate a piece of writing. The rubric on Student page 34 can be used to evaluate a historical episode. It is based on the same historical episode traits listed on Student page 32.

Now point out the terms above each rubric column: *Excelling, Achieving, Developing,* and *Beginning.* Explain that each column symbolizes a degree of writing skill, and that each rubric row focuses on a specific writing trait. When students use the rubric to evaluate their own work at each step of the writing process, they increase the likelihood of producing polished, well-written historical episodes.

Historical Episode
Using the Rubric to Study the Model

Now, let's use the rubric to check Carrie Taylor's historical episode, Ed ie's Other Engagement." How many check marks would you give Carrie for each trait?

Information/Organization
- The story focuses on one historical event.
- Story elements are well organized.

Carrie introduces the major story event—Edie's decision to become an air force pilot—in the opening paragraph. This decision causes conflict with her fiancé and leads to other story events.

[from the writing model]

" . . . No, Edie, I won't allow it. No fiancée of mine is going to be a World War II Fly Girl."

Voice/Audience
- The setting and theme are clearly described for the reader.

Carrie lets the reader know the theme and setting of the story right at the start. Notice how Hank's opening dialogue names the setting (America in 1943) and hints at the theme (women's place on the front lines).

[from the writing model]

"Edie, you must be dreaming!" cried Hank. "This is America in 1943! No matter what you want, they'll never let women fly planes in this war. . . ."

Study the Model
(Student pages 35–37)

Explain that Student pages 35–37 show how the writing model on Student page 33 meets all six traits of the rubric. Read each section with the students. Have them look for other examples of each trait in the writing model.

Ask students how many check marks they would assign the writing model for each trait. Then, as a class, decide how the writing model should be rated overall.

Remind students to use the rubric as they write their own historical episodes, to be sure they are meeting all six writing traits.

Historical Episode

 **Content/Ideas** • Historical details are included throughout.

Carrie includes a lot of historical details that make the reader believe the story really happened. Although it's fiction, the reader learns these real-life details along the way: World War II was going on in 1943, and women pilots were called Fly Girls, WASPs, or Woman Airforce Service Pilots. At graduation, they were given wing-shaped pins.

[from the writing model]

I've finished my WASP training, and I'm graduating. Today—December 17, 1943—I will finally get my wings.

Word Choice/Clarity • Dialogue reflects the time and place in which the characters live.

Carrie's characters sound real because they talk like people who lived during World War II. Americans probably didn't speak much differently in 1943 than they do today. But if you read Hank's words below, you'll see how they reflect an old-fashioned attitude.

[from the writing model]

"Then I guess this is it, Edie," Hank said slowly. "I'm very sorry. But I want my wife at home, not on a plane!"

 Sentence Fluency • Sentence length is varied throughout.

I like how Carrie's sentences aren't all the same length. Check out the paragraph below. It begins with two short sentences, and a long sentence follows. Then, Carrie ends with another short sentence. This variety makes her writing more interesting to read.

[from the writing model]

I always dreamed I would fly someday. And now I'll have the chance. My mission now is to join other women in ferrying planes to bases across the United States so that our male pilots, who are badly needed at the front, will be released from ferrying duties. Just imagine my excitement!

 Grammar/Mechanics • Spelling, punctuation, and capitalization are correct. Dialogue punctuation is also correct.

In her story, Carrie includes both the narrator's thoughts and characters' exact words. Sometimes Edie and Hank speak to each other, and sometimes Edie speaks to the reader. Because the dialogue is always enclosed in quotes, I can easily tell who's speaking to whom.

[from the writing model]

"Then I guess this is it, Edie," Hank said slowly. "I'm very sorry. But I want my wife at home, not on a plane!"

"Then this is good-bye," sighed Edie. "I leave tomorrow for flight school. I'll always remember you, Hank. I hope you'll understand someday."

 My Turn! I'm going to write a historical episode set during an interesting time period. I'll follow the rubric and use good writing strategies. Read on to see how I do it!

Differentiating Instruction

Support Some students may benefit from a closer examination of how the author blends fact and fiction in "Edie's Other Engagement." On the board, write the headings *Fact* and *Fiction*. Then, work with a small group to review the story, asking for examples of each. **Possible responses: FACT—The U.S. was at war in 1943; World War II Fly Girls really did exist; WASP training existed; Women pilots really did perform ferrying duties. FICTION—Edie and Hank are fictional; The dialogue and plot are fictional.**

Enrichment Challenge students to flesh out "Edie's Other Engagement" by expanding upon the existing elements of plot and character. To lengthen the story, students can

- establish a more specific setting for paragraphs 1–4 by lengthening the conversation between Edie and Hank.
- write a scene that shows some of what Edie summarizes in paragraphs 5–6.
- write a scene between Edie and her parents that shows how they support her, as described in paragraph 7.
- expand upon the conversation between Edie and Hank in paragraphs 8–9.
- write a new, longer ending.

Remind students that although they may use many new details to expand the story, they should not contradict its basic elements.

Writing a Historical Episode

Prewriting Gather Information

Information/Organization The story focuses on one historical event.

Writing Strategy Choose a historical event and gather information from several resources, including the Internet and primary sources.

Last year, my family moved to Kansas from New York. So when I was asked to write a historical episode, I decided to write about a family that settles in Kansas in the late 1870s. To gather information, I read a few articles and a book about sod houses. I also got some information from the Internet, including a primary source: a letter written by a guy who lived in a sod house. Here are some of my notes.

Writer's Term

Primary Source
A **primary source** is the person or book that is closest to the information. For example, a primary source about the Revolutionary War would be the journal, diary, or letter of a person who lived through the war.

My Notes on Sod Houses

✔ hardly any trees, so couldn't build log cabins
✔ used blocks of prairie sod to build "soddies"
✔ cheap to build and didn't burn down in prairie fires
✔ dirt roofs leaked
✔ mice, snakes, and bugs—frequent "guests"

Practice!
Now it's your turn. Choose a historical period in which to set your story. Then, think of a story idea. Gather information from a variety of resources.

Prewriting Organize Ideas

Information/Organization Story elements are well organized.

Writing Strategy Make a Story Map to organize story elements.

Writer's Term
Story Map
Use a **Story Map** to organize story elements such as setting, characters, theme, conflict, and resolution.

The rubric says to organize my story elements, so I'll include these on a Story Map. Then, I'll use the Story Map to keep me focused as I write.

Story Map

Setting: Abilene, Kansas, 1876

Major Character(s): The narrator, Jeremy Thompson
Minor Character(s): Jeremy's sister, Lulu

Theme: Adjusting to a new place is often difficult.
Conflict: Jeremy doesn't like his new home in Kansas.

Plot		
Event 1	Event 2	Event 3
When the Thompsons arrive in Kansas, Jeremy hates it and wants to go back home.	After the neighbors help the Thompsons build a soddie, Jeremy discovers some of its pitfalls.	Jeremy gets a good laugh while teasing Lulu about her method of picking up cow chips.

Resolution: Jeremy realizes that teasing Lulu makes him feel more "at home."

Practice!
Now it's your turn. Organize story elements by using your notes to make a Story Map.

Reflect
How did I do? Do you think my Story Map will help me as I write?

Prewriting
(Student pages 38–39)

Ask students what they think they'll need to know before developing plots for their historical episodes. **Possible responses: historical facts, events, information** Then, discuss the Writer's Term box on Student page 38. Ask students to name other resources they might use to help get background information. **Possible responses: history textbooks, encyclopedias, history magazines, the Internet**

Next, point out the notes Ashley made about sod houses. Then, have students review her Story Map on Student page 39. Tell students to structure their own notes by organizing them into a Story Map.

Differentiating Instruction

Support Model how to narrow the scope of a historical episode by saying the following:

"I'm interested in Ancient China, so I'll brainstorm what I already know about this topic. I'll also look at a map and use geography to prompt further ideas. My map shows the Yangtze River and the Great Wall. That's it—I'll write a historical episode about an ordinary person who is working to build the Great Wall. Before I map out my plot, I'll do a little research to find out when the wall was built, who the laborers were, and what the work was like."

More Practice!

For more practice with these writing strategies, you may wish to have students use the Strategy Practice Book. See the appendix for annotated Strategy Practice Book pages.

Work with a Partner

Have students work together to brainstorm ideas for their historical episodes. Suggest that they write these down. Then, have them choose the best one to explore in more depth. To ensure students are on the right track, have them submit their topics for approval before they begin drafting.

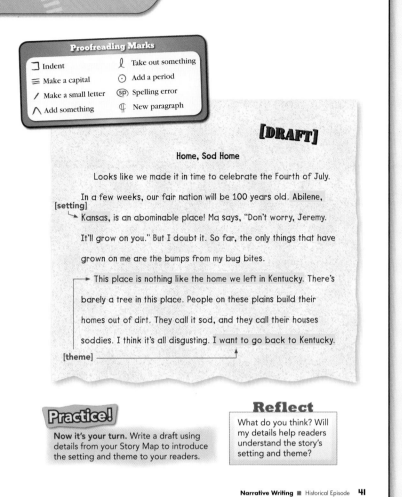

Writing a Historical Episode

Drafting — Write a Draft

Voice/Audience The setting and theme are clearly described for the reader.

Writing Strategy Clearly describe the setting and theme for the reader.

Writer's Term

Setting/Theme
The **setting** is the time and place of the story. Let the audience know the setting as soon as possible to help them understand what's happening. The **theme** is a message about life that the author wants to express in the story.

Now I'll use my Story Map to help me write my draft. According to the rubric, I need to be really clear about the setting and theme. That's because the setting has a big effect on both the plot and the theme. If I don't describe these elements right away, my reader may not understand what's going on or why the characters act in certain ways. See how I included the setting and theme in my first two paragraphs on the next page?

Proofreading Marks

⌐ Indent
≡ Make a capital
/ Make a small letter
∧ Add something
ℓ Take out something
⊙ Add a period
SP Spelling error
¶ New paragraph

[DRAFT]

Home, Sod Home

Looks like we made it in time to celebrate the Fourth of July.

In a few weeks, our fair nation will be 100 years old. Abilene,
[setting]
Kansas, is an abominable place! Ma says, "Don't worry, Jeremy.
It'll grow on you." But I doubt it. So far, the only things that have grown on me are the bumps from my bug bites.

This place is nothing like the home we left in Kentucky. There's barely a tree in this place. People on these plains build their homes out of dirt. They call it sod, and they call their houses soddies. I think it's all disgusting. I want to go back to Kentucky.
[theme]

Practice!
Now it's your turn. Write a draft using details from your Story Map to introduce the setting and theme to your readers.

Reflect
What do you think? Will my details help readers understand the story's setting and theme?

Drafting
(Student pages 40–41)

Remind students that drafting is a chance to get ideas on paper without having to worry about making mistakes.

Read aloud Ashley's words on Student page 40. Then, read the section of her draft on Student page 41. Refer to the Practice and Reflect boxes on Student page 41, which remind students to use the details from their Story Maps to convey specific settings and themes. Ask whether Ashley introduces her setting and theme on Student page 41. **yes** Then, have students find more examples (other than what is highlighted) of these elements in Ashley's draft. Also, discuss whether Ashley's draft includes details from her Story Map. Then, have students use the details in their Story Maps to draft their historical episodes.

Point out that Ashley repeatedly refers to the rubric as she writes. Encourage students to get into the habit of using the rubric to help guide their own writing.

Writing Across the Curriculum

Social Studies Help students benefit from the background information they and their peers have researched by setting aside time for them to share what they have learned. Students may choose to

- make posters highlighting key facts and display them around the classroom.
- compile information in the form of a travel brochure.
- give brief oral reports about the most interesting things they discovered.
- jot down key information as part of a class timeline or map.

Writing a Historical Episode

Revising Extend Writing

 Content/Ideas

Historical details are included throughout.

Writing Strategy Add historical details.

 Writer's Term

Historical Details
Historical details are facts and information about an actual time, place, or event in history. They help the reader understand the time period being described.

After I wrote my draft, something dawned on me: My reader probably doesn't know much about life on the Great Plains in 1876. According to the rubric, I need to use plenty of historical details, so I decided to add some information to help my readers understand what it was like to live in a sod house.

[DRAFT]

I still don't like this place. When it's dry out, the dust is unbearable. I swear, I don't know which is worse.

Dirt drifts down from the ceiling of our soddy and adds an unwelcome flavor to our food. It crumbles from the walls and gets stirred up under our feet until there's a coating of dust over everything. When it rains, the roof leaks for days.

[added historical details]

Practice!

Now it's your turn. Add some historical details to help your readers picture life in the past.

Revising Clarify Writing

 Word Choice/ Clarity

Dialogue reflects the time and place in which the characters live.

Writing Strategy Make sure dialogue reflects the time and place in which the characters live.

The rubric says that I should make my characters sound realistic—like people who could have lived during the time in which I set my story. When I reread my draft, I realized that I could make it sound more authentic. In my research, I came across different words that people used during pioneer times, so I replaced some of my original words with ones that I found. I also corrected an error in verb tense, since I noticed it while adding dialogue.

[DRAFT]

[corrected verb tense] had
The only good laugh that I have in the last two months was when "Girl, tarnation
my little sister was picking up cow chips. What in the world are you doing?" I asked. "Are you trying to pick up those cow chips 'em
or eat them?" [used dialogue that reflects the setting]

Practice!

Now it's your turn. Revise dialogue that sounds unrealistic by using words and speech patterns that fit the historical setting.

Reflect

What do you think of my revisions? Are they true to the setting?

Revising

(Student pages 42–43)

Explain to students that historical details provide a context in which a writer can tell a story, and that they can also help readers understand the time period in which the story is set. To prompt discussion, write the following topic on the board and ask students to name historical details related to it: *Westward Movement in the Nineteenth Century.* **Possible responses: horse-drawn covered wagons, pioneers, lack of electricity and automobiles** While having this discussion, remind students that it's important to check the accuracy of historical details, and that when adding these to their drafts, they should refer to their research notes.

Now, turn students' attention to the revisions Ashley made to her draft on Student page 43. Ask why she replaced the deleted words. **Possible response: because the new words make the dialogue sound like it was spoken by someone from that time period** Then, have students check and revise their drafts for dialogue that could sound more realistic and better reflect the time and place in which the characters live.

Differentiating Instruction

English-Language Learners These students may find it difficult to write and revise dialogue in English. Pair them with native English speakers who can provide feedback on how accurately the dialogue reflects the time period. Coach pairs by suggesting that they read each other's dialogue aloud and then discuss whether the speech sounds authentic. Then, have them suggest specific ways that they can improve their characters' dialogue.

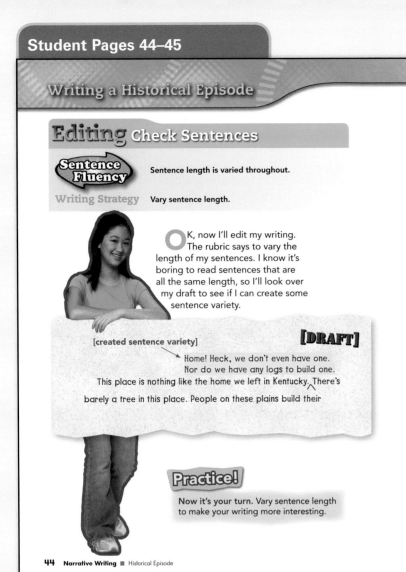

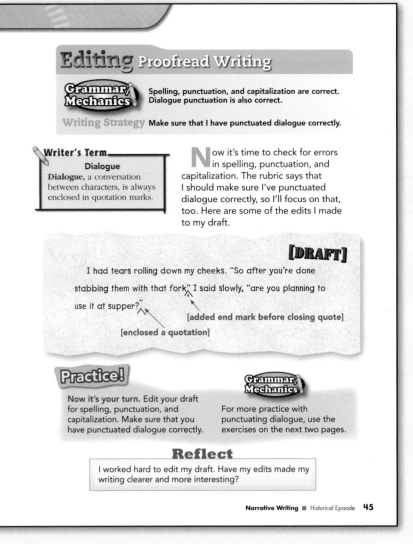

Editing

(Student pages 44–45)

Call students' attention to the sentences Ashley added to her draft on Student page 44. Ask a volunteer to read aloud the added sentences. Then, discuss what effect Ashley's edits have on her writing. Have students begin checking their historical episodes for places where they can vary sentence length to make their writing more interesting.

Next, point out the Writer's Term box on Student page 45, and ask a volunteer to read it aloud. Have students note how, on Student page 45, Ashley edited a section of dialogue for correct punctuation. Ask students what Ashley corrected. **She added a comma before the first closing quotes, and she added a set of closing quotes at the end of the character's speech.** Have students check their drafts to make sure they have punctuated dialogue correctly. Remind them that they should also check for proper spelling and capitalization.

If any of your students are having trouble understanding how to punctuate dialogue, you may wish to teach the Mini-Lesson on pages 48–49 of this Teacher Edition. Then, have students complete the exercises on pages 46–47 of their books. Review the answers and possible rewrites with them.

WORK with a **PARTNER** Have pairs of students read one another's drafts, using sticky notes to mark errors in spelling, punctuation, and grammar. Then, tell students to perform a second read that focuses on the editing strategies they learned in this chapter.

Punctuating Dialogue

KNOW the RULE

- **Dialogue**, a conversation between characters, is always enclosed in **quotation marks**.
- Use **opening quotes** at the beginning of dialogue.
- Use **closing quotes** at the end of dialogue.
- Begin dialogue with a **capital letter**, unless it has been interrupted by an expression such as *she said*. Add **end punctuation** (period, question mark, exclamation point, or comma in place of a period) before the closing quotes. Also, add end punctuation, if necessary, at the end of the sentence containing the dialogue.
- Always begin a new paragraph when the speaker changes.
  Examples:
  "Hey, Jeremy! Why don't you help your sister pick up those cow chips?" asked Pa.
  "Sure thing, Pa," I grinned. "Just let me grab my fork."

Practice the Rule

Number a separate sheet of paper 1–5. Rewrite each sentence, adding quotation marks, commas, and end punctuation in the appropriate places. Use capitalization where needed.

1. Did you know that my great-great-grandfather was a homesteader I asked
2. I didn't Sarah replied tell me about it
3. Well I began his name was Albert, and he moved from Virginia to Nevada in 1861
4. How did he like Nevada Sarah asked
5. They say he liked it quite a bit I said he was, apparently, pretty content.

Apply the Rule

Read the historical episode, looking for errors in dialogue punctuation. Then, rewrite the story correctly on another sheet of paper.

Off From Independence

Betsy's father had told her not to fret. "Don't think about the length of the journey, girl he'd warned. We'll just take it step by step." But amid the crunch of travelers camped on the prairie just outside Independence, Missouri, Betsy could not get her mind off the trek that would take them along the Oregon Trail.

Betsy! Finally, I've found you!" Betsy's older brother, Sam, came running through the crowd. Mama's going to be mad, Betsy told him. "we've been looking for you all over the place"

"Well, I'm back now said Sam. Where's Pa? Sam then ran toward their wagon, with Betsy kicking up dust behind him.

I saw them, Pa" Sam shouted. "Up by the river junction—all heading out at the same time! No one could move. we need to get ready. I don't want to be stuck in the back with the other greenhorns"

"Watch your mouth, Sam," said Mama "Don't be ashamed to come from the city"! "Sorry," said Sam. But listen! The trail boss was making some folks throw things off their wagons. You should see it—cast iron skillets, sacks of flour—just piles of stuff along the road"!

"That's because they overpacked," said Pa "we're lucky your cousins made the journey first. Now we know not to pack house and home!"

Grammar/Mechanics Mini-Lesson

(Student pages 46–47)

Punctuating Dialogue

Write the following sentences on the board, run together as shown:

My family settled in the West in the 1860s, Fred said. Mine did, too, I told him.

Note that because the dialogue does not contain correct punctuation, it may be hard to figure out who's speaking. Then, have students add the correct punctuation and create a new paragraph where necessary:

"My family settled in the West in the 1860s," Fred said.

"Mine did, too," I told him.

Review the Know the Rule box on Student page 46 with students. Then, ask volunteers to list the major definitions. Possible responses: Always use opening and closing quotation marks to enclose dialogue. Begin dialogue with a capital letter. Add end punctuation before the closing quotes. Always begin a new paragraph when the speaker changes.

Remind students to keep these rules in mind when they check their writing for correct punctuation of dialogue.

Answers for Practice the Rule

1. "Did you know that my great-great-grandfather was a homesteader?" I asked.
2. "I didn't," Sarah replied. "Tell me about it."
3. "Well," I began, "his name was Albert, and he moved from Virginia to Nevada in 1861."
4. "How did he like Nevada?" Sarah asked.
5. "They say he liked it quite a bit," I said. "He was, apparently, pretty content."

Answers for Apply the Rule

Off From Independence

Betsy's father had told her not to fret. "Don't think about the length of the journey, girl," he'd warned. "We'll just take it step by step." But amid the crunch of travelers camped on the prairie just outside Independence, Missouri, Betsy could not get her mind off the trek that would take them along the Oregon Trail.

(Answers continue on page 49.)

Writing a Historical Episode

Publishing Share Writing

Dramatize my story.

My historical episode is finished! Now I can think about how to publish it. I could add it to a class anthology, or I could submit it to a history-themed magazine that publishes student writing. But I really like the idea of turning my story into a play. I can get a few classmates to help me perform it—and then my story will really come to life! First though, I want to read through it one last time to make sure it includes all of the items on my checklist.

My Checklist

✔ The story focuses on one historical event and is well organized.

✔ The setting and theme are clear.

✔ Historical details appear throughout.

✔ Dialogue is true to the setting.

✔ Sentence length is varied.

✔ Spelling, capitalization, and punctuation, including dialogue punctuation, are correct.

Practice!

Now it's your turn. Make a checklist and check your historical episode. Then, make a final draft to publish.

Home, Sod Home
by Ashley

Looks like we made it in time to celebrate the Fourth of July. In a few weeks, our fair nation will be 100 years old. Abilene, Kansas, is an abominable place! Ma says, "Don't worry, Jeremy. It'll grow on you." But I doubt it. So far, the only things that have grown on me are the bumps from my bug bites.

This place is nothing like the home we left in Kentucky. Home! Heck, we don't even have one. Nor do we have any logs to build one. There's barely a tree in this place. People on these plains build their homes out of dirt. They call it sod, and they call their houses soddies. I think it's all disgusting. I want to go back to Kentucky.

With help from the neighbors, who are turning out to be a kind and generous bunch, we got our soddy built in pretty good time. Home, sod home. I still don't like this place. When it's dry out, the dust is unbearable. Dirt drifts down from the ceiling of our soddy and adds an unwelcome flavor to our food. It crumbles from the walls and gets stirred up under our feet until there's a coating of dust over everything. When it rains, the roof leaks for days. I swear, I don't know which is worse.

And then there's the matter of fueling the place. Seems we homesteaders must use what we have most of—cow chips. The only good laugh that I have had in the last two months was when my little sister was picking up cow chips. "Girl, what in tarnation are you doing?" I asked. "Are you trying to pick up those cow chips or eat 'em?"

Seems Lulu found the whole chip-picking ordeal distasteful. As she stabbed delicately at each chip with a fork, she said, "I refuse to touch these things. They're foul and dirty and smelly."

I had tears rolling down my cheeks. "So after you're done stabbing them with that fork," I said slowly, "are you planning to use it at supper?"

Lulu glared at me. Then, she glared at her fork. A cow chip was poised on the end. "I'm never eating again!" she cried. "And it's all your fault!" She threw down her fork and stomped off. A cloud of dust danced merrily in her wake.

Well, my sister and I were at it again. At least something was starting to feel like home.

Reflect

Did I use all the traits of a good historical episode in my writing? Check it against the rubric, and don't forget to use the rubric to check your own historical episode.

(Answers continued from page 48.)

"Betsy! Finally, I've found you!" Betsy's older brother, Sam, came running through the crowd.

"Mama's going to be mad," Betsy told him. "We've been looking for you all over the place."

"Well, I'm back now," said Sam. "Where's Pa?" Sam then ran toward their wagon, with Betsy kicking up dust behind him.

"I saw them, Pa!" Sam shouted. "Up by the river junction—all heading out at the same time! No one could move. We need to get ready. I don't want to be stuck in the back with the other greenhorns."

"Watch your mouth, Sam," said Mama. "Don't be ashamed to come from the city!"

"Sorry," said Sam. "But listen! The trail boss was making some folks throw things off their wagons. You should see it—cast iron skillets, sacks of flour—just piles of stuff along the road!"

"That's because they overpacked," said Pa. "We're lucky your cousins made the journey first. Now we know not to pack house and home!"

 For more practice with grammar/mechanics skills, see Zaner-Bloser's *G.U.M.* materials.

Publishing
(Student pages 48–49)

Ask students if they like Ashley's choice for sharing her historical episode. Tell the class that her choice is not the only option for publishing her work. Invite students to name other ways they could publish their own historical episodes.

Have each student make a checklist and perform a final evaluation of his or her historical episode before publishing it. Encourage students to share copies of their historical episodes with friends and relatives who might be interested in reading about what they wrote.

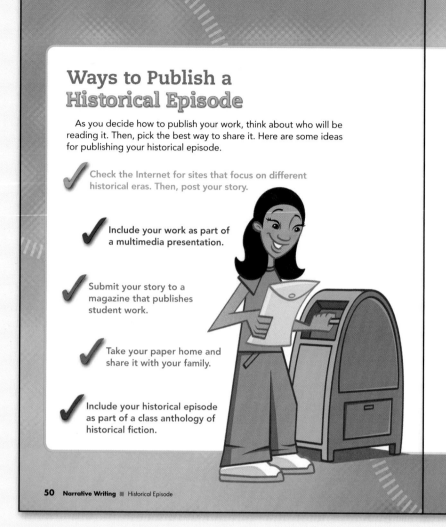

Ways to Publish a
Historical Episode

As you decide how to publish your work, think about who will be reading it. Then, pick the best way to share it. Here are some ideas for publishing your historical episode.

✓ Check the Internet for sites that focus on different historical eras. Then, post your story.

✓ Include your work as part of a multimedia presentation.

✓ Submit your story to a magazine that publishes student work.

✓ Take your paper home and share it with your family.

✓ Include your historical episode as part of a class anthology of historical fiction.

Writing Across the Content Areas
Historical Episode

Choose a school subject and see how many related writing topics you can brainstorm. Check out these examples.

Science
• Choose a famous inventor and write a fictional story about an actual discovery.
• Write about a historical weather-related disaster.

Social Studies
• Write a fictional story based on a major national event.
• Fictionalize an event in the life of a famous historical figure.

Art and/or Music
• Research a specific painting or sculpture. Make up a story about how it was created.
• Fictionalize a day in the life of a famous Renaissance artist.

Ways to Publish
(Student page 50)

Read and discuss with students the different publishing options listed on Student page 50. Encourage students to consider some of these options when publishing their own writing. Remind students that Ashley chose to publish her historical episode by dramatizing it, but they can choose their own way of publishing. Perhaps one student will want to submit his or her historical episode to a magazine that publishes student work, while another will want to include it in a multimedia presentation.

Writing Across the
Content Areas
(Student page 51)

Explain to students that writing is not just for English or language arts class. Many other school subjects contain ideas, issues, and events that students may want to write about. Encourage students to consider using one of the content areas listed on Student page 51 as a springboard for more writing options. Students may also wish to consult with other teachers for more ideas on writing in the content areas.

Books for Professional Development

Routman, Regie. *Invitations: Changing as Teachers and Learners K–12.* **Portsmouth: Heinemann, 1994.**

Both inspirational and practical, this text focuses on authenticity in writing. Routman offers ideas and examples of stories, journals, and letters. There is also information on establishing a whole-school publishing program.

Kashatus, William C. *Past, Present and Personal: Teaching Writing in U.S. History.* **Portsmouth: Heinemann, 2002.**

In this book, Kashatus offers methods to move teenage students from basic descriptive writing to more complex expository essays and term papers on U.S. history. Reflecting his title, Kashatus divides his book into three parts. "Past History" explores interpretation and assessment of historical documents. "Present History" examines research-based writing. "Personal History" offers experiential techniques to create a "living history classroom."

Harvey, Stephanie. *Nonfiction Matters: Reading, Writing, and Research in Grades 3–8.* **Portland: Stenhouse, 1998.**

Full of practical suggestions, Harvey's book presents strategies for research, ideas for organizing and writing, suggestions for facilitating project-based learning and assessment, and guided practice in modeling instruction. It also includes bibliographies of nonfiction books and magazines, and a list of inquiry tools and resources—both print and electronic.

Wood, Karen D., and Janis M. Harmon. *Strategies for Integrating Reading and Writing in Middle and High School Classrooms.* **Westerville: NMSA, 2001.**

These easy-to-use, research-based strategies are designed to improve students' performance and interest in course content by increasing the time they spend reading and writing. Each chapter addresses a topic relevant to middle school and high school literacy, and offers sample lessons to illustrate the application to various subject areas.

Biography Overview

In this chapter, students will learn how to write a biography. They will learn the elements of a biography—third-person narrator, characters, logical sequence, and direct quotations—and some reasons why they might want to write one. Students will then use a biography rubric to study a model writing sample.

Students will follow the student guide as she goes through the writing stages—prewriting, drafting, revising, editing, and publishing. As the student guide learns new writing strategies in each step, students will be directed to practice the strategies in their own writing.

During prewriting and drafting, students will
- choose a person as their focus.
- gather information by writing interview questions and conducting an interview.
- plot important events on a Timeline.
- grab the reader's attention in the introduction.

During revising and editing, students will
- add direct quotations.
- use a dictionary to check word use.
- reorder awkwardly placed information.
- edit their drafts for spelling, capitalization, and punctuation, making sure there are no sentence fragments or run-ons.

Finally, students will publish a final draft. You may wish to send to families the School-Home Connection Letter for this chapter, located at the end of this unit in the Teacher Edition.

Biography Writing Traits

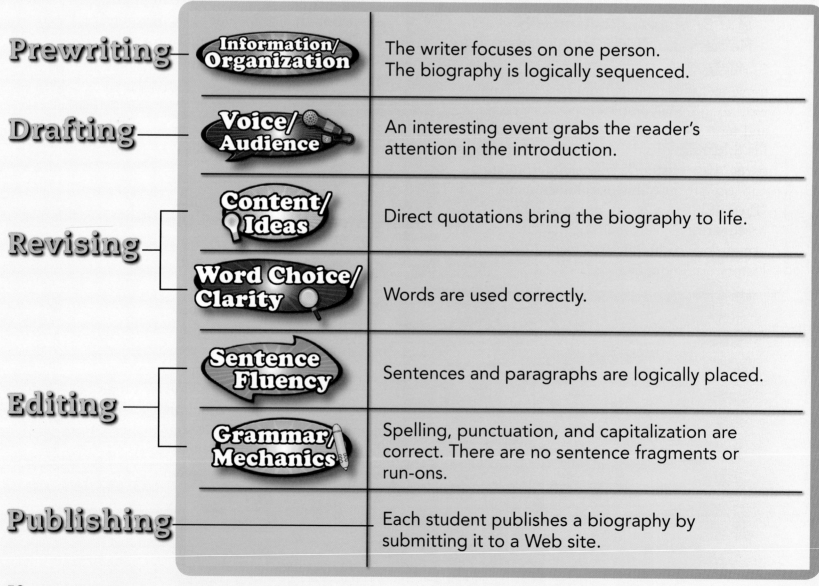

Prewriting	Information/Organization	The writer focuses on one person. The biography is logically sequenced.
Drafting	Voice/Audience	An interesting event grabs the reader's attention in the introduction.
Revising	Content/Ideas	Direct quotations bring the biography to life.
	Word Choice/Clarity	Words are used correctly.
Editing	Sentence Fluency	Sentences and paragraphs are logically placed.
	Grammar/Mechanics	Spelling, punctuation, and capitalization are correct. There are no sentence fragments or run-ons.
Publishing		Each student publishes a biography by submitting it to a Web site.

Biography Time Management

	Day 1	Day 2	Day 3	Day 4	Day 5
Learning Objectives					
	Students will: • learn the components of a biography.	Students will: • learn how to gather information for a biography.	Students will: • practice gathering information for their own biographies.	Students will: • learn how to plot important events on a Timeline.	Students will: • practice plotting important events on a Timeline.
Activities					
	• Discuss the elements and traits of a biography (Student pages 52–54). • Use the rubric to study the model (Student pages 55–59).	• Read and discuss **Prewriting: Gather Information** (Student page 60).	• Brainstorm ideas and choose a subject. • Gather information by writing interview questions and conducting an interview.	• Read and discuss **Prewriting: Organize Ideas** (Student page 61).	• Review the information gathered from interviews. • Plot important events on a Timeline.

	Day 1	Day 2	Day 3	Day 4	Day 5
Learning Objectives					
	Students will: • learn how to use an interesting event to grab the reader's attention in the introduction.	Students will: • practice writing their own drafts.	Students will: • learn how adding direct quotations can bring their biographies to life.	Students will: • practice adding direct quotations to their drafts.	Students will: • learn how to use a dictionary to make sure words are used correctly.
Activities					
	• Read and discuss **Drafting: Write a Draft** (Student pages 62–63).	• Use a Timeline to write a draft. • Begin the draft with an interesting event.	• Read and discuss **Revising: Extend Writing** (Student page 64).	• Add direct quotations.	• Read and discuss **Revising: Clarify Writing** (Student page 65).

	Day 1	Day 2	Day 3	Day 4	Day 5
Learning Objectives					
	Students will: • practice using a dictionary to make sure words are used correctly.	Students will: • learn how to reorder awkwardly placed sentences and paragraphs.	Students will: • learn how to correct sentence fragments and run-ons.	Students will: • practice editing their drafts for spelling, capitalization, punctuation, and sentence fragments/run-ons.	Students will: • learn different ways to publish their biographies.
Activities					
	• Reread drafts, looking for places where words are not used correctly. • Use a dictionary to check word use.	• Read and discuss **Editing: Check Sentences** (Student page 66). • Make sure to place sentences and paragraphs in a logical order.	• Read and discuss **Editing: Proofread Writing** (Student page 67).	• Fix any spelling, capitalization, or punctuation errors. • Fix sentence fragments and run-ons.	• Read and discuss **Publishing: Share Writing** (Student page 70).

To complete the chapter in fewer days, teach the learning objectives and activities for two days in one day.

This planning chart, correlated to your state's writing standards, is available on-line at http://www.zaner-bloser.com/sfw.

What's a Biography?

It's a story about a real person's life. I'm looking forward to writing a biography because there's a world of people I can write about. I can choose someone who really interests me—and become a biographer!

What's in a Biography?

Third-Person Narrator
The writer of a biography narrates the story but is not involved in the action. I'll use the third-person point of view to narrate and objectively present my biography.

Characters
These are the important people in my subject's life. They are often more than story characters: They can also function as great sources of information about the subject of a biography.

Logical Sequence
It makes perfect sense for a writer to start a biography at the beginning of a subject's life and move through it in chronological order. But as long as the sequence is logical, a writer can also flash back and flash forward between key moments in the subject's life.

Direct Quotations
I can include direct quotations from important people in my subject's life. This will help bring my biography to life.

Why write a Biography?

There are many reasons for writing a biography. As I made this list, I realized my purpose for writing will probably depend on the subject of my biography.

Entertainment
Reading a biography can be fun. If I make sure I focus on what's most interesting about my subject, I'll be sure to entertain my readers.

Lessons
Some people have played important roles in history, or have lived their lives as examples for others. If this applies to my subject, my biography can teach valuable lessons to my readers.

Connections
A good biography should tell a story about a real person—someone who is probably like other people in many ways. As I write, I'll remember to think about what my readers might have in common with my subject. That way, my audience can connect with the story.

Information
There are many people I've heard of, but don't know much about. The purpose of my biography could be to inform my readers with details about a familiar face or name. Or I could inform my audience about a lesser-known person.

Define the Genre
(Student page 52)

Biography

Discuss with students the definition of a biography. Ask students whether they have ever written about another person. **Possible response: yes** Point out that any time they tell the story of a real person's life, they are using the biography genre.

Elements of the Genre

Biography

Read and discuss with students the various elements of a biography. Ask volunteers which elements are also common to other forms of writing. **Possible responses: Third-Person Narrator—magazine features, short stories; Characters—fantasy, plays; Logical Sequence— historical writing, instructions; Direct Quotations— newspaper articles, speeches** Discuss why each element may be important to writing a biography.

Authentic Writing
(Student page 53)

Biography

Read and discuss with students the reasons for writing a biography listed on Student page 53. Point out that all writing has a purpose and is aimed at a specific audience. These authentic purposes help authors shape their writing. Ask a volunteer to read aloud the Entertainment box. Then, have students discuss other reasons someone might write a biography for entertainment. Repeat this process for the Lessons, Connections, and Information boxes. Then, have students brainstorm other purposes for writing a biography that are not listed on Student page 53. Encourage students to think about their own reasons for writing a biography, and how these reasons will affect the tone and focus of their writing.

Biography Writing Traits

I know that there are six traits of good writing. Here's a list of what makes a good biography. I'll use it to help me write.

Information/Organization	The writer focuses on one person. The biography is logically sequenced.
Voice/Audience	An interesting event grabs the reader's attention in the introduction.
Content/Ideas	Direct quotations bring the biography to life.
Word Choice/Clarity	Words are used correctly.
Sentence Fluency	Sentences and paragraphs are logically placed.
Grammar/Mechanics	Spelling, punctuation, and capitalization are correct. There are no sentence fragments or run-ons.

I can use Stewart Chase's biography on the next page as a model for my own writing. Later, we'll check out how he used the traits to help him write.

Biography Model

Characters

GILBERT CHASE: A MAN ON THE MOVE
by Stewart Chase

On the day my Great-Grandpa Gilbert was born, fate was in the mood for practical jokes. You see, Gilbert Chase was born breech on April Fools' Day, 1905. My mother told me that his mother always used to say, "Baby Gil was born breech 'cause he wanted to hit the ground running." **Logical Sequence**

Third-Person Narrator And run he did! It seemed his friends and family could never keep up with him. All through school he was the fastest boy in any race, and his grades were better than everyone else's, too. After he graduated from high school in 1923, he was accepted into the University of Illinois. Four years later, he graduated at the top of his class. In 1928, Gil opened a chain of stores that sold all kinds of electrical appliances. By that time, about two thirds of the country had electricity, and people were buying things on credit. Gil made tons of money.

His first major purchase, a Model T Ford sedan, cost him $295 right off the assembly line. Great-Grandpa Gil loved his new Model T. He drove it all over town. His friends would see him coming, and he'd pick them up for rides. Often, he'd stop at the ice cream parlor and treat them to their favorite flavors. "He's generous to a fault, that Gil," his friend Bruce would always say.

And Gil would always reply, "Brucie! What's the fun of having money if you can't share it with your friends?" **Direct Quotation**

Those trips to the ice cream parlor paid off because that's where Gil met his future wife. Her name was Alice Smith, and according to Gil, "She was the most beautiful gal I had ever seen." Gil married her, and their wedding took place on July 19, 1929—exactly six months from the day they met.

Gil and Alice lived a very good life, though things got a bit lean during the Great Depression. They had two children—Scott, born in 1931, and Fay, born in 1934—and gave them the best of everything.

On his 40th birthday, Gil's friends and family threw him a huge surprise party at the country club. Gil was so shocked that he sat in a chair and cried.

He said he felt wonderful after the party, but Great-Grandma Alice said he didn't look right. She took him home and put him to bed. When she checked on him just before midnight, Great-Grandpa Gil was dead.

The doctor said that Gil had had a stroke and died in his sleep. My mom says that her Grandpa Gil was just in a hurry to meet his maker.

Writing Traits
(Student pages 54-55)

Biography

Have students discuss famous people who spark their interest. Then, ask students to name sources they might turn to for more information about these people. **Possible responses: the Internet, newspapers, magazines, TV news, biographies** Note that, of all these sources, a biography often provides the most accurate and in-depth information about a person.

Remind students that biographies do not always have to feature famous people and that when writing, they should focus on an interesting person that they know.

Tell students that they are going to study and use strategies for writing biographies, and that a good biography has the traits listed on Student page 54.

Differentiating Instruction

English-Language Learners Preteach key words and concepts to help these students better understand "Gilbert Chase: A Man on the Move." Read the biography aloud, stopping at each of the following phrases. Before explaining each definition (included in parentheses after each phrase), have students use context to try figuring out what each one means.

- *April Fools' Day* (A day, sometimes called All Fools' Day, that is marked by the playing of practical jokes.)
- *The Great Depression* (A period of time in America during the 1930s that was marked by mass unemployment and poverty.)
- *born breech* (born feet first)
- *generous to a fault* (overly kind, so as to potentially cause problems)
- *paid off* (was successful or went well)

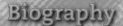

Biography
Rubric

The traits of a good biography from page 54 have been used to make the rubric below. By using 1, 2, 3, or 4 check marks to judge each trait, you can decide how well any biography was written.

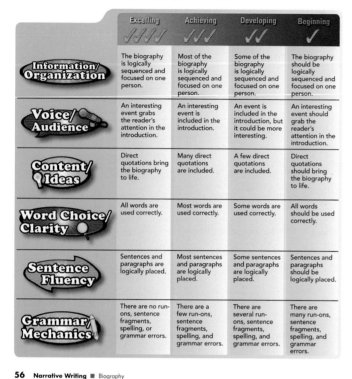

	Excelling ✓✓✓✓	Achieving ✓✓✓	Developing ✓✓	Beginning ✓
Information/ Organization	The biography is logically sequenced and focused on one person.	Most of the biography is logically sequenced and focused on one person.	Some of the biography is logically sequenced and focused on one person.	The biography should be logically sequenced and focused on one person.
Voice/ Audience	An interesting event grabs the reader's attention in the introduction.	An interesting event is included in the introduction.	An event is included in the introduction, but it could be more interesting.	An interesting event should grab the reader's attention in the introduction.
Content/ Ideas	Direct quotations bring the biography to life.	Many direct quotations are included.	A few direct quotations are included.	Direct quotations should bring the biography to life.
Word Choice/ Clarity	All words are used correctly.	Most words are used correctly.	Some words are used correctly.	All words should be used correctly.
Sentence Fluency	Sentences and paragraphs are logically placed.	Most sentences and paragraphs are logically placed.	Some sentences and paragraphs are logically placed.	Sentences and paragraphs should be logically placed.
Grammar/ Mechanics	There are no run-ons, sentence fragments, spelling, or grammar errors.	There are a few run-ons, sentence fragments, spelling, and grammar errors.	There are several run-ons, sentence fragments, spelling, and grammar errors.	There are many run-ons, sentence fragments, spelling, and grammar errors.

Using the Biography Rubric to Study the Model

Let's use the rubric to check Stewart Chase's biography, "Gilbert Chase: A Man on the Move." How many check marks would you give Stewart for each trait?

Information/ Organization
- The writer focuses on one person.
- The biography is logically sequenced.

Stewart focuses his biography on Gilbert Chase, telling the key events of his subject's life in logical order. He even uses transitional phrases (underlined in the passage below) to tell how much time passed between one key event and the next.

[from the writing model]

<u>After he graduated</u> from high school in 1923, he was accepted into the University of Illinois. <u>Four years later</u>, he graduated at the top of his class. <u>In 1928</u>, Gil opened a chain of stores that sold all kinds of electrical appliances.

Voice/ Audience
- An interesting event grabs the reader's attention in the introduction.

Stewart introduces his great-grandfather by describing his unusual birth on April Fools' Day. This is great because the reader immediately knows that the biography is going to be unique in some way.

[from the writing model]

On the day my Great-Grandpa Gilbert was born, fate was in the mood for practical jokes. You see, Gilbert Chase was born breech on April Fools' Day, 1905. My mother told me that his mother always used to say, "Baby Gil was born breech 'cause he wanted to hit the ground running."

Using the Rubric
(Student page 56)

Explain that a rubric is a tool that can be used to evaluate a piece of writing. The rubric on Student page 56 can be used to evaluate a biography. It is based on the same biography traits listed on Student page 54.

Point out the terms above each rubric column: *Excelling, Achieving, Developing,* and *Beginning.* Explain that each column symbolizes a degree of writing skill, and that each rubric row focuses on a specific writing trait. When students use the rubric to evaluate their own work at each step of the writing process, they increase the likelihood of producing polished, well-written biographies.

Study the Model
(Student pages 57-59)

Explain that Student pages 57–59 show how the writing model on Student page 55 meets all six traits of the rubric. Read each section with the students. Have them look for other examples of each trait in the writing model.

Ask students how many check marks they would assign the writing model for each trait. Then, as a class, decide how the writing model should be rated overall.

Remind students to use the rubric as they write their own biographies, to be sure they are meeting all six writing traits.

Biography

Content/Ideas
• Direct quotations bring the biography to life.

I like how Stewart includes direct quotes to help the reader understand what Gilbert Chase was really like. Some of the quotes are from people who knew him, and some are from Gilbert himself. Look at this example.

[from the writing model]

"He's generous to a fault, that Gil," his friend Bruce would always say. And Gil would always reply, "Brucie! What's the fun of having money if you can't share it with your friends?"

Word Choice/Clarity
• Words are used correctly.

Stewart's writing is easy to read because he uses words correctly. In this next passage, Stewart uses the word *lean*. This word has several different meanings (incline, rest against, thin, lacking in fullness), but Stewart uses it to express the idea that Gilbert's family had to do without many things.

[from the writing model]

Gil and Alice lived a very good life, though things got a bit lean during the Great Depression. They had two children—Scott, born in 1931, and Fay, born in 1934—and gave them the best of everything.

Sentence Fluency
• Sentences and paragraphs are logically placed.

The paragraphs in Stewart's biography are well placed. Also, the sentences within each paragraph flow from one to the next in a way that makes sense. This makes the biography easy to follow.

[from the writing model]

Those trips to the ice cream parlor paid off because that's where Gil met his future wife. Her name was Alice Smith, and according to Gil, "She was the most beautiful gal I had ever seen." Gil married her, and their wedding took place on July 19, 1929—exactly six months from the day they met.

Grammar/Mechanics
• Spelling, punctuation, and capitalization are correct. There are no sentence fragments or run-ons.

If Stewart's biography ever contained any sentence fragments or run-ons, he made sure to correct them before publishing his work. You can tell Stewart's sentences are complete because each one contains both a subject and a predicate.

[from the writing model]

The doctor said that Gil had had a stroke and died in his sleep. My mom says that her Grandpa Gil was just in a hurry to meet his maker.

My Turn!

I'm going to write a biography about someone I'd like to know more about. I'll follow the rubric and use good writing strategies. Read on to see how I do it!

Differentiating Instruction

Support Some students may benefit from extra instruction on how to write an interesting introduction. Make sure they understand that some forms of writing, including biographies, memoirs, and magazine features, contain introductions that differ from the standard format. The standard format is straightforward and introduces the topic and the thesis.

The introduction in a biography is often more creative, starting with an interesting event, or a "hook." Remind students that they can "hook" readers with
• a quotation that is funny, provocative, or intriguing.
• a question that sparks readers' curiosity.
• a description that paints a vivid picture.
• a recap of an interesting event.
• a technique called *in media res* (Latin for "in the middle"), which involves joining an event, conversation, or other situation right in the middle of the action. Rather than a recap, in media res gives readers a peek at action or dialogue as it is happening.

Discuss each type of beginning. Then, ask students to share examples of how they might use one of these techniques to introduce their biographies.

Writing a Biography

Prewriting Gather Information

Information/Organization The writer focuses on one person.

Writing Strategy Choose a person as the focus of my biography. Then, write interview questions and conduct an interview.

When my teacher said to write a biography, the first thing I did was choose a subject. I chose my grandmother because everyone says I look and act a lot like her. Then, I wanted to do some research about her. Because she died before I was born, I decided to interview her children: my father and my aunt. Finally, I wrote some interview questions.

My Interview Questions

✔ What do you remember most about my grandma, Mai Chaw?

✔ What would you like other people to know about her?

✔ What memories do you have of Mai Chaw and of leaving Laos?

✔ Do you have any memories of Mai Chaw in the refugee camp?

Practice!

Now it's your turn. Choose a person to be the focus of your biography. Gather information by writing interview questions and conducting an interview.

60 **Narrative Writing** ■ Biography

Prewriting Organize Ideas

Information/Organization The biography is logically sequenced.

Writing Strategy Plot important events on a Timeline.

Writer's Term
Timeline
A **Timeline** can help you sequence key events in chronological order, the order in which they happened.

I know from the rubric that organization is important in a biography. If I don't describe the key events of Grandma Mai's life in order, my reader could get confused. After I conducted my interviews, I took all the information I gathered and plotted the most important events on a Timeline.

Timeline

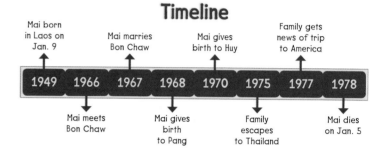

Mai born in Laos on Jan. 9		Mai marries Bon Chaw		Mai gives birth to Huy		Family gets news of trip to America	
1949	1966	1967	1968	1970	1975	1977	1978
	Mai meets Bon Chaw		Mai gives birth to Pang		Family escapes to Thailand		Mai dies on Jan. 5

Practice!

Now it's your turn. Organize your biography by plotting the most important events on a Timeline.

Reflect

Do you think my interview questions were helpful? Will my Timeline help me stay focused as I write?

Narrative Writing ■ Biography 61

Prewriting

(Student pages 60–61)

Discuss Ashley's words on Student page 60. Then, point out her interview questions and note that because her grandmother is deceased, Ashley will interview others who knew her. Remind students that after they choose a subject, they must decide where they can go for information.

Point out Ashley's Timeline on Student page 61, and discuss with students how Ashley plotted the major events from her interviews. Remind students to refer to these pages as they organize and plan their own biographies.

Differentiating Instruction

Support Help students prepare for their interviews. First, remind them that conducting an interview will not necessarily result in a lot of interesting information. The key to a good interview is preparation. Explain that if students don't know basic information about their subject, they should research it before the interview. That way, they can ask more interesting questions.

Also, coach students in writing interview questions. Explain that if students can't think of good questions, they should apply the question starters _Who, What, When, Where, Why,_ and _How_ to dig more deeply for interview answers.

More Practice!

For more practice with these writing strategies, you may wish to have students use the Strategy Practice Book. See the appendix for annotated Strategy Practice Book pages.

WORK with a PARTNER

Encourage students to try their interview questions out on partners. Have partners share what they know about their subjects and then offer their questions for feedback. Pairs should evaluate questions based on whether they will get the interviewee to reveal useful information.

Writing a Biography

Drafting Write a Draft

Voice/Audience
An interesting event grabs the reader's attention in the introduction.

Writing Strategy Grab the reader's attention with an interesting event in the introduction.

OK, now I'm ready to begin writing. The rubric says that I should introduce Grandma Mai in an interesting way. I'll start with the family's escape to Thailand and then flash forward, telling the story in chronological order from that point on. I won't worry too much about punctuation and spelling errors. The important thing is to get my ideas down.

After I started writing though, I noticed that I used simple and perfect tense verbs correctly. Verb tense has given me trouble in the past, so I'm happy to see that's not the case anymore.

Proofreading Marks

⌐ Indent
≡ Make a capital
/ Make a small letter
∧ Add something
ℓ Take out something
⊙ Add a period
SP Spelling error
¶ New paragraph

[DRAFT]

The Courage of Mai Chaw

by Ashley

"Still, children, stay very still!" said Mai Chaw. "We must keep the raft nice and steady." Her desperate voice repeated those words until she could no longer speak. She and her children were running for their lives, and their lives depended on keeping that raft afloat and unnoticed. As they glided across the Mekong River, away from Laos, Mai wondered if they'd make it to Thailand. ← **[attention-grabbing event]**

She was num with fear, but she had to go on. Only hours before, she had seen her husband dragged away by communist soldiers. — **[correct use of past perfect tense]** Though it was 1975, and the fighting in Vietnam had ended, Mai's battle was only beginning. She was in for the fight of her life. She had to protect herself and her children from the communist soldiers. They would face certain death if they were found.

My father told us that our mother was very strong. ← **[correct use of simple past tense]**

Practice!

Now it's your turn. Write a draft using a key event from your Timeline to grab your readers' attention.

Reflect

What do you think? Is the event that I used to begin my biography interesting enough to hook my readers?

Drafting
(Student pages 62–63)

Remind students that drafting is a chance to get ideas on paper without having to worry about making mistakes.

Read aloud Ashley's words on Student page 62. Then, read the first part of her draft on Student page 63. Refer to the Practice and the Reflect boxes on Student page 63, which remind students to use a key event from their Timelines to grab readers' attention. Then, have students use the events on their Timelines to draft their biographies.

Point out that Ashley repeatedly refers to the rubric as she writes. Encourage students to get into the habit of using the rubric to help guide their own writing.

Writing Across the Curriculum

Social Studies Many students will probably choose family members or ancestors as biography subjects. These people might have come from another country or era.

Have students explore background information about their subjects by adding details to their biographies in the form of

- a family tree.
- family photos.
- a map.
- a travel brochure.
- an illustrated cover.

Students may also wish to display family mementos or artifacts, present a slide show, or give an oral report.

Writing a Biography

Revising Extend Writing

Content/Ideas Direct quotations bring the biography to life.

Writing Strategy Add direct quotations to bring the biography to life.

Writer's Term

Direct Quotations
Direct quotations are the exact words that someone says. They are enclosed in quotation marks, just like dialogue.

After I drew my audience into Grandma Mai's story, I decided to go back and describe her. Instead of using my own words, I decided to use some direct quotations from my interviews. I guess I was right on track because the rubric says quotations will bring my biography to life. I had to be careful, though. I know quotations are similar to dialogue, and I've had trouble with dialogue punctuation before. That's why I added a quotation mark as soon as I saw that it was missing!

[DRAFT]

[added a direct quote]

"Our mother survived the journey because she was a very strong person," said my father, Huy Chaw.

~~My father told us that our mother was very strong.~~

"Yes, she was very strong," agreed his sister (my aunt) Pang, "and she was the bravest person I've ever known."

[corrected dialogue punctuation]

Practice!

Now it's your turn. Add some direct quotations to bring your biography to life.

Revising Clarify Writing

Word Choice/Clarity Words are used correctly.

Writing Strategy Use a dictionary to make sure I have used words correctly.

I had my teacher look over my draft. She said my story was interesting, but she reminded me to check what the rubric says about using words correctly. It's a good thing, too, because I spotted some errors.

[DRAFT]

[corrected word usage]

Mai arrived in the world on January 9, 1949. She was born in Laos, a small country in Southeast Asia. As soon as she ~~aged,~~ was old enough she began working in the rice paddies with her family. They farmed their paddies from sunup until sundown. Planting and harvesting rice was ~~complicated~~ backbreaking work that left them exhausted. But Mai was strong. And happy.

Practice!

Now it's your turn. Replace words that are used incorrectly with words that better fit the ideas you want to get across.

Reflect

Have my revisions created a clearer picture of my story?

Revising

(Student pages 64–65)

Write the words *dialogue* and *direct quotations* on the board. Make sure students understand that dialogue usually refers to conversation between characters in a fictional or narrative story, and that direct quotations are a real person's actual words.

Have a volunteer read the Writer's Term box on Student page 64. Then, ask what is similar about dialogue and direct quotations. **They are both enclosed in quotation marks.** Explain that direct quotations help writers convey characters' feelings, making writing more lively and interesting. Have students note how Ashley added a direct quotation to her draft on Student page 64. Remind them to look for places in their own draft where direct quotations can make their writing livelier.

Now, direct students' attention to Ashley's words on Student page 65. Note the edits she made to her draft. Then, ask students why she replaced the first deleted word. **Possible response: because we don't usually say that people age** Finally, remind students to use a dictionary to make sure they have used words correctly in their drafts.

Differentiating Instruction

English-Language Learners Pair English-language learners with native English speakers who can provide feedback on their choice of words. Have pairs review each other's drafts, checking for proper word use. Provide guidance by telling them to

- underline any sentences that seem confusing.
- reread each sentence to see if any words are used incorrectly.
- ask their partner what he or she is trying to say.
- use a dictionary to check the use of words in context.
- offer suggestions about how to make suggestions.

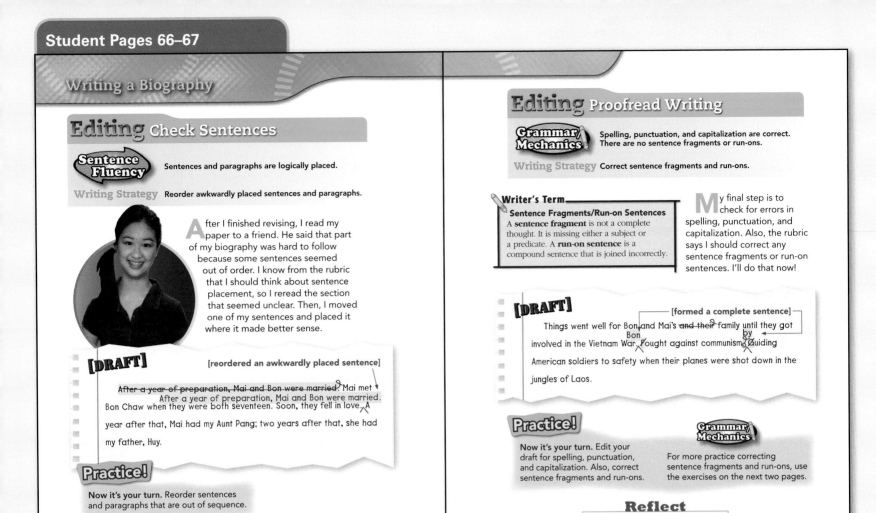

Writing a Biography

Editing Check Sentences

Sentence Fluency Sentences and paragraphs are logically placed.

Writing Strategy Reorder awkwardly placed sentences and paragraphs.

After I finished revising, I read my paper to a friend. He said that part of my biography was hard to follow because some sentences seemed out of order. I know from the rubric that I should think about sentence placement, so I reread the section that seemed unclear. Then, I moved one of my sentences and placed it where it made better sense.

[DRAFT] [reordered an awkwardly placed sentence]

After a year of preparation, Mai and Bon were married. Mai met Bon Chaw when they were both seventeen. Soon, they fell in love. A year after that, Mai had my Aunt Pang; two years after that, she had my father, Huy.

Practice!

Now it's your turn. Reorder sentences and paragraphs that are out of sequence.

66 Narrative Writing ■ Biography

Editing Proofread Writing

Grammar/Mechanics Spelling, punctuation, and capitalization are correct. There are no sentence fragments or run-ons.

Writing Strategy Correct sentence fragments and run-ons.

Writer's Term__
Sentence Fragments/Run-on Sentences
A **sentence fragment** is not a complete thought. It is missing either a subject or a predicate. A **run-on sentence** is a compound sentence that is joined incorrectly.

My final step is to check for errors in spelling, punctuation, and capitalization. Also, the rubric says I should correct any sentence fragments or run-on sentences. I'll do that now!

[DRAFT] [formed a complete sentence]

Things went well for Bon and Mai's and their family until they got involved in the Vietnam War. Fought against communism Guiding American soldiers to safety when their planes were shot down in the jungles of Laos.

Practice!

Now it's your turn. Edit your draft for spelling, punctuation, and capitalization. Also, correct sentence fragments and run-ons.

Grammar/Mechanics

For more practice correcting sentence fragments and run-ons, use the exercises on the next two pages.

Reflect

Have my edits helped my writing? Are my ideas clearer now?

Narrative Writing ■ Biography 67

Editing

(Student pages 66–67)

Write the following paragraph on the board:

During the Great Depression, my grandfather, an artist, traveled the country painting scenes of ordinary Americans. He studied art at New York University. His work took him to both town and country, and from coast to coast. He was born in 1906. Many of his paintings depict impoverished neighborhoods in Chicago.

Have a volunteer read the paragraph aloud. Then, ask students to explain whether the text works as a paragraph. Through discussion, make sure students understand that the sentences do not all speak to the same main idea. Ask students to state the main idea. **Possible response: My grandfather painted scenes of the Great Depression.** Then, ask students how they would edit the paragraph. **Possible response: Sentences 2 and 4 could be moved to another paragraph.**

Call students' attention to Ashley's words on Student page 66, and to the edits she made to her draft. Explain why Ashley made this revision, noting that the opening sentences seem out of sequence. Have students look for places in their own biographies where they can improve the placement of sentences and paragraphs.

Turn students' attention to the revisions Ashley made to her draft on Student page 67. Ask why she inserted the highlighted words. **to turn two sentence fragments into a complete sentence** Have students review the Writer's Term box on the same page. Then, have them check their drafts to make sure there are no sentence fragments or run-ons. Remind them that they should also check for proper spelling, capitalization, and punctuation.

If any of your students are having trouble understanding how to edit sentence fragments and run-ons, you may wish to teach the Mini-Lesson on pages 62–63 of this Teacher Edition.

WORK with a PARTNER Have pairs of students read one another's drafts, using sticky notes to mark errors in spelling, punctuation, and grammar. Then, tell students to perform a second read that focuses on the editing strategies they learned in this chapter.

Sentence Fragments and Run-ons

KNOW the RULE

A group of words that is missing a subject or a predicate is a **sentence fragment**. Correct a fragment by adding the missing subject or predicate.

Fragment: Born in Laos. (subject missing)
Correct: Mai Chaw was born in Laos.
Fragment: The fighting in Vietnam. (predicate missing)
Correct: The fighting in Vietnam had ended.

A **run-on sentence** is a compound sentence that is joined incorrectly. Correct a run-on sentence by adding a semicolon or a comma and a conjunction. You may also break it into two sentences.

Run-on: The United States said they would help they never did.
Correct: The United States said they would help; they never did.
Correct: The United States said they would help, but they never did.
Correct: The United States said they would help. They never did.

Practice the Rule

Number a separate sheet of paper 1–5. Then, read each item below. Write *F* if the item is a fragment or *R* if the item is a run-on. Then, rewrite each item correctly.

1. Some people think that Laos is located in Africa it is actually in Southeast Asia.
2. Laos is bordered by China to the north the western border lies along the Mekong River.
3. Governed by a single party.
4. More than fifty ethnic groups live in Laos they are officially divided into three categories.
5. Rugged mountains in northern Laos.

Apply the Rule

Read the biography, looking for sentence fragments and run-ons. Then, rewrite the story correctly on another sheet of paper.

Helie Lee: Author or Adventurer?

In 1996, when Scribner published <u>Still Life With Rice: A Young American Woman Discovers the Life and Legacy of Her Korean Grandmother</u>, Helie Lee saw a dream fulfilled: understanding her Korean legacy. As it turned out, however, the dream came at great price her book's international popularity put the lives of North Korean relatives in danger.

Lee was born in 1964 in Seoul, South Korea originally, her family had lived in North Korea. In 1953, many people fled the North. When the communists took power after the Korean War, Lee's uncle did not make it to the South.

<u>Still Life With Rice</u> ends with Lee's grandmother's dearest wish: to see her son again. She would get her wish, but only after Lee, by naming her uncle in her book, unwittingly made him and other North Korean relatives targets of the repressive government. Living in Los Angeles at the time, Lee could only think of one thing to do: rescue her uncle. She and other relatives. Embarked on a dangerous mission. And in December 1997, the family was united in South Korea.

(Student pages 68–69)

Sentence Fragments and Run-ons

Ask students to read the first part of the Know the Rule box on Student page 68 and then define *sentence fragment*. **A sentence fragment is not a complete sentence.** Explain that a complete sentence contains both a subject and a predicate, and that a fragment can be missing either part.

Write the following sentence on the board: *The midterm exam contained fifty questions.* Ask a student to name the verb. **contained** Ask another student to name the subject. **The midterm exam** Then, ask yet another student to circle the predicate. **contained fifty questions**

Then, have students read the second half of the Know the Rule box, noting that a run-on sentence is a compound sentence that is joined incorrectly. Next, write this sentence on the board: *Jen studied hard for the test afterward she thought she did well.* Have students suggest three ways to fix this run-on. **Place a semicolon after test. Place a** comma followed by *and* after *test*. Place a period after *test* and capitalize *afterward*.

Answers for Practice the Rule

1. R; Some people think that Laos is located in Africa, but it is actually in Southeast Asia.
2. R; Laos is bordered by China to the north; the western border lies along the Mekong River.
3. F; Some nations are governed by a single party.
4. R; More than fifty ethnic groups live in Laos. They are officially divided into three categories.
5. F; There are rugged mountains in northern Laos.

Answers for Apply the Rule

Helie Lee: Author or Adventurer?

In 1996, when Scribner published <u>Still Life With Rice: A Young American Woman Discovers the Life and Legacy of Her Korean Grandmother</u>, Helie Lee saw a dream fulfilled: understanding her Korean legacy. As it turned out, however, the dream came at great price. Her book's international popularity put the lives of North Korean relatives in danger.

(Answers continue on page 63.)

Writing a Biography

Publishing Share Writing

Submit my biography to a Web site.

Now that I've finished my biography, I want to publish it. I could add it to a class anthology or I could see if a magazine would publish it. I really want people to know my grandmother's story because it's so much like the stories of other Hmong refugees in America. So I think I'll publish it on a Web site about the Hmong people. First though, I want to read through it one last time to make sure it includes all of the items on my checklist.

My Checklist

✔ The story focuses on one person and is logically sequenced.

✔ An interesting event draws the reader in.

✔ Direct quotations add life to the biography.

✔ Words are used correctly.

✔ Sentences and paragraphs are well placed.

✔ Spelling, capitalization, and punctuation are all correct. There are no run-ons or fragments.

Practice!

Now it's your turn. Make a checklist and check your biography. Then, make a final draft to publish.

The Courage of Mai Chaw
by Ashley

"Still, children, stay very still!" said Mai Chaw. "We must keep the raft nice and steady." Her desperate voice repeated those words until she could no longer speak. She and her children were running for their lives, and their lives depended on keeping that raft afloat and unnoticed. As they glided across the Mekong River, away from Laos, Mai wondered if they'd make it to Thailand.

She was numb with fear, but she had to go on. Only hours before, she had seen her husband dragged away by communist soldiers. Though it was 1975, and the fighting in Vietnam had ended, Mai's battle was only beginning. She was in for the fight of her life. She had to protect herself and her children from the communist soldiers. They would face certain death if they were found.

"Our mother survived the journey because she was a very strong person," said my father, Huy Chaw.

"Yes, she was very strong," agreed his sister (my aunt) Pang, "and she was the bravest person I've ever known." That's how Mai Chaw's children describe her. They say she had been that way from the day she was born.

Mai arrived in the world on January 9, 1949. She was born in Laos, a small country in Southeast Asia. As soon as she was old enough, she began working in the rice paddies with her family. They farmed

---

(Answers continued from page 62.)

Lee was born in 1964 in Seoul, South Korea, but originally, her family had lived in North Korea. In 1953, many people fled the North. When the communists took power after the Korean War, Lee's uncle did not make it to the South.

Still Life With Rice ends with Lee's grandmother's dearest wish: to see her son again. She would get her wish, but only after Lee, by naming her uncle in her book, unwittingly made him and other North Korean relatives targets of the repressive government. Living in Los Angeles at the time, Lee could only think of one thing to do: rescue her uncle. She and other relatives embarked on a dangerous mission, and in December 1997, the family was united in South Korea.

✔ For more practice with grammar/mechanics skills, see Zaner-Bloser's *G.U.M.* materials.

Differentiating Instruction

Enrichment Help advanced writers submit their biographies for publication by offering guidance on how to write a query letter. After students choose a method of publication, introduce the following points:

- A query letter introduces a piece of writing to an editor. Like the work itself, a query letter must arouse the curiosity of an editor who sees many pieces of mail every day. A great query letter may make the difference between an editor's acceptance or rejection of work.
- Writers approach query letters with the same attention to detail as any other piece of writing. However, a query letter is still a business letter, and it should contain all of the standard parts.
- Use the Internet search *"how to write a query letter"* or use writers' reference books for sample letters.
- After drafting and revising a query letter, submit it to a partner for feedback. Then, revise it again as needed.

Help students by bringing in sample query letters, and by reviewing their own letters.

Writing a Biography

their paddies from sunup until sundown. Planting and harvesting rice was backbreaking work that left them exhausted. But Mai was strong and happy. She was always smiling, and she never complained about hard work.

Mai met Bon Chaw when they were both seventeen. Soon, they fell in love. After a year of preparation, Mai and Bon were married. A year after that, Mai had my Aunt Pang; two years after that, she had my father, Huy.

Things went well for Bon and Mai's family until they got involved in the Vietnam War. Bon fought against communism by guiding American soldiers to safety when their planes were shot down in the jungles of Laos. Bon and several of his countrymen helped save many American soldiers' lives. The United States said they would help

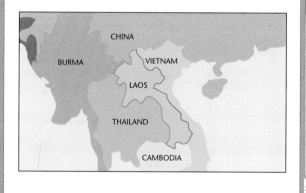

the Laotians in return, but they never did. Instead, they pulled out of Vietnam in 1975 and left the Hmongs to suffer the consequences of having fought against the communists. Many villages were destroyed, and the communists killed anyone who they thought had helped the Americans. Bon, who had helped American soldiers, was labeled a traitor. The communists tied him up and took him away, leaving Mai to protect their children.

Taking what she could, Mai soon found herself on a raft escaping to Thailand with her children. They were all frightened, but Mai stayed brave through it all. It took weeks, but she finally got herself and the children to a refugee camp.

Mai spent the next two years at the refugee camp, waiting to see if she and her family would be relocated to the United States. On December 29, 1977, word finally came; they would soon be leaving for America. She and her children would be safe! One week later, though, Mai had a heart attack and died.

Mai never saw the United States, but her children and grandchildren definitely benefited from her courageous act.

Reflect

What do you think? Did I use all the traits of a good biography in my writing? Check it against the rubric. Don't forget to use the rubric to check your own biography.

Publishing

(Student pages 70–73)

Ask students if they like Ashley's choice for sharing her biography. Tell the class that her choice is not the only option for publishing her work. Invite students to name other ways they could publish their own biographies.

Have each student make a checklist and perform a final evaluation of his or her biography before publishing it. Encourage students to share copies of their biographies with friends and relatives who might be interested in reading about what they wrote.

Call students' attention to the Reflect box on the bottom of Student page 73. Explain that assessing Ashley's biography against the rubric will help them better understand how to apply the traits to their own work. Have students use sticky notes to mark at least one example of each trait in Ashley's writing. Tell them to include an evaluation on each note.

After this process, have students assess how well they were able to identify each trait in Ashley's writing, and how easy or hard it was to use the rubric. Remind them to apply what they learned from Ashley's work when they use the rubric to check their own writing.

TiPS for the Writing Classroom

Committing to a Philosophy of Student Cooperation, Ownership, and Personalization Education (SCOPE)

by Ken Stewart, *Master Teacher*

Through **cooperative** learning, students are guided to cooperate in order to solve problems to achieve a common goal. You, as the teacher, take on the role of facilitator.

Give students **ownership** in how they learn. Establish well-defined criteria (specific to the writing genre being taught), and give your students options as to how to reach those criteria. Within the parameters of your lesson, give your students the freedom to design how they will accomplish their tasks.

Personalization is the ability to make school and the "real" world one and the same. Set aside time for students to share, discuss, and understand how their ideas are part of a larger picture. Help them understand that they are not just writing for a grade, but they are writing to communicate valuable ideas worthy of thought, discussion, and action.

By committing to SCOPE, you will be meeting the needs of most of your students most of the time. You may also find that competition is reduced or replaced entirely with cooperation.

Ways to Publish a

As you decide how to publish your work, think about who will be reading it. Then, you can pick the best way to share it. Here are some ideas for publishing your biography.

✔ Read your biography aloud to the class.

✔ Include your biography as part of a multimedia presentation on famous people or family roots.

✔ Submit your story to a magazine that publishes student work.

✔ Include your biography as part of a class anthology.

✔ Take your biography home and share it with your family.

Writing Across the Content Areas
Biography

School subjects can be great sources for writing ideas. Choose a subject and see how many related topics you can brainstorm. Check out these examples.

Science
- Choose a fascinating science career. Then, write a biography about a person in this field.
- Who made the most significant discovery or developed the most important invention of our time? Write his or her biography.

Language Arts
- Write about the life of your favorite author.
- Tell the story of someone who has impacted the world of Web content. Possibilities include search engine innovators, famous bloggers, and people who have launched Internet forums or networks.

Art and/or Music
- Write about an artist or musician whose style appeals to you.
- How did your favorite artist or musician make it big? Tell his or her story.

Ways to Publish
(Student page 74)

Read and discuss with students the different publishing options listed on Student page 74. Encourage students to consider some of these options when publishing their own writing. Remind students that Ashley chose to publish her biography by submitting it to a Web site, but they can choose their own way of publishing. Perhaps one student will want to submit his or her biography to a magazine that publishes student work, while another will want to include it as part of a class anthology.

Writing Across the Content Areas
(Student page 75)

Explain to students that writing is not just for English or language arts class. Many other school subjects contain ideas, issues, and events that students may want to write about. Encourage students to consider using one of the content areas listed on Student page 75 as a springboard for more writing options. Students may also wish to consult with other teachers for more ideas on writing in the content areas.

Narrative Test Writing

In this chapter, students will learn how to write a personal memoir for a test. They will review the traits of a personal memoir, and will study a test prompt and a scoring guide. Students will then use a model writing prompt and a scoring guide to study a sample personal memoir test.

Students will follow the student guide as she goes through the test writing stages—time planning, studying the writing prompt, prewriting, drafting, revising, and editing. As the student guide reviews the writing strategies in each step, students will be directed to practice the test writing strategies.

During prewriting and drafting, students will
- study the writing prompt.
- respond to the task.
- choose a graphic organizer.
- check the graphic organizer against the scoring guide.
- engage the reader with interesting details.

During revising and editing, students will
- add dialogue to strengthen characterization.
- use clear, concrete words.
- use prepositional phrases to add sentence variety.
- edit their drafts for grammar, punctuation, capitalization, and spelling.

You may wish to send to families the School-Home Connection Letter for this chapter, located at the end of this unit in the Teacher Edition.

Writing Traits in the Scoring Guide

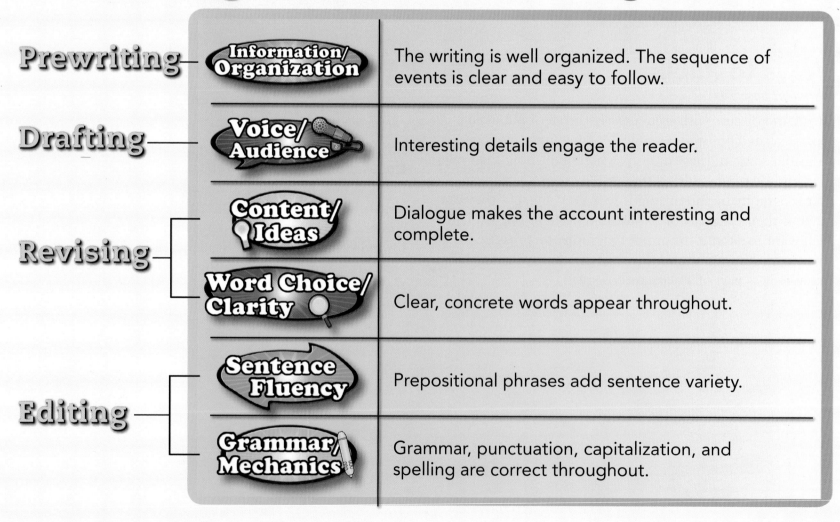

Prewriting	**Information/Organization**	The writing is well organized. The sequence of events is clear and easy to follow.
Drafting	**Voice/Audience**	Interesting details engage the reader.
Revising	**Content/Ideas**	Dialogue makes the account interesting and complete.
	Word Choice/Clarity	Clear, concrete words appear throughout.
Editing	**Sentence Fluency**	Prepositional phrases add sentence variety.
	Grammar/Mechanics	Grammar, punctuation, capitalization, and spelling are correct throughout.

Narrative Test Writing Time Management

WEEK 1

	Day 1	Day 2	Day 3	Day 4	Day 5
Learning Objectives					
	Students will: • learn the components of the writing prompt model.	Students will: • recognize the relationship of the scoring guide to the rubric and the six traits of writing. • read a writing prompt model response.	Students will: • apply the scoring guide to the writing prompt model response.	Students will: • continue to apply the scoring guide to the writing prompt model response.	Students will: • learn how to plan their time during a writing test.
Activities					
	• Discuss the components of the writing prompt model (Student pages 76–77).	• Read and discuss the scoring guide (Student page 78). • Read the writing prompt model response (Student page 79).	• Read and discuss **Using the Scoring Guide to Study the Model** (Student pages 80–81).	• Read and discuss **Using the Scoring Guide to Study the Model** (Student page 82).	• Read and discuss **Planning My Time** (Student page 83).

WEEK 2

	Day 1	Day 2	Day 3	Day 4	Day 5
Learning Objectives					
	Students will: • read a writing prompt for a personal memoir. • apply the six traits of writing to the writing prompt.	Students will: • learn how to respond to the task in the writing prompt.	Students will: • learn how to choose a graphic organizer for narrative test writing.	Students will: • learn how to check the graphic organizer against the scoring guide.	Students will: • learn how to engage the reader with interesting details.
Activities					
	• Read and discuss **Prewriting: Study the Writing Prompt** (Student pages 84–85).	• Read and discuss **Prewriting: Gather Information** (Student page 86).	• Read and discuss **Prewriting: Organize Ideas** (Student page 87).	• Read and discuss **Prewriting: Check the Scoring Guide** (Student pages 88–89).	• Read and discuss **Drafting: Write a Draft** (Student pages 90–91).

WEEK 3

	Day 1	Day 2	Day 3	Day 4	Day 5
Learning Objectives					
	Students will: • add dialogue to strengthen characterization in their writing test.	Students will: • use clear, concrete words in their writing test.	Students will: • use prepositional phrases to add sentence variety to their writing test.	Students will: • edit their writing test for proper grammar and mechanics.	Students will: • learn tips for test writing.
Activities					
	• Read and discuss **Revising: Extend Writing** (Student page 92).	• Read and discuss **Revising: Clarify Writing** (Student page 93).	• Read and discuss **Editing: Check Sentences** (Student page 94).	• Read and discuss **Editing: Proofread Writing** (Student pages 95–96).	• Read and discuss **Test Tips** (Student page 97).

To complete the chapter in fewer days, teach the learning objectives and activities for two days in one day.

This planning chart, correlated to your state's writing standards, is available on-line at http://www.zaner-bloser.com/sfw.

NARRATiVE test writing

Read the Writing Prompt

I know that every writing test starts with a writing prompt. Most writing prompts have three parts:

Setup This part of the writing prompt gives you the background information you need to get ready to write.

Task This part of the writing prompt tells you exactly what you are supposed to write: a personal memoir.

Scoring Guide This section tells how your writing will be scored. To do well on the test, you should include everything on the list.

Remember the rubrics you've been using? When you take a writing test, you don't always have all of the information that's on a rubric. But the scoring guide is a lot like a rubric. It lists everything you need to think about to write a good paper. Like the rubrics you've used, many scoring guides are based on the six important traits of writing:

- Information/Organization
- Content/Ideas
- Sentence Fluency
- Voice/Audience
- Word Choice/Clarity
- Grammar/Mechanics

Writing MODEL Prompt

Think about a time when you helped another person or people in some way.

Write a personal memoir about that experience.

Be sure your writing

- is well organized. The sequence of events should be clear and easy to follow.
- includes details to make the story interesting.
- contains dialogue that makes the account interesting and complete.
- has clear, concrete words.
- includes prepositional phrases for sentence variety.
- contains correct grammar, punctuation, capitalization, and spelling.

Introduce the Writing Prompt

(Student pages 76–77)

Narrative Writing

Write this sentence on the board: *Write a personal memoir about a time when you helped someone else.* Note that sentences such as these—called prompts—often appear on homework assignments. They also appear on writing tests. Ask students to compare how they respond to homework with how they respond to a writing test prompt. **Possible response: I take more time on homework.** Make sure students understand that although they must follow test writing time limits, they should still use the writing steps they have previously learned: prewriting, drafting, revising, and editing.

Read aloud the three parts of the writing prompt listed on Student page 76. Explain that within the scoring guide, students will find traits similar to those they have seen in the rubrics throughout this unit. Note that just as a rubric includes the qualities of a good paper, the scoring guide includes the qualities of a good test.

Read the writing prompt model aloud. Then, write the following correlations on the board and review:

- *Setup: This provides the background information needed in order to write for a test.*
- *Task: This is the assignment, and it often names the type of writing to be done.*
- *Scoring Guide: This is much like a rubric, providing information necessary for doing well on a writing test.*

Writing Traits
in the Scoring Guide

Look back at the scoring guide in the writing prompt on page 77. Not every writing prompt will include each of the six writing traits, but this one does. You can use the following chart to help you better understand the connection between the scoring guide and the writing traits in the rubrics you've been using.

 **Information/Organization**
- Be sure your writing is well organized. The sequence of events should be clear and easy to follow.

 Voice/Audience
- Be sure your writing includes details to make the story interesting.

 Content/Ideas
- Be sure your writing contains dialogue that makes the account interesting and complete.

 **Word Choice/Clarity**
- Be sure your writing has clear, concrete words.

 Sentence Fluency
- Be sure your writing includes prepositional phrases for sentence variety.

 Grammar/Mechanics
- Be sure your writing contains correct grammar, punctuation, capitalization, and spelling.

Look at Eric Weismann's story on the next page. Did he follow the scoring guide?

A New Face
by Eric Weismann

"Students, I'd like to introduce you to Andrew Mancini," said our teacher, Ms. Kennedy, one morning as we began class.

It was midway through my eighth grade year at South Lincoln, and it seemed weird to me that we were getting a new student at this time of year. I wondered how Andrew felt. He was a tall, gangly kid, with a thick mop of brown hair that fell across his eyes. He wore clothes that were too small, showing his sharp wrists and bony ankles. His sneakers looked like they came straight from a garage sale. When Ms. Kennedy introduced him, he half smiled and looked down at his desk.

That first day at school, I noticed that Andrew was really quiet and wasn't very happy. He kept chewing on his pencil and looking out the window. At lunchtime, he sat all by himself. I felt really bad for him. Did he want to be by himself, or did he think that no one wanted to hang out with him? I wanted to say something, but I wasn't sure how to approach him.

That night, I told my parents about Andrew. "It has to be hard to start all over again in a new school, making friends and finding your way around," my mom said, "especially when everyone around you already knows one another."

My dad suggested that I introduce Andrew to some of my friends. "Just start out by saying hello to him," he said. "Ask him if he likes to play basketball."

The next day, I made a point of saying hello to Andrew first thing in the morning. "Did you and your family just move to the area?" I asked him.

Andrew perked up a bit. "Yeah, my dad got transferred here from California."

"Well, I think you'll like it here," I told him. "You want to meet my friends?"

"Yeah!" he said.

At lunch, he sat with my friends and me. We all found out that we had a lot in common.

"Hey," he said, "do you guys like to play basketball?"

"Of course," I said.

He laughed. "You know, maybe this new school isn't so bad after all."

Writing Traits in the Scoring Guide

(Student pages 78–79)

Ask students to recall the six traits of writing they have studied throughout the unit. **Information/Organization, Voice/Audience, Content/Ideas, Word Choice/Clarity, Sentence Fluency, Grammar/Mechanics** If they are having trouble providing a response, remind them that the first trait is Information/Organization. Tell them that when they read a scoring guide, they should try to identify the traits within it. This will help them think about the purpose of each item in the scoring guide. It will also help them relate to what they have already learned about these writing traits.

Read the Model:
Writing Prompt Response

Distribute one copy of the model to each student. As you read it aloud, have each student use a highlighter to identify the traits set forth in the scoring guide.

Differentiating Instruction

English-Language Learners **Preteach** difficult vocabulary and idiomatic expressions in context by writing this summary of "A New Face" on the board:

In this story, Eric wonders why a new student named Andrew is starting school midway through the year. Eric notices that Andrew is tall and gangly. He sees Andrew sitting alone at lunchtime. That night, Eric tells his parents that he doesn't know what to say to Andrew. His father suggests that he should introduce Andrew to some friends and invite him to play basketball. The next day, Eric makes a point of saying hi to Andrew. As they talk, he learns that Andrew transferred from California. Eric also learns that his father is right: Basketball is a good way to make friends.

Read through the summary, stopping to show students how to use context clues to help them figure out the meanings of the underlined words and phrases.

Using the Scoring Guide to Study the Model

Let's use the scoring guide to check Eric's writing test, "A New Face." How well does his essay meet each of the six writing traits?

**Information/Organization**
• The story is well organized. The sequence of events should be clear and easy to follow.

Eric tells the story in a logical order. He uses transitional phrases (underlined below) to tell the reader how much time passes between one event and the next. Here is an example.

> That first day at school, I noticed that Andrew was really quiet and wasn't very happy. He kept chewing on his pencil and looking out the window. At lunchtime, he sat all by himself. I felt really bad for him. Did he want to be by himself, or did he think that no one wanted to hang out with him? I wanted to say something, but I wasn't sure how to approach him.

Voice/Audience
• The writing includes details that make the story interesting.

Eric gets me interested with details about Andrew. I can visualize what Andrew looked like and how he must have felt.

> He was a tall, gangly kid, with a thick mop of brown hair that fell across his eyes. He wore clothes that were too small, showing his sharp wrists and bony ankles. His sneakers looked like they came straight from a garage sale. When Ms. Kennedy introduced him, he half smiled and looked down at his desk.

Content/Ideas
• The writing contains dialogue that makes the account interesting and complete.

Eric uses dialogue in his memoir. This makes the story more interesting, and it tells me exactly how he got to know Andrew. Here's an example.

> "Did you and your family just move to the area?" I asked him.
> Andrew perked up a bit. "Yeah, my dad got transferred here from California."
> "Well, I think you'll like it here," I told him. "You want to meet my friends?"

Word Choice/Clarity
• The writing has clear, concrete words.

Eric uses appropriate language to tell his story. His words are really clear and concrete, and this makes his description vivid and interesting.

> He was a tall, gangly kid, with a thick mop of brown hair that fell across his eyes. He wore clothes that were too small, showing his sharp wrists and bony ankles. His sneakers looked like they came straight from a garage sale. When Ms. Kennedy introduced him, he half smiled and looked down at his desk.

Using the Scoring Guide to Study the Model

(Student pages 80–82)

Review the function of the scoring guide. First, have students review a rubric from one of the earlier chapters in this unit. Then, point out the similarities and differences between that rubric and the scoring guide. Make sure students understand that although a scoring guide does not include criteria for various levels of accomplishment, it does provide guidance in the six key areas of writing: Information/Organization, Voice/Audience, Content/Ideas, Word Choice/Clarity, Sentence Fluency, and Grammar/Mechanics.

Explain that in the same way traits in a rubric are used to assess writing, criteria in a scoring guide are used to assess test writing. Remind students to use the scoring guide when they write for a test to ensure that they meet all of the traits.

Differentiating Instruction

Enrichment Even advanced writers find it challenging to write dialogue that sounds true to life. While writers can rely on guidelines to help them punctuate dialogue correctly, they cannot turn to a set of rules to help them compose realistic conversation. Encourage students to challenge themselves by including extra dialogue in their writing, working to make it sound authentic. Offer these suggestions to students:

• After you finish your draft, read it to yourself or to a partner.
• Listen to how the dialogue sounds: Would the character say these words? Would he or she say them in this particular way?
• Also listen for words that sound like they should be dialogue, or for dialogue that sounds like it should be running text.
• To revise, add or delete the correct punctuation.

Planning My Time

Using the Scoring Guide to Study the Model

Sentence Fluency
- The writing includes prepositional phrases for sentence variety.

Eric uses a variety of sentence patterns. He avoids repetition by starting some of his sentences with a prepositional phrase. He also includes complex sentences. Here's an example.

At lunch, he sat with my friends and me. We all found out that we had a lot in common.

Grammar/ Mechanics
- The writing contains correct grammar, punctuation, capitalization, and spelling.

It looks like Eric spelled correctly and used the right punctuation. Don't forget to check for mistakes in your own work. For example, if you know you often forget to capitalize proper nouns, you should pay close attention to capitalization. Editing for grammar and mechanics at every step of the writing process will help you avoid errors on your final test.

Planning My Time

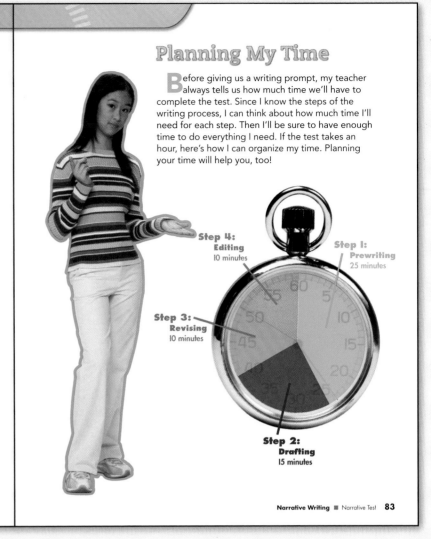

Before giving us a writing prompt, my teacher always tells us how much time we'll have to complete the test. Since I know the steps of the writing process, I can think about how much time I'll need for each step. Then I'll be sure to have enough time to do everything I need. If the test takes an hour, here's how I can organize my time. Planning your time will help you, too!

Step 4: Editing 10 minutes

Step 1: Prewriting 25 minutes

Step 3: Revising 10 minutes

Step 2: Drafting 15 minutes

Planning My Time
(Student page 83)

Explain to students the importance of organizing time when planning for a test. Remind them that they will have a limited amount of time to complete their test, so it is important to set aside a block of time for each one of the steps in the writing process.

Refer to Student page 83, and ask a student volunteer to tell the class which writing step Ashley plans to spend the most time on. **prewriting** Point out that many students do poorly on test writing because they start writing before they develop a plan, and they continue writing until they run out of time. Stress to students the importance of including enough time to prewrite, draft, revise, and edit.

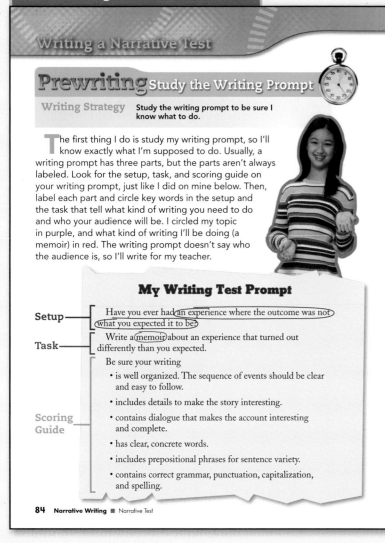

Writing a Narrative Test

Prewriting Study the Writing Prompt

Writing Strategy — Study the writing prompt to be sure I know what to do.

The first thing I do is study my writing prompt, so I'll know exactly what I'm supposed to do. Usually, a writing prompt has three parts, but the parts aren't always labeled. Look for the setup, task, and scoring guide on your writing prompt, just like I did on mine below. Then, label each part and circle key words in the setup and the task that tell what kind of writing you need to do and who your audience will be. I circled my topic in purple, and what kind of writing I'll be doing (a memoir) in red. The writing prompt doesn't say who the audience is, so I'll write for my teacher.

My Writing Test Prompt

Setup — Have you ever had an experience where the outcome was not what you expected it to be?

Task — Write a memoir about an experience that turned out differently than you expected.

Scoring Guide — Be sure your writing

• is well organized. The sequence of events should be clear and easy to follow.

• includes details to make the story interesting.

• contains dialogue that makes the account interesting and complete.

• has clear, concrete words.

• includes prepositional phrases for sentence variety.

• contains correct grammar, punctuation, capitalization, and spelling.

84 **Narrative Writing** ■ Narrative Test

Think about how the scoring guide relates to the six writing traits in the rubrics you've studied. Not all of the traits will be included in every scoring guide, but you need to remember them all to write a good essay.

• Be sure your writing is well organized. The sequence of events should be clear and easy to follow.

I want my reader to be able to follow the story, so organization is important.

• Be sure your writing includes details to make the story interesting.

I want to grab the reader's interest right away, so I'll be sure to include plenty of colorful details.

• Be sure your writing contains dialogue that makes the account interesting and complete.

I have to remember to use dialogue throughout my story. That'll make it more interesting.

• Be sure your writing has clear, concrete words.

I need to be sure that my words are clear and easy to understand.

• Be sure your writing includes prepositional phrases for sentence variety.

I can add life to my writing by using different kinds of sentences. Prepositional phrases will help make my sentences flow.

• Be sure your writing contains correct grammar, punctuation, capitalization, and spelling.

I should always remember to check my grammar and mechanics anytime I write.

Narrative Writing ■ Narrative Test 85

Study the Writing Prompt
(Student pages 84–85)

Read aloud Ashley's words on Student page 84. Tell students that it is important to read and understand their writing prompts before beginning to write. Explain that even if students write a great paper, they won't receive a great score unless they have followed the instructions set forth in the scoring guide.

Ask a student volunteer to tell the class what type of essay Ashley is supposed to write. **a memoir** Explain that Ashley needs to think of an experience that turned out differently than expected, and then she needs to write a memoir about that experience.

Read through the scoring guide portion of the writing prompt shown on Student page 84. Then, review Student page 85 with students. Note how each of the traits relates to the six key areas of assessment. Remind students that if this were a rubric, these traits would be those seen under the Excelling category. Point out that even before Ashley begins to prewrite, she thinks about each of the traits she will need to include in her test.

Writing a Narrative Test

Prewriting Gather Information

Information/Organization — Writing Strategy **Respond to the task.**

Writers always gather information before they begin writing. When you write to take a test, you can find a lot of information in the writing prompt. Let's take another look at the task, since this is the part of the writing prompt that explains what I'm supposed to write. Remember, there's not much time! That's why it's really important to think about how you'll respond before you begin to write.

I see that first I have to come up with a time when an experience turned out differently than I expected. I recently took a surprising visit to a nursing home, so I'll jot down some notes about it.

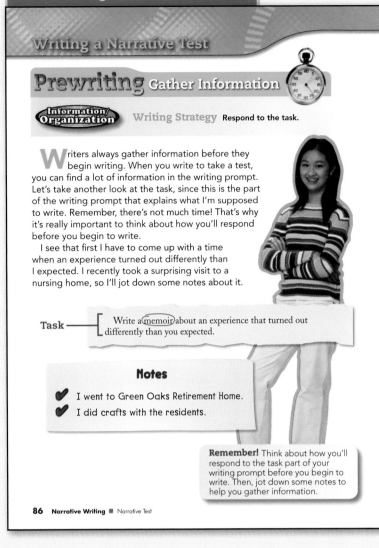

Task —— Write a memoir about an experience that turned out differently than you expected.

Notes

✔ I went to Green Oaks Retirement Home.
✔ I did crafts with the residents.

Remember! Think about how you'll respond to the task part of your writing prompt before you begin to write. Then, jot down some notes to help you gather information.

Prewriting Organize Ideas

Information/Organization — Writing Strategy **Choose a graphic organizer.**

I don't have a lot of time, so I'll begin organizing my ideas right away. I'll start by choosing a graphic organizer. I'm writing my memoir in chronological order, so I'll use a Story Frame to help me record story events.

Setting:	Green Oaks Retirement Home, a local nursing home
Introduction:	supposed to do a community service project at Green Oaks and wasn't happy about it
Rising Action (Event 1):	director took me to room; people waiting seemed bored
Rising Action (Event 2):	director introduced me
Rising Action (Event 3):	residents started making necklaces
Climax:	residents started having a good time
Falling Action (Event 1):	helped Mrs. Fields find pretty beads
Falling Action (Event 2):	Rose did great job
Falling Action (Event 3):	residents were pleased; probably lonely and enjoyed the company
Falling Action (Event 4):	residents thanked me and invited me back
Resolution:	visit Green Oaks once a month

Remember! Choose a graphic organizer that's appropriate for the type of essay you are writing.

Reflect
Did I include enough details on my graphic organizer?

Gather Information and Organize Ideas
(Student pages 86–87)

Ask students to recall what they learned about prewriting in other chapters in this unit. Point out that on a writing test, the prewriting stage is similar: They should consider the assignment and then gather information.

Remind students to use a graphic organizer to organize their ideas. Tell students that during a writing test, they will not be told what kind of graphic organizer to use. Instead, they must think about how they have used graphic organizers in the past, and they must decide which one will be the most useful for a test.

Read through Ashley's Story Frame on Student page 87. Note that even before she started writing, she had already written down much of the information that would appear in her essay.

Differentiating Instruction

Support Help students review how graphic organizers can help them structure their notes. Ask volunteers to name various types of graphic organizers such as those they have used throughout the unit. **Story Frame, Story Map, Timeline** Then, ask students how they might decide which graphic organizer to use on a test. **Possible response: by thinking about which one fits the writing genre** Remind students to look for clues in the writing prompt to help them choose a useful graphic organizer.

Writing a Narrative Test

Prewriting Check the Scoring Guide

Information/Organization

Writing Strategy Check my graphic organizer against the scoring guide.

In a test, there's usually not much time to revise, so that makes prewriting more important than ever! Before I get started, I'll check my Story Frame against the scoring guide in the writing prompt.

Setting:	Green Oaks Retirement Home, a local nursing home
Introduction:	supposed to do a community service project at Green Oaks and wasn't happy about it
Rising Action (Event 1):	director took me to room; people waiting seemed bored
Rising Action (Event 2):	director introduced me
Rising Action (Event 3):	residents started making necklaces
Climax:	residents started having a good time
Falling Action (Event 1):	helped Mrs. Fields find pretty beads
Falling Action (Event 2):	Rose did great job
Falling Action (Event 3):	residents were pleased; probably lonely and enjoyed the company
Falling Action (Event 4):	residents thanked me and invited me back
Resolution:	visit Green Oaks once a month

Information/Organization
- Be sure your writing is well organized. The sequence of events should be clear and easy to follow.

I'll use the introduction from my Story Frame. Then, I'll include the details from the other boxes, since they're already in chronological order.

Voice/Audience
- Be sure your writing includes details to make the story interesting.

I included a bunch of details on my Story Frame.

Content/Ideas
- Be sure your writing contains dialogue that makes the account interesting and complete.

I didn't use any dialogue in my Story Frame, so I'll make sure to include some when I write.

Word Choice/Clarity
- Be sure your writing has clear, concrete words.

I'll be sure to use clear words as I explain the events that are listed on my Story Frame.

Sentence Fluency
- Be sure your writing includes prepositional phrases for sentence variety.

I'll need to remember to do this as I write.

Grammar/Mechanics
- Be sure your writing contains correct grammar, punctuation, capitalization, and spelling.

I'll check for proper grammar and mechanics when I edit my draft.

Remember! Before you start to write, reread the scoring guide in the writing prompt to be sure you know what to do.

Reflect

My Story Frame doesn't include every point in the scoring guide, but I think it covers most of them. Is there anything else that I'm forgetting?

Check the Scoring Guide

(Student pages 88–89)

Ask students why they think Ashley is not yet ready to write even though she has used a graphic organizer to structure her notes. **Possible response: because she needs to check her graphic organizer against the scoring guide** Emphasize the importance of paying attention to the scoring guide throughout test writing. Note that on Student page 89, Ashley once again refers back to each point in the scoring guide to be sure she has met each one. Explain that during this step of the test writing process, students may need to add or change information in their graphic organizers to meet the criteria.

Point out that while the graphic organizer helped Ashley organize her notes and meet the scoring guide criteria, she will continue to think about all of the scoring guide traits as she writes.

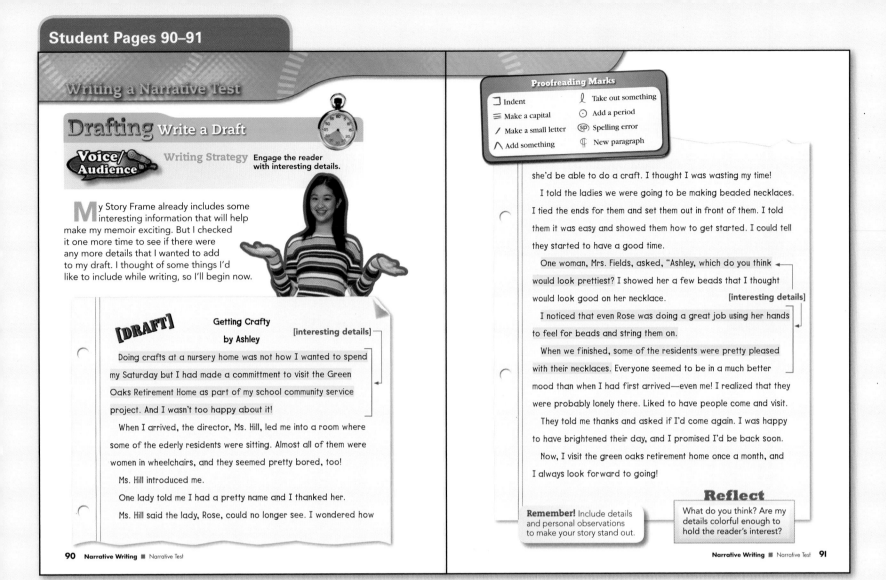

Drafting

(Student pages 90–91)

Read Ashley's words on Student page 90. Point out how she refers to her graphic organizer in order to write her draft. Emphasize to students the importance of using their graphic organizers as guidance during the drafting process. Explain that because of editing, they will want to leave space between the lines so that they will have room to make changes and additions to their work. Also, remind them to write neatly, even in the drafting stage, because the test evaluator should be able to read what they have written.

Then, discuss Ashley's draft. Have students refer back to her graphic organizer to see whether she included the information that she outlined in her Story Frame. Ask students what they think of Ashley's draft, pointing out that although there are mistakes, she has remembered to leave time during the editing stage to go through and change any errors she made in spelling and grammar.

Finally, review proofreading marks with students. Note that these marks will be helpful as they revise and edit their drafts.

Differentiating Instruction

English-Language Learners Remind these students that when drafting, they should concentrate mainly on getting ideas down on paper. Offer the following suggestions:

- If students have trouble coming up with appropriate words or phrases, they can leave blank spots in their writing and come back to them later.
- Tell students not to worry if they cannot come up with an interesting opening: Other ideas may appear as they write their drafts.
- Explain that students can work on sentence variety as they revise: Any repetitive patterns should be easier to spot when they reread their drafts.
- Remind students that at this stage, they should not be overly concerned with spelling and grammar since they can fix mistakes during editing.

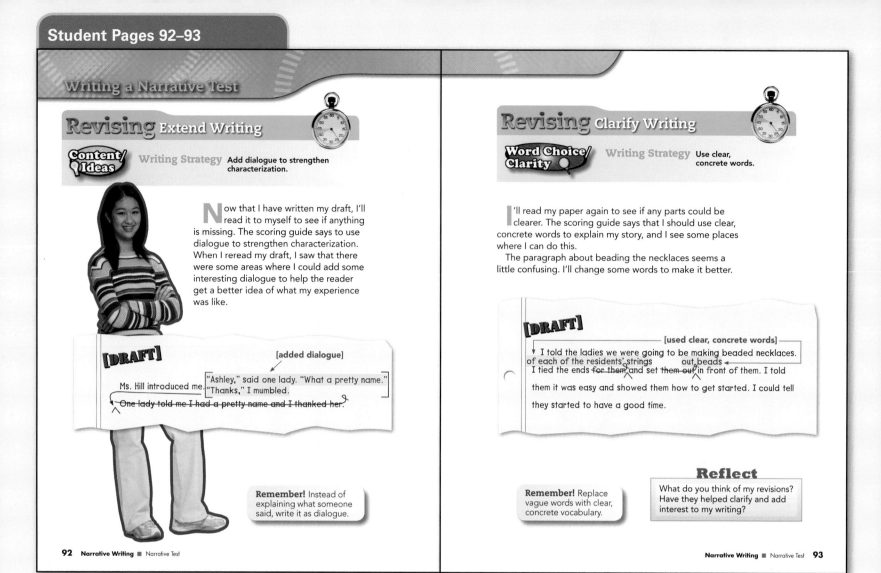

Revising

(Student pages 92–93)

Discuss the revisions Ashley made on Student pages 92–93. She added dialogue and replaced general words with clear, concrete words. Point out that Ashley once again reviewed her scoring guide in order to determine a revision focus. Encourage students to refer back to the scoring guide section of the writing prompt even after they have completed their drafts.

Point out Ashley's revision on Student page 92. Discuss whether the additions help students better understand her experience. Have students point out other places in Ashley's draft where replacing statements with dialogue could help bring her memoir to life.

Next, review with students the ways Ashley replaced general words in her draft on Student page 93 with words that are clear and concrete. Have students explain what they think the new words contribute to the draft. **Possible response: They make the wording clear and concise.**

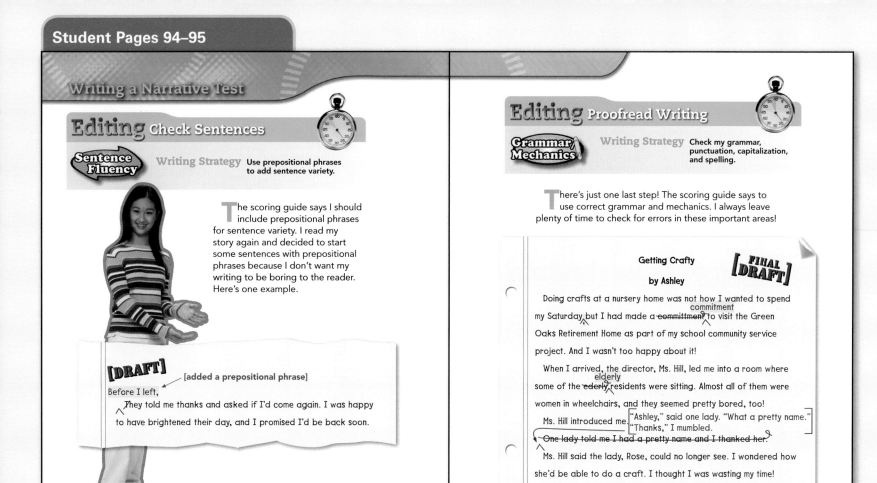

Editing

(Student pages 94–96)

Read aloud the section of Ashley's draft shown on Student page 94, noting how she added a prepositional phrase at the beginning. Point out that in this edit, Ashley added a prepositional phrase to change the sentence structure. Remind students that they can also change the placement of an already existing prepositional phrase. For example, moving a prepositional phrase from the middle or end of a sentence to the beginning can break up a string of sentences that all start the same way.

Emphasize to students that they should always proofread for mistakes, checking for errors in sentence completeness, punctuation, and spelling.

Differentiating Instruction

Support Reinforce students' understanding of prepositional phrases by reviewing the following.

- Remind students that a prepositional phrase consists of a preposition and its object.
- Make sure students understand that a preposition describes how the subject of a sentence relates to another noun, called the object.
- There are many prepositions. Some common ones are *above, across, after, before, beside, between, inside, over, upon,* and *with.*
- Write some prepositional phrases on the board. Then, have students write other examples.
- Explain that while a prepositional phrase may appear anywhere in a sentence, placing it at the beginning can help break up the pattern of starting every sentence with the subject.
- Write examples of sentences that begin with a prepositional phrase such as *Before lunch, I went to the library.* Then, write other sentences that students can revise so that the prepositional phrase comes at the beginning.

[FINAL DRAFT]

I told the ladies we were going to be making beaded necklaces.
of each of the residents strings   out beads
I tied the ends for them and set them out in front of them. I told

them it was easy and showed them how to get started. I could tell

they started to have a good time.

One woman, Mrs. Fields, asked, "Ashley, which do you think

would look prettiest?" I showed her a few beads that I thought

would look good on her necklace.

I noticed that even Rose was doing a great job using her hands

to feel for beads and string them on.

When we finished, some of the residents were pretty pleased

with their necklaces. Everyone seemed to be in a much better

mood than when I had first arrived—even me! I realized that they
                                    and
were probably lonely there, liked to have people come and visit.
Before I left,
They told me thanks and asked if I'd come again. I was happy

to have brightened their day, and I promised I'd be back soon.

Now, I visit the green oaks retirement home once a month, and

I always look forward to going!

Reflect

Is my writing missing anything? Check it against the scoring guide. Remember to use your writing prompt's scoring guide to check your writing anytime you take a test!

I'm finished! You just have to remember to use the writing process when you take a writing test. The process is a little different for a test, but you'll do fine as long as you remember these important tips.

TEST TIPS

1. **Study the writing prompt before you start to write.** Most writing prompts have three parts: the setup, the task, and the scoring guide. The parts probably won't be labeled. You'll have to figure them out for yourself!

2. **Make sure you understand the task before you start to write.**
   • Read all three parts of the writing prompt carefully.
   • Circle key words in the task part of the writing prompt that tell what kind of writing you need to do. The task might also identify your audience.
   • Make sure you know how you'll be graded.
   • Say the assignment in your own words to yourself.

3. **Keep an eye on the clock.** Decide how much time you will spend on each part of the writing process and try to stick to your schedule. Don't spend so much time on prewriting that you don't have enough time left to write.

4. **Reread your writing. Check it against the scoring guide at least twice.** Remember the rubrics you've used? A scoring guide on a writing test is like a rubric. It can help you keep what's important in mind.

5. **Plan, plan, plan!** You don't get much time to revise during a test, so planning is more important than ever.

6. **Write neatly.** Remember, if the people who score your test can't read your writing, it doesn't matter how good your essay is!

Test Tips

(Student page 97)

Ask students to recall the lessons they learned in this chapter. Ask them to name the important steps to take when writing for a test. **Possible responses: follow the writing prompt; plan time; save time for editing and revising**

Remind students that test writing is similar to writing for a class assignment. One big difference, though, is that test writing is timed.

Read aloud the Test Tips on Student page 97. Have students think about how Ashley followed each of these tips during test writing. Point out that they should keep each of the six tips in mind when they write their own tests.

Differentiating Instruction

Support Some students may benefit from a review of capitalization rules. Remind them to capitalize
• the first letter of each word that begins a sentence or direct quotation.
• all proper names.
• family relations when used as part of a proper name; for example, *My Aunt Amy* takes a capital, but *My aunt is named Amy* does not.
• titles that begin names, but not those that come after names; for example, *Mayor Jill Saunders* takes a capital, but *Jill Saunders is our mayor* does not.
• directions that are used as proper names of regions, but not as compass points; for example, *The North has a cold climate* takes a capital, but *Walk north to the bridge* does not.
• the names of days, months, and holidays. Seasons are capitalized only when used as part of a title.
• the names of specific countries, nationalities, and languages.
• the major words in book titles.
• periods, events, and eras, such as *The Great Depression* or *The Colonial Era.*

Books for Professional Development

Anderson, Carl. *How's It Going? A Practical Guide to Conferring With Student Writers.* **Portsmouth: Heinemann, 2000.**

Anderson provides samples that demonstrate various techniques and strategies that will help both teacher and students refine their participation in a conference.

Bromley, Karen, Linda Irwin-De Vitis, and Marcia Modlo. *Graphic Organizers: Visual Strategies for Active Learning.* **New York: Scholastic, 1995.**

The authors share ways of using graphic organizers in teaching across the curriculum as well as organizational techniques that students can use in content areas as they plan their writing.

Clark, Roy Peter. *Free to Write: A Journalist Teaches Young Writers.* **Portsmouth: Heinemann, 1995.**

The key value of this book is its use of the real world as a source of all writing. Clark encourages students to write every day, gathering and sifting information, writing leads, building momentum, rethinking and correcting, and reaching an audience.

King, Laurie, and Dennis Stovall. *Classroom Publishing: A Practical Guide to Enhancing Student Literacy.* **Hillsboro: Blue Heron, 1992.**

This book features six brief chapters that describe classroom publishing projects for grades 6–8.

School-Home
Connection

Dear Family,

Your child is currently learning to write a memoir, which is a reflection about a personal experience. As he or she goes through the steps of writing, here's how you can help:

1. **Prewriting:** Students will begin by jotting down notes about a personal experience. They will then make a Story Frame to organize their notes. You can help your child brainstorm and choose an appropriate topic by reminiscing about past events and friendly gatherings.

2. **Drafting:** Students will make a working draft of their memoir, using a reflective tone to convey meaning and insight to the reader. You can help by having your child read his or her draft to you as it is written. This way, you can point out passages where more reflection is needed.

3. **Revising:** Students will refine their drafts by adding details and using a thesaurus to vary word choice. Help your child by asking for further information about weak passages, or by suggesting alternate terms or phrases for confusing areas.

4. **Editing:** You can help check for errors in spelling, punctuation, and capitalization by listening as your child reads the draft aloud to you, or you can provide further help by reading the draft together.

5. **Publishing:** Students will publish a final copy of their work. Urge them to make copies to send to friends and family members.

Being able to reflect on personal experience is a skill that is required throughout life, in both school and the workplace. If you have any questions as you provide assistance, please let me know.

Thanks for your help in the writing process!

School-Home Connection

Dear Family,

Your child is currently learning to write a historical episode, which is a story that combines both real and fictional details about a historical event. As he or she goes through the steps of writing, here's how you can help:

1. **Prewriting:** Students will begin by choosing one historical event and then gathering information from several resources. They will then organize story elements on a Story Map. You can help your child review and research possible topics by working together to brainstorm interesting eras and events in history. Perhaps you yourself have lived through a certain historical event that could serve as a great writing topic!

2. **Drafting:** Students will make a working draft of their historical episode, clearly describing the setting and theme for the reader. You can help by having your child read his or her draft to you as it is written. This way, you can point out passages where more explanation is needed to expand on the setting or theme.

3. **Revising:** Students will refine their drafts by adding historical details and making sure dialogue reflects the time and place in which the characters live. Help your child by reminding him or her to fact-check the accuracy of historical details. Suggest that he or she use the Internet or an encyclopedia to do this.

4. **Editing:** You can help check for errors in spelling, punctuation, and capitalization by listening as your child reads the draft aloud to you, or you can provide further help by reading the draft together.

5. **Publishing:** Students will be publishing a final copy of their work. Urge them to make copies to send to friends and family members.

Being able to conduct research and synthesize information are skills that are required throughout life, in both school and the workplace. If you have any questions as you provide assistance, please let me know.

Thanks for your help in the writing process!

School-Home Connection

Dear Family,

Your child is currently learning to write a biography, which is a brief history of another person's life events. As he or she goes through the steps of writing, here's how you can help:

1. **Prewriting:** Students will begin by choosing a person as the focus of their writing. They will then conduct an interview to gather information about that person. Finally, students will plot important events on a Timeline. You can help by role-playing the part of your child's interviewee, offering feedback and suggestions for conversation starters and appropriate interview questions.

2. **Drafting:** Students will make a working draft of their biography, remembering to include an introduction that grabs the reader's attention. You can help by suggesting possible ways to begin the draft.

3. **Revising:** Students will refine their drafts by adding direct quotations and using a dictionary to make sure they have used words correctly. Help your child by suggesting alternate word choices and making sure he or she uses a dictionary to double-check spellings and definitions of words.

4. **Editing:** You can help check for errors in spelling, punctuation, and capitalization by listening as your child reads the draft aloud to you, or you can provide further help by reading the draft together.

5. **Publishing:** Students will publish a final copy of their work. Urge them to make copies to send to friends and family members.

Being able to summarize information in an engaging manner is a skill that is required throughout life, in both school and the workplace. If you have any questions as you provide assistance, please let me know.

Thanks for your help in the writing process!

School-Home Connection

Dear Family,

Your child is currently learning to write a narrative test. The test is timed. Here are the necessary steps involved in writing a narrative test, and here's how you can help with each step:

1. **Prewriting:** Students will learn to read a writing prompt to understand the type of writing required. The writing prompt will tell your child what kind of writing to do and what topic to write about. Time management is crucial in test writing. Practice breaking an hour into segments of time with your child, so that he or she has a sense of how long it takes for 10, 15, or 25 minutes of time to pass. Your child will also use a graphic organizer to plan his or her writing. Help him or her decide upon an appropriate graphic organizer by prompting a discussion of organizers used in the past.

2. **Drafting:** Students will use their graphic organizers to write a draft that engages the reader with interesting details. Remind your child that the draft should be written neatly the first time because there will not be enough time to write it again.

3. **Revising:** Students will use the scoring guide in the writing prompt as a reminder to add dialogue and to use clear, concrete words. Help your child by asking for further details about any confusing or weak passages.

4. **Editing:** Students will spend the last part of the timed writing test checking for common errors in punctuation, capitalization, and spelling. Discourage your child from fretting over the "imperfect" appearance of his or her writing test. The pages won't look as neat as usual, and it's OK for students to make corrections right on the page.

If you have any questions, please let me know. Together, we'll help your child master the important skill of writing on demand, a skill that students use in many subjects throughout their school years.

Thanks for your help in the writing process!

DESCRIPTIVE
writing strategies

IN THIS UNIT

1 Business Letter

- List my main idea or topic. Then, list details that support it.
- Make a Main-Idea Table to organize my information.
- Make sure my letter format is correct and my tone is appropriate.
- Look for places to add vivid details.
- Delete or revise details that don't support my main idea.
- Break up wordy sentences to keep my letter flowing.
- Make sure subjects and verbs agree.

2 Scientific Observation

- Observe and take notes.
- Make Cause-and-Effect Links to organize my notes.
- Use scientific language that is appropriate for the audience.
- Add diagrams to enhance the description.
- Use specific words to show important connections.
- Use transitional phrases to help the writing flow.
- Make sure colons and hyphens are used correctly.

3 Descriptive Vignette

- Choose a personal experience. Jot down notes about what I heard, smelled, tasted, and touched.
- Make a Web to organize my notes.
- Help the reader visualize by including plenty of sensory details.
- Add figurative language.
- Replace clichés, vague words, and overused words with precise words.
- Use participial phrases to create sentence variety.
- Make sure comparative and superlative forms are used correctly.

4 Writing for a Test

- Study the writing prompt to be sure I know what to do.
- Respond to the task.
- Choose a graphic organizer.
- Check my graphic organizer against the scoring guide.
- Use an appropriate tone to keep the reader interested.
- Add sensory details.
- Replace vague words with precise words.
- Use clauses to strengthen weak sentences.
- Check my grammar, punctuation, capitalization, and spelling.

DESCRIPTIVE writing describes something to the reader.

Hi, I'm Josh. I'm learning about descriptive writing in school, and I really think I'm going to have fun with it. I like sharing with my friends and family all the things that happen to me, and now I'll learn some strategies to turn those experiences into full-length pieces of descriptive writing.

IN THIS UNIT

1. **Business Letter**
2. **Scientific Observation**
3. **Descriptive Vignette**
4. **Writing for a Test**

Name: Josh
Home: Virginia
Hobbies: going to the movies, playing baseball, spending time at the beach
Favorite Movie: *Star Wars*

98 Descriptive Writing

Descriptive Writing 99

IN THIS UNIT

Business Letter This genre introduces students to important skills that will help them communicate with the world beyond friends and family.

Scientific Observation This genre gives students the opportunity to run and observe experiments, summarize their process, and make inferences about what they learned.

Descriptive Vignette This genre gives students a chance to use sensory details to describe a specific place, thing, or event so that it comes to life on the page.

Descriptive Test Students learn and practice how to read a descriptive test prompt and how to plan their time. They also learn and practice writing strategies for successful test writing in the descriptive mode.

Meet Josh

The student guide for this chapter is Josh, a boy from Virginia. You may wish to explore with students how Josh's background, hobbies, interests, and personality connect with his choices of writing topics. Explain to students that Josh will use what he knows to make decisions about his topics—a process that helps make his writing special and real. Encourage students to follow Josh's lead by using their own background knowledge, interests, and personalities as they write. Descriptive writing describes something to the reader, and your students will have many interesting, unique, and authentic experiences to describe.

by Julie Coiro, Ph.D.
University of Connecticut

Locating Resources: Generating Keyword Searches

There are different keyword strategies you can use to quickly locate the Internet materials you need. If you are using a search engine designed for children, you should get relatively good results by just inserting the topic into the search bar and clicking "search." However, if you or your students are using a more advanced search engine like **Google** or **Yahoo**, you may wish to try the following.

- **Choose your keywords wisely.** Indicate in the search bar a subject area or a specific topic. Use quotations to group two or more words together as a phrase. For example, if you are looking for a lesson on descriptive writing, you would enclose the phrase in quotation marks: "descriptive writing."

- **Narrow your search with a "topic+focus" keyword strategy.** If you preface both topic and focus words/phrases with a plus sign (+lesson+"descriptive writing"), the search engine will only look for hits that have both topic and focus words/phrases on the same Web page.

- **Specify an appropriate grade level, if desired.** If you find your search results are not appropriate for students at your grade level, include the grade level or grade range in quotes before or after your search ("third grade"+"writing lesson").

- **Think of a synonym or skim the search result annotations for more appropriate keywords.** Sometimes reading within the search results or on a few related Web sites creates more familiarity with the language around that topic. This will help you generate more appropriate search terms for your needs.

Here are some examples of the keyword strategies listed above:

"lesson plans" + "descriptive writing"
"fifth grade" + "biography project"
webquest + poetry
quiz + biography
cyberhunt + "Ancient Egypt"

Critical Evaluation: Evaluating Bias

One aspect of reading critically involves the ability to detect bias, or the stance with which an author shapes information for different purposes. Information on the Internet is widely available from people who have strong political, economic, or religious stances, so we must assist students in becoming critical consumers of such information.

One strategy for helping students understand the concept of biased information involves helping them distinguish between facts, opinions, and points of view. A classroom discussion about descriptive writing techniques can provide an excellent context within which to introduce these ideas. Your students are bound to have different opinions about various topics, so you may wish to highlight these differences by selecting a topic that some students really like and others really don't. Ask students to write three factual non-opinionated descriptive statements that describe the topic. Then, ask them to write three opinionated descriptive sentences. Encourage students to share their sentences while others try to guess whether

they're facts or opinions. Categorize the sentences that reflect one point of view (e.g., *I like broccoli*) versus another (e.g., *I don't like broccoli*), and explain that both are valid but come from different perspectives. Thus, the descriptions are biased toward one perspective or another. Explain that a complete description of this topic would include sentences that represent both perspectives.

Point out to students that many Web sites are written from only one perspective. This is important to know so that students do not base their whole thinking about an issue on one person's point of view. For example, take some time to explore **Kids web Japan** at **http://web-japan.org/kidsweb** and ask why students would not find negative information about Japan at this site. Similarly, visit **The National Wildlife Federation** Web site at **http://www.nwf.org** and ask why students would not find information about hunting at this site. If students feel they are not getting "the whole story" from one Web site, they should look for another that offers a different perspective.

Communicating Globally: Publishing Descriptive Writing

There are a number of interesting on-line projects that can prompt descriptive writing ideas as well as provide space for students to publish their final work. Here are two examples.

- **Art Tales** at **http://www.wildlifeart.org/ArtTales** is sponsored by the National Museum of Wildlife Art. Students are invited, via a unique interactive interface, to explore a wide range of stunning wildlife drawings and paintings while playing the role of a frontier explorer, field guide writer, or museum curator. They select the paintings most relevant for their needs and compile them, with support, into a descriptive journal, informational field guide, or an art exhibition. When they finish, their work is published at the Web site.

- **New Moon Blog** at **http://newmoonnews. blogspot.com** is an exciting new publishing opportunity designed for girls to talk and write about things from their perspective. Created by the publishers of *New Moon: The Magazine for Girls and Their*

Dreams at **http://www.newmoon.org**, it provides screened and safe opportunities for girls ages 10 and up to publish their descriptive stories, book reviews, reactions to current events, and other news about girls. Their companion Web site, **For Girls and their Dreams** at **http://www.forgirlsandtheirdreams.org**, hosts additional opportunities for girls to share their dreams and life goals, discuss hot topics, explore others countries, and e-mail their opinions. This site is an example of the new social networking experiences that are quickly becoming part of daily life for adolescents.

Supporting and Extending Writing: Sparking Writing Ideas

As part of this descriptive writing unit, you may wish to spend a few minutes of class time to highlight the following on-line science experiment collections from which your students can select an experiment, try it out at home, and then formally write up their procedures and observations in their scientific observations.

- **PBS Science Activities http://pbskids.org/zoom/ activities/sci** includes experiments especially designed for exploring concepts such as chemistry, engineering, the five senses, and life science.

- **Energy Quest Science Projects http://www. energyquest.ca.gov/projects/index.html** offers fun experiments for exploring chemical, geothermal, and nuclear energy.

- **Exploratorium Science Snacks http://www. exploratorium.edu/snacks/snackintro.html** are mini-versions of the most popular exhibits at the Exploratorium Museum of Science, Art, and Human Perception in San Francisco, California. Each features ideas about what to do after setting up an experiment.

- **Steve Spangler's Easy Science Experiment Projects http://www.stevespanglerscience. com/experiments** features a list of top ten science experiments. Don't miss the videos, too, at **http://www. stevespanglerscience.com/video**.

- **Little Shop of Physics http://littleshop.physics. colostate.edu/onlineexperiments.htm** is part of Colorado State University's hands-on science outreach program, featuring experiments about the physics of objects using household items or a computer.

- **Science Experiments at Home http://members. ozemail.com.au/~macinnis/scifun/miniexp.htm** is a collection of short experiments sure to prompt writing ideas.

- **Wondernet: Science That Matters http://www. chemistry.org/portal/a/c/s/1/wondernetdisplay. html?DOC=wondernet\topics_list\index.html** is sponsored by the American Chemical Society. It combines chemical reactions with graphing activities that can easily be converted into scientific observations.

Business Letter Overview

In this chapter, students will learn how to write a business letter. They will learn the different elements of a business letter—purpose, tone, supporting facts, and vivid details—and some reasons why they might choose to write one. Students will then use a business letter rubric to study a model writing sample.

Students will follow the student guide as he goes through the writing stages—prewriting, drafting, revising, editing, and publishing. As the student guide learns new writing strategies in each step, students will be directed to practice the strategies in their own writing.

During prewriting and drafting, students will

- choose a topic or main idea.
- jot down details that support the topic.

- organize their notes into a Main-Idea Table.
- write a draft in letter format.
- use an appropriate tone.

During revising and editing, students will

- add vivid details to enhance description.
- delete or revise irrelevant details.
- break up wordy sentences to help the writing flow.
- edit their drafts for spelling, capitalization, punctuation, and subject-verb agreement.

Finally, students will write a final draft to be published.

You may wish to send to families the School-Home Connection Letter for this chapter, located at the end of this unit in the Teacher Edition.

Business Letter Writing Traits

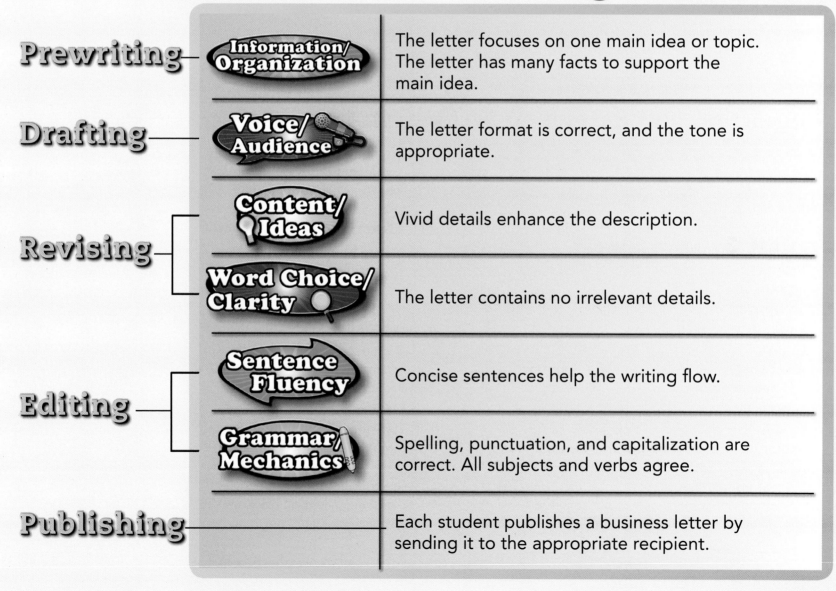

Stage	Trait	Description
Prewriting	Information/Organization	The letter focuses on one main idea or topic. The letter has many facts to support the main idea.
Drafting	Voice/Audience	The letter format is correct, and the tone is appropriate.
Revising	Content/Ideas	Vivid details enhance the description.
Revising	Word Choice/Clarity	The letter contains no irrelevant details.
Editing	Sentence Fluency	Concise sentences help the writing flow.
Editing	Grammar/Mechanics	Spelling, punctuation, and capitalization are correct. All subjects and verbs agree.
Publishing		Each student publishes a business letter by sending it to the appropriate recipient.

Business Letter Time Management

	Day 1	Day 2	Day 3	Day 4	Day 5
Learning Objectives					
	Students will: • learn the components of a business letter.	Students will: • learn how to gather information for a business letter.	Students will: • practice gathering information for their own business letters.	Students will: • learn how to make a Main-Idea Table to organize details.	Students will: • practice organizing details into a Main-Idea Table.
Activities					
	• Discuss the elements and traits of a business letter (Student pages 100–102). • Use the rubric to study the model (Student pages 103–109).	• Read and discuss **Prewriting: Gather Information** (Student page 110).	• Brainstorm ideas and choose a letter topic. • Gather information by jotting down details that support the topic.	• Read and discuss **Prewriting: Organize Ideas** (Student page 111).	• Review the details listed while gathering information. • Make a Main-Idea Table to organize details.

WEEK 2

	Day 1	Day 2	Day 3	Day 4	Day 5
Learning Objectives					
	Students will: • learn how to use an appropriate tone. • learn to write in letter format.	Students will: • practice writing their own drafts.	Students will: • learn how adding vivid details can enhance their descriptions.	Students will: • practice adding vivid details to their drafts.	Students will: • learn how to delete or revise irrelevant details.
Activities					
	• Read and discuss **Drafting: Write a Draft** (Student pages 112–113).	• Use Main-Idea Tables to write drafts. • Use the correct letter format and an appropriate tone.	• Read and discuss **Revising: Extend Writing** (Student page 114).	• Choose vivid details to add to drafts.	• Read and discuss **Revising: Clarify Writing** (Student page 115).

WEEK 3

	Day 1	Day 2	Day 3	Day 4	Day 5
Learning Objectives					
	Students will: • practice deleting or revising irrelevant details.	Students will: • learn how using concise sentences can help their writing flow.	Students will: • learn how to make subjects and verbs agree.	Students will: • practice editing their drafts for spelling, capitalization, and punctuation.	Students will: • learn different ways to publish their business letters.
Activities					
	• Reread drafts, looking for information that does not support the purpose. • Delete or revise irrelevant details to make writing clearer.	• Read and discuss **Editing: Check Sentences** (Student page 116). • Make sure to break up wordy sentences.	• Read and discuss **Editing: Proofread Writing** (Student page 117).	• Fix any spelling, capitalization, or punctuation errors. • Fix any subjects and verbs that do not agree.	• Read and discuss **Publishing: Share Writing** (Student page 120).

To complete the chapter in fewer days, teach the learning objectives and activities for two days in one day.

This planning chart, correlated to your state's writing standards, is available on-line at http://www.zaner-bloser.com/sfw.

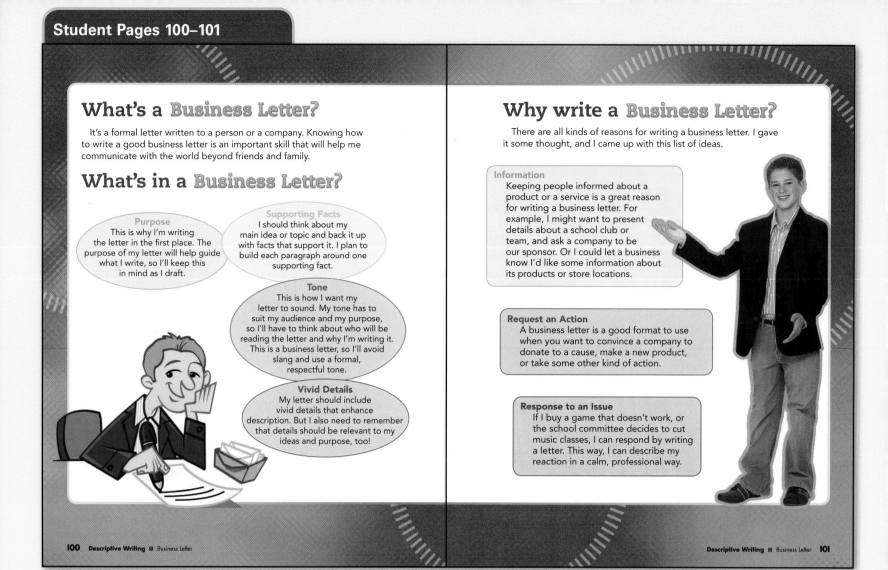

Define the Genre

(Student page 100)

Business Letter

Discuss with students the definition of a business letter. Ask students whether any of them have ever written a letter of request, praise, or complaint. Point out that any time they write a formal letter with a specific purpose, they are using the business letter genre.

Elements of the Genre

Business Letter

Read and discuss with students the elements of a business letter listed on Student page 100. Ask volunteers which elements are also common to other forms of writing. **Possible responses: Purpose—friendly letters, persuasive writing; Supporting Facts—persuasive essays, research papers; Tone—personal narratives, editorials; Vivid Details—stories, vignettes** Discuss why each element may be important to writing a business letter.

Authentic Writing

(Student page 101)

Business Letter

Read and discuss with students the reasons for writing a business letter listed on Student page 101. Point out that all writing has a purpose and is aimed at a specific audience. These authentic purposes help authors shape their writing. Ask a volunteer to read aloud the Information box. Then, have students discuss other reasons someone might write a business letter for information. Repeat this process for the Request an Action and the Response to an Issue boxes. Then, have students brainstorm other purposes for writing a business letter that are not listed on Student page 101. Encourage students to think about their own reasons for writing a business letter, and how these reasons will affect the tone and focus of their writing.

Business Letter Writing Traits

What goes into a good business letter? I can answer this question by focusing on the six traits of good writing. I'll use the list below when I write my letter.

Information/Organization	The letter focuses on one main idea or topic. The letter has many facts to support the main idea.
Voice/Audience	The letter format is correct, and the tone is appropriate.
Content/Ideas	Vivid details enhance the description.
Word Choice/Clarity	The letter contains no irrelevant details.
Sentence Fluency	Concise sentences help the writing flow.
Grammar/Mechanics	Spelling, punctuation, and capitalization are correct. All subjects and verbs agree.

I can use Denny McCabe's business letter on the next three pages as a model for my own writing. Later, I'll analyze how Denny used the traits to help him write.

Business Letter Model

1045 Stonegate Drive
Westmont, IL 60559
August 3, 20--

Mr. Ronald Richards, General Manager
Woodcreek Theaters
1 South Mall Drive
Clarendon Hills, IL 60514

Dear Mr. Richards:

Purpose

I am writing to tell you about the unpleasant experience that I had at your new theater complex this evening. I was expecting an exciting evening, especially after all the publicity about the twelve new screens with plush seating and state-of-the-art sound systems. It was at one of these screens—Theater 6, to be exact—that I arrived to see *Exploring Space*. My experience was disappointing, considering everything that happened tonight.

Supporting Fact

Three problems made it impossible to enjoy the movie. The first relates to the lack of service in the lobby area. A large cinema complex should have more than one concession stand, and this one did. Two circular, glass-topped counters displayed a tempting array of candies, sodas, popcorn, and hot snacks such as nachos.

Vivid Details

Although the lobby was packed with movie-goers, only one counter was open because only two ushers were available to work. The lines were so long that people started pushing and shoving to get to the front. Some particularly impatient people even shouted out their orders before those in front of them could say what they wanted. After someone complained, the second concession stand was opened. This might have eased the problem, if the

Writing Traits
(Student pages 102–105)

Business Letter

Tell students you are going to read aloud the beginning of two different versions of a business letter. Explain that one version has an informal tone, and the other has a formal tone.

Afterward, ask students to compare the two versions. Then, discuss with students the characteristics of formal and informal tones. Explain that an informal tone is often signified by casual language, slang, humor, personal references, sentence fragments, and a distinctive voice. But a formal tone is signified by neutral or polite language, complete sentences, and straightforward description.

Tell students that they are going to study and use strategies for writing business letters, and that a good business letter has the traits listed on Student page 102. Then, ask students to listen for these traits as you read aloud the business letter on Student pages 103–105.

Differentiating Instruction

English-Language Learners Preteach key words and concepts that can help these students understand the business letter model. Explain that the author's purpose is to provide feedback, or a reaction, to an experience at a new cinema. Then, write the following word categories on the board and review their meanings.

feedback	*cinema/theater*
unpleasant	*screens*
disappointing	*lobby*
disgruntled	*concession stand*
littered	*ushers*
understaffing	*manager*
ruined	*technician*

Help increase students' understanding by reviewing additional vocabulary and idioms with them. Focus on the following multiple-meaning words that may cause confusion. Write these word pairs and their definitions on the board, and ask students which meanings are used in the letter.

complex (adj.): having many parts; complicated
complex (n.): a structure made up of individual parts
counter (n.): a table or display case
counter (n.): a person who counts
run (v.): to move quickly
run (n.): a period of being in demand

Business Letter

manager hadn't taken one of the ushers from the first counter to staff it. Now, two stands were functioning, but with only one staffer apiece. After waiting 15 minutes for popcorn, I left empty-handed, only to stand in another disgruntled, slow-moving crowd to get to my film on time. — Supporting Fact

When I finally took my seat, I was immediately confronted with a second problem: the conditions inside Theater 6. For starters, the theater was freezing cold. Before the coming attractions even began, several people asked the manager to adjust the thermostat. She said she would take care of it, but the temperature never changed. Consequently, several people sitting around me got up and left about halfway through the movie. Other people opted to stay, fidgeting endlessly by shrugging on their coats and squirming in their seats, as if keeping in constant motion might keep them warm.

Supporting Fact — In addition, Theater 6 looked and felt as if it had never been cleaned. In my row, empty containers littered the floor, topped with a layer of discarded popcorn puffs stuck to a coating of spilled soda. This was a multi-sensory nightmare. Aside from the horrible sight of it, there was the sticky feel of jelly candies plastered to the back of my chair, and the sucking sound my sneakers made each time I lifted them off the floor. I assume that this problem stemmed from the same cause as the situation in the lobby: understaffing. Perhaps the lack of ushers made it impossible to keep up with between-show cleanings. — Supporting Fact

Vivid Details

The third problem was the presentation of the movie itself. First, there was the sound. Although we could barely hear our own movie, we could clearly hear the one in Theater 5. As soon as *Exploring Space* began, people started asking for the volume to

be adjusted. Even so, we couldn't really hear it until the film's final half hour. Then, the film suddenly stopped right at the high point of the movie! The technician got it started again pretty quickly, but it was too late. Along with everything else that had gone wrong, the interruption ruined any enjoyment I was getting out of the movie. At that point, I gave up and left.

Considering the events of this evening, I may not return to the new Woodcreek Theaters. I hope you consider this feedback because, without certain improvements, the new cinema complex might have an extremely short run. — Tone

Sincerely,

Denny McCabe

Denny McCabe

Differentiating Instruction

Enrichment Tell students that using the active voice is one way to make their sentences more concise. Remind them that in the active voice, the subject of the sentence performs the action. In the passive voice, the subject receives the action expressed by the verb. Write the following on the board and have students note that the passive voice is usually wordier.

Active: Students surveyed movie-goers about the new cinema.

Passive: A survey of movie-goers was taken by students about the new cinema.

Challenge pairs of students to use the passive voice to write sentences about movies. Then, have them exchange sentences and rewrite them using the active voice. Call on volunteers to share their sentence pairs and discuss which ones—active or passive—are more concise.

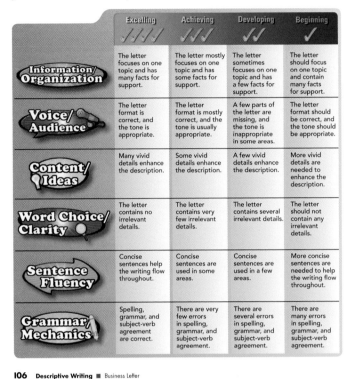

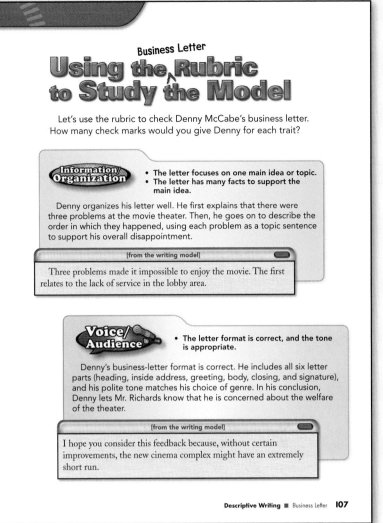

Using the Rubric
(Student page 106)

Explain that a rubric is a tool that can be used to evaluate a piece of writing. The rubric on Student page 106 can be used to evaluate a business letter. It is based on the same business letter traits listed on Student page 102.

Now point out the terms above each rubric column: *Excelling, Achieving, Developing,* and *Beginning.* Explain that each column symbolizes a degree of writing skill, and that each rubric row focuses on a specific writing trait. When students use the rubric to evaluate their own work at each step of the writing process, they increase the likelihood of producing polished, well-written business letters.

Study the Model
(Student pages 107–109)

Explain that Student pages 107–109 show how the writing model on Student pages 103–105 meets all six traits of the rubric. Read each section with the students. Then, have them look for other examples of each trait in the writing model.

Ask students how many check marks they would assign the writing model for each trait. Then, as a class, decide how the writing model should be rated overall.

Remind students to use the rubric as they write their own business letter, to be sure they are meeting all six writing traits.

Business Letter

Content/ Ideas
• Vivid details enhance the description.

Denny states the problems he encountered and describes his experience in detail. Because the details he uses are specific and colorful, they really help him get his point across.

> **[from the writing model]**
>
> In my row, empty containers littered the floor, topped with a layer of discarded popcorn puffs stuck to a coating of spilled soda. This was a multi-sensory nightmare. Aside from the horrible sight of it, there was the sticky feel of jelly candies plastered to the back of my chair, and the sucking sound my sneakers made each time I lifted them off the floor.

Word Choice/ Clarity
• The letter contains no irrelevant details.

Denny's main idea is that his experience at the new theater complex was really unpleasant. He explains why by describing how each problem affected him and the other movie-goers. All these details relate to his purpose, and I didn't read anything that seemed off point. In this section, all the details were necessary to describe how understaffing led to chaos.

> **[from the writing model]**
>
> Although the lobby was packed with movie-goers, only one counter was open because only two ushers were available to work. The lines were so long that people started pushing and shoving to get to the front. Some particularly impatient people even shouted out their orders before those in front of them could say what they wanted.

Sentence Fluency
• Concise sentences help the writing flow.

I enjoyed reading Denny's writing. His sentences aren't choppy, and he doesn't ramble. He gives the reader specific details but not in an overwhelming way. Notice how the sentences below offer just the right amount of information to make the writing flow.

> **[from the writing model]**
>
> For starters, the theater was freezing cold. Before the coming attractions even began, several people asked the manager to adjust the thermostat. She said she would take care of it, but the temperature never changed.

Grammar/ Mechanics
• Spelling, punctuation, and capitalization are correct. All subjects and verbs agree.

Denny also does the little things well—like putting commas and periods in the right places, and checking his spelling. All his subjects and verbs agree, too. I don't see any errors in his writing, do you?

> **[from the writing model]**
>
> The third problem was the presentation of the movie itself. First, there was the sound. Although we could barely hear our own movie, we could clearly hear the one in Theater 5. As soon as *Exploring Space* began, people started asking for the volume to be adjusted. Even so, we couldn't really hear it until the film's final half hour.

My Turn!

Now I'm going to write a business letter, but I'll focus on a positive experience. I'll use the rubric, along with good writing strategies, to help me write a detailed letter. Read along to see how I do it.

Differentiating Instruction

Support Remind students that vivid details can enhance description. Then, read aloud these two sentences, the second of which is from the model on Student page 108:

1. *In my row, there was litter on the floor.*

2. *In my row, empty containers littered the floor, topped with a layer of discarded popcorn puffs stuck to a coating of spilled soda.*

Now, ask students which sentence, the first or the second, is more detailed. **the second**

Have students use the following strategy to help them enhance description with vivid details: First, tell students they will write a paragraph about standing in a ticket line outside a movie theater on a hot summer day. Have them write down this sentence first: *It was hot, smelly, and noisy, and the line was really long.* Then, as a class, brainstorm a list of details that paint more of a vivid picture of the scene. (Possible responses appear below.) Finally, have students use details from the class list to write a brief paragraph about waiting in line.

sight	sound	touch	taste	smell
• people wearing shorts and tank tops	• shouts and horns from parking lot	• heat from concrete seeping through soles of shoes	• salt from sweat	• chemical odor of car exhaust
• sandaled feet in double rows like a centipede	• shuffling feet, smacking gum, kids whining	• shirts stuck to people's backs	• taste of warm bottled water	• buttery aroma wafting from popcorn machine

Writing a Business Letter

Prewriting Gather Information

Information/Organization The letter focuses on one main idea or topic.

Writing Strategy List my main idea or topic. Then, list details that support it.

I enjoy going to the movies, too. So when I read Denny's letter, I understood how he felt. I also remembered an experience at the movie theater that could have been horrible if not for some quick thinking by the theater manager. I knew this would make a great topic for a business letter, so I jotted down the idea. Then, I listed some supporting details.

Main Idea: To thank the manager of my local theater for how she handled a tough situation

Supporting Details:
- Biggest blockbuster of the summer; a lot of people; manager had us form different lines
- Temperature over 90°; many waited outside; manager passed out free water
- Film scheduled to start, and people still filing in; manager held up start time
- Not everyone got into the last show; manager gave free tickets to everyone in line and told them to come back the next day

Practice!

Now it's your turn. Choose a topic for a business letter. Then, write down your main idea and supporting details.

110 Descriptive Writing ■ Business Letter

Prewriting Organize Ideas

Information/Organization The letter has many facts to support the main idea.

Writing Strategy Make a Main-Idea Table to organize my information.

Writer's Term

Main-Idea Table
A **Main-Idea Table** can help you structure a piece of writing by organizing your main idea and supporting details in a logical way. Write your main idea or topic at the top of the table. Then, fill in the "legs" with supporting facts, details, and examples.

According to the rubric, it's important that every fact in my letter supports my main idea. I've already listed some details. Now, I'll organize them in a Main-Idea Table. I'm going to write about how the manager solved problems, so I'll label these details "Problem" and "Solution."

Main-Idea Table

Main Idea: I want to thank the manager of the York Street Theater for how she handled a tough situation.

Problem: When Voyage to Mars opened, the theater was swamped with people. **Solution:** To let the crowd in faster, the manager had us form different lines.	**Problem:** The temperature was over 90°, and many people had to wait outside. **Solution:** The manager had some employees walk down the lines and pass out free ice water.	**Problem:** When the film was scheduled to start, people were still filing into the theater. **Solution:** The manager held up the start time until every seat was filled.	**Problem:** Not everyone in line got into the last show of the night. **Solution:** The manager gave free tickets to everyone still in line and invited them back.

Practice!

Now it's your turn. Organize your main idea and supporting details into a Main-Idea Table.

Reflect
Do you think I included enough details to get started?

Descriptive Writing ■ Business Letter 111

Prewriting
(Student pages 110–111)

Ask volunteers to describe an experience, good or bad, at a theater, a store, a park, or at any other public area. How might this experience prompt a business letter? Have the class consider similar situations as they decide on letter topics.

Point out the notes on Student page 110 that feature the main idea and supporting details for Josh's draft. Remind students that writers are not limited to their notes, and that Josh may think of more details—or delete a few—as he drafts his letter.

Tell students that one good way to structure a business letter is to organize details into paragraphs based on problems and solutions. A Main-Idea Table can help writers organize information in this way.

More Practice!

For more practice with these writing strategies, you may wish to have students use the Strategy Practice Book. See the appendix for annotated Strategy Practice Book pages.

Differentiating Instruction

English-Language Learners Help these students brainstorm letter topics by working in pairs or small groups with English-proficient classmates. Lead groups as necessary to conduct a "Bests and Worsts" discussion in which students list their best and worst experiences at common locations. Which of these experiences might provide the basis for a business letter? What might be the main idea of the letter?

WORK with a PARTNER

Have students choose a personal experience that they could use as the basis for a business letter. Then, have pairs share their stories and brainstorm details. Direct students to help each other choose the best details for their drafts.

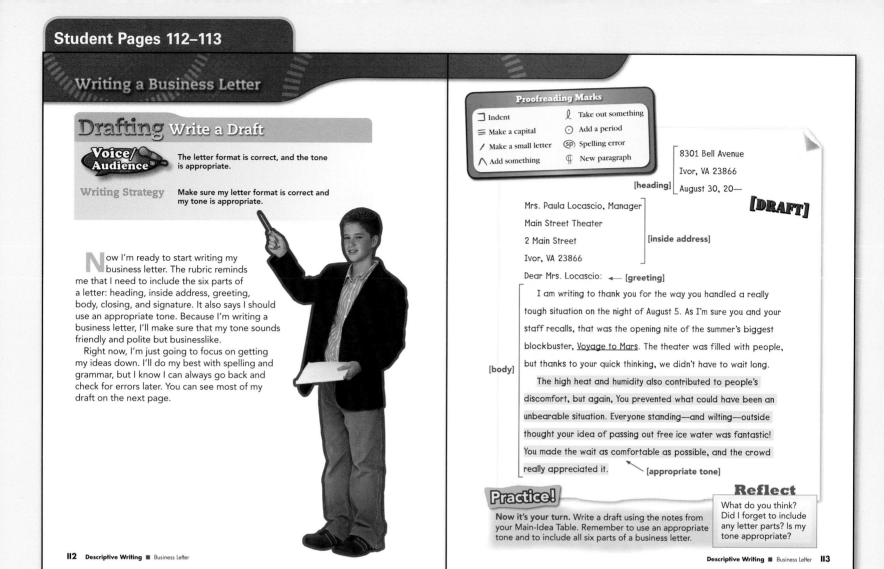

Drafting
(Student pages 112–113)

Remind students that drafting is a chance to get ideas on paper without having to worry about making mistakes.

Read aloud Josh's words on Student page 112. Then, read his draft on Student page 113. Refer to the Practice and the Reflect boxes at the bottom of the page, which remind students to include all six parts of a business letter and to use an appropriate tone. Ask a volunteer to name the six parts of a business letter. **heading, inside address, greeting, body, closing, signature** Point out that Josh already included four of these parts in the beginning of his draft. Then, discuss whether he used an appropriate tone. Have students find words (other than the highlighted ones) that illustrate his tone. Also discuss whether Josh's draft includes information from his Main-Idea Table.

Point out that Josh repeatedly refers to the rubric as he writes. Encourage students to get into the habit of using the rubric to help guide their own writing. Then, have students use the events in their Main-Idea Tables to draft their business letters.

Writing Across the Curriculum

The Arts Josh's letter was prompted by his attendance at the screening of a science-fiction movie. Science fiction—a genre with plots, settings, and themes that draw imaginatively on scientific knowledge and speculation—has resulted in many popular films and TV shows. Have students research the development of science fiction on the big and small screen. Research topics might include famous films (*Star Wars, The X Files*, etc.), famous TV series (*Stargate, Star Trek*, etc.), or other topics (other worlds, space travel, robots, etc.). Students could also compare original movies with their remakes (*War of the Worlds, Invasion of the Body Snatchers*, etc.) or research special effects. Have students write up reports supplemented with visuals such as timelines, photographs, posters, or collages. Allow time for students to share their reports with the class.

Writing a Business Letter

Revising Extend Writing

Content/Ideas Vivid details enhance the description.

Writing Strategy Look for places to add vivid details.

Now that I've written my draft, I think I'll check the rubric again. It says description is important, so I'll look for places to add details that will bring my letter to life. I think my third paragraph could use some work in this area. I'll focus on adding details there for now, but I can always add more to the rest of the draft later on!

[DRAFT]   [added vivid details]

         thoughtfully
    Another problem you took care of was holding up the film's start

time until all the people in the theater was seated. Although you did

your best to make the lines move quickly, not everyone were seated
           witnessed, first hand, the anxiety that began to spread as
by 7:15. I was in this group, and I ~~saw what happened when~~

people realized they might miss part of the movie. But by skipping

the coming attractions and starting the film at 7:30, you allowed

everyone to see the beginning.

Practice!

Now it's your turn. Make sure to include plenty of vivid details that will add energy and life to your writing.

114   Descriptive Writing ■ Business Letter

Revising Clarify Writing

Word Choice/Clarity The letter contains no irrelevant details.

Writing Strategy Delete or revise details that don't support my main idea.

I always reread my draft to myself several times before I'm done. When I did it this time, I realized that my conclusion had some extra information that didn't really do much to support my purpose. Then, I realized the rubric says to avoid using irrelevant details, so I deleted them.

[DRAFT]

    I'm happy to say that I count myself as one of those satisfied

customers. You can be sure that I'll be back at your theater when

one of the next blockbuster movies come to town. ~~I really hope it's~~

~~another science fiction movie because those are my favorite movies~~

~~of all. I also like action movies, but not as much as science fiction~~

~~ones. Anyway!~~ Please keep up the excellent work. I'm sure it will pay

off in the long run!
                [deleted irrelevant details]

Practice!

Now it's your turn. Reread your draft and delete any details that don't relate to your purpose.

Reflect

Is my writing clearer and more vivid now?

Descriptive Writing ■ Business Letter   115

Revising

(Student pages 114–115)

Write the words *vivid details* on the board. Explain that vivid details help writers paint descriptive pictures so that readers can visualize people, places, and things. Model adding vivid details by writing this sentence on the board: *The movie was about to begin.* Invite students to suggest details that could paint a more vivid picture of this image. **Possible responses: theater lights dimmed; screen brightened; sound turned up; theme music began; audience members shushed each other; excited whispering** Then, note how Josh added vivid details to his draft on Student page 114. Have students look for places in their business letters where they can add vivid details.

Turn students' attention to the revisions Josh made to his draft on Student page 115. Ask why he deleted the highlighted sentences. **Possible response: They contained extra information that did not support his purpose.** Make sure students understand Josh's purpose for writing (to thank Mrs. Locascio) and why the deleted sentences are irrelevant. Have students delete or revise details from their drafts that don't support their purpose.

Differentiating Instruction

English-Language Learners Use visual tools to help these students understand the concept of vivid details. Individually or in a small group, show students a large picture of a dramatic storm scene. Above it, write a general sentence such as *The storm blew through town.* Ask volunteers for details that describe the picture. **Possible responses: snow, trees, rain, waves, roof, house, trailer** Together with students, use sticky notes to label the picture. Then, ask volunteers for vivid details that more precisely describe specific elements of the picture. Label these with a second color of sticky notes. **Possible responses: swirling snow; trees bending like rubber; sleeting rain; angry waves; shattered roof; flattened house; upturned trailer** Work with students to write descriptive sentences that use these details. Leave time for students to read their sentences aloud.

Adapt this activity by using a picture of another dramatic scene, eye-catching individual, or interesting animal.

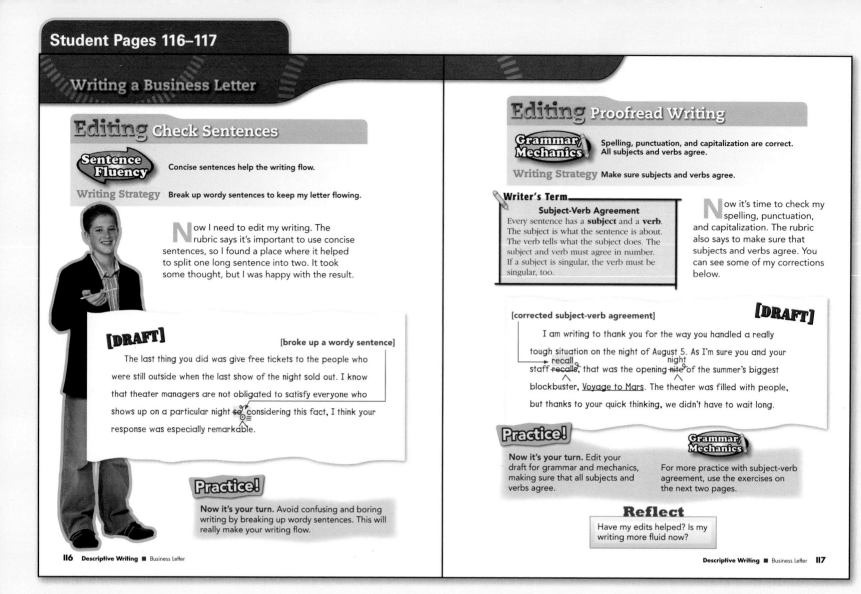

Editing

(Student pages 116–117)

Call students' attention to the edits Josh made to his draft on Student page 116. Ask a volunteer to read aloud the sentence as it was first written. Have another student read aloud the text after Josh's edit. Ask students how Josh fixed the wordy sentence. **He broke it into two sentences.** Discuss why this was effective. Have students check their business letters for wordy sentences that could be more concise.

Point out the Writer's Term box on Student page 117, and ask a volunteer to read it aloud. Then, have students note how Josh edited his draft on the same page. Finally, have them check their drafts to make sure all subjects and verbs agree. Remind them that they should also check their spelling, capitalization, and punctuation.

If any of your students are having trouble with subject-verb agreement, you may wish to teach the Mini-Lesson on pages 99–100 of this Teacher Edition. Then, have students complete the exercises on Student pages 118–119. Review the answers and possible rewrites with them.

WORK with a **PARTNER** Have pairs of students read one another's drafts, using sticky notes to mark errors in spelling, punctuation, and grammar. Then, tell students to perform a second read that focuses on the editing strategies they learned in this chapter.

Practice!

Subject-Verb Agreement

KNOW the RULE

The **subject** and **verb** in every sentence must agree in number, but figuring out whether a subject is singular or plural can be tricky.

- A **collective noun,** such as *crowd, group,* or *team* names more than one person or object acting together as a group. Collective nouns are almost always singular.
  Example: The **crowd forms** different lines.
- Most **indefinite pronouns,** including *everyone, nobody, nothing, something,* and *anything,* are singular, except for *many* and *several,* which are considered plural.
  Example: Everyone has money for a ticket.
  Example: Many have tickets already.
- A **compound subject** that includes the conjunction *and* is plural, but if the compound subject includes *or* or *nor,* the verb agrees with the last item in the subject.
  Example: Sam and Jerry take people's tickets.
  Example: Either popcorn or **nachos are** fine.
- Every verb must agree with its subject, and not with the object of the preposition that comes before the verb.
  Example: My **favorite** of all movies **is playing** at this theater.

Practice the Rule

Rewrite the paragraph below on a separate sheet of paper, using the verb in parentheses that agrees with the subject of the sentence.

When my mother and I (go/goes) to the grocery store, we always (looks/look) for your brand name on the shelves. Seeing one of your products (is/are) always reassuring to her. Everybody (know/knows) that your label means good quality and good taste. That's why my mother (know/knows) she can always count on you!

Apply the Rule

Read the following excerpt, looking for errors in subject-verb agreement. Then, rewrite the excerpt correctly on another sheet of paper.

17 West Washington Drive
Woodland Hills, CA 91364
March 13, 20—

Mr. Maxwell Jackson
Jackson Toy Company
1346 Industrial Drive
Hanover Park, IL 60103

Dear Mr. Jackson:

I am writing to tell you how much I enjoy your new game Do Tell. My family and I plays games every night, and we is always looking for good ones. One thing that are so great about Do Tell is that it have so many playing cards. My parents often buys a game, only to find that we use up all the cards in no time at all. But this is not the case with Do Tell. We'll definitely be playing it for a long time.

Another good thing about the game is its durability and its easy-to-read format. The vinyl-coated board help us keep it clean. Everyone like to eat while playing games in my house, and my little brother often spill things on the board. My mother tries to keep him from eating while he is playing, but it get pretty hard.

By far, my family's favorite thing about the game is that it is fun to play! My family laugh harder while playing Do Tell than during any other game we own. One thing that makes it so funny are the face in the middle of the game board. It almost looks as funny as some of the faces people makes while playing! My dad just scratches his head in amazement when he watch all of us laugh, and my mother and brother sometimes laughs so hard that they can't even breathe!

Mini-Lesson

(Student pages 118–119)

Subject-Verb Agreement

Explain to students that when writers check their drafts for subject-verb agreement, they must first determine whether a subject is singular or plural.

Explain that figuring out whether a subject is singular or plural is sometimes complicated. Turn students' attention to the Know the Rule box on Student page 118. Ask students to name the three types of subjects listed in the box. **collective noun, indefinite pronoun, compound subject** Write these on the board as headings.

Ask students to name examples of each of the three types of subjects and to use each example in a sentence. Write these on the board. For each sentence, discuss whether or not the subject and verb agree. With the class, edit as necessary.

Possible responses:

collective noun: team—Our team wears the colors red and blue.

indefinite pronoun: everyone—Everyone notices my sister's fiery red hair.

compound subject: cats and dogs—Cats and dogs make the best pets.

Ask students to read the final bulleted point in the box on Student page 118. Explain that when a sentence contains an object and a preposition, it may confuse subject-verb agreement. Remind students to avoid mistaking the object of the preposition for the subject.

Answers for Practice the Rule

When my mother and I go to the grocery store, we always look for your brand name on the shelves. Seeing one of your products is always reassuring to her. Everybody knows that your label means good quality and good taste. That's why my mother knows she can always count on you!

(Answers continue on page 100.)

 For more practice with grammar/mechanics skills, see Zaner-Bloser's *G.U.M.* materials.

Writing a Business Letter

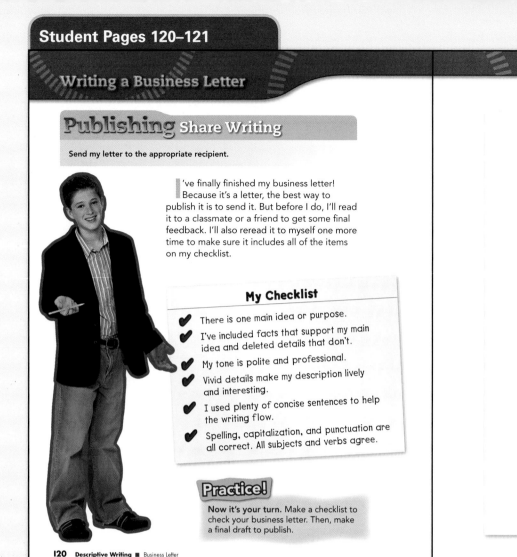

Publishing Share Writing

Send my letter to the appropriate recipient.

I've finally finished my business letter! Because it's a letter, the best way to publish it is to send it. But before I do, I'll read it to a classmate or a friend to get some final feedback. I'll also reread it to myself one more time to make sure it includes all of the items on my checklist.

My Checklist

✔ There is one main idea or purpose.

✔ I've included facts that support my main idea and deleted details that don't.

✔ My tone is polite and professional.

✔ Vivid details make my description lively and interesting.

✔ I used plenty of concise sentences to help the writing flow.

✔ Spelling, capitalization, and punctuation are all correct. All subjects and verbs agree.

Practice!

Now it's your turn. Make a checklist to check your business letter. Then, make a final draft to publish.

120 Descriptive Writing ■ Business Letter

8301 Bell Avenue
Ivor, VA 23866
August 30, 20—

Mrs. Paula Locascio, Manager
Main Street Theater
2 Main Street
Ivor, VA 23866

Dear Mrs. Locascio:

I am writing to thank you for the way you handled a really tough situation on the night of August 5. As I'm sure you and your staff recall, that was opening night of the summer's biggest blockbuster, *Voyage to Mars*. The theater was filled with people, but thanks to your quick thinking, we didn't have to wait long.

The high heat and humidity also contributed to people's discomfort, but again, you prevented what could have been an unbearable situation. Everyone standing—and wilting—outside thought your idea of passing out free ice water was fantastic! You made the wait as comfortable as possible, and the crowd really appreciated it.

Another problem you thoughtfully took care of was holding up the film's start time until all of the people in the theater were seated. Although you did your best to make the lines move quickly, not everyone was seated by 7:15. I was in this group, and I witnessed, first hand, the anxiety that began to spread as people realized they might miss part of the movie. But by skipping the coming attractions and starting the film at 7:30, you allowed everyone to see the beginning.

Descriptive Writing ■ Business Letter 121

(Answers continued from page 100.)

Answers for Apply the Rule

Dear Mr. Jackson:

I am writing to tell you how much I enjoy your new game Do Tell. My family and I play games every night, and we are always looking for good ones. One thing that is so great about Do Tell is that it has so many playing cards. My parents often buy a game, only to find that we use up all the cards in no time at all. But this is not the case with Do Tell. We'll definitely be playing it for a long time.

Another good thing about the game is its durability and its easy-to-read format. The vinyl-coated board helps us keep it clean. Everyone likes to eat while playing games in my house, and my little brother often spills things on the board. My mother tries to keep him from eating while he is playing, but it gets pretty hard.

By far, my family's favorite thing about the game is that it is fun to play! My family laughs harder while playing Do Tell than during any other game we own. One thing that makes it so funny is the face in the middle of the game board. It almost looks as funny as some of the faces people make while playing! My dad just scratches his head in amazement when he watches all of us laugh, and my mother and brother sometimes laugh so hard that they can't even breathe!

Publishing

(Student pages 120–123)

Ask students if they like Josh's choice for sharing his business letter. Tell the class that his choice is not the only option for publishing his work. Invite students to name other ways they could publish their own business letters.

Have each student make a checklist and perform a final evaluation of his or her letter before publishing it. Encourage students to share copies of their letters with friends and relatives who might be interested in reading about what they wrote.

Then, call students' attention to the way Josh addressed his envelope on Student page 123. If students want to send their letters by mail, have them use this format as a guide when they address their own envelopes. If possible, have students use a computer printer, selecting the appropriate envelope setting on the print menu.

Writing a Business Letter

The last thing you did was give free tickets to the people who were still outside when the last show of the night sold out. I know that theater managers are not obligated to satisfy everyone who shows up on a particular night. Considering this fact, I think your response was especially remarkable. By inviting those people back the next day and assuring them that they'd be the first ones allowed into the theater, you hung on to many customers.

I'm happy to say that I count myself as one of those satisfied customers. You can be sure that I'll be back at your theater when the next blockbuster movie comes to town. Please keep up the excellent work. I'm sure it will pay off in the long run!

Sincerely,

Josh Greene

Josh Greene

Josh Greene
8301 Bell Avenue
Ivor, VA 23866

Mrs. Paula Locascio
Main Street Theater
2 Main Street
Ivor, VA 23866

Reflect

What do you think? I hope I used all the traits of a good business letter. Check my work against the rubric, and don't forget to use the rubric, to check your own business letter, too!

Differentiating Instruction

Support Some students may benefit from direct instruction and repetition in evaluating use of the writing traits. While other students are working independently on peer reviews, organize a small group of students to use the traits to study each other's letters. Begin by making enough copies of students' business letters for each student in the group. Then, do the following:

- Display the rubric in an enlarged form on chart paper. Highlight the Content/Ideas trait.

- Choose one business letter to review together first. Then, use words like the following to model the Content/Ideas trait: *When I look at the rubric, the Content/Ideas trait says that many vivid details should enhance the description. I'll review the letter with this in mind. In the second paragraph, I see one place where I'd like to know more about . . .*

- Using the same business letter, go around the group and have each student model the other traits. Coach students as needed, discussing together how to apply the rubric.

- Convene each day until the group finishes reviewing all the letters.

Ways to Publish a Business Letter

As you decide how to publish your work, make sure you think about who will be reading it. Then, pick the best way to share it. Of course, publishing a letter usually means sending it to the recipient. But here are some other ways you can publish it.

✔ **Submit it to the "Letter to the Editor" page of your local newspaper.**

✔ **Post it on your blog or Web page, along with an explanation of why you wrote it.**

✔ Take your business letter home and share it with your family.

✔ E-mail it to the intended recipient!

124 Descriptive Writing ■ Business Letter

Writing Across the Content Areas Business Letter

Your school subjects can be a source of writing ideas. So pick a subject and brainstorm as many topics that relate to it as you can. Here are some examples.

Language Arts
- Write a letter to your favorite author, describing what you liked best about one of his or her books.
- Want to publish a story or an article? First, write a letter to a newspaper or magazine, asking if they publish student work.

Social Studies
- Are you concerned about an issue in your community? Write your elected official about your thoughts.
- Write a company to give feedback on one of its products.

Art and/or Music
- Write to your favorite musician or band member, describing what you like best about his or her music.
- Do you want more community art, sculptures, murals, or other works in your city or town? Write your mayor and describe the situation.

Descriptive Writing ■ Business Letter 125

Ways to Publish
(Student page 124)

Read and discuss with students the publishing options listed on Student page 124. Encourage students to consider some of these options when publishing their own writing. Remind students that Josh chose to publish his letter by sending it to the intended recipient, but they can choose their own way of publishing. Perhaps one student will want to submit his or her letter to a "Letter to the Editor" page, while another will want to post it on a blog or a Web page.

Writing Across the Content Areas
(Student page 125)

Explain to students that writing is not just for English or language arts class. Many other school subjects contain ideas, issues, and events that students may want to write about. Encourage students to consider using one of the content areas listed on Student page 125 as a springboard for more writing options. Students may also wish to consult with other teachers for more ideas on writing in the content areas.

Books for Professional Development

Gallagher, Kelly. *Teaching Adolescent Writers.* **Portland: Stenhouse, 2006.**

Gallagher draws on his classroom experience as co-director of a regional writing project to offer teachers practical ways to incorporate writing instruction into their day.

Tompkins, Gail E. *Teaching Writing: Balancing Process and Product.* **4th ed. Upper Saddle River: Prentice Hall, 2004.**

This book contains information on teaching writing strategies for grades K–8, covering prewriting, drafting, revising, editing, and publishing. It also offers techniques for helping children develop ideas, organize writing, choose vocabulary, apply stylistic devices, and correct mechanical errors. Numerous authentic children's writing samples are interspersed throughout the material, along with the author's well-respected mini-lessons and thoughtful discussion of performance-based tools for assessment.

Cole, Ardith Davis. *Better Answers: Written Performance That Looks Good and Sounds Smart.* **Portland: Stenhouse, 2002.**

This book offers step-by-step protocol for helping students focus on acquiring the basic literacy skills to meet state standards for writing. Each of these five progressive steps to teaching writing are laid out in individual chapters: Restate the Questions; Construct a Gist Answer; Use Details to Support Your Answer; Stay on the Topic; Use Proper Conventions. The book also contains many samples of student responses, lesson plans, and other valuable resources.

Soven, Margot Iris. *Teaching Writing in Middle and Secondary Schools: Theory, Research and Practice.* **Boston: Allyn & Bacon, 1998.**

This book contains practical explanations of teaching strategies, many examples of assignments and student writing, novel methods through which to teach the writing process, and new techniques to effectively evaluate and respond to student writers.

Scientific Observation Overview

In this chapter, students will learn how to write a scientific observation. They will learn the elements of a scientific observation—organization, cause and effect, voice, and conclusions—and some reasons why they might choose to write one. Students will then use a scientific observation rubric to study a model writing sample.

Students will follow the student guide as he goes through the writing stages—prewriting, drafting, revising, editing, and publishing. As the student guide learns new writing strategies in each step, students will be directed to practice the strategies in their own writing.

During prewriting and drafting, students will

- observe and take notes.
- make Cause-and-Effect Links.

- write a draft using scientific language that is appropriate for the audience.

During revising and editing, students will

- add diagrams to enhance the description.
- use specific words to show connections.
- use transitional phrases.
- edit their drafts for spelling, capitalization, and punctuation, making sure that colons and hyphens are used correctly.

Finally, students will write a final draft to be published.

You may wish to send to families the School-Home Connection Letter for this chapter, located at the end of this unit in the Teacher Edition.

Scientific Observation Writing Traits

Prewriting	**Information/Organization**	The writer describes several experiments. The observation includes causes and effects.
Drafting	**Voice/Audience**	Scientific language is appropriate for the audience.
Revising	**Content/Ideas**	Diagrams enhance the description.
	Word Choice/Clarity	Specific words show important connections throughout.
Editing	**Sentence Fluency**	Transitional phrases help the writing flow.
	Grammar/Mechanics	Spelling, punctuation, and capitalization are correct. Colons and hyphens are used correctly.
Publishing		Each student publishes a scientific observation by including it in a science classroom display.

Scientific Observation Time Management

WEEK 1

Day 1	Day 2	Day 3	Day 4	Day 5
Learning Objectives				
Students will: • learn the components of a scientific observation.	Students will: • learn how to gather information for a scientific observation.	Students will: • practice gathering information for their scientific observations.	Students will: • learn how to make Cause-and-Effect Links to organize their notes.	Students will: • practice organizing their notes into Cause-and-Effect Links.
Activities				
• Discuss the elements and traits of a scientific observation (Student pages 126–128). • Use the rubric to study the model (Student pages 129–135).	• Read and discuss **Prewriting: Gather Information** (Student page 136).	• Brainstorm ideas and choose experiments to run. • Make observations and take notes.	• Read and discuss **Prewriting: Organize Ideas** (Student page 137).	• Review notes about what was observed. • Make Cause-and-Effect Links to organize notes.

WEEK 2

Day 1	Day 2	Day 3	Day 4	Day 5
Learning Objectives				
Students will: • learn how to use scientific language appropriate for the audience.	Students will: • practice writing their own drafts.	Students will: • learn how adding diagrams can enhance their descriptions.	Students will: • practice adding diagrams to their drafts.	Students will: • learn how to use specific words to show important connections.
Activities				
• Read and discuss **Drafting: Write a Draft** (Student pages 138–141).	• Use Cause-and-Effect Links to write drafts. • Use scientific language appropriate for the audience.	• Read and discuss **Revising: Extend Writing** (Student page 142).	• Draw diagrams to add to drafts.	• Read and discuss **Revising: Clarify Writing** (Student page 143).

WEEK 3

Day 1	Day 2	Day 3	Day 4	Day 5
Learning Objectives				
Students will: • practice using specific words to show important connections.	Students will: • learn how using transitional phrases can help their writing flow.	Students will: • learn how to use colons and hyphens correctly.	Students will: • practice editing their drafts for spelling, capitalization, and punctuation.	Students will: • learn different ways to publish their scientific observations.
Activities				
• Reread drafts, looking for places where connections are unclear. • Add specific words to make connections clearer.	• Read and discuss **Editing: Check Sentences** (Student page 144). • Make sure to use transitional phrases to help writing flow.	• Read and discuss **Editing: Proofread Writing** (Student page 145).	• Fix any spelling, capitalization, or punctuation errors. • Fix any colons or hyphens that are not used correctly.	• Read and discuss **Publishing: Share Writing** (Student page 148).

To complete the chapter in fewer days, teach the learning objectives and activities for two days in one day.

This planning chart, correlated to your state's writing standards, is available on-line at http://www.zaner-bloser.com/sfw.

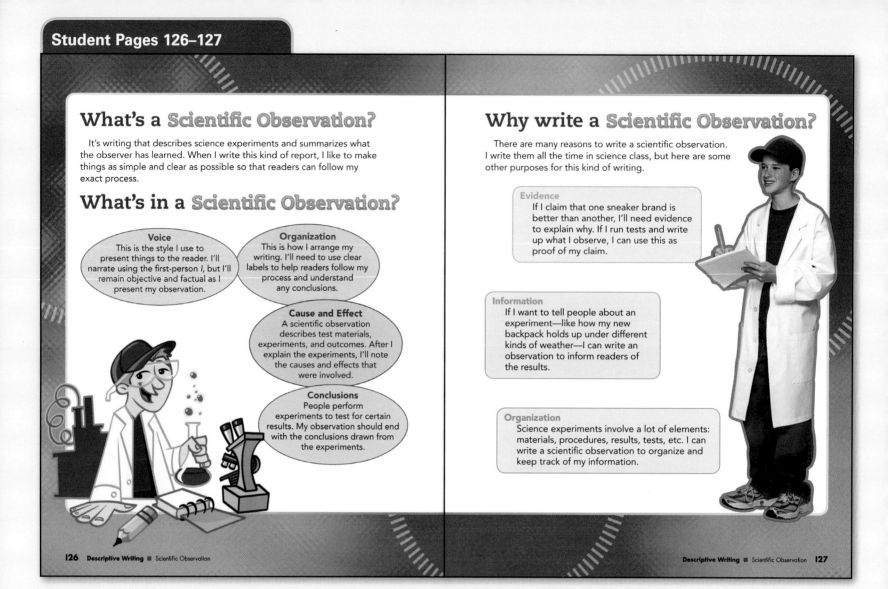

What's a Scientific Observation?

It's writing that describes science experiments and summarizes what the observer has learned. When I write this kind of report, I like to make things as simple and clear as possible so that readers can follow my exact process.

What's in a Scientific Observation?

Voice
This is the style I use to present things to the reader. I'll narrate using the first-person *I*, but I'll remain objective and factual as I present my observation.

Organization
This is how I arrange my writing. I'll need to use clear labels to help readers follow my process and understand any conclusions.

Cause and Effect
A scientific observation describes test materials, experiments, and outcomes. After I explain the experiments, I'll note the causes and effects that were involved.

Conclusions
People perform experiments to test for certain results. My observation should end with the conclusions drawn from the experiments.

Why write a Scientific Observation?

There are many reasons to write a scientific observation. I write them all the time in science class, but here are some other purposes for this kind of writing.

Evidence
If I claim that one sneaker brand is better than another, I'll need evidence to explain why. If I run tests and write up what I observe, I can use this as proof of my claim.

Information
If I want to tell people about an experiment—like how my new backpack holds up under different kinds of weather—I can write an observation to inform readers of the results.

Organization
Science experiments involve a lot of elements: materials, procedures, results, tests, etc. I can write a scientific observation to organize and keep track of my information.

126 **Descriptive Writing** ■ Scientific Observation

Descriptive Writing ■ Scientific Observation 127

Define the Genre
(Student page 126)

Scientific Observation

Discuss with students the definition of a scientific observation. Ask students whether they have ever written up an experiment for science class. **Possible response: yes** Point out that any time they describe a scientific process, they are using the scientific observation genre.

Elements of the Genre

Scientific Observation

Read and discuss with students the elements of a scientific observation listed on Student page 126. Ask volunteers which elements are also common to other forms of writing. **Possible responses: Voice—first-person narration, memoirs; Organization—research papers, directions; Cause and Effect—historical writing, mysteries; Conclusions—summaries, persuasive writing** Discuss why each element may be important to writing a scientific observation.

Authentic Writing
(Student page 127)

Scientific Observation

Read and discuss with students the reasons for writing a scientific observation listed on Student page 127. Point out that all writing has a purpose and is aimed at a specific audience. These authentic purposes help authors shape their writing. Ask a volunteer to read aloud the Evidence box. Then, have students discuss other reasons someone might write a scientific observation to provide evidence. Repeat this process for the Information and the Organization boxes. Then, have students brainstorm other purposes for writing a scientific observation that are not listed on Student page 127. Encourage students to think about their own reasons for writing a scientific observation, and how these reasons will affect the tone and focus of their writing.

Scientific Observation Writing Traits

You can analyze a scientific observation in the same way that you look at other types of writing: by focusing on the six traits of good writing. I'll use these traits to help me write my observation.

Information/Organization	The writer describes several experiments. The observation includes causes and effects.
Voice/Audience	Scientific language is appropriate for the audience.
Content/Ideas	Diagrams enhance the description.
Word Choice/Clarity	Specific words show important connections throughout.
Sentence Fluency	Transitional phrases help the writing flow.
Grammar/Mechanics	Spelling, punctuation, and capitalization are correct. Colons and hyphens are used correctly.

I can use Hannah Prince's scientific observation on the next three pages as a model for my own writing. Later, we'll analyze how Hannah used the traits to help her write.

128 Descriptive Writing ■ Scientific Observation

Scientific Observation Model

Observing Solar Collectors

By Hannah Prince

Did you know that solar energy doesn't cost a penny? Well, when I heard that, I decided to conduct a series of experiments to find out how to improve the collection of solar energy. I predicted that the more insulation a collector was given the more heat it would collect.

Voice

MATERIALS
shoebox, larger box, masking tape, thermometer, clock or watch, black construction paper, clear plastic wrap, packing peanuts

PROCEDURES ← Organization

Experiment 1
First, I taped a thermometer inside one of the long sides of a shoebox. (See Diagram 1.) Then, I placed the uncovered shoebox outside and turned it so that the bottom of the box was directly in the sun, and the thermometer bulb was in the shade. I left the box in that position for 15 minutes.

I recorded the temperature inside the box at the start of the experiment and again 15 minutes later. Here are my observations. The temperature inside the box at the start of the experiment was 72°F (24°C). The temperature inside the box after 15 minutes was 98°F (36°C).

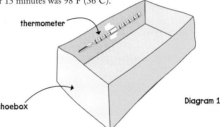

thermometer

shoebox

Diagram 1

Descriptive Writing ■ Scientific Observation **129**

Writing Traits

(Student pages 128–131)

Scientific Observation

Share with students a time when you made a scientific observation outside of a formal science class. Examples might include seeing which kind of bat hits a baseball farther, testing different methods for teaching your pets tricks, and determining which ingredients make better cookies.

Ask students if they have ever made informal observations or tested a theory about something. Explain that these informal experiments are forms of scientific observation.

Turn students' attention to the traits of a good scientific observation listed on Student page 128. Have one or more volunteers read aloud the traits and their descriptions. Discuss why someone might use these traits when sharing their findings in writing.

Tell students that they are going to study and use strategies for writing scientific observations, and that a good scientific observation has the traits listed on Student page 128.

Differentiating Instruction

English-Language Learners Preteach key words and concepts that can help these students understand the scientific observation model.

Explain that the author performed experiments to find out how to improve the collection of solar energy. Review with students the following concepts about solar energy: Solar energy is the use of sunlight to produce heat or electricity; although the sun produces a lot of energy, it is spread out over a large area; solar energy has to be collected in order to be used.

Help students visualize the experiments by reviewing the materials list. Read aloud the words and discuss their meanings. Many English-Language learners benefit from the use of visual aids. If possible, display the following: masking tape, black construction paper, clear plastic wrap, and packing peanuts.

Scientific Observation

Experiment 2

I did the experiment again, only this time I covered the inside of the shoebox with black construction paper. Then, I left the box for 15 minutes in the same position as before. (I did have to turn the box slightly to adjust for the movement of the sun.)

I again recorded the temperatures before and after the experiment. Here is what I observed. The temperature inside the box at the start of the experiment was 98°F (36°C). The temperature inside the box after 15 minutes was 98.5°F (36.25°C).

Experiment 3 ← Organization

I did the experiment again. For this third time, however, I covered the top of the shoebox with clear plastic wrap. Then, I sealed the plastic wrap with masking tape so that no air could enter or leave the box. Next, I left the box for 15 minutes in the same position as before. (Again, I turned the box slightly to adjust for the movement of the sun.)

Once again, I recorded the temperatures and made these observations. The temperature inside the box at the start of the experiment was 98.5°F (36.25°C). The temperature inside the box after 15 minutes was 105°F (42°C).

Experiment 4

I did the experiment one last time. For this fourth time, I placed the shoebox inside another, larger box and then placed a layer of packing peanuts between the shoebox and the larger box. (See Diagram 2.) Next, I left the box for 15 minutes in the same position as before, again turning the box slightly to adjust for the movement of the sun.

Again, I recorded the temperatures and made these observations. The temperature inside the box at the start of the experiment was 105°F (42°C). The temperature inside the box after 15 minutes was 120+°F (50+°C).

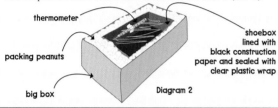

thermometer

packing peanuts

big box

shoebox lined with black construction paper and sealed with clear plastic wrap

Diagram 2

OBSERVATIONS

Each change that I made to my solar collector caused the inside of the shoebox to get hotter, resulting in a rise in temperature on the thermometer. When I placed the plain, uncovered shoebox in the sun, the Fahrenheit temperature increased 26°. When I covered the inside of the shoebox with black construction paper, the temperature increased another 0.5°. When I sealed the top of the box with plastic wrap, the temperature increased another 6.5°. When I placed the shoebox inside another box and put packing peanuts between them, the temperature increased another 15° before the thermometer topped out. Had my little thermometer gone beyond 120°F, I wonder how hot it would have gotten inside the shoebox! When I put my hand inside, the temperature change was pretty amazing. It felt almost twice as hot inside the shoebox as it felt outside that day.

Cause and Effect

CONCLUSIONS

Conclusions

I learned several things from my experiments: For one thing, I now understand the basics of collecting solar energy. For another, I learned that solar energy really is a clean, efficient, and cost-effective way to heat a space. I also learned that the best way to gather the most heat with a solar collector is to place it inside a larger, well-insulated space. (I drew this conclusion because the insulation in Experiment 4 sent the temperature in the shoebox sky-high.) I was able to prove that my prediction was correct by doing these experiments. Since solar energy can be so powerful, I guess it's no wonder that people in regions where there is a lot of winter sun have been harnessing the sun's energy for centuries.

Differentiating Instruction

Support If students have trouble understanding the ideas presented in the model, they might not be able to grasp the use of the writing strategies. To aid students' comprehension, convene a small strategies group. Use the following process:

Before Reading On chart paper or on individual cards, display the following skills and strategies. Read them aloud and review their use with students.

- *Understanding Causes and Effects: This helps me explain why things happen. To understand causes and effects, I should look for connections.*

- *Summarizing: This helps me understand and remember important points. When I summarize, I should state only the main ideas and details.*

- *Drawing Conclusions: This helps me understand what I learned. When I draw conclusions, I should use evidence to develop new ideas.*

Gather materials from the list on Student page 129 that can serve as visuals for understanding the model. Then, preview the organization of the model by reading the headings. Tell students they will be using the three strategies to read each section. Finally, have each student set a purpose for reading.

During Reading Read aloud Student page 129. Restate the Summarizing strategy. Then, model its use by summarizing the page. Write the important parts on chart paper or on the chalkboard and discuss them with students. Next, have students revise their purposes for reading. After reading Student page 130 together, have a student model Summarizing. Coach him or her as needed. Then, repeat the process by modeling the other two strategies after reading Student page 131.

After Reading Have students assess their understanding of the strategies. How well were they able to apply them? Which one was easiest or most difficult? Did using the strategies help them better understand the content?

Reading to Writing Remind students that they will be using strategies to write their own scientific observations. Discuss how they might best organize their writing. Review how Hannah Prince described causes and effects. Then, ask students to make such connections in their own writing.

Scientific Observation
Rubric

The traits of a good scientific observation from page 128 have been used to make the rubric below. By using 1, 2, 3, or 4 check marks to judge each trait, you can decide how well any scientific observation was written.

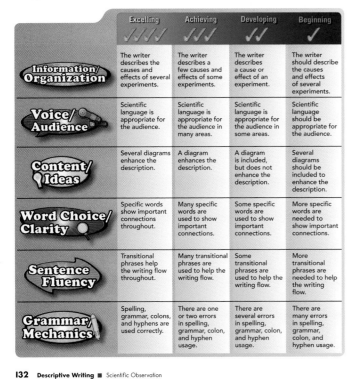

	Excelling ✓✓✓✓	Achieving ✓✓✓	Developing ✓✓	Beginning ✓
Information/ Organization	The writer describes the causes and effects of several experiments.	The writer describes a few causes and effects of some experiments.	The writer describes a cause or effect of an experiment.	The writer should describe the causes and effects of several experiments.
Voice/ Audience	Scientific language is appropriate for the audience.	Scientific language is appropriate for the audience in many areas.	Scientific language is appropriate for the audience in some areas.	Scientific language should be appropriate for the audience.
Content/ Ideas	Several diagrams enhance the description.	A diagram enhances the description.	A diagram is included, but does not enhance the description.	Several diagrams should be included to enhance the description.
Word Choice/ Clarity	Specific words show important connections throughout.	Many specific words are used to show important connections.	Some specific words are used to show important connections.	More specific words are needed to show important connections.
Sentence Fluency	Transitional phrases help the writing flow throughout.	Many transitional phrases are used to help the writing flow.	Some transitional phrases are used to help the writing flow.	More transitional phrases are needed to help the writing flow.
Grammar/ Mechanics	Spelling, grammar, colons, and hyphens are used correctly.	There are one or two errors in spelling, grammar, colon, and hyphen usage.	There are several errors in spelling, grammar, colon, and hyphen usage.	There are many errors in spelling, grammar, colon, and hyphen usage.

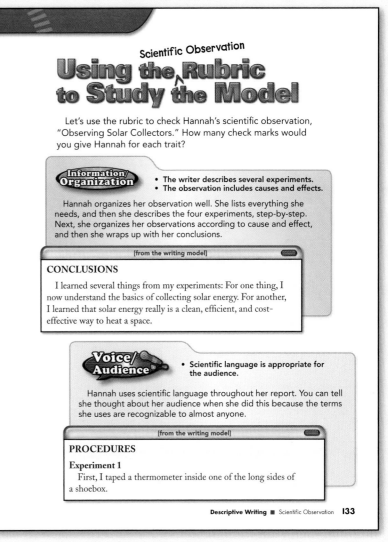

Scientific Observation
Using the Rubric to Study the Model

Let's use the rubric to check Hannah's scientific observation, "Observing Solar Collectors." How many check marks would you give Hannah for each trait?

Information/ Organization
• The writer describes several experiments.
• The observation includes causes and effects.

Hannah organizes her observation well. She lists everything she needs, and then she describes the four experiments, step-by-step. Next, she organizes her observations according to cause and effect, and then she wraps up with her conclusions.

[from the writing model]

CONCLUSIONS

I learned several things from my experiments: For one thing, I now understand the basics of collecting solar energy. For another, I learned that solar energy really is a clean, efficient, and cost-effective way to heat a space.

Voice/ Audience
• Scientific language is appropriate for the audience.

Hannah uses scientific language throughout her report. You can tell she thought about her audience when she did this because the terms she uses are recognizable to almost anyone.

[from the writing model]

PROCEDURES
Experiment 1
First, I taped a thermometer inside one of the long sides of a shoebox.

Using the Rubric
(Student page 132)

Explain that a rubric is a tool that can be used to evaluate a piece of writing. The rubric on Student page 132 can be used to evaluate a scientific observation. It is based on the same scientific observation traits listed on Student page 128.

Now point out the terms above each rubric column: *Excelling, Achieving, Developing,* and *Beginning.* Explain that each column symbolizes a degree of writing skill, and that each rubric row focuses on a specific writing trait. When students use the rubric to evaluate their own work at each step of the writing process, they increase the likelihood of producing polished, well-written scientific observations.

Study the Model
(Student pages 133–135)

Explain that Student pages 133–135 show how the writing model on Student pages 129–131 meets all six traits of the rubric. Read each section with the students. Have them look for other examples of each trait in the writing model.

Ask students how many check marks they would assign the writing model for each trait. Then, as a class, decide how the writing model should be rated overall.

Remind students to use the rubric as they write their own scientific observation, to be sure they are meeting all six writing traits.

Scientific Observation

Content/Ideas
- Diagrams enhance the description.

Hannah includes two labeled diagrams that illustrate what happened during the experiments. Diagram 1 shows exactly where in the shoebox Hannah placed the thermometer. Diagram 2 (shown below) shows how she placed the shoebox in the larger box.

[from the writing model]

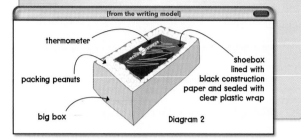

thermometer

packing peanuts

big box

shoebox lined with black construction paper and sealed with clear plastic wrap

Diagram 2

Word Choice/Clarity
- Specific words show important connections throughout.

I like how Hannah uses specific words to show important connections. This helps me understand the relationship between cause and effect. Take a look at the words I underlined below. See what I mean?

[from the writing model]

Each change that I made to my solar collector <u>caused</u> the inside of the shoebox to get hotter, <u>resulting</u> in a rise in temperature on the thermometer. <u>When</u> I placed the plain, uncovered shoebox in the sun, the Fahrenheit temperature increased 26°.

Sentence Fluency
- Transitional phrases help the writing flow.

I also like how Hannah uses transitional phrases such as *15 minutes later* and *after 15 minutes* to show the order of events. This puts everything in order and makes the observation easy to follow.

[from the writing model]

I recorded the temperature inside the box at the start of the experiment and again 15 minutes later. Here are my observations. The temperature inside the box at the start of the experiment was 72°F (24°C). The temperature inside the box after 15 minutes was 98°F (36°C).

Grammar/Mechanics
- Spelling, punctuation, and capitalization are correct. Colons and hyphens are used correctly.

In the passage below, Hannah uses a colon to separate the first two sentences, since the second one explains the first. She also uses a hyphen to connect *cost* and *effective*, which together, act as an adjective. I also think she must have edited for spelling and grammar because as far as I can tell, there are no mistakes.

[from the writing model]

I learned several things from my experiments: For one thing, I now understand the basics of collecting solar energy. For another, I learned that solar energy really is a clean, efficient, and cost-effective way to heat a space.

My Turn!

I'm going to write a scientific observation that describes something I'm curious about. I'll follow the rubric and use good writing strategies. Read on to see how I do it!

Differentiating Instruction

English-Language Learners To help students understand how to make connections between causes and effects, review these common words and phrases:

because	therefore
due to	as a result/resulted in
since	for this reason
so that	cause/caused/causing
thus	if…then
leads to	when…then

Read the terms aloud with students. Point out examples of their use from the model. Together with students, use these specific words and phrases to write sentences that explain causes and effects. *Hint: This process may be easier for students if they are given common topics such as food, hunger, sleep, energy, pollution, school, sports, computers, music, etc. Start students off by writing the following cause-and-effect sentences on the board:

- *Because I stayed up until midnight last night, I am very tired today.*
- *If you eat spicy peppers, then your mouth will burn.*
- *The noise outside caused Carl to shut the window.*
- *Nora hit Save so that she would not lose her document.*
- *Marco's hand injury resulted in a low batting average.*
- *Since Tony studied for the test, he got a good grade.*

Remind students to use specific words to make connections like these when they write their scientific observations.

Writing a Scientific Observation

Prewriting Gather Information

Information/Organization The writer describes several experiments.

Writing Strategy Observe and take notes.

Recently, my teacher asked us to record and write a scientific observation. I'm a total baseball freak, so I decided to do some baseball experiments. I recently read an article on how baseballs act under different conditions, so I decided to do a few of the experiments. I even got my brother Brian to help so that I could observe and take notes. I wrote down the question I wanted to answer, and then I continued from there.

My Notes

- **Question:** At what temperature (frozen, heated, or room temperature) will the rebound rate of a baseball be highest?
- **Prediction:** The warm baseball's rebound rate will be highest.
- **What I did:** Brian stood on a chair, held a tape measure 72 inches off the ground, and dropped a baseball straight down. I then observed and recorded how high the ball bounced. I then divided that amount by 72 inches to get the rebound rate. We repeated the experiment three times with a cold baseball, a warm baseball, and a baseball at room temperature.
- **The Results:** The cold baseball had a rebound rate of 0.305. The warm baseball had a rebound rate of 0.236. The baseball at room temperature had a rebound rate of 0.292.
- **Conclusion:** My prediction was wrong. The cold baseball had the highest rebound rate, not the warm one.

Practice!

Now it's your turn. Choose a few experiments about something that interests you. Gather what you need. Then, run the experiments and describe what you observe.

136 Descriptive Writing ■ Scientific Observation

Prewriting Organize Ideas

Information/Organization The observation includes causes and effects.

Writing Strategy Make Cause-and-Effect Links to organize my notes.

Writer's Term
Cause-and-Effect Links
Sometimes a single cause brings about a single effect. When this happens, you can use **Cause-and-Effect Links** to show each pair of events.

There are two kinds of organization in a scientific observation. Sequence is important because you need to follow the proper order of steps in an experiment so that your results will be accurate. Cause and effect are important because each cause can result in a different outcome. To track these causes and effects, I'll use Cause-and-Effect Links.

CAUSE-AND-EFFECT LINKS

 Cause: I refrigerated a baseball for eight hours. **Effect:** It rebounded 22 inches for a rebound rate of 0.305.

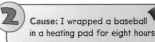 **Cause:** I wrapped a baseball in a heating pad for eight hours. **Effect:** It rebounded 17 inches for a rebound rate of 0.236.

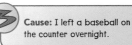 **Cause:** I left a baseball on the counter overnight. **Effect:** It rebounded 21 inches for a rebound rate of 0.292.

Practice!

Now it's your turn. Use Cause-and-Effect Links to organize your notes.

Reflect
Do you think my Cause-and-Effect Links will help me?

Descriptive Writing ■ Scientific Observation 137

Prewriting

(Student pages 136–137)

Ask students if they've ever been curious about the way something works. **Possible response: yes** Discuss their interests. Then, explore topics they might investigate that could provide the basis for a scientific observation.

Have a volunteer summarize how Josh turned his interest in baseball into an experiment. Point out Josh's notes on Student page 136, focusing on how he organized these into categories.

Remind students that sometimes they'll need more than one form of organization to help structure writing. Then, discuss why they'll need both sequence and cause and effect to structure their scientific observations. Point out how Josh used the Cause-and-Effect Links on Student page 137 to help organize his notes, and encourage students to do the same.

More Practice!

For more practice with these writing strategies, you may wish to have students use the Strategy Practice Book. See the appendix for annotated Strategy Practice Book pages.

Differentiating Instruction

Support Some students may find it difficult to design an experiment. Remind them to use the Internet, science texts, or periodicals for experiment ideas. Offer further help by providing these options:

- Observe what happens to carnations when placed in jars filled with different food coloring.
- Discover whether plants lose water through their leaves by placing a plant outside in the sun. Cover some leaves with a plastic bag, watch what happens, and compare this to the uncovered leaves.
- Use a balloon, a fluorescent light bulb, a wool sweater, and yourself to find out whether a human can generate electricity.

WORK with a PARTNER

Encourage students to run experiments and write scientific observations with partners. Make sure pairs work together from start to finish, beginning with brainstorming ideas and ending with publishing their work. Help each pair set up a schedule and division of labor. Follow up with conferences that ensure students are meeting each benchmark and sharing the work.

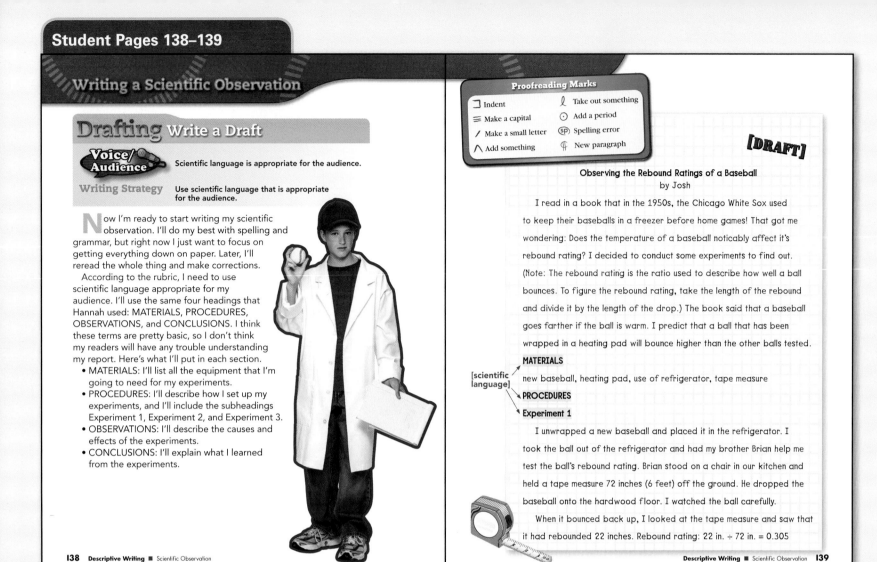

Drafting

(Student pages 138–139)

Remind students that drafting is a chance to get ideas on paper without having to worry about making mistakes.

Read aloud Josh's words on Student page 138. Point out that he refers to the rubric as he thinks about how to begin his draft. Encourage students to get into the habit of using the rubric to help guide their own writing.

Then, read aloud the drafting strategy on Student page 138, and have a student read aloud the portion of Josh's draft shown on Student page 139. Ask students which words he used to label each section of the draft on this page. **Materials, Procedures, Experiment** Point out that these words are scientific language, and that Josh kept them basic enough so that the average reader could understand them.

Finally, ask what types of information Josh included in his opening paragraph. **Possible responses: the questions he wanted his experiments to answer; his predictions** Note that students might wish to include similar information in their own introductions. Then, remind them to use their Cause-and-Effect Links while drafting their own scientific observations.

Writing Across the Curriculum

Science Have students write research papers, essays, or editorials that explore ideas raised in their scientific observations. Introduce this option by referring to Josh's draft together, noting the following ideas that could be further explored: how a baseball's construction has changed over the years, the materials used in different kinds of baseballs, and the effect of wind on a traveling baseball.

[scientific language]   [DRAFT]

▶ **Experiment 2**

 I let the ball return to room temperature. I wrapped a heating pad around it and set the temperature on "low." I took the ball out of the heating pad and had Brian help me test the ball's rebound rating. Brian had to stands on the same chair in the same spot in our kitchen. He held a tape measure 72 inches (6 feet) off the ground. Then he dropped the baseball onto the hardwood floor. I watched the ball carefully.

 When it bounced back up, I looked at the tape measure and saw that it had rebounded 17 inches. Rebound rating: 17 in. ÷ 72 in. = 0.236

▶ **Experiment 3**

 I let the ball return to room temperature by letting it sit untouched on a counter. I had Brian help me test the ball's rebound rating. Brian stood on the same chair in the same spot in our kitchen. Again, he held a tape measure 72 inches (6 feet) off the ground. Then he dropped the baseball onto the hardwood floor. Again, I watched the ball carefully.

 When it bounced back up, I looked at the tape measure and saw that it had rebounded 21 inches. Rebound rating: 21 in. ÷ 72 in. = 0.292

[scientific language]   [DRAFT]

▶ **OBSERVATIONS**

 The baseball rebounded very differently under cold and hot conditions. When refrigerated, it rebounded to 22 inches (about a third of the height from which it was dropped). When heated, however, it only rebounded to 17 inches (about a fourth of the height from which it was dropped). That was a difference of 5 inches. When the ball returned to room temperature, its rebound rating was closer to the rating of the cold ball, but it wasn't quite as high.

▶ **CONCLUSIONS**

 I learned that the temperature of a baseball really does affect its variations in rebound rating, a colder ball has a grater rebound. In a baseball game, this would mean that when hit off a bat, a colder baseball would go farther than a warm one. So that must mean that a team that plays in a cool weather city would hit the ball farther than a team that plays in a warm weather city. I had predicted that the warmer ball would bounce higher. This is weird. How did I get these results? I'll repeat my experiments next week to see if I get the same results.

Practice!

Now it's your turn. Make sure to use scientific language that your readers will understand.

Reflect

Do you think my scientific language is appropriate for my audience?

Drafting

(Student pages 140–141)

Direct students to the two headings in Josh's draft on Student page 141. Make sure students understand that in OBSERVATIONS, Josh described the results of each different experiment, and that in CONCLUSIONS, he made inferences about the meaning of his results.

Explain that making inferences involves combining facts, details, or evidence with personal experience to develop ideas that go beyond what is explicitly known. Remind students that they will be making inferences about causes and effects as they write, and that they may wish to include a CONCLUSIONS section in their own drafts.

Listening Skills

by Ken Stewart, *Master Teacher*

Emphasize to your students the importance of developing good listening skills. They must understand that attentive listening is just as important as clearly voicing their ideas. Since listening is at least fifty percent of effective oral communication, then it is imperative that you establish good listening skills in your classroom.

With your guidance, have your class discuss the rules of good listening. Use the following questions to guide the discussion:

• *How important is listening?*

• *What are some rules about listening that we should observe in our classroom?*

List responses on the board or on an overhead projector. Then, transfer them to a poster board to be displayed and referred to throughout the year.

Note: Rules should include remaining silent while another person speaks, looking at the speaker, nodding or smiling to show understanding, asking for clarification when necessary, and restating what you heard or think you heard.

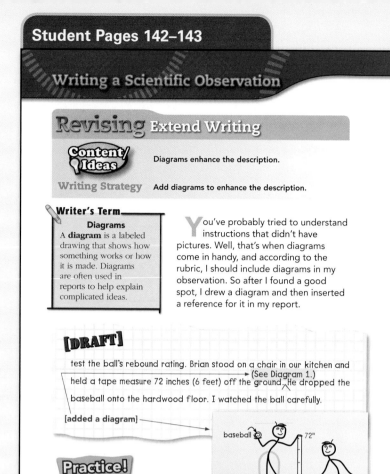

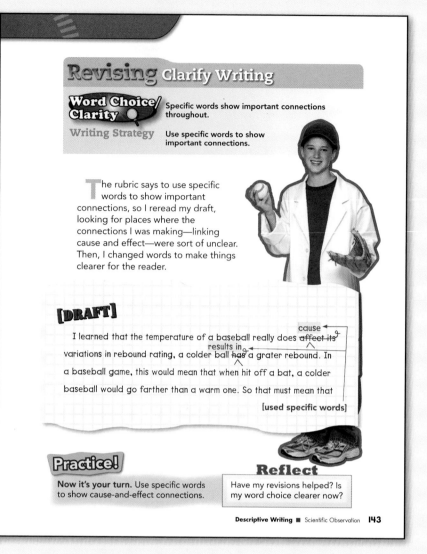

Revising

(Student pages 142–143)

Ask students if they have ever had to assemble something. **Possible response: yes** Have volunteers share their experiences. Were instructions included? Did they include diagrams?

Have students imagine putting something together without the aid of diagrams. Then, discuss the role of diagrams in descriptions. Point out that visual aids can often help to clarify wordy or confusing passages.

Call students' attention to the diagram that Josh added to his draft on Student page 142. Discuss whether this visual enhances his description. Have students skim Josh's draft on Student pages 139–141, noting other places where diagrams might help clarify the text. Then, have students add diagrams to enhance the descriptions in their own scientific observations.

Now, turn students' attention to the revisions Josh made to his draft on Student page 143. Ask why he inserted the words *cause* and *results in*. **Possible response: because**

they clarify the cause-and-effect connection Review other specific words that show cause-and-effect connections. Then, have students use specific words to show important connections in their own drafts.

Differentiating Instruction

Enrichment Students who are skilled at drawing can apply their talents in several ways. They can

- include multiple hand-drawn diagrams in their own scientific observations.
- publish their finished product by including small decorative illustrations that portray materials used in the experiments.
- help other students by drawing final illustrations based on their rough sketches.

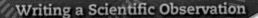

Writing a Scientific Observation

Editing Check Sentences

Sentence Fluency

Transitional phrases help the writing flow.

Writing Strategy Use transitional phrases to help the writing flow.

Now I need to edit my writing. The rubric says to use transitional phrases to help my writing flow. This is important because I have to describe the experiments, step-by-step, and that can make the writing sound a little choppy. So I looked over my draft and found a few places where the writing seemed rough because each sentence started with the subject. I smoothed things out with some transitional phrases, and I even fixed an error in subject-verb agreement since I know that's important, too!

[DRAFT]

[used transitional phrases]

The next day,
I let the ball return to room temperature. I wrapped a heating pad
Eight hours later,
around it and set the temperature on "low." I took the ball out of the

heating pad and had Brian help me test the ball's rebound rating. Brian
stands
had to ~~stands~~ on the same chair in the same spot in our kitchen. He

[corrected subject-verb agreement]

Practice!

Now it's your turn. Use transitional phrases to make your writing flow.

144 **Descriptive Writing** ■ Scientific Observation

Editing Proofread Writing

Grammar/Mechanics

Spelling, punctuation, and capitalization are correct. Colons and hyphens are used correctly.

Writing Strategy Make sure colons and hyphens are used correctly.

Writer's Term

Colons and Hyphens

A **colon (:)** is used to separate two independent clauses when the second one explains the first. It can also be used to introduce a list at the end of a sentence. A **hyphen (-)** is used to separate words at the end of a line or to link two words that, when used together, act as an adjective.

The last thing to do is check my observation for incorrect spelling, punctuation, and capitalization. The rubric also says to make sure that colons and hyphens are used correctly. I checked my draft and fixed any errors that I saw.

[DRAFT]

[correctly used a colon]

cause
I learned that the temperature of a baseball really does ~~affect its~~
results in greater
variations in rebound rating: a colder ball ~~has a grater~~ rebound. In

a baseball game, this would mean that when hit off a bat, a colder

baseball would go farther than a warm one. So that must mean that

a team that plays in a cool weather city would hit the ball farther

than a team that plays in a warm weather city. I had predicted that

[correctly used hyphens]

Practice!

Now it's your turn. Make sure that colons, hyphens, grammar, and mechanics are used correctly.

Grammar/Mechanics

For more practice with colons and hyphens, use the exercises on the next two pages.

Reflect

Did my edits make my writing clearer?

Descriptive Writing ■ Scientific Observation 145

Editing

(Student pages 144–145)

Call students' attention to the edits Josh made to his draft on Student page 144. Ask a volunteer to read aloud the sentences without the edits. Then, have another student read aloud the text with Josh's edits. Ask students which version sounds better and why. **Possible response: The edited version sounds better because the transitional phrases help the writing flow.** Have students check their own scientific observations for places where transitional phrases will help the writing flow.

Then, ask a volunteer to read aloud the Writer's Term box on Student page 145. Have students note how Josh edited his writing for proper use of hyphens and colons. Ask students to note what he corrected and why. **He changed a comma into a colon to separate two related independent clauses. He inserted a hyphen between *cool* and *weather* and *warm* and *weather* because these words are used together as adjectives.** Have students begin checking their drafts to make sure they have used all colons and hyphens correctly. Remind them that they should also check their spelling, capitalization, and punctuation.

If any of your students are having trouble understanding how to use colons and hyphens correctly, you may wish to teach the Mini-Lesson on pages 116–117 of this Teacher Edition. Then, have students complete the exercises on Student pages 146–147. Review the answers and possible rewrites with them.

WORK with a PARTNER

Have pairs of students read one another's drafts, using sticky notes to mark errors in spelling, punctuation, and grammar. Then, tell students to perform a second read that focuses on the editing strategies they learned in this chapter.

Grammar/Mechanics Practice!

Colons and Hyphens

KNOW the RULE

A **colon** is used to separate two independent clauses when the second one explains the first.
   Example: I conducted an awesome experiment: I observed various items under a black light.
A **colon** can also be used to introduce a list at the end of a sentence.
   Example: Here is what I used: a white shirt, a pink shirt, nail polish, and fluorescent paint.
A **hyphen** is used to separate words at the end of a line or to link two words that, when used together, act as an adjective.
   Examples: black-light experiment; greenish-yellow tint

Practice the Rule

Copy the sentences below on a separate sheet of paper, inserting colons and hyphens where needed.

1. I will conduct an experiment I will observe the rebound ratings of three balls.
2. I predict that two balls will have similar rebound ratings the tennis ball and the basketball.
3. A golf ball is a lightning fast ball.
4. The golf ball's diameter is the smallest 1.68 inches.
5. British made golf balls are slightly smaller than American ones, so they probably have an even higher rebound rating.

Apply the Rule

Read the following passage, looking for colon and hyphen errors. Rewrite the corrected text on another sheet of paper.

Experiment

To begin my liquid density experiment, I filled three glasses with equal amounts of water. I also set out the following vegetable oil, soy sauce, and skim milk. Then, I measured out one teaspoonful of oil and poured it into a glass of water. I repeated this same process with the soy sauce and milk, making sure to rinse the liquid coated teaspoon after each different liquid.

OBSERVATIONS

The liquids behaved in the following ways Each one either floated on top of the water or sank to the bottom of the glass. When I poured in the oil, it floated on top of the water in little circles. But the soy sauce sank, and so did the milk.

CONCLUSIONS

I learned that oil was the least dense. Because it floated on top of the water, oil has a density of less than 1. Both the soy sauce and the skim milk sank, meaning they both have densities that are greater than 1. The experiment did leave me with one question What would happen if I tested the density of whole milk? Whole milk has fat in it, similar to that in oil. Will it float?

Grammar/Mechanics Mini-Lesson

(Student pages 146–147)

Colons and Hyphens

Explain to students that it helps to keep a few simple rules in mind when checking to see if colons and hyphens have been used correctly. Have them read the Know the Rule box on Student page 146. Then, discuss its contents together.

Note that a colon can be used to separate two independent clauses. Ask a volunteer to define an independent clause. **It contains both a subject and a verb, and it expresses a complete thought.** Write the following on the board: *Josh ran a series of experiments: He tested the rebound rate of a baseball.* Ask students whether the colon is used correctly, and have them explain their answer. **Yes, because it separates two independent clauses, the second of which explains the first.** Remind students that a colon can also be used to introduce a list at the end of a sentence.

Explain that one correct use of a hyphen is to link two words that work together as an adjective. Write the following phrases on the board and ask students to add hyphens where appropriate:

1. *a one-way street*
2. *a coat of many colors*
3. *a hair-raising chase*
4. *a slow-moving turtle*
5. *a small brown bird*
6. *sugar-coated candy*

Make sure students understand that the second phrase does not take a hyphen because the adjectives come *after* the noun, and the fifth phrase does not take a hyphen because the two adjectives work separately rather than together.

Answers for Practice the Rule

1. I will conduct an experiment: I will observe the rebound ratings of three balls.
2. I predict that two balls will have similar rebound ratings: the tennis ball and the basketball.
3. A golf ball is a lightning-fast ball.
4. The golf ball's diameter is the smallest: 1.68 inches.
5. British-made golf balls are slightly smaller than American ones, so they probably have an even higher rebound rating.

(Answers continue on page 117.)

Writing a Scientific Observation

Publishing Share Writing

Include my observation in a display in my science classroom.

My scientific observation is done! Now I want to publish it. I could post it on the Web or read it to a friend. But a lot of kids like baseball, so I think my classmates will be interested in my results. That's why I want to include my final draft in a display in my science class. I'll read through it again right now to make sure it includes all of the items on my checklist.

My Checklist

- ✔ The observation describes several experiments.
- ✔ It includes causes and effects.
- ✔ Scientific language is appropriate for the audience.
- ✔ Diagrams clarify the description.
- ✔ Transitional phrases and specific words make the writing flow.
- ✔ Spelling, capitalization, and punctuation are all correct. Colons and hyphens are used correctly.

Practice!

Now it's your turn. Make a checklist to check your scientific observation. Then, make a final draft to publish.

Observing the Rebound Ratings of a Baseball

by Josh

I read in a book that in the 1950s, the Chicago White Sox used to keep their baseballs in a freezer before home games! That got me wondering: Does the temperature of a baseball noticeably affect its rebound rating? I decided to conduct some experiments to find out. (Note: The rebound rating is the ratio used to describe how well a ball bounces. To figure the rebound rating, take the length of the rebound and divide it by the length of the drop.) The book said that a baseball goes farther if the ball is warm. I predict that a ball that has been wrapped in a heating pad will bounce higher than the other balls tested.

MATERIALS

new baseball, heating pad, use of refrigerator, tape measure

PROCEDURES

Experiment 1

To begin my experiment, I unwrapped a new baseball and placed it in the refrigerator. After eight hours, I took the ball out of the refrigerator and had my brother Brian help me test the ball's rebound rating. Brian stood on a chair in our kitchen and held a tape measure 72 inches (6 feet) off the ground. (See Diagram 1.) Then, he dropped the baseball onto the hardwood floor. I watched the ball carefully.

When it bounced back up, I looked at the tape measure and saw that it had rebounded 22 inches. Rebound rating: 22 in. ÷ 72 in. = 0.305

(Answers continued from page 116.)

Answers for Apply the Rule

Experiment

To begin my liquid density experiment, I filled three glasses with equal amounts of water. I also set out the following: vegetable oil, soy sauce, and skim milk. Then, I measured out one teaspoonful of oil and poured it into a glass of water. I repeated this same process with the soy sauce and milk, making sure to rinse the liquid-coated teaspoon after each different liquid.

OBSERVATIONS

The liquids behaved in the following ways: Each one either floated on top of the water or sank to the bottom of the glass. When I poured in the oil, it floated on top of the water in little circles. But the soy sauce sank, and so did the milk.

CONCLUSIONS

I learned that oil was the least dense. Because it floated on top of the water, oil has a density of less than 1. Both the soy sauce and the skim milk sank, meaning they both have densities that are greater than 1. The experiment did leave me with one question: What would

happen if I tested the density of whole milk? Whole milk has fat in it, similar to that in oil. Will it float?

Publishing

(Student pages 148–149)

Ask students if they like Josh's choice for sharing his scientific observation. Tell the class that his choice is not the only option for publishing his work. Invite students to name other ways they could publish their own writing.

Have each student make a checklist and perform a final evaluation of his or her scientific observation before publishing it. Encourage students to share copies of their work with friends and relatives who might be interested in reading about what they wrote.

 For more practice with grammar/mechanics skills, see Zaner-Bloser's *G.U.M.* materials.

Writing a Scientific Observation

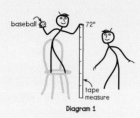
Diagram 1

Experiment 2

I let the ball return to room temperature. The next day, I wrapped a heating pad around it and set the temperature on "low." Eight hours later, I took the ball out of the heating pad and had Brian help me test the ball's rebound rating. Brian had to stand on the same chair in the same spot in our kitchen. Again, he held a tape measure 72 inches (6 feet) off the ground. Then, he dropped the baseball onto the hardwood floor. Again, I watched the ball carefully.

When it bounced back up, I looked at the tape measure and saw that it had rebounded 17 inches. Rebound rating: 17 in. ÷ 72 in. = 0.236

Experiment 3

I let the ball return to room temperature by letting it sit untouched on a counter. After school the next day, I had Brian help me test the ball's rebound rating. Brian stood on the same chair in the same spot in our kitchen. Again, he held a tape measure 72 inches (6 feet) off the ground. Then, he dropped the baseball onto the hardwood floor. Again, I watched the ball carefully.

When it bounced back up, I looked at the tape measure and saw that it had rebounded 21 inches. Rebound rating: 21 in. ÷ 72 in. = 0.292

OBSERVATIONS

The baseball rebounded differently under cold and hot conditions. When refrigerated, it rebounded to 22 inches (about a third of the height from which it was dropped). When heated, however, it only rebounded to 17 inches (about a fourth of the height from which it was dropped). That was a difference of 5 inches. When the ball returned to room temperature, its rebound rating was closer to the rating of the cold ball, but it wasn't quite as high.

CONCLUSIONS

I learned that the temperature of a baseball really does cause variations in rebound rating: A colder ball results in a greater rebound. In a baseball game, this would mean that when hit off a bat, a colder baseball would go farther than a warm one. So that must mean that a team that plays in a cool-weather city would hit the ball farther than a team that plays in a warm-weather city. I had predicted that the warmer ball would bounce higher. This is weird. How did I get these results? I'll repeat my experiments next week to see if I get the same results.

Reflect

What do you think? Did I use all the traits of a good scientific observation in my writing? Check it against the rubric. Don't forget to use the rubric to check your own report, too.

Publishing

(Student pages 150–151)

Call students' attention to the Reflect box on the bottom of Student page 151. Explain that assessing Josh's scientific observation against the rubric will help them better understand how to apply the traits to their own work. Then, have students use sticky notes to mark at least one example of each trait in Josh's writing. Tell them to include an evaluation on each note.

After this process, have students assess how well they were able to identify each trait in Josh's writing, and how easy or hard it was to use the rubric. Remind them to apply what they learned from Josh's work when they use the rubric to check their own writing.

Differentiating Instruction

Support Some students may benefit from direct instruction and repetition in evaluating the use of the writing traits. While other students are working independently on peer reviews, organize a small group of students to use the traits to study each other's work. Begin by making enough copies of students' scientific observations for each student in the group. Then, do the following.

- Display the rubric in an enlarged form on chart paper. Highlight the Content/Ideas trait.

- Choose one observation to review together first. Then, use words like the following to model the Content/Ideas trait: *When I look at the rubric, the Content/Ideas trait says diagrams should enhance the description. I'll review the observation with this in mind. In the third paragraph, I see one place where the text does not completely explain . . .*

- Using the same observation, go around the group and have each student model the other traits. Coach students as needed, discussing together how to apply the rubric.

- Convene each day until the group finishes reviewing all the observations.

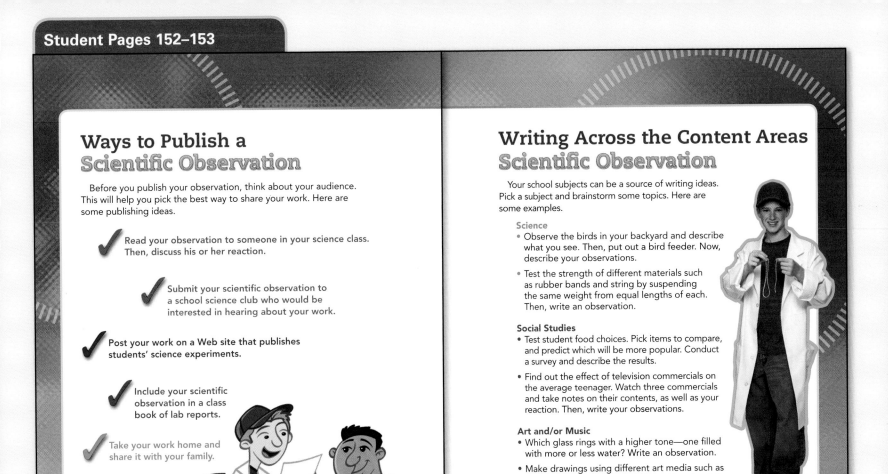

Ways to Publish
(Student page 152)

Read and discuss with students the publishing options listed on Student page 152. Encourage students to consider some of these options when publishing their own writing. Remind students that Josh chose to publish his scientific observation by including it in a display in his science classroom, but they can choose their own way of publishing. Perhaps one student will want to submit his or her observation to a school science club, while another will want to post it on a Web site that publishes students' science experiments.

Writing Across the Content Areas
(Student page 153)

Explain to students that writing is not just for English or language arts class. Many other school subjects contain ideas, issues, and events that students may want to write about. Encourage students to consider using one of the content areas listed on Student page 153 as a springboard for more writing options. Students may also wish to consult with other teachers for more ideas on writing in the content areas.

Descriptive Vignette Overview

In this chapter, students will learn how to write a descriptive vignette. They will study some of the elements of a descriptive vignette—organization, narration, sensory details, and figurative language—and some reasons why they might choose to write one. Students will then use a descriptive vignette rubric to study a model writing sample.

Students will follow the student guide as he goes through the writing stages—prewriting, drafting, revising, editing, and publishing. As the student guide learns new writing strategies in each step, students will be directed to practice the strategies in their own writing.

During prewriting and drafting, students will
- choose an experience and jot down notes.
- make a Web to organize their notes.
- write a draft that includes plenty of sensory details for the reader.

During revising and editing, students will
- add figurative language.
- replace clichés, vague words, and overused words with precise words.
- use participial phrases for sentence variety.
- edit their drafts for spelling, capitalization, and punctuation, making sure that comparative and superlative forms are correct.

Finally, students will write a final draft to be published.

You may wish to send to families the School-Home Connection Letter for this chapter, located at the end of this unit in the Teacher Edition.

Descriptive Vignette Writing Traits

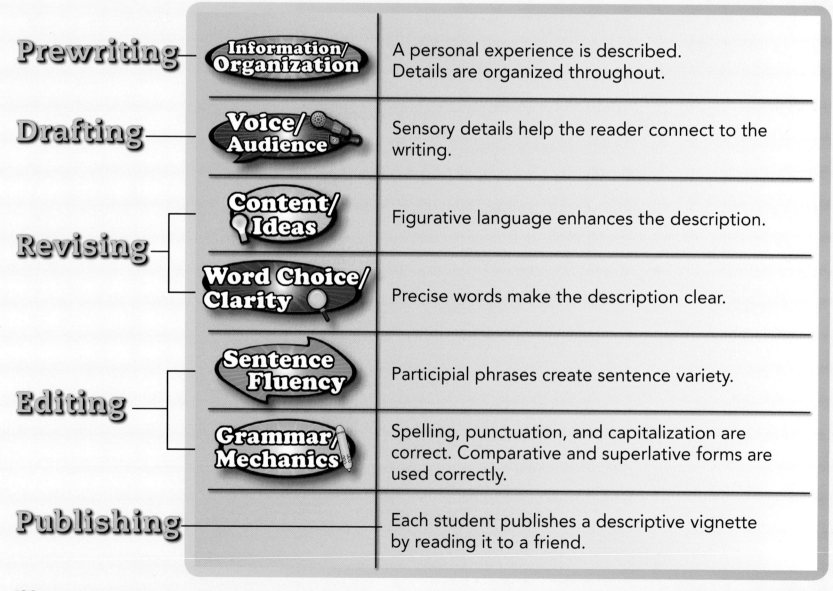

Stage	Trait	Description
Prewriting	Information/Organization	A personal experience is described. Details are organized throughout.
Drafting	Voice/Audience	Sensory details help the reader connect to the writing.
Revising	Content/Ideas	Figurative language enhances the description.
Revising	Word Choice/Clarity	Precise words make the description clear.
Editing	Sentence Fluency	Participial phrases create sentence variety.
Editing	Grammar/Mechanics	Spelling, punctuation, and capitalization are correct. Comparative and superlative forms are used correctly.
Publishing		Each student publishes a descriptive vignette by reading it to a friend.

Descriptive Vignette Time Management

Day 1	Day 2	Day 3	Day 4	Day 5
Learning Objectives				
Students will: • learn the components of a descriptive vignette.	Students will: • learn how to gather information for a descriptive vignette.	Students will: • practice gathering information for their descriptive vignettes.	Students will: • learn how to make a Web to organize their notes.	Students will: • practice making a Web to organize their notes.
Activities				
• Discuss the elements and traits of a descriptive vignette (Student pages 154–156). • Use the rubric to study the model (Student pages 157–161).	• Read and discuss **Prewriting: Gather Information** (Student page 162).	• Brainstorm ideas and choose a personal experience to write about. • Jot down detailed notes.	• Read and discuss **Prewriting: Organize Ideas** (Student page 163).	• Review notes made while gathering information. • Make a Web to organize notes.

WEEK 2

Day 1	Day 2	Day 3	Day 4	Day 5
Learning Objectives				
Students will: • learn how sensory details can help the reader connect to the writing.	Students will: • practice writing their own drafts.	Students will: • learn how figurative language can enhance description.	Students will: • practice adding figurative language to their drafts.	Students will: • learn how to use precise words to clarify description.
Activities				
• Read and discuss **Drafting: Write a Draft** (Student pages 164–165).	• Use Webs to write drafts. • Include plenty of sensory details for the reader.	• Read and discuss **Revising: Extend Writing** (Student page 166).	• Add figurative language to drafts.	• Read and discuss **Revising: Clarify Writing** (Student page 167).

WEEK 3

Day 1	Day 2	Day 3	Day 4	Day 5
Learning Objectives				
Students will: • practice using precise words to clarify description.	Students will: • learn how participial phrases can help create sentence variety.	Students will: • learn how to use comparative and superlative forms correctly.	Students will: • practice editing their drafts for spelling, capitalization, and punctuation.	Students will: • learn different ways to publish their descriptive vignettes.
Activities				
• Reread drafts, looking for clichés, vague words, and overused words. • Replace these with precise words to make the description clearer.	• Read and discuss **Editing: Check Sentences** (Student page 168). • Use participial phrases to create sentence variety.	• Read and discuss **Editing: Proofread Writing** (Student page 169).	• Fix any spelling, capitalization, or punctuation errors. • Fix any comparative and superlative forms that are not used correctly.	• Read and discuss **Publishing: Share Writing** (Student page 172).

To complete the chapter in fewer days, teach the learning objectives and activities for two days in one day.

This planning chart, correlated to your state's writing standards, is available on-line at http://www.zaner-bloser.com/sfw.

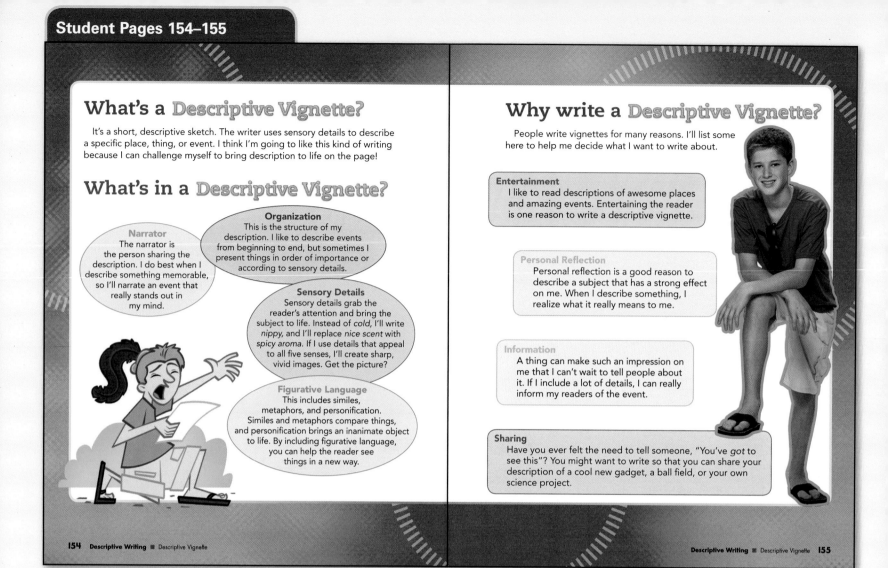

Define the Genre
(Student page 154)

Descriptive Vignette

Discuss with students the definition of a descriptive vignette. Ask students whether they have ever described a setting, person, or experience in detail. **Possible response: yes** Point out that any time they write a short, in-depth description about a personal experience, they are using the descriptive vignette genre.

Elements of the Genre
Descriptive Vignette

Read and discuss with students the elements of a descriptive vignette listed on Student page 154. Ask volunteers which elements are also common to other forms of writing. **Possible responses: Narrator—memoirs, short stories; Organization—biographies, directions; Sensory Details—poems, mysteries; Figurative Language—narratives, poems** Discuss why each element may be important to writing a descriptive vignette.

Authentic Writing
(Student page 155)

Descriptive Vignette

Read and discuss with students the reasons for writing a descriptive vignette listed on Student page 155. Point out that all writing has a purpose and is aimed at a specific audience. These authentic purposes help authors shape their writing. Ask a volunteer to read aloud the Entertainment box. Then, have students discuss what kinds of descriptions might be the most entertaining. Repeat this process for the Personal Reflection, Information, and Sharing boxes. Then, have students brainstorm other purposes for writing a descriptive vignette that are not listed on Student page 155. Encourage students to think about their own reasons for writing a descriptive vignette, and how these reasons will affect the tone and focus of their writing.

Descriptive Vignette Writing Traits

I know that there are six traits of good writing. But what makes a good descriptive vignette? This list will help me write my description.

Information/Organization	A personal experience is described. Details are organized throughout.
Voice/Audience	Sensory details help the reader connect to the writing.
Content/Ideas	Figurative language enhances the description.
Word Choice/Clarity	Precise words make the description clear.
Sentence Fluency	Participial phrases create sentence variety.
Grammar/Mechanics	Spelling, punctuation, and capitalization are correct. Comparative and superlative forms are used correctly.

I can use Gina Bedow's descriptive vignette on the next page as a model for my own writing. Later, we'll check out how Gina used these traits to help her write.

Descriptive Vignette Model

The Concert

By Gina Bedow

Narrator

Last night I went to the most deafening concert I've ever attended. My ears are still ringing from the music, and my throat is still sore from screaming above the crowd. I guess you could say that I experienced the concert with all five of my senses! *Personification*

The concert was outdoors, and there were food tents set up everywhere. The smoke from the barbecue ribs rose above the crowd. It curled a finger under Jackson's nose, beckoning him to eat. The pizza tent was next door, and Sharon couldn't resist the smell of fresh mozzarella. I chose corn on the cob. As I ate, butter dripped down my hand with each sweet, crunchy bite, and salt stung my lips like a thousand tiny bees. *Simile* *Sensory Details*

Personification Hunger satisfied, we found a place to sit about halfway up a hill. The grass felt cool and stiff as we spread out our blanket. Stretching drowsily, the sun soon sank behind the hill. I felt a little chilly, so I untied my sweater from around my waist and slipped it over my head. Its gentle caress felt soft and warm, and I secretly thanked my mom for making me take it along.

Organization After a while, the concert began. When the band hit the stage, the crowd sprang to its feet. I saw two girls, arms locked, in a jerky kind of square dance. To their right, a boy stood playing an imaginary drum set. To his right, a group of people clapped in time with the music.

And then it started raining—hard. Within minutes, we were all drenched, and so was the ground. It was now a toboggan run of mud. *Metaphor* I couldn't stand it anymore. I took off my shoes and socks, rolled up my jeans, and went flailing down the hill. There's nothing quite like the feel of cold, wet mud against the skin. By the time I finished, I looked like *Simile* someone had turned me upside down and dipped me in a vat of chocolate.

The band tried to get everyone's attention by playing louder than the roar of the crowd. The bass was so loud that it rattled my bones. I plugged my ears with cotton, and it's a good thing I did! A few hours later, my ears were still ringing, and I practically had to shout to hear myself.

When I got home, my parents asked how the night had gone. I just laughed and shouted, "I'll tell you tomorrow, when I get my hearing back!"

Writing Traits

(Student pages 156–157)

Descriptive Vignette

Ask volunteers to talk about their favorite place, a memorable experience, or someone important in their lives. After students share, ask them questions to draw out more detailed descriptions, and invite others to share descriptions as well.

Next, ask students what might motivate someone to write a descriptive vignette. **Possible response: to share something interesting, exciting, or entertaining** Turn students' attention to the traits of a good descriptive vignette listed on Student page 156. Have one or more volunteers read aloud the traits and their descriptions. Discuss why someone might use these traits when writing a description. What kinds of traits would *not* belong in a descriptive vignette? **Possible responses: arguments/counterarguments; citing of sources; sales techniques**

Tell students that they are going to study and use strategies for writing descriptive vignettes, and that a good descriptive vignette has the traits listed on Student page 156.

Differentiating Instruction

English-Language Learners **Preteach** idioms and other forms of figurative language to help these students better understand the model.

Explain that an idiom is an expression with meaning that cannot be predicted from the meanings of its individual parts. Point out these idioms from the model: *My ears are still ringing* and *the band hit the stage.* Explain their meanings, using sounds and gestures as needed.

Students may also be confused by the personification, *It curled a finger under Jackson's nose, beckoning him to eat.* Explain that this phrase is an example of personification because it gives human qualities to a lifeless object: smoke.

Point out the metaphor *It was now a toboggan run of mud.* Explain that a toboggan is a long, flat-bottomed sled. A metaphor may be more confusing than a simile to these students because it is a direct comparison that, at first glance, might not make sense. Explain that a metaphor is a literary comparison that calls one thing another.

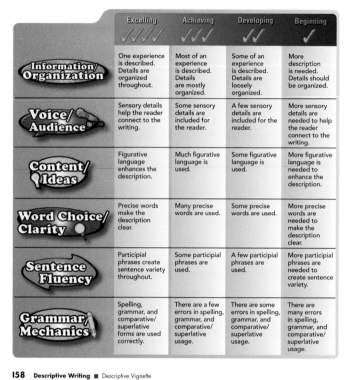

Using the Rubric
(Student page 158)

Explain that a rubric is a tool that can be used to evaluate a piece of writing. The rubric on Student page 158 can be used to evaluate a descriptive vignette. It is based on the same descriptive vignette traits listed on Student page 156.

Now point out the terms above each rubric column: *Excelling, Achieving, Developing,* and *Beginning.* Explain that each column symbolizes a degree of writing skill, and that each rubric row focuses on a specific writing trait. When students use the rubric to evaluate their own work at each step of the writing process, they increase the likelihood of producing polished, well-written descriptive vignettes.

Study the Model
(Student pages 159–161)

Explain that Student pages 159–161 show how the writing model on Student page 157 meets all six traits of the rubric. Read each section with the students. Have them look for other examples of each trait in the writing model.

Ask students how many check marks they would assign the writing model for each trait. Then, as a class, decide how the writing model should be rated overall.

Remind students to use the rubric as they write their own descriptive vignettes, to be sure they are meeting all six writing traits.

Descriptive Vignette

Content/Ideas
• Figurative language enhances the description.

Gina makes her description even more vivid by using similes, metaphors, and other figurative language. In the passage below, Gina uses personification to describe both the sun and her sweater as if they were living beings. I realize these are just objects that don't have the ability to act, but Gina finds a creative way to bring them to life.

[from the writing model]

Stretching drowsily, the sun soon sank behind the hill. I felt a little chilly, so I untied my sweater from around my waist and slipped it over my head. Its gentle caress felt soft and warm, and I secretly thanked my mom for making me take it along.

Word Choice/Clarity
• Precise words make the description clear.

I really appreciate the way Gina keeps her writing interesting. Instead of using vague, generic words that readers see all the time, she picks the exact words for what she wants to say. Check out the precise details in this passage. Instead of *wet*, Gina uses *drenched*. She could have written *went down the hill*, but *flailing down the hill* says it so much better.

[from the writing model]

Within minutes, we were all drenched, and so was the ground. It was now a toboggan run of mud. I couldn't stand it anymore. I took off my shoes and socks, rolled up my jeans, and went flailing down the hill.

Sentence Fluency
• Participial phrases create sentence variety.

I remember what a participle is! It's a verb form that ends in *–ing* or *–ed*, and when it's included in a group of words or a phrase that acts as an adjective, it's called a participial phrase. In the passage below, Gina uses the participial phrase *Hunger satisfied* to describe the group of concert-goers.

[from the writing model]

Hunger satisfied, we found a place to sit about halfway up a hill.

Grammar/Mechanics

• Spelling, punctuation, and capitalization are correct. Comparative and superlative forms are used correctly.

Gina knows how to use the correct comparative and superlative forms of adjectives and adverbs. She uses the comparative form to compare two objects or people, and the superlative form to compare three or more. Notice her use of the superlative adjective form *most deafening* to explain that this was the loudest concert she has ever attended.

[from the writing model]

Last night I went to the most deafening concert I've ever attended.

Gina also uses the comparative adverb form *louder* to explain how loud the band played.

[from the writing model]

The band tried to get everyone's attention by playing louder than the roar of the crowd.

My Turn!

I'm going to write a descriptive vignette about something that's meaningful to me. I'll follow the rubric and use good writing strategies. Read on to see how I do it!

Differentiating Instruction

English-Language Learners Help these students increase their vocabulary by working together to compile lists of precise words. Write the following words on the board, and have students copy them. Tell them to leave 3–5 lines of space underneath each word.

Nouns	Verbs	Adjectives
tree	speak	bad
book	run	pretty
room	make	heavy
light	cook	messy
shirt	fall	loud

Have pairs of students look up each word in a thesaurus, and then write several synonyms under each one. Then, have pairs write five sentences that use at least one synonym in each.

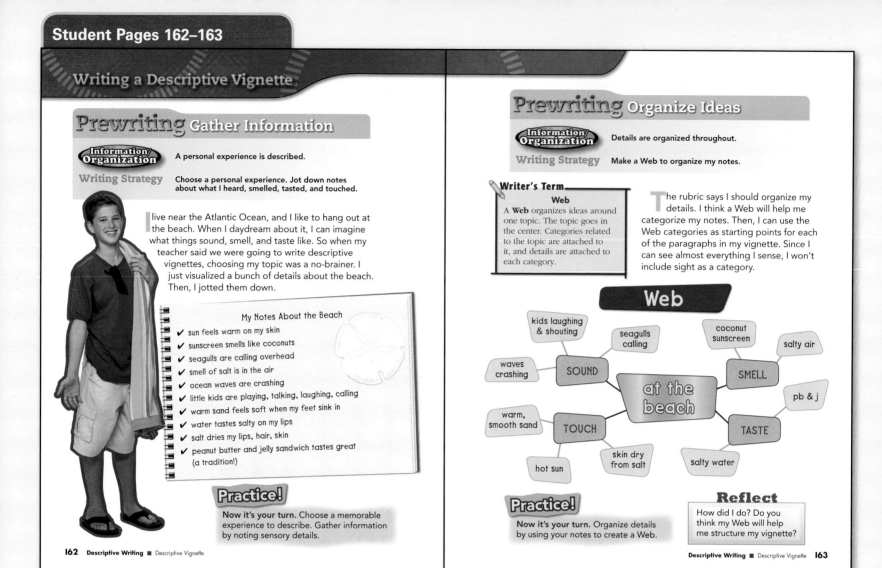

Writing a Descriptive Vignette

Prewriting Gather Information

Information/Organization A personal experience is described.

Writing Strategy Choose a personal experience. Jot down notes about what I heard, smelled, tasted, and touched.

I live near the Atlantic Ocean, and I like to hang out at the beach. When I daydream about it, I can imagine what things sound, smell, and taste like. So when my teacher said we were going to write descriptive vignettes, choosing my topic was a no-brainer. I just visualized a bunch of details about the beach. Then, I jotted them down.

My Notes About the Beach
- ✓ sun feels warm on my skin
- ✓ sunscreen smells like coconuts
- ✓ seagulls are calling overhead
- ✓ smell of salt is in the air
- ✓ ocean waves are crashing
- ✓ little kids are playing, talking, laughing, calling
- ✓ warm sand feels soft when my feet sink in
- ✓ water tastes salty on my lips
- ✓ salt dries my lips, hair, skin
- ✓ peanut butter and jelly sandwich tastes great (a tradition!)

Practice!
Now it's your turn. Choose a memorable experience to describe. Gather information by noting sensory details.

162 Descriptive Writing ■ Descriptive Vignette

Prewriting Organize Ideas

Information/Organization Details are organized throughout.

Writing Strategy Make a Web to organize my notes.

Writer's Term
Web
A **Web** organizes ideas around one topic. The topic goes in the center. Categories related to it, and details are attached to each category.

The rubric says I should organize my details. I think a Web will help me categorize my notes. Then, I can use the Web categories as starting points for each of the paragraphs in my vignette. Since I can see almost everything I sense, I won't include sight as a category.

Web

kids laughing & shouting — seagulls calling — SOUND — waves crashing — at the beach — coconut sunscreen — salty air — SMELL — pb & j — warm, smooth sand — TOUCH — hot sun — skin dry from salt — TASTE — salty water

Practice!
Now it's your turn. Organize details by using your notes to create a Web.

Reflect
How did I do? Do you think my Web will help me structure my vignette?

Descriptive Writing ■ Descriptive Vignette 163

Prewriting
(Student pages 162–163)

Ask volunteers to share a favorite place, interesting person, or memorable experience that they plan to feature in their descriptive vignettes. Tell students that before they draft their vignettes, they should visualize details about their chosen topic and jot down notes. Have students read Josh's notes on Student page 162 and ask what—besides the beach—the details have in common. **Possible response: They all appeal to the senses.** Then, ask whether or not Josh can use his notes—as is—to organize his draft. **Possible response: No, because they seem to be in random order.**

Turn students' attention to the Writer's Term box on Student page 163, and ask a volunteer to read it aloud. Then, have students review Josh's Web and compare it to his notes. Ask what is different about the Web. **Possible response: The Web organizes the notes into categories.** Remind students to plan their own drafts by organizing their notes into a Web. Explain that although Josh sorted his notes into four different senses, their own details might fit into different categories.

More Practice!

For more practice with these writing strategies, you may wish to have students use the Strategy Practice Book. See the appendix for annotated Strategy Practice Book pages.

WORK with a PARTNER
Pair English-Language learners with English-proficient students to work on prewriting tasks. Have partners share their topics and brainstorm ideas for individual notes. Then, have them trade notes and assess whether
- the notes contain enough details to form the basis for a first draft.
- the details feature enough variety.

If necessary, have partners prompt further details by asking each other questions about their topic. Encourage English-proficient students to help their partners by offering synonyms and other vocabulary suggestions. Finally, have pairs check each other's Webs for accuracy and completeness.

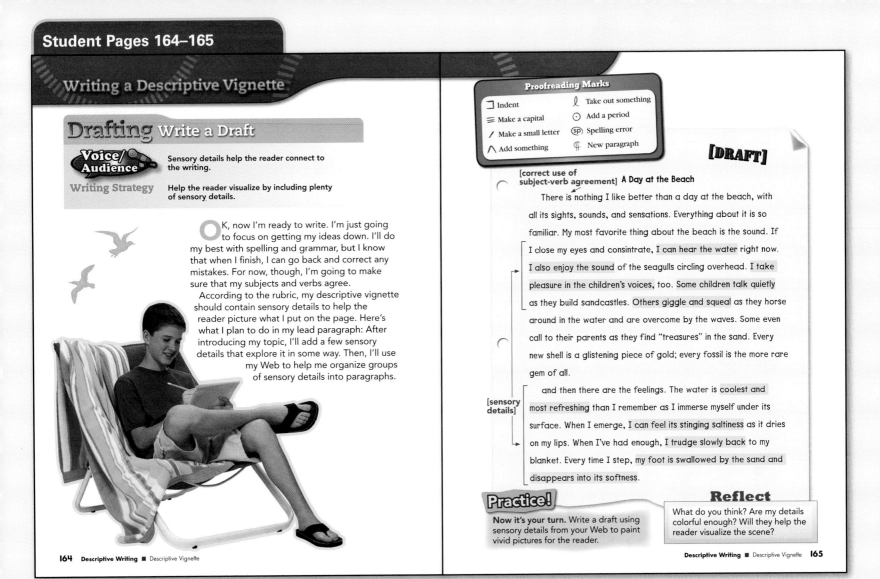

Writing a Descriptive Vignette

Drafting Write a Draft

Voice/Audience
Sensory details help the reader connect to the writing.

Writing Strategy
Help the reader visualize by including plenty of sensory details.

OK, now I'm ready to write. I'm just going to focus on getting my ideas down. I'll do my best with spelling and grammar, but I know that when I finish, I can go back and correct any mistakes. For now, though, I'm going to make sure that my subjects and verbs agree.

According to the rubric, my descriptive vignette should contain sensory details to help the reader picture what I put on the page. Here's what I plan to do in my lead paragraph: After introducing my topic, I'll add a few sensory details that explore it in some way. Then, I'll use my Web to help me organize groups of sensory details into paragraphs.

Proofreading Marks

⌐ Indent
≡ Make a capital
/ Make a small letter
∧ Add something
ℓ Take out something
⊙ Add a period
SP Spelling error
¶ New paragraph

[DRAFT]

[correct use of subject-verb agreement] **A Day at the Beach**

There is nothing I like better than a day at the beach, with all its sights, sounds, and sensations. Everything about it is so familiar. My most favorite thing about the beach is the sound. If I close my eyes and consintrate, I can hear the water right now. I also enjoy the sound of the seagulls circling overhead. I take pleasure in the children's voices, too. Some children talk quietly as they build sandcastles. Others giggle and squeal as they horse around in the water and are overcome by the waves. Some even call to their parents as they find "treasures" in the sand. Every new shell is a glistening piece of gold; every fossil is the more rare gem of all.

[sensory details] and then there are the feelings. The water is coolest and most refreshing than I remember as I immerse myself under its surface. When I emerge, I can feel its stinging saltiness as it dries on my lips. When I've had enough, I trudge slowly back to my blanket. Every time I step, my foot is swallowed by the sand and disappears into its softness.

Practice!

Now it's your turn. Write a draft using sensory details from your Web to paint vivid pictures for the reader.

Reflect

What do you think? Are my details colorful enough? Will they help the reader visualize the scene?

164 **Descriptive Writing** ■ Descriptive Vignette

Descriptive Writing ■ Descriptive Vignette **165**

Drafting
(Student pages 164–165)

Remind students that drafting is a chance to get ideas on paper without having to worry about making mistakes.

Read aloud Josh's words on Student page 164. Point out that Josh refers to the rubric as he thinks about how to begin his draft. Encourage students to get into the habit of using the rubric to help guide their own writing.

Then, refer to the Practice and the Reflect boxes on Student page 165, which remind students to use sensory details to help the reader visualize what's being described. Ask if Josh included details from his Web. **yes** Then, remind students to use details from their Webs to draft their own descriptive vignettes.

Writing Across the Curriculum

Science Have students find out more about one of the five senses of sight, touch, taste, hearing, and smell. Have them briefly research the topic in reference books or on the Internet. Suggest that they consider any of the following formats in which to share their findings: a collage or a poster, a multi-media presentation, a song or a poem, a Web site, a diorama, a drawing or a painting, or a written report.

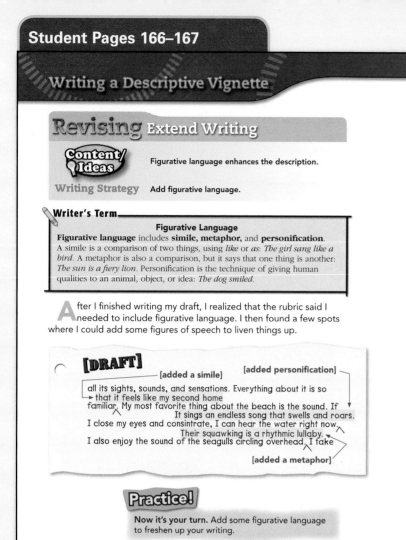

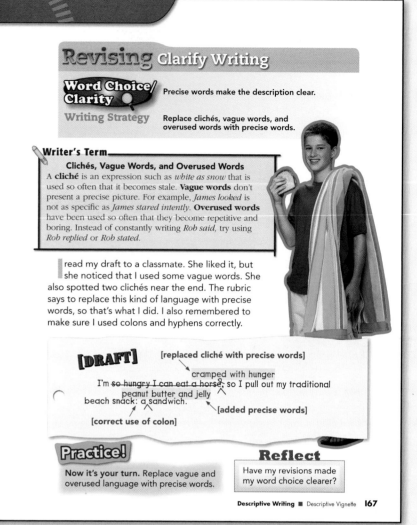

Revising

(Student pages 166–167)

Read aloud the Writer's Term box on Student page 166. To ensure that students understand the difference between a simile and a metaphor, write the following sentences on the board, and have students classify each one.

The dog bounded along the path like a kangaroo. **simile**

The dog was a kangaroo bounding along the path. **metaphor**

Then, have a volunteer offer examples of personification. **Possible responses:** *The computer glared back at me. The tree cradled me in its branches.*

Next, call students' attention to Josh's edits on Student page 166, and discuss whether these changes enhance his description. Have students look for places in their own drafts where they can add figurative language.

Read aloud the Writer's Term box on Student page 167. Have students share other examples of clichés, vague words, and overused words. **Possible responses: cliché—as black as night; vague word—nice** Then, turn their attention to the revisions Josh made to his draft. Discuss whether these improved the text, and have students replace clichés, vague words, and overused words in their own drafts with words that are more precise.

Differentiating Instruction

English-Language Learners These students may need extra help identifying English clichés as well as vague and overused words. Explain that a cliché is similar to an idiom. Review these common English clichés and their meanings:

- *I've had it up to here! / That makes my blood boil!*

- *That's as easy as pie. / It's a slam dunk.*

Have students share clichés from their own native languages, and challenge them to use a Web to make lists of other English clichés.

Tip: Explain that vague and overused words are usually more general words. Tell students that as they write, they can avoid these words by using visualization and asking themselves, "What does the 'word' look like? Can I describe it with a more specific word?"

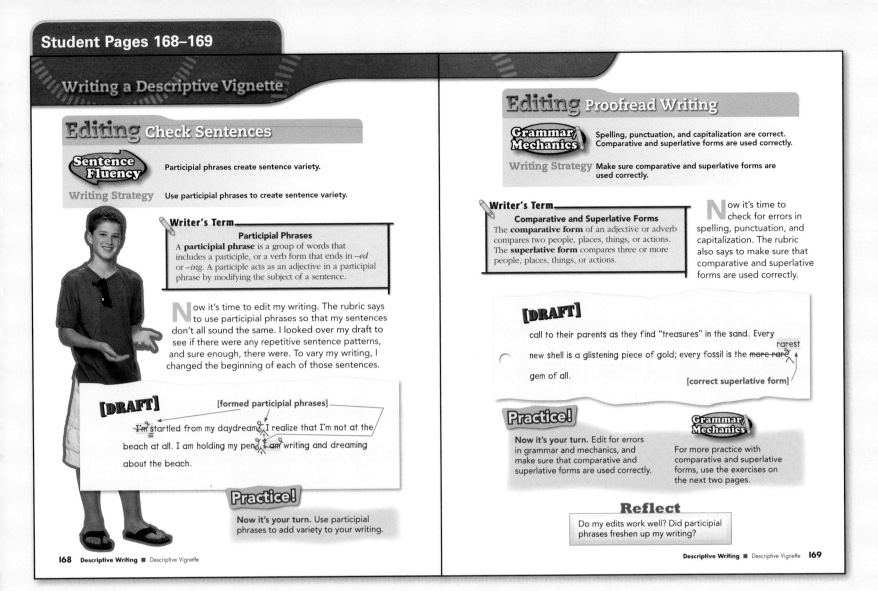

Writing a Descriptive Vignette

Editing Check Sentences

Sentence Fluency

Participial phrases create sentence variety.

Writing Strategy Use participial phrases to create sentence variety.

Writer's Term

Participial Phrases

A **participial phrase** is a group of words that includes a participle, or a verb form that ends in *–ed* or *–ing*. A participle acts as an adjective in a participial phrase by modifying the subject of a sentence.

Now it's time to edit my writing. The rubric says to use participial phrases so that my sentences don't all sound the same. I looked over my draft to see if there were any repetitive sentence patterns, and sure enough, there were. To vary my writing, I changed the beginning of each of those sentences.

[DRAFT]

[formed participial phrases]

I'm startled from my daydream, I realize that I'm not at the beach at all. I am holding my pen, I am writing and dreaming about the beach.

Practice!

Now it's your turn. Use participial phrases to add variety to your writing.

168 Descriptive Writing ■ Descriptive Vignette

Editing Proofread Writing

Grammar/ Mechanics Spelling, punctuation, and capitalization are correct. Comparative and superlative forms are used correctly.

Writing Strategy Make sure comparative and superlative forms are used correctly.

Writer's Term

Comparative and Superlative Forms

The **comparative form** of an adjective or adverb compares two people, places, things, or actions. The **superlative form** compares three or more people, places, things, or actions.

Now it's time to check for errors in spelling, punctuation, and capitalization. The rubric also says to make sure that comparative and superlative forms are used correctly.

[DRAFT]

call to their parents as they find "treasures" in the sand. Every new shell is a glistening piece of gold; every fossil is the more rare gem of all. rarest [correct superlative form]

Practice!

Now it's your turn. Edit for errors in grammar and mechanics, and make sure that comparative and superlative forms are used correctly.

Grammar/ Mechanics For more practice with comparative and superlative forms, use the exercises on the next two pages.

Reflect

Do my edits work well? Did participial phrases freshen up my writing?

Descriptive Writing ■ Descriptive Vignette **169**

Editing

(Student pages 168–169)

Call students' attention to the edits Josh made to his draft on Student page 168. Ask a volunteer to read aloud the text without the edits. Then, ask students why they think Josh decided to revise this passage. **Possible response: because all the sentences have the same structure**

Read aloud the Writer's Term box on Student page 168. To further students' understanding of participial phrases, write these sample sentences on the board:

• *Having been chosen to start the game, the pitcher was nervous.*

• *Lungs heaving, Maya stumbled toward the finish line.*

• *Straining against its leash, the dog tried to escape.*

• *Disappointed in my grade, I vowed to study harder.*

Now, have students underline the participial phrase in each sentence. Some students may mistake the verb in the sentence for the participle. Point out the verb and explain why this word conveys the action in the sentence. Tell students to use participial phrases to create sentence variety in their own drafts.

Read aloud the Writer's Term box on Student page 169, and ask a volunteer to explain the difference between the comparative and the superlative form. **The comparative form compares two items, and the superlative form compares three or more.** Remind students to check their drafts, making sure they have used all comparative and superlative forms correctly. Remind them that they should also check their spelling, capitalization, and punctuation.

You may wish to teach the Mini-Lesson on pages 130–131 of this Teacher Edition. Then, have students complete the exercises on Student pages 170–171. Review with them the answers and possible rewrites.

WORK with a PARTNER Have pairs of students read one another's drafts, using sticky notes to mark errors in spelling, punctuation, and grammar. Then, tell students they should conduct a second read that focuses on the editing strategies they learned in this chapter.

Comparative and Superlative Forms

KNOW the RULE

The **comparative form** of an adjective or adverb compares two people, places, things, or actions.
- Add an *–er* ending to short adjectives and adverbs to create the comparative form.
  Examples: loud, loud**er**; small, small**er**
- Use the word *more* or *less* before long adjectives and adverbs (of three or more syllables) to create the comparative form.
  Examples: wonderful, **more** wonderful, **less** wonderful

The **superlative form** compares three or more people, places, things, or actions.
- Add an *–est* ending to short adjectives and adverbs to create the superlative form.
  Examples: loud, loud**est**; small, small**est**
- Use the word *most* or *least* before long adjectives and adverbs (of three or more syllables) to create the superlative form.
  Examples: wonderful, **most** wonderful, **least** wonderful

Practice the Rule

On a separate sheet of paper, write the word or phrase in parentheses that correctly completes each sentence. Then, write whether that form is comparative or superlative.

1. The (more memorable/most memorable) teacher I've ever known was my swim instructor.
2. I swim (more skillfully/most skillfully) than my brother.
3. When I swam (slower/slowest) than he did, he used to tease me.
4. I've heard that Mediterranean beaches have the (more beautiful/most beautiful) sand.
5. Though the butterfly is (harder/more hard) than the breaststroke, I still want to learn it.

Apply the Rule

Read the following vignette, watching for errors in comparative and superlative usage. On a separate sheet of paper, rewrite the corrected text.

I went to the more wonderful restaurant in the whole world last night! Their menu had more items than I've ever seen before. There were seven kinds of pasta dishes, and each one sounded deliciouser than the next. Just when I thought I had chosen the one that sounded more delectable, the waiter told me about the evening's special, which sounded even most luscious.

The special was something called surf and turf. The "surf" was a whole lobster. I would have to crack it open and dip each piece in my own cup of melted butter. The "turf" was a small steak, called a filet mignon, that was wrapped in bacon. My mom told me that filet mignon is tenderer than any other steak she has eaten. The surf and turf sounded so good that I decided to order it.

When the food came, it smelled wonderful. My lobster was the most sweet seafood I've ever eaten! Sometimes I had trouble cracking open the hard shell, but my dad helped me out. His hands are more strong than mine. Oh, and my mom was right about the filet mignon. It seemed to melt in my mouth.

Boy, was I full! I didn't think I could eat another thing . . . until I saw that there was chocolate cake for dessert!

(Student pages 170–171)
Comparative and Superlative Forms

Explain to students that it helps to keep a few simple rules in mind when checking to see if they have used comparative and superlative forms correctly. Have them read the Know the Rule box on Student page 170. Then, discuss its contents together.

Write the following sentences on the board to model the correct use of the comparative and superlative forms.

- *Fred's dog collar was brighter than Fido's.*
- *Fred's collar was the brightest of all.*
- *Dave's joke was more ridiculous than Ron's.*
- *Dave's joke was the most ridiculous I have ever heard.*

Call on a volunteer to explain which sentences contain the comparative form. **The first and third sentences contain the comparative form.** Now, ask which ones contain the superlative form. **The second and fourth sentences contain the superlative form.**

Then, write the following categories and words on the board, and call on volunteers to come up and write either their comparative or superlative form.

Comparative	Superlative
pretty **prettier**	*noisy* **noisiest**
slow **slower**	*blue* **bluest**
likeable **more likeable**	*talented* **most talented**
complicated **more complicated**	*beautiful* **most beautiful**

Answers for Practice the Rule
1. most memorable; superlative
2. more skillfully; comparative
3. slower; comparative
4. most beautiful; superlative
5. harder; comparative

Answers for Apply the Rule
I went to the most wonderful restaurant in the whole world last night! Their menu had more items than I've ever seen before. There were seven kinds of pasta dishes, and each one sounded more delicious than the next. Just when I thought I had chosen the one that sounded the most

(Answers continue on page 131.)

Publishing Share Writing

Read my vignette to a friend.

My descriptive vignette is finished! Now it's time to publish it. I could publish my work in one of several ways. I could submit it to a magazine or newspaper for publication, post it on the Web, or even add it to our class journal. But I'd like to read this one to a friend. Before sharing my vignette, I want to read through it one last time to make sure it includes all of the items on my checklist.

My Checklist

✓ My vignette describes a personal experience.

✓ The details are organized.

✓ Sensory details and figurative language paint vivid pictures.

✓ Clichés and vague language have been replaced with precise words.

✓ Participial phrases add variety.

✓ Spelling, capitalization, and punctuation are all correct. Comparative and superlative forms are used correctly.

Practice!

Now it's your turn. Make a checklist to check your descriptive vignette. Then, make a final draft to publish.

A Day at the Beach
By Josh

There is nothing I like better than a day at the beach, with all its sights, sounds, and sensations. Everything about it is so familiar that it feels like my second home. My favorite thing about the beach is the sound. If I close my eyes and concentrate, I can hear the water right now. It sings an endless song that swells and roars. I also enjoy the sound of the seagulls circling overhead. Their squawking is a rhythmic lullaby. I take pleasure in the children's voices, too. Some children talk quietly as they build sandcastles. Others giggle and squeal as they frolic in the water and are overcome by the waves. Some even call to their parents as they find "treasures" in the sand. Every new shell is a glistening piece of gold; every fossil is the rarest gem of all.

And then there are the feelings. The water is cooler and more refreshing than I remember as I immerse myself under its surface. When I emerge, I can feel its stinging saltiness as it dries on my lips. When I've had enough, I trudge slowly back to my blanket. Every time I step, my foot is swallowed by the sand and disappears into its softness.

The sun beams down at me like a loving friend. Its hot breath warms my skin and hair and dries me again. As I dry, the saltwater parches my skin. It feels as tight on my body as shrink-wrap.

I'm cramped with hunger, so I pull out my traditional beach snack: a peanut butter and jelly sandwich. It is a savory blend of sweet, nutty, and salty flavors. Sticking to the roof of my mouth, the peanut butter prompts me to wash it down with some water.

Startled from my daydream, I realize that I'm not at the beach at all. I am holding my pen, writing and dreaming about the beach.

Reflect

Did I use all the traits of a good vignette in my writing? Check it against the rubric. Don't forget to use the rubric to check your own work, too.

(Answers continued from page 130.)

delectable, the waiter told me about the evening's special, which sounded even more luscious.

The special was something called surf and turf. The "surf" was a whole lobster. I would have to crack it open and dip each piece in my own cup of melted butter. The "turf" was a small steak, called a filet mignon, that was wrapped in bacon. My mom told me that filet mignon is the tenderest steak she has eaten. The surf and turf sounded so good that I decided to order it.

When the food came, it smelled wonderful. My lobster was the sweetest seafood I've ever eaten! Sometimes I had trouble cracking open the hard shell, but my dad helped me out. His hands are stronger than mine. Oh, and my mom was right about the filet mignon. It seemed to melt in my mouth.

Boy, was I full! I didn't think I could eat another thing . . . until I saw that there was chocolate cake for dessert!

✓ For more practice with grammar/mechanics skills, see Zaner-Bloser's *G.U.M.* materials.

Publishing
(Student pages 172–173)

Tell the class that Josh's choice for sharing his descriptive vignette is not the only option for publishing. Invite students to name other ways they could publish their own writing.

Have each student make a checklist and perform a final evaluation of his or her work before publishing it. Encourage students to share copies with friends and relatives.

Call students' attention to the Reflect box on the bottom of Student page 173. Explain that assessing Josh's vignette against the rubric will help them better understand how to apply the traits to their own work. Have students use sticky notes to mark at least one example of each trait in Josh's writing.

After this process, have students assess how well they were able to identify each trait in Josh's writing. Remind them to apply what they learned from Josh's work when they use the rubric to check their own writing.

Ways to Publish a Descriptive Vignette

While trying to decide how to publish your work, you should also think about who will be reading it. Then, you can pick the best way to share it. Here are some publishing ideas.

✓ Read your work to your writing partner. Then, discuss his or her reaction.

✓ Submit your vignette to a local newspaper or magazine that publishes student work.

✓ If you have a Web page or a blog, post your description there. Then, wait for feedback.

✓ Include your vignette in a class anthology or journal.

✓ Add your work to a personal scrapbook or your writing journal.

174 **Descriptive Writing** ■ Descriptive Vignette

Writing Across the Content Areas Descriptive Vignette

You can get all kinds of writing ideas at school. Pick your favorite subject, and brainstorm some related topics. Check out these examples.

Math
• Write about a sporting event during which your favorite team won by making the final tie-breaking score.
• Describe what you would do with your paycheck. Would you save the money or spend it?

Social Studies
• Describe an important local statue, monument, or memorial.
• Watch a debate between political candidates, or follow a political campaign. Then, describe the highlights.

Art and/or Music
• Review a local concert or a new CD. Describe the band or singer and the type of music played.
• Visit an art museum and describe your favorite exhibit, painting, or sculpture.

Descriptive Writing ■ Descriptive Vignette 175

Ways to Publish
(*Student page 174*)

Read and discuss with students the publishing options on Student page 174. Encourage students to consider some of these options when publishing their own writing. Remind students that Josh chose to publish his work by reading it to a friend, but they can choose their own way of publishing. Perhaps one student will want to submit his or her vignette to a local newspaper or magazine that publishes student work, while another will want to include it in a class anthology or journal.

Writing Across the Content Areas
(*Student page 175*)

Explain to students that writing is not just for English or language arts class. Many other school subjects contain ideas, issues, and events that students may want to write about. Encourage students to consider using one of the content areas listed on Student page 175 as a springboard for more writing options. Students may also wish to consult with other teachers for more ideas on writing in the content areas.

Books for Professional Development

Graves, Donald H. *Build a Literate Classroom.* The Reading/Writing Teacher's Companion. Portsmouth: Heinemann, 1991.

Reading and writing processes have historically been kept apart, but this book unites them. It also helps teachers learn how to uncover students' potential to be lifelong readers and writers.

Harris, Karen R., and Steve Graham. *Making the Writing Process Work: Strategies for Composition and Self-Regulation.* Cognitive Strategies Training Ser. Cambridge: Brookline, 1996.

Emphasizing "strategy instruction," these authors offer teachers of grades 4–8 explicit teaching instruction in the areas of generating content, planning, writing, and revising. The focus is on the narrative genre, but instruction applies to other areas as well.

Lane, Barry. *After the End: Teaching and Learning Creative Revision.* Portsmouth: Heinemann, 1992.

This author stresses the importance of helping students take charge of their own writing in this "idea book" for upper elementary through high school grade levels. The book guides the teacher in using specific revising techniques as part of the writing process.

Stewig, John Warren. *Read to Write: Using Children's Literature as a Springboard for Teaching Writing.* 3rd ed. Katonah: Richard C. Owen, 1990.

This resource for teachers of grades 3–8 offers strategies for teaching characterization, point of view, setting, plot, and conflict. The book also contains editing strategies that students can use to improve their stories.

Descriptive Test Writing

In this chapter, students will learn how to write a descriptive vignette for a test. They will review the traits of a descriptive vignette, and will study a test prompt and a scoring guide. Students will then use a model writing prompt and a scoring guide to study a sample descriptive vignette test.

Students will follow the student guide as he goes through the test writing stages—time planning, studying the writing prompt, prewriting, drafting, revising, and editing. As the student guide reviews the writing strategies in each step, students will be directed to practice the test writing strategies.

During prewriting and drafting, students will

- study the writing prompt.
- respond to the task.

- choose a graphic organizer.
- check the graphic organizer against the scoring guide.
- use an appropriate tone to keep the reader interested.

During revising and editing, students will

- add sensory details.
- replace vague words with precise words.
- use clauses to strengthen weak sentences.
- edit their drafts for proper grammar, punctuation, capitalization, and spelling.

You may wish to send to families the School-Home Connection Letter for this chapter, located at the end of this unit in the Teacher Edition.

Writing Traits in the Scoring Guide

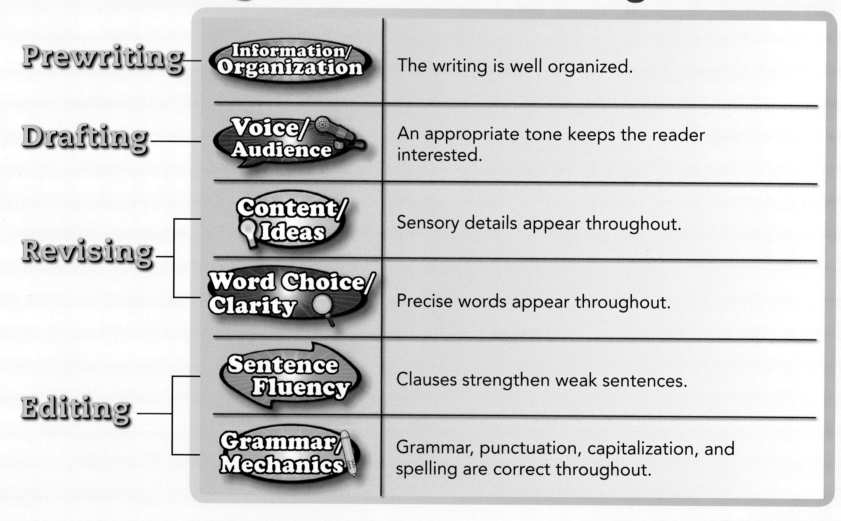

Prewriting	Information/ Organization	The writing is well organized.
Drafting	Voice/ Audience	An appropriate tone keeps the reader interested.
Revising	Content/ Ideas	Sensory details appear throughout.
	Word Choice/ Clarity	Precise words appear throughout.
Editing	Sentence Fluency	Clauses strengthen weak sentences.
	Grammar/ Mechanics	Grammar, punctuation, capitalization, and spelling are correct throughout.

Descriptive Test Writing Time Management

WEEK 1

Day 1	Day 2	Day 3	Day 4	Day 5
Learning Objectives				
Students will: • learn the components of the writing prompt model.	Students will: • recognize the relationship of the scoring guide to the rubric and the six traits of writing. • read a writing prompt model response.	Students will: • apply the scoring guide to the writing prompt model response.	Students will: • continue to apply the scoring guide to the writing prompt model response.	Students will: • learn how to plan their time during a writing test.
Activities				
• Discuss the components of the writing prompt model (Student pages 176–177).	• Read and discuss the scoring guide (Student page 178). • Read the writing prompt model response (Student page 179).	• Read and discuss **Using the Scoring Guide to Study the Model** (Student pages 180–181).	• Read and discuss **Using the Scoring Guide to Study the Model** (Student page 182).	• Read and discuss **Planning My Time** (Student page 183).

WEEK 2

Day 1	Day 2	Day 3	Day 4	Day 5
Learning Objectives				
Students will: • read a writing prompt for a descriptive vignette. • apply the six traits of writing to the writing prompt.	Students will: • learn how to respond to the task in the writing prompt.	Students will: • learn how to choose a graphic organizer for descriptive test writing.	Students will: • learn how to check the graphic organizer against the scoring guide.	Students will: • learn how to use an appropriate tone to keep the reader interested.
Activities				
• Read and discuss **Prewriting: Study the Writing Prompt** (Student pages 184–185).	• Read and discuss **Prewriting: Gather Information** (Student page 186).	• Read and discuss **Prewriting: Organize Ideas** (Student page 187).	• Read and discuss **Prewriting: Check the Scoring Guide** (Student pages 188–189).	• Read and discuss **Drafting: Write a Draft** (Student pages 190–191).

WEEK 3

Day 1	Day 2	Day 3	Day 4	Day 5
Learning Objectives				
Students will: • add sensory details to their writing test.	Students will: • replace vague words in their writing test with precise words.	Students will: • use clauses to strengthen weak sentences in their writing test.	Students will: • edit their writing test for proper grammar and mechanics.	Students will: • learn tips for test writing.
Activities				
• Read and discuss **Revising: Extend Writing** (Student page 192).	• Read and discuss **Revising: Clarify Writing** (Student page 193).	• Read and discuss **Editing: Check Sentences** (Student page 194).	• Read and discuss **Editing: Proofread Writing** (Student pages 195–196).	• Read and discuss **Test Tips** (Student page 197).

To complete the chapter in fewer days, teach the learning objectives and activities for two days in one day.

This planning chart, correlated to your state's writing standards, is available on-line at http://www.zaner-bloser.com/sfw.

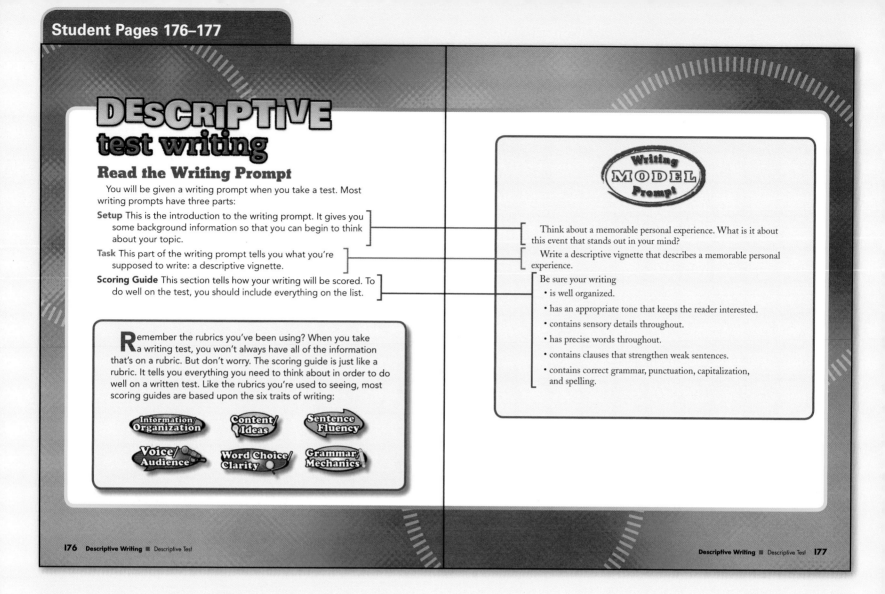

Introduce the Writing Prompt
(Student pages 176–177)

Descriptive Writing

Tell students that they are going to apply what they have learned about descriptive writing to the feat of writing a descriptive test. Note that when they write for a test, they will receive a writing prompt and a certain amount of time in which to write. Then, their writing will be evaluated, as with any test. Assure students that they do not need to be anxious about writing a test, because the skills they have already practiced will help them do a good job.

Read aloud the three parts of the writing prompt listed on Student page 176. Explain that within the scoring guide, students will find traits similar to those they have seen in the rubrics throughout this unit. Note that just as a rubric includes the qualities of a good paper, the scoring guide includes the qualities of a good writing test.

Read the writing prompt model aloud. Then, write the following correlations on the board and review:

- *Setup: This provides the background information needed in order to write for a test.*

- *Task: This is the assignment, and it often names the type of writing to be done.*

- *Scoring Guide: This is much like a rubric, providing information necessary for doing well on a writing test.*

Writing Traits
in the Scoring Guide

Not every writing prompt will include each of the six writing traits, but the one on page 177 does. Study the chart below to help you understand how this scoring guide relates to the writing traits in the rubrics you're used to using.

 **Information/Organization**
- Be sure your writing is well organized.

 Voice/Audience
- Be sure your writing has an appropriate tone that keeps the reader interested.

 **Content/Ideas**
- Be sure your writing contains sensory details throughout.

 Word Choice/Clarity
- Be sure your writing has precise words throughout.

 Sentence Fluency
- Be sure your writing contains clauses that strengthen weak sentences.

Grammar/Mechanics
- Be sure your writing contains correct grammar, punctuation, capitalization, and spelling.

Amy Lee's vignette is on the next page. Did she follow the scoring guide?

Summer at the Park
by Amy Lee

It was the second week of summer vacation, but the weather had been chilly and wet. Today, however, the clouds were nowhere to be seen. The sun's rays shone through my bedroom window and woke me from my slumber. It finally felt as though summer had arrived.

My sister, my mom, and I decided to start the season with a picnic at the park. When we arrived, we discovered we were not the only ones lured by the warm weather. Kids were riding their bikes along the winding paths while mothers pushed babies and toddlers along in strollers. The picnic tables were taken, so we laid out our big, comfy blanket on the grass.

I sat for a few minutes and watched the young children running through the fountains, splashing and laughing. Then, I kicked off my flip-flops and moved them from the blanket to the grass. Although the sun was warm, the grass was still cool and damp.

I got out my book of poems, which I had checked out from the library. As soon as school had ended, I went straight to the library to load up on reading material. Amber, on the other hand, put on her headphones so she could listen to the new CD she had just purchased. It was time to settle in, so I rolled over on my stomach and started to read.

"Amy," my mother said, "wake up. It's lunchtime."

Without realizing it, I had fallen asleep, lulled by the warmth of the sun and the sounds of children playing. I stretched my body from head to toe and sat back up. Mom had packed sweet, juicy honey chicken and a thermos of tangy, homemade lemonade. For dessert, she brought fresh, sweet purple plums. "The first of the season," she told us.

After lunch, Amber and I ran down to the fountains. Water squirted up and drenched us, and we laughed and screamed, just like the other kids.

It didn't take long for us to dry off in the sun. By now, even the grass was dry. Eventually, we packed up our bags and headed back to the car. Even though I was sad the day was over, I was happy that summer had finally come!

Writing Traits in the Scoring Guide
(Student pages 178–179)

Ask students to recall the six traits of writing they have studied throughout the unit. **Information/Organization, Voice/Audience, Content/Ideas, Word Choice/Clarity, Sentence Fluency, Grammar/Mechanics** If they are having trouble providing a response, remind them that the first trait is Information/Organization. Tell them that when they read a scoring guide, they should try to identify the traits within it. This will help them think about the purpose of each item in the scoring guide. It will also help them relate to what they have already learned about these writing traits.

Ask a student volunteer to read the traits in the scoring guide on Student page 178. Then, tell students that they are going to study and use strategies for descriptive test writing and that a good descriptive test has all of the traits listed on Student page 178.

Read the Model:
Writing Prompt Response

Distribute one copy of the model to each student. As you read it aloud, have each student use a highlighter to identify the traits set forth in the scoring guide.

Differentiating Instruction

English-Language Learners Preteach key vocabulary in context by writing this summary of "Summer at the Park" on the board and then reading it aloud: *The author enjoys one of the first days of summer by going on a picnic with her family. When they get to the park, they see that others have been lured there by the warm weather. They walk down a winding path and find a spot to lay their big comfy blanket. The author is then lulled by the sun's warmth and falls asleep. Her mother wakes her for a lunch of chicken and lemonade. Then, the author and her sister get drenched in the fountain. The picnic ends, but the author is glad that summer finally arrived.*

As you read through the summary, stop and show students how to use context clues to figure out the meanings of the underlined words.

Using the Scoring Guide to Study the Model

Now let's use the scoring guide to check Amy's writing test, "Summer at the Park." How well does her vignette meet each of the six writing traits?

Information/Organization
• The vignette is well organized.

Amy's story is well organized. Because she describes events in chronological order, her vignette is easy to follow.

> My sister, my mom, and I decided to start the season with a picnic at the park. When we arrived, we discovered we were not the only ones lured by the warm weather. Kids were riding their bikes along the winding paths while mothers pushed babies and toddlers along in strollers. The picnic tables were taken, so we laid out our big, comfy blanket on the grass.

Voice/Audience
• The vignette has an appropriate tone that keeps the reader interested.

Since this is a vignette about an upbeat, informal event, Amy uses a friendly tone to capture her reader's interest. She uses words and images that make me feel like I'm part of the story. I mean, who can't relate to a summertime nap in the sun?

> Without realizing it, I had fallen asleep, lulled by the warmth of the sun and the sounds of children playing. I stretched my body from head to toe and sat back up.

Content/Ideas
• The vignette contains sensory details throughout.

Amy uses plenty of sensory details to help the reader visualize her day at the park. Her description of the picnic lunch really makes my mouth water!

> Mom had packed sweet, juicy honey chicken and a thermos of tangy, homemade lemonade. For dessert, she brought fresh, sweet purple plums. "The first of the season," she told us.

Word Choice/Clarity
• The vignette has precise words throughout.

Amy is not vague with her description. She uses precise words to describe her day. In the passage below, she doesn't just say the kids were playing; she says they were "splashing and laughing." She could've said she took off her shoes, but instead, she says, "I kicked off my flip-flops."

> I sat for a few minutes and watched the young children running through the fountains, splashing and laughing. Then, I kicked off my flip-flops and moved them from the blanket to the grass. Although the sun was warm, the grass was still cool and damp.

Using the Scoring Guide to Study the Model

(Student pages 180–182)

Review the function of the scoring guide. First, have students review a rubric from one of the earlier chapters in this unit. Then, point out the similarities and differences between that rubric and the scoring guide. Make sure students understand that although a scoring guide does not include criteria for various levels of accomplishment, it does provide guidance in the six key areas of assessment: Information/Organization, Voice/Audience, Content/Ideas, Word Choice/Clarity, Sentence Fluency, and Grammar/Mechanics.

Explain that in the same way traits in a rubric are used to assess writing, criteria in a scoring guide are used to assess test writing. Remind students to use the scoring guide when they write for a test to ensure that they meet all of the traits.

Differentiating Instruction

English-Language Learners To help these students increase vocabulary, point out the following words in "Summer at the Park": *slumber, discovered, splashing, laughing, flip-flops, plums,* and *drenched.* Explain that the author might have used a thesaurus to find precise words such as these. Note that students will not be allowed to use a thesaurus on most tests. But students should continue to build their knowledge of English vocabulary so that they will be better prepared at test time. This way, they can work to replace vague words in their test writing with synonyms that are more precise.

Using the Scoring Guide to Study the Model

Sentence Fluency

- The vignette contains clauses that strengthen weak sentences.

Amy uses clauses to add detail to her sentences and strengthen her writing. I think the clauses also add good sentence variety. What do you think?

I got out my book of poems, which I had checked out from the library. As soon as school had ended, I went straight to the library to load up on reading material. Amber, on the other hand, put on her headphones so she could listen to the new CD she had just purchased. It was time to settle in, so I rolled over on my stomach and started to read.

Grammar/ Mechanics

- The vignette contains correct grammar, punctuation, capitalization, and spelling.

It looks like Amy used correct grammar, spelling, capitalization, and punctuation. I know it's important to check for these kinds of mistakes, and I'll be sure to keep that in mind as I write. But you should check for proper grammar and mechanics in your writing, too. Don't forget that this can be done at every step of the writing process!

Planning My Time

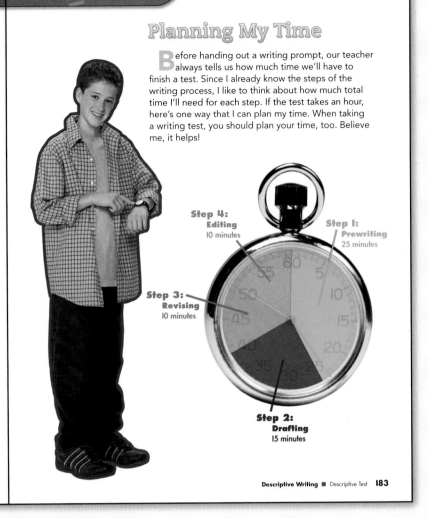

Before handing out a writing prompt, our teacher always tells us how much time we'll have to finish a test. Since I already know the steps of the writing process, I like to think about how much total time I'll need for each step. If the test takes an hour, here's one way that I can plan my time. When taking a writing test, you should plan your time, too. Believe me, it helps!

Step 4: Editing 10 minutes

Step 1: Prewriting 25 minutes

Step 3: Revising 10 minutes

Step 2: Drafting 15 minutes

Planning My Time
(Student page 183)

Explain to students the importance of organizing time when planning for a test. Remind them that they will have a limited amount of time to complete their test, so it is important to set aside a block of time for each one of the steps in the writing process.

Refer to Student page 183, and ask a student volunteer to tell the class which writing step Josh plans to spend the most time on. **prewriting** Point out that many students do poorly on test writing because they start writing before they develop a plan, and they continue writing until they run out of time. Stress to students the importance of including enough time to prewrite, draft, revise, and edit.

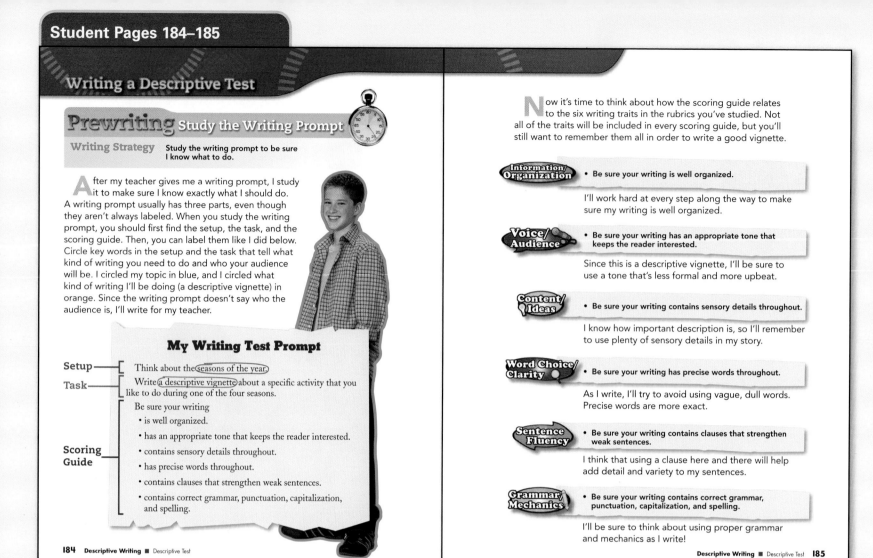

Study the Writing Prompt

(Student pages 184–185)

Read aloud Josh's words on Student page 184. Tell students that it is important to read and understand their writing prompts before beginning to draft. Explain that even if students write a great paper, they won't receive a great score unless they have followed the instructions set forth in the scoring guide.

Ask a student volunteer to tell the class what type of essay Josh is supposed to write. **a descriptive vignette** Explain that Josh needs to decide upon an activity he likes to do during one of the four seasons, and then he needs to write a descriptive vignette about that activity.

Read through the scoring guide portion of the writing prompt shown on Student page 184. Then, review Student page 185 with students. Note how each of the traits relate to the six key areas of assessment. Remind students that if they were using a rubric, these traits would be those seen under the Excelling category. Point out that even before Josh begins to prewrite, he thinks about each of the traits he will need to include in his test.

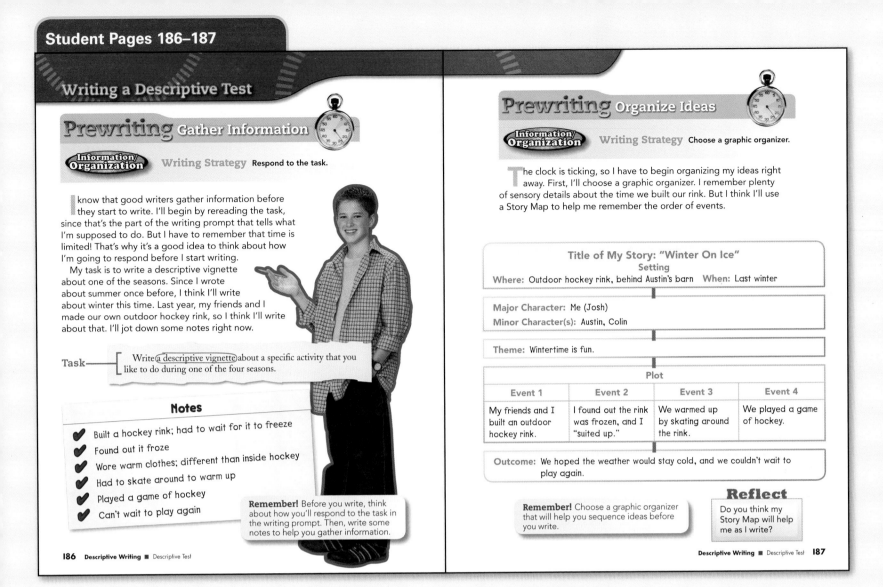

Writing a Descriptive Test

Prewriting Gather Information

Information/Organization

Writing Strategy **Respond to the task.**

I know that good writers gather information before they start to write. I'll begin by rereading the task, since that's the part of the writing prompt that tells what I'm supposed to do. But I have to remember that time is limited! That's why it's a good idea to think about how I'm going to respond before I start writing.

My task is to write a descriptive vignette about one of the seasons. Since I wrote about summer once before, I think I'll write about winter this time. Last year, my friends and I made our own outdoor hockey rink, so I think I'll write about that. I'll jot down some notes right now.

Task —— [Write a descriptive vignette about a specific activity that you like to do during one of the four seasons.

Notes

✔ Built a hockey rink; had to wait for it to freeze
✔ Found out it froze
✔ Wore warm clothes; different than inside hockey
✔ Had to skate around to warm up
✔ Played a game of hockey
✔ Can't wait to play again

Remember! Before you write, think about how you'll respond to the task in the writing prompt. Then, write some notes to help you gather information.

186 **Descriptive Writing** ■ Descriptive Test

Prewriting Organize Ideas

Information/Organization

Writing Strategy **Choose a graphic organizer.**

The clock is ticking, so I have to begin organizing my ideas right away. First, I'll choose a graphic organizer. I remember plenty of sensory details about the time we built our rink. But I think I'll use a Story Map to help me remember the order of events.

Title of My Story: "Winter On Ice"
Setting
Where: Outdoor hockey rink, behind Austin's barn **When:** Last winter

Major Character: Me (Josh)
Minor Character(s): Austin, Colin

Theme: Wintertime is fun.

Plot			
Event 1	Event 2	Event 3	Event 4
My friends and I built an outdoor hockey rink.	I found out the rink was frozen, and I "suited up."	We warmed up by skating around the rink.	We played a game of hockey.

Outcome: We hoped the weather would stay cold, and we couldn't wait to play again.

Remember! Choose a graphic organizer that will help you sequence ideas before you write.

Reflect
Do you think my Story Map will help me as I write?

Descriptive Writing ■ Descriptive Test 187

Gather Information and Organize Ideas

(Student pages 186–187)

Ask students to recall what they learned about prewriting in other chapters in this unit. Point out that on a writing test, the prewriting stage is similar: They should consider the assignment and then gather information.

Remind students to use a graphic organizer to organize their ideas. Tell students that during a writing test, they will not be told what kind of graphic organizer to use. Instead, they must think about how they have used graphic organizers in the past, and they must decide which one will be the most useful for a test.

Read through Josh's Story Map on Student page 187. Note that even before he started writing, Josh had already written down much of the information that would appear in his essay.

Differentiating Instruction

Support Remind students that graphic organizers can help them structure their notes. Ask volunteers to name the graphic organizers that they used throughout the unit. **Main-Idea Table, Cause-and-Effect Links, Web** Then, ask students how they might decide which graphic organizer to use on a test. **Possible response: by thinking about which one fits the writing genre** Remind students to look for clues in the writing prompt to help them choose a useful graphic organizer.

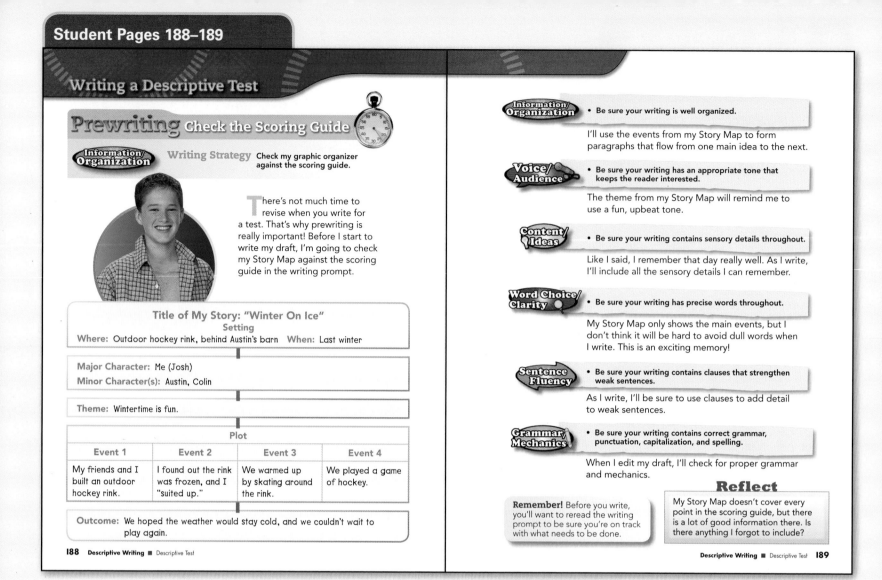

Check the Scoring Guide

(Student pages 188–189)

Ask students why they think Josh is not yet ready to write even though he has used a graphic organizer to structure his notes. **Possible response: because he needs to check his graphic organizer against the scoring guide** Emphasize the importance of paying attention to the scoring guide throughout test writing. Note that on Student page 189, Josh once again refers back to each point in the scoring guide to be sure he has met them all. Explain that during this step of the test writing process, students may need to add or change information in their graphic organizers to meet the criteria.

Point out that while the graphic organizer helped Josh organize his notes and meet the scoring guide criteria, he will continue to think about all of the scoring guide traits as he writes.

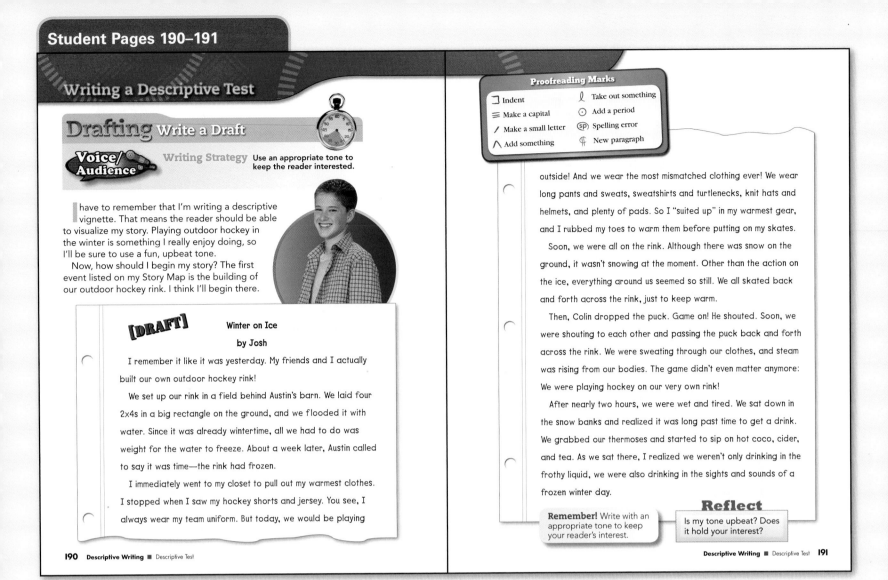

Drafting
(Student pages 190–191)

Read Josh's words on Student page 190. Point out that he refers to his graphic organizer in order to write his draft. Emphasize to students the importance of using their graphic organizers as guidance during the drafting process. Explain that because of editing, they will want to leave space between the lines so that they will have room to make changes and additions to their work. Also remind them to write neatly, even in the drafting stage, because the test evaluator should be able to read what they have written.

Then, discuss Josh's draft. Have students refer back to his graphic organizer to see whether he included the information that he outlined in his Story Map. Ask students what they think of his draft, pointing out that although there are mistakes, Josh has remembered to leave time during the editing stage to go through and change any errors he made in spelling and grammar.

Finally, review proofreading marks with students. Note that these marks will be helpful as they revise and edit their drafts.

Differentiating Instruction

English-Language Learners Remind these students that when drafting, they should concentrate on getting ideas down on paper. Note that if they have trouble coming up with appropriate words or phrases, they can leave blank spots in their writing and come back to them later. Also, remind students that at this stage, they should not be overly concerned with spelling or grammar since they can fix mistakes during editing.

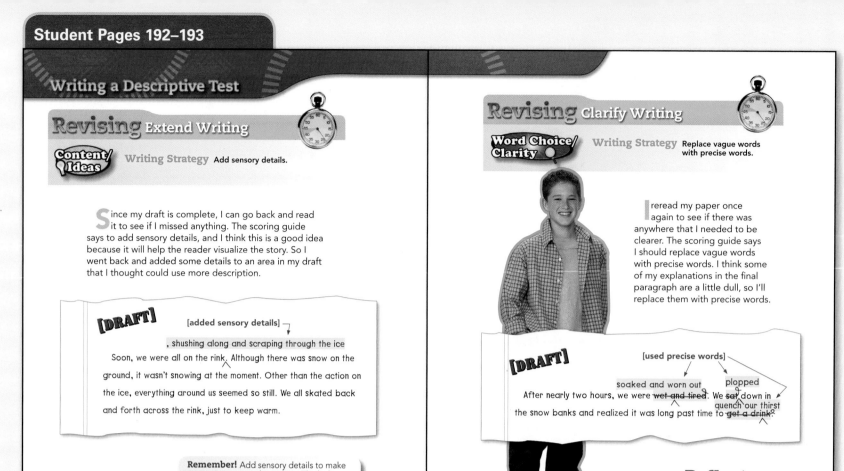

Revising

(Student pages 192–193)

Discuss the revisions Josh made on Student pages 192–193. He added sensory details and replaced vague words with more precise words. Point out that Josh once again reviewed his scoring guide in order to determine a revision focus. Encourage students to refer back to the scoring guide section of the writing prompt even after they have completed their drafts.

Point out Josh's revision on Student page 192. Ask students whether they feel the addition enhanced his description. Have them point out other places in Josh's draft where more sensory details could bring the description to life.

Next, review with students the ways Josh replaced vague words on Student page 193 with words that are more precise. Have students explain what they feel the revisions contribute to the draft. **Possible response: They make the description more precise.**

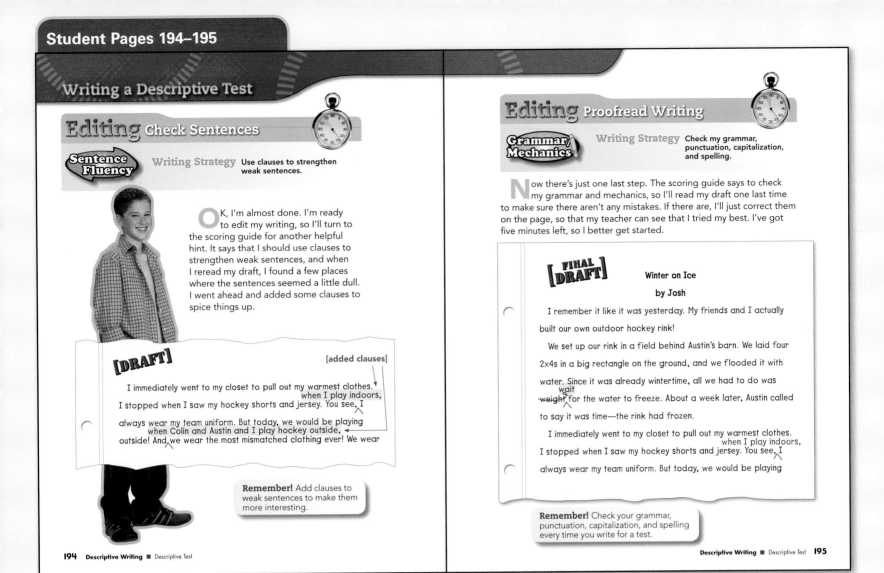

Editing Check Sentences

Sentence Fluency

Writing Strategy Use clauses to strengthen weak sentences.

OK, I'm almost done. I'm ready to edit my writing, so I'll turn to the scoring guide for another helpful hint. It says that I should use clauses to strengthen weak sentences, and when I reread my draft, I found a few places where the sentences seemed a little dull. I went ahead and added some clauses to spice things up.

[DRAFT]

[added clauses]

I immediately went to my closet to pull out my warmest clothes.

when I play indoors,

I stopped when I saw my hockey shorts and jersey. You see, I always wear my team uniform. But today, we would be playing

when Colin and Austin and I play hockey outside,

outside! And we wear the most mismatched clothing ever! We wear

Remember! Add clauses to weak sentences to make them more interesting.

Editing Proofread Writing

Grammar Mechanics

Writing Strategy Check my grammar, punctuation, capitalization, and spelling.

Now there's just one last step. The scoring guide says to check my grammar and mechanics, so I'll read my draft one last time to make sure there aren't any mistakes. If there are, I'll just correct them on the page, so that my teacher can see that I tried my best. I've got five minutes left, so I better get started.

[FINAL DRAFT]

Winter on Ice

by Josh

I remember it like it was yesterday. My friends and I actually built our own outdoor hockey rink!

We set up our rink in a field behind Austin's barn. We laid four 2x4s in a big rectangle on the ground, and we flooded it with water. Since it was already wintertime, all we had to do was

wait

~~weight~~ for the water to freeze. About a week later, Austin called to say it was time—the rink had frozen.

I immediately went to my closet to pull out my warmest clothes.

when I play indoors,

I stopped when I saw my hockey shorts and jersey. You see, I always wear my team uniform. But today, we would be playing

Remember! Check your grammar, punctuation, capitalization, and spelling every time you write for a test.

Editing

(Student pages 194–196)

Have students recall how they edited sentences for improvement during earlier lessons in this unit. Remind them of how they edited sentence structure, adding transitional and participial phrases to help their writing flow more smoothly.

Call students' attention to the edits Josh made to his draft on Student page 194. Read aloud the text without the edits. Ask a volunteer to read the same section aloud—this time including Josh's edits. Ask students how the added clauses helped Josh improve his sentences. **Possible response: The first clause explains when Josh wears his team uniform. The second clause explains when he wears mismatched clothing.** Explain that because these clauses begin with the relative adverb *when,* they are relative clauses that cannot stand alone as sentences.

Emphasize to students that they should always proofread for mistakes, checking for errors in sentence completeness, punctuation, and spelling.

Differentiating Instruction

Support Have students practice editing by writing sample sentences for correction on the board. Then, ask them to take turns using the appropriate editing marks from Student page 191 to edit the sentences.

FINAL DRAFT

when Colin and Austin and I play hockey outside,
outside! And we wear the most mismatched clothing ever! We wear
long pants and sweats, sweatshirts and turtlenecks, knit hats and
helmets, and plenty of pads. So I "suited up" in my warmest gear,
and I rubbed my toes to warm them before putting on my skates.
, shushing along and scraping through the ice
Soon, we were all on the rink. Although there was snow on the
ground, it wasn't snowing at the moment. Other than the action on
the ice, everything around us seemed so still. We all skated back
and forth across the rink, just to keep warm.

Then, Colin dropped the puck. "Game on! He shouted. Soon, we
were shouting to each other and passing the puck back and forth
across the rink. We were sweating through our clothes, and steam
was rising from our bodies. The game didn't even matter anymore:
We were playing hockey on our very own rink!
soaked and worn out   plopped
After nearly two hours, we were wet and tired. We sat down in
quench our thirst
the snow banks and realized it was long past time to get a drink.
cocoa
We grabbed our thermoses and started to sip on hot coco, cider,
and tea. As we sat there, I realized we weren't only drinking in the
frothy liquid, we were also drinking in the sights and sounds of a
frozen winter day.

Reflect

Did I miss anything? I'll check my writing against
the scoring guide one last time before turning it
in. Remember to use your writing prompt's scoring
guide to check your writing when you take a test.

I'm done! I never knew taking a test
could be so easy! I guess when you
use the scoring guide, it really helps out.
But also remember to keep in mind these
important tips when you write for a test.

TEST TIPS

1. **Study the writing prompt before you start to write.** Most
   writing prompts have three parts: the setup, the task, and the
   scoring guide. The parts probably won't be labeled. You'll have
   to figure them out for yourself!

2. **Make sure you understand the task before you start
   to write.**
   - Read all three parts of the writing prompt carefully.
   - Circle key words in the task part of the writing prompt that tell
     what kind of writing you need to do. The task might also identify
     your audience.
   - Make sure you know how you'll be graded.
   - Say the assignment in your own words to yourself.

3. **Keep an eye on the clock.** Decide how much time you will
   spend on each part of the writing process and try to stick to your
   schedule. Don't spend so much time on prewriting that you don't
   have enough time left to write.

4. **Reread your writing. Compare it to the scoring guide
   at least twice.** Remember the rubrics you've used? A scoring
   guide on a writing test is like a rubric. It can help you keep what's
   important in mind.

5. **Plan, plan, plan!** You don't get much time to revise during a
   test, so planning is more important than ever.

6. **Write neatly.** Remember, if the people who score your test can't
   read your writing, it doesn't matter how good your essay is!

Test Tips
(Student page 197)

Ask students to recall the lessons they learned in this
chapter. Ask them what they feel are the important
steps to take when writing for a test. **Possible responses:
follow the writing prompt; plan time; save time for editing
and revising**

Remind students that test writing is similar to writing for
a class assignment. One big difference, though, is that test
writing is timed.

Read aloud the Test Tips on Student page 197. Have
students think about how Josh followed each of these tips
during test writing. Point out that they should keep each
of the six tips in mind when they write their own tests.

Books for Professional Development

Freeman, Marcia S. *Listen to This: Developing an Ear for Expository.* **Gainesville: Maupin House, 1997.**

This author suggests adding an aural component to writing. She encourages teachers to read aloud sample essays in a variety of informative, narrative, and persuasive genres. Students are guided to analyze these essays and then use them as models for their own writing.

Graves, Donald H. *A Fresh Look at Writing.* **Portsmouth: Heinemann, 1994.**

This book is an informative and useful guide for teachers who want to implement classroom strategies to help students strengthen their writing skills. It explains how the implementation of strategies such as the author's chair and portfolios can help students practice and take pride in their writing.

McCarthy, Tara. *Teaching Genre: Explore 9 Types of Literature to Develop Lifelong Readers and Writers.* **New York: Scholastic, 1996.**

This book is designed to develop lifelong readers and writers. It is accompanied by many reproducible, quality worksheets, and it is filled with interesting and creative writing assignments.

Urquhart, Vickie, and Monett McIver. *Teaching Writing in the Content Areas.* **Alexandria: ASCD, 2005.**

This book shows how to quickly integrate writing assignments into the content areas by using strategic, practical tools. Included in the book are thirty-five classroom strategies that will help teachers guide students through the steps of preparing written assignments, getting their thoughts down, and refining their work.

School-Home Connection

Dear Family,

Your child is currently learning to write a business letter that focuses on a descriptive explanation of one main idea or topic. As he or she goes through the steps of writing this letter, here's how you can help:

1. **Prewriting:** Students will begin by choosing a main idea or topic and listing details that support the topic. They will then organize details into a Main-Idea Table. You can help your child brainstorm and choose an appropriate topic by sharing business letters that you yourself have written.

2. **Drafting:** Students will write a working draft of their business letter, making sure that the letter format is correct and the tone is appropriate. You can help by reviewing with your child the necessary letter parts (heading, inside address, greeting, body, closing, and signature). In addition, it may be helpful to discuss appropriate tone by reminding your child that a business letter should address the reader directly, but in a calm, professional way.

3. **Revising:** Students will refine their drafts by adding vivid details and deleting or revising irrelevant information. You can help by asking for further clarification of any confusing passages in the draft.

4. **Editing:** You can help check for errors in spelling, punctuation, and capitalization by listening as your child reads his or her draft aloud to you, or you can provide further help by reading the draft over together.

5. **Publishing:** Students will be publishing a final copy of their work. Urge them to make copies to send to friends and family members.

The ability to describe a topic or an event while using an appropriate tone is a skill that is required throughout life, in both school and the workplace. If you have any questions as you provide assistance, please let me know.

Thanks for your help in the writing process!

School-Home Connection

Dear Family,

Your child is currently learning to write a scientific observation, which is a descriptive summary of several science experiments. As he or she goes through the steps of writing this observation, here's how you can help:

1. **Prewriting:** Students will begin by describing the causes and effects of several science experiments. They will then organize this information into Cause-and-Effect Links. You can help your child choose a series of experiments to write about. Take him or her to the local library to check out books and other resources on age-appropriate science experiments. Then, offer to help conduct the experiments as he or she observes and takes notes.

2. **Drafting:** Students will make a working draft of their scientific observation, remembering to use scientific language appropriate for the audience. You can help by pointing out areas in the draft that sound too technical. Suggest alternate terms or phrases for these areas, or refer your child to a thesaurus or a dictionary.

3. **Revising:** Students will refine their drafts by adding diagrams and using specific words to show important connections. Help your child by asking for further clarification of any confusing passages in his or her draft—perhaps these are areas where diagrams could be inserted!

4. **Editing:** You can help check for errors in spelling, punctuation, and capitalization by listening as your child reads his or her draft aloud to you, or you can provide further help by reading the draft over together.

5. **Publishing:** Students will be publishing a final copy of their work. Urge them to make copies to send to friends and family members.

The ability to describe technical processes is a skill that is required throughout life, in both school and the workplace. If you have any questions as you provide assistance, please let me know.

Thanks for your help in the writing process!

School-Home Connection

Dear Family,

Your child is currently learning to write a descriptive vignette, which is a short, in-depth description of a personal experience. As he or she goes through the steps of writing this vignette, here's how you can help:

1. **Prewriting:** Students will begin by choosing a personal experience to describe. They will then jot down sensory details about the experience and organize them into a Web. You can help your child brainstorm and choose an experience to write about. Remind him or her of favorite pastimes such as picnics in the park, vacations, or holiday celebrations. In this case, reminiscing is not only fun, but helpful as well!

2. **Drafting:** Students will make a working draft of their descriptive vignette, using plenty of sensory details to help the reader visualize. You can help by having your child read his or her draft to you as it is written. This way, you can point out passages that could use more details.

3. **Revising:** Students will refine their drafts by adding figurative language and replacing clichés, vague words, and overused words with precise words. Help your child by providing him or her with a dictionary or a thesaurus for help with word choice.

4. **Editing:** You can help check for errors in spelling, punctuation, and capitalization by listening as your child reads his or her draft aloud to you, or you can provide further help by reading the draft over together.

5. **Publishing:** Students will be publishing a final copy of their work. Urge them to make copies to send to friends and family members.

The ability to vividly describe personal experiences is a skill that is required throughout life. If you have any questions as you provide assistance, please let me know.

Thanks for your help in the writing process!

School-Home Connection

Dear Family,

Your child is currently learning to write a descriptive test. A descriptive test is an explanation that students write in response to a writing prompt. The test is timed. Here are the necessary steps involved in writing a descriptive test, and here's how you can help with each step:

1. **Prewriting:** Students will learn to read a writing prompt carefully to understand the type of writing required. The prompt will tell your young writer not only what kind of writing to do but also what topic to write about. Time management is crucial in test writing. Practice breaking an hour into segments of time with your child so that he or she has a sense of how long it takes for 25, 15, or 10 minutes of time to pass. Your child will also use a graphic organizer to plan his or her writing. Please help by prompting a discussion of organizers used in the past.

2. **Drafting:** Students will use their graphic organizers to write a draft that has an appropriate tone. Remind your child that the draft should be written neatly the first time because there will not be enough time to write it again.

3. **Revising:** Students will use the scoring guide in the writing prompt as a reminder to add sensory details and to replace vague words with precise words. Help your child by asking for further details about passages that seem vague or weak.

4. **Editing:** Students will spend the last part of the timed writing test checking their drafts for common errors in punctuation, capitalization, and spelling. Encourage your child not to worry about the "imperfect" appearance of his or her writing test. The pages won't look as neat as usual, and it's OK for students to make corrections right on the page.

If you have any questions, please let me know. Together, we'll help your child master the important skill of writing on demand, a skill that students use in many subjects throughout their school years.

Thanks for your help in the writing process!

EXPOSITORY
writing strategies

IN THIS UNIT

1 Book Report: Response to Literature

- Read a book on a topic that interests me. Then, list my responses about the book.
- Make a Pro-and-Con Chart to organize my responses by order of importance.
- State my purpose so the reader will understand why I'm writing.
- Add examples to support my responses.
- Change passive voice to active voice to make the report clearer.
- Use declarative sentences to present facts.
- Make sure introductory verbal phrases are used correctly.

2 Research Report

- Choose a topic, survey some sources, and make a 3 W's Chart. Then, make note cards.
- Make an Outline to organize my information.
- Use my Outline to draft my report. Remember to include an introduction that grabs the reader's attention.
- Add quotes and paraphrased information from experts.
- Make sure I have cited all quotes correctly. Then, make my list of Works Consulted.
- Use introductory verbal phrases to vary my sentences.
- Make sure I've formed compound and complex sentences correctly.

3 How-To Guide: Instructional Text

- Choose a process to explain. List the main steps in the process.
- Make a Sequence Chain to arrange steps in a sequential order.
- Use a friendly tone to explain each step to the reader.
- Add pictures and explanative details.
- Make sure all jargon has been explained.
- Use compound and complex sentences for variety.
- Check to see that appositives have been set off with commas.

4 Writing for a Test

- Study the writing prompt to be sure I know what to do.
- Respond to the task.
- Choose a graphic organizer.
- Check my graphic organizer against the scoring guide.
- Provide plenty of explanative details for the reader.
- Add supporting facts.
- Make sure I have not misused homophones.
- Combine short sentences to make the writing flow smoothly.
- Check my grammar, punctuation, capitalization, and spelling.

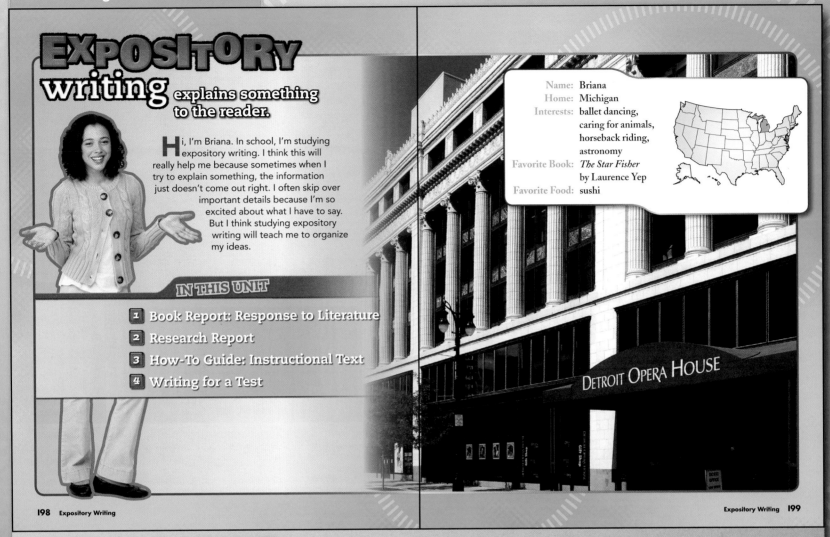

EXPOSITORY writing explains something to the reader.

Hi, I'm Briana. In school, I'm studying expository writing. I think this will really help me because sometimes when I try to explain something, the information just doesn't come out right. I often skip over important details because I'm so excited about what I have to say. But I think studying expository writing will teach me to organize my ideas.

IN THIS UNIT

1 Book Report: Response to Literature
2 Research Report
3 How-To Guide: Instructional Text
4 Writing for a Test

Name: Briana
Home: Michigan
Interests: ballet dancing, caring for animals, horseback riding, astronomy
Favorite Book: *The Star Fisher* by Laurence Yep
Favorite Food: sushi

DETROIT OPERA HOUSE

IN THIS UNIT

Book Report This genre gives students the opportunity to respond to a book by explaining its pros and cons in an organized way.

Research Report This genre gives students the chance to work step by step to investigate a topic and to write a report that incorporates a variety of expert sources.

How-To Guide This genre introduces students to important skills that will help them explain a process so that readers can follow and repeat the steps.

Expository Test Students learn and practice how to read an expository test prompt and how to plan their time. They also learn and practice writing strategies for successful test writing in the expository mode.

Meet Briana

The student guide for this chapter is Briana, a girl from Michigan. You may wish to explore with students how Briana's background, hobbies, interests, and personality connect with her choices of writing topics. Explain to students that Briana will use what she knows to make decisions about her topics—a process that helps make her writing special and real. Encourage students to follow Briana's lead by using their own background knowledge, interests, and personalities as they write. Expository writing informs readers and explains topics to them; in the weeks to come, your students will be writing about many interesting and exciting subjects.

by Julie Coiro, Ph.D.
University of Connecticut

Locating Resources: Reading Within Search Engine Results

One of the most challenging aspects of on-line reading is understanding how to strategically evaluate a long list of search results to determine which link, if any, to pursue. You may wish to share these strategies with students:

- **Read the description, not just the link.** Some students only skim the blue underlined titles that appear in a search list entry. However, the description that follows often contains helpful clues, with keywords from the search in bold print. Students can avoid a link that's not useful by using the available descriptions to more accurately predict if the information actually meets their research needs. Several search engines use ellipses (. . .) at the end of descriptions; students should understand what ellipses mean and try to anticipate what the rest of the description might say.

- **Know how to read the parts of a Web site address.** Information can be gleaned from the dots, slashes, abbreviations, and words in the Web addresses that appear in search results. Show students how Web addresses can be broken down, with each part providing identification of the path leading to the Web site host, as follows:

http://	school. discovery. com/	schooladventures/	geogame. html
type of protocol	domain name, or host	path or directory to the file	name and type of file

Once students understand these "clues," they can use them to determine which Web sites will be useful.

- **Use the clues to try a different search.** If nothing useful is found in the first ten or twenty sites in the search result list, it's time to try a new search with different keywords. Encourage students to think about words that appeared in the descriptions or within the Web sites they visited. Sometimes reading more about the topic on one Web site will help generate synonyms for different keywords that might yield better results in a new search.

Critical Evaluation: Evaluating Accuracy

Students should know that it is possible for credible individuals to make an inaccurate statement or a mistake. For this reason, you may wish to discuss strategies to help students evaluate the accuracy of on-line information. *Accuracy* refers to the extent to which information contains factual details that can be verified by another reliable source. Here are three tips you may wish to model for your students:

- **Read the Web site.** Read carefully. Searching for information requires skimming and scanning. Reading for accuracy requires close reading. Ask yourself the following questions: *Does the information make sense? When was it last updated? Is it free from spelling or grammatical errors? Does the author list the bibliographic sources for the information?*

- **Read other Web sites.** Can the information be verified at another Web site? Use a search engine and the keyword strategies covered in Unit 2 to search for other sites that contain similar facts.

- **Read a primary source Web site.** You may wish to spend a class period talking about the differences between primary sources and secondary sources. Then, you can recommend that students include at least one primary source in their research report. **The Library of Congress American Memory Database Learning Page** at **http://memory.loc.gov/learn/lessons/psources/pshome. html** provides excellent lessons on primary sources for older students. A search for "Primary Sources" on the **ReadWriteThink** Web site at **www.readwritethink. org** also results in several comprehensive lessons using the American Memory Database. These include **Slave Narratives: Constructing U.S. History Through Analyzing Primary Sources** at **http://edsitement. neh.gov/view_lesson_plan.asp?id=364** and the **Boston Tea Party: Costume Optional?** at **http://edsitement.neh.gov/view_lesson_plan. asp?id=397**.

Finally, **QUICK (The QUality Information CheckList)** from the United Kingdom at **http://www.quick.org.uk/ menu.htm** is an additional resource for evaluating accuracy.

Communicating Globally: Publishing With Classroom Blogs and Podcasts

Blogs and podcasts are two exciting new ways for students to share their work with others around the world. *Blog* is short for *weblog*, which is an on-line journal that displays entries in reverse chronological order. You can publish a blog on the Internet without knowing hypertext code or having to upload anything on a special server. A podcast is an audio or video file that is broadcast on the Internet. You may wish to explore the links in this section to get an idea of how teachers and students have begun using these on-line publishing tools.

Examples of Classroom Blogs

- Mark Ahlness is a veteran teacher who has experience with integrating technology, including blogs, into his classroom. One example of his work is **Mighty Writers 2006–07** at **http://roomtwelve.com**.

- Anne Davis of Georgia State University created **The Write Weblog** at **http://itc.blogs.com/thewriteweblog** with staff and students from J.H. House Elementary School in Conyers, Georgia. Anne's

work at the school inspired Hillary Meeler to begin her own classroom blog project called **Blog Write** at **http://jhh.blogs.com/blogwrite**.

Examples of Classroom Podcasts

- **Podcast Central** at **http://mabryonline.org/podcasts** features video-enhanced podcasts and a series of blogs by middle school students and their teachers, including **Sixceed** at **http://mabryonline.org/sixceed**.

- Students at Sandaig Primary School in Glasgow, Scotland, have joined together to publish both **Radio Sandaig Podcasts** at **http://www.sandaigprimary.co.uk/radio_sandaig/index.php** and **Sandaig Otters Weblog** at **http://www.sandaigprimary.co.uk/pivot/index.php**.

If the above examples inspired you, you may wish to use the following introductory tutorial: "Introduction to Blogs and Blogging," written by Michael Stach of **TechLearning** at **http://www.techlearning.com/story/showArticle.php?articleID=18400984**.

Supporting and Extending Writing: Internet Project

Students can share what they are learning with others around the world through Internet Project. Internet Project may take place as you work with another class on a common learning activity. It may also take place when classes contribute data to a common site and then analyze and compare results. One way to get involved with Internet Project is to join one of the following projects that have already demonstrated success.

- **Monarch Watch** at **http://www.monarchwatch.org** invites students to raise, tag, and release butterflies; record observations about them; and sit back and watch while the data is used to track their annual migration.

- **Square of Life: Studies in Local and Global Environments** at **http://www.k12science.org/curriculum/squareproj** invites students to investigate their local environment, share their findings with other participating classes, look for similarities and differences in the reported data, and prepare a final presentation to share with other students from around the world.

- **Journey North: A Global Study of Wildlife Migration and Seasonal Change** at **http://www.learner.org/jnorth** provides opportunities to explore animal migration or to track the growth patterns of tulips.

For access to a large database of other existing Internet projects across the curriculum, try **Global SchoolNet's Internet Projects Registry** at **http://www.globalschoolnet.org/GSH/pr/index.cfm**. This site enables you to search by grade level, content area, and collaboration type through projects conducted by teachers worldwide. This site's **Collaborative Learning Center** at **http://www.globalschoolnet.org/center** also provides an excellent overview of how to select partner classes.

For more information, you may wish to read Donald J. Leu, Jr.'s article titled "Internet Project: Preparing Students for New Literacies in a Global Village" at **http://www.readingonline.org/electronic/RT/3-01_Column/index.html**.

Book Report Overview

In this chapter, students will learn how to write a book report. They will learn the different elements of a book report—summary, viewpoint, pros and cons, and examples—and some reasons why they might want to write one. Students will then use a book report rubric to study a model writing sample.

Students will follow the student guide as she goes through the writing stages—prewriting, drafting, revising, editing, and publishing. As the student guide learns new writing strategies in each step, students will be directed to practice the strategies in their own writing.

During prewriting and drafting, students will
- read a book and list responses to it.
- make a Pro-and-Con Chart to organize responses by order of importance.
- draft a book report that contains a clear purpose.

During revising and editing, students will
- add examples to support responses.
- change passive voice to active voice.
- use declarative sentences to present facts.
- edit their drafts for spelling, capitalization, and punctuation, making sure introductory verbal phrases are used correctly.

Finally, students will write a final draft to be published.

You may wish to send to families the School-Home Connection Letter for this chapter, located at the end of this unit in the Teacher Edition.

Book Report Writing Traits

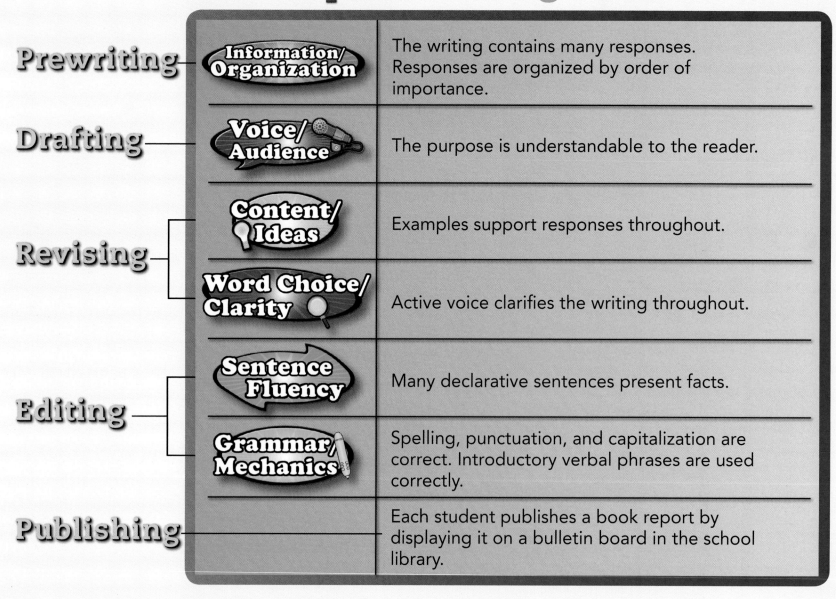

Prewriting	Information/ Organization	The writing contains many responses. Responses are organized by order of importance.
Drafting	Voice/ Audience	The purpose is understandable to the reader.
Revising	Content/ Ideas	Examples support responses throughout.
	Word Choice/ Clarity	Active voice clarifies the writing throughout.
Editing	Sentence Fluency	Many declarative sentences present facts.
	Grammar/ Mechanics	Spelling, punctuation, and capitalization are correct. Introductory verbal phrases are used correctly.
Publishing		Each student publishes a book report by displaying it on a bulletin board in the school library.

Book Report Time Management

WEEK 1

Day 1	Day 2	Day 3	Day 4	Day 5
Learning Objectives				
Students will: • learn the components of a book report.	Students will: • learn how to gather information for a book report.	Students will: • practice gathering information for their own book reports.	Students will: • learn how to organize their responses into a Pro-and-Con Chart.	Students will: • practice organizing their responses into a Pro-and-Con Chart.
Activities				
• Discuss the elements and traits of a book report (Student pages 200–202). • Use the rubric to study the model (Student pages 203–207).	• Read and discuss **Prewriting: Gather Information** (Student page 208).	• Read a book of interest. • Gather information by listing responses about the book.	• Read and discuss **Prewriting: Organize Ideas** (Student page 209).	• Review responses. • Make a Pro-and-Con Chart to organize responses by order of importance.

WEEK 2

Day 1	Day 2	Day 3	Day 4	Day 5
Learning Objectives				
Students will: • learn how to state a purpose so that it is understandable to the reader.	Students will: • practice writing their own drafts.	Students will: • learn how adding examples can help support their opinions.	Students will: • practice adding examples to their drafts.	Students will: • learn how to change passive voice to active voice to make their reports clearer.
Activities				
• Read and discuss **Drafting: Write a Draft** (Student pages 210–211).	• Use a Pro-and-Con Chart to write a draft. • State the purpose for the reader.	• Read and discuss **Revising: Extend Writing** (Student page 212).	• Add examples to drafts.	• Read and discuss **Revising: Clarify Writing** (Student page 213).

WEEK 3

Day 1	Day 2	Day 3	Day 4	Day 5
Learning Objectives				
Students will: • practice changing passive voice to active voice.	Students will: • learn how to use declarative sentences to present facts.	Students will: • learn how to use introductory verbal phrases correctly.	Students will: • practice editing their drafts for spelling, capitalization, and punctuation.	Students will: • learn different ways to publish their book reports.
Activities				
• Reread drafts, looking for passive voice. • Change passive voice to active voice.	• Read and discuss **Editing: Check Sentences** (Student page 214). • Use declarative sentences to present facts.	• Read and discuss **Editing: Proofread Writing** (Student page 215).	• Fix any spelling, capitalization, or punctuation errors. • Make sure introductory verbal phrases are used correctly.	• Read and discuss **Publishing: Share Writing** (Student page 218).

To complete the chapter in fewer days, teach the learning objectives and activities for two days in one day.
This planning chart, correlated to your state's writing standards, is available on-line at http://www.zaner-bloser.com/sfw.

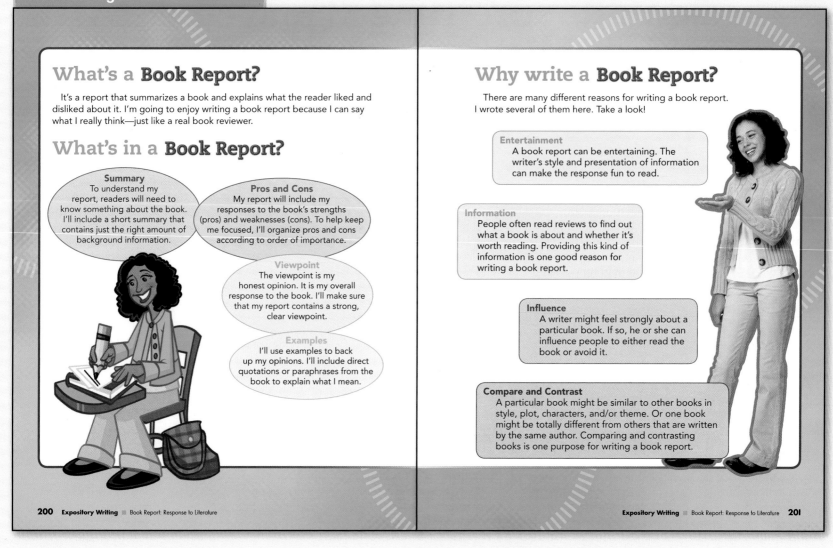

What's a **Book Report?**

It's a report that summarizes a book and explains what the reader liked and disliked about it. I'm going to enjoy writing a book report because I can say what I really think—just like a real book reviewer.

What's in a **Book Report?**

Summary
To understand my report, readers will need to know something about the book. I'll include a short summary that contains just the right amount of background information.

Pros and Cons
My report will include my responses to the book's strengths (pros) and weaknesses (cons). To help keep me focused, I'll organize pros and cons according to order of importance.

Viewpoint
The viewpoint is my honest opinion. It is my overall response to the book. I'll make sure that my report contains a strong, clear viewpoint.

Examples
I'll use examples to back up my opinions. I'll include direct quotations or paraphrases from the book to explain what I mean.

Why write a **Book Report?**

There are many different reasons for writing a book report. I wrote several of them here. Take a look!

Entertainment
A book report can be entertaining. The writer's style and presentation of information can make the response fun to read.

Information
People often read reviews to find out what a book is about and whether it's worth reading. Providing this kind of information is one good reason for writing a book report.

Influence
A writer might feel strongly about a particular book. If so, he or she can influence people to either read the book or avoid it.

Compare and Contrast
A particular book might be similar to other books in style, plot, characters, and/or theme. Or one book might be totally different from others that are written by the same author. Comparing and contrasting books is one purpose for writing a book report.

200 **Expository Writing** ▪ Book Report: Response to Literature

Expository Writing ▪ Book Report: Response to Literature 201

Define the Genre

(Student page 200)

Book Report

Discuss with students the definition of a book report. Ask students to recall times they have expressed opinions about a particular book. Have they ever recommended a certain book—or told others *not* to read it? Point out that any time they respond to a book in writing, they are using the book report genre.

Elements of the Genre

Book Report

Read and discuss with students the elements of a book report listed on Student page 200. Ask volunteers which elements are also common to other forms of writing. **Possible responses: Summary—history writing, newspaper article; Pros and Cons—persuasion, comparing and contrasting; Viewpoint—editorial, speech; Examples— research report, biography** Discuss why each element may be important to writing a book report.

Authentic Writing

(Student page 201)

Book Report

Read and discuss with students the reasons for writing a book report listed on Student page 201. Point out that all writing has a purpose and is aimed at a specific audience. These authentic purposes help authors shape their writing. Ask a volunteer to read aloud the Entertainment box. Then, have students discuss other reasons someone might write a book report for entertainment. Repeat this process for the Information, Influence, and Compare and Contrast boxes. Then, have students brainstorm other purposes for writing a book report that are not listed on Student page 201. Encourage students to think about their own reasons for writing a book report, and how these reasons will affect the tone and focus of their writing.

Book Report: Response to Literature
Writing Traits

I know that there are six traits of good writing. Here's a list of what makes a good book report. I'll use it to help me write.

Information/ Organization	The writing contains many responses. Responses are organized by order of importance.
Voice/ Audience	The purpose is understandable to the reader.
Content/ Ideas	Examples support responses throughout.
Word Choice/ Clarity	Active voice clarifies the writing throughout.
Sentence Fluency	Many declarative sentences present facts.
Grammar/ Mechanics	Spelling, punctuation, and capitalization are correct. Introductory verbal phrases are used correctly.

I can use Lizzie Webber's book report on the next page as a model for my own writing. Later, we'll check out how Lizzie used the traits to help her write.

202 Expository Writing ■ Book Report: Response to Literature

Book Report Model

King of Shadows
A book report by Lizzie Webber

Summary

I would like to tell you about a really interesting book. *King of Shadows* was written by Newbery winner Susan Cooper. The book is about a group of young American actors called the Company of Boys. They travel to London's new Globe Theatre to put on Shakespeare's play *A Midsummer Night's Dream*. One of the actors, Nathan Field, gets seriously ill. He falls asleep one night and awakens the next morning to find that he's still in London, only now the year is 1599. No longer acting in the Company of Boys, Nat is now in the Lord Chamberlain's Men, performing alongside William Shakespeare.

Pros — Several things appeal to me about this book. I like the way that Cooper seamlessly weaves fact and fiction together. Using the same play as the backdrop for both time periods, she moves Nat, as well as her readers, back and forth between the present and the past. For example, Nat is rehearsing to play Puck in the present, so he fits Puck's role in the past. ← Examples

Cooper also changes the characters' speech from modern American English (in the present) to Elizabethan English (in the past). This clarifies when and where the action takes place.

Cons — But I have to admit that there were also times when I was frustrated by *King of Shadows*. For example, I didn't know until the very end why Nat had to go back to 1599. Once I knew, the whole story made perfect sense. I also didn't know why the author spent so much time on details that, at the time, seemed unimportant. For example, near the beginning of the book, Cooper takes a whole paragraph to describe a muscle twitch under Richard Burbage's left eye. When I got to the end of the book, however, I realized why that twitch was so important. That's when I realized that all of Cooper's details are intentional, right down to the names of the directors: Richard Burbage in the past, and Arby (RB), which stands for Richard Babbage, in the present. Viewpoint

Overall, I highly recommend *King of Shadows*, as I'm sure everyone will be delighted when the secret of the book is revealed.

Expository Writing ■ Book Report: Response to Literature **203**

Writing Traits
(Student pages 202–203)

Book Report

Ask students whether they have ever read a book review or a book report. Make sure they understand that some book reviewers are well known to many readers and have earned their respect. However, even unknown writers—and students—can present authoritative, well-supported opinions about a book.

Now, turn students' attention to the traits of a good book report listed on Student page 202. Have one or more volunteers read aloud the traits and their descriptions. Then, tell students that they are going to study and use strategies for writing book reports, and that a good book report has the traits listed on Student page 202.

Differentiating Instruction

English-Language Learners **Preteach** key words and concepts to help students understand "King of Shadows." Explain that the author begins by summarizing the plot, which centers on a group of young American actors who travel to London to perform *A Midsummer Night's Dream* by William Shakespeare. Tell students that William Shakespeare, a sixteenth-century poet and playwright, is regarded by many as the greatest writer of the English language.

Now, write the following words/phrases and their meanings on the board.

appeal: please   *clarifies: makes clear*
seamlessly: smoothly   *frustrated: bothered; disappointed*
backdrop: setting   *muscle twitch: nervous tic or spasm*
rehearsing: practicing   *intentional: purposeful*

Next, say each word/phrase aloud, immediately followed by its meaning. Then, read aloud "King of Shadows," pointing out the pretaught words in context to reinforce their meanings.

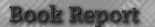

Book Report Rubric

The traits of a good book report from page 202 have been used to make the rubric below. By using 1, 2, 3, or 4 check marks to judge each trait, you can decide how well any book report was written.

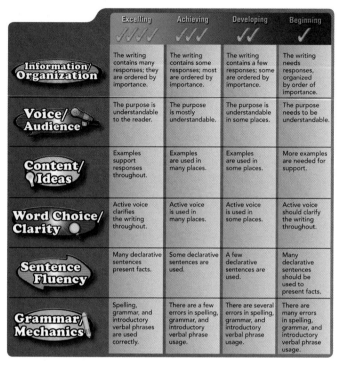

	Excelling ✓✓✓✓	Achieving ✓✓✓	Developing ✓✓	Beginning ✓
Information/Organization	The writing contains many responses; they are ordered by importance.	The writing contains some responses; most are ordered by importance.	The writing contains a few responses; some are ordered by order of importance.	The writing needs responses, organized by order of importance.
Voice/Audience	The purpose is understandable to the reader.	The purpose is mostly understandable.	The purpose is understandable in some places.	The purpose needs to be understandable.
Content/Ideas	Examples support responses throughout.	Examples are used in many places.	Examples are used in some places.	More examples are needed for support.
Word Choice/Clarity	Active voice clarifies the writing throughout.	Active voice is used in many places.	Active voice is used in some places.	Active voice should clarify the writing throughout.
Sentence Fluency	Many declarative sentences present facts.	Some declarative sentences are used.	A few declarative sentences are used.	Many declarative sentences should be used to present facts.
Grammar/Mechanics	Spelling, grammar, and introductory verbal phrases are used correctly.	There are a few errors in spelling, grammar, and introductory verbal phrase usage.	There are several errors in spelling, grammar, and introductory verbal phrase usage.	There are many errors in spelling, grammar, and introductory verbal phrase usage.

Using the Rubric to Study the Book Report Model

Now, let's use the rubric to check Lizzie Webber's book report, "King of Shadows." How many check marks would you give Lizzie for each trait?

Information/Organization
- The writing contains many responses.
- Responses are organized by order of importance.

After Lizzie summarizes the book, she describes some of its pros, or strengths. Then, she describes some of its cons, or weaknesses. She begins with the more important points and works down to the less important points. Here's how she begins the body of her response.

[from the writing model]

Several things appeal to me about this book. I like the way that Cooper seamlessly weaves fact and fiction together. Using the same play as the backdrop for both time periods, she moves Nat, as well as her readers, back and forth between the present and the past.

Voice/Audience
- The purpose is understandable to the reader.

Lizzie states her purpose in the first sentence of the lead paragraph. This way, her audience knows that what follows is the author's opinion about a specific book, which is named in the second sentence.

[from the writing model]

I would like to tell you about a really interesting book. *King of Shadows* was written by Newbery winner Susan Cooper.

Using the Rubric
(Student page 204)

Explain to students that a rubric is a tool that can be used to evaluate a piece of writing, and that the rubric on Student page 204 can be used to evaluate a book report. Have students note that it is based on the same book report traits listed on Student page 202.

Now point out the terms above each rubric column: *Excelling, Achieving, Developing,* and *Beginning.* Explain that each rubric column symbolizes a degree of writing skill, and that each rubric row focuses on a specific writing trait. When students use the rubric to evaluate their own work at each step of the writing process, they increase the likelihood of producing polished, well-written book reports.

Study the Model
(Student pages 205–207)

Explain that Student pages 205–207 show how the writing model on Student page 203 meets all six traits of the rubric. Read each section with the students. Then, have them look for other examples of each trait in the writing model.

Ask students how many check marks they would assign the writing model for each trait. Then, as a class, decide how the writing model should be rated overall.

To be sure they are meeting all six writing traits, remind students to use the rubric as they write their own book reports.

Book Report

• Examples support responses throughout.

Whether she is writing about the book's pros or cons, Lizzie uses examples to support her responses. Here's a passage where she begins with a response and then supports it with a specific example from the book.

> [from the writing model]
>
> I also didn't know why the author spent so much time on details that, at the time, seemed unimportant. For example, near the beginning of the book, Cooper takes a whole paragraph to describe a muscle twitch under Richard Burbage's left eye. When I got to the end of the book, however, I realized why that twitch was so important.

Word Choice/Clarity

• Active voice clarifies the writing throughout.

Lizzie uses the active voice to present her report. This makes her writing clear and easy to read. For instance, she could've used this wordy, passive construction in her report: The characters' speech was changed by Cooper from modern American English (in the present) to Elizabethan English (in the past). But she used the following active sentence instead.

> [from the writing model]
>
> Cooper also changes the characters' speech from modern American English (in the present) to Elizabethan English (in the past).

Sentence Fluency

• Many declarative sentences present facts.

Lizzie uses declarative sentences to present facts. She makes clear statements and keeps the writing simple. These declarative sentences from her opening paragraph show what I mean.

> [from the writing model]
>
> The book is about a group of young American actors called the Company of Boys. They travel to London's new Globe Theatre to put on Shakespeare's play *A Midsummer Night's Dream.*

Grammar/Mechanics

• Spelling, punctuation, and capitalization are correct. Introductory verbal phrases are used correctly.

I know that a verbal is a verb form that acts like a noun, adjective, or adverb, and I appreciate how Lizzie uses verbal phrases to begin some of her sentences. This pattern adds variety to her writing. Look at the following example, in which the introductory verbal phrase *Using the same play as the backdrop for both time periods* clearly describes the subject *she.*

> [from the writing model]
>
> Using the same play as the backdrop for both time periods, she moves Nat, as well as her readers, back and forth between the present and the past.

My Turn!

I'm going to write a book report about a book I recently read. I'll follow the rubric and use good writing strategies. Read along to find out how I do it!

TiPS for the Writing Classroom

Establishing a Cooperative Atmosphere
by Ken Stewart, *Master Teacher*

If you establish a cooperative atmosphere from the first day of school, students will be encouraged to communicate openly in their writing and class discussions. An important component of the cooperative classroom is cooperative learning groups. However, placing students in groups without established guidelines or without practicing how to work with group members may be a prescription for failure. Follow these simple steps to give students experience in becoming cooperative learners.

1. Post five easy-to-follow classroom rules:

   Rule 1: Always do your best work.

   Rule 2: When you think you have done your best, challenge yourself to do better.

   Rule 3: Stay on task and be responsible for your own actions.

   Rule 4: When working in a group, speak softly.

   Rule 5: Share information and respect others' ideas. If one member of your group understands the lesson, all the members should understand.

2. Create mini-lessons that give your students opportunities to use cooperative learning in a variety of ways.

3. When introducing a cooperative learning style, allow at least five minutes for the whole class to process the positives and negatives of the experience. Offer encouragement for positive behaviors; allow students to suggest improvements.

4. Create fun activities to help students process why working on a team is often better than working individually.

Writing a Book Report

Prewriting Gather Information

Information/Organization The writing contains many responses.

Writing Strategy Read a book on a topic that interests me. Then, list my responses about the book.

When my teacher said to write a book report, the first thing I did was choose a book. I take ballet, and I absolutely love to dance. So I chose *Another Way to Dance* by Martha Southgate. After I finished reading, I looked back through the book and jotted down some things that I liked and disliked about it. I put smiley faces next to the pros and frowns next to the cons.

Another Way to Dance

- ☺ interesting and well-developed main characters
- ☹ the same things said too many times
- ☹ too much obsessing on Vicki's part
- ☺ very good/accurate descriptions of Vicki's ballet classes
- ☺ realistic feelings and actions toward Vicki's family members
- ☹ corny and overused ending

Practice!
Now it's your turn. Choose a book to read. Then, jot down notes about the things you liked and disliked.

Prewriting Organize Ideas

Information/Organization Responses are organized by order of importance.

Writing Strategy Make a Pro-and-Con Chart to organize my responses by order of importance.

Writer's Term___
Pro-and-Con Chart
A **Pro-and-Con Chart** can help you organize your opinions about a book. By presenting a book's **pros** (good points) and **cons** (bad points) in order of their importance, you can tell your reader what the book is about, as well as why you liked and/or disliked it.

The rubric says my responses should be organized by order of importance, so I took my list of likes and dislikes and made it into a Pro-and-Con Chart. You can see how I put the most important ideas at the top of each column and worked down from there.

PRO-AND-CON CHART

PROS	CONS
very good/accurate descriptions of Vicki's ballet classes	the same things said too many times
realistic feelings and actions toward Vicki's family members	too much obsessing on Vicki's part
interesting and well-developed main characters	corny and overused ending

Practice!
Now it's your turn. Organize your book report by making a Pro-and-Con Chart that lists your responses in order of importance.

Reflect
Is my Pro-and-Con Chart clearly organized? Do you think it will help me stay focused as I write?

Prewriting

(Student pages 208–209)

Discuss with students a book that affected you in some way. Share what the book is about and why it was important to you. Then, discuss options for sharing your ideas about the book, including telling a friend, loaning it to another reader, or writing about it in a book report.

Refer to Briana's description on Student page 208 of how she chose a book for her report. Note that although Briana knew immediately what she wanted to read about, many people often need to search to find a book that sparks their interest. Then, discuss various methods students could use to search for a good book.

More Practice!

For more practice with these writing strategies, you may wish to have students use the Strategy Practice Book. See the appendix for annotated Strategy Practice Book pages.

Differentiating Instruction

Enrichment Challenge students to widen the scope of their book reports by choosing one of the following.

- Compare and contrast two books with similar topics or themes.
- Compare and contrast two books written by the same author.
- Read a book by a familiar author and then write a report that evaluates this book in the context of the author's other works.
- Compare and contrast two books with opposing views on the same subject.

WORK with a PARTNER

Students who need help finding a good book to review may benefit from searching with a partner. Suggest that pairs of students begin by drawing up lists of books they know. They should then work together to seek out other resources—such as teachers, librarians, booksellers, older siblings, or the Internet—to help them find appropriate books for their reports.

Writing a Book Report

Drafting Write a Draft

Voice/Audience The purpose is understandable to the reader.

Writing Strategy State my purpose so the reader will understand why I'm writing.

Writer's Term

Purpose
Sometimes an author has more than one **purpose**. An author's purpose can include any one or more of the following:
- to inform or explain
- to entertain or amuse
- to persuade or convince
- to express a feeling, an idea, or an opinion

I'll use my Pro-and-Con Chart to help me write my draft. According to the rubric, my purpose needs to be clear. I could write in favor of the book I read, or I could write against it. But in this case, my purpose is more neutral: I'd like to summarize the book and then share my opinions about the way the author presented her information. Of course, the reader will want to know which book I'm reporting on, so I'll begin by naming it.

I'll do my best with grammar and spelling errors. But mainly, I just want to concentrate on getting my ideas down. I can always go back later to proofread.

210 Expository Writing ■ Book Report: Response to Literature

Proofreading Marks

⊐ Indent	ℓ Take out something
≡ Make a capital	⊙ Add a period
/ Make a small letter	(SP) Spelling error
∧ Add something	¶ New paragraph

[DRAFT]

[purpose for writing]

<u>Another Way to Dance</u>
A book report by Briana

After reading <u>Another Way to Dance</u> by Martha Southgate, I had mixed opinions. I'd like to share some of them with you now. Having studied ballet myself, I found the premise of the book particularly interesting. A fourteen-year-old African American girl named Vicki is accepted into the summer dance program at the School of American Ballet in New York City. The book chronicles everything that happens to her Vicki that summer. She experiences several things that help her mature, including an exciting first date and a devastating encounter with a racist schoolmate.

In many ways, I think the author does a good job of describing Vicki and her experiences. As I read them, I could almost smell the dance studio, hear the music and activity, and feel my muscles straining to move along with Vicki's.

Practice!
Now it's your turn. When you write your draft, make sure to state your purpose so that it's clear to the reader.

Reflect
What do you think? Is my purpose appropriate for a book report?

Expository Writing ■ Book Report: Response to Literature 211

Drafting

(Student pages 210–211)

Remind students that drafting is a chance to get ideas on paper without having to worry about making mistakes.

Refer to Briana's words and the Writer's Term box on Student page 210. Then, point to the first part of Briana's draft on Student page 211, and ask students to define her purpose for writing. **Possible response: to share her opinions** Make sure students understand that there are many reasons for writing a book report. Sometimes a writer can even have more than one purpose. Explain that figuring out a purpose before writing will help students focus their reports.

Refer to the Practice and Reflect boxes on Student page 211, which remind students to clearly state their purpose for writing their reports. Point out that Briana repeatedly refers to the rubric as she writes. Encourage students to get into the habit of using the rubric to help guide their own writing. Then, have students use the events on their Pro-and-Con Charts to draft their book reports.

Writing Across the Curriculum

Literature Have students research and report on book reviewers and publications. They may choose to focus on one of the following.

- Where is the best place for people to read book reviews? Investigate book review publications such as *The New York Times* book review section, local newspaper reviews, magazines, and the Internet. Then, compare and contrast their quality and target audience.
- Find two book reviews—one that is helpful and one that is not. Analyze their qualities by comparing the elements of the two reviews.

Writing a Book Report

Revising Extend Writing

Content/Ideas

Examples support responses throughout.

Writing Strategy Add examples to support my responses.

Writer's Term

Examples
Examples are pieces of information that support a topic, a statement, an idea, or an opinion. An example can be a fact, a description, a quotation, or a paraphrase of an author's exact words.

In my introduction, I gave my purpose for writing and a brief description of what the book is about. In the body, I presented my opinions of the book, based on my list of pros and cons. The rubric says that I need examples to support my responses, so I added some description from the book to make my opinions even stronger.

[DRAFT]

In many ways, I think the author does a good job of describing Vicki and her experiences. For example, the passages describing Vicki's ballet classes are very accurate and detailed. As I read them, I could almost smell the dance studio, hear the music and activity, and feel my muscles straining to move along with Vicki's. [added an example]

Practice!

Now it's your turn. Add examples that support your opinions.

Revising Clarify Writing

Word Choice/Clarity

Active voice clarifies the writing throughout.

Writing Strategy Change passive voice to active voice to make the report clearer.

Writer's Term
Active Voice/Passive Voice
If the subject of a sentence performs the action, the verb is in the **active voice**. If the subject is acted upon by something else, the verb is in the **passive voice**. The active voice makes sentences stronger.
Active voice: Janice sang a lively song.
Passive voice: A lively song was sung by Janice.

The rubric says that active voice will clarify my writing. So I reread part of my draft where I had used passive voice. Then, I changed it to active voice.

[DRAFT] [changed passive voice to active]

I especially liked Vicki's "Aunt" Hanna, her girlfriend Stacey, her boyfriend Michael, and Michael's mother. Vicki is shown by Michael and Stacey that there's another way to view the world around her. And she show Vicki is shown by Stacey and Michael's mother that there's another way to dance.

Practice!

Now it's your turn. Read through your draft to see where you can change passive voice to active voice to clarify your writing.

Reflect
Did my changes make my writing clearer? Did I use the active voice correctly?

Revising

(Student pages 212–213)

Discuss with students the contents of the Writer's Term box on Student page 212, emphasizing the many ways that a writer can use examples to support his or her opinions. Next, have students note how Briana added an example to her draft on Student page 212. Then, remind them to add examples to support the opinions given in their own drafts.

Read aloud the Writer's Term box on Student page 213. Ask students what voice is used if the subject of a sentence performs the action. **active** Then, ask what voice is used if the subject is acted upon. **passive** Point out the revisions made to Briana's draft on Student page 213, explaining that revising for active voice often requires more than changing a verb tense; rather, it often calls for a restructuring of the sentence. Remind students that active voice is clearer and more exact than passive voice. They should then look for places in their own drafts where they can revise for active voice to make their writing stronger.

Differentiating Instruction

Support Students might be unclear about how to revise for active voice. Help them by offering extra practice. Begin by writing these sentences on the board:

The sentence was written by the teacher.
The teacher wrote the sentence.

Ask students which sentence is active and which is passive. **The first is passive; the second is active.** Make sure students understand that active voice strengthens writing because it makes the subject of a sentence perform the action.

• Note that revising for active voice often means more than changing a single verb tense; it also involves introducing new words and/or restructuring sentences.

• Write the following sentences on the board. Then, have students copy them on a sheet of paper, leaving two lines of empty space underneath each one for revisions. Tell students to revise them using the active voice.

Tonight, dinner was cooked by Tina.
Tonight, Tina cooked dinner.
Dessert was planned by Claire.
Claire planned dessert.

Writing a Book Report

Editing Check Sentences

Sentence Fluency
Many declarative sentences present facts.

Writing Strategy
Use declarative sentences to present facts.

Writer's Term

Declarative Sentences
Different types of sentences have different uses. A **declarative sentence** is a statement that ends with a period.

Now, it's time to edit. The rubric says to use declarative sentences to present facts. When I reread my draft, I ran across a question that would be better stated as a declarative sentence. I didn't change any of my exclamatory sentences, since they express feelings rather than state facts.

[DRAFT]
[used a declarative sentence]

The author kept
~~Doesn't it bug you when an author keeps~~ talking about the same things over and over. Vicki's constant fantasizing about Baryshnikov is one example. I mean, every ballet dancer loves Misha. But please, give me a break!

Practice!
Now it's your turn. Make stronger statements by using declarative sentences to present facts.

Editing Proofread Writing

Grammar/Mechanics
Spelling, punctuation, and capitalization are correct. Introductory verbal phrases are used correctly.

Writing Strategy
Make sure introductory verbal phrases are used correctly.

Writer's Term

Introductory Verbal Phrases
A **verbal** is a verb form that acts like a noun, an adjective, or an adverb. An **introductory verbal phrase** comes at the beginning of a sentence and describes the subject.

According to the rubric, I should pay special attention to introductory verbal phrases. These phrases can make my writing more interesting, but I need to make sure that I use them correctly. Here's how I edited one sentence.

[DRAFT]
[corrected subject of introductory verbal phrase]

I also got tired of the fact that Vicki was such a high-maintenance
she made me wish
character. Constantly crying over one thing or another, ~~I wished~~ she would just stop!

Practice!
Now it's your turn. Edit your draft for spelling, punctuation, and capitalization. Also, make sure each introductory verbal phrase correctly describes its subject.

Grammar/Mechanics
For more practice with introductory verbal phrases, use the exercises on the next two pages.

Reflect
I worked hard to use declarative sentences to present facts and to make sure I used verbal phrases correctly. Did it help my writing?

Editing
(Student pages 214–215)

Discuss with students the contents of the Writer's Term box on Student page 214. Then, point out how Briana revised her draft on the same page. Remind students that they will be making similar editing choices as they review their own drafts for places where declarative sentences might better serve their purpose.

Now, read aloud the Writer's Term box on Student page 215, and then write the following sentences on the board: *Rattling in the wind, I hear the tree move outside my window. Rattling in the wind, the tree moves outside my window.* Ask students to identify the verbal phrase in each. **Rattling in the wind** Then, ask which sentence is correct and why. **Possible response: The second sentence is correct because the introductory verbal phrase should describe the subject *the tree*, not *I*.** Now, remind students to edit their drafts, making sure that each introductory verbal phrase describes the subject of the sentence. While doing this, students should also check their drafts for proper spelling, capitalization, and punctuation.

Differentiating Instruction

Support Review sentence patterns with students by displaying the following:

- *Declarative sentence: makes a statement*
  Example: I will find a mystery to read.
- *Imperative sentence: gives a command*
  Example: Hand me that book.
- *Interrogative sentence: asks a question*
  Example: Did you read that mystery?
- *Exclamatory sentence: shows strong feeling*
  Example: That book was great!

Discuss the differences among the types of sentences, and have students note the various types of sentences used in their book reports.

WORK with a PARTNER
Have pairs of students read one another's drafts, using sticky notes to mark errors in spelling, punctuation, and grammar. Then, have students perform a second read that focuses on the editing strategies they learned in this chapter.

Grammar/Mechanics Practice!

Introductory Verbal Phrases

KNOW the RULE

A **verbal** is a verb that ends in either *–ed* or *–ing* and acts as a noun, an adjective, or an adverb. An **introductory verbal phrase** comes at the beginning of a sentence and describes the subject.

> **Correct:**
> Laughing loudly, Andrew enjoyed the show.
> (The introductory verbal phrase is *Laughing loudly*, and the verbal is *Laughing*. The verbal phrase describes the subject *Andrew*.)

When the introductory verbal phrase doesn't describe the subject, it causes confusion for the reader. Here is an example of a verbal phrase that does not describe the subject.

> **Incorrect:**
> Laughing loudly, the show was enjoyable for Andrew.
> (Here again, the phrase is *Laughing loudly*, but it incorrectly describes *the show*.)

Practice the Rule

Number a separate sheet of paper 1–5. Then, write the introductory verbal phrase from each sentence, underlining the verbal in each. If the verbal correctly describes the subject of the sentence, write the subject after the phrase. If the verbal does not describe the subject, rewrite the rest of the sentence correctly.

1. Sitting on the couch like a friend, my favorite book awaits me.
2. Filled with humorous stories, I can hear its pages call to me.
3. Salvaged by several tapings, I see its cover wink at me.
4. Smiling in anticipation, I pick up the book.
5. Slowly spinning on my heel, I turn and sit down.

Apply the Rule

Read the following passage, noting any mistakes in the use of introductory verbal phrases. Then, rewrite the passage correctly on a separate sheet of paper.

To Kill a Mockingbird
a book report

It's not often that a book surprises me, but To Kill a Mockingbird by Harper Lee sure did. As soon as I finished the last page, I wanted to tell people about it. Suggesting I read it independently, my teacher gave me this book. Knowing it was famous, the book had to be boring and irrelevant, I figured. Boy, was I wrong! To Kill a Mockingbird has got to be the best book I've ever read.

To Kill a Mockingbird is set during the Great Depression in the South. The main character is a girl named Scout Finch, who lives with her brother, Jem, and her father, Atticus. The two children befriend Dill and Boo Radley, and the story gets interesting when Atticus Finch defends a black man who has been unjustly accused of a serious crime.

Discovering that the book was first published back in 1960, the story would contain nothing I could relate to. But I got hooked on the first page because the author gives Scout, who narrates in the first person, such a strong voice. Piquing my interest on the first page, I included interesting questions that made me want to read further.

Grammar/Mechanics Mini-Lesson

(Student pages 216–217)

Introductory Verbal Phrases

Ask students to read the Know the Rule box on Student page 216. Then, discuss the terms *verbal* and *introductory verbal phrase* with the students. Finally, display these pairs of sentences on the board:

Taking his seat, Andrew waited for the show to begin.
Taking his seat, the show couldn't begin soon enough for Andrew.

Feeling hungry, the intermission allowed Andrew to get a snack.
Feeling hungry, Andrew got a snack during intermission.

Now, have students tell which sentences are correct and which are incorrect. **The first and fourth sentences are correct, and the second and third are incorrect.**

Answers for Practice the Rule

1. <u>Sitting</u> on the couch like a friend; my favorite book
2. <u>Filled</u> with humorous stories, its pages call to me.
3. <u>Salvaged</u> by several tapings, its cover winks at me.
4. <u>Smiling</u> in anticipation; I
5. Slowly <u>spinning</u> on my heel; I

Answers for Apply the Rule

To Kill a Mockingbird
a book report

It's not often that a book surprises me, but To Kill a Mockingbird by Harper Lee sure did. As soon as I finished the last page, I wanted to tell people about it. Suggesting I read it independently, my teacher gave me this book. Knowing it was famous, I figured the book had to be boring and irrelevant. Boy, was I wrong! To Kill a Mockingbird has got to be the best book I've ever read.

To Kill a Mockingbird is set during the Great Depression in the South. The main character is a girl named Scout Finch, who lives with her brother, Jem, and her father, Atticus. The two children befriend Dill and Boo

(Answers continue on page 167.)

Writing a Book Report

Publishing Share Writing

Display my book report on a bulletin board in the school library.

Now that I've finished my book report, how should I publish it? I could read it to a friend or post it in the classroom, but I'd reach a larger audience if I posted it in the school library. First, I'll get permission from the school librarian. Then, I'll make a clean copy that's easy to read. I should remember to print each page on one side only, in case I have to pin my report to the bulletin board. Before I post it, though, I'll read through it one last time to make sure it includes all of the items on my checklist.

My Checklist

✓ My responses are organized by order of importance.

✓ My purpose is easy to understand.

✓ Examples from the book support my opinions.

✓ Active voice makes the writing clear.

✓ Declarative sentences present facts.

✓ Spelling, capitalization, and punctuation are all correct. Introductory verbal phrases are used correctly.

Practice!

Now it's your turn. Make a checklist to check your book report. Then, make a final draft to publish.

Another Way to Dance
A book report by Briana

After reading *Another Way to Dance* by Martha Southgate, I had mixed opinions. I'd like to share some of them with you now. Having studied ballet myself, I found the premise of the book particularly interesting. A fourteen-year-old African American girl named Vicki is accepted into the summer dance program at the School of American Ballet in New York City. The book chronicles everything that happens to Vicki that summer. She experiences several things that help her mature, including an exciting first date and a devastating encounter with a racist schoolmate.

In many ways, I think the author does a good job of describing Vicki and her experiences. For example, the passages describing Vicki's ballet classes are very accurate and detailed. As I read them, I could almost smell the dance studio, hear the music and activity, and feel my muscles straining to move along with Vicki's.

I also think that the author does a good job of capturing Vicki's complicated feelings toward her family. Since her

---

(Answers continued from page 166.)

Radley, and the story gets interesting when Atticus Finch defends a black man who has been unjustly accused of a serious crime.

Discovering that the book was first published back in 1960, I thought the story would contain nothing I could relate to. But I got hooked on the first page because the author gives Scout, who narrates in the first person, such a strong voice. Piquing my interest on the first page, the book included interesting questions that made me want to read further.

 For more practice with grammar/mechanics skills, see Zaner-Bloser's *G.U.M.* materials.

Publishing
(Student pages 218–219)

Ask students if they like Briana's choice for sharing her book report. Tell the class that her choice is not the only option for publishing her report. Invite students to name other ways they could publish their own book reports.

Have each student make a checklist and perform a final evaluation of his or her report before publishing it. Encourage students to share copies of their reports with friends and relatives who might be interested in reading about what they wrote.

Writing a Book Report

parents are newly divorced, Vicki feels a mixture of sympathy and resentment toward them. She also feels that she can't be entirely honest with her mother, so she bottles up her emotions. I think all of this is quite realistic.

One more thing I think the author does well is reveal the personalities of some of the characters. I especially liked Vicki's "Aunt" Hannah, her girlfriend Stacey, her boyfriend Michael, and Michael's mother. Michael and Stacey show Vicki that there's another way to view the world around her. Stacey and Michael's mother show Vicki that there's another way to dance.

There were, however, some things that I didn't like about the book. The author kept talking about the same things over and over. Vicki's constant fantasizing about Baryshnikov is one example. I mean, every ballet dancer loves Misha. But please, give me a break! After a while, I was bored with all that fantasizing. I was much more interested in Vicki's real relationship with Michael than the one that goes on in her head.

I also got tired of the fact that Vicki was such a high-maintenance character. Constantly crying over one thing or another, she made me wish she would just stop! It's not that some of her problems weren't completely valid. It's just that

after a while, they got really old. Many times, I just wanted to tell her, "Calm down, girl! Just get over yourself and relax! And join the real world while you're at it."

After all that reading, the thing that disappointed me the most was the ending. It sounded like such a cliché. I was really hoping that the author would include a juicy morsel to chew on for a while after I finished the book—some theme or life lesson that Vicki learned after all that obsessing. Instead, I got a corny and overused ending.

Well, if you love ballet—and you really love Baryshnikov—*Another Way to Dance* is worth the read. But if you tend to get impatient with reading about the struggles of a confused and insecure adolescent, you might want to pass on this one.

Reflect
What do you think? Did I use all the traits of a good book report in my writing? Check it against the rubric. Don't forget to use the rubric to check your own book report, too.

Publishing
(Student pages 220–221)

Call students' attention to the Reflect box on the bottom of Student page 221. Explain that assessing Briana's book report against the rubric will help them better understand how to apply the traits to their own work. Then, have students use sticky notes to mark at least one example of each trait in Briana's writing. Tell them to include an evaluation on each note.

After this process, have students assess how well they were able to identify each trait in Briana's writing and how easy or difficult it was to use the rubric. Remind them to apply what they learned from Briana's work when they use the rubric to check their own writing.

Differentiating Instruction

Enrichment Have students use their book reports to convene one or more "book group" sessions. Encourage students to review each others' reports and then choose several of the books for group reading and discussion. Help each group develop discussion questions that focus on the following:

• Characters' problems, actions, motivations, or traits
• Plot development
• Major themes or issues
• Narrative voice
• Writing style

Have each group choose a discussion leader for each meeting.

Ways to Publish a
Book Report

As you decide how to publish your work, it's a good idea to think about who might want to read it. That way, you can figure out the best way to share it. Here are some ideas for publishing your book report.

✓ Read your paper aloud to the class. Then, discuss whether other students have read the same book.

✓ Find a Web site where others have posted reviews of your book. Then, upload your work.

✓ Mail your work to a newspaper or book review publication that accepts student work.

✓ Include your report as part of a multimedia presentation.

✓ Include your report as part of a class publication called "Should You Read This Book?"

Writing Across the Content Areas
Book Report

Your school subjects can be a great source of writing ideas. Choose a subject and see how many related topics you can brainstorm. Check out these examples.

Science
• Read a biography about a famous scientist. Then, write a book report.
• Write about a science-fiction book.

Social Studies
• Read a nonfiction book on an era you'd like to know more about. Then, respond by writing a book report.
• Write about a historical fiction book.

Art and/or Music
• Read a biography about an artist or musician. Then, respond by writing a book report.
• Read a book about your favorite form of art. Then, write a book report.

Ways to Publish
(Student page 222)

Read and discuss with students the publishing options listed on Student page 222. Encourage students to consider some of these options when publishing their own writing. Remind students that Briana chose to publish her book report by displaying it on a bulletin board in the school library, but they can choose their own way of publishing. Perhaps one student will want to submit his or her report to a newspaper or book review publication that publishes student work, while another will want to post it on a Web site where others have posted reviews of the same book.

Writing Across the Content Areas
(Student page 223)

Explain to students that writing is not just for English or language arts class. Many other school subjects contain ideas, issues, and events that students may want to write about. Encourage students to consider using one of the content areas listed on Student page 223 as a springboard for more writing options. Students may also wish to consult with other teachers for more ideas on writing in the content areas.

Research Report Overview

In this chapter, students will learn how to write a research report. They will learn the different elements of a research report—narrow topic, attention-grabbing introduction, quotes and paraphrases, and a list of Works Consulted—and some reasons why they might want to write one. Students will then use a research report rubric to study a model writing sample.

Students will follow the student guide as she goes through the writing stages—prewriting, drafting, revising, editing, and publishing. As the student guide learns new writing strategies in each step, students will be directed to practice the strategies in their own writing.

During prewriting and drafting, students will
- choose a topic, survey sources, make a 3 W's Chart, and make note cards.
- make an Outline to organize information.
- draft a report including an attention-grabbing introduction.

During revising and editing, students will
- add quotes and paraphrased information from experts.
- make sure quotes are cited correctly and then make a list of Works Consulted.
- use introductory verbal phrases to vary sentences.
- edit their drafts for spelling, capitalization, punctuation, and compound and complex sentences.

Finally, students will publish a final draft.

You may wish to send to families the School-Home Connection Letter for this chapter, located at the end of this unit in the Teacher Edition.

Research Report Writing Traits

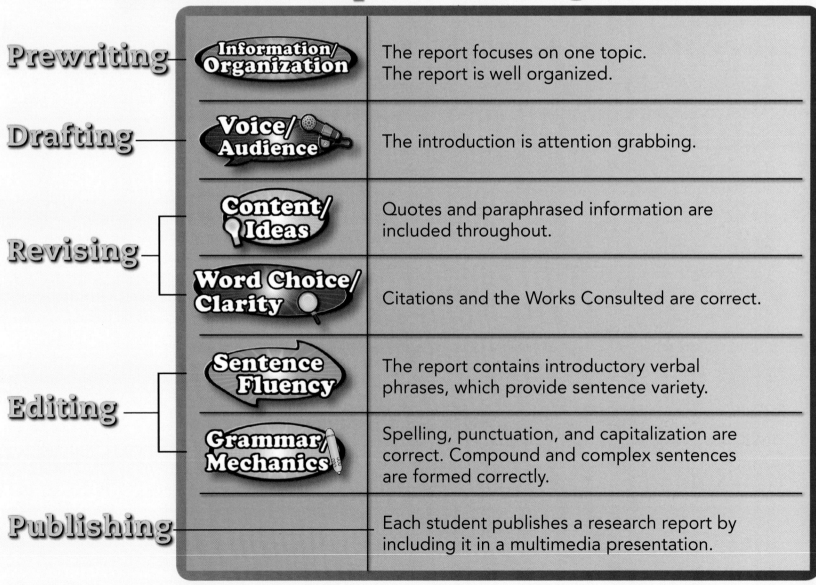

Prewriting	Information/Organization	The report focuses on one topic. The report is well organized.
Drafting	Voice/Audience	The introduction is attention grabbing.
Revising	Content/Ideas	Quotes and paraphrased information are included throughout.
	Word Choice/Clarity	Citations and the Works Consulted are correct.
Editing	Sentence Fluency	The report contains introductory verbal phrases, which provide sentence variety.
	Grammar/Mechanics	Spelling, punctuation, and capitalization are correct. Compound and complex sentences are formed correctly.
Publishing		Each student publishes a research report by including it in a multimedia presentation.

Research Report Time Management

WEEK 1

	Day 1	Day 2	Day 3	Day 4	Day 5
Learning Objectives	Students will: • learn the components of a research report.	Students will: • learn how to gather information for a research report.	Students will: • practice gathering information for their own research reports.	Students will: • learn how to organize their information into an Outline.	Students will: • practice organizing their notes into an Outline.
Activities	• Discuss the elements and traits of a research report (Student pages 224–226). • Use the rubric to study the model (Student pages 227–233).	• Read and discuss **Prewriting: Gather Information** (Student pages 234–236).	• Choose a topic, survey sources, and make a 3 W's Chart. • Make note cards.	• Read and discuss **Prewriting: Organize Ideas** (Student pages 237–239).	• Review note cards. • Make an Outline to organize information.

WEEK 2

	Day 1	Day 2	Day 3	Day 4	Day 5
Learning Objectives	Students will: • learn how to include an attention-grabbing introduction in their drafts.	Students will: • practice writing their own drafts.	Students will: • learn how to add quotes and paraphrased information from experts.	Students will: • practice adding quotes and paraphrased information from experts.	Students will: • learn how to cite quotes correctly. • learn how to make a list of Works Consulted.
Activities	• Read and discuss **Drafting: Write a Draft** (Student pages 240–243).	• Use an Outline to write a draft. • Include an introduction that grabs the reader's attention.	• Read and discuss **Revising: Extend Writing** (Student pages 244–245).	• Add quotes and paraphrased information from experts.	• Read and discuss **Revising: Clarify Writing** (Student pages 246–247).

WEEK 3

	Day 1	Day 2	Day 3	Day 4	Day 5
Learning Objectives	Students will: • practice citing quotes correctly. • practice making a list of Works Consulted.	Students will: • learn how to use introductory verbal phrases to vary sentences.	Students will: • learn how to form compound and complex sentences correctly.	Students will: • practice editing their drafts for spelling, capitalization, and punctuation.	Students will: • learn different ways to publish their research reports.
Activities	• Reread drafts, making sure quotes are cited correctly. • Make a list of Works Consulted.	• Read and discuss **Editing: Check Sentences** (Student page 248). • Use introductory verbal phrases to vary sentences.	• Read and discuss **Editing: Proofread Writing** (Student page 249).	• Fix any spelling, capitalization, or punctuation errors. • Use compound and complex sentences correctly.	• Read and discuss **Publishing: Share Writing** (Student page 252).

To complete the chapter in fewer days, teach the learning objectives and activities for two days in one day.

This planning chart, correlated to your state's writing standards, is available on-line at http://www.zaner-bloser.com/sfw.

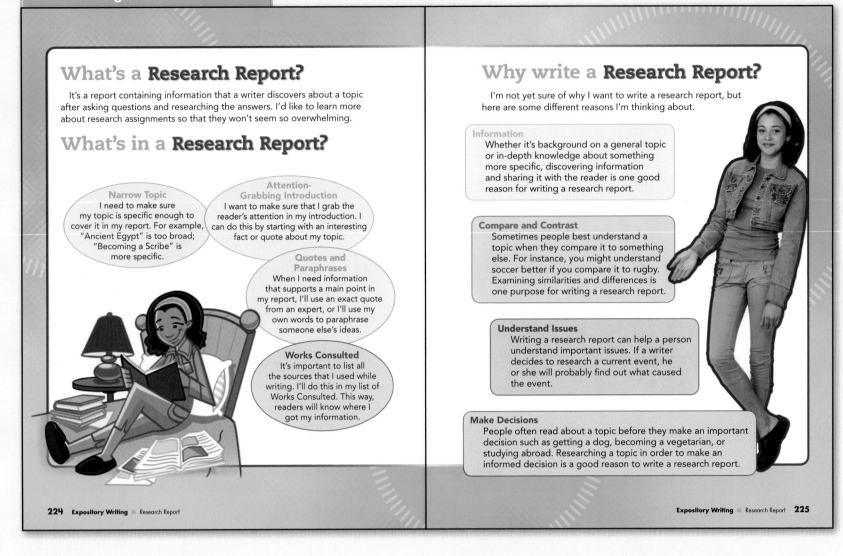

Define the Genre
(Student page 224)

Research Report

Discuss with students the definition of a research report. Explain that a research report involves posing questions about a topic, consulting sources for answers, and then writing up the findings.

Elements of the Genre

Research Report

Read and discuss with students the elements of a research report. Ask volunteers which elements are also common to other forms of writing. **Possible responses: Narrow Topic—essay, science writing; Attention-Grabbing Introduction—news article, short story; Quotes and Paraphrases—biography, memoir; Works Consulted— historical writing, biography** Discuss why each element may be important to writing a research report.

Authentic Writing
(Student page 225)

Research Report

Read and discuss with students the reasons for writing a research report listed on Student page 225. Point out that all writing has a purpose and is aimed at a specific audience. These authentic purposes help authors shape their writing. Ask a volunteer to read aloud the Information box. Then, have students discuss other reasons someone might write a research report to provide information. Repeat this process for the Compare and Contrast, Understand Issues, and Make Decisions boxes. Then, have students brainstorm other purposes for writing a research report that are not listed on Student page 225. Encourage students to think about their own reasons for writing a research report, and how these reasons will affect the tone and focus of their writing.

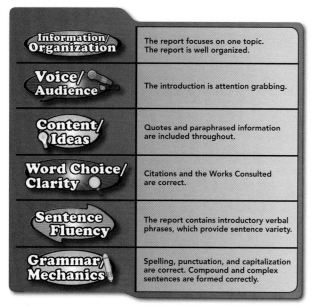

Research Report
Writing Traits

I know that there are six traits of good writing. Here's a list of what makes a good research report. I'll use this list to help me write.

Information/Organization	The report focuses on one topic. The report is well organized.
Voice/Audience	The introduction is attention grabbing.
Content/Ideas	Quotes and paraphrased information are included throughout.
Word Choice/Clarity	Citations and the Works Consulted are correct.
Sentence Fluency	The report contains introductory verbal phrases, which provide sentence variety.
Grammar/Mechanics	Spelling, punctuation, and capitalization are correct. Compound and complex sentences are formed correctly.

I can use Julie Fleming's research report on the next three pages as a model for my own writing. Later, we'll check out how Julie used the traits to help her write.

Research Report Model

UNDERSTANDING PHOBIAS
by Julie Fleming

Narrow Topic

Attention-Grabbing Introduction

Fears—we all have them. Walking alone at night, crossing dangerous intersections, and speaking in front of a crowd are all common fears. However, fears become abnormal when they become so irrational or exaggerated that a person never leaves the house. That's when fears turn into phobias.

Fear is a normal response to a scary situation. A phobia is an unreasonable response and is not normal. A phobia keeps people from doing the things that they want or need to do, such as going to work, school, or attending social functions. Judy Monroe, author of *Phobias: Everything You Wanted to Know, But Were Afraid to Ask,* quotes Anne Marie Albana at the Center of Stress and Anxiety Disorders at the State University of New York at Albany: "A phobia is an unrealistic fear that is all out of proportion to the actual threat. The fear of spiders, for instance, would be present even when there were no spiders around" (15–16). There are more than 500 phobias currently listed on the Internet. They fall into three common types: specific phobia, social phobia, and agoraphobia. Let's look at them one at a time.

Quote

The most common type is a specific phobia, or a simple phobia. As the name suggests, a specific phobia is an unreasonable fear of a specific thing, animal, or situation. Most specific phobias are related to the fear of animals, environments, or bodily harm or injury. Fear of animals is the most common. Which animal is feared most? The results of a 2001 Gallup poll put snakes at the top of the list.

Specific environmental phobias include fear of storms, lightning, thunder, and earthquakes. Others include the fear of school, elevators, cars, airplanes, open spaces, closed spaces, and heights. Specific body phobias include the fear of pain, germs, blood, and terminal illnesses.

The second type of phobia is related to social fear. People with social phobias have intense fear of social situations. An example of an especially difficult social phobia is a situation in which a person thinks that he or she will be watched and judged by others. People with social phobias spend great amounts of time trying to avoid public situations. For some, drinking a cup of coffee or writing a check in public is enough to cause immense fear.

Writing Traits
(Student pages 226–229)

Research Report

Share with students a time when you were motivated to find answers to an important question. Note that people often do not need class deadlines to conduct research. Sometimes our own personal interests drive us to seek out answers.

Ask students to share examples of subjects they have researched on their own. Acknowledge that an assigned report might seem more demanding than independent research; however, any kind of research report can proceed more smoothly if writers first learn specific skills and traits.

Turn students' attention to the traits of a good research report listed on Student page 226. Have one or more volunteers read aloud the traits and their descriptions. Then, discuss with students why someone might use these traits when sharing their findings in writing.

Tell students that they are going to study and use strategies for writing research reports, and that a good research report has the traits listed on Student page 226.

Differentiating Instruction

English-Language Learners **Preteach** key words and concepts that may prevent students from focusing on the writing traits modeled in "Understanding Phobias." Begin by telling students that this report describes types of exaggerated, or overstated, fears called phobias. Point out the quoted definition of *phobia* near the end of the second paragraph. Then, explain that the author organizes her report into three types of phobias:

- Simple, or specific phobias involve the fear of a specific thing or place. For example, some people fear spiders or elevators.
- Social phobias involve peoples' anxiety, or mental distress, about certain social situations, such as giving a speech or going to a party.
- Agoraphobia, in which peoples' fears keep them from leaving home, is the most extreme phobia.

Point out that after describing these phobias, the author discusses their causes, noting that one may be hereditary, or passed from parent to child through genes.

Research Report

According to the American Psychological Association (APA), the most common social phobia is giving a speech in public. However, others include eating in restaurants, attending parties, dating, playing sports, and dancing.

Paraphrase

The third kind of phobia, and the most disabling one, is agoraphobia. Of the people with agoraphobia, women outnumber men two to one. The most common fears suffered by these people are the fear of leaving home and the fear of being in a public place that would be difficult to leave quickly.

Agoraphobia sounds quite similar to social phobia, but they differ in one major way. Although people with social phobias fear looking foolish in public, people with agoraphobia fear having anxiety attacks and losing control. Symptoms of an anxiety attack could include chest pains and a racing heart, shortness of breath, hot or cold flashes, nausea, sweating, and fainting. These symptoms can last from several minutes to several hours. Fearing these symptoms, many people with this phobia do not ever leave home.

What are the causes of all of these phobias? Several theories exist. Among them is the belief that phobias are psychological. Judy Monroe states: *Quote*

Some researchers say that phobias arise when people ignore unresolved problems and conflicts. If someone has a stressful home life, for example, and never gets any help, then that person's anxiety will grow. Over time, that anxiety can change into a phobia. The phobia is the way that person manages the fearful situation. It symbolizes the real fear and allows the person to focus all fear onto one situation or thing. (70–71)

Other researchers believe that people's body chemistry makes them more prone to phobias. Still other researchers say that phobias are hereditary. A person with agoraphobia, for example, often has a parent or other relative who also has the condition.

Another theory states that phobias can be learned, either by watching a family member or by having an unpleasant personal experience. If a person were to become frightened while trapped in an elevator, he or she might develop claustrophobia, an irrational fear of closed spaces.

Yet another theory, offered by Dr. Harold Levinson, states that 90 percent of all phobias are caused by physical problems with the inner ear. Levinson reports that he has helped many patients with a combination of therapy and medicines for inner-ear disorders.

The good news about phobias is that there are many effective ways to treat and to cure them. One of the newest is virtual-reality therapy. The virtual-reality simulator, which works like an arcade game, gradually and safely exposes a person to the situation they most fear. In this way, patients can be exposed to airplanes, elevators, balconies, footbridges, different kinds of audiences, and even a jungle in Vietnam, all without leaving the room.

Well before virtual-reality therapy was invented, therapists were taking their patients on trips to real places. Through the USAir (currently US Airways) Fearful Flyer Program, people with aerophobia actually worked on their fear of flying by taking a short flight with their instructor and classmates.

Doctors prescribe antidepressants and anti-anxiety drugs to some people with phobias. Other treatments include individual therapy, group therapy, and self-help books. Also effective are programs that combine breathing and meditation exercises with vitamins, herbs, and foods that fight stress.

Many researchers feel that the most important way for people to overcome their phobias is to seek help in confronting them. According to an article in *Time International*, "The harder phobics work to avoid the things they fear, the more the brain grows convinced that the threat is real" (60).

Confronting fears helps people with phobias get rid of them. This works in much the same way that turning on the light helps children see that the "monster" in the corner is really a chair piled with clothes. Of course, facing fears isn't easy for patients with phobias. But if done gradually and gently, many can greatly decrease their fears, if not overcome them completely.

Works Consulted *Works Consulted*

Dolliver, Mark. "These Are a Few of Our Least-Favorite Things." *AdWeek* 26 Mar. 2001, eastern ed.: 15.

"Fear Not! PHOBIAS: For Millions of Sufferers, Science Is Offering New Treatments—and New Hope." *Time International* 14 May 2001: 60.

Heller, Sharon, Ph.D. *The Complete Idiot's Guide to Conquering Fear and Anxiety.* New York: Alpha Books, 1999.

Monroe, Judy. *Phobias: Everything You Wanted to Know, But Were Afraid to Ask.* Springfield: Enslow, 1996.

Stern, Richard. *Mastering Phobias: Cases, Causes, and Cures.* New York: Penguin, 1996.

Differentiating Instruction

Support Explain to students that analyzing the structure of "Understanding Phobias" can help them better understand text organization. Help students figure out the purpose of each paragraph within the model by working together to form the Outline below. Remind students that when forming an Outline, Roman numerals stand for main ideas, capital letters stand for paragraph topics, and numbers stand for supporting details.

I. Introduction
   A. Grab attention
II. Fears vs. phobias
   A. Compare definitions
      1. expert quote
      2. types of phobias
III. Types of phobias
   A. Specific phobia
      1. definition and examples
      2. statistic
   B. Specific environmental/body phobias
      1. examples
   C. Social phobia
      1. definition and examples
   D. Most common social phobia
      1. expert paraphrase
   E. Agoraphobia
      1. definition
      2. symptoms
IV. Causes
   A. Psychological
      1. expert quote
   B. Physical/hereditary
      1. example
   C. Learned
      1. example
   D. Inner-ear problems
      1. statistic
      2. expert paraphrase
V. Treatment
   A. Virtual-reality therapy
      1. definition and examples
   B. Therapy
      1. example
   C. Prescription drug therapy
      1. examples
   D. Confrontational help
      1. expert quote
VI. Conclusion
   A. Wrap-up

Research Report
Rubric

The traits of a good research report from page 226 have been used to make the rubric below. By using 1, 2, 3, or 4 check marks to judge each trait, you can decide how well any research report was written.

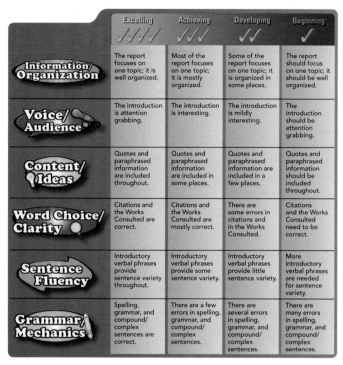

	Excelling ✓✓✓✓	Achieving ✓✓✓	Developing ✓✓	Beginning ✓
Information/Organization	The report focuses on one topic; it is well organized.	Most of the report focuses on one topic; it is mostly organized.	Some of the report focuses on one topic; it is organized in some places.	The report should focus on one topic; it should be well organized.
Voice/Audience	The introduction is attention grabbing.	The introduction is interesting.	The introduction is mildly interesting.	The introduction should be attention grabbing.
Content/Ideas	Quotes and paraphrased information are included throughout.	Quotes and paraphrased information are included in some places.	Quotes and paraphrased information are included in a few places.	Quotes and paraphrased information should be included throughout.
Word Choice/Clarity	Citations and the Works Consulted are correct.	Citations and the Works Consulted are mostly correct.	There are some errors in citations and in the Works Consulted.	Citations and the Works Consulted need to be correct.
Sentence Fluency	Introductory verbal phrases provide sentence variety throughout.	Introductory verbal phrases provide some sentence variety.	Introductory verbal phrases provide little sentence variety.	More introductory verbal phrases are needed for sentence variety.
Grammar/Mechanics	Spelling, grammar, and compound/complex sentences are correct.	There are a few errors in spelling, grammar, and compound/complex sentences.	There are several errors in spelling, grammar, and compound/complex sentences.	There are many errors in spelling, grammar, and compound/complex sentences.

Research Report
Using the Rubric to Study the Model

Now, let's use the rubric to check Julie Fleming's research report, "Understanding Phobias." How many check marks would you give Julie for each trait?

Information/Organization
- The report focuses on one topic.
- The report is well organized.

Julie focuses her report on the topic of phobias. Her paper has a clear introduction, body, and conclusion, and she puts information in a logical order, including subpoints for all of her main points. In this excerpt, Julie breaks the main topic into three subpoints: specific phobias, social phobias, and agoraphobia.

> **[from the writing model]**
>
> There are more than 500 phobias currently listed on the Internet. They fall into three common types: specific phobia, social phobia, and agoraphobia. Let's look at them one at a time.

Voice/Audience
- The introduction is attention grabbing.

Julie captures the audience's interest in her introduction. She describes something everyone can relate to—fears. Then, she hooks readers with specific details.

> **[from the writing model]**
>
> Fears—we all have them. Walking alone at night, crossing dangerous intersections, and speaking in front of a crowd are all common fears. However, fears become abnormal when they become so irrational or exaggerated that a person never leaves the house. That's when fears turn into phobias.

Using the Rubric
(Student page 230)

Explain to students that a rubric is a tool that can be used to evaluate a piece of writing, and that the rubric on Student page 230 can be used to evaluate a research report. Have students note that it is based on the same research report traits listed on Student page 226.

Now point out the terms above each rubric column: *Excelling, Achieving, Developing,* and *Beginning.* Explain that each rubric column symbolizes a degree of writing skill, and that each rubric row focuses on a specific writing trait. When students use the rubric to evaluate their own work at each step of the writing process, they increase the likelihood of producing polished, well-written research reports.

Study the Model
(Student pages 231–233)

Explain that Student pages 231–233 show how the writing model on Student pages 227–229 meets all six traits of the rubric. Read each section with the students. Then, have them look for other examples of each trait in the writing model.

Ask students how many check marks they would assign the writing model for each trait. Then, as a class, decide how the writing model should be rated overall.

To be sure they are meeting all six writing traits, remind students to use the rubric as they write their own research reports.

Research Report

 Content/Ideas
- Quotes and paraphrased information are included throughout.

Julie quotes experts as she discusses different definitions and theories about phobias. She also paraphrases ideas by putting them in her own words. By including ideas from several specialists in the field of mental health, Julie makes her report more credible.

[from the writing model]

According to the American Psychological Association (APA), the most common social phobia is giving a speech in public. However, others include eating in restaurants, attending parties, dating, playing sports, and dancing.

 **Word Choice/Clarity**
- Citations and the Works Consulted are correct.

When Julie uses an exact quotation in the body of her report, she always makes sure to first provide a brief introduction to the quote. Then, she uses parentheses to indicate the page number(s) on which the information can be found in its original source. Julie also includes a list of Works Consulted at the end of her report, so that readers can view full source information.

[from the writing model]

Judy Monroe, author of *Phobias: Everything You Wanted to Know, But Were Afraid to Ask*, quotes Anne Marie Albana at the Center of Stress and Anxiety Disorders at the State University of New York at Albany: "A phobia is an unrealistic fear that is all out of proportion to the actual threat. The fear of spiders, for instance, would be present even when there were no spiders around" (15–16).

 Sentence Fluency
- The report contains introductory verbal phrases, which provide sentence variety.

I appreciate the way Julie uses different types of sentences to make her writing more interesting. This example shows how she uses an introductory verbal phrase to avoid an otherwise wordy sentence.

[from the writing model]

Fearing these symptoms, many people with this phobia do not ever leave home.

 Grammar/Mechanics
- Spelling, punctuation, and capitalization are correct. Compound and complex sentences are formed correctly.

Julie uses the proper conjunctions and punctuation to join compound and complex sentences. Notice how she uses a comma and the conjunction *but* to join these two independent clauses into one compound sentence.

[from the writing model]

Agoraphobia sounds quite similar to social phobia, but they differ in one major way.

This next sentence is a complex sentence with both a dependent and an independent clause, and again, Julie uses a comma to separate the two.

[from the writing model]

According to the American Psychological Association (APA), the most common social phobia is giving a speech in public.

My Turn!

I'm going to write a research report about an interesting topic. I'll follow the rubric and use good writing strategies. Read along to see how I do it.

Differentiating Instruction

English-Language Learners Allow students extra instruction and practice in paraphrasing an author's ideas. First, explain that paraphrasing allows writers to avoid exact quotations that may be overly long or wordy. Model this process by paraphrasing the following quote from the second paragraph of "Understanding Phobias" on Student page 227.

Quote: "A phobia is an unrealistic fear that is all out of proportion to the actual threat. The fear of spiders, for instance, would be present even when there were no spiders around."

Paraphrase: A phobia is an extreme and unrealistic fear. One example is the irrational fear of spiders.

Tell students that the first step in paraphrasing an author's exact words is to internalize its meaning. In other words, to restate an idea, a writer must understand what an author is saying. Remind students that a good paraphrase summarizes the most essential ideas.

Have students practice paraphrasing by restating the quote in the fourth paragraph of "Understanding Phobias" on Student page 228.

Writing a Research Report

Prewriting Gather Information

Information/Organization

Writing Strategy

The report focuses on one topic.

Choose a topic, survey some sources, and make a 3 W's Chart. Then, make note cards.

My teacher told us that we'd be writing research reports. I really like watching the night sky with my telescope, so I decided to choose a topic related to astronomy. I just read an article about deadly asteroid threats, so I chose asteroids as my topic. My first step was to look at books and magazine articles, so I went to the library and searched for information about asteroids. Here's a list of some of the information I read for my report.

Source	Why I Chose It
"Deadly Space Threats Get More Attention." The Columbus Dispatch	Newspaper article about asteroids and comets that could hit Earth
"Danger from the Sky." Cricket	Magazine article about asteroids and meteors
The Search for the Killer Asteroid	Book about the times that asteroids have hit Earth

Practice!

Now it's your turn. Choose a topic and gather information from sources.

Writer's Term

3 W's Chart

A **3 W's Chart** organizes your ideas about a topic. It lists **what** your questions are, **what** information you already know, and **where** you might find answers to your questions.

After I chose my topic and began my research, I decided to make a 3 W's Chart to organize the information that I found. Notice on my chart how some of the information can be found in more than one place. This is good because if I find the same information in different sources, it's probably correct.

3 W's CHART

What are some of my questions?	What do I already know?	Where can I find answers/ explanations?
What are asteroids, and where are they found?	They're pieces of rock that move through space.	The Search for the Killer Asteroid
What are the differences among asteroids, meteoroids, meteors, and meteorites?	I'm not sure—will need to find out.	article in Cricket magazine, The Search for the Killer Asteroid
What important meteorites have hit Earth? What were their effects?	One hit Arizona around 50,000 years ago. It left a huge crater.	Web site on Barringer Meteorite Crater, Cricket article
Why are scientists so concerned about asteroids, and why do they study them so closely?	They're afraid one could slam into Earth and cause mass destruction—and possible extinction.	Internet article from Space.com, newspaper article on space threats, MIT Web site, Cricket article
Is there any way to stop asteroids from slamming into Earth?	I don't know—will need to find out.	The Search for the Killer Asteroid, newspaper article on space threats, Cricket article

Practice!

Now it's your turn. Make a 3 W's Chart to decide what you want to know, what you already know, and where you can find the answers.

Prewriting

(Student pages 234–235)

Help students brainstorm a list of possible topics for their research reports by asking the following: "What are your personal interests?" and "What special knowledge do you have about a particular topic or subject?" and "Is there anything about this topic or subject that you'd like to know more about?" Then, direct students' attention to Briana's words on Student page 234. Point out that Briana chose to use a topic of personal interest as the focus of her research report, and that she then narrowed her topic based on an article she recently had read. Remind students that they can make their research process lively and fun by using a topic of personal interest as the focus of their report.

Now, point out Briana's source notes on Student page 234, focusing on the right-hand column. Explain to students that when surveying sources, they should think about the usefulness and validity of the information being presented. Is it relevant to their topic? Will it help them maintain a narrow research focus? Point out that students will want to use the most recent but accurate sources available at the time of their research.

Finally, direct students' attention to Briana's 3 W's Chart on Student page 235. Tell students they will make similar 3 W's Charts to help them think about what they want to know, what they already know, and where they can find further information about their topic.

More Practice!

For more practice with these writing strategies, you may wish to have students use the Strategy Practice Book. See the appendix for annotated Strategy Practice Book pages.

WORK with a PARTNER

Students with similar interests may benefit from working on their reports in pairs. Make sure partners work together from start to finish, beginning with brainstorming ideas and ending with publishing their work. Help each pair set up an agreeable schedule and division of labor. Follow up with "check-in" conferences as necessary.

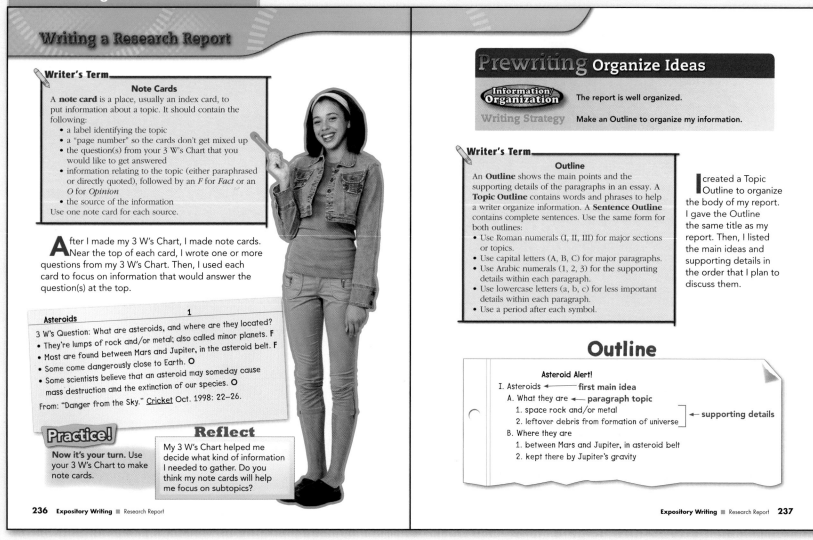

Writing a Research Report

Writer's Term
Note Cards

A **note card** is a place, usually an index card, to put information about a topic. It should contain the following:
- a label identifying the topic
- a "page number" so the cards don't get mixed up
- the question(s) from your 3 W's Chart that you would like to get answered
- information relating to the topic (either paraphrased or directly quoted), followed by an *F* for *Fact* or an *O* for *Opinion*
- the source of the information

Use one note card for each source.

After I made my 3 W's Chart, I made note cards. Near the top of each card, I wrote one or more questions from my 3 W's Chart. Then, I used each card to focus on information that would answer the question(s) at the top.

Asteroids   1

3 W's Question: What are asteroids, and where are they located?
- They're lumps of rock and/or metal; also called minor planets. **F**
- Most are found between Mars and Jupiter, in the asteroid belt. **F**
- Some come dangerously close to Earth. **O**
- Some scientists believe that an asteroid may someday cause mass destruction and the extinction of our species. **O**

From: "Danger from the Sky." *Cricket* Oct. 1998: 22–26.

Practice!
Now it's your turn. Use your 3 W's Chart to make note cards.

Reflect
My 3 W's Chart helped me decide what kind of information I needed to gather. Do you think my note cards will help me focus on subtopics?

Prewriting — Organize Ideas

Information/Organization   The report is well organized.

Writing Strategy   Make an Outline to organize my information.

Writer's Term
Outline

An **Outline** shows the main points and the supporting details of the paragraphs in an essay. A **Topic Outline** contains words and phrases to help a writer organize information. A **Sentence Outline** contains complete sentences. Use the same form for both outlines:
- Use Roman numerals (I, II, III) for major sections or topics.
- Use capital letters (A, B, C) for major paragraphs.
- Use Arabic numerals (1, 2, 3) for the supporting details within each paragraph.
- Use lowercase letters (a, b, c) for less important details within each paragraph.
- Use a period after each symbol.

I created a Topic Outline to organize the body of my report. I gave the Outline the same title as my report. Then, I listed the main ideas and supporting details in the order that I plan to discuss them.

Outline

Asteroid Alert!

I. Asteroids ◄—— first main idea
  A. What they are ◄—— paragraph topic
    1. space rock and/or metal
    2. leftover debris from formation of universe ◄—— supporting details
  B. Where they are
    1. between Mars and Jupiter, in asteroid belt
    2. kept there by Jupiter's gravity

Prewriting
(Student pages 236–237)

Have students read the Writer's Term box on Student page 236 and then review the note card underneath it. Tell students to check the note card against the definition in the box. Then, ask if Briana followed the directions. **yes** Remind students to review the definition and examples on this page as they make their own note cards.

Point out the labels *F* and *O* on Briana's note card and ask students what these letters refer to. **F stands for *Fact*, and O stands for *Opinion*.** Make sure students understand that a fact is a statement that can be proven, whereas an opinion states a writer's thoughts or feelings. Remind students to evaluate their sources as they read to determine whether statements are facts or opinions.

Then, direct students to read the Writer's Term box on Student page 237. Next, have students look over the first part of Briana's Outline on the same page. Point out the difference between the information labeled in Roman numerals, capital letters, and Arabic numbers. Finally, remind students to refer to the Writer's Term box on this page as they draft their own Outlines from the information on their note cards.

Writing a Research Report

II. Differences among asteroids, meteoroids, meteors, meteorites
  A. Meteoroids: pieces of asteroids that have collided
  B. Meteors: meteoroids that fall into Earth's atmosphere
    1. meteors that pass near/over Earth: near-Earth objects (NEOs)
    2. meteors that make bright streaks across sky: shooting, or falling, stars
  C. Meteorites: meteors that fall to Earth
III. Important meteorites that have damaged Earth
  A. Barringer Meteorite Crater, Arizona (a.k.a. Meteor Crater)
    1. hit Earth 50,000 years ago
    2. was traveling 45,000 mph
    3. made a crater 4,150 feet wide and 570 feet deep
    4. meteorite estimated at 100 feet in diameter and 60,000 tons
  B. Tunguska Valley, Siberia
    1. exploded above Earth in 1908
    2. could be seen 466 miles away in daylight
    3. could be felt 50 miles away
    4. started a 30-mile area on fire
  C. Yucatán Peninsula, Mexico
    1. hit Earth 65 million years ago
    2. was 5 miles wide
    3. was traveling 150,000 mph
    4. changed Earth's climate
    5. believed to have caused extinction of dinosaurs
  D. The moon
    1. hit Earth 4.5 billion years ago
    2. was the size of Mars
    3. was traveling 25,000 mph
    4. sent rubble into orbit
    5. orbiting rubble formed the moon
IV. Why scientists are concerned about asteroid activity
  A. Two NEOs passed less than 500,000 miles (6 hours) away
    1. March 1989
    2. October 2001

  B. One NEO passed within 280,000 miles
    1. June 1996
    2. would have been as destructive as all nuclear weapons at once
  C. Earth will be threatened by asteroids again
    1. asteroids 1 kilometer (0.62 miles) across
      a. hit every 100,000 to 300,000 years
      b. would disrupt global climate
      c. could cause extinction of some species
    2. asteroids 100 meters (328 feet) across or larger
      a. hit every 1,000 to 3,000 years
      b. could eliminate a city
      c. could create a tsunami
V. Actions scientists are taking to avoid disaster
  A. Researchers are locating, recording, and rating new asteroids
  B. Scientists are proposing ways of destroying or averting asteroids
    1. attach rocket engine to asteroid and alter its orbit
    2. destroy asteroid with an atomic bomb

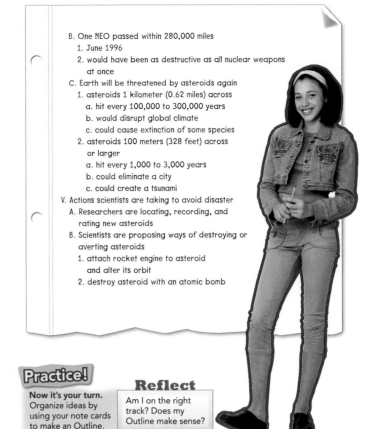

Practice!

Now it's your turn. Organize ideas by using your note cards to make an Outline.

Reflect

Am I on the right track? Does my Outline make sense?

Differentiating Instruction

Support Students may need to review and practice the concepts of fact and opinion. Write the following definitions on the board:

Fact: a statement that can be verified
Opinion: a statement of feeling or belief that cannot be verified

Assess students' understanding by stating the following sentence: *The Ravens won fourteen games this year; the Redwings won ten.* Then, ask whether the following statement is a fact or an opinion: *The Ravens are a better team than the Redwings.* **opinion**

Note that although it can be documented that the Ravens won more games, they are not necessarily a better team.

Explain that the word *better* expresses a subjective judgment and signals that the statement is an opinion. Ask students to reword the sentence and state it as a fact. **Possible response: The Ravens won more games than the Redwings.**

Ask students to name some other words that express opinions. **Possible responses:** *think, feel, usually, beautiful, incredible, awesome, good, awful, sad, great*

Write additional sentences on the board and ask students to identify each one as fact or opinion.

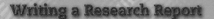

Writing a Research Report

Drafting Write a Draft

Voice/Audience The introduction is attention grabbing.

Writing Strategy Use my Outline to draft my report. Remember to include an introduction that grabs the reader's attention.

Now, I'm ready to write my research report. It's going to be pretty long, so for now, I'll just focus on getting my ideas down. I'll do my best with spelling and grammar, but I can fine-tune everything later on.

I checked the rubric, and it says that my introduction should grab the reader's attention. But how should I do that? I could start with a surprising quote or fact, but since I plan on including a lot of facts in the body of my writing, I don't really want to begin that way. I mean, I know this is a fact-based research paper, but that doesn't mean my opening paragraph can't be fun.

I've got an idea! I've always thought it would be fun to be a TV news announcer, so I think I'll open with a news scene.

Proofreading Marks

⌐ Indent	ℓ Take out something
≡ Make a capital	⊙ Add a period
/ Make a small letter	(SP) Spelling error
∧ Add something	¶ New paragraph

[DRAFT]

Asteroid Alert! [attention-grabbing introduction]

by Briana

"We interupt this program to bring you a special report. Scientists at the University of Arizona's Spacewatch center have downgraded their previous Torino Scale rating of Asteroid 2003CB from 1 to 0. This means that the likelihood of the asteroid's collision with Earth is less likely than something the same size hitting Earth within the next few decades. Citizens all over the globe can now breathe easier as they look into friendlier skies. . . . And now we return you to your regularly scheduled program."

Is the paragraph fact or fiction? It's hard to tell. That's because it's filled with facts. For one, there really is a Spacewatch center in Arizona where scientists study the skies for asteroid "attacks" and near misses. For another, the torino scale exists, too. Adopted in 1999 the scale is used to measure and categorize the risk that asteroids and other near Earth objects (NEOs) pose to Earth.

Practice!

Now it's your turn. Draft an introduction using interesting details to capture your reader's attention.

Drafting

(Student pages 240–243)

Remind students that drafting is a chance to get ideas on paper without having to worry about making mistakes.

Read aloud Briana's words on Student page 240. Then, refer to the Practice box on Student page 241 that reminds students to use interesting details to capture readers' attention. Discuss with students various ways to spark readers' interest. Then, have them work in pairs or small groups to brainstorm ideas for interesting introductions.

Also point out how Briana used her Outline to draft her research report. Suggest that students review both the Outline and the report, side by side. This method will help them evaluate how well Briana stuck to her Outline and whether she made adjustments as she wrote. Remind students to use their Outlines to draft their own research reports, keeping in mind that they should feel free to change the order of details as they write.

Finally, point out that Briana repeatedly refers to the rubric as she writes. Encourage students to get into the habit of using the rubric to help guide their own writing.

Writing Across the Curriculum

Science/Social Studies Encourage students who are writing science or social-studies related reports to note questions raised by their research. Explain that keeping track of these questions can help them get more out of their research as well as provide possible topics for future research assignments. Remind students that these further research topics should be ones that go beyond the scope of their current reports. To illustrate this concept, ask students to identify the information in Briana's research report that could prompt further research. **Possible responses: the Spacewatch center in Arizona; careers in astronomy; a day in the life of a scientist at a space observatory**

Writing a Research Report

[DRAFT]

Just what are asteroids, and why are they important? Simply put, asteroids are pieces of space rock, or metal, or both. Also called planetoids or minor planets, they range in size from just a few yards across to several hundred miles across.

Many scientists believe that asteroids are leftover "space debris" from some heavenly bodies that collided when the universe formed. Most asteroids are located between the orbits of Mars and Jupiter in an area known as the asteroid belt. They are located there because Jupiter's gravitational pull on the asteroids is stronger than any other planet's. When Jupiter's orbit changes, an asteroid's orbit also will change, and it will be pulled into another planet's orbit. When an asteroid gets pulled into Earth's orbit, it will begin to travel toward Earth. This is why an asteroid sometimes gets close to, or even crashes into, Earth.

What are meteoroids, meteors, and meteorites? When asteroids collide with each other they shatter into smaller pieces called meteoroids. These meteoroids sometimes fall into Earth's atmosphere. When they do they are called meteors. Meteors that pass near Earth are called near Earth objects, or NEOs. The ones that burn up as they streak brightly across the sky are called shooting stars. The ones that hit Earth before they burn up are called meteorites.

[DRAFT]

Some meteorites have been large enough to form craters when they hit Earth. The best example of a crater is the Barringer Meteorite Crater in Arizona. (It is also known as the Meteor Crater.) About 50,000 years ago, a meteorite traveling almost 45,000 miles per hour struck Arizona in the area between what are now the towns of Winslow and Flagstaff. It created a crater about 4,150 feet wide and 570 feet deep. Scientists estimate that the meteorite was 100 feet in diameter and 60,000 tons in weight.

Another meteorite exploded several miles above the Tunguska Valley in Siberia in 1908. This explosion was so bright that it could be seen 466 miles away in broad daylight. The explosion was so powerful that it could be felt as far as 50 miles away. It also started a forest fire 30 miles wide.

Practice!

Now it's your turn. Use the information in your Outline to draft your research report.

Reflect

What do you think? Will my introduction grab the reader's attention?

Differentiating Instruction

Support Some students may benefit from extra help in developing an attention-grabbing introduction. Prompt students' creativity by providing the following ideas for alternative introductions to Briana's report.

- Create an alternative imaginary scene in which astronauts in a spaceship encounter asteroids while on a mission.
- Draw readers in by posing an interesting question such as, *Do you think it's possible for an asteroid to collide with Earth?*
- Find and include a controversial quote about the possibility of an asteroid attack.

- Create a brief conversation in which two scientists are studying an asteroid that's heading for Earth.
- Include an intriguing description of the Meteor Crater.

Have pairs of students brainstorm introductions for their own research reports. Suggest that they develop one idea based on each of the techniques listed above. Then, they can choose the best one to use in their reports.

Writing a Research Report

Revising Extend Writing

Content/Ideas Quotes and paraphrased information are included throughout.

Writing Strategy Add quotes and paraphrased information from experts.

Writer's Term

Paraphrase/Plagiarize
To **paraphrase** is to restate the meaning of a particular passage in your own words. Don't **plagiarize**! To plagiarize means to present another person's writing as your own work.

The rubric says that a good research report includes quotes and paraphrased information. When I finished my draft, I reread it and realized that I hadn't included any quotes at all. I'm no expert, so quoting specialists should make my report more credible. But I didn't want to add just any old quotes. I knew they should add to the information I already had, so I went back through my note cards and found some good information.

I know I have to be careful not to use an author's words without giving proper credit, so I'll make sure to introduce quotes properly. After all, I don't want to get into trouble for stealing another person's work!

244 Expository Writing ■ Research Report

[DRAFT]

Although scientists often disagree on how much money and time should be spent tracking NEOs, most agree that Earth could someday be threatened by a devastating asteroid.

What actions are being taken to avoid NEO crashes? Researchers all over the world are continuing to locate new asteroids. Once located, each asteroid's size and orbit is measured and recorded.

[added quotes] According to an article written by Robert Roy Britt, a collision with a large asteroid "would rock the planet, disrupt the global climate for years, and could render some species extinct." Britt also says, "Such an event could eliminate a city or create a tsunami that might inundate shore communities and even large cities along multiple coastlines."

Practice!

Now it's your turn. Add quotes and paraphrased information to support your main points.

Reflect

What do you think? Did the added quotes help strengthen the point I was trying to make?

Expository Writing ■ Research Report **245**

Revising

(Student pages 244–245)

Ask students to consider their reactions when they come across quotations in a piece of informational writing. Note that ideas and quotes from experts lend an air of authority to a report.

Refer students to the Writer's Term box on Student page 244. Then, ask a volunteer to describe the difference between an exact quotation and a paraphrased statement. **A quotation is a person's exact words, and a paraphrase is a restatement of someone else's ideas in the writer's own words.** Remind students that whenever they use someone else's exact words in their writing, they must put them in quotation marks and credit the source. Point out that even when they paraphrase text, they must credit the source (without the use of quotes) to avoid accusations of plagiarism.

Have students read Briana's words on Student page 244 and the section of her draft on Student page 245. Call attention to the exact quotes that Briana added to her draft, and discuss what these revisions add to Briana's writing. Then, have students look for places in their own research reports where they can add quotations or paraphrases.

Differentiating Instruction

Support Explain to students that they will need to decide which resources provide the best information for their report. They should consider the following when selecting their sources: the date of the publication, the author's credentials, the tone and bias of the source, and the documentation that backs up the information. Also, students should scrutinize Internet sources to avoid opinionated sites in lieu of sites that are backed up by credible organizations or universities.

Have students use these guidelines to evaluate sources. Then you can review their findings, using any questionable choices as examples for the whole group.

Writing a Research Report

Revising Clarify Writing

Word Choice/Clarity   Citations and the Works Consulted are correct.

Writing Strategy   Make sure I have cited all quotes correctly. Then, make my list of Works Consulted.

After I added quotes and paraphrased information, I checked the rubric one more time. It says to make sure all quotes are cited correctly. Anytime I use a quote without introducing it with the author's name, article, or book title, I know I should add that information in parentheses at the end of the quote. I should also include a list of Works Consulted at the end of my report, so that readers will know the full source information for each source I used in my report.

Writer's Term

Citing Sources: Works Consulted

When **citing sources,** list where you found borrowed information. The examples below show how to present this information in a list of **Works Consulted**. Place the list at the end of your paper, and include each source used, regardless of whether direct quotes were pulled from that source. Pay special attention to the order of the information and the use of punctuation. Listings in a Works Consulted are arranged alphabetically according to authors' last names. When there is no author, use the first word in the title. In addition, use the styles shown here.

To cite a book:
Author's last name, author's first name. *Book title.* City of publication: Publisher, date of publication.

To cite a magazine or a newspaper article:
Author's last name, author's first name. "Article title." *Magazine/newspaper title* Date of publication: page number(s).

To cite an article in an on-line periodical:
Author's last name, author's first name. "Article title." *On-line periodical title* Date of publication. Date of access <Web address>.

To cite a Web site:
Author's last name, author's first name. *Web site title.* Date of last update. Sponsor of Web site. Date of access <Web address>.

[DRAFT]   [added Works Consulted]

Works Consulted ←

Bridges, Andrew. "Deadly Space Threats Get More Attention." The Columbus Dispatch 13 May 2001: C4.
Britt, Robert Roy. "Asteroid Discoveries May Outpace Ability to Assess Threat to Earth." Space.com 19 Oct. 2001. 20 Oct. 2006 <http://www.space.com/scienceastronomy/solarsystem/asteroid.html>.
"Danger from the Sky." Cricket Oct. 1998: 22–26.
"MIT Researcher Creates Scale to Assess Earth-Asteroid Close Encounters." MIT News 22 July 1999. 20 Oct. 2006 <http://web.mit.edu/newsoffice/nr/1999/asteroid.html>.
Vogt, Gregory L. The Search for the Killer Asteroid. Brookfield: Millbrook, 1994.
What is the Barringer Meteorite Crater? 1998. The Cyrus Company. 20 Oct. 2006 <http://www.barringercrater.com/science/main/htm>.

Practice!

Now it's your turn. Make sure that you correctly cite quotes and include a Works Consulted at the end of your report.

Reflect
Did I format my Works Consulted correctly?

Revising

(Student pages 246–247)

Have students review Briana's words at the top of Student page 246. Ask students to summarize the two main points Briana makes. 1) If a quote is introduced without information about the author or source, include those facts in parentheses at the end of the quote. 2) Include a list of Works Consulted at the end of the report.

Refer students to the Writer's Term box on Student page 246. Have them review the text and read Briana's draft on Student page 247. Ask students to check each source on the list against the guidelines on the previous Student page. For each item, have students note the type of source and whether it is formatted correctly. Remind students to refer to Student pages 246–247 as they draft their own lists of Works Consulted.

Differentiating Instruction

Support   Some students may benefit from direct instruction and repetition of the writing traits. Begin by dividing the class into groups of three and making enough copies of students' research reports for each student in the group. Then, display the rubric in an enlarged form on chart paper, highlighting the Content/Ideas trait. Choose one report to review together first. Then, use words like the following to model the trait:

When I look at the rubric, the Content/Ideas trait says quotes and paraphrased information should be included throughout. I'll review my report with this in mind. In the fourth paragraph, I see one place where a quote could add specific detail and reinforce the main idea . . .

Using the same report, go around the group, having each student model the other traits. Coach students as needed, discussing together how to apply the rubric. Convene this "trait group" each day until the group finishes reviewing all the research reports.

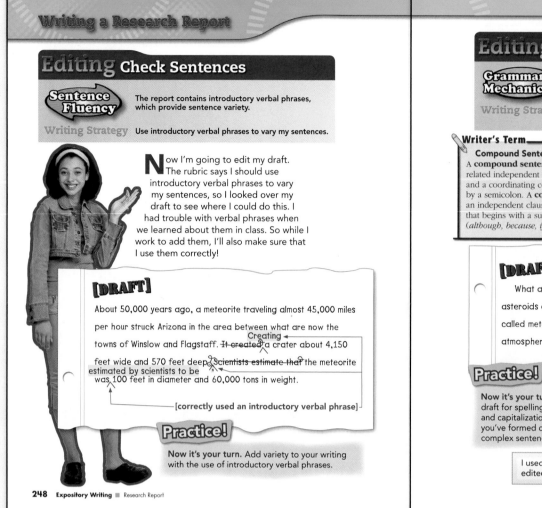

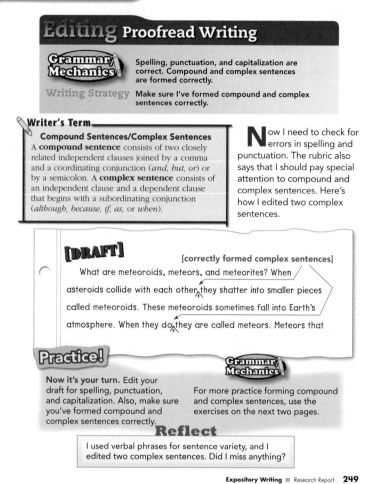

Editing

(Student pages 248–249)

Call students' attention to the edits Briana made to her draft on Student page 248. Note that in the process of editing, she made several changes. Explain to students that when creating an introductory verbal phrase, they will often have to make several edits to make sure the phrase describes the subject of the sentence and not the object. Remind students that the focus of the last chapter's grammar lesson was introductory verbal phrases and that they should refer to Student pages 215–217 if they need further help. Have students begin checking their own research reports for places where adding introductory verbal phrases will create more variety. Remind them to revise correctly, making sure that the subject in any edited sentence remains consistent.

Now, point out the Writer's Term box on Student page 249, and ask a volunteer to read it aloud. Then, have students note how Briana edited her draft so that complex sentences were punctuated correctly. Have them review her edits and discuss whether or not these changes match the guidelines in the box. Finally, have students check

their drafts to make sure they have formed compound and complex sentences correctly. Remind them that they should also check their spelling, capitalization, and punctuation.

If any of your students are having trouble understanding how to form compound and complex sentences, you may wish to teach the Mini-Lesson on pages 185–186 of this Teacher Edition. Then, have students complete the exercises on Student pages 250–251. Review the answers and possible rewrites with them.

WORK with a PARTNER
Have pairs of students read one another's drafts, using sticky notes to mark errors in spelling, punctuation, and grammar. Tell students to perform a second read that focuses on the editing strategies they learned in this chapter.

Compound and Complex Sentences

KNOW the RULE

A **compound sentence** consists of two closely related independent clauses. An independent clause can stand alone as a sentence, but two independent clauses should be joined by a comma and a coordinating conjunction (*and, but, or*) or by a semicolon.

Example: An NEO passes Earth, **but** a meteorite hits it.
Example: An NEO passes Earth; a meteorite hits it.

A **complex sentence** consists of an independent clause and a dependent clause joined by a comma. A dependent clause cannot stand alone as a sentence because it begins with a subordinating conjunction such as *although, because,* or *when.*

Example: Because some asteroids are potentially harmful, scientists keep watching the skies.
Example: When an asteroid poses no threat to Earth, it gets a Torino rating of 0.

Practice the Rule

Number a separate sheet of paper 1–5. Read the sentences below. Write *CX* if the sentence is complex. Write *CD* if the sentence is compound. Then, copy each dependent clause onto the paper.

1. The Torino Impact Hazard Scale is relatively new; it was adopted in 1999.
2. It was developed by Richard Binzel; he worked on it for several years.
3. Because so many new asteroids were being discovered, Binzel felt the need to help the public understand them.
4. When a new asteroid is discovered, scientists gather information about it.
5. They calculate where the asteroid will be in the future, and they assign a rating to it.

Apply the Rule

Read the research report, looking for errors in the use of compound/complex sentences. Then, rewrite the passage correctly on a separate sheet of paper.

A meteor is the streak of light that appears when a meteorite, an actual piece of falling rock, enters Earth's atmosphere. Meteorites are genuine bits of our solar system. Most of them have broken off of asteroids, which are space rocks that are too small to be classified as planets. Some meteorites come from comets, which are balls of ice and frozen gas.

When a meteor shower occurs the sky lights up with thousands of meteor trails. Scientists use the path of Earth's rotation to predict these spectacular light shows, which repeat each year as the planet crosses the path of a comet.

Regular meteor showers have names that come from the constellations that produce them. Because it originates in the constellation Leo one shower is called the Leonids. You can find out when the Leonids and other regular meteor showers are scheduled to appear by checking one of several sources. Weather forecasters keep track of these displays and you can also check for schedules on Web sites such as www.nasa.com.

(Student pages 250–251)

Compound and Complex Sentences

Explain to students that when checking to see if they have formed compound and complex sentences correctly, they should understand basic sentence parts. Have them read the Know the Rule box on Student page 250. Then, discuss its contents with the students.

Ask students to define a compound sentence. **It consists of two closely related independent clauses joined by either a semicolon or a comma and a coordinating conjunction.** Make sure students understand that an independent clause is a simple sentence. Then, have students reread the first half of the Know the Rule box, noting the guidelines for how to join two independent clauses.

Now, write the following complex sentence on the board: *Because Amy loves astronomy, she plans to study science in college.* Have students name the two parts of this sentence. **The first half is a dependent clause, and the second** half is an independent clause. Then, ask how a dependent clause differs from an independent clause. **A dependent clause cannot stand alone as a sentence.** Underline the word *Because* and note that this word is a subordinating conjunction. Display other subordinating conjunctions such as *although, if, as,* and *when.* Note that a dependent clause always begins with a subordinating conjunction. Remind students that when a complex sentence begins with a dependent clause, the clause is always followed by a comma.

Answers for Practice the Rule

1. CD
2. CD
3. CX; Because so many new asteroids were being discovered,
4. CX; When a new asteroid is discovered,
5. CD

 For more practice with grammar/mechanics skills, see Zaner-Bloser's *G.U.M.* materials.

(Answers continue on page 186.)

Writing a Research Report

Publishing Share Writing

Include my report as part of a multimedia presentation.

I finished my research report, and now I want to publish it. I could show it to some classmates or read it aloud. But I think my report begs for multimedia! I can sit at a desk in the front of the classroom like a TV reporter and deliver the special announcement in the beginning of my report. Then, I can move away from the desk and present the rest of my report as a slide show. Before I do this, though, I'll read through my paper one last time to make sure it includes all of the items on my checklist.

My Checklist

✓ The report includes one well-organized topic.

✓ The introduction grabs the reader's attention.

✓ Quotes and paraphrased information support main points.

✓ All quotes are cited correctly, and the Works Consulted is well formatted.

✓ Introductory verbal phrases add sentence variety.

✓ Spelling, capitalization, and punctuation are all correct. Compound and complex sentences are also used correctly.

Practice!

Now it's your turn. Make a checklist to check your research report. Then, make a final draft to publish.

Asteroid Alert!

by Briana

"We interrupt this program to bring you a special report. Scientists at the University of Arizona's Spacewatch center have downgraded their previous Torino Scale rating of Asteroid 2003CB from 1 to 0. This means that the likelihood of the asteroid's collision with Earth is less likely than something the same size hitting Earth within the next few decades. Citizens all over the globe can now breathe easier as they look into friendlier skies. . . . And now we return you to your regularly scheduled program."

Is the paragraph fact or fiction? It's hard to tell. That's because it's filled with facts. For one, there really is a Spacewatch center in Arizona where scientists study the skies for asteroid "attacks" and near-misses. For another, the Torino Scale exists, too. Adopted in 1999, the scale is used to measure and categorize the risk that asteroids and other near-Earth objects (NEOs) pose to Earth.

Just what are asteroids, and why are they important? Simply put, asteroids are pieces of space rock, or metal, or both. Also called planetoids or minor planets, they range in size from just a few yards across to several hundred miles across.

Many scientists believe that asteroids are leftover "space debris" from some heavenly bodies that collided when the universe formed. Most asteroids are located between the orbits of Mars and Jupiter in an area known as the asteroid belt. They are located there because Jupiter's gravitational pull on the asteroids is stronger than any other planet's. When Jupiter's orbit changes, an asteroid's orbit will also change, and it will be pulled into another planet's orbit. When an asteroid gets pulled into Earth's orbit, it will begin to travel toward Earth. This is why an asteroid sometimes gets close to, or even crashes into, Earth.

What are meteoroids, meteors, and meteorites? When asteroids collide with each other, they shatter into smaller pieces called meteoroids. These meteoroids sometimes fall into Earth's atmosphere. When they do, they are called meteors. Meteors that pass near Earth are called near-Earth objects, or NEOs. The ones that burn up as they streak brightly across the sky are called shooting stars. The ones that hit Earth before they burn up are called meteorites.

Some meteorites have been large enough to form craters when they hit Earth. The best example of a crater is the Barringer Meteorite Crater in Arizona. (It is also known as the Meteor Crater.) About 50,000 years ago, a meteorite traveling almost 45,000 miles per hour struck Arizona in the area between what

---

(Answers continued from page 185.)

Answers for Apply the Rule

A meteor is the streak of light that appears when a meteorite, an actual piece of falling rock, enters Earth's atmosphere. Meteorites are genuine bits of our solar system. Most of them have broken off of asteroids, which are space rocks that are too small to be classified as planets. Some meteorites come from comets, which are balls of ice and frozen gas.

When a meteor shower occurs, the sky lights up with thousands of meteor trails. Scientists use the path of Earth's rotation to predict these spectacular light shows, which repeat each year as the planet crosses the path of a comet.

Regular meteor showers have names that come from the constellations that produce them. Because it originates in the constellation Leo, one shower is called the Leonids. You can find out when the Leonids and other regular meteor showers are scheduled to appear by checking one of several sources. Weather forecasters keep track of these displays; you can also check for schedules on Web sites such as www.nasa.com.

Publishing

(Student pages 252–253)

Ask students if they like Briana's choice for sharing her research report. Tell the class that her choice is not the only option for publishing her report. Invite students to name other ways they could publish their own research reports.

Have each student make a checklist and peform a final evaluation of his or her report before publishing it. Encourage students to share copies of their reports with friends and relatives who might be interested in reading about what they wrote.

Writing a Research Report

are now the towns of Winslow and Flagstaff. Creating a crater about 4,150 feet wide and 570 feet deep, the meteorite was estimated by scientists to be 100 feet in diameter and 60,000 tons in weight.

Another meteorite exploded several miles above the Tunguska Valley in Siberia in 1908. This explosion was so bright that it could be seen 466 miles away in broad daylight. The explosion was so powerful that it could be felt as far as 50 miles away. It also started a forest fire 30 miles wide.

An even more important impact happened 65 million years ago. Scientists believe that an asteroid at least five miles wide crashed into Mexico's Yucatán Peninsula at about 150,000 miles per hour. This crash sent dust and other debris high into Earth's atmosphere. The debris blocked so much of the sunlight for so long that Earth's climate changed entirely. Much of the plant life died. This caused the plant-eating dinosaurs to die off. This, in turn, caused the meat-eating dinosaurs to die off because their food supply had disappeared.

Many astronomers believe that the most violent asteroid impact of all might have occurred 4.5 billion years ago. At that time, an asteroid the size of Mars traveled more than 25,000 miles per hour before smashing into Earth. This sent a huge amount of rubble into orbit. For a while, the rubble just continued to orbit Earth. Over time, however, due in part to Earth's gravitational pull, the rubble came together and formed the moon.

Because of many NEOs' potential for destruction, scientists all over the world have become concerned about asteroids. Two particularly frightening NEOs, sighted in March 1989 and October 2001, sped past Earth at a distance of less than 500,000 miles—twice the distance to the moon—and missed a collision with Earth by a mere six hours.

In June 1996, an even scarier near-miss occurred when Asteroid 1996 JA1 passed within only 280,000 miles of Earth. Scientists estimate that if that asteroid had crashed into Earth, it would have had as much destructive power as all the nuclear weapons on Earth exploding at the same time.

Although scientists often disagree on how much money and time should be spent tracking NEOs, most agree that Earth could someday be threatened by a devastating asteroid. According to an article written by Robert Roy Britt, a collision with a large asteroid "would rock the planet, disrupt the global climate for years, and could render some species extinct." Britt also says, "Such an event could eliminate a city or create a tsunami that might inundate shore communities and even large cities along multiple coastlines."

What actions are being taken to avoid NEO crashes? Researchers all over the world are continuing to locate new asteroids. Once located, each asteroid's size and orbit is measured and recorded. Then, the asteroid is assigned a rating on the Torino Scale, which, according to Carl Pilcher, Science Director for solar system exploration in the NASA Office of Space Science in Washington, D.C., "is a major advance in our ability to explain the hazard posed by a particular NEO." Carl further explains, "If we ever find an object with a greater value than one, the scale will be an effective way to communicate the resulting risk" ("MIT").

Scientists are also proposing ways to destroy or avert devastating NEOs that might be on their way to Earth. One proposal is to attach rocket engines to the asteroids to alter their orbit and move them out of Earth's path. Another proposal is to destroy the asteroids with spacecraft loaded with atomic bombs.

Scientists remain alert, but fortunately, Earth has not had to take on an NEO yet. Thankfully, "the attack of the killer asteroid" is still only fiction.

Works Consulted

Bridges, Andrew. "Deadly Space Threats Get More Attention." *The Columbus Dispatch* 13 May 2001: C4.

Britt, Robert Roy. "Asteroid Discoveries May Outpace Ability to Assess Threat to Earth." *Space.com* 19 Oct. 2001. 20 Oct. 2006 <http://www.space.com/scienceastronomy/solarsystem/asteroid.html>.

"Danger from the Sky." *Cricket* Oct. 1998: 22–26.

"MIT Researcher Creates Scale to Assess Earth-Asteroid Close Encounters." *MIT News* 22 July 1999. 20 Oct. 2006 <http://web.mit.edu/newsoffice/nr/1999/asteroid.html>.

Vogt, Gregory L. *The Search for the Killer Asteroid.* Brookfield: Millbrook, 1994.

What is the Barringer Meteorite Crater? 1998. The Cyrus Company. 20 Oct. 2006 <http://www.barringercrater.com/science/main/htm>.

Reflect

What do you think? Did I use all of the traits of a good research report in my writing? Check it against the rubric. Don't forget to use the rubric to check your own report, too.

Publishing

(Student pages 254–255)

Call students' attention to the Reflect box on the bottom of Student page 255. Explain that assessing Briana's research report against the rubric will help them better understand how to apply the traits to their own work. Then, have students use sticky notes to mark at least one example of each trait in Briana's writing. Tell them to include an evaluation on each note.

After this process, have students assess how well they were able to identify each trait in Briana's writing and how easy or difficult it was to use the rubric. Remind them to apply what they learned from Briana's work when they use the rubric to check their own writing.

Designing an Interdisciplinary Unit

by Ken Stewart, *Master Teacher*

In an interdisciplinary unit, two or more educational disciplines are connected. With this in mind, always look for natural connections in all subject areas to show students that what they are learning is meaningful. When planning such a unit, follow these helpful hints:

1. Decide on an appropriate theme/topic for your grade level.

2. Establish your goals and objectives.

3. Decide how many disciplines the unit will encompass.

4. Meet with other teachers involved to get a general understanding of their goals and objectives.

5. Write out detailed lesson plans (with dates) including a culminating event that brings all disciplines together. (Each teacher must do this.)

6. Meet a second time with everyone involved to discuss specific plans and assignments.

7. Decide on your evaluation methods.

8. Present the unit to your class and ask for their suggestions.

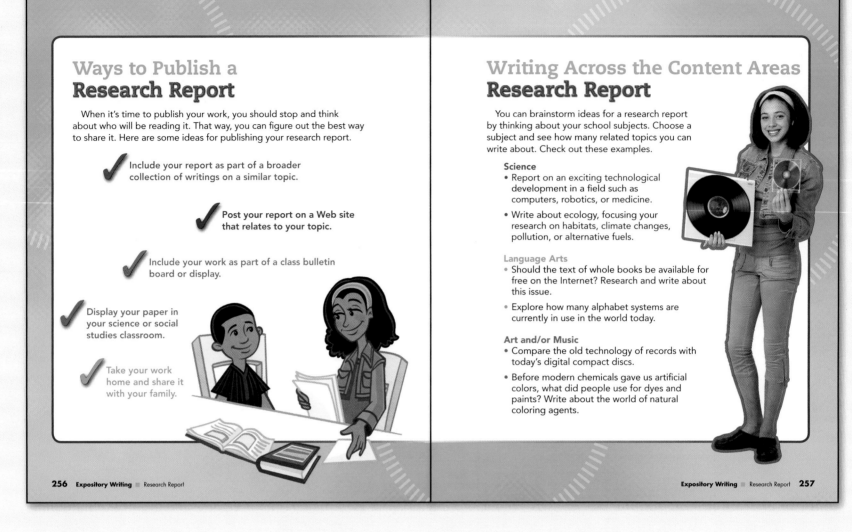

Ways to Publish a
Research Report

When it's time to publish your work, you should stop and think about who will be reading it. That way, you can figure out the best way to share it. Here are some ideas for publishing your research report.

✓ Include your report as part of a broader collection of writings on a similar topic.

✓ Post your report on a Web site that relates to your topic.

✓ Include your work as part of a class bulletin board or display.

✓ Display your paper in your science or social studies classroom.

✓ Take your work home and share it with your family.

256   Expository Writing ▪ Research Report

Writing Across the Content Areas
Research Report

You can brainstorm ideas for a research report by thinking about your school subjects. Choose a subject and see how many related topics you can write about. Check out these examples.

Science
• Report on an exciting technological development in a field such as computers, robotics, or medicine.
• Write about ecology, focusing your research on habitats, climate changes, pollution, or alternative fuels.

Language Arts
• Should the text of whole books be available for free on the Internet? Research and write about this issue.
• Explore how many alphabet systems are currently in use in the world today.

Art and/or Music
• Compare the old technology of records with today's digital compact discs.
• Before modern chemicals gave us artificial colors, what did people use for dyes and paints? Write about the world of natural coloring agents.

Expository Writing ▪ Research Report   257

Ways to Publish
(Student page 256)

Read and discuss with students the publishing options listed on Student page 256. Encourage students to consider some of these options when publishing their own writing. Remind students that Briana chose to publish her research report by including it as part of a multimedia presentation, but they can choose their own way of publishing. Perhaps one student will want to include his or her report as part of a class bulletin board or display, while another will want to post it on a Web site.

Writing Across the Content Areas
(Student page 257)

Explain to students that writing is not just for English or language arts class. Many other school subjects contain ideas, issues, and events that students may want to write about. Encourage students to consider using one of the content areas listed on Student page 257 as a springboard for more writing options. Students may also wish to consult with other teachers for more ideas on writing in the content areas.

Books for Professional Development

McCarthy, Tara. *Expository Writing (Grades 4–8).* **New York: Scholastic, 1999.**

This complete resource includes great activities, models, and reproducibles for helping students with their expository writing skills. They'll learn how to write accurate messages and announcements, well-organized expository paragraphs, and successful reports. The book includes independent learning ideas, reinforcement activities, and self-assessment pages.

Strausser, Jeffrey. *Painless Writing.* **Hauppauge: Barron's Educational Series, 2001.**

This textbook supplement is designed especially for classroom use with middle school and high school students. Its approach is meant to appeal to students who find the subject of writing boring, too difficult, or both. The author is an experienced educator who gives practical advice that transforms essay writing into a satisfying experience for students. He offers tips on enlivening writing by adding vivid words and rhythm, smoothing out sentences, and silencing the dull passive voice.

Peha, Steve, and Margot Carmichael Lester. *Be a Better Writer: Power Tools for Young Writers!* **Bend: The Leverage Factory, 2006.**

Packed with practical tips and techniques to help young writers build a solid foundation, this fun, easy-to-use guide is a comprehensive introduction to the world of the written word. Students will learn how to generate interesting ideas, how to use descriptive detail, and how to beat writer's block. They will also learn how to perform the five most important types of revision.

Murray, Donald M. *Shoptalk: Learning to Write with Writers.* **Portsmouth: Boynton/Cook, 1990.**

This collection of quotations is taken from a wide variety of writers on all aspects of the writing process. It includes comments from writers both famous and obscure. One example is James Thurber's "Don't get it right, get it written."

How-To Guide Overview

In this chapter, students will learn how to write a how-to guide. They will learn the different elements of a how-to guide—explanation, sequence, friendly tone, and visual aids—and some reasons why they might choose to write one. Students will then use a how-to guide rubric to study a model writing sample.

Students will follow the student guide as she goes through the writing stages—prewriting, drafting, revising, editing, and publishing. As the student guide learns new writing strategies in each step, students will be directed to practice the strategies in their own writing.

During prewriting and drafting, students will

- choose a process to explain, and list the main steps in the process.
- make a Sequence Chain to sequence steps.

- write a draft using a friendly tone to explain each step to the reader.

During revising and editing, students will

- add pictures and explanative details.
- make sure all jargon has been explained.
- use compound and complex sentences for variety.
- edit their drafts for spelling, capitalization, and punctuation, making sure appositives have been set off with commas.

Finally, students will write a final draft to be published.

You may wish to send to families the School-Home Connection Letter for this chapter, located at the end of this unit in the Teacher Edition.

How-To Guide Writing Traits

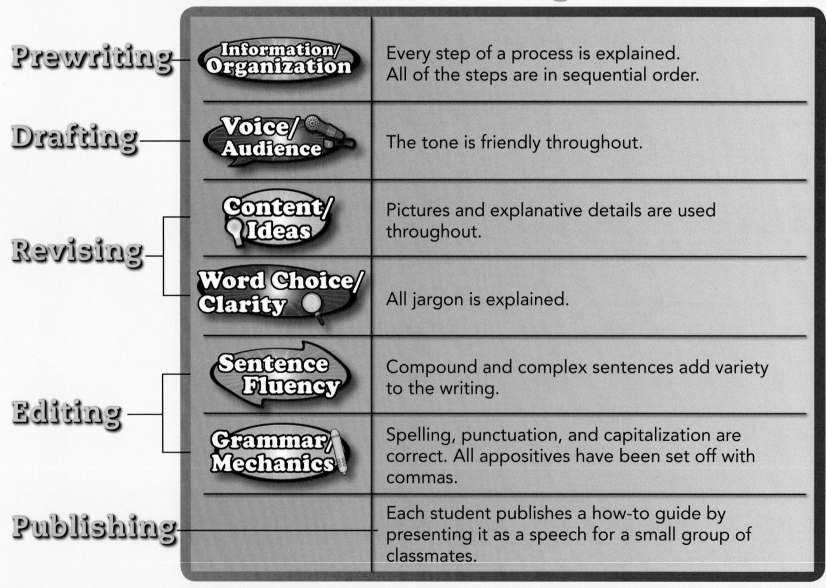

Prewriting	**Information/Organization**	Every step of a process is explained. All of the steps are in sequential order.
Drafting	**Voice/Audience**	The tone is friendly throughout.
Revising	**Content/Ideas**	Pictures and explanative details are used throughout.
	Word Choice/Clarity	All jargon is explained.
Editing	**Sentence Fluency**	Compound and complex sentences add variety to the writing.
	Grammar/Mechanics	Spelling, punctuation, and capitalization are correct. All appositives have been set off with commas.
Publishing		Each student publishes a how-to guide by presenting it as a speech for a small group of classmates.

How-To Guide Time Management

WEEK 1

Day 1	Day 2	Day 3	Day 4	Day 5
Learning Objectives				
Students will: • learn the components of a how-to guide.	Students will: • learn how to gather information for a how-to guide.	Students will: • practice gathering information for their own how-to guides.	Students will: • learn how to make a Sequence Chain to sequence steps.	Students will: • practice making a Sequence Chain to sequence steps.
Activities				
• Discuss the elements and traits of a how-to guide (Student pages 258–260). • Use the rubric to study the model (Student pages 261–267).	• Read and discuss **Prewriting: Gather Information** (Student page 268).	• Choose a process to explain. • List the main steps in the process.	• Read and discuss **Prewriting: Organize Ideas** (Student page 269).	• Review the steps listed while gathering information. • Make a Sequence Chain to arrange steps.

WEEK 2

Day 1	Day 2	Day 3	Day 4	Day 5
Learning Objectives				
Students will: • learn how to use a friendly tone.	Students will: • practice writing their own drafts.	Students will: • learn how to add pictures and explanative details.	Students will: • practice adding pictures and explanative details.	Students will: • learn how to explain jargon.
Activities				
• Read and discuss **Drafting: Write a Draft** (Student pages 270–271).	• Use a Sequence Chain to write a draft. • Use a friendly tone to explain each step to the reader.	• Read and discuss **Revising: Extend Writing** (Student pages 272–273).	• Add pictures and explanative details.	• Read and discuss **Revising: Clarify Writing** (Student pages 274–275).

WEEK 3

Day 1	Day 2	Day 3	Day 4	Day 5
Learning Objectives				
Students will: • practice explaining jargon.	Students will: • learn how to use compound and complex sentences for variety.	Students will: • learn how to set off appositives with commas.	Students will: • practice editing their drafts for spelling, capitalization, and punctuation.	Students will: • learn different ways to publish their how-to guides.
Activities				
• Reread drafts, making sure to explain all jargon.	• Read and discuss **Editing: Check Sentences** (Student page 276). • Use compound and complex sentences for variety.	• Read and discuss **Editing: Proofread Writing** (Student page 277).	• Fix any spelling, capitalization, or punctuation errors. • Make sure that all appositives have been set off with commas.	• Read and discuss **Publishing: Share Writing** (Student page 280).

* To complete the chapter in fewer days, teach the learning objectives and activities for two days in one day.

This planning chart, correlated to your state's writing standards, is available on-line at http://www.zaner-bloser.com/sfw.

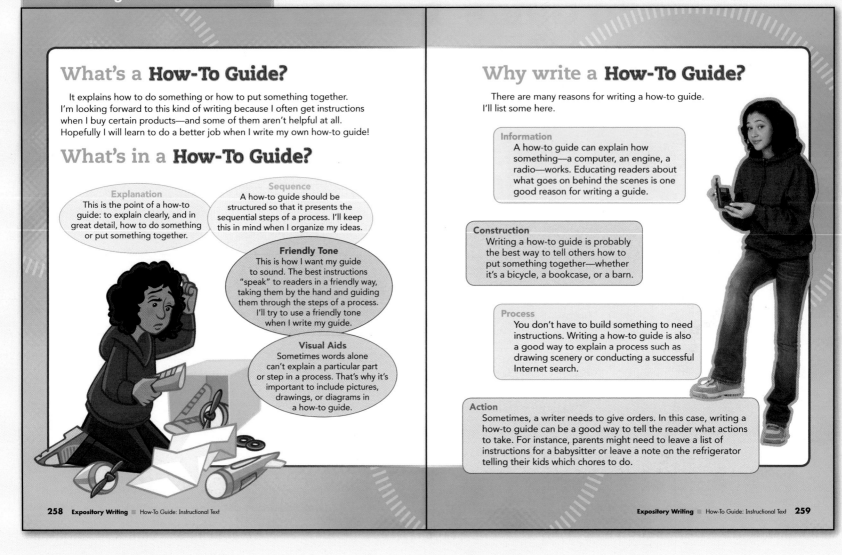

What's a **How-To Guide?**

It explains how to do something or how to put something together. I'm looking forward to this kind of writing because I often get instructions when I buy certain products—and some of them aren't helpful at all. Hopefully I will learn to do a better job when I write my own how-to guide!

What's in a **How-To Guide?**

Explanation
This is the point of a how-to guide: to explain clearly, and in great detail, how to do something or put something together.

Sequence
A how-to guide should be structured so that it presents the sequential steps of a process. I'll keep this in mind when I organize my ideas.

Friendly Tone
This is how I want my guide to sound. The best instructions "speak" to readers in a friendly way, taking them by the hand and guiding them through the steps of a process. I'll try to use a friendly tone when I write my guide.

Visual Aids
Sometimes words alone can't explain a particular part or step in a process. That's why it's important to include pictures, drawings, or diagrams in a how-to guide.

Why write a **How-To Guide?**

There are many reasons for writing a how-to guide. I'll list some here.

Information
A how-to guide can explain how something—a computer, an engine, a radio—works. Educating readers about what goes on behind the scenes is one good reason for writing a guide.

Construction
Writing a how-to guide is probably the best way to tell others how to put something together—whether it's a bicycle, a bookcase, or a barn.

Process
You don't have to build something to need instructions. Writing a how-to guide is also a good way to explain a process such as drawing scenery or conducting a successful Internet search.

Action
Sometimes, a writer needs to give orders. In this case, writing a how-to guide can be a good way to tell the reader what actions to take. For instance, parents might need to leave a list of instructions for a babysitter or leave a note on the refrigerator telling their kids which chores to do.

Define the Genre
(Student page 258)

How-To Guide

Discuss with students the definition of a how-to guide. Point out that a how-to guide explains how to perform an action or put something together; it can also explain how something works. Ask students to list places where they might read a how-to guide. **Possible responses: directions included in toys, electronics, or furniture** Then, have students share examples of how-to guides that they have read.

Elements of the Genre

How-To Guide

Read and discuss with students the elements of a how-to guide. Ask volunteers which elements are also common to other forms of writing. **Possible responses: Explanation— essay, science writing; Sequence—short story, biography; Friendly Tone—personal narrative, memoir; Visual Aids— science observation, research report** Discuss why each element may be important to writing a how-to guide.

Authentic Writing
(Student page 259)

How-To Guide

Read and discuss with students the reasons for writing a how-to guide listed on Student page 259. Point out that all writing has a purpose and is aimed at a specific audience. These authentic purposes help authors shape their writing. Ask a volunteer to read aloud the Information box. Then, have students discuss other reasons someone might write a how-to guide to provide information. Repeat this process for the Construction, Process, and Action boxes. Then, have students brainstorm other purposes for writing a how-to guide that are not listed on Student page 259. Encourage students to think about their own reasons for writing a how-to guide, and how these reasons will affect the tone and focus of their writing.

How-To Guide: Instructional Text
Writing Traits

I know that there are six traits of good writing. Here's a list of what makes a good how-to guide. I'll use it to help me write.

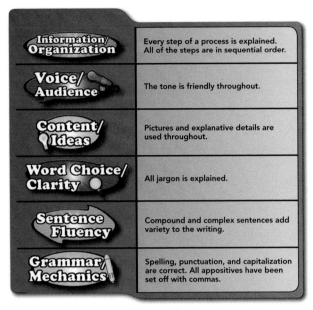

Information/Organization	Every step of a process is explained. All of the steps are in sequential order.
Voice/Audience	The tone is friendly throughout.
Content/Ideas	Pictures and explanative details are used throughout.
Word Choice/Clarity	All jargon is explained.
Sentence Fluency	Compound and complex sentences add variety to the writing.
Grammar/Mechanics	Spelling, punctuation, and capitalization are correct. All appositives have been set off with commas.

I can use Adrian Desmond's how-to guide on the next three pages as a model for my own writing. Later, we'll see how Adrian used the traits to help him write.

How-To Guide Model

"Building" a Sailboat Cake
by Adrian Desmond

For years, my brother has dreamed of owning a sailboat. For his birthday this year, I decided to build him one—well, sort of. I made him a sailboat cake. It was pretty easy once I got started. And if I could do it, so could you! Here are the steps to follow to make a sailboat cake.

First, decide on the kind of cake you want to make. Next, buy a boxed cake mix that will work in a pan that is 13 × 9 × 2 inches, and buy one package, 7.2 ounces, of white frosting mix. Bake the cake according to the directions on the package. When it's done, set the cake pan on a rack until the cake is cool enough to cut. Then, cut the cake diagonally into three pieces, as shown in Diagram 1. (You may want to leave the cake in the pan, which makes the pieces easier to handle.) Finally, place the uncovered pan of cut cake pieces in the freezer, and set a timer for one hour. Freezing the pieces will make them easier to frost.

Sequence

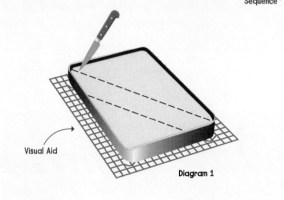

Visual Aid

Diagram 1

Writing Traits
(Student pages 260–263)

How-To Guide

Discuss whether students have ever needed to figure out how to perform an action or put something together. Discuss whether they had access to instructions. Note that a how-to guide probably could have made these activities easier. Then, share an experience in which you had to rely on poor instructions. Point out that a well-written how-to guide would have been very helpful at the time.

Turn students' attention to the traits of a good how-to guide listed on Student page 260. Have one or more volunteers read aloud the traits and their descriptions. Discuss why someone might use these traits when sharing their findings in writing. Then, tell students that they are going to study and use strategies for writing how-to guides.

Differentiating Instruction

English-Language Learners To help students better understand subtle differences in word meanings, write the following verb forms (from the writing model) on the board: *make, prepare, squeeze, fold, roll, blended,* and *mixing.* Then, read aloud the writing model, stopping at each verb form to do the following:

- Explain the different shades of meaning in *make* and *prepare,* as in *to make a sailboat cake* (paragraph one) and *prepare the frosting* (paragraph three). Note that in this case, *make* means "to assemble or put together" and *prepare* means "to assemble or put together in advance or ahead of time."
- Pantomime the different motions involved in *squeeze, fold* (as with a spoon), and *roll,* as in *squeeze the frosting out* (paragraph five), *fold one tablespoon of cocoa into it* (paragraph five), and *Roll up a 14 x 4-inch sheet* (paragraph six).
- Explain the similarity between the root forms *blend* and *mix* as in *When the frosting is well blended* (paragraph five) and *make water by mixing* (paragraph five). Note that *blend* and *mix* are synonyms both meaning "to combine"; however, in this case, *mixing* also means "to add to."

How-To Guide

Friendly Tone

While the cake is in the freezer, you'll need to do two things. First, prepare the frosting according to the directions on the package. When it is nice and fluffy, put one cup of it into a medium-sized bowl. Take a few tablespoons of frosting from there, and put it into a small-sized bowl. Then, set all three bowls aside. Next, make an ocean on which to set your sailboat. You can do this by covering a 20 × 18-inch tray or piece of heavy cardboard with aluminum foil.

When the timer sounds, take the pieces of cake out of the freezer and arrange them into a sailboat, as shown in Diagram 2. As you arrange the sails, leave plenty of space between them for the mast, the pole from which the sails are hung.

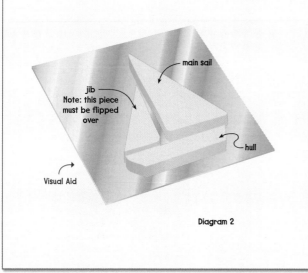

main sail

jib
Note: this piece
must be flipped
over

hull

Visual Aid

Diagram 2

Explanation

Before you add the mast, frost the sails. Use the frosting from the largest bowl to carefully frost the sails. You may want to make a few waves in the frosting to suggest an ocean breeze. If you want, you can put some of the frosting from this bowl into a square plastic bag with one corner cut off. Then, you can squeeze the frosting out to make a cloud and sea gulls. (See Diagram 3.) Next, take the medium-sized bowl of frosting and gently fold one tablespoon of cocoa into it. When the frosting is well blended, spread it over the hull, the long body of the sailboat. Finish off the hull by adding some portholes, or windows: Take five white, ring-shaped candies, and place them as you see them in Diagram 3. Finally, make water by mixing blue food coloring into the small bowl of frosting. Use another square plastic bag with a corner cut off to draw some waves.

Now it's time for the mast. Roll up a 14 × 4-inch sheet of aluminum foil and place it between the sails. If you wish to add a bit of color, attach a red paper flag at the top.

Now your cake is ready to set sail. Wish your "passengers" *bon voyage,* as well as *bon appétit*!

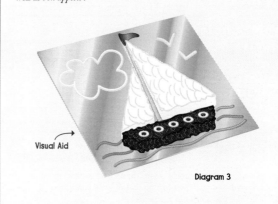

Visual Aid

Diagram 3

Differentiating Instruction

Support Some students may benefit from direct instruction and repetition in evaluating use of the writing traits in the writing model on Student pages 261–263.

• Make a transparency of the traits chart on Student page 260. Display it in the classroom, and highlight the Content/Ideas trait.

• Use words like the following to model the Content/Ideas trait: *The Content/Ideas trait in the rubric says the how-to guide should contain pictures and explanative details throughout. At the bottom of each page of "'Building' a Sailboat Cake," I see helpful diagrams that explain how to . . .*

• Call on volunteers to model the other traits. Coach students as needed, discussing together how to apply the writing traits to the model.

How-To Guide
Rubric

The traits of a good how-to guide from page 260 have been used to make the rubric below. By using 1, 2, 3, or 4 check marks to judge each trait, you can decide how well any how-to guide was written.

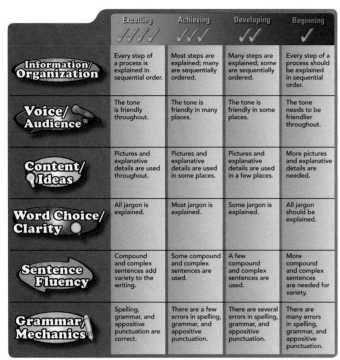

	Excelling	Achieving	Developing	Beginning
Information/Organization	Every step of a process is explained in sequential order.	Most steps are explained; many are sequentially ordered.	Many steps are explained; some are sequentially ordered.	Every step of a process should be explained in sequential order.
Voice/Audience	The tone is friendly throughout.	The tone is friendly in many places.	The tone is friendly in some places.	The tone needs to be friendlier throughout.
Content/Ideas	Pictures and explanative details are used throughout.	Pictures and explanative details are used in some places.	Pictures and explanative details are used in a few places.	More pictures and explanative details are needed.
Word Choice/Clarity	All jargon is explained.	Most jargon is explained.	Some jargon is explained.	All jargon should be explained.
Sentence Fluency	Compound and complex sentences add variety to the writing.	Some compound and complex sentences are used.	A few compound and complex sentences are used.	More compound and complex sentences are needed for variety.
Grammar/Mechanics	Spelling, grammar, and appositive punctuation are correct.	There are a few errors in spelling, grammar, and appositive punctuation.	There are several errors in spelling, grammar, and appositive punctuation.	There are many errors in spelling, grammar, and appositive punctuation.

How-To Guide
Using the Rubric to Study the Model

Now, let's use the rubric to check Adrian Desmond's how-to guide, "'Building' a Sailboat Cake." How many check marks would you give Adrian for each trait?

Information/Organization
- Every step of a process is explained.
- All of the steps are in sequential order.

Adrian does a good job of organizing his guide into sequential steps. The following passage is a good example. Notice how each main step flows smoothly to the next.

[from the writing model]

First, decide on the kind of cake you want to make. Next, buy a boxed cake mix that will work in a pan that is 13 × 9 × 2 inches, and buy one package, 7.2 ounces, of white frosting mix. Bake the cake according to the directions on the package. When it's done, set the cake pan on a rack until the cake is cool enough to cut.

Voice/Audience
- The tone is friendly throughout.

I like the way Adrian's writing sounds sort of chatty, as if he's right there talking the reader through the process of making the cake. This friendly tone helps make the instructions easier to follow.

[from the writing model]

While the cake is in the freezer, you'll need to do two things. First, prepare the frosting according to the directions on the package. When it is nice and fluffy, put one cup of it into a medium-sized bowl. Take a few tablespoons of frosting from there, and put it into a small-sized bowl. Then, set all three bowls aside.

Using the Rubric
(Student page 264)

Explain to students that a rubric is a tool that can be used to evaluate a piece of writing, and that the rubric on Student page 264 can be used to evaluate a how-to guide. Have students note that it is based on the same how-to guide traits listed on Student page 260.

Now point out the terms above each rubric column: *Excelling, Achieving, Developing,* and *Beginning.* Explain that each rubric column symbolizes a degree of writing skill, and that each rubric row focuses on a specific writing trait. When students use the rubric to evaluate their own work at each step of the writing process, they increase the likelihood of producing polished, well-written how-to guides.

Study the Model
(Student pages 265–267)

Explain that Student pages 265–267 show how the writing model on Student pages 261–263 meets all six traits of the rubric. Read each section with the students. Then, have them look for other examples of each trait in the writing model.

Ask students how many check marks they would assign the writing model for each trait. Then, as a class, decide how the writing model should be rated overall.

To be sure they are meeting all six writing traits, remind students to use the rubric as they write their own how-to guides.

How-To Guide

Content/Ideas

• Pictures and explanative details are used throughout.

Adrian uses a lot of details so that the reader can understand each step. It's also good that he includes diagrams because the pictures help make everything clear. In this passage, Adrian uses both details and a reference to the diagram on the page to explain what he means.

[from the writing model]

When the timer sounds, take the pieces of cake out of the freezer and arrange them into a sailboat, as shown in Diagram 2. As you arrange the sails, leave plenty of space between them for the mast, the pole from which the sails are hung.

Word Choice/Clarity

• All jargon is explained.

Adrian's instructions are clear and easy to follow because he defines technical words, or jargon. In this example, I underlined the two words that might be unfamiliar terms to the reader. You can see how Adrian defines each one, right after using it.

[from the writing model]

When the frosting is well blended, spread it over the <u>hull</u>, the long body of the sailboat. Finish off the hull by adding some <u>portholes</u>, or windows.

Sentence Fluency

• Compound and complex sentences add variety to the writing.

Adrian doesn't stick with just one sentence pattern; instead, he uses different kinds of sentences to add variety. Take a look at the passage below. Notice how Adrian uses a complex sentence followed by a compound statement. This makes his writing flow from one point to the next.

[from the writing model]

When it is nice and fluffy, put one cup of it into a medium-sized bowl. Take a few tablespoons of frosting from there, and put it into a small-sized bowl.

Grammar/Mechanics

• Spelling, punctuation, and capitalization are correct. All appositives have been set off with commas.

I can tell that Adrian proofread his writing because I didn't find any mistakes. He also uses appositives correctly. I know that an appositive is a phrase that defines a noun and that it needs to be set off from the rest of the sentence by a comma. In this passage, notice how Adrian correctly inserts a comma to separate the definition of a mast from the rest of the sentence.

[from the writing model]

As you arrange the sails, leave plenty of space between them for the mast, the pole from which the sails are hung.

My Turn!

I'm going to write a how-to guide about something I can do well. I'll follow the rubric and use good writing strategies. Read on to see how I do it!

Differentiating Instruction

Support Some students may fail to explain jargon in their own writing because they have trouble understanding which words fall into this category. Help students identify jargon—and how to explain it—by

• explaining that because a how-to guide often centers on specific or technical material, it is likely to contain jargon. Ask students to define *jargon*, leading them to understand that the word means "vocabulary unique to a particular trade, profession, or group."

• skimming the model how-to guide, together noting examples of jargon as well as how the writer explains these words. Also, have students note whether the author has included jargon that is not explained.

• developing a list of jargon words with the students. Then, have them write explanations for each word or phrase on the list.

• reminding students that as they write their own how-to guides, they should identify jargon by including explanations each time it is used.

Writing a How-To Guide

Prewriting Gather Information

Information/Organization	Every step of a process is explained.
Writing Strategy	Choose a process to explain. List the main steps in the process.

I'm really crazy about horses, and I love to go riding every chance I get. A lot goes into preparing for a safe and enjoyable ride—for both the rider and the horse. Since my assignment was to write a how-to guide, it seemed only natural to write about tacking up. Tacking up involves getting a horse ready to ride by putting on its bridle and saddle. Before I started writing my explanation, I thought it would be useful to make a checklist of the main steps involved in the process. Here's what I came up with.

Tacking Up—Main Steps

✔ Position the bridle, and put the bit in the horse's mouth.

✔ Pull the bridle over the horse's ears.

✔ Buckle the noseband and the throatlatch, making sure they are not too tight.

✔ Position the blanket or saddle pad over the horse's withers.

✔ Place the saddle on top of the blanket.

✔ Fasten and adjust the girth, making sure it is not too tight.

✔ Check the fit one last time to make sure the horse is comfortable.

Now it's your turn. Choose a process to explain. Then, jot down the major steps involved in completing the task.

Prewriting Organize Ideas

Information/Organization	All of the steps are in sequential order.
Writing Strategy	Make a Sequence Chain to arrange steps in a sequential order.

Writer's Term

Sequence Chain
A **Sequence Chain** shows the chronological steps of a complex process. Some of the steps might have substeps. These should be placed, in order, below each step.

Nearly every step I included on my checklist has at least one substep. To keep things organized, I used a Sequence Chain.

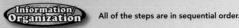

SEQUENCE CHAIN

Topic: Tacking Up

Step 1: Position bridle; put bit in mouth.
  a. Use thumb to guide bit in.
  b. Make sure it clears horse's teeth.

Step 2: Pull bridle over ears.
  a. Pull ears through headstall and browband.
  b. Pull forelock out from under browband.

Step 3: Buckle noseband and throatlatch comfortably.
  a. Fit two fingers under noseband.
  b. Fit width of hand between throatlatch and cheek.

Step 4: Position blanket or pad over withers.
  a. Slide blanket or pad back so hair lies flat.

Step 5: Place saddle on top of blanket.
  a. Unfold girth and let it hang down.
  b. Reach carefully under belly and grab girth strap.

Step 6: Fasten and adjust girth by slipping fingers between girth and horse's body.

Step 7: Make one last check for fit by checking for pinched skin.

Result: The horse is tacked up and ready to ride.

Now it's your turn. Use a Sequence Chain to organize the steps of your process.

Reflect

Do you think my Sequence Chain will help me keep my writing organized?

Prewriting

(Student pages 268–269)

Ask students to share something they do well, such as performing a certain action or putting something together. Help students center on tasks that are sufficiently narrow or specific enough to be covered in a how-to guide. For example, *How to Plan a Party* does not provide as helpful a focus as *How to Plan a Themed Birthday Party*.

Call students' attention to Student page 268, noting how Briana turned her love of horses into a topic for a how-to guide. Refer students to Briana's notes at the bottom of the page, and ask how writing the list might help her prepare to write. **Possible response: It might help her think through the steps of the process.**

WORK with a PARTNER
Have students with similar interests brainstorm topic ideas with partners. Suggest that they discuss general interests and then break them down into specific actions. Conference with pairs as needed to provide guidance.

Differentiating Instruction

Support To help students understand the importance of writing the correct steps in the right order, ask them to write down all the steps involved in making a peanut butter sandwich. Choose a student who left out a step and/or put the steps in the wrong order. Then, using real ingredients as props, ask the student to read his or her steps aloud while you follow the directions. The resulting attempt to make a sandwich should demonstrate the importance of completely thinking through a task before writing a how-to guide. Remind students that their Sequence Chains will also help them with this task.

More Practice!

For more practice with these writing strategies, you may wish to have students use the Strategy Practice Book. See the appendix for annotated Strategy Practice Book pages.

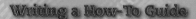

Writing a How-To Guide

Drafting Write a Draft

Voice/Audience The tone is friendly throughout.

Writing Strategy Use a friendly tone to explain each step to the reader.

Now I'll use my Sequence Chain to help me write my draft. According to the rubric, I should use a friendly tone. I know I won't be able to talk to my audience face-to-face, but I can pretend. I can use casual phrases and expressions that I normally use while speaking.

I also know how impersonal directions can be, especially when it sounds like they were written with no particular person in mind. So I'll also use the second person pronoun *you* to address my readers.

Right now, I won't worry too much about grammar and spelling errors. I just want to concentrate on presenting the steps in a way that will keep readers interested. However, I know that I've had trouble with introductory verbal phrases in the past, so I'll make sure to use them correctly.

Proofreading Marks

⬐ Indent	ℓ Take out something
≡ Make a capital	⊙ Add a period
/ Make a small letter	(SP) Spelling error
∧ Add something	¶ New paragraph

[DRAFT]

Tacking Up a Horse

by Briana   [used a friendly tone]

Have you ever watched someone fit a horse with a bridle and a saddle? If you have, you've seen the process of "tacking up." Tacking up properly is very important. Below are the steps involved in the process of tacking up. If you follow these steps carefully, you're sure to make the ride enjoyable, for both horse and rider alike.

First, you will need to put on the horse's bridle. Begin by unfastening all of the buckles. When finished, you should put the bit into the horse's mouth. To insert the bit without hurting the horse, first slide your thumb into its mouth. Then, gently guide the bit into place, making sure it clears the teeth and rests comfterbly on the tongue.

Once the bit is positioned, slide the bridle over the horse's head. Then, pull the forelock out from under the browband.   [correct use of an introductory verbal phrase]

Practice!

Now it's your turn. Use a friendly tone to address your readers.

Reflect

Is my tone friendly enough? Are there any places where I could be friendlier?

Drafting

(Student pages 270–271)

Remind students that drafting is a chance to get ideas on paper without having to worry about making mistakes.

Read Briana's words on Student page 270, which describe how she tried to figure out what a friendly tone might sound like. Ask students to describe the elements of a friendly tone. **Possible responses: casual expressions; sentences that sound like natural speech; use of the second person** Remind them to use these elements to create a friendly tone as they draft their own how-to guides.

Then, point out the highlighted sentences on Student page 271 that show Briana's use of a friendly tone. Encourage students to look for similar examples as they read the rest of her draft. Next, have them compare this section of Briana's draft to her Sequence Chain on Student page 269. As students draft their guides, remind them to follow the order of steps as listed in their own Sequence Chains.

Point out that Briana repeatedly refers to the rubric as she writes. Encourage students to get into the habit of using the rubric to help guide their own writing.

Writing Across the Curriculum

Science/Math Encourage students to use their how-to guides as opportunities for understanding underlying principles of other disciplines. Explain that many how-to guides are practical applications of science, math, and other subjects. For example, a how-to guide titled "How to Make a Picture Frame" would probably rely on mathematical concepts including measurements, fractions, and geometric angles.

Suggest that students examine their how-to guides for relationships to other disciplines. Then, help them identify any underlying principles that are at work.

Writing a How-To Guide

Revising Extend Writing

Content/Ideas Pictures and explanative details are used throughout.

Writing Strategy Add pictures and explanative details.

I just reread my draft, and it feels like something is missing. The rubric says to use pictures and explanative details, so I'll reread my draft, looking for places to further my explanation with helpful diagrams and specific details.

[DRAFT]

Have you ever watched someone fit a horse with a bridle and a saddle? If you have, you've seen the process of "tacking up." Tacking up properly is very important. Below are the steps involved in the process of tacking up. If you follow these steps carefully, you're sure to make the ride enjoyable, for both horse and rider alike.

If the process is not followed correctly, a person could cause a horse discomfort or injury. **[added explanative details]**

272 Expository Writing ■ How-To Guide: Instructional Text

[DRAFT]

[added explanative details]

(Remember to always stand to the left of the horse.)
First, you will need to put on the horse's bridle. Begin by unfastening all of the buckles. When finished, you should put the bit into the horse's mouth. To insert the bit without hurting the horse, first slide your thumb, behind its teeth into its mouth. Then, gently guide the bit into place, making sure it clears the teeth and rests comfterbly on the tongue.
Be careful not to hurt its ears as you pull them through the headstall Once the bit is positioned, slide the bridle over the horse's head. and browband.
Then, pull the forelock out from under the browband.

Next, position the noseband and throatlatch and buckle them by slipping two fingers between it and the horse's nose securely. Check that the noseband is not too tight. Check the throatlatch by putting a hand's width between it and the horse's cheek. (See Diagram 1.)

[added a picture]

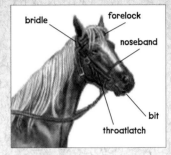

Diagram 1

bridle forelock noseband bit throatlatch

Practice!

Now it's your turn. Add explanative details and pictures to make your guide easier to understand.

Expository Writing ■ How-To Guide: Instructional Text 273

Revising

(Student pages 272–273)

Have students review Briana's words and the edits she made to her draft on Student page 272. Ask students what the highlighted sentence adds to her explanation. **Possible response: It explains why tacking up properly is very important.** Then, point out the illustration at the bottom of Student page 273, and ask how it helps readers. **Possible response: It helps them visualize the various parts being described.** Finally, have students look for places in their own how-to guides where they can add pictures and explanative details.

Differentiating Instruction

Enrichment Give students with art skills the opportunity to emphasize illustrations and diagrams in their how-to reports. Suggest that they

- pay special attention to the artwork in their guides, spending extra time on illustrations.
- choose some of the best examples of their work to display for the class as models.
- coach others who are having difficulty drawing illustrations or diagrams.
- experiment with new styles. If they have not tried computer illustration methods, encourage them to include at least one example in their guides.

Writing a How-To Guide

Revising Clarify Writing

Word Choice/Clarity ● All jargon is explained.

Writing Strategy Make sure all jargon has been explained.

I read my how-to guide to a classmate who told me that he'd never tacked up a horse before. He was confused by some of the terms I used. The rubric says that I should explain all jargon used in my writing, so I defined any terms that I thought were specific to horseback riding.

Writer's Term

Jargon

Jargon is the language used by a group of people to describe their profession, trade, or hobby. One group (such as nurses or horseback riders) might not understand the jargon used by another group (such as athletes or skydivers). For this reason, whenever jargon is used, it should always be carefully explained.

[DRAFT]

(Remember to always stand to the left of the horse.)

First, you will need to put on the horse's bridle. Begin by unfastening [explained jargon] ——→ , or headgear, all of the buckles. When finished, you should put the bit into the horse's (The bit helps the rider control the horse.) mouth. To insert the bit without hurting the horse, first slide your thumb behind its teeth into its mouth. Then, gently guide the bit into place, making sure it clears the teeth and rests comfterbly on the tongue.

[DRAFT]

Be careful not to hurt its ears as you pull them through the headstall Once the bit is positioned, slide the bridle over the horse's head. , the long hair between the horse's ears, and browband. Then, pull the forelock out from under the browband. , the straps across the horse's nose and face, Next, position the noseband and throatlatch, and buckle them by slipping two fingers between it and the horse's nose securely. Check that the noseband is not too tight. Check the

throatlatch by putting a hand's width between it and the horse's (See Diagram 1.) cheek.

[explained jargon]

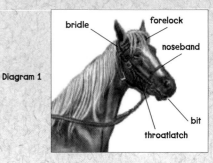

bridle
forelock
noseband
Diagram 1
bit
throatlatch

Practice!

Now it's your turn. Review your draft to see if you've included jargon. If so, add an explanation for each term.

Reflect

I added a diagram and some explanative details to clarify jargon and important steps. Do my additions help? Do they make things clearer?

Revising

(Student pages 274–275)

Write these words on the board: *bridle, bit, forelock,* and *throatlatch.* Ask if students are familiar with these words or their meanings. Explain that the words are examples of jargon. Then, refer students to the Writer's Term box on Student page 274, and ask a volunteer to define *jargon.* **Jargon is the language used by a group of people to describe their profession, trade, or hobby.**

Have students read Briana's words at the top of Student page 274. Then, have them review her draft on Student pages 274–275, noting the four examples of jargon listed on the board. Discuss with students how Briana explains these words. As they revise their own how-to guides, remind students to make sure all jargon has been explained.

Differentiating Instruction

English-Language Learners These students may need extra help understanding compound sentences. Remind them that a compound sentence contains two independent clauses (simple sentences) joined by either a semicolon or a comma and a coordinating conjunction such as *for, and, nor, but, or, yet,* or *so.* Then, write the following on the board:

The goal is far away. I can run fast.

John likes ice cream. Bob likes milk shakes.

The dog barks a lot. The neighbors complain.

Call on volunteers to come up and join each sentence pair with a comma and a coordinating conjunction.

Writing a How-To Guide

Editing Check Sentences

Sentence Fluency

Compound and complex sentences add variety to the writing.

Writing Strategy

Use compound and complex sentences for variety.

Now I'm going to edit my draft. The rubric says to include compound and complex sentences for variety. I remember learning about these kinds of sentences not too long ago. Since I already know how to use them correctly, I'll focus on using them to add variety to my writing, just like the rubric says. Take a look at the passage below to see how I created variety by forming a complex sentence out of two closely related statements that both started with the same subject: *You.*

[DRAFT]

[added variety by forming a complex sentence]

Before
~~You are almost finished tacking up.~~ You should check one last time to make sure everything fits the horse comfterbly.

Practice!

Now it's your turn. Use compound and complex sentences to add variety to your writing.

Editing Proofread Writing

Grammar/Mechanics

Spelling, punctuation, and capitalization are correct. All appositives have been set off with commas.

Writing Strategy

Check to see that appositives have been set off with commas.

Writer's Term

Appositives
An **appositive** is a word or a phrase that identifies a noun. An appositive usually follows the noun it identifies, and it is usually separated from the rest of the sentence by one or more commas.

Now I need to check for errors. I always check spelling, punctuation, and capitalization, but the rubric says I should also check to see if appositives have been set off with commas. I used appositives to explain jargon, and lucky for me, I remembered to use the correct punctuation.

[DRAFT]

Be careful not to hurt its ears as you pull them through the headstall Once the bit is positioned, slide the bridle over the horse's head. and browband.
, the long hair between the horse's ears,
Then, pull the forelock out from under the browband.

[correct use of appositive]

Practice!

Now it's your turn. Edit your draft for spelling, punctuation, and capitalization. Make sure that appositives have been set off with commas.

Grammar/Mechanics

For more practice with appositives, use the exercises on the next two pages.

Reflect

What do you think of my edits? I tried hard to vary my writing, and I think I used all appositives correctly. Does my writing flow better now?

Editing

(Student pages 276–277)

Call students' attention to the edits Briana made to her draft on Student page 276. Remind students that they learned about compound and complex sentences in the last chapter. Then, have them check their own how-to guides for places where using compound or complex sentences will create variety.

Now, point out the Writer's Term box on Student page 277, and ask a volunteer to read it aloud. Have students note how Briana edited her writing, adding appositives to explain jargon. Then, discuss with students whether these changes match the guidelines in the Writer's Term box on the page. Finally, remind students to check their own guides to make sure they have used appositives correctly. Remind them that they should also check their spelling, capitalization, and punctuation.

If any of your students are having trouble understanding how to use appositives correctly, you may wish to teach the Mini-Lesson on pages 202–203 of this Teacher Edition. Then, have students complete the exercises on Student pages 278–279. Review the answers and possible rewrites with them.

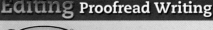

WORK with a PARTNER Have pairs of students read one another's drafts, using sticky notes to mark errors in spelling, punctuation, and grammar. Then, tell students to perform a second read that focuses on the editing strategies they learned in this chapter.

Grammar Mechanics Practice!

Appositives

KNOW the RULE

An **appositive** is a word or a phrase that identifies a noun. An appositive usually follows the noun it identifies, and it is usually separated from the rest of the sentence by one or more commas.

If the appositive appears at the end of a sentence, put a comma right after the noun being identified.
Example: I usually ride Daisy, **my favorite horse**.

If the appositive appears mid-sentence, put one comma before it and one comma after it.
Example: Daisy, **my favorite horse**, has brown and white spots.

Practice the Rule

Number a separate sheet of paper 1–5. Then, copy each of these sentences. After each one, write the appositive and the noun it identifies.

1. My family, the Mirabelli family, loves to have lots of parties.
2. Whenever there's a party at my house, I like to make my favorite appetizer, "The Ball."
3. The Ball, a cheese ball made with cream cheese, was named by my cousin Patty.
4. Patty, the daughter of Uncle Wes and Aunt Mary, says that The Ball is her favorite food.
5. The recipe, a six-step process, is really quite easy to follow.

Apply the Rule

Read the passage below, looking for errors in appositive punctuation. Then, rewrite the text correctly on a separate sheet of paper.

How To Make a Paperweight

Do you want to liven up your desk or study area? This guide will show you how to turn an ordinary rock, some paints, and a little imagination into a colorful paperweight.

The first step in this process finding a good rock is easy. The best one for the job is about the size of a baseball. However, your rock does not have to be perfectly round. After you've found a rock you like, the next step is to clean it. Hold it under running water or soak it for 5–10 minutes until its surface is free of all visible dirt. Rub it with a towel, and then let it sit in the open until it feels dry to the touch.

While your rock dries, prepare your work area a table or the floor, by covering it with newspapers or an old sheet. Gather paints and brushes. You may also want to gather ideas from books that show appealing designs or patterns. Plan out your design by sketching a few ideas on paper. You can turn your rock into something animate a pet or a funny face. You can paint pictures of leaves or ladybugs, or you can drip on random doodles—anything goes!

Grammar Mechanics Mini-Lesson

(Student pages 278–279)

Appositives

Display this list of classroom-related nouns on the board. Then, work with students to write phrases that identify something about each noun.

desk	*a sturdy surface*
textbook	*a grammar manual*
thesaurus	*a reference book*

Explain that each identifier phrase is called an appositive. Then, have students read the Know the Rule box on Student page 278.

Point out that an appositive usually comes directly after the noun it identifies and that it is usually set off by one or more commas. Then, ask students how they can tell whether to use one or two commas to separate an appositive. If the appositive appears in the middle of the sentence, it needs two commas; if it appears at the end, it needs only one.

Answers for Practice the Rule

1. the Mirabelli family; My family
2. "The Ball"; my favorite appetizer
3. a cheese ball made with cream cheese; The Ball
4. the daughter of Uncle Wes and Aunt Mary; Patty
5. a six-step process; The recipe

Answers for Apply the Rule

How to Make a Paperweight

Do you want to liven up your desk or study area? This guide will show you how to turn an ordinary rock, some paints, and a little imagination into a colorful paperweight.

The first step in this process, finding a good rock, is easy. The best one for the job is about the size of a baseball. However, your rock does not have to be perfectly round. After you've found a rock you like, the next step is to clean it. Hold it under running water or soak it for 5–10 minutes until its surface is free of all visible dirt. Rub it with a towel, and then let it sit in the open until it feels dry to the touch.

(Answers continue on page 203.)

Writing a How-To Guide

Publishing Share Writing

Present my guide as a speech for a small group of classmates.

Now that I've finished my how-to guide, I need to decide how to publish it. I could post it on-line or on a class bulletin board. But my classmates know I love to horseback ride, so I think it would be fun to read my paper as a speech. I can enlarge the diagrams and make them into posters, and I can use a model of a tacked up horse while I talk. To prepare, I'm going to practice in front of a mirror until I feel comfortable. But before I present, I'll read through my guide one last time to make sure it includes all of the items on my checklist.

My Checklist

- ✔ Every step of a process is explained.
- ✔ The tone is friendly and inviting.
- ✔ Pictures and details help explain complicated steps.
- ✔ All jargon is explained.
- ✔ Compound and complex sentences add variety to the writing.
- ✔ Spelling, punctuation, and capitalization are correct. Appositives are set off with commas.

Practice!

Now it's your turn. Make a checklist to check your how-to guide. Then, make a final draft to publish.

Tacking Up a Horse
by Briana

Have you ever watched someone fit a horse with a bridle and a saddle? If you have, you've seen the process of "tacking up." Tacking up properly is very important. If the process is not followed correctly, a person could cause a horse discomfort or injury. Below are the steps involved in the process of tacking up. If you follow these steps carefully, you're sure to make the ride enjoyable, for both horse and rider alike.

First, you will need to put on the horse's bridle, or headgear. (Remember to always stand to the left of the horse.) Begin by unfastening all of the buckles. When finished, you should put the bit into the horse's mouth. (The bit helps the rider control the horse.) To insert the bit without hurting the horse, first slide your thumb into its mouth, behind its teeth. Then, gently guide the bit into place, making sure it clears the teeth and rests comfortably on the tongue.

Once the bit is positioned, slide the bridle over the horse's head. Be careful not to hurt its ears as you pull them through the headstall and browband. Then, pull the forelock, the long hair between the horse's ears, out from under the browband.

(Answers continued from page 202.)

While your rock dries, prepare your work area, a table or the floor, by covering it with newspapers or an old sheet. Gather paints and brushes. You may also want to gather ideas from books that show appealing designs or patterns. Plan out your design by sketching a few ideas on paper. You can turn your rock into something animate, a pet or a funny face. You can paint pictures of leaves or ladybugs, or you can drip on random doodles—anything goes!

 For more practice with grammar/mechanics skills, see Zaner-Bloser's *G.U.M.* materials.

Publishing

(Student pages 280–281)

Ask students if they like Briana's choice for sharing her how-to guide. Tell the class that her choice is not the only option for publishing her work. Invite students to name other ways they could publish their own how-to guides.

Have each student make a checklist and perform a final evaluation of his or her guide before publishing it. Encourage students to share copies of their guides with friends and relatives who might be interested in reading what they wrote.

Writing a How-To Guide

Next, position the noseband and throatlatch, the straps across the horse's nose and face, and buckle them securely. Check that the noseband is not too tight by slipping two fingers between it and the horse's nose. Check the throatlatch by putting a hand's width between it and the horse's cheek. (See Diagram 1.)

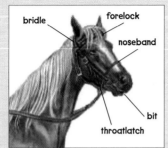

Diagram 1

Now, it is time to put on the saddle. To begin, position a blanket or saddle pad over the horse's withers, or shoulders. Slide the blanket or pad back so that the horse's hair lies flat and doesn't get pulled the wrong way. Place the saddle on top of it. Unfold the girth, the strap that goes underneath the horse, and let it hang down. Then, reach under the horse's belly and grab the girth strap. Fasten the girth and then adjust it. Again, make sure it's not too tight by running your hand between it and the horse's body.

282 Expository Writing ■ How-To Guide: Instructional Text

Before you finish tacking up, you should check one last time to make sure everything fits the horse comfortably. Then, gently pull the horse's forelegs forward to release any skin that might be pinched or wrinkled. And there you have it—your horse is tacked up! Now, you're ready for a wonderful ride.

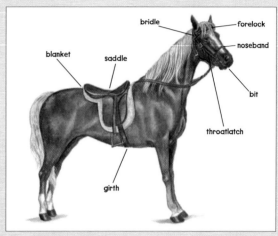

Diagram 2

Reflect

What do you think? Did I use all of the traits of a good how-to guide in my writing? Check it against the rubric. Don't forget to use the rubric to check your own guide, too.

Expository Writing ■ How-To Guide: Instructional Text 283

Publishing

(Student pages 282–283)

Call students' attention to the Reflect box on the bottom of Student page 283. Explain that assessing Briana's how-to guide against the rubric will help them better understand how to apply the traits to their own work. Then, have students use sticky notes to mark at least one example of each trait in Briana's writing. Tell them to include an evaluation on each note.

After this process, have students assess how well they were able to identify each trait in Briana's writing and how easy or difficult it was to use the rubric. Remind them to apply what they learned from Briana's work when they use the rubric to check their own writing.

Differentiating Instruction

Support Encourage students to assess their understanding of the writing strategies taught in this chapter by discussing how they used them to help write their how-to guides. Begin by displaying the strategies from this chapter. Then, model the process of self-assessment as follows:

I know that a friendly tone sounds casual and informal. At first, though, I wasn't sure how to make a piece of nonfiction writing sound friendly. Then, I decided to write my how-to guide as if I were talking to someone and explaining the steps in person. This really helped! I learned a lot about how to write using a friendly tone, and I'm confident I can apply this success to future writing.

Have students assess their use of each strategy—either verbally or in writing. Encourage students to be specific about their experiences, and to note any difficulties or successes.

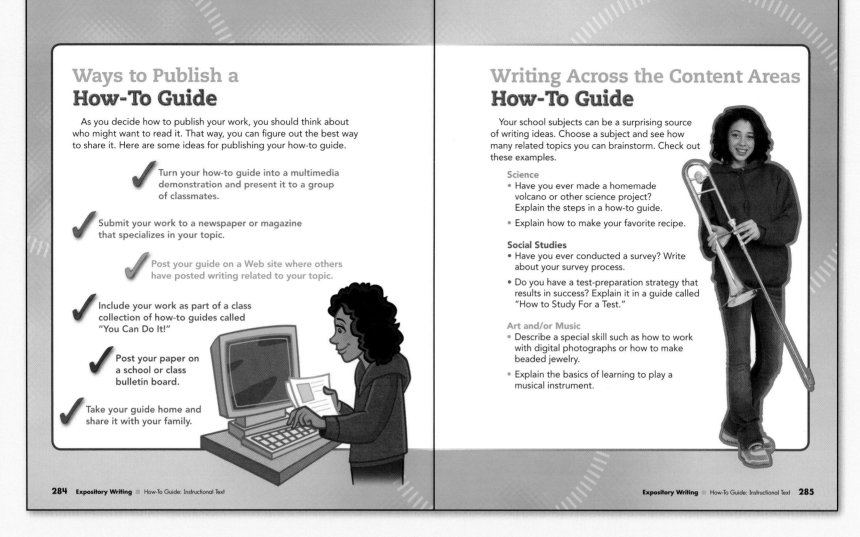

Ways to Publish a How-To Guide

As you decide how to publish your work, you should think about who might want to read it. That way, you can figure out the best way to share it. Here are some ideas for publishing your how-to guide.

✓ Turn your how-to guide into a multimedia demonstration and present it to a group of classmates.

✓ Submit your work to a newspaper or magazine that specializes in your topic.

✓ Post your guide on a Web site where others have posted writing related to your topic.

✓ Include your work as part of a class collection of how-to guides called "You Can Do It!"

✓ Post your paper on a school or class bulletin board.

✓ Take your guide home and share it with your family.

284 Expository Writing ■ How-To Guide: Instructional Text

Writing Across the Content Areas How-To Guide

Your school subjects can be a surprising source of writing ideas. Choose a subject and see how many related topics you can brainstorm. Check out these examples.

Science
- Have you ever made a homemade volcano or other science project? Explain the steps in a how-to guide.
- Explain how to make your favorite recipe.

Social Studies
- Have you ever conducted a survey? Write about your survey process.
- Do you have a test-preparation strategy that results in success? Explain it in a guide called "How to Study For a Test."

Art and/or Music
- Describe a special skill such as how to work with digital photographs or how to make beaded jewelry.
- Explain the basics of learning to play a musical instrument.

Expository Writing ■ How-To Guide: Instructional Text 285

Ways to Publish
(Student page 284)

Read and discuss with students the publishing options listed on Student page 284. Encourage students to consider some of these options when publishing their own writing. Remind students that Briana chose to publish her how-to guide by presenting it as a speech for a small group of classmates, but they can choose their own way of publishing. Perhaps one student will want to post his or her how-to guide on a school or class bulletin board, while another will want to post it on a Web site where others have posted writing related to the same topic.

Writing Across the Content Areas
(Student page 285)

Explain to students that writing is not just for English or language arts class. Many other school subjects contain ideas, issues, and events that students may want to write about. Encourage students to consider using one of the content areas listed on Student page 285 as a springboard for more writing options. Students may also wish to consult with other teachers for more ideas on writing in the content areas.

Expository Test Writing

In this chapter, students will learn how to write a how-to guide for a test. They will review the traits of a how-to guide and will study a test prompt and a scoring guide. Students will then use a model writing prompt and a scoring guide to study a sample expository test.

Students will follow the student guide as she goes through the test writing stages—time planning, studying the writing prompt, prewriting, drafting, revising, and editing. As the student guide reviews the writing strategies in each step, students will be directed to practice the test writing strategies.

During prewriting and drafting, students will

- study the writing prompt.
- respond to the task.

- choose a graphic organizer.
- check the graphic organizer against the scoring guide.
- use a lot of explanative details to help the reader understand the process.

During revising and editing, students will

- support their writing with factual information.
- check for proper use of homophones.
- make sure their writing flows smoothly.
- edit their drafts for proper grammar, punctuation, capitalization, and spelling.

You may wish to send to families the School-Home Connection Letter for this chapter, located at the end of this unit in the Teacher Edition.

Writing Traits in the Scoring Guide

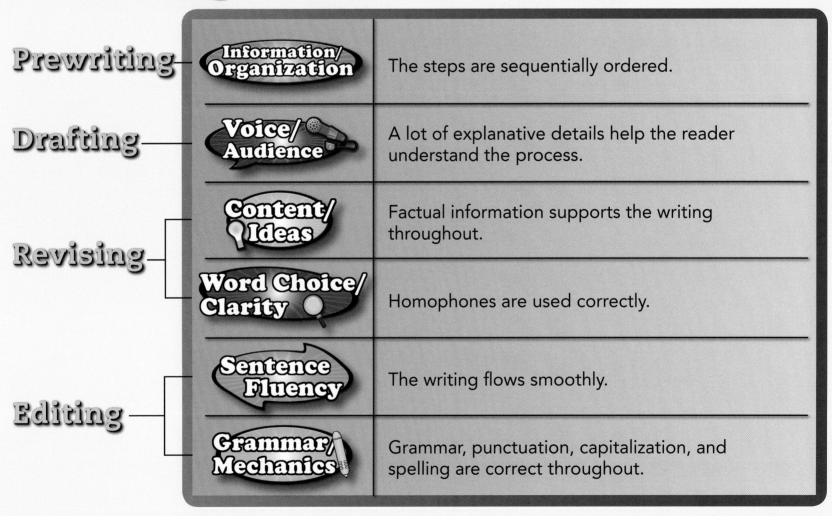

Prewriting — **Information/Organization** — The steps are sequentially ordered.

Drafting — **Voice/Audience** — A lot of explanative details help the reader understand the process.

Revising — **Content/Ideas** — Factual information supports the writing throughout.

Revising — **Word Choice/Clarity** — Homophones are used correctly.

Editing — **Sentence Fluency** — The writing flows smoothly.

Editing — **Grammar/Mechanics** — Grammar, punctuation, capitalization, and spelling are correct throughout.

Expository Test Writing Time Management

WEEK 1

Day 1	Day 2	Day 3	Day 4	Day 5
Learning Objectives				
Students will: • learn the components of the writing prompt model.	Students will: • recognize the relationship of the scoring guide to the rubric and the six traits of writing. • read a writing prompt model response.	Students will: • apply the scoring guide to the writing prompt model response.	Students will: • continue to apply the scoring guide to the writing prompt model response.	Students will: • learn how to plan their time during a writing test.
Activities				
• Discuss the components of the writing prompt model (Student pages 286–287).	• Read and discuss the scoring guide (Student page 288). • Read the writing prompt model response (Student page 289).	• Read and discuss **Using the Scoring Guide to Study the Model** (Student pages 290–291).	• Read and discuss **Using the Scoring Guide to Study the Model** (Student page 292).	• Read and discuss **Planning My Time** (Student page 293).

WEEK 2

Day 1	Day 2	Day 3	Day 4	Day 5
Learning Objectives				
Students will: • read a writing prompt for a how-to guide. • apply the six traits of writing to the writing prompt.	Students will: • learn how to respond to the task in the writing prompt.	Students will: • learn how to choose a graphic organizer for expository test writing.	Students will: • learn how to check the graphic organizer against the scoring guide.	Students will: • learn how to provide plenty of explanative details for the reader.
Activities				
• Read and discuss **Prewriting: Study the Writing Prompt** (Student pages 294–295).	• Read and discuss **Prewriting: Gather Information** (Student page 296).	• Read and discuss **Prewriting: Organize Ideas** (Student page 297).	• Read and discuss **Prewriting: Check the Scoring Guide** (Student pages 298–299).	• Read and discuss **Drafting: Write a Draft** (Student pages 300–301).

WEEK 3

Day 1	Day 2	Day 3	Day 4	Day 5
Learning Objectives				
Students will: • add supporting facts to their writing test.	Students will: • make sure they have not misused homophones in their writing test.	Students will: • combine short sentences to make the writing flow smoothly.	Students will: • edit their writing test for proper grammar and mechanics.	Students will: • learn tips for test writing.
Activities				
• Read and discuss **Revising: Extend Writing** (Student page 302).	• Read and discuss **Revising: Clarify Writing** (Student page 303).	• Read and discuss **Editing: Check Sentences** (Student page 304).	• Read and discuss **Editing: Proofread Writing** (Student pages 305–306).	• Read and discuss **Test Tips** (Student page 307).

To complete the chapter in fewer days, teach the learning objectives and activities for two days in one day.

This planning chart, correlated to your state's writing standards, is available on-line at http://www.zaner-bloser.com/sfw.

EXPOSITORY test writing

Read the Writing Prompt

When you take a writing test, you will be given a writing prompt. Most writing prompts have three parts:

Setup This part of the writing prompt gives you the background information you need to get ready to write.

Task This part of the writing prompt tells you exactly what you are supposed to write: a how-to guide.

Scoring Guide This section tells how your writing will be scored. To do well on the test, you should include everything on the list.

Remember the rubrics you've used? When you take a writing test, you don't always have all of the information that's on a rubric, but the scoring guide is a lot like a rubric. It lists everything you should think about as you write. Like the rubrics you've previously used, most scoring guides are based on the six traits of writing:

- Information/Organization
- Content/Ideas
- Sentence Fluency
- Voice/Audience
- Word Choice/Clarity
- Grammar/Mechanics

Writing MODEL Prompt

Think of a chore that you enjoy. This should be something that others normally find dull or routine. For example, do you like to tinker around, cleaning, washing, and/or organizing things? Do you enjoy cooking, baking, or washing the family car?

Write a how-to guide explaining how to accomplish a chore that you actually enjoy.

Be sure your writing

- is sequentially ordered.
- contains a lot of explanative details that help the reader understand the process.
- is supported with factual information.
- has been checked for proper use of homophones.
- flows smoothly.
- contains correct grammar, punctuation, capitalization, and spelling.

Introduce the Writing Prompt

(Student pages 286–287)

Expository Writing

Tell students that they are going to apply what they have learned about expository writing to the challenge of writing an expository test. Note that when they write for a test, they will receive a writing prompt and a certain amount of time in which to write. Then, their writing will be evaluated, as with any test. Assure students that they do not need to be anxious about writing a test, because the skills they have already practiced will help them do a good job.

Read aloud the three parts of the writing prompt listed on Student page 286. Explain that within the scoring guide, students will find traits similar to those they have seen in the rubrics throughout this unit. Note that just as a rubric highlights the qualities of a good paper, the scoring guide highlights the qualities of a good writing test.

Read the writing prompt model aloud. Then, write the following correlations on the board and review:

- *Setup: This provides the background information needed in order to write for a test.*

- *Task: This is the assignment, and it often names the type of writing to be done.*

- *Scoring Guide: This is much like a rubric, providing information necessary for doing well on a writing test.*

Writing Traits in the Scoring Guide

Reread the scoring guide in the writing prompt on page 287. Not every test prompt will include each of the six writing traits, but this one does. You can use the following chart to help you better understand the connection between the scoring guide and the writing traits in the rubrics you've used.

 **Information/Organization**
- Be sure your writing is sequentially ordered.

 Voice/Audience
- Be sure your writing contains a lot of explanative details that help the reader understand the process.

Content/Ideas
- Be sure your writing is supported with factual information.

 Word Choice/Clarity
- Be sure your writing has been checked for proper use of homophones.

Sentence Fluency
- Be sure your writing flows smoothly.

Grammar/Mechanics
- Be sure your writing contains correct grammar, punctuation, capitalization, and spelling.

Look at Kyle Greer's how-to guide on the next page. Did he follow the scoring guide?

 **Writing Prompt MODEL Response**

HOW TO MOW A LAWN

by Kyle Greer

Are you looking for a great way to earn extra money? If so, I have the perfect job for you: mowing other people's lawns. Here are the steps to take to mow a great lawn.

First, you'll need to get your equipment ready. You can use a gas mower, an electric mower, or a push mower. I think the gas and electric mowers are better because they are easier to handle. If you use a gas mower, be sure that it has enough gas and oil. An electric mower, like the one that I use, needs to be charged, so be sure to charge yours. Also, most mowers have settings for grass length, so make sure your mower is set properly.

Then, you'll need to walk through the yard that you're going to mow, picking up items that will get in your way, such as rocks and sticks or toys. It's important to do this because otherwise it can wreak havoc on your mower's blades, ruin the items that you mow over, and/or cause things to fly up toward you as you mow.

Before you start your mower, you'll want to put on safety glasses or goggles, as well as sneakers or work boots to protect your feet. Now, you're ready to start the power. You do this by either pushing a button or using the pull cord. Once the mower is started, mow along the outside of the lawn. Go in one direction across the lawn and then back in the other direction right beside where you first mowed. Repeat this again and again until you reach the edge of the lawn opposite to where you first began.

I use a mulching mower that cuts up the grass clippings and puts them back into the grass as I mow. But if you use a mower that has a grass collector, you will periodically need to check the bag on the mower to see how full it is getting. When it gets full, you will need to empty the clippings into a bag that you can leave for the homeowner to either use as compost or properly dispose of. Be sure to turn the mower off or make sure that the blade is stopped before emptying the bag.

Now the lawn is mowed. Turn off the mower and check your work one last time to be sure you didn't miss anything. Good job!

Writing Traits in the Scoring Guide

(Student pages 288–289)

Ask students to recall the six traits of writing they have studied throughout the unit. **Information/Organization, Voice/Audience, Content/Ideas, Word Choice/Clarity, Sentence Fluency, Grammar/Mechanics** If they are having trouble providing a response, remind them that the first trait is Information/Organization. Tell them that when they read a scoring guide, they should try to identify the traits within it. This will help them think about the purpose of each item in the scoring guide. It will also help them relate to what they have already learned about these writing traits.

Ask a student volunteer to read the traits in the scoring guide on Student page 288. Then, tell students they are going to study and use strategies for expository test writing and that a good expository test has all of the traits listed on Student page 288.

Read the Model:
Writing Prompt Response

Distribute one copy of "How to Mow a Lawn" to each student. As you read the model aloud, have each student use a highlighter to identify the traits set forth in the scoring guide.

Differentiating Instruction

English-Language Learners **Preteach** key vocabulary in context by previewing the writing prompt model response. As you preview the essay, note the following multiple-meaning words—*charge, handle,* and *blade*—and challenge students to use context to figure out the meanings used in this essay.

Using the Scoring Guide to Study the Model

Now we'll use the scoring guide to check Kyle's writing test, "How to Mow a Lawn." Let's see how well his essay meets each of the six writing traits.

Information/Organization • The guide is sequentially ordered.

Kyle wrote the steps in his guide in the order that they are to be followed. He begins with a short explanation of equipment preparation. Then, he explains the importance of removing items from the grass and putting on safety gear before mowing the lawn. I like the way Kyle ordered his guide, and the way he stresses safety, too.

> Before you start your mower, you'll want to put on safety glasses or goggles, as well as sneakers or work boots to protect your feet. Now, you're ready to start the power.

Voice/Audience • The writing contains a lot of explanative details that help the reader understand the process.

Kyle tells his readers what to do and why they should do it. To help his readers better understand the process, he also talks about how he does these things.

> Now, you're ready to start the power. You do this by either pushing a button or using the pull cord. Once the mower is started, mow along the outside of the lawn. Go in one direction across the lawn and then back in the other direction right beside where you first mowed. Repeat this again and again until you reach the edge of the lawn opposite to where you first began.

Content/Ideas • The guide is supported with factual information.

Kyle doesn't just give his opinion or point of view when he explains how to mow a lawn; he also points out the facts, such as what is needed to prepare equipment.

> If you use a gas mower, be sure that it has enough gas and oil. An electric mower, like the one that I use, needs to be charged, so be sure to charge yours. Also, most mowers have settings for grass length, so make sure your mower is set properly.

Word Choice/Clarity • The writing has been checked for proper use of homophones.

Kyle uses homophones correctly. He uses *It's* instead of *Its*, and he uses the word *wreak* instead of *reek*, which has a totally different meaning!

> It's important to do this because otherwise it can wreak havoc on your mower's blades, ruin the items that you mow over, and/or cause things to fly up toward you as you mow.

Using the Scoring Guide to Study the Model

(Student pages 290–292)

Review the function of the scoring guide with students. First, have them review a rubric from one of the earlier chapters in this unit. Then, point out the similarities and differences between that rubric and the scoring guide. Make sure students understand that although a scoring guide does not include criteria for various levels of accomplishment, it does provide guidance in the six key areas of assessment: Information/Organization, Voice/Audience, Content/Ideas, Word Choice/Clarity, Sentence Fluency, and Grammar/Mechanics.

Explain that in the same way traits in a rubric are used to assess writing, criteria in a scoring guide are used to assess test writing. Remind students to use the scoring guide when they write for a test to ensure that they meet all of the traits.

Differentiating Instruction

English-Language Learners To help these students increase their vocabulary, point out the following words from the first paragraph of How to Mow a Lawn." As you note each word, write it on the board. Then, write homophones for each word and discuss word meanings.

story word	homophone(s)
you	ewe, yew
great	grate
way	weigh
to	too, two
earn	urn
so	sew, sow
I	eye
for	four
here	hear

Using the Scoring Guide to Study the Model

Sentence Fluency

• The writing flows smoothly.

Kyle's story flows smoothly. Even though it's step-by-step, the writing still contains enough sentence variety to make it interesting and easy to read.

I use a mulching mower that cuts up the grass clippings and puts them back into the grass as I mow. But if you use a mower that has a grass collector, you will periodically need to check the bag on the mower to see how full it is getting. When it gets full, you will need to empty the clippings into a bag that you can leave for the homeowner to either use as compost or properly dispose of.

Grammar/Mechanics

• The writer correctly uses grammar, punctuation, capitalization, and spelling.

I think Kyle's how-to guide is error-free. But I know it's important to check for mistakes in my own work, so I'll be sure to do this as I write. And remember, you should check for proper grammar and mechanics at every step of the writing process so that you can avoid having errors on your final test, too!

Planning My Time

When our teacher gives us a writing prompt, she always tells us how much time we'll have to complete the test. I'm already familiar with the writing process, so I'll think about how much time I need for each step. Then, I'll add it all up to see if it meets the amount of time my teacher has given us. She has allowed us an hour for this test, so here's how I plan to organize my time. Remember, planning your time will help you, too!

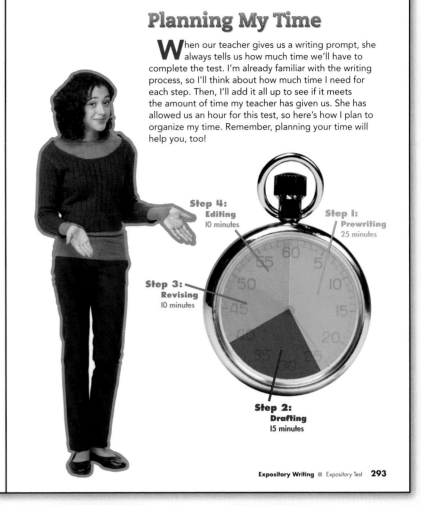

Step 4: Editing 10 minutes

Step 1: Prewriting 25 minutes

Step 3: Revising 10 minutes

Step 2: Drafting 15 minutes

Planning My Time
(Student page 293)

Explain to students the importance of organizing time when planning for a test. Remind them that they will have a limited amount of time to complete their test, so it is important to set aside a block of time for each one of the steps in the writing process.

Refer students to Student page 293, and ask a volunteer to tell the class which writing step Briana plans to spend the most time on. **prewriting** Point out that many students do poorly on test writing because they start writing before they develop a plan, and they continue writing until they run out of time. Stress to students the importance of including time to prewrite, draft, revise, and edit.

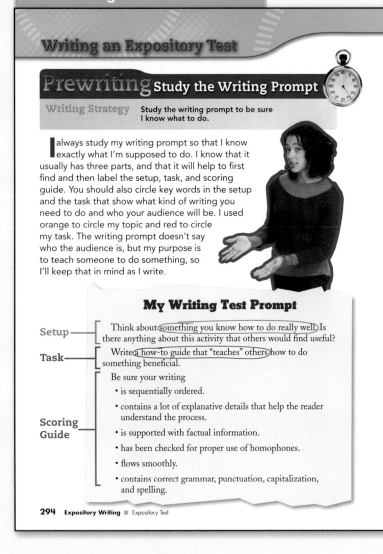

Writing an Expository Test

Prewriting Study the Writing Prompt

Writing Strategy Study the writing prompt to be sure I know what to do.

I always study my writing prompt so that I know exactly what I'm supposed to do. I know that it usually has three parts, and that it will help to first find and then label the setup, task, and scoring guide. You should also circle key words in the setup and the task that show what kind of writing you need to do and who your audience will be. I used orange to circle my topic and red to circle my task. The writing prompt doesn't say who the audience is, but my purpose is to teach someone to do something, so I'll keep that in mind as I write.

My Writing Test Prompt

Setup — Think about (something you know how to do really well.) Is there anything about this activity that others would find useful?

Task — Write (a how-to guide that "teaches" others) how to do something beneficial.

Be sure your writing

Scoring Guide
- is sequentially ordered.
- contains a lot of explanative details that help the reader understand the process.
- is supported with factual information.
- has been checked for proper use of homophones.
- flows smoothly.
- contains correct grammar, punctuation, capitalization, and spelling.

Think about how the scoring guide meets the writing traits in the rubrics you've used. All of the traits might not be included in every scoring guide, but you'll want to think about each of them in order to write a good essay.

Information/Organization
- Be sure your writing is sequentially ordered.

I want to be sure I write all the steps in the correct order.

Voice/Audience
- Be sure your writing contains a lot of explanative details that help the reader understand the process.

I need to include details that explain each step of the process. This way, my readers will really understand what I'm talking about.

Content/Ideas
- Be sure your writing is supported with factual information.

I'd better include facts for credibility.

Word Choice/Clarity
- Be sure your writing has been checked for proper use of homophones.

Sometimes it's easy to mix up words while writing, so I'll make sure that I've used homophones correctly.

Sentence Fluency
- Be sure your writing flows smoothly.

I can make my writing flow smoothly by using different kinds of sentence patterns.

Grammar/Mechanics
- Be sure your writing contains correct grammar, punctuation, capitalization, and spelling.

I'll remember to check grammar and mechanics throughout the writing process.

Study the Writing Prompt
(Student pages 294–295)

Read aloud Briana's words on Student page 294. Tell students that it is important to read and understand their writing prompts before beginning to draft. Explain that even if students write a great paper, they won't receive a great score unless they have followed the instructions set forth in the scoring guide.

Ask a student volunteer to tell the class what type of essay Briana is supposed to write. **a how-to guide** Explain that Briana needs to think about something she knows how to do well, and then she needs to ask herself what is useful about this activity.

Read through the scoring guide portion of the writing prompt shown on Student page 294. Then, review Student page 295 with students. Note how the traits relate to the six key areas of assessment. Remind students that if they were using a rubric, these traits would be those seen under the Excelling category. Point out that even before Briana begins to prewrite, she thinks about each of the traits she will need to include in her test.

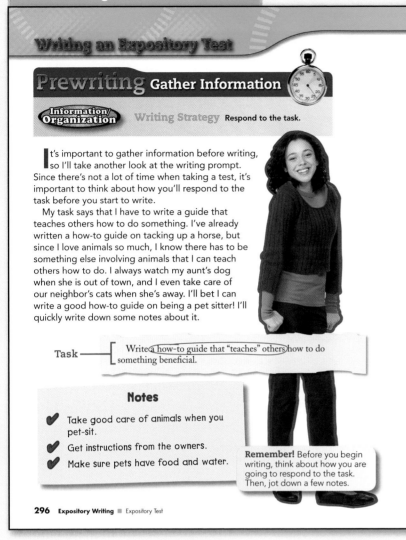

Writing an Expository Test

Prewriting Gather Information

Information/Organization

Writing Strategy Respond to the task.

It's important to gather information before writing, so I'll take another look at the writing prompt. Since there's not a lot of time when taking a test, it's important to think about how you'll respond to the task before you start to write.

My task says that I have to write a guide that teaches others how to do something. I've already written a how-to guide on tacking up a horse, but since I love animals so much, I know there has to be something else involving animals that I can teach others how to do. I always watch my aunt's dog when she is out of town, and I even take care of our neighbor's cats when she's away. I'll bet I can write a good how-to guide on being a pet sitter! I'll quickly write down some notes about it.

Task — Write a how-to guide that "teaches" others how to do something beneficial.

Notes

- Take good care of animals when you pet-sit.
- Get instructions from the owners.
- Make sure pets have food and water.

Remember! Before you begin writing, think about how you are going to respond to the task. Then, jot down a few notes.

296 Expository Writing ▪ Expository Test

Prewriting Organize Ideas

Information/Organization

Writing Strategy Choose a graphic organizer.

Since I don't have much time, I'll start organizing my ideas. The scoring guide says my writing should be in sequential order, so I'll use a Sequence Chain to organize the steps in my how-to guide.

Topic: How to be a good pet sitter
Step 1: Ask the pet owners for details. a. Visit the pet owner's home. b. Write down a list of important instructions. c. Find out when they'll leave and when they'll return. d. Ask how often you need to stop by and what you need to do. e. Get the keys so you can get in the house. f. Get emergency numbers.
Step 2: When it's time for your visit, call the pet by name. a. Give the pet some love and attention while you're there.
Step 3: Give the pet its food and water.
Step 4: If the owners requested it, take the pet for a walk. a. Make sure to take waste bags with you. b. Remember to put the pet on a leash.
Step 5: Repeat the above steps for as many times as the owners requested. a. Leave the owners a note to tell them how things went.
Result: The pet is well cared for, and the owners appreciate it!

Remember! Choose a graphic organizer to arrange steps in the order that they should be followed.

Reflect

Did I include enough steps on my Sequence Chain?

Expository Writing ▪ Expository Test 297

Gather Information and Organize Ideas

(Student pages 296–297)

Ask students to recall what they learned about prewriting in other chapters in this unit. Point out that on a writing test, the prewriting stage is similar: They should consider the assignment and then gather information.

Remind students to use a graphic organizer to organize their ideas. Tell students that during a writing test, they will not be told what kind of graphic organizer to use. Instead, they must think about how they have used graphic organizers in the past, and they must decide which one will be the most useful for their test.

Read through Briana's Sequence Chain on Student page 297. Note that even before she starts writing, she has already written down much of the information that will appear in her how-to guide.

Differentiating Instruction

Support Help students review how the use of graphic organizers can help them structure their notes. Ask volunteers to name the graphic organizers used throughout the unit. **Pro-and-Con Chart, Outline, Sequence Chain** Then, ask students how they might decide which graphic organizer to use on a test. **Possible response: Think about which one fits the writing genre.** Remind students to look for clues in the writing prompt to help them choose. Then, discuss whether Briana's choice on Student page 297 fits the genre for which she is writing.

Writing an Expository Test

Prewriting Check the Scoring Guide

Information/Organization   Writing Strategy   Check my graphic organizer against the scoring guide.

You won't have much time to revise during a writing test, so prewriting is more important than ever. Before I start writing, I'll check my Sequence Chain against the scoring guide in the writing prompt.

Topic: How to be a good pet sitter
Step 1: Ask the pet owners for details. a. Visit the pet owner's home. b. Write down a list of important instructions. c. Find out when they'll leave and when they'll return. d. Ask how often you need to stop by and what you need to do. e. Get the keys so you can get in the house. f. Get emergency numbers.
Step 2: When it's time for your visit, call the pet by name. a. Give the pet some love and attention while you're there.
Step 3: Give the pet its food and water.
Step 4: If the owners requested it, take the pet for a walk. a. Make sure to take waste bags with you. b. Remember to put the pet on a leash.
Step 5: Repeat the above steps for as many times as the owners requested. a. Leave the owners a note to tell them how things went.
Result: The pet is well cared for, and the owners appreciate it!

298 Expository Writing ■ Expository Test

 Information/Organization
- Be sure your writing is sequentially ordered.

I'll mention my topic in my introduction, and I'll use my Sequence Chain to help me write the body of my guide. This will help me keep things in order.

 Voice/Audience
- Be sure your writing contains a lot of explanative details that help the reader understand the process.

I'll explain the steps from my Sequence Chain in detail, and I'll talk about my own experiences, too.

 Content/Ideas
- Be sure your writing is supported with factual information.

I've already written some facts on my Sequence Chain, but I'll be sure to include even more in my guide.

 Word Choice/Clarity
- Be sure your writing has been checked for proper use of homophones.

As I write, I'll make sure to use the correct words.

 Sentence Fluency
- Be sure your writing flows smoothly.

I'll use different kinds of sentences to make one step flow to the next.

 Grammar/Mechanics
- Be sure your writing contains correct grammar, punctuation, capitalization, and spelling.

I'll pay close attention to this as I write. Then, I'll go back and edit my draft before turning it in.

Remember! Check your graphic organizer against the scoring guide before you start to write. This will help you remember what to do once you begin the writing process.

Reflect

My Sequence Chain has given me a good start. Do you think I'm missing anything?

Expository Writing ■ Expository Test **299**

Check the Scoring Guide
(Student pages 298–299)

Ask students why they think Briana is not yet ready to write even though she has used a graphic organizer to structure her notes. **Possible response: She needs to check her notes against the scoring guide.** Emphasize the importance of paying attention to the scoring guide throughout test writing. Note that on Student page 299, Briana once again refers back to each point in the scoring guide to be sure she has met them all. Explain that during this step of the test writing process, students may need to add or change information in their graphic organizers to meet the criteria.

Point out that while the graphic organizer helped Briana organize her notes and meet the scoring guide criteria, she will continue to think about all of the scoring guide traits as she writes.

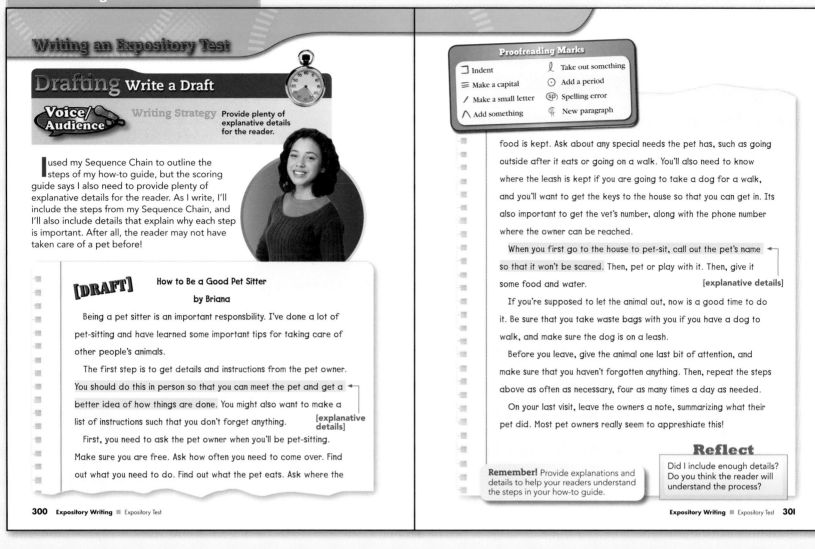

Writing an Expository Test

Drafting Write a Draft

Voice/Audience

Writing Strategy Provide plenty of explanative details for the reader.

I used my Sequence Chain to outline the steps of my how-to guide, but the scoring guide says I also need to provide plenty of explanative details for the reader. As I write, I'll include the steps from my Sequence Chain, and I'll also include details that explain why each step is important. After all, the reader may not have taken care of a pet before!

[DRAFT]

How to Be a Good Pet Sitter
by Briana

Being a pet sitter is an important responsbility. I've done a lot of pet-sitting and have learned some important tips for taking care of other people's animals.

The first step is to get details and instructions from the pet owner. You should do this in person so that you can meet the pet and get a better idea of how things are done. You might also want to make a list of instructions such that you don't forget anything. **[explanative details]**

First, you need to ask the pet owner when you'll be pet-sitting. Make sure you are free. Ask how often you need to come over. Find out what you need to do. Find out what the pet eats. Ask where the

Proofreading Marks

⨅ Indent
≡ Make a capital
/ Make a small letter
∧ Add something
ℓ Take out something
⊙ Add a period
(SP) Spelling error
¶ New paragraph

food is kept. Ask about any special needs the pet has, such as going outside after it eats or going on a walk. You'll also need to know where the leash is kept if you are going to take a dog for a walk, and you'll want to get the keys to the house so that you can get in. Its also important to get the vet's number, along with the phone number where the owner can be reached.

When you first go to the house to pet-sit, call out the pet's name so that it won't be scared. Then, pet or play with it. Then, give it some food and water. **[explanative details]**

If you're supposed to let the animal out, now is a good time to do it. Be sure that you take waste bags with you if you have a dog to walk, and make sure the dog is on a leash.

Before you leave, give the animal one last bit of attention, and make sure that you haven't forgotten anything. Then, repeat the steps above as often as necessary, four as many times a day as needed.

On your last visit, leave the owners a note, summarizing what their pet did. Most pet owners really seem to appreshiate this!

Remember! Provide explanations and details to help your readers understand the steps in your how-to guide.

Reflect
Did I include enough details? Do you think the reader will understand the process?

Drafting
(Student pages 300–301)

Read Briana's words on Student page 300. Point out how she refers to her graphic organizer as she writes her draft. Emphasize to students the importance of using their graphic organizers as guidance during the drafting process. Explain that because of editing, they will want to leave space between the lines so that they will have room to make changes and additions to their work. Also, remind them to write neatly, even in the drafting stage, because the test evaluator should be able to read what they have written.

Then, discuss Briana's draft. Have students refer back to her graphic organizer to see how she included the information that she outlined in her Sequence Chain. Ask students what they think of Briana's draft, pointing out that although there are mistakes, she has remembered to leave time during the editing stage to go through and change any errors she made in spelling and grammar.

Point out the writing strategy at the top of Student page 300, and discuss how well Briana applied this strategy. Have students skim the draft, looking for places where explanative details are particularly helpful in describing parts of the process. Have students also note any spots that need further explanation.

Finally, review proofreading marks with students. Note that these marks will be helpful as they revise and edit their drafts.

Differentiating Instruction

English-Language Learners Stress that it is particularly important for these students to leave time for revising and editing. Remind them that when drafting, they should concentrate on getting ideas from their graphic organizers down on paper. Note that if they have trouble coming up with appropriate words or phrases, they can leave blank spots in their writing and come back to them later. Also remind students that at this stage, they should not be overly concerned with spelling or grammar since they can fix mistakes during editing.

Expository Writing ■ Expository Test **215**

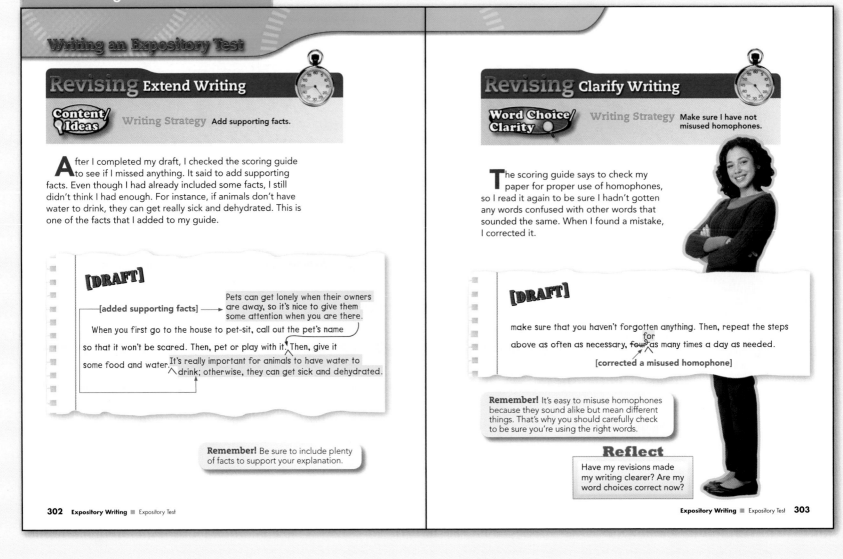

Writing an Expository Test

Revising Extend Writing

Content/Ideas

Writing Strategy Add supporting facts.

After I completed my draft, I checked the scoring guide to see if I missed anything. It said to add supporting facts. Even though I had already included some facts, I still didn't think I had enough. For instance, if animals don't have water to drink, they can get really sick and dehydrated. This is one of the facts that I added to my guide.

[DRAFT]

[added supporting facts] → Pets can get lonely when their owners are away, so it's nice to give them some attention when you are there.

When you first go to the house to pet-sit, call out the pet's name so that it won't be scared. Then, pet or play with it. Then, give it some food and water. It's really important for animals to have water to drink; otherwise, they can get sick and dehydrated.

Remember! Be sure to include plenty of facts to support your explanation.

302 **Expository Writing** ■ Expository Test

Revising Clarify Writing

Word Choice/Clarity

Writing Strategy Make sure I have not misused homophones.

The scoring guide says to check my paper for proper use of homophones, so I read it again to be sure I hadn't gotten any words confused with other words that sounded the same. When I found a mistake, I corrected it.

[DRAFT]

make sure that you haven't forgotten anything. Then, repeat the steps above as often as necessary, four as many times a day as needed.

for

[corrected a misused homophone]

Remember! It's easy to misuse homophones because they sound alike but mean different things. That's why you should carefully check to be sure you're using the right words.

Reflect

Have my revisions made my writing clearer? Are my word choices correct now?

Expository Writing ■ Expository Test 303

Revising

(Student pages 302–303)

Discuss the ways Briana has revised her test: she added supporting facts and checked to make sure homophones were not misused. Point out that Briana once again reviewed her scoring guide in order to determine a revision focus. Encourage students to refer back to the scoring guide section of the writing prompt even after they have completed their drafts.

Discuss the new information that Briana added to her draft on Student page 302. Have students point out other places in Briana's draft where additional supporting facts could help strengthen her explanations.

Next, review with students the way Briana replaced the word *four* with the homophone *for* on Student page 303. Discuss why she made this revision.

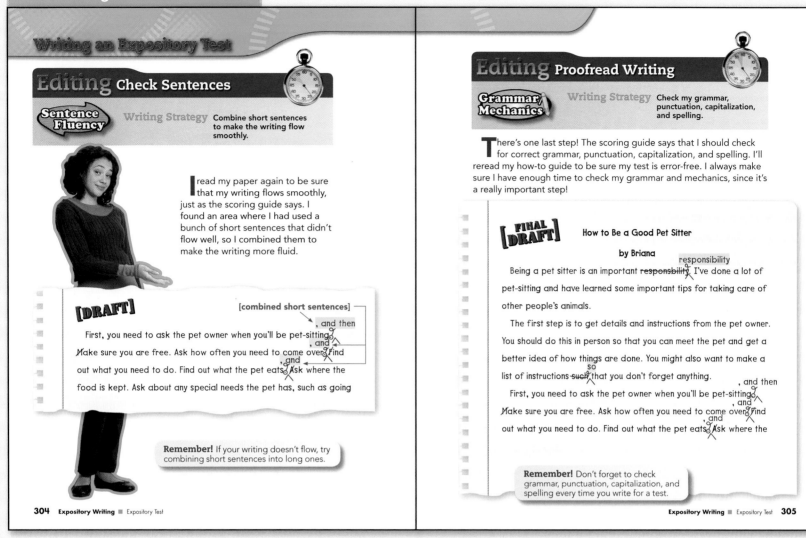

304 Expository Writing ■ Expository Test

Expository Writing ■ Expository Test 305

Editing

(Student pages 304–306)

Ask a volunteer to read aloud Briana's draft on Student page 304—without the edits. Then, ask students to describe the sound of these sentences. **Possible responses: short, repetitive, choppy** Discuss how Briana changed her draft and whether these edits made her writing flow more smoothly. Note that Briana combined short sentences with a comma and the conjunction *and*. Ask students to describe other ways they can combine short sentences. **Possible response: with other conjunctions such as *but*, *so*, *yet*, *because*, *since*, or *while***

Emphasize to students that although they should always proofread for mistakes, basic errors in sentence completeness, punctuation, and spelling will likely affect their scores more than minor errors.

Differentiating Instruction

Support Have students practice combining short sentences by writing these sample sentences on the board. Then, ask students to take turns combining the sentences. Discuss each revision, suggesting alternatives or corrections as needed.

- *I don't like winter. It is too snowy and cold.*
- *My dog Lucky has long fur. He never gets cold.*
- *Mia goes ice skating on Saturdays. Jon plays soccer.*
- *It was stormy today. Mom drove Dad's car.*
- *Some people look forward to winter. Others can't wait for spring.*

[FINAL DRAFT]

food is kept. Ask about any special needs the pet has, such as going

outside after it eats or going on a walk. You'll also need to know

where the leash is kept if you are going to take a dog for a walk,

and you'll want to get the keys to the house so that you can get in. It's

also important to get the vet's number, along with the phone number

where the owner can be reached. Pets can get lonely when their owners are away, so it's nice to give them some attention when you are there.

When you first go to the house to pet-sit, call out the pet's name

so that it won't be scared. Then, pet or play with it. Now, the pet give it

some food and water. It's really important for animals to have water to drink; otherwise, they can get sick and dehydrated.

If you're supposed to let the animal out, now is a good time to do

it. Be sure that you take waste bags with you if you have a dog to

walk, and make sure the dog is on a leash.

Before you leave, give the animal one last bit of attention, and

make sure that you haven't forgotten anything. Then, repeat the steps

above as often as necessary, four as many times a day as needed. for

On your last visit, leave the owners a note, summarizing what their

pet did while they were away. Most pet owners really seem to appreshiate this! appreciate

Reflect

> I'm ready to turn my test in, but before I do, I'll check it against the scoring guide one more time. Remember to use your writing prompt's scoring guide to check your writing anytime you take a test.

Well now, that wasn't so bad! Just remember to use the writing process when you take a writing test. The process is just a little different for a test, but if you keep in mind these important tips, I'm sure you'll do just fine!

TEST TIPS

1. **Study the writing prompt before you start to write.** Most writing prompts have three parts: the setup, the task, and the scoring guide. The parts probably won't be labeled. You'll have to figure them out for yourself!

2. **Make sure you understand the task before you start to write.**
   - Read all three parts of the writing prompt carefully.
   - Circle key words in the task part of the writing prompt that tell what kind of writing you need to do. The task might also identify your audience.
   - Make sure you know how you'll be graded.
   - Say the assignment in your own words to yourself.

3. **Keep an eye on the clock.** Decide how much time you will spend on each part of the writing process and try to stick to your schedule. Don't spend so much time on prewriting that you don't have enough time left to write!

4. **Reread your writing. Compare it to the scoring guide at least twice.** Remember the rubrics you've used? A scoring guide on a writing test is like a rubric. It can help you keep what's important in mind.

5. **Plan, plan, plan!** You don't get much time to revise during a test, so planning is more important than ever.

6. **Write neatly.** Remember, if the people who score your test can't read your writing, it doesn't matter how good your essay is!

Test Tips

(Student page 307)

Ask students to recall the lessons they learned in this chapter. Ask them what they feel are important steps to take when writing for a test. **Possible responses: follow the writing prompt; plan time; save time for editing and revising**

Remind students that test writing is similar to writing for a class assignment. One big difference is that test writing is timed.

Read aloud the Test Tips on Student page 307. Have students think about the ways Briana followed each of these tips during test writing. Point out that they should keep each of the six tips in mind when they write their own tests.

Books for Professional Development

Atwell, Nancie. *Lessons That Change Writers.* Portsmouth: Heinemann, 2002.

In this book, the author focuses on the mini-lesson as a vehicle for helping students improve their writing. She shares over a hundred of these writing lessons.

Harvey, Stephanie. *Nonfiction Matters: Reading, Writing, and Research in Grades 3–8.* Portland: Stenhouse, 1998.

Full of practical suggestions, Harvey's book presents strategies for research, ideas for organizing and writing, suggestions for facilitating project-based learning and assessment, and guided practice in modeling instruction. It also includes bibliographies of nonfiction books and magazines and a list of inquiry tools and resources—both print and electronic.

Freeman, Marcia S. *Listen to This: Developing an Ear for Expository.* Gainesville: Maupin, 1997.

This author suggests adding an aural component to writing. She encourages teachers to read aloud sample essays in a variety of informative, narrative, and persuasive genres. Students are guided to analyze these essays and then use them as models for their own writing.

Portalupi, JoAnn, and Ralph Fletcher. *Nonfiction Craft Lessons: Teaching Information Writing K–8.* Portland: Stenhouse, 2001.

Portalupi and Fletcher present a series of one-page descriptions of strategies that address all aspects of the writing process. Focusing on informative writing in general, the book includes some lessons specific to persuasion, comparison, and how-to writing.

School-Home Connection

Dear Family,

Your child is currently learning to write a book report, which is an explanative summary and review of a book of choice. As he or she goes through the steps of writing this report, here's how you can help:

1. **Prewriting:** Students will begin by reading a book of interest. They will then list their responses to the book, organizing them in a Pro-and-Con Chart. You can help your child brainstorm and choose an appropriate book for such a purpose.

2. **Drafting:** Students will make a working draft of their book report, stating their purpose so the reader will understand why they're writing. You can help by discussing with your child possible reasons for writing.

3. **Revising:** Students will refine their drafts by adding examples to support their responses and by changing passive voice to active voice. Help your child by asking for further clarification of any confusing passages in his or her draft.

4. **Editing:** You can help check for errors by listening as your child reads the draft aloud to you, or you can provide further help by reading the draft over together.

5. **Publishing:** Students will publish a final copy of their work. Urge them to make copies to send to friends and family members.

Being able to summarize writing and appropriately express personal opinions are skills that are required throughout life, in both school and the workplace. If you have any questions as you provide assistance, please let me know.

Thanks for your help in the writing process!

School-Home Connection

Dear Family,

Your child is currently learning to write a research report, which is an account based on factual information gathered and compiled from several other sources. As he or she goes through the steps of writing this report, here's how you can help:

1. **Prewriting:** Students will begin by choosing a topic, surveying some sources, and making a 3 W's Chart. They will then make note cards, the information from which will later be organized into an Outline. You can help your child brainstorm and choose a topic, and then you can aid in research selection.

2. **Drafting:** Students will make a working draft of their research report, remembering to include an introduction that grabs the reader's attention. You can help by discussing possible ways to begin the draft.

3. **Revising:** Students will refine their drafts by adding quotes and paraphrased information from experts and by making sure they've included a list of Works Consulted as well as cited all quotes correctly. Help your child by asking for further clarification of any confusing passages in his or her draft—perhaps these are areas where more quotes are needed!

4. **Editing:** You can help check for errors by listening as your child reads the draft aloud to you, or you can provide further help by reading the draft over together.

5. **Publishing:** Students will publish a final copy of their work. Urge them to make copies to send to friends and family members.

Being able to summarize research and integrate quotes are skills that will be required throughout your child's educational journey. If you have any questions as you provide assistance, please let me know.

Thanks for your help in the writing process!

School-Home Connection

Dear Family,

Your child is currently learning to write a how-to guide, which is a step-by-step explanation of a specific process. As he or she goes through the steps of writing this guide, here's how you can help:

1. **Prewriting:** Students will begin by choosing a process to explain. They will then list the sequential steps in the process. You can help your child brainstorm and choose a process to explain, reminding him or her to list every step in sequential order.

2. **Drafting:** Students will make a working draft of their how-to guide, using a friendly tone to explain each step to the reader. You can help by having your child read his or her draft to you as it is written. This way, you can point out any parts that seem distant or harsh.

3. **Revising:** Students will refine their drafts by adding pictures and explanative details and by making sure all jargon has been explained. Help your child by asking for further clarification of any steps or specific words that seem confusing.

4. **Editing:** You can help check for errors by listening as your child reads the draft aloud to you, or you can provide further help by reading the draft over together.

5. **Publishing:** Students will publish a final copy of their work. Urge them to make copies to send to friends and family members.

Being able to logically and sequentially explain details are skills that are required throughout life, in both school and the workplace. If you have any questions as you provide assistance, please let me know.

Thanks for your help in the writing process!

School-Home Connection

Dear Family,

Your child is currently learning to write an expository test. An expository test is an explanation that students write in response to a writing prompt. The test is timed. Here are the necessary steps involved in writing an expository test, and here's how you can help with each step:

1. **Prewriting:** Students will learn to read a writing prompt to understand the type of writing required. The prompt will tell your child not only what kind of writing to do but also what topic to write about. Time management is crucial in test writing. Practice breaking an hour into segments of time with your child so that he or she has a sense of how long it takes for 25, 15, or 10 minutes of time to pass. Your child will also use a graphic organizer to plan his or her writing. Help him or her decide upon an appropriate graphic organizer by prompting a discussion of organizers used in the past.

2. **Drafting:** Students will use their graphic organizers to write a draft containing plenty of explanative details for the reader. Remind your child to write neatly the first time because there will not be enough time to rewrite the draft.

3. **Revising:** Students will use the scoring guide in the writing prompt as a reminder to add supporting facts and check the use of homophones (words that sound the same but mean different things) in their drafts. Help your child by reviewing common homophones such as *to, too,* and *two*. Refer to a dictionary if needed.

4. **Editing:** Students will spend the last part of the timed writing test checking for common errors in punctuation, capitalization, and spelling in their drafts. Encourage your child not to worry about the "imperfect" appearance of his or her writing test. The pages won't look as neat as usual, and it's OK for students to make corrections right on the page.

If you have any questions, please let me know. Together, we'll help your child master the important skill of writing on demand, a skill that students use in many subjects throughout their school years.

Thanks for your help in the writing process!

PERSUASIVE writing strategies

IN THIS UNIT

1 Editorial

- State the problem. List the pros and cons of several solutions.
- Make a Problem-Solution Frame to organize the pros and cons of several solutions.
- State a problem and offer some helpful solutions for the reader.
- Add detail sentences that accurately support their topic sentences.
- Use quotation marks to clarify catch phrases.
- Use a variety of sentence patterns.
- Make sure each compound personal pronoun refers back to the subject of its sentence.

2 TV Commercial Script

- Choose a type of product to advertise. Search the Internet and take notes on the product.
- Choose a sales technique. Make a Storyboard to sequence ideas.
- Begin with words and images that grab the audience's attention.
- Add a clear call to action at the end of my script.
- Delete any unnecessary, irrelevant, or confusing words and images.
- Use short, exclamatory sentences to create a fast pace.
- Make sure each pronoun and its antecedent has been used correctly.

3 Persuasive Speech

- Choose a problem that I feel strongly about. List a call to action, along with several reasons for the request.
- Make a Persuasion Map to organize the reasons for my call to action.
- Use a convincing tone to persuade the audience.
- Add persuasive details throughout.
- Replace biased or loaded words with neutral words.
- Make use of the question-and-answer sentence pattern.
- Make sure that progressive tense verbs are used correctly.

4 Writing for a Test

- Study the writing prompt to be sure I know what to do.
- Respond to the task.
- Choose a graphic organizer.
- Check my graphic organizer against the scoring guide.
- Clearly state my opinion for the reader.
- Add facts and examples to support each reason.
- Delete unnecessary ideas.
- Use conditional sentences.
- Check my grammar, punctuation, capitalization, and spelling.

PERSUASIVE writing convinces the reader of something.

Hi, my name is Luis. We're studying persuasive writing in school. I'm excited about trying to convince readers of my opinions. I can't wait to try it!

IN THIS UNIT

1 **Editorial**
2 **TV Commercial Script**
3 **Persuasive Speech**
4 **Writing for a Test**

308 Persuasive Writing

Name: Luis
Home: New Hampshire
Hobbies: writing, listening to music, playing video games, watching TV
Favorite Sport: snowboarding
Favorite Book: *The Encyclopedia of the Winter Olympics* by John F. Wukovits

Persuasive Writing 309

IN THIS UNIT

Editorial This genre gives students the opportunity to state a viewpoint and back it up with explanative details.

TV Commercial Script This genre helps students create and sell a product, using a specific sales technique.

Persuasive Speech This genre allows students to put forth a call to action, using well-supported reasoning to motivate an audience.

Persuasive Test Students learn and practice how to read a persuasive test prompt and how to plan their time. They will also learn and practice writing strategies for successful test writing in the persuasive mode.

Meet Luis

The student guide for this chapter is Luis, a boy from New Hampshire. You may wish to explore with students how Luis's background, hobbies, interests, and personality connect with his choices of writing topics. Explain to students that Luis will use what he knows to make decisions about his topics—a process that helps make his writing special and real. Encourage students to follow Luis's lead by using their own background knowledge, interests, and personalities as they write. Persuasive writing convinces the reader of something; in the weeks to come, your students will be writing about many interesting and exciting subjects.

by Julie Coiro, Ph.D.
University of Connecticut

Locating Resources: Reading Within Web Sites

Once students have located a relevant Web site, the challenge is to decide what to attend to first. Like previewing a book, scanning a Web site's homepage can give readers a sense of the structure and intended connections among different content linked within the site. Unlike reading a book, readers cannot rapidly page through large sections to get a sense of the text; they must think strategically about how to preview multiple levels of a Web site for their reading purposes.

The following strategy lesson invites students to stop, think, and anticipate where important information about a Web site's content might be found. Initially, you may wish to model for students these seven steps for previewing a Web site, thinking out loud to show the decision-making that accompanies each step.

1. Read both the title of the page and the title of the Web site in the margin at the top of the window.

2. To get a big picture of the information within the site, scan menu choices by holding your mouse over the navigational or topical menus that often appear along the sides of the frame or across the top of the window, but don't click yet.

3. Explore interactive features of dynamic images (animated images or images that change as a viewer holds the mouse over them), pop-up menus, and scroll bars that may reveal additional levels of information.

4. Identify the creator of the Web site and when the site was last updated. You can often find this information by clicking on a button on the homepage labeled "About This Site." Consider what this information indicates about the site.

5. Decide whether or not the site seems worthwhile. If the site looks worthwhile, decide which areas to explore first.

After several effective demonstrations, you may wish to have students practice these previewing strategies in their own on-line reading.

Critical Evaluation: Evaluating Commercial Bias

Many Web sites contain information that appears to be influenced by commercial interests for or against a certain product. Often, advertising is artfully woven into factual information or interactive games. This is known as commercial bias. It is critical that students, even young students, recognize the techniques businesses use to persuade and influence others who use the Internet for information.

Commercially biased Web sites share information with readers, but they also sell products.

When determining commercial bias, encourage your students to consider questions such as the following:

*   *Whose opinion does the information represent?*
*   *What techniques does the business use to attract children to its Web site?*
*   *What techniques does the business use to attract children to its products?*
*   *Are there attempts to offer new ideas or teach something new?*

*   *Why did the authors use these techniques?*
*   *How does the advertising influence your opinions of the products sold on the site?*
*   *Who benefits most from the different types of information provided at this site?*

For additional practice in considering persuasive marketing techniques, you may wish to have students explore **Kids. Gov: The Official Kids' Portal for the U.S. Government** at **http://www.kids.gov**. Here, resources for each topic are divided into categories, including Government, Organizations, Education, and Commercial Sites to help children distinguish among the different points of view. Encourage students to consider the questions above as they explore several Web sites in each category. Take time to compare and contrast the ways information is presented about the topic on Web sites created for education as compared to commercial sites, for example.

Communicating Globally: Persuasive Writing Opportunities

The Internet provides a number of opportunities for students to practice their persuasive writing techniques for a larger audience. One idea is to have students share their opinions about a book they have read in ways that persuade others to read (or perhaps not to read) the same book. Web sites that allow children to add their book reviews to a collection maintained by someone outside your school include the following:

- **The Book Zone** at **http://www.rif.org/readingplanet/bookzone** is sponsored by Reading is Fundamental, Inc., the nation's oldest and largest nonprofit children's literacy organization. Children are invited to publish their book reviews by simply clicking on the "Review This Book" icon featured as part of the on-line book search tool. Other students can then search for their favorite book and compare the range of reviews available before they select what book they'd like to read next. Students can visit another part of the Web site to learn more about many popular authors and illustrators before or after writing their review.

- **Bookhooks** at **http://www.bookhooks.com/index.cfm**, created by Adrian Hoad-Reddick, is a free on-line book-reporting tool kit for young readers. A simple pop-up form allows one to compose his or her book review, add an illustration, rate the emotional impact of the book, and have it published alongside a growing list of other reviews sorted by genre and author. The site is rounded out by an on-line style guide and invitations to add a book-related quotation or word search puzzle to the collection.

- **World of Reading** at **http://www.worldreading.org**, sponsored by the Ann Arbor District Library in Ann Arbor, Michigan, accepts book reviews from students all around the world. Teachers are asked to e-mail the site's creators so that they can help set up the form for the appropriate school. Then, an on-line form walks students through the process of publishing their book reviews.

Supporting and Extending Writing: On-line Instructional Resources

Teaching students about issues related to persuasion and commercial bias are complex and challenging. The Internet provides a number of comprehensive Web sites dedicated to helping teachers and parents understand these issues in order to better support children as they develop critical reading skills. One useful resource is called **Web Awareness** at **http://www.media-awareness.ca/english/special_initiatives/web_awareness/index.cfm**. It was developed by the Canadian group Media Awareness Network to help parents, teachers, and librarians teach children how to locate good information, as well as how to question and evaluate on-line sources. The section for teachers focuses on teaching students about Internet safety, authenticating on-line information, and dealing with on-line marketing and privacy issues. The site also features links to background articles and to three interactive games that teach students how to make smart and ethical decisions about the Internet. This site is great for parents, too.

A second on-line resource you may find helpful is titled **Information and Its Counterfeits: Propaganda, Misinformation, and Disinformation** at **http://www.library.jhu.edu/researchhelp/general/evaluating/counterfeit.html**. Library media expert Elizabeth Kirk at Johns Hopkins University wrote this helpful summary to review important strategies useful for distinguishing real information from three look-alikes.

Many Web sites also offer on-line lesson plans to extend the writing curriculum. A favorite among teachers is **ReadWriteThink** at **http://www.readwritethink.org**, established in partnership with several organizations including the International Reading Association. Each lesson is designed by a classroom teacher and grounded in research. Each also integrates helpful handouts, scoring rubrics, and Internet resources.

Editorial Overview

In this chapter, students will learn how to write an editorial. They will learn the elements of an editorial—opinions, pros and cons, details, and problems and solutions—and some reasons why they might choose to write one. Students will then use an editorial rubric to study a model writing sample.

Students will follow the student guide as he goes through the writing stages—prewriting, drafting, revising, editing, and publishing. As the student guide learns new writing strategies in each step, students will be directed to practice the strategies in their own writing.

During prewriting and drafting, students will
- state a problem and list the pros and cons of several solutions.
- make a Problem-Solution Frame to organize the pros and cons of several solutions.

- write a draft that states the problem and offers helpful solutions for the reader.

During revising and editing, students will
- add detail sentences to support topic sentences.
- use quotation marks to clarify catch phrases.
- use a variety of sentence patterns.
- edit their drafts for spelling, capitalization, and punctuation, making sure each compound personal pronoun refers back to the subject of its sentence.

Finally, students will write a final draft to be published.

You may wish to send to families the School-Home Connection Letter for this chapter, located at the end of this unit in the Teacher Edition.

Editorial Writing Traits

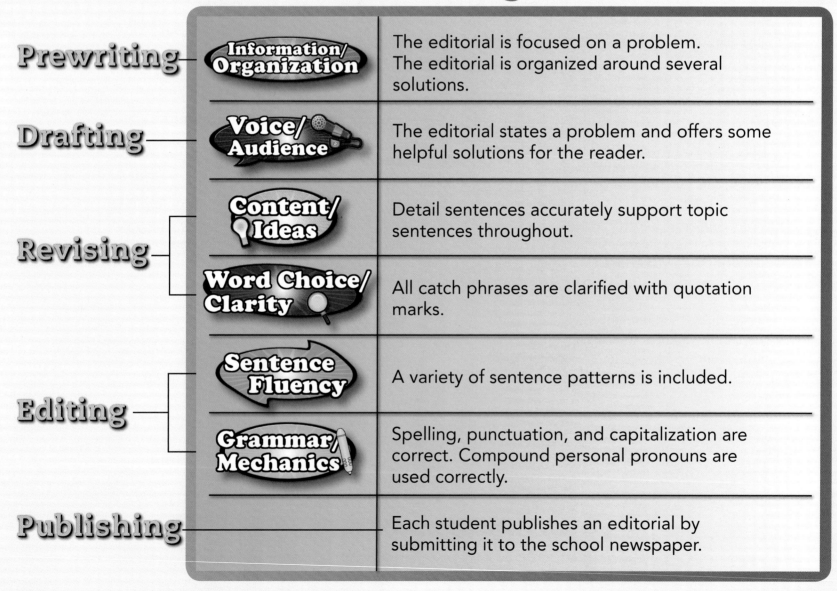

Prewriting	**Information/ Organization**	The editorial is focused on a problem. The editorial is organized around several solutions.
Drafting	**Voice/ Audience**	The editorial states a problem and offers some helpful solutions for the reader.
Revising	**Content/ Ideas**	Detail sentences accurately support topic sentences throughout.
	Word Choice/ Clarity	All catch phrases are clarified with quotation marks.
Editing	**Sentence Fluency**	A variety of sentence patterns is included.
	Grammar/ Mechanics	Spelling, punctuation, and capitalization are correct. Compound personal pronouns are used correctly.
Publishing		Each student publishes an editorial by submitting it to the school newspaper.

Editorial Time Management

WEEK 1

	Day 1	Day 2	Day 3	Day 4	Day 5
Learning Objectives	Students will: • study the components of an editorial.	Students will: • learn how to gather information for an editorial.	Students will: • practice gathering information for their own editorials.	Students will: • learn how to organize pros and cons on a Problem-Solution Frame.	Students will: • practice organizing pros and cons on a Problem-Solution Frame.
Activities	• Discuss the elements and traits of an editorial. (Student pages 310–312). • Use the rubric to study the model (Student pages 313–317).	• Read and discuss **Prewriting: Gather Information** (Student pages 318–319).	• State a problem. • List the pros and cons of several solutions.	• Read and discuss **Prewriting: Organize Ideas** (Student pages 320–321).	• Review the pros and cons listed while gathering information. • Make a Problem-Solution Frame to organize pros and cons.

WEEK 2

	Day 1	Day 2	Day 3	Day 4	Day 5
Learning Objectives	Students will: • learn how to state a problem and offer helpful solutions for the reader.	Students will: • practice writing their own drafts.	Students will: • learn to add detail sentences in support of topic sentences.	Students will: • practice adding detail sentences to their drafts.	Students will: • learn how to clarify catch phrases with quotation marks.
Activities	• Read and discuss **Drafting: Write a Draft** (Student pages 322–323).	• Use Problem-Solution Frames to write drafts. • State the problem and offer helpful solutions for the reader.	• Read and discuss **Revising: Extend Writing** (Student page 324).	• Add detail sentences in support of topic sentences.	• Read and discuss **Revising: Clarify Writing** (Student page 325).

WEEK 3

	Day 1	Day 2	Day 3	Day 4	Day 5
Learning Objectives	Students will: • practice clarifying catch phrases with quotation marks.	Students will: • learn how to use a variety of sentence patterns.	Students will: • learn how to use compound personal pronouns correctly.	Students will: • practice editing their drafts for spelling, capitalization, and punctuation.	Students will: • learn different ways to publish their editorials.
Activities	• Reread drafts, looking for catch phrases. • Clarify each catch phrase with quotation marks.	• Read and discuss **Editing: Check Sentences** (Student page 326). • Make sure to use a variety of sentence patterns.	• Read and discuss **Editing: Proofread Writing** (Student page 327).	• Fix any spelling, capitalization, or punctuation errors. • Fix any compound personal pronoun errors.	• Read and discuss **Publishing: Share Writing** (Student page 330).

* To complete the chapter in fewer days, teach the learning objectives and activities for two days in one day.

This planning chart, correlated to your state's writing standards, is available on-line at http://www.zaner-bloser.com/sfw.

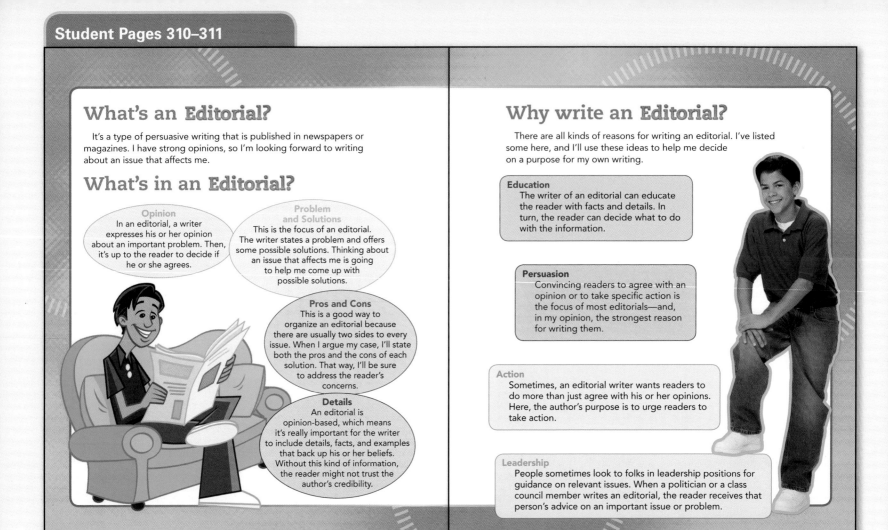

What's an **Editorial?**

It's a type of persuasive writing that is published in newspapers or magazines. I have strong opinions, so I'm looking forward to writing about an issue that affects me.

What's in an **Editorial?**

Opinion
In an editorial, a writer expresses his or her opinion about an important problem. Then, it's up to the reader to decide if he or she agrees.

Problem and Solutions
This is the focus of an editorial. The writer states a problem and offers some possible solutions. Thinking about an issue that affects me is going to help me come up with possible solutions.

Pros and Cons
This is a good way to organize an editorial because there are usually two sides to every issue. When I argue my case, I'll state both the pros and the cons of each solution. That way, I'll be sure to address the reader's concerns.

Details
An editorial is opinion-based, which means it's really important for the writer to include details, facts, and examples that back up his or her beliefs. Without this kind of information, the reader might not trust the author's credibility.

Why write an **Editorial?**

There are all kinds of reasons for writing an editorial. I've listed some here, and I'll use these ideas to help me decide on a purpose for my own writing.

Education
The writer of an editorial can educate the reader with facts and details. In turn, the reader can decide what to do with the information.

Persuasion
Convincing readers to agree with an opinion or to take specific action is the focus of most editorials—and, in my opinion, the strongest reason for writing them.

Action
Sometimes, an editorial writer wants readers to do more than just agree with his or her opinions. Here, the author's purpose is to urge readers to take action.

Leadership
People sometimes look to folks in leadership positions for guidance on relevant issues. When a politician or a class council member writes an editorial, the reader receives that person's advice on an important issue or problem.

Define the Genre
(Student page 310)

Editorial

Discuss with students the definition of an editorial. Ask whether they have ever expressed their opinions in writing. **Possible response: yes** Point out that any time students write about a problem—and offer opinionated solutions—they are using the editorial genre.

Elements of the Genre

Editorial

Read and discuss with students the elements of an editorial listed on Student page 310. Ask volunteers which elements are also common to other forms of writing. **Possible responses: Opinion—book review, speech; Problem and Solutions—persuasive argument, letter to the editor; Pros and Cons—book report, expository writing; Details—description, fiction** Discuss why each element may be important to writing an editorial.

Authentic Writing
(Student page 311)

Editorial

Read and discuss with students the reasons for writing an editorial listed on Student page 311. Point out that all writing has a purpose and is aimed at a specific audience. These authentic purposes help authors shape their writing. Ask a volunteer to read aloud the Education box. Then, have students discuss other reasons someone might write an editorial to educate. Repeat this process for the Persuasion, Action, and Leadership boxes. Then, have students brainstorm other purposes for writing an editorial that are not listed on Student page 311. Encourage students to think about their own reasons for writing an editorial and how these reasons will affect the tone and focus of their writing.

Editorial Writing Traits

I know that there are six traits of good writing. Here's a list of what makes a good editorial. I'll use it later to help me write.

Information/ Organization	The editorial is focused on a problem. The editorial is organized around several solutions.
Voice/ Audience	The editorial states a problem and offers some helpful solutions for the reader.
Content/ Ideas	Detail sentences accurately support topic sentences throughout.
Word Choice/ Clarity	All catch phrases are clarified with quotation marks.
Sentence Fluency	A variety of sentence patterns is included.
Grammar/ Mechanics	Spelling, punctuation, and capitalization are correct. Compound personal pronouns are used correctly.

I can use Julia Powell's editorial on the next page as a model for my own writing. Later, we'll check out how Julia used the traits to help her write.

Editorial Model

The Fate of the Main Street Theater

by Julia Powell

Problem

In three weeks, the city of Springside is planning to tear down its oldest landmark, the Main Street Theater. First opened in 1927, this historical building has deteriorated to such a degree that it is too expensive to save. The theater, which stood empty for years, is situated in a prime location in the center of downtown. Two groups have their eye on that location and are fighting to gain support for their plans. One group wants a multilevel parking garage. The other wants a park with an amphitheater. Both groups want support from the people of Springside in the upcoming election. Therefore, we must educate ourselves about the pros and cons of both proposals. **Pro**

Solutions

Details

First, let's look at the park proposal. The best thing about it is that it would give people some much-needed green space downtown. During the day, downtown workers would have a place to relax and eat lunch. Plays and concerts in the amphitheater would draw people downtown in the evening. This would provide business and income for the stores and restaurants in the area. The park itself would not make money for the city, but its existence would benefit the entire downtown area in other ways, both financially and ecologically. **Con**

On the negative side, however, the costs of designing and building the park would come from our pockets, possibly from a tax levy. The additional cost to maintain the park would be covered by various garden clubs in Springside. **Pro**

Now, let's look at the garage. What would be good about it? If people know they have a convenient place to park, they're much more likely to come downtown and frequent the businesses there. This would attract new businesses, which might consider Springside a good place to call home. **Con**

What's the downside? Some people say a garage would be an eyesore, especially if it's not well maintained. Others say it would be a "crime magnet" that would invite trouble if not well guarded. Yes, hiring people to maintain and guard the garage would create a few jobs. However, I doubt that the hourly fees charged for parking would be enough to pay these workers and maintain the facility.

Personally, I'm in favor of using the site for a downtown park. How about you? Which side will you take when you vote? Choose carefully now! The vote you cast in the upcoming election will affect Springside for years.

Opinion

Writing Traits

(Student pages 312–313)

Editorial

Ask students to share issues or problems that are common to their school or community. Discuss whether everyone agrees on the source of these problems—and how they might be solved. Then, discuss the various ways that people come together to express their opinions. Note that reading and writing editorials are good ways to learn about issues, express opinions, and debate possible solutions.

Next, ask students to describe what they look for in a good editorial. **Possible responses: clear statement of a problem; two or more possible solutions; discussion of all sides of the issue; strong arguments supported by facts** Then, turn students' attention to the traits listed on Student page 312, and discuss why someone might use these traits when writing an editorial.

Finally, tell students that they are going to study and use strategies for writing editorials and that a good editorial has the traits listed on Student page 312.

Differentiating Instruction

English-Language Learners **Preteach** the following key words and definitions to help these students better understand the writing model, "The Fate of the Main Street Theater."

landmark (n.): a building of special historical importance
deteriorated (v.): fallen apart
amphitheater (n.): an open-air theater
benefit (v.): to be good for
financially (adv.): concerning money
ecologically (adv.): with relation to living things and their environment
convenient (adj.): easy to use; handy
frequent (v.): to visit often
eyesore (n.): something that is ugly

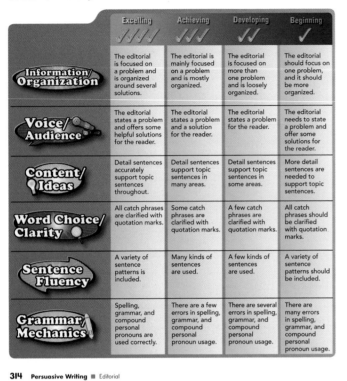

Editorial Rubric

The traits of a good editorial from page 312 have been used to make the rubric below. By using 1, 2, 3, or 4 check marks to judge each trait, you can decide how well any editorial was written.

	Excelling ✓✓✓✓	Achieving ✓✓✓	Developing ✓✓	Beginning ✓
Information/ Organization	The editorial is focused on a problem and is organized around several solutions.	The editorial is mainly focused on a problem and is mostly organized.	The editorial is focused on more than one problem and is loosely organized.	The editorial should focus on one problem, and it should be more organized.
Voice/ Audience	The editorial states a problem and offers some helpful solutions for the reader.	The editorial states a problem and a solution for the reader.	The editorial states a problem for the reader.	The editorial needs to state a problem and offer some solutions for the reader.
Content/ Ideas	Detail sentences accurately support topic sentences throughout.	Detail sentences support topic sentences in many areas.	Detail sentences support topic sentences in some areas.	More detail sentences are needed to support topic sentences.
Word Choice/ Clarity	All catch phrases are clarified with quotation marks.	Some catch phrases are clarified with quotation marks.	A few catch phrases are clarified with quotation marks.	All catch phrases should be clarified with quotation marks.
Sentence Fluency	A variety of sentence patterns is included.	Many kinds of sentences are used.	A few kinds of sentences are used.	A variety of sentence patterns should be included.
Grammar/ Mechanics	Spelling, grammar, and compound personal pronouns are used correctly.	There are a few errors in spelling, grammar, and compound personal pronoun usage.	There are several errors in spelling, grammar, and compound personal pronoun usage.	There are many errors in spelling, grammar, and compound personal pronoun usage.

Using the Rubric to Study the Model

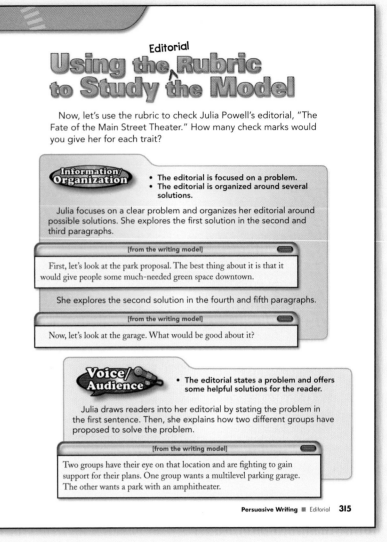

Now, let's use the rubric to check Julia Powell's editorial, "The Fate of the Main Street Theater." How many check marks would you give her for each trait?

Information/ Organization
- The editorial is focused on a problem.
- The editorial is organized around several solutions.

Julia focuses on a clear problem and organizes her editorial around possible solutions. She explores the first solution in the second and third paragraphs.

[from the writing model]

First, let's look at the park proposal. The best thing about it is that it would give people some much-needed green space downtown.

She explores the second solution in the fourth and fifth paragraphs.

[from the writing model]

Now, let's look at the garage. What would be good about it?

Voice/ Audience
- The editorial states a problem and offers some helpful solutions for the reader.

Julia draws readers into her editorial by stating the problem in the first sentence. Then, she explains how two different groups have proposed to solve the problem.

[from the writing model]

Two groups have their eye on that location and are fighting to gain support for their plans. One group wants a multilevel parking garage. The other wants a park with an amphitheater.

Using the Rubric
(Student page 314)

Explain that a rubric is a tool that can be used to evaluate a piece of writing. The rubric on Student page 314 can be used to evaluate an editorial. It is based on the same traits for an editorial listed on Student page 312.

Now, point out the terms above each rubric column: *Excelling, Achieving, Developing,* and *Beginning.* Explain that each column symbolizes a degree of writing skill and that each rubric row focuses on a specific writing trait. When students use the rubric to evaluate their own work at each step of the writing process, they increase the likelihood of producing polished, well-written editorials.

Study the Model
(Student pages 315–317)

Explain that Student pages 315–317 show how the writing model on Student page 313 meets all six traits of the rubric. Read each section with the students. Then, have them look for other examples of each trait in the writing model.

Ask students how many check marks they would assign the writing model for each trait. Then, as a class, decide how the writing model should be rated overall.

Remind students to use the rubric as they write their own editorials, to be sure they are meeting all six writing traits.

Editorial

Content/Ideas
- Detail sentences accurately support topic sentences throughout.

Julia uses detail sentences to support each topic sentence. In this paragraph, she begins with the following: "First, let's look at the park proposal." Then, she adds detail sentences that describe the advantages of putting a park downtown.

> **[from the writing model]**
>
> The best thing about it is that it would give people some much-needed green space downtown. During the day, downtown workers would have a place to relax and eat lunch. Plays and concerts in the amphitheater would draw people downtown in the evening.

Word Choice/Clarity
- All catch phrases are clarified with quotation marks.

Julia uses the catch phrase *crime magnet* in her editorial. Normally, I wouldn't know what she means by this, but she uses quotation marks to show that the phrase has become popularly associated with the issue of the Main Street Theater.

> **[from the writing model]**
>
> Some people say a garage would be an eyesore, especially if it's not well maintained. Others say it would be a "crime magnet" that would invite trouble if not well guarded.

Sentence Fluency
- A variety of sentence patterns is included.

Julia uses sentence patterns that vary in length, pattern, and type. This adds interest to the editorial, since it keeps readers from being lulled by repetition in tone and rhythm. Check out this paragraph to see what I mean.

> **[from the writing model]**
>
> Personally, I'm in favor of using the site for a downtown park. How about you? Which side will you take when you vote? Choose carefully now! The vote you cast in the upcoming election will affect Springside for years.

Grammar/Mechanics
- Spelling, punctuation, and capitalization are correct. Compound personal pronouns are used correctly.

I know that a compound personal pronoun like *herself, themselves,* or *yourself* must refer to its antecedent. Julia makes sure each compound personal pronoun refers back to the subject of its sentence. This eliminates any confusion and makes the editorial easy to follow.

> **[from the writing model]**
>
> The park itself would not make money for the city, but its existence would benefit the entire downtown area in other ways, both financially and ecologically.

My Turn! I'm going to write an editorial about something I feel strongly about. I'll follow the rubric and use good writing strategies. Read on to see how I do it!

316 Persuasive Writing ■ Editorial

Persuasive Writing ■ Editorial 317

Differentiating Instruction

English-Language Learners Help build these students' English vocabulary by introducing synonyms for the words *pro* and *con*. Explain to students that using a variety of words will help make their editorials more interesting.

- Display *Pro* and *Con* as separate headings. Then, list words (and their parts of speech) that have similar meanings for the headings.

	Pro	Con
adj.	positive	negative
adj.	useful	useless
adj.	practical	impractical
adv.	helpful/beneficial	harmful
n.	strength	weakness
n.	plus	minus
n.	advantage	disadvantage

- Explain to students that these word pairs represent different parts of speech as well as varying shades of meaning. Help them learn how to use the synonyms

appropriately by writing the following items on the board and having volunteers complete them.

1. Building a fence around that huge field is just <u>impractical</u>.
2. Using the extra funds for new equipment will give our team a huge <u>advantage</u>.
3. One <u>strength</u> of the new cafeteria is its larger size.
4. Don's proposal to build a pool next to the beach is totally <u>useless</u>.
5. Putting the department store on our crowded street will be <u>harmful</u> to the community.
6. Hiring new teachers to reduce class sizes is a <u>positive</u> thing.

- Work with students to rewrite the sentences so that the opposite word is used in each pair.

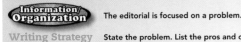

Writing an Editorial

Prewriting Gather Information

Information/Organization The editorial is focused on a problem.

Writing Strategy State the problem. List the pros and cons of several solutions.

I'm on the staff of our school newspaper. I contribute poems, articles, and editorials. So when my teacher said we were going to write an editorial about an important school or community problem, I knew exactly what to write about: Our administration is upset about the clothes some kids are wearing to school. They want us to start wearing uniforms.

To begin working on my editorial, I jotted down the issue. Next, I wrote down possible ways to solve it. Then, I started listing some positives and negatives (pros and cons) about each solution. I also gathered more information by interviewing a friend who has to wear a uniform to school. Several of my arguments came out of that interview.

Problem: Our administration is upset about the clothes that some students wear to school.

Why it's a problem: They feel that the students' clothing causes discipline problems.

Possible solutions:

1. School uniforms for all students

Pros
It's the "great equalizer."
You never have to wonder/worry about what to wear to school.
It saves parents money on kids' wardrobe and accessories.

Cons
Everyone looks the same every day.
Students can't express individuality through clothing.
You get singled out in public—and ridiculed!

2. Dress code that restricts certain clothing

Pros
It allows for individual expression, within limits.
Students can wear different outfits every day.
Parents don't waste money on new uniforms for their kids.

Cons
Dress code guidelines would be set per administration's personal opinions.
Some kids will try to test/abuse the rules.
Their rebellion could end up proving the administration's point.

Practice!

Now it's your turn. Think about a problem, along with several possible solutions. Gather information by jotting down the pros and cons of each solution.

318 Persuasive Writing ■ Editorial

Persuasive Writing ■ Editorial 319

Prewriting
(Student pages 318–319)

Direct students' attention to Luis's words on Student page 318. Note that although Luis knew immediately what he wanted to write about, students might need to brainstorm to come up with an issue that sparks their interest.

Point out Luis's notes on Student page 319, and ask students to state the problem along with Luis's explanation of why it is a problem. **Administration is upset about students' clothing choices; they feel the clothing causes discipline problems.** Point out that Luis structures his notes by stating two possible solutions to the problem, followed by a list of the pros and cons for each. Explain that Luis will use these notes to help organize his editorial. Remind students that when making their own notes, they might want to follow Luis's lead by stating a problem, listing the pros and cons of several solutions, and then using their notes to organize their editorials.

More Practice!

For more practice with these writing strategies, you may wish to have students use the Strategy Practice Book. See the appendix for annotated Strategy Practice Book pages.

WORK with a PARTNER Students who need help identifying a writing topic may benefit from brainstorming with a partner. Suggest that students work in pairs to draw up lists of issues. They should then choose the best two or three for you to review.

Writing an Editorial

Prewriting Organize Ideas

Information/Organization

The editorial is organized around several solutions.

Writing Strategy

Make a Problem-Solution Frame to organize the pros and cons of several solutions.

According to the rubric, my editorial should be organized around several solutions. I'll use a Problem-Solution Frame to organize the ideas from my list. This will allow me to make a side-by-side comparison of the pros and cons of a dress code versus school uniforms.

First, I'll write details about the problem in the problem box. Then, I'll write each solution in its own box. Finally, I'll list the pros and cons under their related solutions.

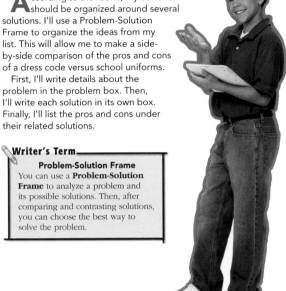

Writer's Term

Problem-Solution Frame
You can use a **Problem-Solution Frame** to analyze a problem and its possible solutions. Then, after comparing and contrasting solutions, you can choose the best way to solve the problem.

Problem-Solution Frame

Problem Box

| What is the problem? | Our administration is upset about the clothes that some students wear to school. |
| Why is it a problem? | They feel that the students' clothing causes discipline problems. |

Solution Box

Solution 1	Solution 2
School uniforms for all students	Dress code that restricts certain clothing

Pros	Cons	Pros	Cons
It's the "great equalizer."	Everyone looks the same every day.	It allows for individual expression, within limits.	Dress code guidelines would be set per the administration's personal opinions.
You never have to wonder/worry about what to wear to school.	Students can't express individuality through clothing.	Students can wear different outfits every day.	Some kids will try to test/abuse the rules.
It saves parents money on kids' wardrobe and accessories.	You get singled out in public—and ridiculed!	Parents don't waste money on new uniforms for their kids.	Student rebellion could end up proving the administration's point.

Practice!

Now it's your turn. Make a Problem-Solution Frame to organize your ideas.

Reflect

How did I do? Do you think my Problem-Solution Frame will help me write a well-organized editorial?

Prewriting

(Student pages 320–321)

Have a volunteer read aloud the Writer's Term box on Student page 320. Then, ask students to compare Luis's Problem-Solution Frame on Student page 321 with the notes he made on Student page 319.

Explain to students that transferring their notes onto a Problem-Solution Frame will make it easier to organize their editorials. Note that if students are having trouble deciding on which solution to promote, a Problem-Solution Frame can help them weigh the pros and cons of each.

Remind students to refer to Student pages 318–321 for help while gathering information and organizing ideas for their own editorials.

Differentiating Instruction

Support Some students may have trouble dissecting their chosen problem and coming up with multiple solutions. Encourage these students to work in pairs to stage "arguments" that can help develop ideas.

- Begin by asking a student to state his or her problem and offer a solution. Then, have the partner argue against the proposal, even if he or she really agrees, stating its negative aspects.
- This partner should then offer a counter proposal, which the first student should rebut.
- As pairs "argue," have students take notes, listing new solutions along with their pros and cons.
- Repeat this process until all students have had a chance to develop their topics.

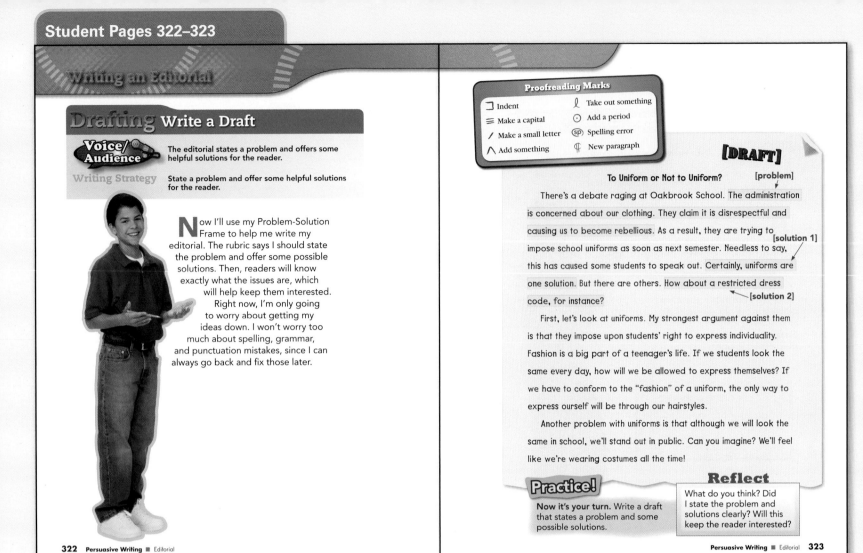

Drafting

(Student pages 322–323)

Remind students that drafting is a chance to get ideas on paper without having to worry about making mistakes.

Refer to Luis's words on Student page 322 and ask students to describe his focus. **Possible response: to state the problem and offer some solutions** Then, turn to Luis's draft on Student page 323 and ask a volunteer to read aloud Luis's problem statement. Ask other volunteers to read aloud solutions 1 and 2. Point out that Luis defined the problem and the solutions in his opening paragraph. Remind students to include these statements in the beginning of their own editorials to help focus readers' attention.

Have students summarize the focus of the second and third paragraphs on Student page 323. **Possible response: The second and third paragraphs argue against school uniforms.** Then, have them predict what information Luis will provide next. **Possible response: Luis will argue in favor of school uniforms.** Note that Luis used the information from his Problem-Solution Frame to write the beginning of his draft. Remind students to use the information from their Problem-Solution Frames to draft their own editorials.

Point out that Luis repeatedly refers to the rubric as he writes. Encourage students to get into the habit of using the rubric to help guide their own writing.

Writing Across the Curriculum

Social Studies Have students read and discuss several editorials from local newspapers. Begin by choosing editorials on a variety of subjects and making copies for students. Then, have students read the editorials and respond briefly to the following questions:

- *What is the problem?*
- *What solutions are proposed?*
- *Which do you agree with, and why?*
- *How well did the writer present the issues?*

Have students form small discussion groups and share their opinions. Then, have volunteers survey the class-wide results and present the findings.

Writing an Editorial

Revising Extend Writing

Content/Ideas — Detail sentences accurately support topic sentences throughout.

Writing Strategy — Add detail sentences that accurately support their topic sentences.

Writer's Term

Topic Sentences/Detail Sentences
A **topic sentence** states the main idea of a paragraph or a piece of writing. **Detail sentences** contain information that supports a topic sentence. This support can be in the form of facts, explanations, illustrations, or examples.

After I finished my draft, I checked the rubric. It says topic sentences should be accurately supported by detail sentences. A lot of the details in my editorial are based on the experiences of a friend, so I feel that most of my information is accurate. But I did find one paragraph in my draft that could use more detail.

[DRAFT]

There are a few advantages to wearing uniforms, however. The most important one is that uniforms are the "great equalizer."

The amount of money a family has is all but indistinguishable when everyone's clothing looks the same.

[added a detail sentence]

Practice!

Now it's your turn. Add accurate information to strengthen your topic sentences.

Revising Clarify Writing

Word Choice/Clarity — All catch phrases are clarified with quotation marks.

Writing Strategy — Use quotation marks to clarify catch phrases.

I want to make sure my writing is clear, so I checked the rubric one more time. It says to use quotation marks to clarify catch phrases. I know that quotation marks can be used around a term or an expression to show that it has a specific meaning. I used a few catch phrases in my draft, so I'll be sure to add the proper punctuation now.

[DRAFT]

[clarified a catch phrase]

For example, T-shirts endorsing tobacco or alcohol products would be forbidden, as would shirts with "suggestive slogans."

Practice!

Now it's your turn. Review your draft to see if you have included any catch phrases. If you have, clarify them with quotation marks.

Reflect

Have my revisions made my writing clearer and more interesting?

Revising

(Student pages 324–325)

Have a volunteer read aloud the Writer's Term box on Student page 324. Then, have students review the detail sentence that Luis added to his draft on Student page 324. Ask what type of detail it provides. **an explanation** Remind students to look for places in their own drafts where topic sentences need more supportive details.

Read aloud Luis's words on Student page 325 and discuss the meaning of the term *catch phrase*. Make sure students understand that a catch phrase is a term that has a meaning that is specific to a particular person, profession, culture, or other area of interest. Have students note how Luis added quotes to the catch phrase in his draft shown on Student page 325. Remind them to use quotation marks to clarify catch phrases in their own drafts.

Differentiating Instruction

Support Some students may benefit from extra practice in adding detail sentences to support topic sentences. Remind students that detail sentences can include facts, explanations, illustrations, and examples. Then, write the following topic sentences on the board and have them add detail sentences for support.

1. *Many teenagers like to skateboard.* **Possible response:** *Statistics show that teenagers are the largest percentage of skateboarders.*
2. *Many school cafeteria foods are high in fat and calories.* **Possible response:** *For example, common menu items are cheeseburgers, pizza, and macaroni and cheese.*
3. *Some teachers give video assignments as an alternative to term papers.* **Possible response:** *One English teacher gave students the option of videotaping a scene from Romeo and Juliet.*
4. *Essentials for a teenage wardrobe are often way too expensive.* **Possible response:** *Many popular sneakers cost more than $100.*

Editing Check Sentences

Sentence Fluency

A variety of sentence patterns is included.

Writing Strategy Use a variety of sentence patterns.

Now it's time to edit. I read my draft again and realized that many of my sentences were the same length and pattern. Then, I looked to the rubric for help. It says to include a variety of sentence patterns, so I rewrote some sentences to mix things up a little. Here's one example.

[DRAFT]

[formed a complex sentence for variety]

Because of their behavior,

~~This would be problematic.~~ These teens just might prove the administration correct in saying that clothing causes disruptive behavior!

Practice!

Now it's your turn. Make your writing more interesting by using a variety of sentence patterns.

Editing Proofread Writing

Grammar/Mechanics

Spelling, punctuation, and capitalization are correct. Compound personal pronouns are used correctly.

Writing Strategy Make sure each compound personal pronoun refers back to the subject of its sentence.

Writer's Term

Compound Personal Pronouns

A **compound personal pronoun** is a pronoun that ends in *–self* or *–selves*. A compound personal pronoun always refers back to the subject of the sentence, usually indicating that the subject is doing something to itself. Because of this, a compound personal pronoun must match its subject in number and gender.

Now it's time to proofread my editorial. I always check for spelling and punctuation errors, but the rubric reminds me to make sure each compound personal pronoun refers back to the subject of its sentence. I know I used some compound personal pronouns in my draft, so I'll make sure they're used correctly right now.

[DRAFT] [corrected a compound personal pronoun error]

Nonetheless, I'd like to ask for your support in fighting for a ourselves dress code. Let us prove ~~ourself~~ to the administration. Let us show responsible that we can be ~~responsible~~ and mature.

Practice!

Now it's your turn. Edit your draft for spelling, punctuation, and capitalization. Also, make sure that you've used compound personal pronouns correctly.

Grammar/Mechanics

For more practice with compound personal pronouns, use the exercises on the next two pages.

Reflect

I tried hard to add variety to my sentence patterns. Did this make my writing more interesting? How are my grammar and mechanics? Did you find any mistakes?

Editing

(Student pages 326–327)

Have students read Luis's words on Student page 326 and note how he revised his draft. Then, ask them to explain what Luis did to revise the second sentence. **He added a subordinating clause to form a complex sentence for variety.** Now, have students check their drafts for places where they can edit for sentence variety.

Next, turn students' attention to the Writer's Term box on Student page 327. Then, write the following on the board:

A compound personal pronoun
- *is a pronoun that ends in –self or –selves.*
- *always refers back to the subject of the sentence.*
- *must match its subject in number and gender.*

Help students better understand this definition by also displaying the following: *Toby told his dad that he could fix his bike himself.* Have students point out the compound personal pronoun and the subject of this sentence. ***himself; Toby*** Then, have them check their drafts to make sure all compound personal pronouns have been used correctly. Remind them that they should also check their spelling, capitalization, and punctuation.

WORK with a PARTNER

Have pairs of students read one another's drafts, using sticky notes to mark errors in spelling, punctuation, and grammar. Then, tell students to perform a second read that focuses on the editing strategies they learned in this chapter.

Grammar/Mechanics Practice!

Compound Personal Pronouns

KNOW the RULE

A **compound personal pronoun** is a pronoun that ends in *–self* or *–selves*. It usually shows that the subject of a sentence is doing something to or for itself.

Example: I made **myself** a cup of tea.

Sometimes, a compound personal pronoun is used for emphasis.
Examples: Mrs. Jenkins built the table **herself**.
Carson changed the tire **himself**.

A compound personal pronoun always refers back to the subject of the sentence; therefore, it must match its subject in number and gender.

Practice the Rule

Number a separate piece of paper 1–6. For sentences 1–3, write the compound personal pronoun and the subject to which it refers. For sentences 4–6, write the compound personal pronoun that correctly completes each sentence.

1. I sat myself down last night to write an editorial for our school newspaper.
2. We have been talking among ourselves about the cafeteria food.
3. The cafeteria employees themselves are unhappy with it.
4. In an editorial, you can really express _____.
5. The students _____ have written many editorials.
6. Coach Decker can get _____ a lot of attention by writing an editorial.

Apply the Rule

Read the editorial below, noting any errors in compound personal pronouns. On a separate sheet of paper, rewrite the editorial correctly.

Avoiding Summer School

Winter glee turns to June gloom when schools have to make up snow days at the end of the year. Last June, kids found theirself in class until the last day of the month. The classrooms were hot, and many summer camps had already begun. Families delayed vacations, and teachers theirselves had to rearrange summer plans.

State laws require that students attend school for a certain amount of calendar days each year, and educators have proposed solutions for making up snow days. One idea is to begin school before Labor Day. Another is to lower the state attendance standards.

An earlier start would add 7–12 days to the beginning of the year. If kids have to make up lost time, they will do so at the beginning of school instead of at the end of June. I myselves am not used to starting school before September. But if others have adjusted to this change, we themselves can, too.

The other option, lowering attendance standards, would allow school administrators ourself to shorten the number of "make-up" days. Some critics believe this option would lower education standards. That's why this proposal would be difficult to attain. Changing the required number of days would necessitate the state legislature to pass a new law.

I herself think the earlier start is the best idea. It's a far better option than staring out the classroom window on a beautiful day in late June!

Grammar/Mechanics Mini-Lesson

(Student pages 328–329)

Compound Personal Pronouns

Ask students to read the Know the Rule box on Student page 328. Then, after writing the following chart on the board, call on volunteers to name the singular and plural compound personal pronouns.

Compound Personal Pronouns	Singular	Plural
First Person	myself	ourselves
Second Person	yourself	yourselves
Third Person	herself, himself	themselves

Make sure students understand why the commonly misused *ourself*, *themself*, and *theirselves* are incorrect by separating them into base words. Note that the plural *our* and *them* do not match the singular *self*. Although *their* and *selves* seem to agree, the word *their* is a possessive pronoun and is not used in a compound personal pronoun.

Answers for Practice the Rule

1. myself/I
2. ourselves/We
3. themselves/employees
4. yourself
5. themselves
6. himself

Answers for Apply the Rule

Avoiding Summer School

Winter glee turns to June gloom when schools have to make up snow days at the end of the year. Last June, kids found themselves in class until the last day of the month. The classrooms were hot, and many summer camps had already begun. Families delayed vacations, and teachers themselves had to rearrange summer plans.

State laws require that students attend school for a certain amount of calendar days each year, and educators have proposed solutions for making up snow days. One idea is to begin school before Labor Day. Another is to lower the state attendance standards.

(Answers continue on page 240.)

Writing an Editorial

Publishing Share Writing

Publish my editorial in the school newspaper.

Now that I'm done, I need to publish my editorial. I could read it to a friend or display it on a class bulletin board. But I feel strongly about this issue, so I want to reach as many readers as possible. That's why I'm going to submit my editorial for publication in our school newspaper. Then, maybe we can all work together to convince the administration to adopt a dress code.

Before I submit my work, I'll read through it one last time to make sure it includes all of the items on my checklist.

My Checklist

✓ One problem is discussed.

✓ Several solutions are proposed.

✓ Detail sentences support topic sentences.

✓ Catch phrases are set off with quotation marks.

✓ Sentences are varied and interesting.

✓ Spelling, capitalization, and punctuation are all correct. Compound personal pronouns are used correctly.

Practice!

Now it's your turn. Make a checklist to check your editorial. Then, make a final draft to publish.

To Uniform or Not to Uniform?
by Luis

There's a debate raging at Oakbrook School. The administration is concerned about our clothing. They claim it is disrespectful and causing us to become rebellious. As a result, they are trying to impose school uniforms as soon as next semester. Needless to say, this has caused some students to speak out. Certainly, uniforms are one solution. But there are others. How about a restricted dress code, for instance?

First, let's look at uniforms. My strongest argument against them is that they impose upon students' right to express individuality. Fashion is a big part of a teenager's life. If we students look the same every day, how will we be allowed to express ourselves? If we have to conform to the "fashion" of a uniform, the only way to express ourselves will be through our hairstyles.

Another problem with uniforms is that although we will look the same in school, we'll stand out in public. Can you imagine? We'll feel like we're wearing costumes all the time!

There are a few advantages to wearing uniforms, however. The most important one is that uniforms are the "great equalizer." The amount of money a family has is all but indistinguishable when everyone's clothing looks the same. Uniforms are also time-savers. They take the guesswork out of what to wear. They are also cost-effective since they eliminate the need for elaborate wardrobes and accessories. I know of a girl who said her parents saved at least $300 in clothing costs because she wears a uniform to school!

Before I sound like I'm in favor of school uniforms, let me propose another solution: a dress code that prohibits certain clothing. This would let students know exactly which items are no-noes. This solution still allows students to express their individuality, but it sets certain limitations. For example, T-shirts endorsing tobacco or alcohol products would be forbidden, as would shirts with "suggestive" slogans.

Of course, this solution has a downside. Some students might abuse the dress code and try to test its limits. They might argue that what they're wearing does not violate the rules. This would be problematic. Because of their behavior, these teens just might prove the administration correct in saying that clothing causes disruptive behavior!

Nonetheless, I'd like to ask for your support in fighting for a dress code. Let us prove ourselves to the administration. Let us show that we can be responsible and mature. We can "dress for success" in this effort. We can win—and keep—our right to choose our own clothes!

Reflect

What do you think? Did I use all the traits of a good editorial in my writing? Check it against the rubric, and don't forget to use the rubric to check your own editorial.

(Answers continued from page 239.)

An earlier start would add 7–12 days to the beginning of the year. If kids have to make up lost time, they will do so at the beginning of school instead of at the end of June. I myself am not used to starting school before September. But if others have adjusted to this change, we ourselves can, too.

The other option, lowering attendance standards, would allow school administrators themselves to shorten the number of "make-up" days. Some critics believe this option would lower education standards. That's why this proposal would be difficult to attain. Changing the required number of days would necessitate the state legislature to pass a new law.

I myself think the earlier start is the best idea. It's a far better option than staring out the classroom window on a beautiful day in late June!

✓ For more practice with grammar/mechanics skills, see Zaner-Bloser's *G.U.M.* materials.

Publishing
(Student pages 330–331)

Ask students if they like Luis's choice for sharing his editorial. Tell the class that his choice is not the only option for publishing his work. Invite students to name other ways they could publish their own editorials.

Have each student make a checklist and perform a final evaluation of his or her editorial before publishing it. Encourage students to share copies of their editorials with friends and relatives who might be interested in reading about what they wrote.

Then, call students' attention to the Reflect box on the bottom of Student page 331. Explain that assessing Luis's editorial against the rubric will help students better understand how to apply the traits to their own work. Have students use sticky notes to mark at least one example of each trait in Luis's writing. Tell them to include an evaluation on each note.

After this process, have students assess how well they were able to identify each trait in Luis's writing and how easy or difficult it was to use the rubric. Remind them to apply what they learned from Luis's work when they use the rubric to check their own writing.

Ways to Publish an
Editorial

As you decide how to publish your work, it's a good idea to think about who might want to read it. That way, you can figure out the best way to share it. Here are some ideas for publishing your editorial.

✓ Present your editorial in a class debate.

✓ Post your work on a Web site where others have submitted opinions on the same subject.

✓ Include your editorial as part of a "Class Opinions" publication.

✓ Post your editorial, along with an editorial that takes the opposite view, on a "Pro and Con" class bulletin board.

✓ Take your editorial home and share it with your family.

Writing Across the Content Areas
Editorial

Your school subjects can be a surprising source of writing ideas. Choose a subject and see how many related topics you can brainstorm. Check out these examples.

Science
• Should recycling be mandatory in your community? Take a stand on this issue.

• Write an editorial that agrees or disagrees with a scientific theory you have learned in school.

Social Studies
• Do teenagers watch too much TV? Should parents set TV limits? State your opinion in an editorial.

• Should all young people be required to serve in the military? Write an editorial that argues for or against an enforced draft.

Art and/or Music
• What can musicians do to enforce copyrights on their works? Propose a solution in an editorial.

• Should art and/or music remain part of the curriculum? Take a stand in an editorial.

Ways to Publish
(Student page 332)

Read and discuss with students the publishing options listed on Student page 332. Encourage students to consider some of these options when publishing their own writing. Remind students that Luis chose to publish his editorial in the school newspaper, but they can choose their own way of publishing. Perhaps one student will want to post his or her work on a "Pro and Con" bulletin board, while another will want to share it with his or her family.

Writing Across the
Content Areas
(Student page 333)

Explain to students that writing is not just for English or language arts class. Many other school subjects contain ideas, issues, and events that students may want to write about. Encourage students to consider using one of the content areas listed on Student page 333 as a springboard for more writing options. Students may also wish to consult with other teachers for more ideas on writing in the content areas.

TV Commercial Script Overview

In this chapter, students will learn how to write a TV commercial script. They will learn the elements of a TV commercial script—product, sales technique, attention-grabber, and call to action—and reasons why they might choose to write one. Students will use a TV commercial script rubric to study a writing model.

Students will follow the student guide as he goes through the writing stages—prewriting, drafting, revising, editing, and publishing. As the student guide learns writing strategies in each step, students will practice these strategies.

During prewriting and drafting, students will
- choose a type of product to advertise and search the Internet to take notes.
- choose a sales technique and make a Storyboard to sequence ideas.
- write a draft containing words and images that grab the audience's attention.

During revising and editing, students will
- end their script with a clear call to action.
- delete unnecessary words and images.
- use short, exclamatory sentences to create a fast pace.
- edit their drafts for spelling, capitalization, and punctuation, making sure pronouns and antecedents have been used correctly.

Finally, students will publish a final draft. You may wish to send to families the School-Home Connection Letter for this chapter, located at the end of this unit in the Teacher Edition.

TV Commercial Script Writing Traits

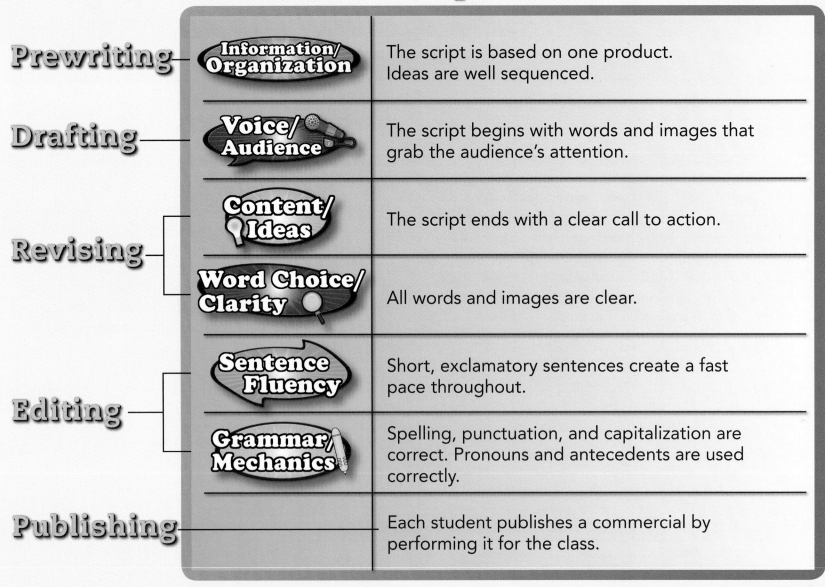

Stage	Trait	Description
Prewriting	Information/Organization	The script is based on one product. Ideas are well sequenced.
Drafting	Voice/Audience	The script begins with words and images that grab the audience's attention.
Revising	Content/Ideas	The script ends with a clear call to action.
Revising	Word Choice/Clarity	All words and images are clear.
Editing	Sentence Fluency	Short, exclamatory sentences create a fast pace throughout.
Editing	Grammar/Mechanics	Spelling, punctuation, and capitalization are correct. Pronouns and antecedents are used correctly.
Publishing		Each student publishes a commercial by performing it for the class.

TV Commercial Script Time Management

WEEK 1

Day 1	Day 2	Day 3	Day 4	Day 5
Learning Objectives				
Students will: • learn the components of a TV commercial script.	Students will: • learn how to gather information for a TV commercial script.	Students will: • practice gathering information for their own TV commercial scripts.	Students will: • learn how to sequence ideas on a Storyboard.	Students will: • practice sequencing ideas on a Storyboard.
Activities				
• Discuss the elements and traits of a TV commercial script (Student pages 334–336). • Use the rubric to study the model (Student pages 337–343).	• Read and discuss **Prewriting: Gather Information** (Student pages 344–345).	• Choose a type of product to advertise. • Search the Internet and take notes on the product.	• Read and discuss **Prewriting: Organize Ideas** (Student pages 346–349).	• Choose a sales technique. • Make a Storyboard to sequence ideas.

WEEK 2

Day 1	Day 2	Day 3	Day 4	Day 5
Learning Objectives				
Students will: • learn how to use words and images to grab the audience's attention.	Students will: • practice writing their own drafts.	Students will: • learn how to add a clear call to action at the end of their scripts.	Students will: • practice adding a clear call to action at the end of their scripts.	Students will: • learn how to delete unnecessary, irrelevant, or confusing words and images.
Activities				
• Read and discuss **Drafting: Write a Draft** (Student pages 350–351).	• Use Storyboards to write drafts. • Begin with words and images that grab the audience's attention.	• Read and discuss **Revising: Extend Writing** (Student page 352).	• Add a clear call to action at the end of the scripts.	• Read and discuss **Revising: Clarify Writing** (Student page 353).

WEEK 3

Day 1	Day 2	Day 3	Day 4	Day 5
Learning Objectives				
Students will: • practice deleting unnecessary, irrelevant, or confusing words and images.	Students will: • learn how to use short, exclamatory sentences to create a fast pace.	Students will: • learn how to make sure each pronoun and its antecedent have been used correctly.	Students will: • practice editing their drafts for spelling, capitalization, and punctuation.	Students will: • learn different ways to publish their TV commercial scripts.
Activities				
• Reread drafts, looking for unclear words and images. • Delete unnecessary, irrelevant, or confusing words and images.	• Read and discuss **Editing: Check Sentences** (Student page 354). • Use short, exclamatory sentences to create a fast pace.	• Read and discuss **Editing: Proofread Writing** (Student page 355).	• Fix any spelling, capitalization, or punctuation errors. • Fix any errors in pronoun-antecedent agreement.	• Read and discuss **Publishing: Share Writing** (Student page 358).

To complete the chapter in fewer days, teach the learning objectives and activities for two days in one day.

This planning chart, correlated to your state's writing standards, is available on-line at http://www.zaner-bloser.com/sfw.

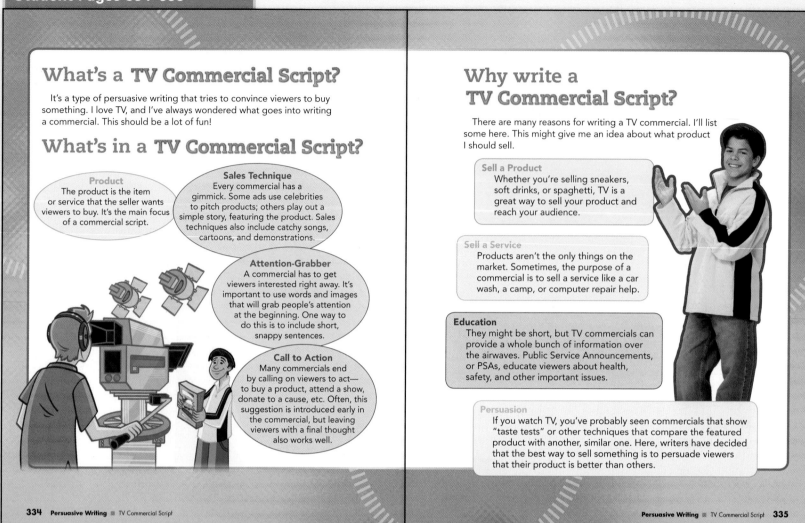

Define the Genre
(Student page 334)

TV Commercial Script

Discuss with students the definition of a TV commercial script. Ask students to recall memorable TV commercials. Can they remember the products being advertised? What about these particular commercials sticks in their minds? Point out that writers of TV commercial scripts rely heavily on sales techniques and attention-grabbing devices to persuade their audiences to act.

Elements of the Genre

TV Commercial Script

Read and discuss with students the elements of a TV commercial script. Ask volunteers which elements are also common to other forms of writing. **Possible responses: Product—speeches; Sales Technique—persuasive arguments, radio and magazine commercials; Attention-Grabber—suspense, narrative writing; Call to Action—editorials, speeches** Discuss why each element may be important to writing a TV commercial script.

Authentic Writing
(Student page 335)

TV Commercial Script

Read and discuss with students the reasons for writing a TV commercial script listed on Student page 335. Point out that all writing has a purpose and is aimed at a specific audience. These authentic purposes help authors shape their writing. Ask a volunteer to read aloud the Sell a Product box. Then, have students discuss other reasons someone might write a TV commercial script to sell a product. Repeat this process for the Sell a Service, Education, and Persuasion boxes. Then, have students brainstorm other purposes for writing a TV commercial script that are not listed on Student page 335. Encourage students to think about their own reasons for writing a TV commercial script and how these reasons will affect the tone and focus of their writing.

TV Commercial Script Writing Traits

I know that there are six traits of good writing. Here's a list of the traits for a good TV commercial script. Later, I'll use this list to help me write.

Information/ Organization	The script is based on one product. Ideas are well sequenced.
Voice/ Audience	The script begins with words and images that grab the audience's attention.
Content/ Ideas	The script ends with a clear call to action.
Word Choice/ Clarity	All words and images are clear.
Sentence Fluency	Short, exclamatory sentences create a fast pace throughout.
Grammar/ Mechanics	Spelling, punctuation, and capitalization are correct. Pronouns and antecedents are used correctly.

I can use Lori Kaspar's TV commercial script on the next three pages as a model for my own writing. Later, we'll check out how Lori used the traits to help her write.

336 Persuasive Writing ■ TV Commercial Script

TV Commercial Script Model

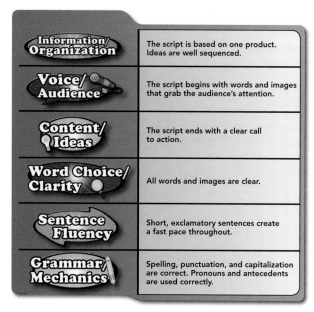

SuperMegaBlast
a TV Commercial by Lori Kaspar

1 (Roger and Bill are hiking in the woods. They enter a clearing and decide to rest. Roger opens his backpack and pulls out some water. Bill opens his pack and pulls out a bottle of green liquid. He shakes it, opens it, and begins gulping the contents.)

2 *Attention-Grabber*
Roger: Hey! Hold on there, buddy! What's that green stuff you're drinking? It looks like spinach juice.

Bill: Spinach juice? No way! This is SuperMegaBlast. It's much better than spinach! *Product*

3 **Roger:** Better than spinach? How's that, Bill?

Bill: Well, you see, SuperMegaBlast is made with spirulina.

Roger: Spiru—what?

4 **Bill:** Spirulina. It's one of the oldest foods on the planet. It's blue-green algae, and it has fifty-eight times more iron than spinach!

Roger: Why, that's incredible!

Persuasive Writing ■ TV Commercial Script **337**

Writing Traits
(Student pages 336–339)

TV Commercial Script

Discuss how students find out about products and how they go about choosing a particular brand. Then, compare and contrast advertisement methods such as pamphlets, newspaper and magazine ads, commercials, Web sites, word-of-mouth, free samples, and taste tests. Have students discuss which are most effective, and why.

Next, ask students to name what goes into a good TV commercial script. **Possible responses: clear sales technique, humor, fast pace, interesting images, good acting** Turn students' attention to the traits of a TV commercial script listed on Student page 336. Have one or more volunteers read aloud the traits and their descriptions. Then, discuss why someone might use these traits when writing.

Finally, tell students that they are going to study and use strategies for writing TV commercial scripts.

Differentiating Instruction

English-Language Learners Preview the format, content, and vocabulary of "SuperMegaBlast" with English-language learners in the class.

Explain that each box of text represents a TV camera shot. This helps the director, actors, and camerapersons visualize how the written dialogue should be presented. Point out that the italicized text in boxes 1, 8, 10, and 11 convey stage directions.

Explain that in this commercial, Roger praises SuperMegaBlast by explaining its health benefits. Discuss the following words in context, making sure students understand their meanings.

- *endurance (n.): the strength to continue or last*
- *essential (adj.): necessary*
- *relieve (v.): to ease*
- *arthritis pain (n.): an uncomfortable swelling of the joints*
- *beneficial (adj.): helpful; giving an advantage*
- *nutritious (adj.): healthful*

TV Commercial Script

(5) **Bill:** Yes, it is. But iron isn't the only good thing in spirulina. It's also nature's richest source of vitamin B12. It's got so much, as a matter of fact, that Olympic athletes use it to improve their energy and endurance. It's also a great source of vitamin E and beta carotene, which are essential for healthy skin and eyes.

(6) **Roger:** Wow, Bill! What else does SuperMegaBlast do?

Bill: Well, it helps relieve arthritis pain. And SuperMegaBlast with spirulina is so beneficial and nutritious that NASA might take it into space some day!

↖ Sales Technique

(7) **Roger:** Space food, eh? I'll bet it tastes awful. It sure doesn't look very good.

Bill: Awful? No way! SuperMegaBlast is delicious. It contains fruit juices—strawberry and banana—so it's sweet and refreshing, especially when chilled.

Roger: Hmm. Say, Bill, would you happen to have another SuperMegaBlast in that backpack of yours?

(8) **Bill:** Sure do, Rog.

(Bill takes another bottle from his backpack and hands it to Roger. Roger shakes the bottle, opens it, and takes a tiny sip. He smacks his lips and smiles. Then, he takes a much bigger sip.)

(9) **Roger:** Hey! This SuperMegaBlast is really good stuff!

Bill: I thought you'd like it.

Roger: Like it? I love it!

(10) *(Roger takes another long sip and looks at the bottle. Then, he suddenly jumps to his feet.)*

Bill: Whoa, Rog! Where are you going?

Roger: To the store! I want to get my own SuperMegaBlast before everyone buys it all. I'd hate to wait so long that the only place I can get it is in outer space!

(11) *(Bill laughs. The two put on their backpacks and hike away briskly. As they do, the camera points above them and into the sky. A SuperMegaBlast bottle appears.)*

(12) **Announcer's Voice:** SuperMegaBlast. It's out of this world. Get it at your local grocer's . . . while supplies last.

Call to Action ↗

Differentiating Instruction

Enrichment Encourage students to investigate popular "health" drinks on the market today. Suggest that they focus on one of the projects below.

• Select two or more brands. Then, compare drinks that contain similar ingredients. List the ingredients and investigate their properties. Analyze the drinks using graphs or other visuals, drawing conclusions about which is best.

• Choose one brand. Then, compare and contrast two or more of its individual products. Describe and analyze ingredients, noting which drinks might be suitable for various purposes.

• Run taste tests that compare individual drinks within one brand. For each drink, document ingredients and properties, keeping this information on hand. Make sure you cover the labels of the drinks to be tested so that subjects do not know which drink they are sampling. For each product tested, have subjects fill out feedback cards. After the taste test, analyze the results and publish your findings.

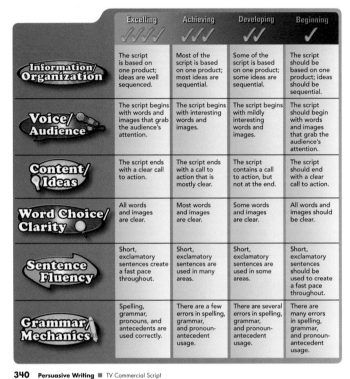

TV Commercial Script
Rubric

The traits of a good TV commercial from page 336 have been used to make the rubric below. By using 1, 2, 3, or 4 check marks to judge each trait, you can decide how well any TV commercial was written.

	Excelling ✓✓✓✓	Achieving ✓✓✓	Developing ✓✓	Beginning ✓
Information/ Organization	The script is based on one product; ideas are well sequenced.	Most of the script is based on one product; most ideas are sequential.	Some of the script is based on one product; some ideas are sequential.	The script should be based on one product; ideas should be sequential.
Voice/ Audience	The script begins with words and images that grab the audience's attention.	The script begins with interesting words and images.	The script begins with mildly interesting words and images.	The script should begin with words and images that grab the audience's attention.
Content/ Ideas	The script ends with a clear call to action.	The script ends with a call to action that is mostly clear.	The script contains a call to action, but not at the end.	The script should end with a clear call to action.
Word Choice/ Clarity	All words and images are clear.	Most words and images are clear.	Some words and images are clear.	All words and images should be clear.
Sentence Fluency	Short, exclamatory sentences create a fast pace throughout.	Short, exclamatory sentences are used in many areas.	Short, exclamatory sentences are used in some areas.	Short, exclamatory sentences should be used to create a fast pace throughout.
Grammar/ Mechanics	Spelling, grammar, pronouns, and antecedents are used correctly.	There are a few errors in spelling, grammar, and pronoun-antecedent usage.	There are several errors in spelling, grammar, and pronoun-antecedent usage.	There are many errors in spelling, grammar, and pronoun-antecedent usage.

TV Commercial Script
Using the Rubric to Study the Model

Let's use the rubric to check Lori Kaspar's TV commercial script, "SuperMegaBlast." How many check marks would you give her for each trait?

Information/ Organization
- The script is based on one product.
- Ideas are well sequenced.

Lori focuses her commercial on one product: SuperMegaBlast. She also does a good job of sequencing the script. First, Bill pulls out the product, sparking Roger's curiosity. Next, Roger and Bill have a conversation during which facts about the product are revealed. It's like the reader of the script is actually watching the commercial!

[from the writing model]

Roger: Better than spinach? How's that, Bill?

Bill: Well, you see, SuperMegaBlast is made with spirulina.

Voice/ Audience
- The script begins with words and images that grab the audience's attention.

Lori's script grabs the audience's attention right from the beginning. The opening scene paints a mental image for the reader.

[from the writing model]

(Roger and Bill are hiking in the woods. They enter a clearing and decide to rest. Roger opens his backpack and pulls out some water. Bill opens his pack and pulls out a bottle of green liquid. He shakes it, opens it, and begins gulping the contents.)

Using the Rubric
(Student page 340)

Explain that a rubric is a tool that can be used to evaluate a piece of writing. The rubric on Student page 340 can be used to evaluate a TV commercial script. It is based on the same traits for a TV commercial script listed on Student page 336.

Now, point out the terms above each rubric column: *Excelling, Achieving, Developing,* and *Beginning.* Explain that each column symbolizes a degree of writing skill and that each rubric row focuses on a specific writing trait. When students use the rubric to evaluate their own work at each step of the writing process, they increase the likelihood of producing polished, well-written TV commercial scripts.

Study the Model
(Student page 341–343)

Explain that Student pages 341–343 show how the writing model on Student pages 337–339 meets all six traits of the rubric. Read each section with the students. Then, have them look for other examples of each trait in the writing model.

Ask students how many check marks they would assign the writing model for each trait. Then, as a class, decide how the writing model should be rated overall.

Remind students to use the rubric as they write their own TV commercial scripts, to be sure they are meeting all six writing traits.

TV Commercial Script

 **Content/Ideas**
• The script ends with a clear call to action.

Lori includes a clear call to action at the end of her script. Leading up to this, Roger says he's hurrying off to buy some SuperMegaBlast before it's too late. This sets up the announcer's final words, which hold viewers' attention until the end.

[from the writing model]

Announcer's Voice: SuperMegaBlast. It's out of this world. Get it at your local grocer's . . . while supplies last.

Word Choice/Clarity
• All words and images are clear.

The commercial is descriptive and clear because Lori does not include any information that would confuse viewers. When Bill tells Roger about spirulina, he uses a lot of clear, precise details.

[from the writing model]

Bill: Spirulina. It's one of the oldest foods on the planet. It's blue-green algae, and it has fifty-eight times more iron than spinach!

Roger: Why, that's incredible!

Bill: Yes, it is. But iron isn't the only good thing in spirulina. It's also nature's richest source of vitamin B12. It's got so much, as a matter of fact, that Olympic athletes use it to improve their energy and endurance. It's also a great source of vitamin E and beta carotene, which are essential for healthy skin and eyes.

 Sentence Fluency
• Short, exclamatory sentences create a fast pace throughout.

A commercial writer needs to get the point across in an extremely short amount of time. So it's good that Lori uses a lot of short exclamations to create a fast pace. Here's an example of what I mean.

[from the writing model]

Roger: Hey! This SuperMegaBlast is really good stuff!

Bill: I thought you'd like it.

Roger: Like it? I love it!

 Grammar/Mechanics
• Spelling, punctuation, and capitalization are correct. Pronouns and antecedents are used correctly.

Lori's script seems to be free of errors. She also makes sure that each pronoun has a clear antecedent. In this excerpt, I can tell that the pronoun *it* replaces the word *bottle*.

[from the writing model]

(Bill takes another bottle from his backpack and hands it to Roger. Roger shakes the bottle, opens it, and takes a tiny sip. He smacks his lips and smiles. Then, he takes a much bigger sip.)

 My Turn!
I'm going to write a TV commercial script about a fun product. I'll follow the rubric and use good writing strategies. Follow along to see how I do it!

Differentiating Instruction

Support Review with students the purpose of graphic design images in commercials. To begin, ask students to think about commercials they have seen. Note that TV commercials often display brand names, slogans, informational text, labels, icons, cartoons, and other graphics.

Ask students to explain the purpose of these graphics. **Possible responses: to familiarize viewers with the product; to present and emphasize information; to support what commercial characters are saying** As students visualize what their commercial will look like onscreen, remind them to include graphic images in their scripts. Point out that they can "spec" these images by including instructions, similar to stage directions, at the points they want the images to appear. Explain that these specs will help students remember which images they wanted to include in which location.

Writing a TV Commercial Script

Prewriting Gather Information

Information/Organization

Writing Strategy

The script is based on one product.

Choose a type of product to advertise. Search the Internet and take notes on the product.

I totally love snowboarding, so I always read up on the best new equipment. When I found out that I had to write a TV commercial, it didn't take me long to decide what kind of product to advertise. You really need the right kind of clothes to stay warm, dry, and safe on the slopes, so I decided to make my commercial about a made-up brand of snowboarding pants called ChillSnowriders.

The first thing I did was log onto the Internet and search for some Web sites that sell snowboarding clothes. I looked at the special features and fabrics of several styles of pants. After deciding what I wanted my product to be like, I wrote down my ideas.

344 **Persuasive Writing** ■ TV Commercial Script

Information About Snowboarding Pants

- highback waist that keeps the snow out
- large front pockets
- need extra padding or fabric around knees and seat
- reinforced knees

- elastic cuffs
- leg vents with zipper

General Notes:
- must be loose fitting and comfortable
- must be waterproof, windproof, and breathable
- outer shell: nylon
- lining: wicking mesh and taffeta

Practice!

Now it's your turn. Choose an interesting product or service to advertise. Then, do some basic research and take useful notes.

Persuasive Writing ■ TV Commercial Script 345

Prewriting

(Student pages 344–345)

Remind students that they will need to "create" products to advertise in their TV commercial scripts. Encourage them to use their imaginations to develop products that relate to areas of interest.

Have students review Luis's words on Student page 344. Note that he chose to advertise a product of special interest and then he did Internet research to take notes on product information. Then, turn students' attention to Student page 345. Point out the various kinds of information that Luis gathered, along with the way in which he chose to organize his notes.

Help students use a similar prewriting process, breaking it down into the following steps:

1. Brainstorm a product that relates to an area of personal interest.
2. Use the Internet to gather product information and help spark other ideas. Take notes while gathering information.

3. Organize the most important information on a "design sheet" that includes visual images.

Remind students to refer to their design sheets as they plan their own TV commercial scripts.

More Practice!

For more practice with these writing strategies, you may wish to have students use the Strategy Practice Book. See the appendix for annotated Strategy Practice Book pages.

WORK with a PARTNER
Students who need extra help developing a product to advertise may benefit from working with a partner. Suggest that students work together to brainstorm areas of interest, focusing on potential product ideas. Check in on pairs from time to time, offering guidance as needed.

Writing a TV Commercial Script

Prewriting Organize Ideas

Information/Organization

Ideas are well sequenced.

Writing Strategy

Choose a sales technique. Make a Storyboard to sequence ideas.

> ✏️ **Writer's Term**
>
> **Sales Technique**
> A **sales technique** is the method used to persuade people to buy a product.

In order to sell my product, I need to choose the right sales technique. I'll use the chart on the next page to help me get started.

I'm selling snowboarding pants, so my audience will probably consist of kids like me. I know the "scientific approach" would be boring to them, so I won't use it. The "animated ad" could work, but that would be hard for me to produce. I think that I'd be a great salesperson, so I'm going to use the "testimonial," featuring me—the famous Luis Rios—as the expert on my product. After I write my script, I'll get to star in my own commercial!

346 Persuasive Writing ■ TV Commercial Script

Common Sales Techniques

The Bandwagon Ad	pictures a group of people using and enjoying a product. The message is usually "EVERYBODY'S using this product, and so should you! Join the crowd!"
The Testimonial	uses familiar faces—sports figures, actors, and other famous people—to endorse a product. The message is usually "You know me, and you can trust me. I use this product, and you should, too!"
The Good Times/ Good Friends Ad	pictures happy people enjoying themselves and each other's company. The setting for these ads is generally a warm, cozy environment or an exciting, exotic location where people are engaged in lively activities. The message is usually "If you use this product, you will have good times and good friends, too."
The Humorous Ad	includes jokes, funny situations, or catch phrases that entertain the audience. This is a "feel good" approach. Because the audience enjoys the advertisement, some viewers are likely to have positive thoughts about the product.
The Animated Ad	uses cartoonlike animals, people, or fictional creatures to sell a product. The audience is usually familiar with the animated character (from a movie, a comic strip, or other advertising). But sometimes a new character is introduced and used instead.
Scientific Approach	uses many scientific-sounding terms and charts to impress the audience. The message is usually "You can believe us because we have scientific evidence to back up our claims."

Now it's your turn. Read the sales techniques on this page. Then, pick the best one for your commercial.

Persuasive Writing ■ TV Commercial Script 347

Prewriting

(Student pages 346–347)

Have students review the Writer's Term box on Student page 346. Then, turn students' attention to the list of common sales techniques on Student page 347 and ask them to explain why it is important to choose specific sales techniques for their commercials. **Possible response: because sales techniques determine the tone and story line of commercials**

Help students better understand the sales techniques listed on Student page 347 by discussing which techniques would be appropriate for which products. Students may draw on their knowledge of specific commercials or products. List the techniques on the board as headings. Then, add students' suggestions. Make sure students understand that there are no right or wrong answers and that one product may be advertised in many different ways.

Remind students to decide on appropriate sales techniques and then use them to help develop Storyboards. Note that they can refer to Student page 347 for help as needed.

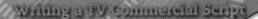

Writing a TV Commercial Script

Prewriting Organize Ideas

Information/Organization
Ideas are well sequenced.

Writing Strategy
Choose a sales technique. Make a Storyboard to sequence ideas.

Writer's Term

Storyboard
A **Storyboard** can help you sequence the main points of a TV commercial. Each frame represents a new idea or event.

TV is visual, so I have to get an idea of what people will "see" when they hear the words in my script. First, I'll use a Storyboard to organize my ideas into six key scenes. Then, I'll draw a picture for each scene.

STORYBOARD

① At start of commercial, announcers introduce themselves along with Luis Rios, who is competing in a halfpipe event. The announcer says Rios is being sponsored by ChillSnowriders pants.

② Rios comes to a dramatic stop in front of the camera. The crowd is cheering wildly. A fan shouts, "Hey, dude! Nice ChillSnowriders!"

③ Rios steps out of his bindings and picks up his board. As he walks toward the camera, a TV announcer tells him that he's won and asks about the secret of his success.

④ Rios talks about how ChillSnowriders are essential to his performance. He praises their fit, their warmth, and their ability to wick away moisture.

⑤ He steps up to the center platform and receives his gold medal. The crowd begins cheering again. TV announcer: "Be unbeatable! Wear ChillSnowriders—the only choice of champions."

⑥ The camera zooms in on Rios. He smiles and holds up his board. A big ChillSnowriders logo appears on it. Freeze frame.

Practice!
Now it's your turn. Make a Storyboard to plan your commercial.

Reflect
What do you think of my sales technique? Is my Storyboard convincing?

Prewriting
(Student pages 348–349)

Have students read and evaluate Luis's Storyboard on Student pages 348–349. Encourage them to assess whether they can visualize each scene. Ask whether Luis includes enough information to guide each scene. **Possible response: yes** Point out that similar to a traditional outline, Luis's Storyboard provides notes and summaries rather than exact words or actual lines of dialogue. Explain that Luis will refer to his Storyboard as he adds details to his script. Remind students to use their own Storyboards to organize ideas into scenes. They can refer to Student pages 348–349 for help as needed.

Differentiating Instruction

Support Some students may need extra help developing their Storyboards. Break down the process by explaining the following steps.

1. Before creating each frame, make notes that answer the following questions:
   Where and when does the scene take place?
   Who is in the scene?
   What happens in the scene?
2. Use the answers to create the text for each frame.
3. Visualize what each scene will look like onscreen to help draw the sketch that appears in each frame.
4. After completing the Storyboard, review it by asking the following questions:
   Does the first frame have the potential to develop into an attention-grabbing opener?
   Does each frame clearly describe a specific scene?
   Will each scene flow smoothly into the next?
   Does the final frame outline a strong ending?

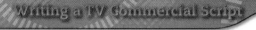

Writing a TV Commercial Script

Drafting Write a Draft

The script begins with words and images that grab the audience's attention.

Writing Strategy Begin with words and images that grab the audience's attention.

I'm ready to write my script. The rubric says that I should begin with words and images that grab my audience's attention. I'll begin with an exciting setting—a snowboarding competition. Then, I'll have two sportscasters address the audience. To draw viewers in further, I'll use words that are common to the snowboarding scene.

While drafting, I'll use my Storyboard to keep my writing on track. I'll do my best with spelling and grammar, but I won't focus too much on mistakes right now. I can always go back and fix those later.

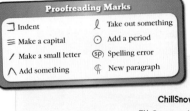

Proofreading Marks

⌐ Indent	ℓ Take out something
≡ Make a capital	⊙ Add a period
/ Make a small letter	SP Spelling error
∧ Add something	¶ New paragraph

[DRAFT]

ChillSnowriders [attention-grabbing image]
a TV Commercial by Luis Rios

First Sportscaster: A great good afternoon, Extreme fans! I'm Jim Smith, and this is Carol Jones. We're here at the Annual Big Air Competition in beautiful New Hampshire, and the crowd is really stoked. Right now you're watching the current champion, Luis Rios, shredding his way to a sure victory in the halfpipe competition. As always, Rios is sponsored by ChillSnowriders, makers of the world's finest snowboarding pants. [attention-grabbing words]

Second Sportscaster: Whoa! Rios caught some really big air there! Did you see that amazing burger flip? This guy is unbelievable! I think he's done it again, Jim!

(Rios comes to a dramatic stop right in front of the camera.)

Fan: Hey, dude! Nice ChillSnowriders!

(Rios nods to the fan, steps out of his bindings, picks up his board, and begins walking toward the winners platform.)

Smith: Hey, Luis! You've won! What's the secret of your success?

Practice!

Now it's your turn. Write a draft that begins with attention-grabbing words and images.

Reflect

What do you think? Did I choose an interesting setting? Will my words and images draw the audience in?

Drafting

(Student pages 350–351)

Remind students that drafting is a chance to get ideas on paper without having to worry about making mistakes.

Refer students to Luis's words on Student page 350. Note that he plans to begin his commercial with an exciting snowboarding scene. Then, turn students' attention to Luis's draft on Student page 351, and have them note the highlighted words and images.

Have students compare Luis's draft to his Storyboard. Ask which scenes are included in this section. 1–3 Remind students to refer to their own Storyboards as they draft their scripts.

Refer to the Practice and Reflect boxes on Student page 351, which remind students to use attention-grabbing words and images at the beginning of their scripts. Then, point out that Luis repeatedly refers to the rubric as he writes. Encourage students to get into the habit of using the rubric to help guide their own writing.

Writing Across the Curriculum

Social Studies: Media Have students explore sales techniques by watching and analyzing TV commercials, then summarizing their findings.

- Give students one week to view TV commercials.
- Encourage them to use a pen and paper for taking notes, a list of sales techniques and their definitions, and a chart with the following headings: *Product Name; Setting; Characters; Story Line; Attention-Grabber; Call to Action; Sales Technique.*
- As students view commercials, have them take notes on their charts.
- After the viewing period, have students summarize their findings by totaling the number of commercials viewed, as well as the number of times each sales technique was used.
- Then, have students make a list of personal "Bests and Worsts." Students may also have fun giving awards for commercials in various categories, such as Funniest Commercial.
- Finally, have students display their findings in a multimedia presentation for the class.

Writing a TV Commercial Script

Revising Extend Writing

Content/Ideas — The script ends with a clear call to action.

Writing Strategy — Add a clear call to action at the end of my script.

Writer's Term

Call to Action
A **call to action** is an appeal to the audience to buy, try, or use whatever is being advertised. A call to action contains strong words and images that persuade the audience.

According to the rubric, my commercial needs to end with a clear call to action. Earlier in the commercial, I used the words *champion* and *unbeatable* to describe the character of Luis. I think I'll use these words again in my call to action to convince my audience that if they wear ChillSnowriders, they can be unbeatable champions, too!

[DRAFT]

(The camera zooms in on Rios. ~~Him~~ looks into the camera, smiles broadly, and holds his board over his head. The ChillSnowriders logo appears across the board, and the frame freezes.)

Jones: You can be unbeatable, too! Wear ChillSnowriders. They're the only choice of champions!

[added a clear call to action]

Practice!
Now it's your turn. Add a clear call to action at the end of your script.

Reflect
Have my revisions made my commercial stronger?

352 **Persuasive Writing** ■ TV Commercial Script

Revising Clarify Writing

Word Choice/Clarity — All words and images are clear.

Writing Strategy — Delete any unnecessary, irrelevant, or confusing words and images.

I read my draft to my classmate Jack. He liked it, but he was a little confused about one part that didn't seem to fit. The rubric says all my words and images should be clear, so I'll get rid of the unnecessary information now.

[DRAFT]
[deleted an unclear image]

Rios: Well, ChillSnowriders are loose fitting, which means that it allows great freedom of movement and the ability to layer in extreme weather conditions. ~~I remember getting caught in a blizzard once. Man, that was intense! It was so white out that I couldn't see my hand in front of my face.~~ ChillSnowriders are waterproof, windproof, and they have a special lining that wicks moisture away from my body.

Practice!
Now it's your turn. Review your draft to see if you have included any unnecessary or irrelevant parts that should be deleted.

Persuasive Writing ■ TV Commercial Script 353

Revising
(Student pages 352–353)

Have students review Luis's words and the section of his draft shown on Student page 352. Note that Luis's call to action serves a dual purpose: It calls on viewers to wear ChillSnowriders while emphasizing the association between the product and the image of an unbeatable champion.

Remind students that in writing his call to action, Luis picked up on ideas conveyed earlier in the commercial. Note that students may wish to follow a similar process when revising their own scripts.

Then, have students review Luis's words and the section of his draft shown on Student page 353. Ask students why they think Luis deleted the highlighted text. **because the information is not necessary** Have students review their scripts, deleting any information that is confusing or irrelevant to the story line.

Differentiating Instruction

Support Some students may benefit from learning a variety of strategies that can help them spot confusing or unnecessary words and images. As they review their drafts, have students

- color-code similar ideas. They should highlight the topic sentence or main idea of each paragraph in one color and then work paragraph by paragraph, using the same color to highlight each sentence that explains something about the main idea. If a sentence doesn't seem to fit, have students skim the draft to see if it belongs in another paragraph. If not, they should delete it.

- underline and analyze. If a sentence doesn't make sense when read two or three times, students should underline it, reread it to determine the source of the confusion, and then delete it or revise it as necessary.

- self-question. When a confusing sentence is spotted, students should ask themselves, *Is the sentence awkwardly written? If so, is it worth rewriting?* To determine the answers, students should ask, *Does the sentence add important information? If so, does it belong here, or does it support an idea in another paragraph?*

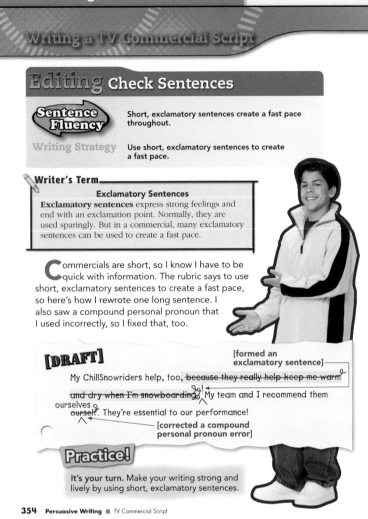

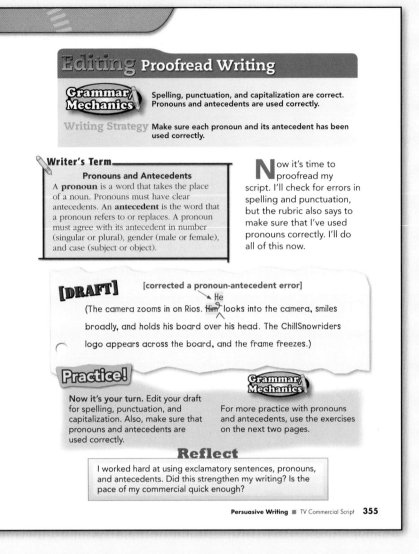

Editing Check Sentences

Sentence Fluency

Short, exclamatory sentences create a fast pace throughout.

Writing Strategy Use short, exclamatory sentences to create a fast pace.

Writer's Term

Exclamatory Sentences
Exclamatory sentences express strong feelings and end with an exclamation point. Normally, they are used sparingly. But in a commercial, many exclamatory sentences can be used to create a fast pace.

Commercials are short, so I know I have to be quick with information. The rubric says to use short, exclamatory sentences to create a fast pace, so here's how I rewrote one long sentence. I also saw a compound personal pronoun that I used incorrectly, so I fixed that, too.

[DRAFT] [formed an exclamatory sentence]

My ChillSnowriders help, too, ~~because they really help keep me warm and dry when I'm snowboarding.~~! My team and I recommend them ourselves ~~ourself~~. They're essential to our performance!

[corrected a compound personal pronoun error]

Practice!
It's your turn. Make your writing strong and lively by using short, exclamatory sentences.

Editing Proofread Writing

Grammar Mechanics

Spelling, punctuation, and capitalization are correct. Pronouns and antecedents are used correctly.

Writing Strategy Make sure each pronoun and its antecedent has been used correctly.

Writer's Term

Pronouns and Antecedents
A **pronoun** is a word that takes the place of a noun. Pronouns must have clear antecedents. An **antecedent** is the word that a pronoun refers to or replaces. A pronoun must agree with its antecedent in number (singular or plural), gender (male or female), and case (subject or object).

Now it's time to proofread my script. I'll check for errors in spelling and punctuation, but the rubric also says to make sure that I've used pronouns correctly. I'll do all of this now.

[DRAFT] [corrected a pronoun-antecedent error]
He
(The camera zooms in on Rios. ~~Him~~ looks into the camera, smiles broadly, and holds his board over his head. The ChillSnowriders logo appears across the board, and the frame freezes.)

Practice!

Now it's your turn. Edit your draft for spelling, punctuation, and capitalization. Also, make sure that pronouns and antecedents are used correctly.

Grammar Mechanics

For more practice with pronouns and antecedents, use the exercises on the next two pages.

Reflect
I worked hard at using exclamatory sentences, pronouns, and antecedents. Did this strengthen my writing? Is the pace of my commercial quick enough?

Editing

(Student pages 354–355)

Have students read the Writer's Term box on Student page 354. Write a variety of sample sentences on the board, and have students point out the ones that are exclamatory. Make sure students understand that an exclamatory sentence states strong feelings and ends with an exclamation point. Remind students that short, exclamatory sentences are appropriate in a TV commercial script because they create a fast pace, a sense of urgency, and a commanding tone.

Then, have students note how Luis revised the section of his draft shown on Student page 354. Ask them to explain how Luis made this revision. **Possible response: He formed an exclamatory sentence by deleting repetitive information.** Remind students to revise their own drafts for places where exclamatory sentences can help strengthen their writing.

Now, turn students' attention to the Writer's Term box on Student page 355. Help students understand pronoun-antecedent agreement by displaying the following sentence: *Jen told Dad that she would be home after soccer practice.* Point out the pronoun *she* and the antecedent *Jen*, and ask students whether this is a case of proper pronoun-antecedent agreement. **yes**

Finally, have students check their drafts to make sure each pronoun and antecedent have been used correctly. If any of your students are having trouble with pronoun-antecedent agreement, you may wish to teach the Mini-Lesson on pages 255–256 of this Teacher Edition.

WORK with a PARTNER Have pairs of students read one another's drafts, using sticky notes to mark errors in spelling, punctuation, and grammar. Then, tell students to perform a second read that focuses on the editing strategies they learned in this chapter.

Pronouns and Antecedents

KNOW the RULE

A **pronoun** is a word that can take the place of a noun. It must have a clear **antecedent**. An antecedent is the word that a pronoun refers to or replaces. A pronoun must agree with its antecedent in number (singular or plural), gender (male or female), and case (subject or object).

Example: My aunt uses that shampoo. **She** says **it** works well.

Subject pronouns include *I, he, she, we,* and *they.* Use a subject pronoun as the subject of a clause or sentence.

Example: Jack and **I** like it, too.

Object pronouns include *me, him, her, us,* and *them.* Use an object pronoun after an action verb or preposition.

Example: Mom paid Tim and Todd. She paid **them** $10.

The pronouns *it* and *you* can be either subjects or objects.

Example: You bought **it. It** belongs to **you.**

Practice the Rule

On a separate sheet of paper, rewrite each of the following sentences. Then, circle the antecedent in each sentence and write the correct pronoun on the blank line.

1. My friends and I were in a restaurant, and _____ were eating lunch.
2. We heard this man behind us, and _____ had the greatest voice.
3. The man was telling a story, and _____ sounded like an announcer.
4. Christa and Peter thought _____ might know him.
5. His voice sounded familiar because _____ was rich and deep.

Apply the Rule

Read this script, noting any pronoun and antecedent errors. On a separate sheet of paper, rewrite the commercial correctly.

Tug-a-Bone
a TV Commercial

(The scene is a family room. The camera shows a dog, sad and bored, with its head on its paws. Then, the camera zooms out to show two girls.)

Jill: What's wrong with Molly? Is she sick?

Rose: No, it is just bored.

Jill: I know what Molly needs—a Tug-a-Bone!

(The camera shows Molly suddenly picking up his head, as if she understands the conversation.)

Rose: What's a Tug-a-Bone?

Jill: She is a new dog toy. I just got one for my dog Toby, and I forgot to take them out of my coat pocket.

(Jill holds up a Tug-a-Bone, which looks like a small, bone-shaped pillow. Rose grabs one end, and Jill tugs on the other. As the bone is tugged, he lights up in the middle. Molly leaps up and runs over, barking. Rose lets Molly tug on the toy.)

Rose: Here, Molly! Get the Tug-a-Bone! Hey, Jill, her really likes it!

Jill: I knew she would! Uh . . . Rose? Is him ever going to let go?

(Suddenly, Molly tugs the toy out of Rose's grasp and runs off.)

Rose: Molly! Come back here with that Tug-a-Bone!

Announcer: Get a new Tug-a-Bone today. Your dog might never let her go! Available wherever pet products are sold.

(Student pages 356–357)

Pronouns and Antecedents

Make sure students understand antecedents by displaying the following sentence: *Dan made a sandwich and put it in his backpack.* Point out the pronoun *it.* Then, circle the antecedent *sandwich,* and remind students that an antecedent is the word that a pronoun refers to or replaces.

Review the concept of pronoun-antecedent agreement by reading aloud the following sentence: *A pronoun must agree with its antecedent in number, gender, and case.* Display a sample sentence for each circumstance, asking students to point out the pronouns and antecedents:

number: **Mom and Dad** said **they** would take me out to dinner.

gender: **Julie** decided **she** would buy a prom dress on Saturday.

case: Dad told **the twins** that Mom would buy **them** new uniforms.

Answers for Practice the Rule

1. (My friends and I) were in a restaurant, and __we__ were eating lunch.
2. We heard (this man) behind us, and __he__ had the greatest voice.
3. (The man) was telling a story, and __he__ sounded like an announcer.
4. (Christa and Peter) thought __they__ might know him.
5. (His voice) sounded familiar because __it__ was rich and deep.

Answers for Apply the Rule

Tug-a-Bone
a TV Commercial

(The scene is a family room. The camera shows a dog, sad and bored, with its head on its paws. Then, the camera zooms out to show two girls.)

Jill: What's wrong with Molly? Is she sick?

Rose: No, she is just bored.

Jill: I know what Molly needs—a Tug-a-Bone!

(The camera shows Molly suddenly picking up her head, as if she understands the conversation.)

(Answers continue on page 256.)

Writing a TV Commercial Script

Publishing Share Writing

Perform the commercial for my class.

Now that I've finished my script, I want to publish it. I could include it in a class anthology or post it on a bulletin board, but that isn't lively enough. A TV commercial is meant to be viewed, so I'll perform mine for my class. I'll need to get some classmates to act in my commercial, and then I'll need to make copies of my script. I should also show everyone my Storyboard. We'll need to rehearse the lines and figure out what actions to use. Before all that, I'll read through my work one last time to make sure it includes all of the items on my checklist.

My Checklist

✓ The script "sells" one product.

✓ The opening grabs the audience's attention.

✓ There is a clear call to action at the end.

✓ All words and images are focused on the sales goal.

✓ Short, exclamatory sentences provide a fast, commercial-like pace.

✓ Spelling, capitalization, and punctuation are all correct. Pronouns and antecedents are used correctly.

Practice!

Now it's your turn. Make a checklist to check your TV commercial script. Then, make a final draft to publish.

ChillSnowriders

a TV Commercial by Luis Rios

First Sportscaster: A great good afternoon, Extreme fans! I'm Jim Smith, and this is Carol Jones. We're here at the Annual Big Air Competition in beautiful New Hampshire, and the crowd is really stoked. Right now you're watching the current champion, Luis Rios, shredding his way to a sure victory in the halfpipe competition. As always, Rios is sponsored by ChillSnowriders, makers of the world's finest snowboarding pants.

Second Sportscaster: Whoa! Rios caught some really big air there! Did you see that amazing burger flip? This guy is unbelievable! I think he's done it again, Jim!

(Rios comes to a dramatic stop right in front of the camera.)

Fan: Hey, dude! Nice ChillSnowriders!

(Answers continued from page 255.)

Rose: What's a Tug-a-Bone?

Jill: It is a new dog toy. I just got one for my dog Toby, and I forgot to take it out of my coat pocket.

(Jill holds up a Tug-a-Bone, which looks like a small, bone-shaped pillow. Rose grabs one end, and Jill tugs on the other. As the bone is tugged, it lights up in the middle. Molly leaps up and runs over, barking. Rose lets Molly tug on the toy.)

Rose: Here, Molly! Get the Tug-a-Bone! Hey, Jill, she really likes it!

Jill: I knew she would! Uh . . . Rose? Is she ever going to let go?

(Suddenly, Molly tugs the toy out of Rose's grasp and runs off.)

Rose: Molly! Come back here with that Tug-a-Bone!

Announcer: Get a new Tug-a-Bone today. Your dog might never let it go! Available wherever pet products are sold.

✓ For more practice with grammar/mechanics skills, see Zaner-Bloser's *G.U.M.* materials.

Differentiating Instruction

Support Some students may benefit from analyzing Luis's final script more closely. Use the following process to map out the elements of Luis's final commercial script.

1. As a class, read the script aloud, frame by frame.
2. Stop after each frame to address the answers to the following questions:
   What is Luis's purpose in this frame?
   How does he get across his main point?
   What does the viewer see in this frame?
3. After discussing the script, ask students to rate the commercial in the following areas: audience interest, quality and quantity of information, entertainment value, and persuasiveness.

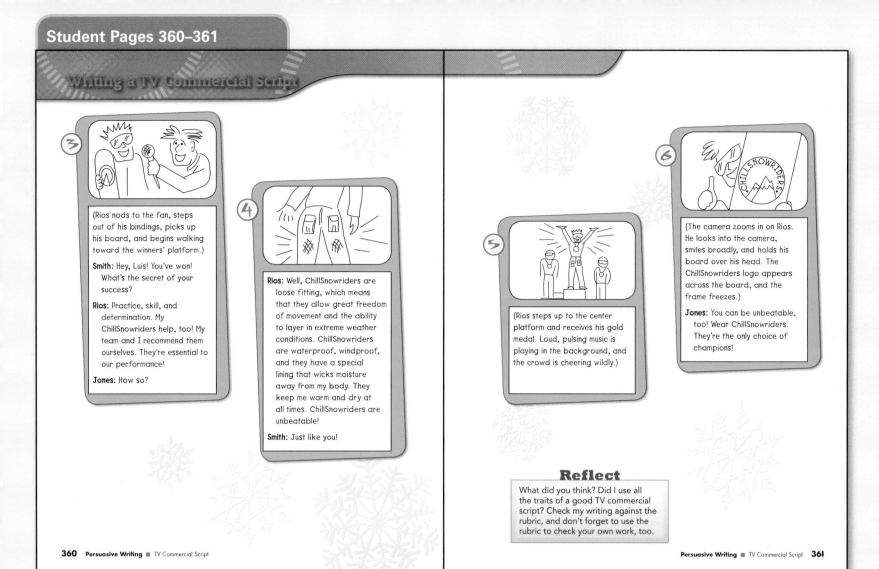

Publishing

(Student pages 358–361)

Ask students if they like Luis's choice for sharing his TV commercial script. Tell the class that his choice is not the only option for publishing his work. Invite students to name other ways they could publish their own scripts.

Have each student make a checklist and perform a final evaluation of his or her TV commercial script before publishing it. Encourage students to share copies of their scripts with friends and relatives who might be interested in reading about their product.

Call students' attention to the Reflect box on the bottom of Student page 361. Explain that assessing Luis's TV commercial script against the rubric will help them better understand how to apply the traits to their own work. Have students use sticky notes to mark at least one example of each trait in Luis's writing. Tell them to include an evaluation on each note.

After this process, have students assess how well they were able to identify each trait in Luis's writing and how easy or difficult it was to use the rubric. Remind them to apply what they learned from Luis's work when they use the rubric to check their own writing.

Tips for the Writing Classroom

Using Student Writing Samples

by Ken Stewart, *Master Teacher*

If your students are having a problem understanding the criteria you are looking for in a piece of writing, use a "not-so-perfect" student sample to model the revision process with their input. Follow these simple steps:

1. Choose a sample piece of student writing to use while you model the revision process. (Ask the student for permission first.)
2. Make copies for each student to correct.
3. Display an overhead transparency of the writing.
4. As a class, read the entire piece aloud and then reread it sentence by sentence. Ask students to note any changes that could be made.
5. Using the appropriate proofreading marks from the Student Edition, mark the changes on your overhead sample and have each student mark the changes on his or her copy as well.
6. After you and the class have made your changes, reread the piece and analyze why the revised version is better.

Your modeling will show students how this process works, and it will show them what they need to do to improve their own writing.

Ways to Publish a TV Commercial Script

As you decide how to publish your work, it's a good idea to think about who might want to read it. Then, you can figure out the best way to share it. Here are some ideas for publishing your TV commercial.

✓ **Read your script to your school's business teacher.** Then, discuss his or her feedback.

✓ Perform your script as a commercial break during a school assembly, variety show, or other performance.

✓ Perform your commercial on videotape.

✓ Include your commercial as part of a "Class Ads" publication.

✓ Take your script home and share it with your family.

Writing Across the Content Areas TV Commercial Script

Your school subjects can be a great source of writing ideas. Choose a subject and see how many related topics you can brainstorm. Check out these examples.

Math
- Write a commercial that compares the costs of two similar items, focusing on how much viewers will save if they buy one of them.
- Develop an idea for a math board game. Then, write a TV commercial about it.

Language Arts
- Do you have a favorite author? Write a script for a TV commercial that advertises his or her latest book.
- Write a TV commercial for computer software that promises to help viewers learn a foreign language.

Art and/or Music
- Advertise a concert by your favorite musical artist.
- Make up a new musical instrument. Then, write a TV commercial about it.

Ways to Publish
(Student page 362)

Read and discuss with students the publishing options listed on Student page 362. Encourage students to consider some of these options when publishing their own writing. Remind students that Luis chose to publish his commercial by performing it for the class, but they can choose their own way of publishing. Perhaps one student will want to perform his or her commercial on videotape, while another will want to include it as part of a "Class Ads" publication.

Writing Across the Content Areas
(Student page 363)

Explain to students that writing is not just for English or language arts class. Many other school subjects contain ideas, issues, and events that students may want to write about. Encourage students to consider using one of the content areas listed on Student page 363 as a springboard for more writing options. Students may also wish to consult with other teachers for more ideas on writing in the content areas.

Books for Professional Development

Fletcher, Ralph. *Live Writing: Breathing Life Into Your Words.* New York: Avon Books, 1999.

This book is based on the simple idea that every writer has a "toolbox." Fletcher's toolbox contains words, imagination, a love of books, a sense of story, and ideas for how to make writing live and breathe. This book contains strategies for improving the toolbox approach.

Kiester, Jane Bell. *Blowing Away the State Writing Assessment Test: Four Steps to Better Scores for Teachers of All Levels.* 2nd ed. Gainesville: Maupin House, 2000.

The author offers reproducible pages for narrative, expository, and persuasive topics in elementary and middle school, as well as information about having students use rubrics to evaluate their work.

Hyerle, David. *Visual Tools for Constructing Knowledge.* Alexandria: ASCD, 1996.

This book provides a deeper understanding of the use and application of graphic organizers. The author also offers many possible variations on the more familiar organizers.

Young, Art. *Teaching Writing Across the Curriculum.* 4th ed. Upper Saddle River: Prentice Hall, 2006.

This edition provides a comprehensive, accessible discussion of writing across the curriculum.

Persuasive Speech Overview

In this chapter, students will learn how to write a persuasive speech. They will learn the elements of a persuasive speech—evidence, convincing tone, questions and answers, and call to action—and reasons why they might choose to write one. Students will then use a persuasive speech rubric to study a model writing sample.

Students will follow the student guide as he goes through the writing stages—prewriting, drafting, revising, editing, and publishing. As the student guide learns new writing strategies in each step, students will be directed to practice the strategies in their own writing.

During prewriting and drafting, students will

- choose a problem that they feel strongly about.

- list a call to action, along with several reasons for the request.
- make a Persuasion Map to organize the reasons for their call to action.
- write a draft, using a convincing tone to persuade the audience.

During revising and editing, students will

- add persuasive details.
- replace biased words with neutral words.
- use the question-and-answer pattern.
- edit their drafts for spelling, capitalization, and punctuation, making sure that progressive tense verbs are used correctly.

Finally, students will publish a final draft.

You may wish to send to families the School-Home Connection Letter for this chapter, located at the end of this unit in the Teacher Edition.

Persuasive Speech Writing Traits

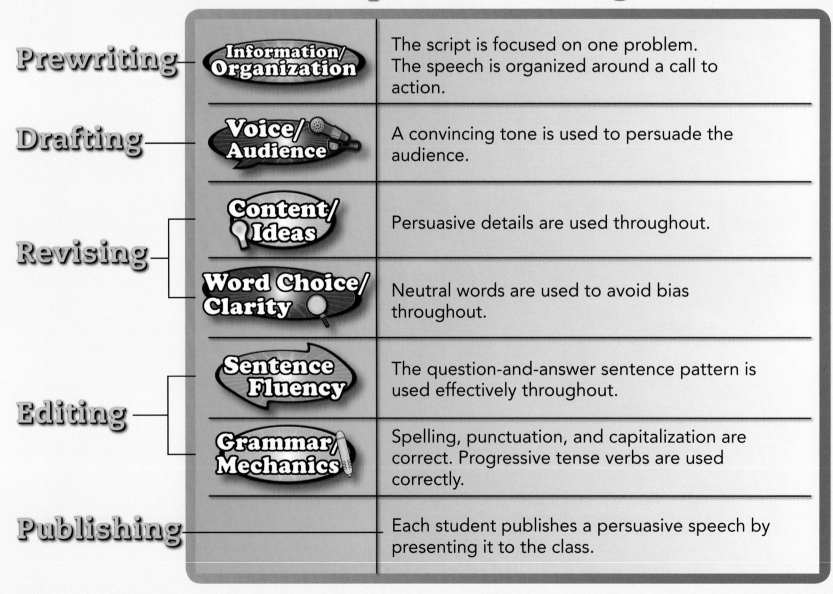

Prewriting	Information/ Organization	The script is focused on one problem. The speech is organized around a call to action.
Drafting	Voice/ Audience	A convincing tone is used to persuade the audience.
Revising	Content/ Ideas	Persuasive details are used throughout.
	Word Choice/ Clarity	Neutral words are used to avoid bias throughout.
Editing	Sentence Fluency	The question-and-answer sentence pattern is used effectively throughout.
	Grammar/ Mechanics	Spelling, punctuation, and capitalization are correct. Progressive tense verbs are used correctly.
Publishing		Each student publishes a persuasive speech by presenting it to the class.

Persuasive Speech Time Management

WEEK 1

	Day 1	Day 2	Day 3	Day 4	Day 5
Learning Objectives	Students will: • study the components of a persuasive speech.	Students will: • learn how to gather information for a persuasive speech.	Students will: • practice gathering information for their persuasive speeches.	Students will: • learn how to make a Persuasion Map to organize their reasons.	Students will: • practice organizing their reasons on a Persuasion Map.
Activities	• Discuss the elements and traits of a persuasive speech (Student pages 364–366). • Use the rubric to study the model (Student pages 367–371).	• Read and discuss **Prewriting: Gather Information** (Student page 372).	• Choose a problem to focus on. • List a call to action, along with several reasons for the request.	• Read and discuss **Prewriting: Organize Ideas** (Student page 373).	• Review the reasons listed while gathering information. • Make a Persuasion Map to organize reasons.

WEEK 2

	Day 1	Day 2	Day 3	Day 4	Day 5
Learning Objectives	Students will: • learn how to use a convincing tone to persuade the audience.	Students will: • practice writing their own drafts.	Students will: • learn how to add persuasive details.	Students will: • practice adding persuasive details.	Students will: • learn how to replace biased or loaded words with neutral words.
Activities	• Read and discuss **Drafting: Write a Draft** (Student pages 374–375).	• Use Persuasion Maps to write drafts. • Use a convincing tone to persuade the audience.	• Read and discuss **Revising: Extend Writing** (Student page 376).	• Add persuasive details throughout.	• Read and discuss **Revising: Clarify Writing** (Student page 377).

WEEK 3

	Day 1	Day 2	Day 3	Day 4	Day 5
Learning Objectives	Students will: • practice replacing biased or loaded words with neutral words.	Students will: • learn how to use the question-and-answer sentence pattern.	Students will: • learn how to use progressive tense verbs correctly.	Students will: • practice editing their drafts for spelling, capitalization, and punctuation.	Students will: • learn different ways to publish their persuasive speeches.
Activities	• Reread drafts, looking for biased or loaded words. • Replace biased or loaded words with neutral words.	• Read and discuss **Editing: Check Sentences** (Student page 378). • Use the question-and-answer sentence pattern.	• Read and discuss **Editing: Proofread Writing** (Student page 379).	• Fix any spelling, capitalization, or punctuation errors. • Fix any progressive tense verbs that are not used correctly.	• Read and discuss **Publishing: Share Writing** (Student page 382).

To complete the chapter in fewer days, teach the learning objectives and activities for two days in one day.

This planning chart, correlated to your state's writing standards, is available on-line at http://www.zaner-bloser.com/sfw.

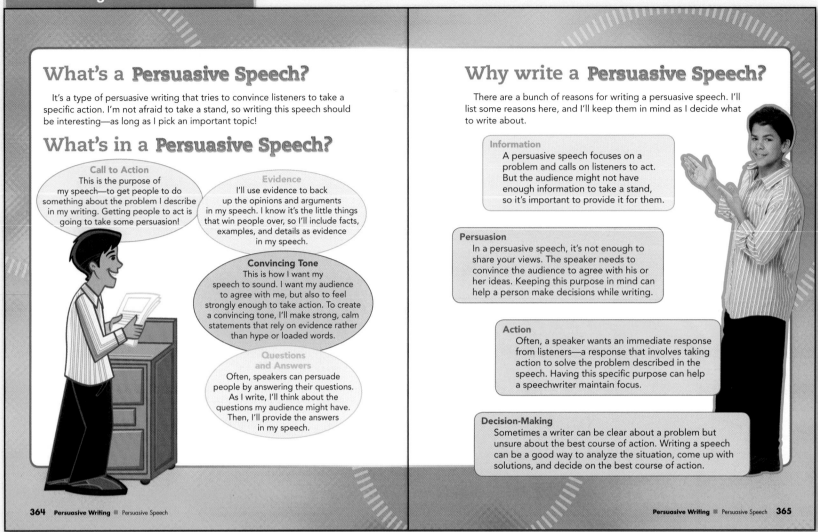

Define the Genre

(Student page 364)

Persuasive Speech

Discuss with students the definition of a persuasive speech. Point out that a speech writer tries to reach large numbers of people to convince them about ideas or persuade them to act. Explain that a persuasive speech usually has a single focus that is linked to an issue that the writer feels strongly about.

Elements of the Genre

Persuasive Speech

Read and discuss with students the elements of a persuasive speech listed on Student page 364. Ask volunteers which elements are also common to other forms of writing. **Possible responses: Call to Action—editorials, commercials; Evidence—persuasive arguments, mysteries; Convincing Tone—letters to the editor, book reviews; Questions and Answers—editorials, commercials** Discuss why each element may be important to writing a persuasive speech.

Authentic Writing

(Student page 365)

Persuasive Speech

Read and discuss with students the reasons for writing a persuasive speech listed on Student page 365. Point out that all writing has a purpose and is aimed at a specific audience. These authentic purposes help authors shape their writing. Ask a volunteer to read aloud the Information box. Then, have students discuss other reasons someone might write a persuasive speech to provide information. Repeat this process for the Persuasion, Action, and Decision-Making boxes. Then, have students brainstorm other purposes for writing a persuasive speech that are not listed on Student page 365. Encourage students to think about their own reasons for writing a persuasive speech and how these reasons will affect the tone and focus of their writing.

Persuasive Speech Writing Traits

I know that there are six traits of good writing. Here's a list of what makes a good persuasive speech. I'll use it later to help me write my speech.

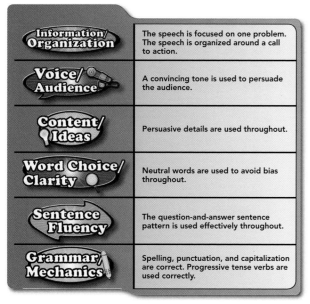

Information/ Organization	The speech is focused on one problem. The speech is organized around a call to action.
Voice/ Audience	A convincing tone is used to persuade the audience.
Content/ Ideas	Persuasive details are used throughout.
Word Choice/ Clarity	Neutral words are used to avoid bias throughout.
Sentence Fluency	The question-and-answer sentence pattern is used effectively throughout.
Grammar/ Mechanics	Spelling, punctuation, and capitalization are correct. Progressive tense verbs are used correctly.

I can use Nola Fabian's persuasive speech on the next page as a model for my own writing. Later, we'll check out how Nola used the traits to help her write.

Persuasive Speech Model

Save Our Books
by Nola Fabian

Imagine an ordinary bookcase filled with your favorite books. Smell the worn pages? Are the titles beckoning you? See the crinkled jacket covers and ragged spines? Well, savor that thought because publishing companies are starting to post books on-line, which means that hand-held books might become obsolete. That's why I'm asking you to take action by demanding that publishers continue to develop and support "real" books. ← Call to Action

Am I sounding a false alarm? I don't think so. Recently, publishers have made a startling number of titles available on-line, and growing numbers of authors are also allowing some form of on-line publication. Questions and Answers

Soon, publishers may even find ways to post books on the Internet after they go out of print. Just think of the devastating effect this will have on book collectors (and traders) worldwide. Many of these people have spent the better part of their lives collecting out-of-print titles and valuable old books.

So you may ask, what has led to this recent trend in publishing? In a word: technology. Word processing software makes it easy to manage massive amounts of text. The Internet has become a literate community, and advances in computer systems include a variety of portable gadgets.

OK, so it is possible to move the world of literature onto the Web. But is it probable? In some areas, it is becoming more profitable to publish solely on the Web. This summer, a handful of magazine publishers announced that they will be posting some issues exclusively on-line. ← Evidence

So if publishing on-line is cheaper and easier, why fight it? Well, a book is more than a collection of words. Many readers enjoy the weight of the book, the texture of the cover, the smell of the ink, and the sound of the pages rustling. Hand-held books are often associated with meaningful memories of a person's journey into the literate world. Not to mention, some people cannot afford to access books on-line. While computers are readily available in most schools and libraries, not everyone owns a home PC. ← Convincing Tone

For these reasons, we need to act now to keep books from being destroyed by the Internet. I have here a petition that calls on publishers to pledge their commitment to hand-held books. Please sign it before you leave, and don't forget to stop by your local bookstore on your way home and buy a hand-held book. You never know—it could be the last "real" book you ever buy! ← Call to Action

Writing Traits
(Student pages 366–367)

Persuasive Speech

Ask students to share problems or issues that they are concerned about. Then, discuss whether they have shared their views with others, and if so, how. Compare and contrast various ways people confront and discuss common problems. Explain that when an issue affects many people, individuals often give speeches to promote ideas and persuade others to act.

Next, turn students' attention to the traits of a persuasive speech listed on Student page 366. Have one or more volunteers read aloud the traits and their descriptions. Discuss why someone might use these traits when writing a persuasive speech.

Tell students that they are going to study and use strategies for writing persuasive speeches and that a good persuasive speech has the traits listed on Student page 366.

Differentiating Instruction

English-Language Learners Preteach the following key words to help these students better understand the writing model.

beckoning (v.): attracting; inviting, as by nodding
savor (v.): to enjoy
obsolete (adj.): outdated or no longer used
startling (adj.): surprising; alarming
devastating (adj.): potentially harmful
trend (n.): a craze or a fad
literate (adj.): educated
portable gadgets (n.): small machines or computers that can be easily carried or transported
texture (n.): the physical feel of a surface
associated (v.): connected
petition (n.): an application to change current policy; an appeal
pledge (v.): to guarantee; to vow
commitment (n.): a promise; an obligation

Persuasive Speech
Rubric

The traits of a good persuasive speech from page 366 have been used to make the rubric below. By using 1, 2, 3, or 4 check marks to judge each trait, you can decide how well any persuasive speech was written.

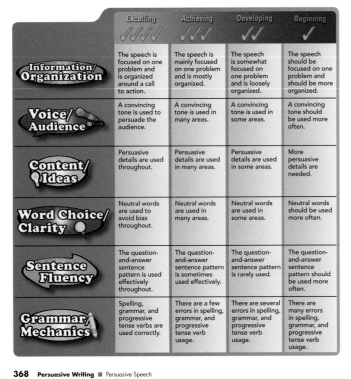

	Excelling ✓✓✓✓	Achieving ✓✓✓	Developing ✓✓	Beginning ✓
Information/ Organization	The speech is focused on one problem and is organized around a call to action.	The speech is mainly focused on one problem and is mostly organized.	The speech is somewhat focused on one problem and is loosely organized.	The speech should be focused on one problem and should be more organized.
Voice/ Audience	A convincing tone is used to persuade the audience.	A convincing tone is used in many areas.	A convincing tone is used in some areas.	A convincing tone should be used more often.
Content/ Ideas	Persuasive details are used throughout.	Persuasive details are used in many areas.	Persuasive details are used in some areas.	More persuasive details are needed.
Word Choice/ Clarity	Neutral words are used to avoid bias throughout.	Neutral words are used in many areas.	Neutral words are used in some areas.	Neutral words should be used more often.
Sentence Fluency	The question-and-answer sentence pattern is used effectively throughout.	The question-and-answer sentence pattern is sometimes used effectively.	The question-and-answer sentence pattern is rarely used.	The question-and-answer sentence pattern should be used more often.
Grammar/ Mechanics	Spelling, grammar, and progressive tense verbs are used correctly.	There are a few errors in spelling, grammar, and progressive tense verb usage.	There are several errors in spelling, grammar, and progressive tense verb usage.	There are many errors in spelling, grammar, and progressive tense verb usage.

Persuasive Speech
Using the Rubric to Study the Model

Now, let's use the rubric to check Nola Fabian's persuasive speech, "Save Our Books." How many check marks would you give Nola for each trait?

Information/ Organization
- The speech is focused on one problem.
- The speech is organized around a call to action.

Nola introduces a problem early in her speech, and she remains focused on the issue throughout. She also introduces a call to action early on.

[from the writing model]

Well, savor that thought because publishing companies are starting to post books on-line, which means that hand-held books might become obsolete. That's why I'm asking you to take action by demanding that publishers continue to develop and support "real" books.

Voice/ Audience
- A convincing tone is used to persuade the audience.

Nola persuades her audience with reasons and details. This contributes to a strong, convincing tone that doesn't sound wildly excited or desperate for support. See if you are convinced by the tone Nola uses in the following paragraph.

[from the writing model]

Soon, publishers may even find ways to post books on the Internet after they go out of print. Just think of the devastating effect this will have on book collectors (and traders) worldwide. Many of these people have spent the better part of their lives collecting out-of-print titles and valuable old books.

Using the Rubric
(Student page 368)

Explain that a rubric is a tool that can be used to evaluate a piece of writing. The rubric on Student page 368 can be used to evaluate a persuasive speech. It is based on the same traits for a persuasive speech that are listed on Student page 366.

Now, point out the terms above each rubric column: *Excelling, Achieving, Developing,* and *Beginning.* Explain that each column symbolizes a degree of writing skill and that each rubric row focuses on a specific writing trait. When students use the rubric to evaluate their own work at each step of the writing process, they increase the likelihood of producing polished, well-written persuasive speeches.

Study the Model
(Student pages 369–371)

Explain that Student pages 369–371 show how the writing model on Student page 367 meets all six traits of the rubric. Read each section with the students. Then, have them look for other examples of each trait in the writing model.

Ask students how many check marks they would assign the writing model for each trait. Then, as a class, decide how the writing model should be rated overall.

Remind students to use the rubric as they write their own persuasive speeches, to be sure they are meeting all six writing traits.

Persuasive Speech

Content/Ideas
• Persuasive details are used throughout.

Nola's speech is effective because she explains each reason with facts, examples, and other details that persuade her audience. In this example, she includes several persuasive details to explain why the audience should fight against on-line books.

[from the writing model]

Many readers enjoy the weight of the book, the texture of the cover, the smell of the ink, and the sound of the pages rustling. Hand-held books are often associated with meaningful memories of a person's journey into the literate world. Not to mention, some people cannot afford to access books on-line. While computers are readily available in most schools and libraries, not everyone owns a home PC.

Word Choice/Clarity
• Neutral words are used to avoid bias throughout.

I appreciate how Nola uses persuasive reasoning without resorting to biased or loaded words. For example, in the lines below, she uses *profitable* instead of *lucrative*, which can sometimes imply greed. And she uses the neutral word *publishers* rather than *big corporations*, which can have a negative meaning.

[from the writing model]

In some areas, it is becoming more profitable to publish solely on the Web. This summer, a handful of magazine publishers announced that they will be posting some issues exclusively on-line.

Sentence Fluency
• The question-and-answer sentence pattern is used effectively throughout.

I like how Nola sharpens the focus of her speech by predicting her audience's questions about the topic. She spends most of her speech posing these questions and then answering them, creating effective question-and-answer patterns.

[from the writing model]

Am I sounding a false alarm? I don't think so. Recently, publishers have made a startling number of titles available on-line, and growing numbers of authors are also allowing some form of on-line publication.

Grammar/Mechanics
• Spelling, punctuation, and capitalization are correct. Progressive tense verbs are used correctly.

Nola's speech flows smoothly because there aren't any mistakes. When she shifts from one verb tense to another, she always gets it right. In the passage below, notice how she switches from the present tense *is possible* to the present progressive tense *is becoming* in one smooth transition.

[from the writing model]

OK, so it is possible to move the world of literature onto the Web. But is it probable? In some areas, it is becoming more profitable to publish solely on the Web.

My Turn!
I'm going to write a persuasive speech about something I feel strongly about. I'll follow the rubric and use good writing strategies. Read on to see how I do it!

Differentiating Instruction

Enrichment Encourage students to explore some of the issues in "Save Our Books" by comparing on-line and hand-held books. Students can examine texts for free on sites that post books with expired copyrights.

• Suggest that students use the key phrase *literature and public domain* to conduct an Internet search. They can then click on links to access texts in a variety of genres.
• Have students browse the offerings, then choose a section or a chapter to read.

• Next, have students read a section from a hand-held book. (For comparison purposes, suggest that they choose a book in the same genre as the on-line text.)
• Have students write a brief comparison of their reading experiences.
• Finally, ask students to write a paragraph stating whether they agree with the opinion expressed in "Save Our Books." Students should also explain their reasons in this paragraph.

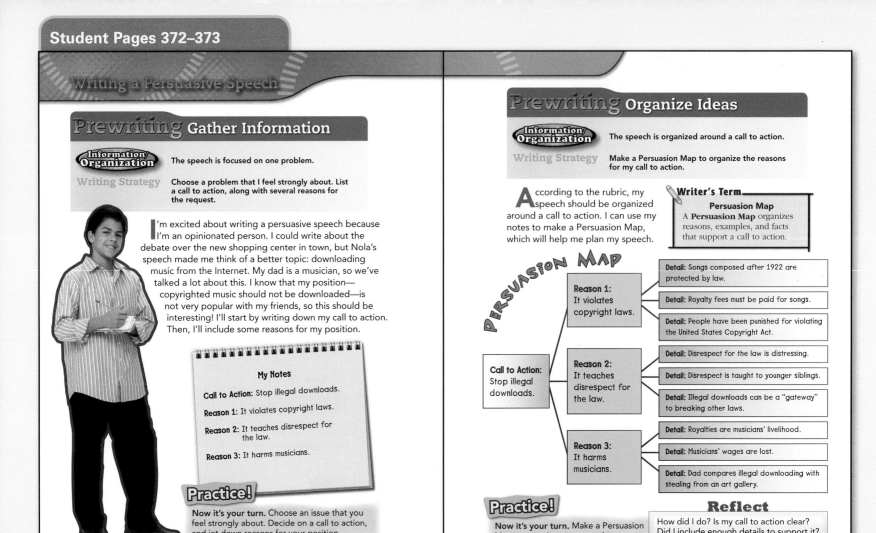

Prewriting

(Student pages 372–373)

Invite students to share issues that are important to them. Then, discuss whether speeches can help spread ideas about these issues and prompt people to act upon possible solutions.

Have students review Luis's notes on Student page 372 and his Persuasion Map on Student page 373. Ask students to describe how the Map differs from the notes. **Possible response: It contains the notes, but it also lists three details for each reason.**

Help students understand how to plan a persuasive speech. Explain that they will follow Luis's lead by

- brainstorming an issue of interest.
- choosing a position and deciding on a call to action.
- writing down a call to action, along with several supporting reasons for the request.
- using their notes to create a Persuasion Map that contains details in support of each reason.

More Practice!

For more practice with these writing strategies, you may wish to have students use the Strategy Practice Book. See the appendix for annotated Strategy Practice Book pages.

WORK with a PARTNER

Students who need help brainstorming a topic or choosing a position may benefit from working with a partner. Have pairs discuss ideas and write down those that seem most promising. Each student should choose an issue and decide on a position. Then, have students make notes and create their Persuasion Maps, offering feedback to their partners. Check in with each pair, offering guidance as needed.

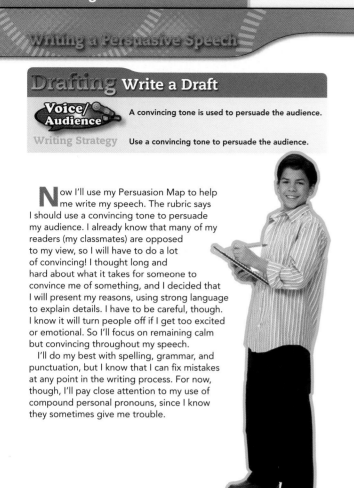

Writing a Persuasive Speech

Drafting — Write a Draft

Voice/Audience A convincing tone is used to persuade the audience.

Writing Strategy Use a convincing tone to persuade the audience.

Now I'll use my Persuasion Map to help me write my speech. The rubric says I should use a convincing tone to persuade my audience. I already know that many of my readers (my classmates) are opposed to my view, so I will have to do a lot of convincing! I thought long and hard about what it takes for someone to convince me of something, and I decided that I will present my reasons, using strong language to explain details. I have to be careful, though. I know it will turn people off if I get too excited or emotional. So I'll focus on remaining calm but convincing throughout my speech.

I'll do my best with spelling, grammar, and punctuation, but I know that I can fix mistakes at any point in the writing process. For now, though, I'll pay close attention to my use of compound personal pronouns, since I know they sometimes give me trouble.

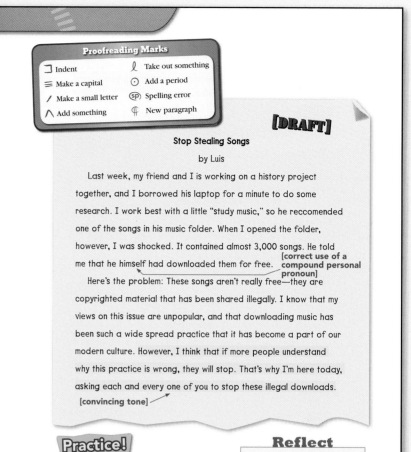

Proofreading Marks

⌐ Indent	ℓ Take out something
≡ Make a capital	⊙ Add a period
/ Make a small letter	(SP) Spelling error
∧ Add something	¶ New paragraph

[DRAFT]

Stop Stealing Songs

by Luis

Last week, my friend and I is working on a history project together, and I borrowed his laptop for a minute to do some research. I work best with a little "study music," so he reccomended one of the songs in his music folder. When I opened the folder, however, I was shocked. It contained almost 3,000 songs. He told me that he himself had downloaded them for free. [correct use of a compound personal pronoun]

Here's the problem: These songs aren't really free—they are copyrighted material that has been shared illegally. I know that my views on this issue are unpopular, and that downloading music has been such a wide spread practice that it has become a part of our modern culture. However, I think that if more people understand why this practice is wrong, they will stop. That's why I'm here today, asking each and every one of you to stop these illegal downloads. [convincing tone]

Practice! Now it's your turn. Write a draft using a convincing tone to persuade your audience.

Reflect What do you think? Is my tone convincing? Will it help persuade my audience?

Drafting
(Student pages 374–375)

Remind students that drafting is a chance to get ideas on paper without having to worry about making mistakes.

Refer to Luis's words on Student page 374, pointing out that he plans to focus on using a convincing tone as he begins his draft. Note that an audience can be moved by emotions if a speech connects to their concerns in an appropriate way. Explain that preparing arguments and offering evidence can help speakers be persuasive.

Turn students' attention to the highlighted text in Luis's draft on Student page 375. Ask a volunteer to read the text aloud. Then, as a class, discuss whether the tone is convincing. Have several other volunteers read the same sentences, varying their delivery. Explain that the tone of a speech can be affected by the way in which it is delivered.

Have students use their Persuasion Maps to draft their speeches, making sure to use a convincing tone as they write.

Writing Across the Curriculum

Science: Technology Have students use Luis's speech topic—and the topic of the writing model—as spring-boards for exploring the effects of technology on society. Encourage students to research and report on aspects of technology, including
- the Internet and people's reading habits.
- file-sharing and the music industry.
- a brief history of the cell phone.
- wireless technology.
- how these technologies may affect our future.

Students may also investigate a technology-related field of their own choosing. After they decide on a topic, help them devise a manageable thesis. Remind students to include details about their chosen technology's effect on society.

Suggest that students use technology to present their findings, giving video presentations or highlighting their reports with digital slide shows and music.

Writing a Persuasive Speech

Revising Extend Writing

Content/Ideas — Persuasive details are used throughout.

Writing Strategy — Add persuasive details throughout.

After I finished my draft, I checked the rubric. It reminded me to use persuasive details throughout my speech. I knew that this would help explain my reasons in a convincing way, so I added some persuasive details to a part of my draft that sounded a little vague.

[DRAFT]

Because my dad is a musician, I know that any song composed by an American before 1922 is in the public domain. That means that it belongs to everyone and can be shared or performed freely. So when you download songs on the Internet, you are violating the United States Copyright Act.

[added persuasive details] → But music composed after 1922 cannot be used without permission. And even with permission, royalties must be paid.

Practice!

Now it's your turn. Add persuasive details to your draft to help convince readers of your opinions.

Revising Clarify Writing

Word Choice/Clarity — Neutral words are used to avoid bias throughout.

Writing Strategy — Replace biased or loaded words with neutral words.

Writer's Term
Biased Words/Loaded Words
Loaded words and **biased words** express unfair judgment. For example, *shack* might be used as a biased or negatively loaded word for the more neutral term *house*.

I checked the rubric again and was reminded how important it is to avoid biased and loaded words. I want to persuade my audience with facts and details, not with tricky language. But when I reread my draft, I was surprised to see that I had included some biased words. Here's an example of how I changed them to neutral words. I also checked my use of pronouns since they've given me trouble in the past.

[DRAFT] ← [used neutral words]

Many of these ~~criminals~~ defendants, some of whom are teenagers just like us, are currently on trial. If convicted, they will have to pay hundreds of thousands of dollars in fines. Now, you're probably thinking there's no way that the government can prosecute all ~~thieves~~ file-sharers. But are you really willing to take that chance?
[correct use of a pronoun]

Practice!

Now it's your turn. Review your draft to see if you used any biased or loaded words. If so, replace them with neutral words.

Reflect
Is my word choice persuasive but unbiased? Are my revisions convincing without being offensive?

Revising
(Student pages 376–377)

Direct students' attention to Student page 376. Explain that persuasive details serve a dual purpose: to support the writer's opinions and to persuade the audience. Have students revise their drafts, looking for places where persuasive details can strengthen their arguments. Note that while revising, students should consider their intended audience by asking themselves the following questions: *How much do my listeners know about my topic? What questions might they have about my viewpoint? How many details will I need to convince them to take action?*

Read aloud the Writer's Term box on Student page 377. Explain that when someone is speaking to those who already agree with his or her position, biased words can be used to excite the crowd and prompt them to act. However, in a persuasive speech, the speaker usually addresses a mixed crowd; therefore, biased words may interfere with the speaker's ability to win over listeners. Then, have students revise their drafts, replacing any biased or loaded words with neutral words.

Differentiating Instruction

Support Some students may benefit from a more detailed explanation of biased and loaded words.

- Write the words *connotation* and *denotation* on the board. Explain that *denotation* refers to a word's literal meaning, and *connotation* refers to the emotional associations that people make when they read or hear a word.

- Next, write the headings *Positive*, *Negative*, and *Neutral* on the board, explaining that words can convey any of these connotations. To illustrate, write the phrase *person with no home* under the *Neutral* heading. Then, ask students to name words that carry the same denotation, but positive or negative connotations. Write appropriate suggestions on the board as shown below:

Positive	Negative
free spirit	vagrant
nonconformist	bum
happy traveler	tramp

- Remind students that as they write their speeches, they should consider the connotations of words and the effect that these may have on their intended audience.

Writing a Persuasive Speech

Editing Check Sentences

Sentence Fluency

The question-and-answer sentence pattern is used effectively throughout.

Writing Strategy

Make use of the question-and-answer sentence pattern.

After once again comparing my speech to the rubric, I realized that I often used the question-and-answer sentence pattern to address my audience's concerns. However, I know that I can also use the question-and-answer sentence pattern to convince listeners to think further about the consequences of their actions. Here's a portion of my draft where I used the pattern for this purpose.

[DRAFT]

[used the question-and-answer sentence pattern]

Even though people might be "getting away with" illegal file-sharing, it is really a broader issue. Many of us feel that it's somehow OK to break the law.

isn't ?

Practice!

Now it's your turn. Strengthen your speech by using the question-and-answer sentence pattern.

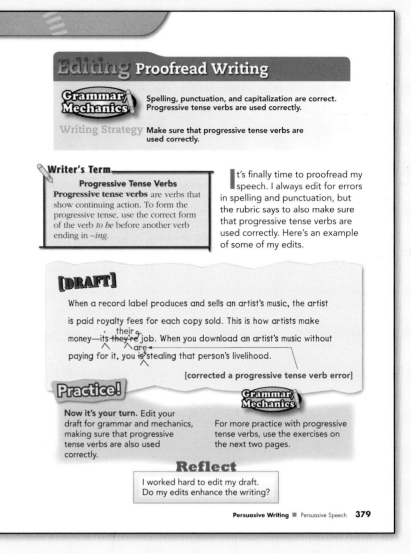

Editing Proofread Writing

Grammar/Mechanics

Spelling, punctuation, and capitalization are correct. Progressive tense verbs are used correctly.

Writing Strategy

Make sure that progressive tense verbs are used correctly.

Writer's Term

Progressive Tense Verbs
Progressive tense verbs are verbs that show continuing action. To form the progressive tense, use the correct form of the verb *to be* before another verb ending in –*ing*.

It's finally time to proofread my speech. I always edit for errors in spelling and punctuation, but the rubric says to also make sure that progressive tense verbs are used correctly. Here's an example of some of my edits.

[DRAFT]

When a record label produces and sells an artist's music, the artist is paid royalty fees for each copy sold. This is how artists make money—its they're job. When you download an artist's music without paying for it, you is stealing that person's livelihood.

their *are*

[corrected a progressive tense verb error]

Practice!

Now it's your turn. Edit your draft for grammar and mechanics, making sure that progressive tense verbs are also used correctly.

Grammar/Mechanics

For more practice with progressive tense verbs, use the exercises on the next two pages.

Reflect

I worked hard to edit my draft. Do my edits enhance the writing?

Editing

(Student pages 378–379)

Direct students' attention to Student page 378. Then, discuss the change Luis made to his draft. To illustrate the effect of this change, have a volunteer read aloud the unedited sentences. Ask another student to read the edited copy. Ask students how the question-and-answer pattern makes a difference. **Possible response: It involves the audience by anticipating their questions and speaking to them directly.** Remind students to review their own drafts for places where using questions and answers can help strengthen their speeches.

Turn students' attention to the Writer's Term box on Student page 379, and ask a volunteer to read aloud the text. Make sure students understand the use of the progressive tense by writing the following sentences on the board:

When you download free music, you steal someone's income.

When you download free music, you are stealing someone's income.

Ask volunteers to read the sentences aloud. Then, discuss the effect of the progressive tense in the second sentence. Explain that the progressive tense in the second sentence makes a stronger point because it emphasizes that the activity is ongoing. Encourage students to use the progressive tense when they want to convey continuous action. Remind them that as they review their drafts, they should make sure they have used the progressive tense correctly.

If any of your students are having trouble with progressive tense verbs, you may wish to teach the Mini-Lesson on pages 270–271 of this Teacher Edition.

WORK with a PARTNER Have pairs of students read one another's drafts, using sticky notes to mark errors in spelling, punctuation, and grammar. Then, tell students to perform a second read that focuses on the editing strategies they learned in this chapter.

Progressive Tense Verbs

KNOW the RULE

The **progressive tense** shows continuing action. To form the **present progressive tense**, add *am, is,* or *are* in front of a present participle verb (a verb ending in *–ing*).
Example: Joe **is walking** home.

To form the **past progressive tense**, add *was* or *were* in front of a present participle verb.
Example: Joe **was walking** home.

To form the **future progressive tense**, add *will be* in front of a present participle verb.
Example: Joe **will be walking** home tomorrow.

Practice the Rule

Number a separate sheet of paper 1–5. Read the sentences below. If a sentence contains a correctly used progressive tense verb, write the word *Correct*. If it contains an error, write the sentence correctly.

1. My friend Nicole is taking voice lessons after school.

2. Currently, her music school will holding auditions for teacher placements.

3. I were thinking about signing up for an audition.

4. Nicole said if I get the job, I will be teaching her class.

5. But last night, I am feeling nervous about it.

Apply the Rule

Read the following persuasive speech, looking for progressive tense verb errors. Then, rewrite the speech correctly on another sheet of paper.

Give Back Our Instruments

This year, we returned to school in September to discover that some changes had been made to our curriculum. Instead of having a full-time music teacher, we is sharing one with another school. Plus, instrumental music class has been dropped.

These cutbacks are upset to many students and parents, so we have started a petition drive. We were aiming to get the school committee to restore instrumental music in our schools, so please sign the petition.

Why is instrumental music important? Well, some young people will grow up to become great musicians, but many will miss their chance if they are not given the opportunity to discover an instrument. The time to be exposed to a wide variety of instrument choices is now, when we be developing our interests.

So what's wrong with learning an instrument outside of school? Some families do not have the resources to rent an instrument. Others don't know enough about music to guide their children in this area. Schools are cut this option and, as a result, creating unequal access to music education.

Let's act before these fresh cutbacks begin to harden and set. This is too important to leave up to a few government leaders. Get involved. Sign the petition, and tell the school committee to restore the cuts.

(Student pages 380–381)

Progressive Tense Verbs

Have students read the Know the Rule box on Student page 380. Ask students to explain the basic purpose of progressive tense verbs. **to show continuing action** To illustrate the present progressive tense, write the following sentences on the board:

Jim and Ann leave for vacation in two days.
Jim and Ann are leaving for vacation in two days.

Ask students which sentence uses the present progressive tense. **the second**

To illustrate the past progressive tense, write the following sentences on the board:

While Jim and Ann were packing, they discussed plans.
When Jim and Ann packed, they discussed plans.

Ask students which sentence uses the past progressive tense. **the first** Note that the first sentence shows that Jim and Ann discussed plans for an *ongoing amount of time* and the second shows that they did so *at one point.*

To illustrate the future progressive tense, write the following sentences on the board:

In two days, Jim and Ann will be sitting on the beach.
In two days, Jim and Ann will sit on the beach.

Ask students which sentence uses the future progressive tense. **the first** Note that the first sentence shows that Jim and Ann will sit on the beach for an *ongoing amount of time,* and the second shows that they will sit on the beach *at one point.*

Answers for Practice the Rule

1. Correct

2. Currently, her music school is holding auditions for teacher placements.

3. I was thinking about signing up for an audition.

4. Correct

5. But last night, I was feeling nervous about it.

(Answers continue on page 271.)

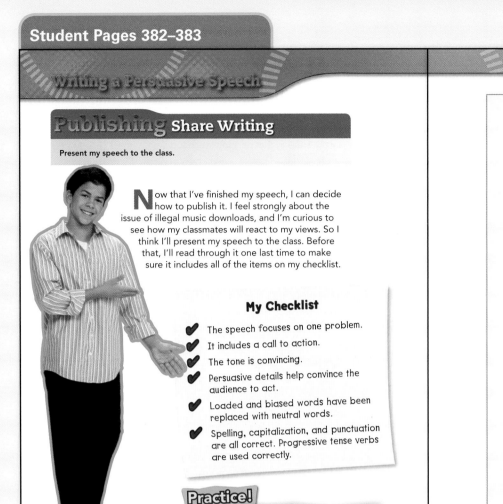

Writing a Persuasive Speech

Publishing Share Writing

Present my speech to the class.

Now that I've finished my speech, I can decide how to publish it. I feel strongly about the issue of illegal music downloads, and I'm curious to see how my classmates will react to my views. So I think I'll present my speech to the class. Before that, I'll read through it one last time to make sure it includes all of the items on my checklist.

My Checklist

✔ The speech focuses on one problem.

✔ It includes a call to action.

✔ The tone is convincing.

✔ Persuasive details help convince the audience to act.

✔ Loaded and biased words have been replaced with neutral words.

✔ Spelling, capitalization, and punctuation are all correct. Progressive tense verbs are used correctly.

Practice!

Now it's your turn. Make a checklist to check your speech. Then, make a final draft to publish.

Stop Stealing Songs

by Luis

Last week, my friend and I were working on a history project together, and I borrowed his laptop for a minute to do some research. I work best with a little "study music," so he recommended one of the songs in his music folder. When I opened the folder, however, I was shocked. It contained almost 3,000 songs. He told me that he himself had downloaded them for free.

Here's the problem: These songs aren't really free—they are copyrighted material that has been shared illegally. I know that my views on this issue are unpopular, and that downloading music has been such a widespread practice that it has become a part of our modern culture. However, I think that if more people understand why this practice is wrong, they will stop. That's why I'm here today, asking each and every one of you to stop these illegal downloads.

Why do I feel so strongly about this issue? First of all, it violates copyright laws, which makes it illegal. Because my dad is a musician, I know that any song composed by an American before 1922 is in the public domain. That means that it belongs to everyone and can be shared or performed freely. But music composed after 1922 cannot be used without permission. And even with permission, royalties must

---

(Answers continued from page 270.)

Answers for Apply the Rule

Give Back Our Instruments

This year, we returned to school in September to discover that some changes had been made to our curriculum. Instead of having a full-time music teacher, we will be sharing one with another school. Plus, instrumental music class has been dropped.

These cutbacks are upsetting to many students and parents, so we have started a petition drive. We are aiming to get the school committee to restore instrumental music in our schools, so please sign the petition.

Why is instrumental music important? Well, some young people will grow up to become great musicians, but many will miss their chance if they are not given the opportunity to discover an instrument. The time to be exposed to a wide variety of instrument choices is now, when we are developing our interests.

So what's wrong with learning an instrument outside of school? Some families do not have the resources to rent an instrument. Others don't know enough about music to guide their children in this area. Schools are cutting this option and, as a result, creating unequal access to music education.

Let's act before these fresh cutbacks begin to harden and set. This is too important to leave up to a few government leaders. Get involved. Sign the petition, and tell the school committee to restore the cuts.

Publishing

(Student pages 382–383)

Ask students if they like Luis's choice for sharing his persuasive speech. Tell the class that his choice is not the only option for publishing his work. Invite students to name other ways they could publish their own speeches.

Have each student make a checklist and perform a final evaluation of his or her persuasive speech before publishing it. Encourage students to read their speeches to friends and relatives who might be interested in hearing about what they wrote.

Writing a Persuasive Speech

be paid. So when you download songs on the Internet, you are violating the United States Copyright Act.

What are the consequences of breaking this law? Most people believe there are none. But tell that to the many people who are being prosecuted and punished. Many of these defendants, some of whom are teenagers just like us, are currently on trial. If convicted, they will have to pay hundreds of thousands of dollars in fines. Now, you're probably thinking there's no way that the government can prosecute all file-sharers. But are you really willing to take that chance?

Even though people might be "getting away with" illegal file-sharing, isn't it really a broader issue? Many of us feel that it's somehow OK to break the law. Even worse, when we download illegal music, we teach this lack of respect to our younger brothers and sisters. And some kids might learn a more dangerous lesson: If it's OK to break one law, maybe it's OK to break others. When you look at it this way, illegal file-sharing could be a "gateway" to breaking other laws.

But the most important reason to stop illegal downloads concerns the songwriters. Music is composed by artists who own the rights to their songs. When a record label produces and sells an artist's music, the artist is paid royalty fees for each copy sold. This is how artists make money—it's their job.

When you download an artist's music without paying for it, you are stealing that person's livelihood.

As I mentioned before, my dad is a musician. Maybe that's why I feel so strongly about this issue. He knows that people find it hard to understand how anyone can actually "own" a piece of music. Once a song is played, it's out there on the public airwaves for everyone to hear, and it's true that no one can stop you from singing or playing a song unless, of course, you charge admission. But my dad recently gave me this analogy: Pirating music is the same as going into a sculptor's studio, deciding which piece of artwork you like, and walking out the door without paying for it. You wouldn't do that, would you? Then you shouldn't download music for free, either.

I hope I've made you think about what you're doing when you download "free" tunes. It's not like you have to give up music entirely. There are a lot of ways to build a great music library without spending tons of money. Start investigating these alternatives. Talk to your friends. And please, stop downloading copyrighted music for free.

Reflect

What do you think? Did I use all the traits of a good persuasive speech in my writing? Check it against the rubric, and don't forget to use the rubric to check your own speech, too.

Publishing

(Student pages 384–385)

Call students' attention to the Reflect box on the bottom of Student page 385. Explain that assessing Luis's speech against the rubric will help them better understand how to apply the traits to their own work. Have students use sticky notes to mark at least one example of each trait in Luis's writing. Tell them to include an evaluation on each note.

After this process, have students assess how well they were able to identify each trait in Luis's writing and how easy or difficult it was to use the rubric. Remind them to apply what they learned from Luis's work when they use the rubric to check their own writing.

Differentiating Instruction

Support   Some students may benefit from examining the structure of Luis's final script. Use the following process to map out the elements of "Stop Stealing Songs."

As a class, read the speech aloud, one paragraph at a time. Stop after each paragraph and discuss

- its purpose and main idea.
- how its main point is conveyed to the audience.
- its tone.
- which words and sentences are most convincing.
- whether students would make changes to strengthen the paragraph.

Encourage students to refer to Luis's Persuasion Map as they review his speech, noting whether his writing follows his initial plan. Remind students that they can refer to Luis's speech for help if they are having trouble organizing their own drafts.

Ways to Publish a Persuasive Speech

When it's time to publish your writing, you should think about your audience. That way, you can figure out the best way to share your work. Here are some ideas for publishing your speech.

✔ Present your work as part of a class lineup of speeches called "Can I Convince You?"

✔ Record your speech on videotape. Then, share it with an appropriate audience.

✔ Include your speech as part of a class booklet called "Persuasive Ideas."

✔ Enter your work in a local speech contest for young people.

✔ Take your speech home and present it to your family.

386   **Persuasive Writing** ■ Persuasive Speech

Writing Across the Content Areas Persuasive Speech

Your school subjects can be a great source of writing ideas. Choose a subject and see how many related topics you can brainstorm. Check out these examples.

Science
• Is there something your community can do to help the environment? Write a speech persuading your audience to think globally.
• Which medical procedures should be covered by insurance? Take a stand and promote it in a speech.

Language Arts
• Should students be required to do summer reading? State your case and present it in a speech.
• Should students be required to learn a foreign language in school? Write a speech convincing others of your position.

Art and/or Music
• Should artists and musicians be subsidized by the government? Write a speech that calls for some form of government funding.
• Think of a way to include more art in your community. Then, promote it in a speech.

Persuasive Writing ■ Persuasive Speech   387

Ways to Publish
(Student page 386)

Read and discuss with students the publishing options listed on Student page 386. Encourage students to consider some of these options when publishing their own writing. Remind students that Luis chose to publish his speech by presenting it to the class, but they can choose their own way of publishing their work. Perhaps one student will want to enter his or her work in a local speech contest, while another will want to record it on videotape and share it with an appropriate audience.

Writing Across the Content Areas
(Student page 387)

Explain to students that writing is not just for English or language arts class. Many other school subjects contain ideas, issues, and events that students may want to write about. Encourage students to consider using one of the content areas listed on Student page 387 as a springboard for more writing options. Students may also wish to consult with other teachers for more ideas on writing in the content areas.

Persuasive Test Writing

In this chapter, students will learn how to write a persuasive essay for a test. They will review traits of a persuasive essay and study a test prompt and a scoring guide. Students will then use a model writing prompt and a scoring guide to study a sample persuasive essay test.

Students will follow the student guide as he goes through the test writing stages—time planning, studying the writing prompt, prewriting, drafting, revising, and editing. As the student guide reviews the writing strategies in each step, students will be directed to practice the test writing strategies.

During prewriting and drafting, students will
- study the writing prompt.
- respond to the task.
- choose a graphic organizer.
- check the graphic organizer against the scoring guide.
- state a clear opinion for the reader.

During revising and editing, students will
- add facts and examples to support each reason.
- delete unnecessary ideas.
- use conditional sentences.
- edit their drafts for proper grammar, punctuation, capitalization, and spelling.

You may wish to send to families the School-Home Connection Letter for this chapter, located at the end of this unit in the Teacher Edition.

Writing Traits in the Scoring Guide

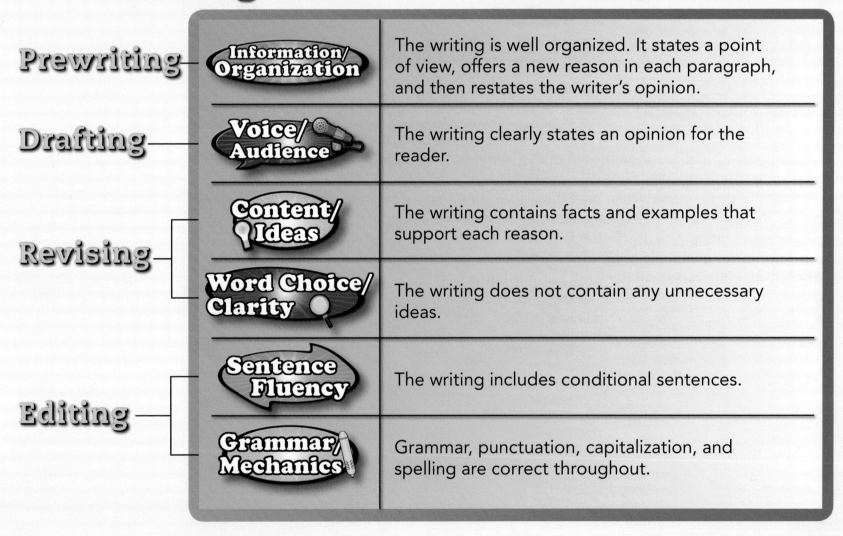

Prewriting

Information/Organization — The writing is well organized. It states a point of view, offers a new reason in each paragraph, and then restates the writer's opinion.

Drafting

Voice/Audience — The writing clearly states an opinion for the reader.

Revising

Content/Ideas — The writing contains facts and examples that support each reason.

Word Choice/Clarity — The writing does not contain any unnecessary ideas.

Editing

Sentence Fluency — The writing includes conditional sentences.

Grammar/Mechanics — Grammar, punctuation, capitalization, and spelling are correct throughout.

Persuasive Test Writing Time Management

WEEK 1

Day 1	Day 2	Day 3	Day 4	Day 5
Learning Objectives				
Students will: • learn the components of the writing prompt model.	Students will: • recognize the relationship of the scoring guide to the rubric and the six traits of writing. • read a writing prompt model response.	Students will: • apply the scoring guide to the writing prompt model response.	Students will: • continue to apply the scoring guide to the writing prompt model response.	Students will: • learn how to plan their time during a writing test.
Activities				
• Discuss the components of the writing prompt model (Student pages 388–389).	• Read and discuss the scoring guide (Student page 390). • Read the writing prompt model response. (Student page 391).	• Read and discuss **Using the Scoring Guide to Study the Model** (Student pages 392–393).	• Read and discuss **Using the Scoring Guide to Study the Model** (Student page 394).	• Read and discuss **Planning My Time** (Student page 395).

WEEK 2

Day 1	Day 2	Day 3	Day 4	Day 5
Learning Objectives				
Students will: • read a writing prompt for a persuasive essay. • apply the six traits of writing to the writing prompt.	Students will: • learn how to respond to the task in the writing prompt.	Students will: • learn how to choose a graphic organizer for persuasive test writing.	Students will: • learn how to check the graphic organizer against the scoring guide.	Students will: • learn how to clearly state their opinion for the reader.
Activities				
• Read and discuss **Prewriting: Study the Writing Prompt** (Student pages 396–397).	• Read and discuss **Prewriting: Gather Information** (Student page 398).	• Read and discuss **Prewriting: Organize Ideas** (Student page 399).	• Read and discuss **Prewriting: Check the Scoring Guide** (Student pages 400–401).	• Read and discuss **Drafting: Write a Draft** (Student pages 402–403).

WEEK 3

Day 1	Day 2	Day 3	Day 4	Day 5
Learning Objectives				
Students will: • add facts and examples to support each reason in their writing test.	Students will: • delete unnecessary ideas in their writing test.	Students will: • use conditional sentences in their writing test.	Students will: • edit their writing test for proper grammar and mechanics.	Students will: • learn tips for test writing.
Activities				
• Read and discuss **Revising: Extend Writing** (Student page 404).	• Read and discuss **Revising: Clarify Writing** (Student page 405).	• Read and discuss **Editing: Check Sentences** (Student page 406).	• Read and discuss **Editing: Proofread Writing** (Student pages 407–408).	• Read and discuss **Test Tips** (Student page 409).

To complete the chapter in fewer days, teach the learning objectives and activities for two days in one day.
This planning chart, correlated to your state's writing standards, is available on-line at http://www.zaner-bloser.com/sfw.

PERSUASIVE test writing

Read the Writing Prompt

When you take a writing test, you will be given a writing prompt. Most writing prompts have three parts:

Setup This part of the writing prompt gives you the background information you need to get ready to write.

Task This part of the writing prompt tells you exactly what you are supposed to write: a persuasive essay.

Scoring Guide This section tells how your writing will be scored. To do well on the test, you should include everything on the list.

Remember the rubrics you've used in writing class this year? When you take a writing test, you don't always have all of the information that's on a rubric. But a scoring guide is a lot like a rubric. It lists everything you need to think about to write a good paper. Like the rubrics you've used, many scoring guides are based on the six traits of writing:

- Information/Organization
- Content/Ideas
- Sentence Fluency
- Voice/Audience
- Word Choice/Clarity
- Grammar/Mechanics

Writing MODEL Prompt

Your school is looking for new ways to raise money to support social programs, such as afterschool sports and band. Some schools accept money from businesses in exchange for placing advertisements around their school facilities. The Super Soda Company has offered to buy your school an expensive scoreboard, provided they can place an advertisement for Super Soda on it. Do you think this is a good idea?

Write a persuasive essay to read to the school board. Decide whether you think the school should accept or reject this offer. Then, give reasons to support your opinion.

Be sure your writing

- is well organized. You should state a point of view, give a new reason in each paragraph, and then restate your opinion.
- clearly states your opinion for your reader.
- includes facts and examples that support each reason.
- does not contain any unnecessary ideas.
- includes conditional sentences.
- contains correct grammar, punctuation, capitalization, and spelling.

Introduce the Writing Prompt
Persuasive Writing

(Student pages 388–389)

Tell students that they are going to apply what they have learned about persuasive writing to the challenge of writing a persuasive test. Note that when they write for a test, they will receive a writing prompt and a certain amount of time in which to write. Then, their writing will be evaluated, as with any test. Assure students that they do not need to be anxious about writing a test, because the skills they have already practiced will help them do a good job.

Make sure students understand that the scoring guide contains traits similar to those they have seen in the rubrics throughout this unit. Note that just as a rubric includes the qualities of a good paper, the scoring guide includes the qualities of a good writing test.

Read aloud the writing prompt model on Student page 389. Then, write the following correlations on the board and review:

- *Setup: This provides the background information needed in order to write for a test.*

- *Task: This is the assignment, and it often names the type of writing to be done.*

- *Scoring Guide: This is much like a rubric, providing information necessary for doing well on a writing test.*

Writing Traits in the Scoring Guide

Take a look at the scoring guide in the writing prompt on page 389. Not every writing prompt will include each of the six writing traits, but this one does. You can use this chart to help you better understand the connection between the scoring guide and the writing traits in the rubrics you've used.

Information/Organization
- Be sure your writing is well organized. You should state a point of view, give a new reason in each paragraph, and then restate your opinion.

Voice/Audience
- Be sure your writing clearly states your opinion for your reader.

Content/Ideas
- Be sure your writing includes facts and examples that support each reason.

Word Choice/Clarity
- Be sure your writing does not contain any unnecessary ideas.

Sentence Fluency
- Be sure your writing includes conditional sentences.

Grammar/Mechanics
- Be sure your writing contains correct grammar, punctuation, capitalization, and spelling.

Look at Mika Peters' story on the next page. Did she follow the scoring guide?

390 **Persuasive Writing** ■ Persuasive Test

Writing Prompt MODEL Response

Say "No, Thanks"

by Mika Peters

I know that Super Soda's offer of a new scoreboard for our school seems like a worthwhile offer, but I think the school board should politely say "no, thanks."

Many middle-school students tend to go along with the crowd. Because they want to do what other kids are doing, some students often have trouble making up their minds about what to wear, how to act, and what to eat. These kids sometimes purchase brand-name clothing to "fit in" with their peers. They buy the same brands of snacks and drinks that everyone else buys, instead of thinking for themselves.

Now, Super Soda has offered to give our school a new scoreboard for the gym. I'm sure the basketball fans would love it. But the scoreboard would probably display a large Super Soda advertisement so that no one would miss it.

You might ask yourself, what's wrong with that? Well, we kids see so many ads for products like Super Soda that we often don't even consider anything else when choosing a product. It's like we've all been brainwashed. When we go to a store or a vending machine, we usually pass up the healthy options and buy the junk food instead. That's because we reach for the product in the familiar package—the one with the same name that everyone else is buying.

I realize that some people are saying that the money the school could get from Super Soda would be enough to support special programs. I'm also aware that the school received over $20,000 last year from beverage sales in the Super Soda vending machines. I understand that the school wouldn't have to pay anything for our new scoreboard if we accept this offer. But wouldn't you agree that students' health is more important? If the scoreboard were free, that would be great. But in my opinion, the cost of the new scoreboard is way too high.

We students are never going to learn to make up our own minds or make smart choices if we keep allowing advertisers to brainwash us. That's why I'm taking a stand (and hoping you'll join me) by saying "no, thanks" to Super Soda's offer!

Persuasive Writing ■ Persuasive Test **391**

Writing Traits in the Scoring Guide

(Student pages 390–391)

Ask students to name the six traits of writing they have studied throughout the unit. **Information/Organization, Voice/Audience, Content/Ideas, Word Choice/Clarity, Sentence Fluency, Grammar/Mechanics** If they are having trouble providing a response, remind them that the first trait is Information/Organization. Tell them that when they read a scoring guide, they should try to identify the traits within it. This will help them think about the purpose of each item in the scoring guide. It will also help them relate to what they have already learned about these writing traits.

Read the Model:
Writing Prompt Response

Ask a student volunteer to read the traits in the scoring guide on Student page 390. Then, tell students that they are going to study and use strategies for persuasive test writing and that a good persuasive test has all of the traits listed on Student page 390.

As students read "Say 'No, Thanks,'" have them look for each trait from the scoring guide.

Differentiating Instruction

English-Language Learners Help English-language learners add to their English vocabulary by encouraging them to review "Say 'No Thanks'" for compound words. Explain that a compound word is formed when two words are joined to make one new word.

Have students review the essay together. As they come across each compound word, have them write it down and discuss its meaning.

Persuasive Writing ■ Persuasive Test **277**

Using the Scoring Guide to Study the Model

Now we'll use the scoring guide to check Mika's writing test, "Say 'No, Thanks.'" Let's see how well her essay meets each of the six writing traits.

Information/Organization
- The essay is well organized.
- It states a point of view, gives a new reason in each paragraph, and then restates the writer's opinion.

Mika begins by stating her opinion on the topic. Then, she gives new reasons in each paragraph to support her point of view. She concludes by restating her opinion.

We students are never going to learn to make up our own minds or make smart choices if we keep allowing advertisers to brainwash us. That's why I'm taking a stand (and hoping you'll join me) by saying "no, thanks" to Super Soda's offer!

Voice/Audience
- The writer clearly states an opinion for the reader.

In the first paragraph, it is clear that Mika understands the argument over the school scoreboard issue. But she clearly states her own opinion: the school should say "no, thanks" to Super Soda's offer.

I know that Super Soda's offer of a new scoreboard for our school seems like a worthwhile offer, but I think the school board should politely say "no, thanks."

Content/Ideas
- The essay contains facts and examples that support each reason.

Mika uses many facts and examples to support her reasons. In this paragraph, she fully explains kids' vulnerability to advertising, citing examples of how they buy clothes and snacks just to "fit in."

Many middle-school students tend to go along with the crowd. Because they want to do what other kids are doing, some students often have trouble making up their minds about what to wear, how to act, and what to eat. These kids sometimes purchase brand-name clothing to "fit in" with their peers. They buy the same brands of snacks and drinks that everyone else buys, instead of thinking for themselves.

Word Choice/Clarity
- The paper does not contain any unnecessary ideas.

Everything Mika includes in her essay is clear and easy to understand. In this passage, she relates everything to her idea of rejecting Super Soda's offer.

Well, we kids see so many ads for products like Super Soda that we often don't even consider anything else when choosing a product. It's like we've all been brainwashed. When we go to a store or a vending machine, we usually pass up the healthy options and buy the junk food instead. That's because we reach for the product in the familiar package—the one with the same name that everyone else is buying.

Using the Scoring Guide to Study the Model

(Student pages 392–394)

Review the function of the scoring guide. First, have students review a rubric from one of the earlier chapters in this unit. Then, point out the similarities and differences between that rubric and the scoring guide. Make sure students understand that although a scoring guide does not include criteria for various levels of accomplishment, it does provide guidance in the six key areas of assessment: Information/Organization, Voice/Audience, Content/Ideas, Word Choice/Clarity, Sentence Fluency, and Grammar/Mechanics.

Explain that in the same way traits in a rubric are used to assess writing, criteria in a scoring guide are used to assess test writing. Remind students to use the scoring guide when they write for a test to ensure that they meet all of the traits.

Differentiating Instruction

Support Some students may need extra help reviewing the structure of the writing prompt model response. Work with students in a small group to outline "Say 'No, Thanks.'" Have students go through the essay together, paragraph by paragraph, noting what the author conveys in each one.

- Paragraph 1 states a clear opinion: The school board should not accept Super Soda's offer of a new scoreboard.
- Paragraph 2 states a supporting reason: Many middle-school students go along with the crowd. Paragraph 2 also provides details: Students follow others' choices in clothes, actions, and brands.
- Paragraphs 3–4 state another supporting reason: Super Soda will probably display a large ad on the scoreboard. Paragraphs 3–4 also provide details: Ads brainwash people into passing up healthier choices.
- Paragraph 5 states another supporting reason: The scoreboard won't be free. Paragraph 5 also provides details: The cost will be brainwashed students.
- Paragraph 6 restates the opinion from Paragraph 1.

Remind students to use a similar structure as they draft their persuasive tests.

Using the Scoring Guide to Study the Model

Sentence Fluency

• The essay contains conditional sentences.

Mika uses conditional sentences to present several convincing and persuasive "what if" scenarios to her reader. The second and third sentences in this passage present the idea that "if" the school accepts Super Soda's offer, it will "probably" have a large advertisement on it.

Now, Super Soda has offered to give our school a new scoreboard for the gym. I'm sure the basketball fans would love it. But the scoreboard would probably display a large Super Soda advertisement so that no one would miss it.

Grammar/Mechanics

• The paper contains correct grammar, punctuation, capitalization, and spelling.

It looks like Mika used correct grammar, spelling, capitalization, and punctuation. I know it's important to check for these kinds of mistakes, so I'll be sure to keep that in mind as I write. Don't forget to check for proper grammar and mechanics in your writing, too. This can be done at every step of the writing process.

Planning My Time

Before giving us a writing prompt, my teacher always tells us how much time we'll have to complete the test. Since I'm already familiar with each step of the writing process, I can plan how much time I'll need for each one. Then, I'll be sure to have enough time to complete the entire process. If the test takes an hour, here's how I'll organize my time. Planning your time will help you, too!

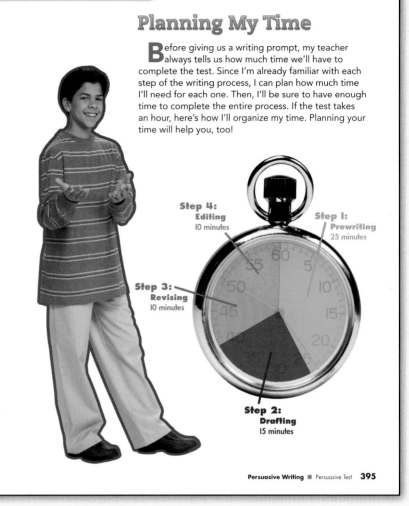

Step 4:
Editing
10 minutes

Step 1:
Prewriting
25 minutes

Step 3:
Revising
10 minutes

Step 2:
Drafting
15 minutes

Planning My Time
(Student page 395)

Explain to students the importance of organizing time when planning for a test. Remind them that they will have a limited amount of time to complete their tests, so it is important to set aside a block of time for each one of the steps in the writing process.

Direct students' attention to Student page 395, and ask a student volunteer to tell the class what writing step Luis plans to spend the most time on. **prewriting** Point out that many students do poorly on test writing because they start writing before they develop a plan, and they continue writing until they run out of time. Stress to students the importance of including enough time to prewrite, draft, revise, and edit.

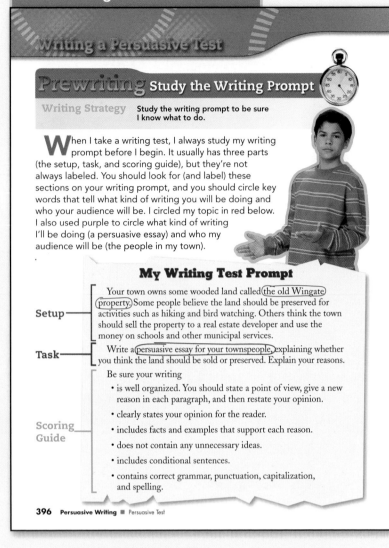

Writing a Persuasive Test

Prewriting Study the Writing Prompt

Writing Strategy Study the writing prompt to be sure I know what to do.

When I take a writing test, I always study my writing prompt before I begin. It usually has three parts (the setup, task, and scoring guide), but they're not always labeled. You should look for (and label) these sections on your writing prompt, and you should circle key words that tell what kind of writing you will be doing and who your audience will be. I circled my topic in red below. I also used purple to circle what kind of writing I'll be doing (a persuasive essay) and who my audience will be (the people in my town).

My Writing Test Prompt

Setup — Your town owns some wooded land called the old Wingate property. Some people believe the land should be preserved for activities such as hiking and bird watching. Others think the town should sell the property to a real estate developer and use the money on schools and other municipal services.

Task — Write a persuasive essay for your townspeople, explaining whether you think the land should be sold or preserved. Explain your reasons.

Scoring Guide — Be sure your writing
- is well organized. You should state a point of view, give a new reason in each paragraph, and then restate your opinion.
- clearly states your opinion for the reader.
- includes facts and examples that support each reason.
- does not contain any unnecessary ideas.
- includes conditional sentences.
- contains correct grammar, punctuation, capitalization, and spelling.

Think about how the scoring guide relates to the six traits of good writing in the rubrics you've studied. Not all of the traits will be included in every scoring guide, but you'll still want to remember them all in order to write a good essay.

Information/Organization
- Be sure your writing is well organized. You should state a point of view, give a new reason in each paragraph, and then restate your opinion.

I want my reader to understand my point of view and the reasons for it, so organization is important.

Voice/Audience
- Be sure your writing clearly states your opinion for the reader.

I'll make sure to clearly state my opinion.

Content/Ideas
- Be sure your writing includes facts and examples that support each reason.

I have to remember to provide plenty of facts and examples to help support my opinion.

Word Choice/Clarity
- Be sure your writing does not contain any unnecessary ideas.

Unnecessary ideas will weaken my argument, so I'll only include what's really important.

Sentence Fluency
- Be sure your writing includes conditional sentences.

I can be more persuasive if I use conditional sentences that describe the "what ifs."

Grammar/Mechanics
- Be sure your writing contains correct grammar, punctuation, capitalization, and spelling.

I know to check my grammar and mechanics whenever I write.

Study the Writing Prompt

(Student pages 396–397)

Read aloud Luis's words on Student page 396. Emphasize the importance of reading and understanding the writing prompt before beginning to draft. Explain that even if students write a great paper, they won't receive a great score unless they have followed the instructions set forth in the scoring guide.

Ask a student volunteer to tell the class what type of test Luis is supposed to write. **a persuasive essay** Explain that before Luis develops a viewpoint, he needs to consider what might be the best use for the old Wingate property.

Read through the scoring guide portion of the writing prompt shown on Student page 396. Then, review Student page 397 with students. Note how each of the traits relates to the six key areas of the scoring guide. Remind students that if they were using a rubric, these traits would be those seen under the Excelling category. Point out that even before Luis begins to prewrite, he thinks about each of the traits he will need to include in his test.

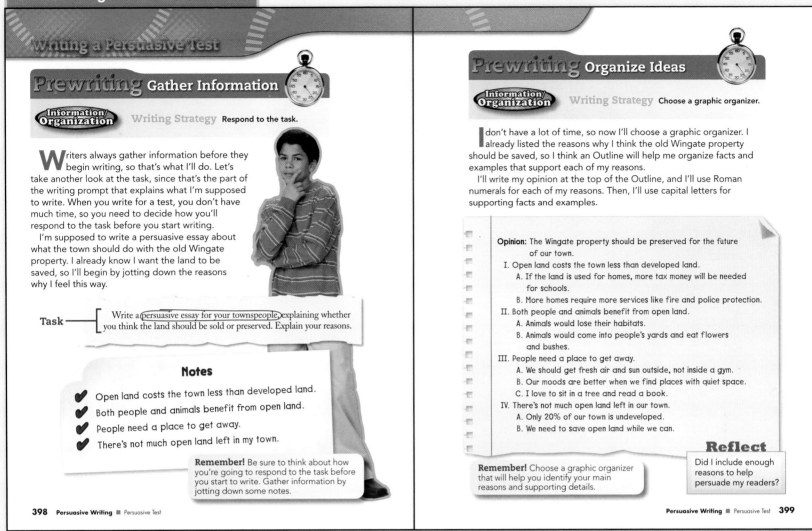

Gather Information and Organize Ideas

(Student pages 398–399)

Ask students to recall what they learned about prewriting in other chapters in this unit. Point out that on a writing test, the prewriting stage is similar. Students should consider the assignment and then gather information.

Remind students to use a graphic organizer to organize their ideas. Tell students that during a writing test, they will not be told what kind of graphic organizer to use. Instead, they must think about how they have used graphic organizers in the past, and then they must decide which one will be the most useful for a persuasive test.

Read through Luis's Outline on Student page 399. Note that even before he started writing, Luis had already written down much of the information that would appear in his essay.

Differentiating Instruction

Support Remind students that graphic organizers can help them structure their notes. Ask volunteers to name the graphic organizers that they used throughout the unit. **Problem-Solution Frame, Storyboard, Persuasion Map** Then, ask students how they might decide which graphic organizer to use on a test. **Possible response: by thinking about which one fits the writing genre** Remind students to look for clues in the writing prompt to help them choose a useful graphic organizer.

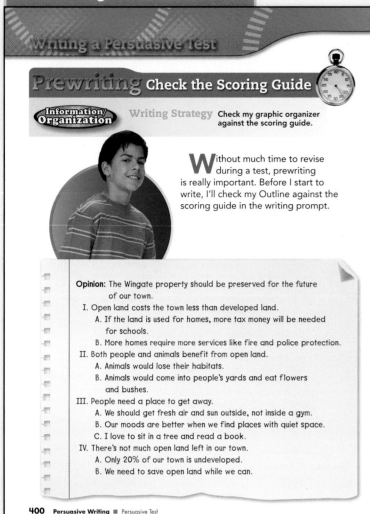

Writing a Persuasive Test

Prewriting Check the Scoring Guide

Information/Organization Writing Strategy Check my graphic organizer against the scoring guide.

Without much time to revise during a test, prewriting is really important. Before I start to write, I'll check my Outline against the scoring guide in the writing prompt.

Opinion: The Wingate property should be preserved for the future of our town.

I. Open land costs the town less than developed land.
  A. If the land is used for homes, more tax money will be needed for schools.
  B. More homes require more services like fire and police protection.

II. Both people and animals benefit from open land.
  A. Animals would lose their habitats.
  B. Animals would come into people's yards and eat flowers and bushes.

III. People need a place to get away.
  A. We should get fresh air and sun outside, not inside a gym.
  B. Our moods are better when we find places with quiet space.
  C. I love to sit in a tree and read a book.

IV. There's not much open land left in our town.
  A. Only 20% of our town is undeveloped.
  B. We need to save open land while we can.

Information/Organization
- Be sure your writing is well organized. You should state a point of view, give a new reason in each paragraph, and then restate your opinion.

I'll just turn my Outline into an essay! I'll state my opinion in my introduction, and I'll use the reasons from each Roman numeral to make a new paragraph. Then, I'll wrap things up in my conclusion.

Voice/Audience
- Be sure your writing clearly states your opinion for the reader.

I'll use the opinion from the top of my Outline to form my lead paragraph.

Content/Ideas
- Be sure your writing includes facts and examples that support each reason.

I'll use the facts and examples from my Outline to support each reason.

Word Choice/Clarity
- Be sure your writing does not contain any unnecessary ideas.

I'll check on this later. I might need to get rid of unnecessary information when I revise my essay.

Sentence Fluency
- Be sure your writing includes conditional sentences.

My Outline already includes a few conditional sentences, but I'll be sure to use more of them as I write.

Grammar/Mechanics
- Be sure your writing contains correct grammar, punctuation, capitalization, and spelling.

I'll check for proper grammar and mechanics when I edit my essay.

Remember! Compare your graphic organizer with the scoring guide before you start to write. This way, you'll know what to do when you begin drafting.

Reflect
My Outline seems pretty complete. Can you think of anything it's missing?

Check the Scoring Guide
(Student pages 400–401)

Ask students why they think Luis is not yet ready to write even though he has used a graphic organizer to structure his notes. **Possible response: because he needs to check his graphic organizer against the scoring guide** Emphasize the importance of paying attention to the scoring guide throughout test writing. Note that on Student page 401, Luis once again refers back to each point in the scoring guide to be sure he has met them all. Explain that during this step of the test writing process, students may need to add or change information in their graphic organizers to meet the criteria.

Point out that while the graphic organizer helped Luis organize his notes and meet the scoring guide criteria, he will continue to think about all of the scoring guide traits as he writes.

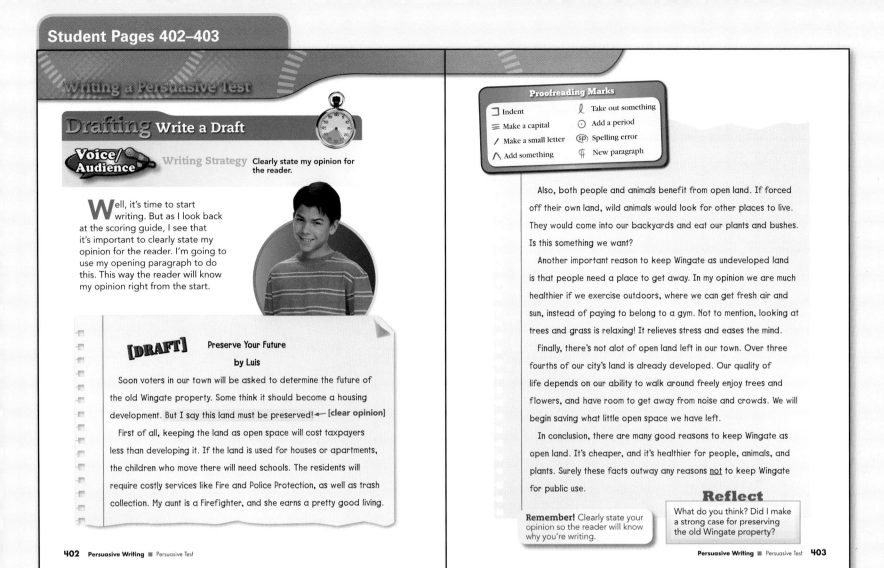

Writing a Persuasive Test

Drafting Write a Draft

Voice/Audience

Writing Strategy Clearly state my opinion for the reader.

Well, it's time to start writing. But as I look back at the scoring guide, I see that it's important to clearly state my opinion for the reader. I'm going to use my opening paragraph to do this. This way the reader will know my opinion right from the start.

[DRAFT]

Preserve Your Future
by Luis

Soon voters in our town will be asked to determine the future of the old Wingate property. Some think it should become a housing development. But I say this land must be preserved! ← [clear opinion]

First of all, keeping the land as open space will cost taxpayers less than developing it. If the land is used for houses or apartments, the children who move there will need schools. The residents will require costly services like Fire and Police Protection, as well as trash collection. My aunt is a Firefighter, and she earns a pretty good living.

Proofreading Marks

⌐ Indent	ℓ Take out something
≡ Make a capital	⊙ Add a period
/ Make a small letter	SP Spelling error
∧ Add something	¶ New paragraph

Also, both people and animals benefit from open land. If forced off their own land, wild animals would look for other places to live. They would come into our backyards and eat our plants and bushes. Is this something we want?

Another important reason to keep Wingate as undeveloped land is that people need a place to get away. In my opinion we are much healthier if we exercise outdoors, where we can get fresh air and sun, instead of paying to belong to a gym. Not to mention, looking at trees and grass is relaxing! It relieves stress and eases the mind.

Finally, there's not alot of open land left in our town. Over three fourths of our city's land is already developed. Our quality of life depends on our ability to walk around freely enjoy trees and flowers, and have room to get away from noise and crowds. We will begin saving what little open space we have left.

In conclusion, there are many good reasons to keep Wingate as open land. It's cheaper, and it's healthier for people, animals, and plants. Surely these facts outway any reasons <u>not</u> to keep Wingate for public use.

Remember! Clearly state your opinion so the reader will know why you're writing.

Reflect
What do you think? Did I make a strong case for preserving the old Wingate property?

402 **Persuasive Writing** ■ Persuasive Test

Persuasive Writing ■ Persuasive Test 403

Drafting

(Student pages 402–403)

Emphasize to students the importance of using their graphic organizers as guidance during the drafting process. Explain that because of editing, they will want to leave space between the lines in their drafts so that they will have room to make changes and additions. Also remind them to write neatly, even in the drafting stage, because the test evaluator should be able to read what they have written.

Then, discuss Luis's draft on Student pages 402–403. Have students refer back to his graphic organizer to see whether he included the information that he noted in his Outline. Ask students what they think of the draft, pointing out that although there are mistakes, Luis has remembered to leave time during the editing stage to go through and change any errors he made in spelling and grammar.

Point out the writing strategy *Clearly state my opinion for the reader* and discuss how well Luis applied this to his draft. Have students skim the draft, looking for places

where Luis's opinion is clearly stated. Have students also note any opinions that need further clarification.

Finally, review proofreading marks with the students. Note that these marks will be helpful as they revise and edit their drafts.

Differentiating Instruction

English-Language Learners Stress that it is particularly important for these students to leave test time for revising and editing. Remind them that when drafting a test essay, they should concentrate on getting ideas down on paper. Note that if they have trouble coming up with appropriate words or phrases, they can leave blank spots in their writing and come back to them later. Also remind students that at this stage, they should not be overly concerned with spelling or grammar since they can fix mistakes during editing.

Writing a Persuasive Test

Revising Extend Writing

Content/Ideas

Writing Strategy Add facts and examples to support each reason.

The scoring guide says to include facts and examples that support each of my reasons. So I reread my essay to see if there were any places where I could add more support. My paragraph about people and animals seems OK as is, but I think I can add even more facts and details to persuade the reader about the dangers of developing wildlife land.

[DRAFT]

Shrubs and gardens are not the only things that could get damaged. Deer, rabbits, and coyotes carry diseases such as Lyme disease, rabies, and rabbit fever. People could get sick from the close contact. ←[added facts]

Also, both people and animals benefit from open land. If forced off their own land, wild animals would look for other places to live. They would come into our backyards and eat our plants and bushes. Is this something we want?

Remember! Don't just state your reasons; add facts and details that support them.

Revising Clarify Writing

Word Choice/Clarity

Writing Strategy Delete unnecessary ideas.

Once I added some new details, I reread my paper to make sure it made sense. The scoring guide says to leave out unnecessary details, which means all of my facts and examples should clearly support my reasons. But there was one sentence that seemed out of place. The fact that my aunt earns a good living has nothing to do with my argument, so I'll get rid of that sentence right now.

[DRAFT]

First of all, keeping the land as open space will cost taxpayers less than developing it. If the land is used for houses or apartments, the children who move there will need schools. The residents will require costly services like Fire and Police Protection, as well as trash collection. ~~My aunt is a Firefighter, and she earns a pretty good living.~~

[deleted an unnecessary idea]

Remember! Delete unnecessary details that weaken your argument.

Reflect

Do all of my details support my argument? Are there enough facts and examples to support each reason?

Revising

(Student pages 404–405)

Discuss the revisions Luis made to his draft on Student pages 404–405. He added facts and deleted an unnecessary idea. Point out that Luis once again reviewed his scoring guide in order to determine a revision focus. Encourage students to refer back to the scoring guide section of the writing prompt even after they have completed their drafts.

Discuss the new information Luis added to his writing on Student page 404. Ask students whether they feel the addition helped support his argument, and if so, how. **Possible response: yes, because it supports the idea that the land should be preserved** Have them point out other places in Luis's draft where additional supporting facts could help strengthen his reasoning.

Next, review with students the highlighted text that Luis deleted from his draft on Student page 405. Discuss whether his decision to delete this sentence was appropriate, and why.

Writing a Persuasive Test

Editing Check Sentences

Sentence Fluency

Writing Strategy Use conditional sentences.

I reread my paper one last time to make sure I included conditional sentences, just as the scoring guide suggests. There was one place in my draft where the existing sentence was kind of confusing to my argument, so I formed a conditional sentence there instead.

[DRAFT]

Finally, there's not alot of open land left in our town. Over three fourths of our city's land is already developed. Our quality of life depends on our ability to walk around freely enjoy trees and flowers, and have room to get away from noise and crowds. ~~We will~~ *That's why we should* begin saving what little open space we have left.

[formed a conditional sentence]

Remember! Use conditional sentences to strengthen your argument.

406 **Persuasive Writing** ■ Persuasive Test

Editing Proofread Writing

Grammar/ Mechanics

Writing Strategy Check my grammar, punctuation, capitalization, and spelling.

I'm almost finished! The scoring guide says to use correct grammar, punctuation, capitalization, and spelling. I always leave plenty of time to check for errors in these important areas.

[FINAL DRAFT] Preserve Your Future
by Luis

Soon voters in our town will be asked to determine the future of the old Wingate property. Some think it should become a housing development. But I say this land must be preserved!

First of all, keeping the land as open space will cost taxpayers less than developing it. If the land is used for houses or apartments, the children who move there will need schools. The residents will require costly services like ~~f~~fire and ~~p~~police protection, as well as trash collection. ~~My aunt is a Firefighter, and she earns a pretty good living.~~

Remember! Check your grammar, punctuation, capitalization, and spelling every time you write for a test.

Persuasive Writing ■ Persuasive Test 407

Editing

(Student pages 406–408)

Ask a volunteer to read aloud the last two sentences of Luis's draft on Student page 406—without the edits. Then, have another volunteer read the edited sentences. Ask whether students think Luis's edit improved his writing, and why. **Possible response: yes, because the conditional sentence restates the idea that it's important to save open land from development** Remind students to review their own writing for places where using conditional sentences can help link ideas and details.

Emphasize to students that they should always proofread for mistakes, checking for errors in sentence completeness, punctuation, and spelling.

Differentiating Instruction

Support Some students may benefit from extra instruction in the use of conditional sentences. Explain that a conditional sentence often consists of a dependent clause immediately followed by an independent clause. Illustrate by displaying the following conditional sentences on the board:

1. *If you don't pick me up, I'll have to walk home.*
2. *If I were mayor, I'd make sure the schools receive more money.*
3. *If my dog hadn't chewed my notes, I wouldn't have failed my test.*

Then, review each of the specific functions of these sentences with the students.

1. The first sentence describes what *will happen* if certain *realistic conditions* are met.
2. The second sentence describes what *might happen* if certain *unrealistic conditions* are met.
3. The third sentence describes what *might have happened* if certain *past conditions* had been different.

Encourage students to be creative with the use of conditional sentences in their own writing.

Shrubs and gardens are not the only things that could get damaged. Deer, rabbits, and coyotes carry diseases such as Lyme disease, rabies, and rabbit fever. People could get sick from the close contact.

Also, both people and animals benefit from open land. If forced off their own land, wild animals would look for other places to live. They would come into our backyards and eat our plants and bushes. Is this something we want?

Another important reason to keep Wingate as undeveloped land is that people need a place to get away. In my opinion, we are much healthier if we exercise outdoors, where we can get fresh air and sun, instead of paying to belong to a gym. Not to mention, looking at trees and grass is relaxing! It relieves stress and eases the mind.

Finally, there's not a~~lot~~ a lot of open land left in our town. Over three fourths of our city's land is already developed. Our quality of life depends on our ability to walk around freely enjoy trees and flowers, and have room to get away from noise and crowds. ~~We will~~ That's why we should begin saving what little open space we have left.

In conclusion, there are many good reasons to keep Wingate as open land. It's cheaper, and it's healthier for people, animals, and plants. Surely these facts ~~outway~~ outweigh any reasons <u>not</u> to keep Wingate for public use.

Reflect

I don't think I missed anything, but I'll check my essay against the scoring guide one more time before I turn it in. Use your writing prompt's scoring guide to check your writing anytime you take a test.

I'm finished! That wasn't so bad. The main thing to remember when you take a writing test is that you use the writing process. The process is a little different when you take a test, but if you keep in mind these important tips, you'll do OK.

TEST TIPS

1. **Study the writing prompt before you start to write.** Most writing prompts have three parts: the setup, the task, and the scoring guide. The parts probably won't be labeled. You'll have to figure them out for yourself!

2. **Make sure you understand the task before you start to write.**
   - Read all three parts of the writing prompt carefully.
   - Circle key words in the task part of the writing prompt that tell what kind of writing you need to do. The task might also identify your audience.
   - Make sure you know how you'll be graded.
   - Say the assignment in your own words to yourself.

3. **Keep an eye on the clock.** Decide how much time you will spend on each part of the writing process and try to stick to your schedule. Don't spend so much time on prewriting that you don't have enough time left to write.

4. **Reread your writing. Check it against the scoring guide at least twice.** Remember the rubrics you've used? A scoring guide on a writing test is like a rubric. It can help you keep what's important in mind.

5. **Plan, plan, plan!** You don't get much time to revise during a test, so planning is more important than ever.

6. **Write neatly.** Remember, if the people who score your test can't read your writing, it doesn't matter how good your essay is!

Test Tips

(Student page 409)

Ask students to recall the lessons they learned in this chapter. Ask them what they feel are the important steps to take when writing for a test. **Possible responses: follow the writing prompt; plan time; save time for editing and revising**

Remind students that test writing is similar to writing for a class assignment. One big difference, though, is that test writing is timed.

Read aloud Student page 409. Have students think about how Luis followed each of these tips during test writing. Point out that they should keep each of the six tips in mind when they write their own tests.

Books for Professional Development

Atwell, Nancie. *Lessons That Change Writers*. Portsmouth: Heinemann, 2002.

This book focuses on the mini-lesson as a vehicle for helping students improve their writing. It also contains over a hundred helpful mini-lessons.

McCarthy, Tara. *Narrative Writing (Grades 4–8)*. New York: Scholastic, 1998.

This book contains great ideas for helping students become better and more imaginative writers. It includes everything needed to teach them how to tell a fiction or a nonfiction story: literary modes, prewriting activities, mini-lessons on plot development, editing and revising tips, and rubrics and evaluation ideas.

Parsons, Les. *Revising and Editing: Using Models and Checklists to Promote Successful Writing Experiences*. Markham, ON: Pembroke, 2001.

This source provides reproducible pages for eight series of revision models labeled "junior" or "intermediate." The author covers narratives, essays, projects or extended assignments, poetry, the entire drafting process, and peer conferencing.

Van Zile, Susan. *Awesome Hands-on Activities for Teaching Literary Elements: 30 Easy, Learning-Rich Activities That Tap Into Students' Multiple Intelligences to Teach Plot, Setting, Character, and Theme*. New York: Scholastic, 2001.

The author of this book shares thirty hands-on activities for instructing students about literary elements. These activities build on students' multiple intelligences, giving all students a chance to learn information in the way that they learn best. It includes reproducible student-direction sheets and rubrics.

School-Home Connection

Dear Family,

Your child is currently learning to write an editorial, which is a persuasive piece that focuses on the pros and cons of several solutions to a problem. As he or she goes through the steps of writing, here's how you can help:

1. **Prewriting:** Students will begin by stating a problem and then listing the pros and cons of several solutions. They will then make a Problem-Solution Frame to organize these pros and cons. You can help your child brainstorm and choose an appropriate topic for such a purpose.

2. **Drafting:** Students will make a working draft of their editorial, stating a problem and offering some helpful solutions to the reader. You can help by discussing possible solutions with your child.

3. **Revising:** Students will refine their drafts by adding detail sentences to support topic sentences, and by using quotation marks to clarify catch phrases. Help your child by asking for further details about any confusing or weak passages in his or her draft.

4. **Editing:** You can help check for errors by listening as your child reads the draft aloud to you, or you can provide further help by reading the draft over together.

5. **Publishing:** Students will publish a final copy of their work. Urge them to make copies to send to friends and family members.

Being able to express opinions and convince an audience to act are skills that are required throughout life, in both school and the workplace. If you have any questions as you provide assistance, please let me know.

Thanks for your help in the writing process!

School-Home Connection

Dear Family,

Your child is currently learning to write a TV commercial script, which uses a specific sales technique to persuade viewers to buy a product. As he or she goes through the steps of writing, here's how you can help:

1. **Prewriting:** Students will begin by choosing a type of product to advertise, searching the Internet for product information, and then taking notes. They will then choose a sales technique and make a Storyboard to sequence ideas. You can help your child brainstorm and choose an appropriate product to "sell." Encourage him or her to be creative and imaginative during this process, expanding on a product concept that already exists in today's marketplace. You may also want to discuss appropriate sales techniques for this product. (See Student page 347 for help.)

2. **Drafting:** Students will make a working draft of their commercial, beginning with words and images that grab the audience's attention. You can help by offering suggestions on possible ways to begin the draft.

3. **Revising:** Students will refine their draft by adding a clear call to action at the end of their script, and by deleting any confusing or irrelevant information. Help your child by asking for further clarification of any confusing passages in his or her draft.

4. **Editing:** You can help check for errors by listening as your child reads the draft aloud to you, or you can provide further help by reading the draft over together.

5. **Publishing:** Students will publish a final copy of their work. Urge them to make copies to send to friends and family members.

Being able to convince readers to act is a skill that is required throughout life, in both school and the workplace. If you have any questions as you provide assistance, please let me know.

Thanks for your help in the writing process!

School-Home Connection

Dear Family,

Your child is currently learning to write a persuasive speech that focuses on a problem and persuades the audience to act upon a solution. As he or she goes through the steps of writing, here's how you can help:

1. **Prewriting:** Students will begin by stating a problem and listing a call to action, along with several reasons for the request. They will then make a Persuasion Map to organize the reasons for their call to action. You can help your child brainstorm and choose an appropriate topic for such a purpose. Encourage him or her to focus on a problem or issue that is of special significance.

2. **Drafting:** Students will make a working draft of their persuasive speech, using a convincing tone to persuade their audience. You can help by having your child read his or her draft to you as it is written, listening for any areas that seem too emotional. Then, you can suggest alternate language choices that are strong and convincing.

3. **Revising:** Students will refine their drafts by adding persuasive details and replacing biased or loaded words with neutral words. Help your child by asking for further details about any passages that seem weak or unconvincing. Also, suggest alternate terms or phrases for biased language, or refer your child to a thesaurus for extra help.

4. **Editing:** You can help check for errors by listening as your child reads the draft aloud to you, or you can provide further help by reading the draft over together.

5. **Publishing:** Students will publish a final copy of their work. Urge them to make copies to send to friends and family members.

Being able to express opinions and convince an audience to act are skills that are required throughout life, in both school and the workplace. If you have any questions as you provide assistance, please let me know.

Thanks for your help in the writing process!

School-Home Connection

Dear Family,

Your child is currently learning to write a persuasive test. A persuasive test is a convincing piece that students write in response to a writing prompt. The test is timed. Here are the necessary steps involved in writing a persuasive test, and here's how you can help with each step:

1. **Prewriting:** Students will learn to read a writing prompt to understand the type of writing required. The writing prompt will tell your child what kind of writing to do and what topic to write about. Time management is crucial in test writing. Practice breaking an hour into segments of time with your child so that he or she has a sense of how long it takes for 25, 15, or 10 minutes of time to pass. Your child will also use a graphic organizer to plan his or her writing. Help him or her decide upon an appropriate graphic organizer by prompting a discussion of organizers used in the past.

2. **Drafting:** Students will use their graphic organizers to write a draft containing a clearly stated opinion for the reader. Remind your child that the draft should be written neatly the first time because there will not be enough time to write it again.

3. **Revising:** Students will use the scoring guide in the writing prompt as a reminder to add supporting facts and examples and to delete any unnecessary ideas. Help your child by asking for further details about confusing or weak passages and by pointing out irrelevant passages.

4. **Editing:** Students will spend the last part of the timed writing test checking for common errors in punctuation, capitalization, and spelling. Discourage your child from fretting over the "imperfect" appearance of his or her writing test. The pages won't look as neat as usual, and it's OK for students to make corrections right on the page.

If you have any questions, please let me know. Together, we'll help your child master the important skill of writing on demand, a skill that students use in many subjects throughout their school years.

Thanks for your help in the writing process!

WRITER'S HANDBOOK

The Writer's Handbook will give you more help and some great hints for making your writing the best it can be. Use the Writer's Handbook any time you have more questions or just need a little extra help.

Table of Contents

Writer's Handbook

Writer's Terms

Active Voice shows that the subject of a sentence is doing the action.

Biased Words are words that show favor for one person or point of view over another.

Call to Action is an appeal to the audience to buy, try, or use a product.

Cause-and-Effect Links can be used to show the relation between cause and effect.

Citing Sources is the act of telling readers where you found certain information.

Clichés are boring and overused expressions such as *white as snow* and *black as night*.

Details are facts, examples, and anecdotes used to support main ideas.

Diagrams are pictures that show how something works, how it's made, or how it's done.

Dialogue is the conversation between characters in a story.

Examples are pieces of information that support a topic, a statement, an idea, or an opinion.

Figurative Language is an expression in which words are used to create a mental picture for the reader.

Historical Details are facts about a particular time, place, or historical event.

Jargon is the specialized language of a particular business or trade.

Loaded Words cause the reader to have a strong positive or negative reaction.

Main-Idea Table can be used to show how a main idea is supported by details.

Metaphor is a comparison that calls one thing another.

Note Cards contain organized information about a topic.

Outline can be used to show the main idea and supporting details of a piece of writing.

Overused Words are used so often that they sound stale.

Paraphrase is a restatement of another person's words or ideas as one's own.

Participial Phrase is a phrase containing a participle, or verb form that ends in *–ed* or *–ing*. The participle in the phrase acts as an adjective because it describes the subject of the sentence.

Passive Voice shows that the subject of a sentence is not doing the action.

Personification is the writing technique of applying human qualities to an animal, object, or idea.

Persuasion Map can be used to show how examples and facts support the reasons in a piece of writing.

Plagiarizing is the act of copying another's words and presenting them as one's own.

Primary Source is a person or book that provides first-hand information about a topic.

Pro-and-Con Chart can be used to organize the positive and negative aspects of an argument.

Problem-Solution Frame can be used to define a problem and organize information to solve it.

Purpose is the author's reason for writing.

Sales Technique is the method used to make people want to buy a product.

Sequence Chain can be used to show the order of steps in a complex process.

Setting is the time and place in which a story takes place.

Simile is a comparison using the word *like* or *as*.

Storyboard can be used to plot the chronological order of a story's main points.

Story Frame can be used to organize the key events in a story, frame by frame.

Story Map can be used to organize the setting, characters, plot, major events, and outcome of a story.

Theme is the message about life that the author wants to convey.

Thesaurus is a reference book containing an alphabetical list of synonyms and antonyms.

Three W's Chart can be used to organize what you already know, what you want to know, and where you can look for further information about a topic.

Timeline can be used to sequence key events.

Tone is the way that the writing sounds.

Vague Words are words that aren't clear or distinct.

Web can be used to organize information about one main topic.

Works Consulted is a list containing the bibliographic information for the sources used in a piece of writing.

Writer's Handbook

Grammar / Mechanics

Sentence Structure

Complex Sentence consists of an independent clause and a dependent clause. The dependent clause begins with a subordinating conjunction such as *although* or *because*.

Compound Sentence consists of two related independent clauses. The clauses can be joined by a semicolon or a comma and a coordinating conjunction such as *or, and,* or *but*.

Declarative Sentence is a sentence that states a fact or an opinion.

Exclamatory Sentence is a sentence that has a sense of urgency and ends with an exclamation mark.

Run-on Sentence is an incorrectly written sentence containing simple sentences that are run together without the proper adjoining punctuation and/or conjunction.

Sentence Fragment is an incomplete sentence that begins with a capital letter and ends with final punctuation.

Subject-Verb Agreement is when the subject and verb of a sentence agree with each other in number and tense. The verb in each sentence should agree with its subject and not with an object of a preposition that comes before the verb.

Quotations

Direct Quotation consists of the exact words of a speaker.
- Begin and end a direct quotation with quotation marks.
- If a direct quotation stands alone as a sentence, begin it with a capital letter.
- If the quotation does not stand alone as a sentence, do not begin it with a capital letter.
- Place the punctuation that ends a quote inside the closing quotation marks.
- Use a comma to set off a phrase that identifies the speaker.
- If a quotation is divided by such a phrase, enclose both parts within quotation marks.

Indirect Quotation consists of a retelling of the speaker's words.
- Do not use quotation marks around an indirect quotation.
- The speaker's words in an indirect quotation are often preceded by the word *that*.

Punctuation

Colon is a type of punctuation used
- when the second clause states a direct result of or further explains the first.
- to introduce a list or series.
- after the greeting in a business letter.
- to separate hours and minutes in an expression of time.
- between the city of publication and the publisher in a bibliographic reference.

Hyphen is a type of punctuation used
- to separate syllables when you break a word at the end of a line.
- to link the parts of certain compound words.
- to link two or more words that precede a noun and act as an adjective.
- to link certain spelled-out numbers.

Parts of Speech

Verbs

Verbs have three simple tenses: present, past, and future.
- The present tense states what currently happens.
- The past tense states what happened in the past. To form the past tense, add *–ed* to the end of most present tense verbs.
- The future tense states what will happen in the future. To form the future tense, add *will* in front of a present tense verb.

Perfect Tense Verbs also have three forms: present, past, and future.
- The present perfect tense states what began in the past and may still be happening. To form the present perfect tense, add *has* or *have* in front of a past tense verb.
- The past perfect tense states what began in the past and was completed. To form the past perfect tense, add *had* in front of a past tense verb.
- The future perfect tense states what will begin in the future and end in the future. To form the future perfect tense, add *will* in front of a present perfect tense verb.

Present Participle Verbs show continuing action. To form the present participle form of a verb, add *–ing* to the end of most present tense verbs.

Progressive Tense Verbs also have three forms: present, past, and future.
- The present progressive tense also states continuing action. To form the present progressive tense, add *am, is,* or *are* in front of a present participle verb.

Writer's Handbook

Grammar / Mechanics continued

- The past progressive tense states action that continually happened in the past. To form the past progressive tense, add *was* or *were* in front of a present participle verb.
- The future progressive tense states action that will continually happen in the future. To form the future progressive tense, add *will be* in front of a present participle verb.

Introductory Verbal Phrase comes at the beginning of a sentence and describes the subject. It contains a verbal that acts like a noun, adjective, or adverb.

Pronouns

Subject Pronouns such as *I, we, she,* and *they* should be used as the subjects of sentences.

Object Pronouns such as *me, us, you, him, her, it,* and *them* should be used as objects following verbs and as objects of prepositions.

Indefinite Pronouns such as *everyone, nobody, nothing, something,* and *anything* are all considered singular.

Possessive Pronouns such as *my, mine, our, ours, your, yours, his, her, hers, its, their,* and *theirs* show ownership or possession but do not contain apostrophes.

Compound Personal Pronouns always end in *–self* or *–selves (himself, yourself, themselves).*

Antecedent is the noun that a pronoun replaces.
- Each pronoun must have a clear antecedent.
- Pronouns must agree with their antecedents in number and gender.

Adjectives/Adverbs

Comparative Form compares two people, places, things, or actions.
- Add *–er* to short adjectives and adverbs to create comparative forms.
- Use the word *more* before long adjectives and adverbs to create comparative forms.

Superlative Form compares three or more people, places, things, or actions.
- Add *–est* to create superlative forms.
- Use the word *most* before long adjectives and adverbs to create superlative forms.

Appositives

Appositive is a word or phrase following a noun that describes the noun.

416 Writer's Handbook

APPENDIX

Table of Contents

Using the Mode-Specific Rubrics

Rubrics are central to instruction in *Strategies for Writers.* Each chapter includes a genre-specific rubric that guides students' writing and measures their performance on the six writing traits.

More general, mode-specific rubrics are included on the following pages. One rubric is included for each of the four writing modes: narrative, descriptive, expository, and persuasive. You may wish to duplicate these rubrics and use them as instruments to guide and assess students' writing both before (as a pretest rubric) and after (as a posttest rubric) instruction within that mode.

The writing traits on each of the rubrics are:

	meaning the way in which the writer chooses an appropriate topic, gathers information, and organizes the writing.
	meaning the way in which the writer identifies, addresses, and relates to the audience intended for the writing.
	meaning the way in which the writer includes relevant content and supporting information to flesh out the writing.
	meaning the way in which the writer chooses appropriate words to convey meaning and clarify writing.
	meaning the way in which sentence variety and patterns contribute to the flow of the writing.
	meaning the ways in which the writer observes grammar, usage, mechanics, and spelling guidelines.

Narrative Rubric

	Achieving ✓✓✓	Developing ✓✓✓	Excelling ✓✓	Beginning ✓
Information/ Organization	Events follow one another in order.	Most events follow one another.	Some events follow one another.	Events need to follow one another.
Voice/ Audience	The writer's voice connects with the audience.	The writer's voice connects with the audience most of the time.	The writer's voice sometimes connects with the audience.	The writer's voice needs to connect with the audience.
Content/ Ideas	The writing contains all elements of narrative writing, including well developed characters, setting, and plot.	The writing contains most of the elements of narrative writing, and they are fairly well developed.	The writing contains some of the elements of narrative writing.	The writing needs all elements of narrative writing, such as characters, setting, and plot.
Word Choice/ Clarity	Vivid wording and interesting details bring the writing to life.	The writing contains interesting details and some vivid wording.	The writing contains a few interesting details.	The writing needs vivid wording and interesting details.
Sentence Fluency	Sentence lengths and patterns vary to make the writing flow.	There is some variety in sentence patterns and length.	There is little variety in sentence patterns and length.	Sentences need to be varied to make the writing flow.
Grammar/ Mechanics	The writing contains no errors in spelling, punctuation, grammar, or mechanics.	The writing contains very few errors in spelling, punctuation, grammar, and mechanics.	The writing contains some errors in spelling, punctuation, grammar, and mechanics.	The writing contains many errors in spelling, punctuation, grammar, and mechanics.

Descriptive Rubric

	Achieving ✓✓✓	Developing ✓✓	Excelling ✓	Beginning ✓
Information/ Organization	The description focuses on one topic. It is organized according to the five senses.	The description focuses on one topic. It is mostly organized around the five senses.	The description sometimes focuses on one topic. It is loosely organized.	The description needs to focus on one topic and be organized around the five senses.
Voice/ Audience	The description captures the audience's attention and keeps it throughout.	The description gets the audience's attention and keeps it most of the time.	The description gets the audience's attention, but doesn't keep it.	The description needs to get the audience's attention.
Content/ Ideas	Many details make the description interesting.	Some details make the description interesting.	A few details make the description somewhat interesting.	The description needs details to make it interesting.
Word Choice/ Clarity	The description contains effective use of figurative language.	The description contains some figurative language.	The description contains little figurative language.	The description needs figurative language.
Sentence Fluency	Variety in sentence beginnings makes the description flow.	Some variety in sentence beginnings makes the description flow.	There is little variety in sentence beginnings to make the description flow.	The description needs variety in sentence beginnings.
Grammar/ Mechanics	The description contains no errors in spelling, punctuation, grammar, or mechanics.	The description contains very few errors in spelling, punctuation, grammar, and mechanics.	The description contains some errors in spelling, punctuation, grammar, and mechanics.	The description contains many errors in spelling, punctuation, grammar, and mechanics.

Expository Rubric

	Achieving ✓✓✓	Developing ✓✓	Excelling ✓✓	Beginning ✓
Information/Organization	The writing focuses on one topic. It is well organized with an introduction, a body, and a conclusion.	The writing is focused on one topic. It is mostly organized.	The writing is sometimes focused on a topic. It is loosely organized.	The writing needs to focus on a topic and contain an introduction, body, and conclusion.
Voice/Audience	The tone of the writing is appropriate for the audience and the purpose.	The tone of the writing is appropriate most of the time.	The tone of the writing is sometimes appropriate.	The tone of the writing needs to be appropriate for the audience and the purpose.
Content/Ideas	The writing contains many facts and details about the topic.	The writing contains some facts and details about the topic.	The writing contains a few facts and details about the topic.	The writing needs facts and details about the topic.
Word Choice/Clarity	Effective use of signal/transition words clarifies ideas.	Signal/transition words sometimes clarify ideas.	Signal/transition words are rarely used to clarify ideas.	Signal/transition words are needed to clarify ideas.
Sentence Fluency	Sentences flow logically to reflect the purpose of the writing.	Most sentences flow logically.	Some sentences flow logically.	Sentences need to flow logically.
Grammar/Mechanics	The writing contains no errors in spelling, punctuation, grammar, or mechanics.	The writing contains very few errors in spelling, punctuation, grammar, and mechanics.	The writing contains some errors in spelling, punctuation, grammar, and mechanics.	The writing contains many errors in spelling, punctuation, grammar, and mechanics.

Persuasive Rubric

	Achieving ✓✓✓	Developing ✓✓	Excelling ✓✓	Beginning ✓
Information/Organization	The opinion is stated clearly. The writing is organized to support the opinion.	The opinion is stated clearly. Most of the writing is organized to support the opinion.	The opinion is stated, but is not clear. Some of the writing is organized.	The opinion needs to be clearly stated. The writing needs to be organized.
Voice/Audience	The writer uses a sincere and persuasive tone throughout.	The writer uses a sincere and persuasive tone most of the time.	The writer sometimes uses a sincere and persuasive tone.	The writer needs to use a sincere and persuasive tone throughout.
Content/Ideas	Many reasons and facts support the writer's opinion.	Some reasons and facts support the writer's opinion.	A few reasons and facts support the writer's opinion.	Reasons and facts are needed to support the writer's opinion.
Word Choice/Clarity	The writing contains clear wording throughout. There are no loaded words.	The writing is mostly clear and unbiased. There are very few loaded words.	The writing is sometimes clear and unbiased. There are some loaded words.	The writing needs to be clear and unbiased. It has many loaded words.
Sentence Fluency	Sentence patterns are effectively repeated for emphasis.	Sentence patterns are sometimes repeated for emphasis.	Sentence patterns are rarely repeated for emphasis.	Sentence patterns need to be repeated for emphasis.
Grammar/Mechanics	The writing contains no errors in spelling, punctuation, grammar, or mechanics.	The writing contains very few errors in spelling, punctuation, grammar, and mechanics.	The writing contains some errors in spelling, punctuation, grammar, and mechanics.	The writing contains many errors in spelling, punctuation, grammar, and mechanics.

This page may be duplicated for classroom use.

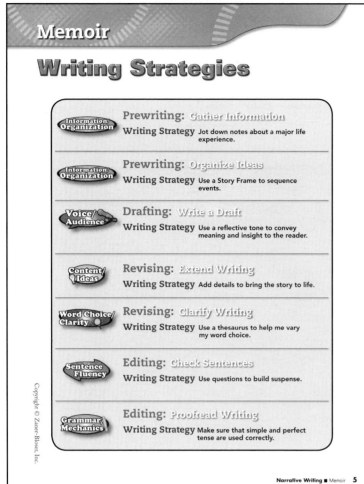

Memoir

Writing Strategies

Information/Organization — **Prewriting: Gather Information**
Writing Strategy Jot down notes about a major life experience.

Information/Organization — **Prewriting: Organize Ideas**
Writing Strategy Use a Story Frame to sequence events.

Voice/Audience — **Drafting: Write a Draft**
Writing Strategy Use a reflective tone to convey meaning and insight to the reader.

Content/Ideas — **Revising: Extend Writing**
Writing Strategy Add details to bring the story to life.

Word Choice/Clarity — **Revising: Clarify Writing**
Writing Strategy Use a thesaurus to help me vary my word choice.

Sentence Fluency — **Editing: Check Sentences**
Writing Strategy Use questions to build suspense.

Grammar/Mechanics — **Editing: Proofread Writing**
Writing Strategy Make sure that simple and perfect tense are used correctly.

Copyright © Zaner-Bloser, Inc.

Narrative Writing ■ Memoir   5

Memoir

Rubric

Use this rubric to help write your memoir. Then, use it again to check your writing.

	Excelling ✓✓✓	Achieving ✓✓	Developing ✓✓	Beginning ✓
Information/Organization	The memoir is focused on one experience and is well sequenced.	The memoir is mainly focused on one experience and is mostly sequential.	Some of the memoir is focused on one experience and is somewhat sequential.	The memoir needs to be well sequenced and focused on one experience.
Voice/Audience	A reflective tone consistently conveys meaning and insight.	A reflective tone conveys meaning and insight in many areas.	A reflective tone conveys meaning and insight in some areas.	The tone needs to be more reflective throughout.
Content/Ideas	Many details bring the story to life.	Some details are included.	A few details are included.	More details are needed to bring the story to life.
Word Choice/Clarity	Word choice is varied.	Word choice is varied in some areas.	Word choice is varied in a few areas.	Word choice should be more varied.
Sentence Fluency	Well-chosen questions build suspense throughout.	Some questions build suspense in some areas.	A few questions build suspense in a few areas.	Well-chosen questions should be used to build suspense throughout.
Grammar/Mechanics	Spelling, grammar, and the use of simple/perfect tense are correct.	There are a few errors in spelling, grammar, and simple/perfect tense usage.	There are several errors in spelling, grammar, and simple/perfect tense usage.	There are many errors in spelling, grammar, and simple/perfect tense usage.

Copyright © Zaner-Bloser, Inc.

6   Narrative Writing ■ Memoir

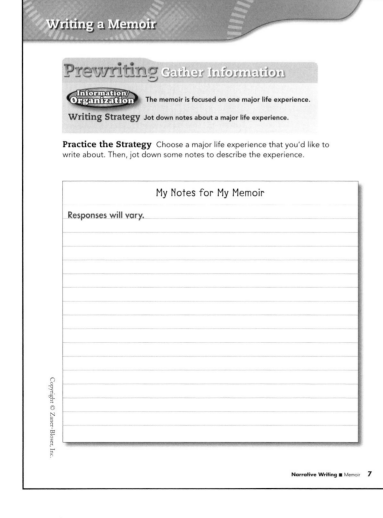

Writing a Memoir

Prewriting Gather Information

Information/Organization The memoir is focused on one major life experience.

Writing Strategy Jot down notes about a major life experience.

Practice the Strategy Choose a major life experience that you'd like to write about. Then, jot down some notes to describe the experience.

My Notes for My Memoir

Responses will vary.

Copyright © Zaner-Bloser, Inc.

Narrative Writing ■ Memoir   7

Writing a Memoir

Prewriting Organize Ideas

Information/Organization The memoir is well sequenced.

Writing Strategy Use a Story Frame to sequence events.

Practice the Strategy Use a Story Frame to organize the notes you took on page 7.

Story Frame	
Setting:	Responses will vary.
Introduction:	
Rising Action (Event 1):	
Rising Action (Event 2):	
Rising Action (Event 3):	
Climax:	
Falling Action (Event 1):	
Resolution:	

Copyright © Zaner-Bloser, Inc.

8   Narrative Writing ■ Memoir

Historical Episode

Writing Strategies

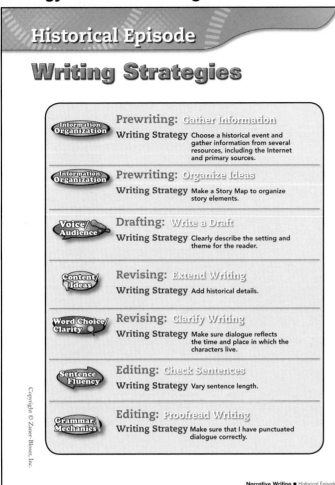

Information/Organization

Prewriting: Gather Information

Writing Strategy Choose a historical event and gather information from several resources, including the Internet and primary sources.

Information/Organization

Prewriting: Organize Ideas

Writing Strategy Make a Story Map to organize story elements.

Voice/Audience

Drafting: Write a Draft

Writing Strategy Clearly describe the setting and theme for the reader.

Content/Ideas

Revising: Extend Writing

Writing Strategy Add historical details.

Word Choice/Clarity

Revising: Clarify Writing

Writing Strategy Make sure dialogue reflects the time and place in which the characters live.

Sentence Fluency

Editing: Check Sentences

Writing Strategy Vary sentence length.

Grammar/Mechanics

Editing: Proofread Writing

Writing Strategy Make sure that I have punctuated dialogue correctly.

Copyright © Zaner-Bloser, Inc.

Narrative Writing ■ Historical Episode **9**

Historical Episode

Rubric

Use this rubric to help write your historical episode. Then, use it again to check your writing.

	Excelling ✓✓✓	Achieving ✓✓	Developing ✓✓	Beginning ✓
Information/Organization	The story focuses on one event and is well organized throughout.	Most of the story focuses on one event and is mostly organized.	The story focuses on several events and is loosely organized.	The story should focus on one event and should be better organized.
Voice/Audience	The setting and theme are clear to the reader.	The setting and theme are mostly clear to the reader.	The setting and theme are clear in a few places.	The setting and theme need to be clearer.
Content/Ideas	Historical details are included throughout.	Many historical details are included.	Some historical details are included.	More historical details are needed throughout.
Word Choice/Clarity	All of the dialogue is true to the setting.	Most of the dialogue is true to the setting.	Some of the dialogue is true to the setting.	The dialogue needs to be more true to the setting.
Sentence Fluency	Sentence length is varied throughout.	Sentence length is varied in some areas.	Sentence length is varied in a few areas.	Sentence length should be varied throughout.
Grammar/Mechanics	Spelling, grammar, and dialogue punctuation are correct.	There are a few errors in spelling, grammar, and dialogue punctuation.	There are several errors in spelling, grammar, and dialogue punctuation.	There are many errors in spelling, grammar, and dialogue punctuation.

10 Narrative Writing ■ Historical Episode

Copyright © Zaner-Bloser, Inc.

Writing a Historical Episode

Prewriting Gather Information

Information/Organization The story focuses on one historical event.

Writing Strategy Choose a historical event and gather information from several resources, including the Internet and primary sources.

Practice the Strategy Choose a historical event to write about. Then, jot down notes while conducting research on the event.

My Notes for My Historical Episode

Responses will vary.

Copyright © Zaner-Bloser, Inc.

Narrative Writing ■ Historical Episode **11**

Writing a Historical Episode

Prewriting Organize Ideas

Information/Organization Story elements are well organized.

Writing Strategy Make a Story Map to organize story elements.

Practice the Strategy Use a Story Map to organize the notes you took on page 11.

Story Map

Setting: Responses will vary.

Major Character(s):

Minor Character(s):

Theme:

Conflict:

	Plot	
Event 1	Event 2	Event 3

Resolution:

12 Narrative Writing ■ Historical Episode

Copyright © Zaner-Bloser, Inc.

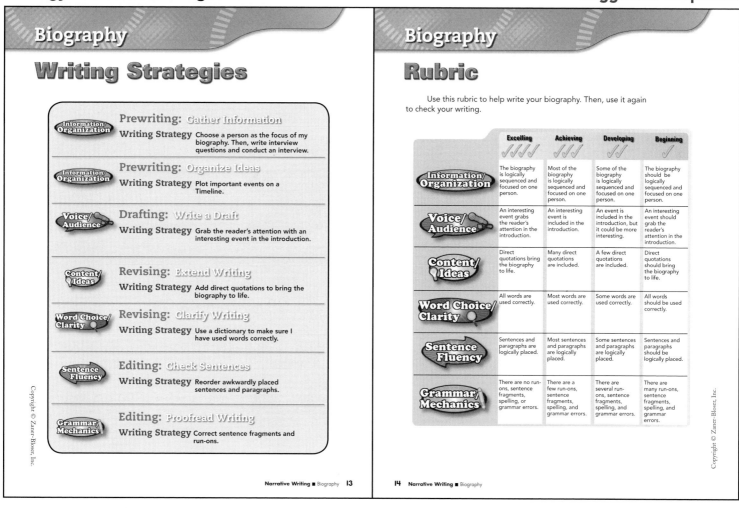

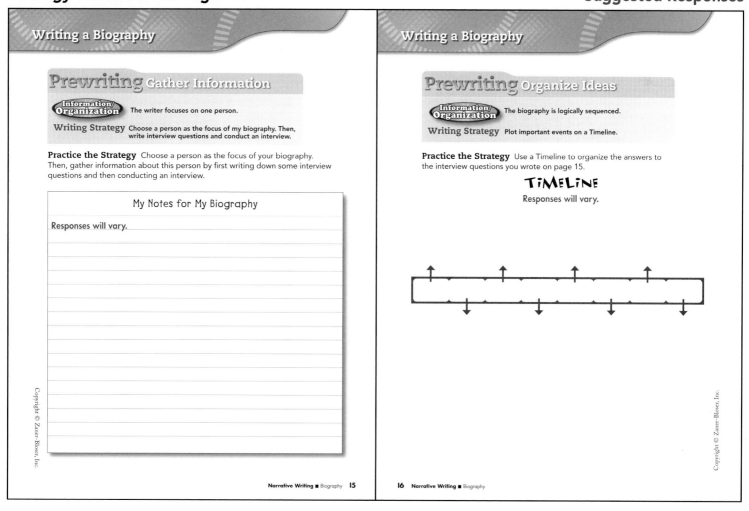

Business Letter

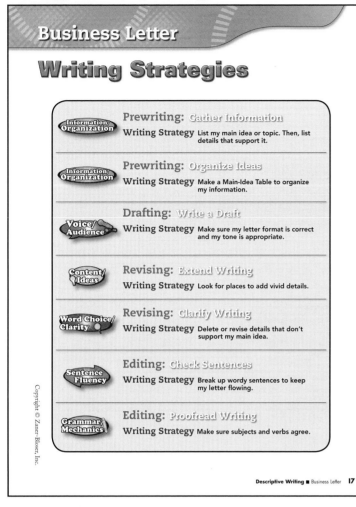

Writing Strategies

Prewriting: Gather Information
Information/Organization
Writing Strategy List my main idea or topic. Then, list details that support it.

Prewriting: Organize Ideas
Information/Organization
Writing Strategy Make a Main-Idea Table to organize my information.

Drafting: Write a Draft
Voice/Audience
Writing Strategy Make sure my letter format is correct and my tone is appropriate.

Revising: Extend Writing
Content/Ideas
Writing Strategy Look for places to add vivid details.

Revising: Clarify Writing
Word Choice/Clarity
Writing Strategy Delete or revise details that don't support my main idea.

Editing: Check Sentences
Sentence Fluency
Writing Strategy Break up wordy sentences to keep my letter flowing.

Editing: Proofread Writing
Grammar/Mechanics
Writing Strategy Make sure subjects and verbs agree.

Descriptive Writing ■ Business Letter **17**

Business Letter

Rubric

Use this rubric to help write your business letter. Then, use it again to check your writing.

	Excelling	Achieving	Developing	Beginning
Information/Organization	The letter focuses on one topic and has many facts for support.	The letter mostly focuses on one topic and has some facts for support.	The letter sometimes focuses on one topic and has a few facts for support.	The letter should focus on one topic and contain many facts for support.
Voice/Audience	The letter format is correct, and the tone is appropriate.	The letter format is mostly correct, and the tone is usually appropriate.	A few parts of the letter are missing, and the tone is inappropriate in some areas.	The letter format should be correct, and the tone should be appropriate.
Content/Ideas	Many vivid details enhance the description.	Some vivid details enhance the description.	A few vivid details enhance the description.	More vivid details are needed to enhance the description.
Word Choice/Clarity	The letter contains no irrelevant details.	The letter contains very few irrelevant details.	The letter contains several irrelevant details.	The letter should not contain any irrelevant details.
Sentence Fluency	Concise sentences help the writing flow throughout.	Concise sentences are used in some areas.	Concise sentences are used in a few areas.	More concise sentences are needed to help the writing flow throughout.
Grammar/Mechanics	Spelling, grammar, and subject-verb agreement are correct.	There are very few errors in spelling, grammar, and subject-verb agreement.	There are several errors in spelling, grammar, and subject-verb agreement.	There are many errors in spelling, grammar, and subject-verb agreement.

18 Descriptive Writing ■ Business Letter

Writing a Business Letter

Prewriting Gather Information

Information/Organization The letter focuses on one main idea or topic.

Writing Strategy List my main idea or topic. Then, list details that support it.

Practice the Strategy Gather information by listing your main idea or topic below. Then, list some supporting details.

My Notes for My Business Letter

Responses will vary.

Descriptive Writing ■ Business Letter **19**

Writing a Business Letter

Prewriting Organize Ideas

Information/Organization The letter has many facts to support the main idea.

Writing Strategy Make a Main-Idea Table to organize my information.

Practice the Strategy Use a Main-Idea Table to organize the notes you took on page 19.

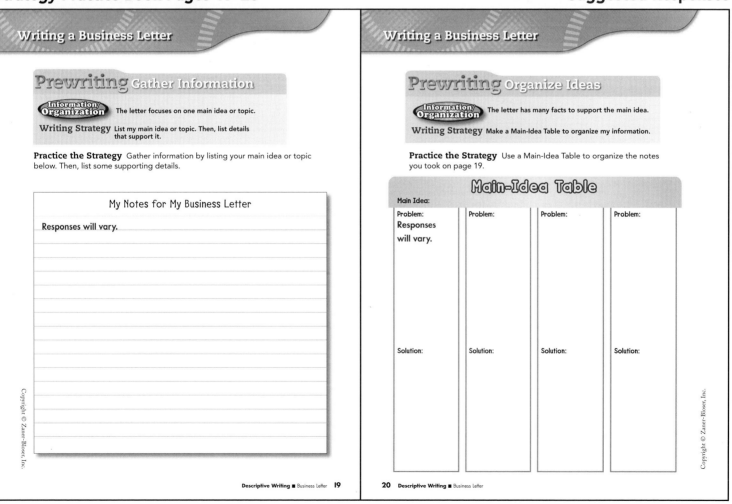

Main-Idea Table

Main Idea:

Problem: Responses will vary.	Problem:	Problem:	Problem:
Solution:	Solution:	Solution:	Solution:

20 Descriptive Writing ■ Business Letter

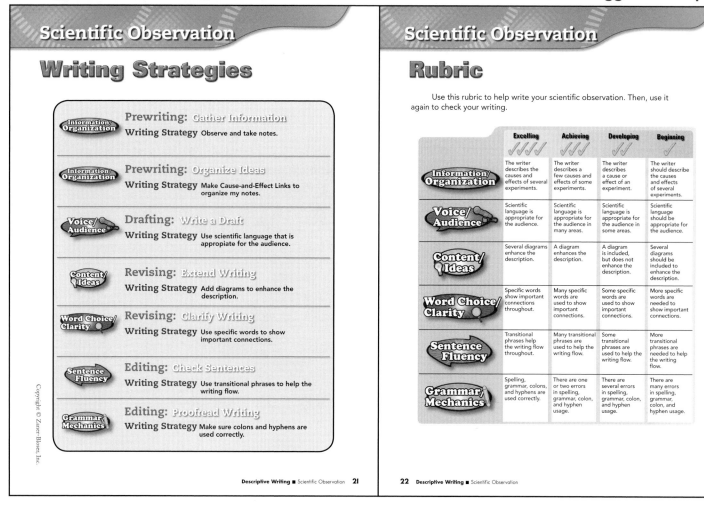

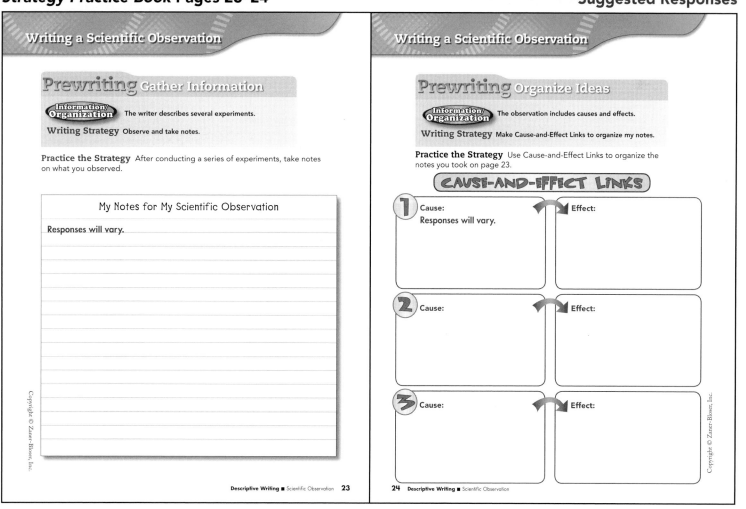

Descriptive Vignette

Writing Strategies

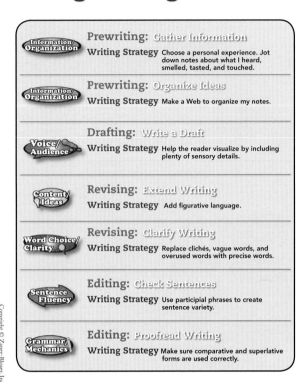

Information/Organization
Prewriting: Gather Information
Writing Strategy Choose a personal experience. Jot down notes about what I heard, smelled, tasted, and touched.

Information/Organization
Prewriting: Organize Ideas
Writing Strategy Make a Web to organize my notes.

Voice/Audience
Drafting: Write a Draft
Writing Strategy Help the reader visualize by including plenty of sensory details.

Content/Ideas
Revising: Extend Writing
Writing Strategy Add figurative language.

Word Choice/Clarity
Revising: Clarify Writing
Writing Strategy Replace clichés, vague words, and overused words with precise words.

Sentence Fluency
Editing: Check Sentences
Writing Strategy Use participial phrases to create sentence variety.

Grammar/Mechanics
Editing: Proofread Writing
Writing Strategy Make sure comparative and superlative forms are used correctly.

Descriptive Vignette

Rubric

Use this rubric to help write your descriptive vignette. Then, use it again to check your writing.

	Excelling	Achieving	Developing	Beginning
Information/Organization	One experience is described. Details are organized throughout.	Most of an experience is described. Details are mostly organized.	Some of an experience is described. Details are loosely organized.	More description is needed. Details should be organized.
Voice/Audience	Sensory details help the reader connect to the writing.	Some sensory details are included for the reader.	A few sensory details are included for the reader.	More sensory details are needed to help the reader connect to the writing.
Content/Ideas	Figurative language enhances the description.	Much figurative language is used.	Some figurative language is used.	More figurative language is needed to enhance the description.
Word Choice/Clarity	Precise words make the description clear.	Many precise words are used.	Some precise words are used.	More precise words are needed to make the description clear.
Sentence Fluency	Participial phrases create sentence variety throughout.	Some participial phrases are used.	A few participial phrases are used.	More participial phrases are needed to create sentence variety.
Grammar/Mechanics	Spelling, grammar, and comparative/superlative forms are used correctly.	There are a few errors in spelling, grammar, and comparative/superlative usage.	There are some errors in spelling, grammar, and comparative/superlative usage.	There are many errors in spelling, grammar, and comparative/superlative usage.

Writing a Descriptive Vignette

Prewriting Gather Information

Information/Organization A personal experience is described.

Writing Strategy Choose a personal experience. Jot down notes about what I heard, smelled, tasted, and touched.

Practice the Strategy Think of a personal experience you'd like to write about. Then, jot down sensory details about what you heard, smelled, tasted, and touched.

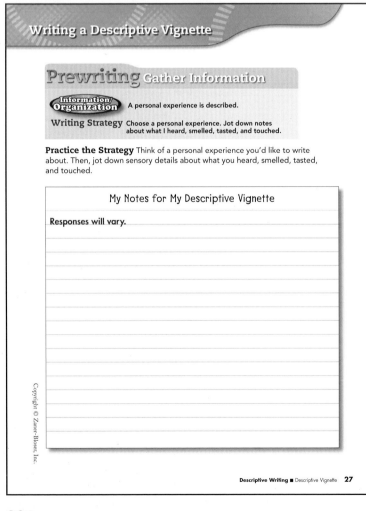

My Notes for My Descriptive Vignette

Responses will vary.

Writing a Descriptive Vignette

Prewriting Organize Ideas

Information/Organization Details are organized throughout.

Writing Strategy Make a Web to organize my notes.

Practice the Strategy Make a Web to organize the notes you took on page 27.

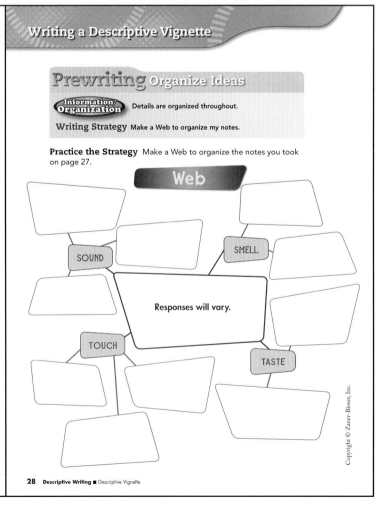

Web

SOUND

SMELL

Responses will vary.

TOUCH

TASTE

Book Report

Writing Strategies

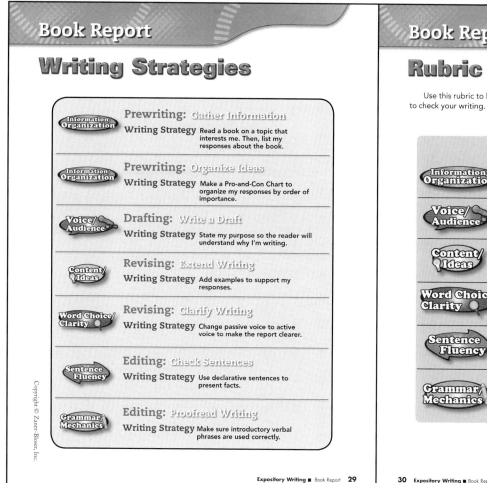

Information/Organization
Prewriting: Gather Information
Writing Strategy Read a book on a topic that interests me. Then, list my responses about the book.

Information/Organization
Prewriting: Organize Ideas
Writing Strategy Make a Pro-and-Con Chart to organize my responses by order of importance.

Voice/Audience
Drafting: Write a Draft
Writing Strategy State my purpose so the reader will understand why I'm writing.

Content/Ideas
Revising: Extend Writing
Writing Strategy Add examples to support my responses.

Word Choice/Clarity
Revising: Clarify Writing
Writing Strategy Change passive voice to active voice to make the report clearer.

Sentence Fluency
Editing: Check Sentences
Writing Strategy Use declarative sentences to present facts.

Grammar/Mechanics
Editing: Proofread Writing
Writing Strategy Make sure introductory verbal phrases are used correctly.

Expository Writing ■ Book Report **29**

Book Report

Rubric

Use this rubric to help write your book report. Then, use it again to check your writing.

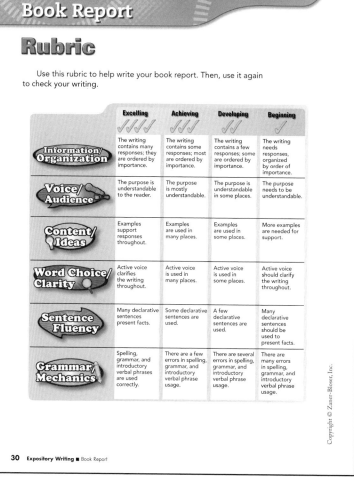

	Excelling ✓✓✓✓	Achieving ✓✓✓	Developing ✓✓	Beginning ✓
Information/Organization	The writing contains many responses; they are ordered by importance.	The writing contains some responses; most are ordered by importance.	The writing contains a few responses; some are ordered by importance.	The writing needs responses, organized by order of importance.
Voice/Audience	The purpose is understandable to the reader.	The purpose is mostly understandable.	The purpose is understandable in some places.	The purpose needs to be understandable.
Content/Ideas	Examples support responses throughout.	Examples are used in many places.	Examples are used in some places.	More examples are needed for support.
Word Choice/Clarity	Active voice clarifies the writing throughout.	Active voice is used in many places.	Active voice is used in some places.	Active voice should clarify the writing throughout.
Sentence Fluency	Many declarative sentences present facts.	Some declarative sentences are used.	A few declarative sentences are used.	Many declarative sentences should be used to present facts.
Grammar/Mechanics	Spelling, grammar, and introductory verbal phrases are used correctly.	There are a few errors in spelling, grammar, and introductory verbal phrase usage.	There are several errors in spelling, grammar, and introductory verbal phrase usage.	There are many errors in spelling, grammar, and introductory verbal phrase usage.

30 Expository Writing ■ Book Report

Writing a Book Report

Prewriting Gather Information

Information/Organization The writing contains many responses.

Writing Strategy Read a book on a topic that interests me. Then, list my responses about the book.

Practice the Strategy After reading a book of interest, jot down some pros and cons about the writing.

My Pros and Cons for My Book Report

Responses will vary.

Expository Writing ■ Book Report **31**

Writing a Book Report

Prewriting Organize Ideas

Information/Organization Responses are organized by order of importance.

Writing Strategy Make a Pro-and-Con Chart to organize my responses by order of importance.

Practice the Strategy Use a Pro-and-Con Chart to organize the notes you took on page 31.

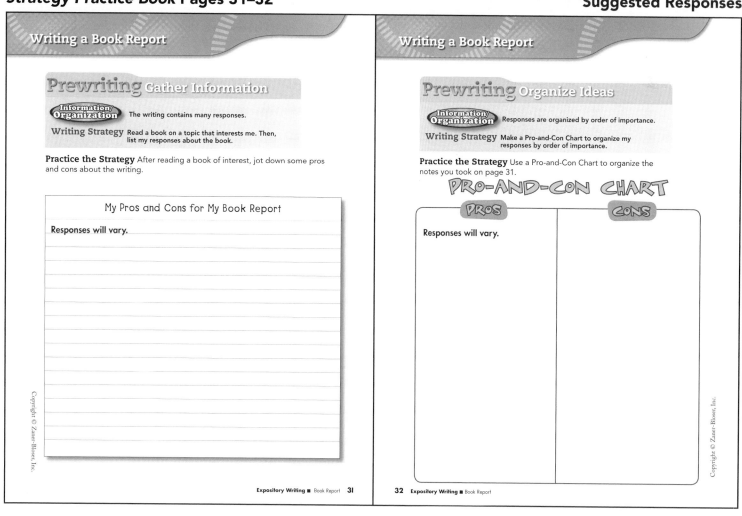

PRO-AND-CON CHART

PROS	CONS
Responses will vary.	

32 Expository Writing ■ Book Report

Research Report

Writing Strategies

Prewriting: Gather Information

Information/Organization

Writing Strategy Choose a topic, survey some sources, and make a 3 W's Chart. Then, make note cards.

Prewriting: Organize Ideas

Information/Organization

Writing Strategy Make an Outline to organize my information.

Drafting: Write a Draft

Voice/Audience

Writing Strategy Use my Outline to draft my report. Remember to include an introduction that grabs the reader's attention.

Revising: Extend Writing

Content/Ideas

Writing Strategy Add quotes and paraphrased information from experts.

Revising: Clarify Writing

Word Choice/Clarity

Writing Strategy Make sure I have cited all quotes correctly. Then, make my list of Works Consulted.

Editing: Check Sentences

Sentence Fluency

Writing Strategy Use introductory verbal phrases to vary my sentences.

Editing: Proofread Writing

Grammar/Mechanics

Writing Strategy Make sure I've formed compound and complex sentences correctly.

Research Report

Rubric

Use this rubric to help write your research report. Then, use it again to check your writing.

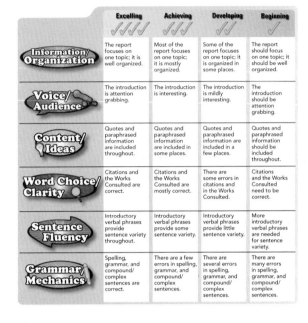

	Excelling ✓✓✓	Achieving ✓✓✓	Developing ✓✓	Beginning ✓
Information/Organization	The report focuses on one topic; it is well organized.	Most of the report focuses on one topic; it is mostly organized.	Some of the report focuses on one topic; it is organized in some places.	The report should focus on one topic; it should be well organized.
Voice/Audience	The introduction is attention grabbing.	The introduction is interesting.	The introduction is mildly interesting.	The introduction should be attention grabbing.
Content/Ideas	Quotes and paraphrased information are included throughout.	Quotes and paraphrased information are included in some places.	Quotes and paraphrased information are included in a few places.	Quotes and paraphrased information should be included throughout.
Word Choice/Clarity	Citations and the Works Consulted are correct.	Citations and the Works Consulted are mostly correct.	There are some errors in citations and in the Works Consulted.	Citations and the Works Consulted need to be correct.
Sentence Fluency	Introductory verbal phrases provide sentence variety throughout.	Introductory verbal phrases provide some sentence variety.	Introductory verbal phrases provide little sentence variety.	More introductory verbal phrases are needed for sentence variety.
Grammar/Mechanics	Spelling, grammar, and compound/complex sentences are correct.	There are a few errors in spelling, grammar, and compound/complex sentences.	There are several errors in spelling, grammar, and compound/complex sentences.	There are many errors in spelling, grammar, and compound/complex sentences.

Writing a Research Report

Prewriting Gather Information

Information/Organization The report focuses on one topic.

Writing Strategy Choose a topic, survey some sources, and make a 3 W's Chart. Then, make note cards.

Practice the Strategy Survey sources and make a 3 W's Chart for the topic you've chosen. Then, make note cards by writing one or more questions from your 3 W's Chart near the top of each card. Use each card to help gather information that answers the question(s) at the top.

My 3 W's Question(s):
Responses will vary.

My 3 W's Question(s):
Responses will vary.

Apply the Strategy Continue making note cards until you've found the answer to each of the questions on your 3 W's Chart.

Writing a Research Report

Prewriting Organize Ideas

Information/Organization The report is well organized.

Writing Strategy Make an Outline to organize my information.

Practice the Strategy Organize the information on your note cards by including it on an Outline. **OUTLINE**

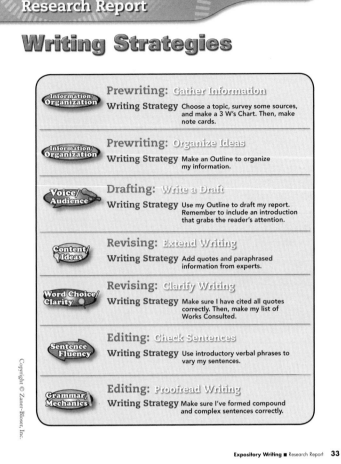

I. Responses will vary.
   A. _____
      1. _____
      2. _____
   B. _____
      1. _____
      2. _____
II. _____
   A. _____
      1. _____
      2. _____
   B. _____
      1. _____
      2. _____
III. _____
   A. _____
      1. _____
      2. _____
   B. _____
      1. _____
      2. _____
IV. _____
   A. _____
      1. _____
      2. _____
   B. _____
      1. _____
      2. _____

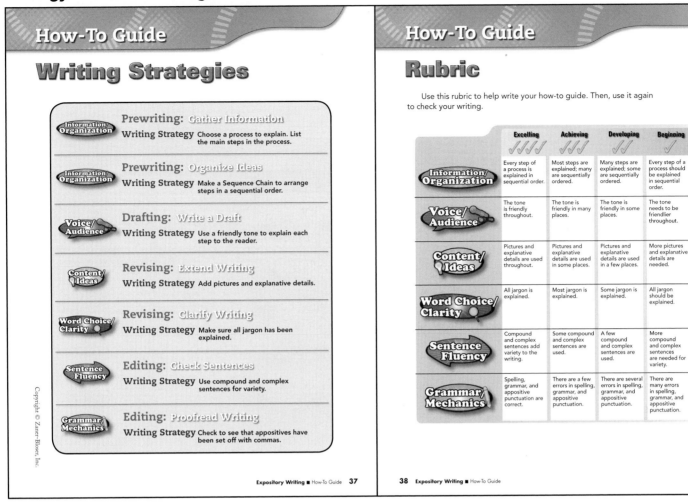

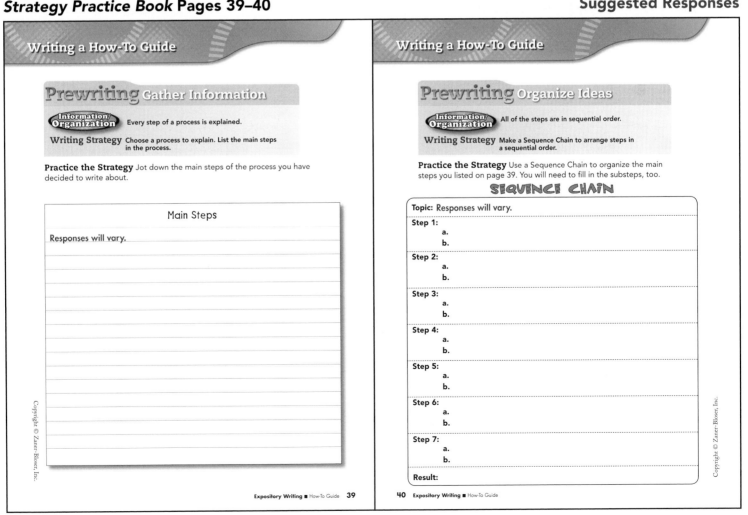

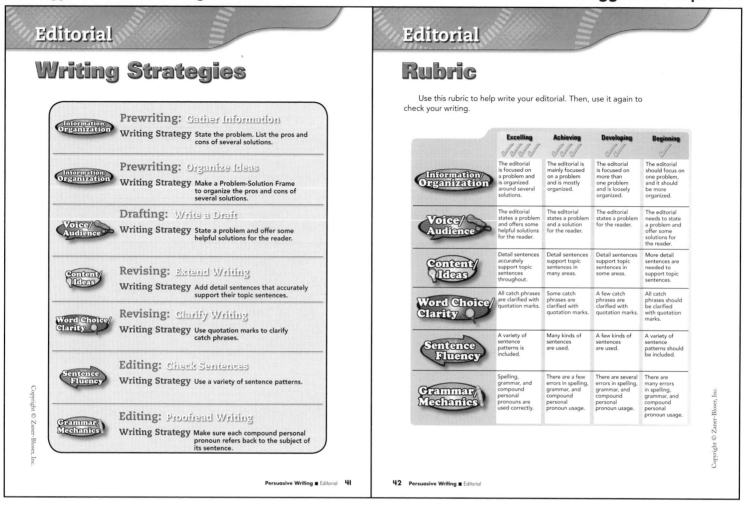

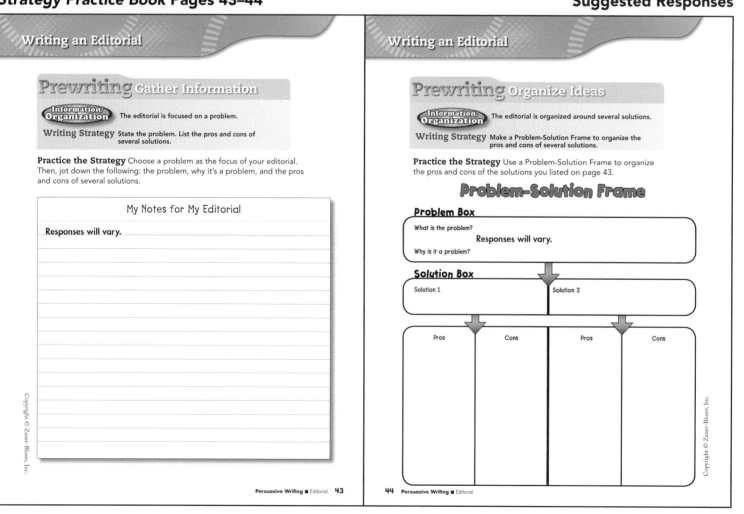

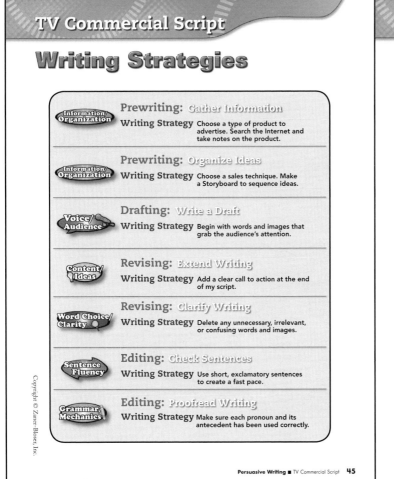

TV Commercial Script
Writing Strategies

Information/Organization
Prewriting: Gather Information
Writing Strategy Choose a type of product to advertise. Search the Internet and take notes on the product.

Information/Organization
Prewriting: Organize Ideas
Writing Strategy Choose a sales technique. Make a Storyboard to sequence ideas.

Voice/Audience
Drafting: Write a Draft
Writing Strategy Begin with words and images that grab the audience's attention.

Content/Ideas
Revising: Extend Writing
Writing Strategy Add a clear call to action at the end of my script.

Word Choice/Clarity
Revising: Clarify Writing
Writing Strategy Delete any unnecessary, irrelevant, or confusing words and images.

Sentence Fluency
Editing: Check Sentences
Writing Strategy Use short, exclamatory sentences to create a fast pace.

Grammar/Mechanics
Editing: Proofread Writing
Writing Strategy Make sure each pronoun and its antecedent has been used correctly.

Copyright © Zaner-Bloser, Inc.

Persuasive Writing ■ TV Commercial Script **45**

TV Commercial Script
Rubric

Use this rubric to help write your TV commercial script. Then, use it again to check your writing.

	Excelling ✓✓✓	Achieving ✓✓✓	Developing ✓✓	Beginning ✓
Information/Organization	The script is based on one product; ideas are well sequenced.	Most of the script is based on one product; most ideas are sequential.	Some of the script is based on one product; some ideas are sequential.	The script should be based on one product; ideas should be sequential.
Voice/Audience	The script begins with words and images that grab the audience's attention.	The script begins with interesting words and images.	The script begins with mildly interesting words and images.	The script should begin with words and images that grab the audience's attention.
Content/Ideas	The script ends with a clear call to action.	The script ends with a call to action that is mostly clear.	The script contains a call to action, but not at the end.	The script should end with a clear call to action.
Word Choice/Clarity	All words and images are clear.	Most words and images are clear.	Some words and images are clear.	All words and images should be clear.
Sentence Fluency	Short, exclamatory sentences create a fast pace throughout.	Short, exclamatory sentences are used in many areas.	Short, exclamatory sentences are used in some areas.	Short, exclamatory sentences should be used to create a fast pace throughout.
Grammar/Mechanics	Spelling, grammar, pronouns, and antecedents are used correctly.	There are a few errors in spelling, grammar, and pronoun-antecedent usage.	There are several errors in spelling, grammar, and pronoun-antecedent usage.	There are many errors in spelling, grammar, and pronoun-antecedent usage.

Copyright © Zaner-Bloser, Inc.

46 Persuasive Writing ■ TV Commercial Script

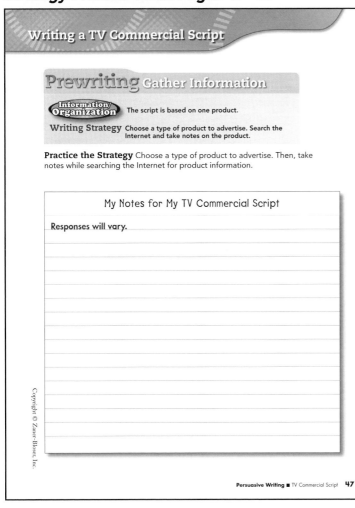

Writing a TV Commercial Script

Prewriting Gather Information

Information/Organization The script is based on one product.

Writing Strategy Choose a type of product to advertise. Search the Internet and take notes on the product.

Practice the Strategy Choose a type of product to advertise. Then, take notes while searching the Internet for product information.

My Notes for My TV Commercial Script

Responses will vary.

Copyright © Zaner-Bloser, Inc.

Persuasive Writing ■ TV Commercial Script **47**

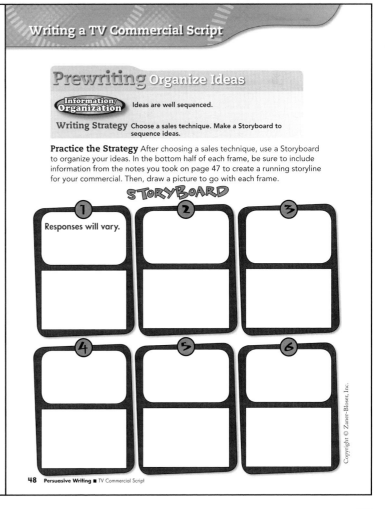

Writing a TV Commercial Script

Prewriting Organize Ideas

Information/Organization Ideas are well sequenced.

Writing Strategy Choose a sales technique. Make a Storyboard to sequence ideas.

Practice the Strategy After choosing a sales technique, use a Storyboard to organize your ideas. In the bottom half of each frame, be sure to include information from the notes you took on page 47 to create a running storyline for your commercial. Then, draw a picture to go with each frame.

STORYBOARD

1. Responses will vary.
2.
3.
4.
5.
6.

Copyright © Zaner-Bloser, Inc.

48 Persuasive Writing ■ TV Commercial Script

Persuasive Speech

Writing Strategies

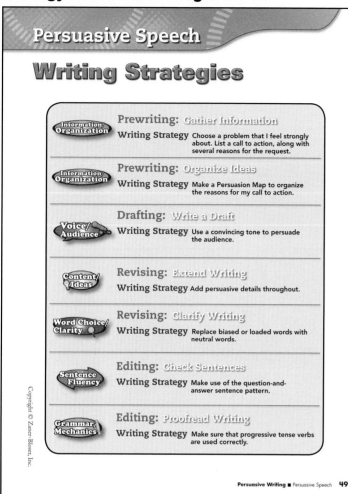

Information/Organization
Prewriting: Gather Information
Writing Strategy Choose a problem that I feel strongly about. List a call to action, along with several reasons for the request.

Information/Organization
Prewriting: Organize Ideas
Writing Strategy Make a Persuasion Map to organize the reasons for my call to action.

Voice/Audience
Drafting: Write a Draft
Writing Strategy Use a convincing tone to persuade the audience.

Content/Ideas
Revising: Extend Writing
Writing Strategy Add persuasive details throughout.

Word Choice/Clarity
Revising: Clarify Writing
Writing Strategy Replace biased or loaded words with neutral words.

Sentence Fluency
Editing: Check Sentences
Writing Strategy Make use of the question-and-answer sentence pattern.

Grammar/Mechanics
Editing: Proofread Writing
Writing Strategy Make sure that progressive tense verbs are used correctly.

Persuasive Writing ■ Persuasive Speech **49**

Persuasive Speech

Rubric

Use this rubric to help write your persuasive speech. Then, use it again to check your writing.

	Excelling	Achieving	Developing	Beginning
Information/Organization	The speech is focused on one problem and is organized around a call to action.	The speech is mainly focused on one problem and is mostly organized.	The speech is somewhat focused on one problem and is loosely organized.	The speech should be focused on one problem and should be more organized.
Voice/Audience	A convincing tone is used to persuade the audience.	A convincing tone is used in many areas.	A convincing tone is used in some areas.	A convincing tone should be used more often.
Content/Ideas	Persuasive details are used throughout.	Persuasive details are used in many areas.	Persuasive details are used in some areas.	More persuasive details are needed.
Word Choice/Clarity	Neutral words are used to avoid bias throughout.	Neutral words are used in many areas.	Neutral words are used in some areas.	Neutral words should be used more often.
Sentence Fluency	The question-and-answer sentence pattern is used effectively throughout.	The question-and-answer sentence pattern is sometimes used effectively.	The question-and-answer sentence pattern is rarely used.	The question-and-answer sentence pattern should be used more often.
Grammar/Mechanics	Spelling, grammar, and progressive tense verbs are used correctly.	There are a few errors in spelling, grammar, and progressive tense verb usage.	There are several errors in spelling, grammar, and progressive tense verb usage.	There are many errors in spelling, grammar, and progressive tense verb usage.

50 Persuasive Writing ■ Persuasive Speech

Writing a Persuasive Speech

Prewriting Gather Information

Information/Organization The speech is focused on one problem.

Writing Strategy Choose a problem that I feel strongly about. List a call to action, along with several reasons for the request.

Practice the Strategy Choose a problem to write about. Then, gather information by listing a call to action and several reasons for the request.

My Notes for My Persuasive Speech

Responses will vary.

Persuasive Writing ■ Persuasive Speech **51**

Writing a Persuasive Speech

Prewriting Organize Ideas

Information/Organization The speech is organized around a call to action.

Writing Strategy Make a Persuasion Map to organize the reasons for my call to action.

Practice the Strategy Use a Persuasion Map to organize the reasons for the call to action you listed on page 51.

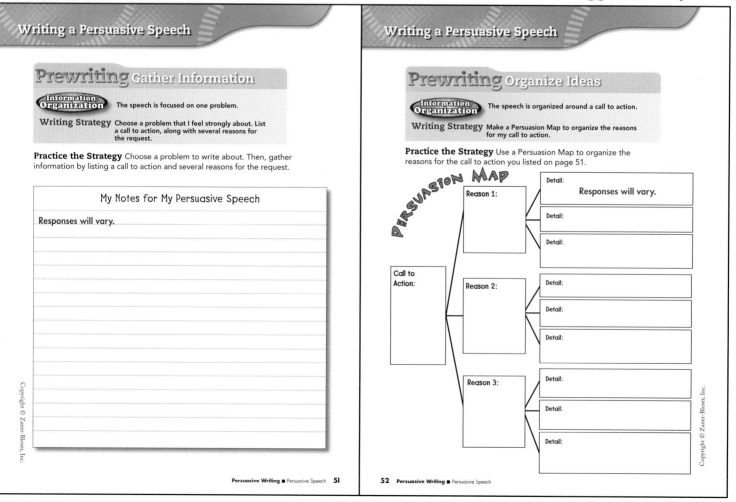

PERSUASION MAP

Call to Action:

Reason 1:
Detail: Responses will vary.
Detail:
Detail:

Reason 2:
Detail:
Detail:
Detail:

Reason 3:
Detail:
Detail:
Detail:

52 Persuasive Writing ■ Persuasive Speech

Scope and Sequence

	K	Level A	Level B	Level C	Level D	Level E	Level F	Level G	Level H
Writing Genres									
Adventure Story					●				
Biographic Sketch		●			●	●		●	●
Book Report		●		●	●	●	●		●
Cause-and-Effect Report							●	●	
Character Sketch					●				
Compare-and-Contrast Essay/Paper	●		●		●	●			
Contemporary Story					●				
Descriptive Essay/Paper		●	●	●		●	●		●
Descriptive Sentence/Paragraph	●	●	●	●	●				
E-mail								●	
Editorial					●			●	●
Eyewitness Account							●		
Fable			●			●			
Factual Report			●	●	●				
Folktale	●			●					
Geographic Description								●	
Historical Fiction/Episode							●	●	●
How-to Essay/Paper			●	●	●	●			●
Invitation	●								
Letters: Friendly, Business		●	●	●	●	●	●	●	●
List	●								
Mystery						●			
Observation Report				●		●	●	●	●
Once Upon a Time Story	●								
Personal Narrative	●	●	●	●	●	●		●	●
Persuasive Essay/Paper		●	●	●	●	●	●		
Persuasive Paragraph				●					
Persuasive Speech			●						●
Poem	●								
Problem-Solution Essay			●	●					
Recipe	●								
Research Report		●				●	●	●	●
Short Story							●		
Summary							●	●	
TV Commercial Script									●
Web Site Review								●	
Graphic Organizers									
Attribute Chart			●		●	●		●	
Cause-and-Effect Chain						●	●	●	●
Character Chart								●	
Fact-and-Opinion Chart			●						

Scope and Sequence (continued)

	K	LEVEL A	LEVEL B	LEVEL C	LEVEL D	LEVEL E	LEVEL F	LEVEL G	LEVEL H
Graphic Organizers (continued)									
5 Senses Chart			●				●	●	
5 W's Chart; 3 W's Chart				●			●	●	●
K-W-S Chart								●	
Main Idea Table				●	●			●	●
Network Tree			●	●	●	●	●		
Observation Chart				●				●	
Opinion Chart		●	●					●	
Order-of-Importance Organizer					●		●		
Outline					●	●	●	●	●
Persuasion Map								●	●
Problem-Solution Frame				●				●	●
Pros-and-Cons Chart						●		●	●
Sequence Chain/Order Chain			●	●	●	●	●		●
Spider Map				●	●	●	●		
Storyboard		●	●			●	●		
Story Frame									●
Story Map			●	●	●	●	●	●	●
Support Pattern						●			
Timeline					●				●
Venn Diagram		●	●				●		
Web		●	●	●	●	●		●	●
Writing Readiness Strategies									
Alphabet Review	●	●							
Big Books	●	●							
High-Frequency Words	●	●							
Left-to-Right Concept	●	●							
Letter Formation	●	●							
Letter Recognition	●	●							
Making Sentences	●	●							
Making Words	●	●							
Phonics	●	●							
Spacing	●	●							
Sound-Letter Correspondence	●	●							
Top-Bottom Concept	●	●							
Word Families	●	●							
Writing Strategies									
Adding Dialogue/Quotations	●			●	●	●	●	●	●
Adding Figurative Language						●	●	●	●
Adding or Rewriting Details/Facts/Examples		●	●	●	●	●	●	●	●
Adding Transition/Signal Words		●	●	●	●	●	●	●	●

Writing Strategies (continued)

	K	A	B	C	D	E	F	G	H
Assessing Personal Experience/Knowledge		●	●	●	●	●	●	●	●
Assessing Personal Interests		●	●	●	●	●	●	●	●
Clear Beginning, Middle, End; Introduction, Conclusion	●	●	●	●	●	●	●	●	
Correcting Sentence Fragments/Run-Ons/Confusing Sentences			●	●	●	●	●	●	●
Deleting Unnecessary or Confusing Information/Wordy Phrases		●	●	●	●	●	●	●	●
Determining Audience	●	●	●	●	●	●	●	●	●
End Notes, Bibliography								●	●
Generating Ideas/Statements/Questions	●	●	●	●	●	●	●	●	●
Interviewing				●	●	●	●	●	●
Listing	●	●	●	●	●	●	●	●	●
Making Notecards							●	●	●
Paraphrasing								●	●
Recognizing and Developing Parts of Genre	●	●	●	●	●	●	●	●	●
Recognizing and Using Genre Conventions	●	●	●	●	●	●	●	●	●
Reordering Sentences/Paragraphs		●	●	●	●	●	●	●	●
Replacing Vague/Loaded/Cliché Language				●	●	●	●	●	●
Restating Opinion, Purpose		●	●	●	●	●	●		●
Rewriting Unclear/Confusing/Incorrect Information		●	●	●	●	●	●	●	●
Selecting a Topic		●	●	●	●	●	●	●	●
Syntax of Oral Language	●								
Taking Notes	●	●	●	●	●	●	●	●	●
Thesis Statement						●	●	●	
Topic and Detail Sentences		●	●	●	●	●	●	●	●
Using Appropriate Text Structure	●	●	●	●	●	●	●	●	●
Using Appropriate Voice/Tone/Point of View		●	●	●	●	●	●	●	●
Using a Thesaurus			●		●	●		●	●
Using Exact/Precise/Interesting Words		●	●	●	●	●	●	●	●
Using Graphic Organizers to Generate Draft		●	●	●	●	●	●	●	●
Using References/Resources		●	●	●	●	●	●	●	●
Visual Aids/Illustrations	●	●	●	●	●	●	●	●	●
Writing Effective Sentences	●	●	●	●	●	●	●	●	●
Writing Paragraphs		●	●	●	●	●	●	●	●

Sharing Writing

	K	A	B	C	D	E	F	G	H
Author's Circle	●			●	●				
Big Books	●	●			●				
Mail to Appropriate Person or Publication		●	●	●	●	●	●	●	●

	K	LEVEL A	LEVEL B	LEVEL C	LEVEL D	LEVEL E	LEVEL F	LEVEL G	LEVEL H
Sharing Writing (continued)									
Multimedia Presentation						●	●	●	●
Observation Journal						●			
Part of a Display		●	●	●			●	●	●
Perform as Play/Newscast/Commercial				●					●
Post on Web Site		●	●	●	●	●		●	
Post on Bulletin Board	●	●	●	●	●		●	●	●
Present as Speech or Read Aloud		●	●	●	●	●	●		●
Publish for Class Library	●	●	●	●	●	●	●		
Publish in Class or School Newspaper/Collection/Magazine/Newsletter/Journal/Diary		●	●	●	●	●	●	●	●
Record on Audiotape				●					
Send as E-mail								●	
Time Capsule						●			
Travel Brochure					●				
Grammar, Usage, and Mechanics									
Active and Passive Voice							●	●	●
Adjectives	●		●	●	●	●	●	●	●
Adverbs					●	●	●	●	●
Apostrophes	●		●	●			●	●	●
Appositives					●		●	●	●
Capitalization	●	●	●	●	●	●	●	●	●
Clauses					●	●	●	●	●
Complete Sentences	●	●	●	●	●		●	●	
Conjunctions			●			●	●	●	●
Contractions			●				●	●	
Dangling Modifiers								●	
Double Negatives						●		●	
Easily Confused Words/Homophones				●	●		●	●	
Introductory Verbal Phrases									●
Letters: Friendly, Business	●	●	●	●	●	●	●	●	●
Nouns: Plural, Possessive	●		●	●	●	●	●	●	
Pronoun Forms/Antecedents			●		●	●	●	●	●
Punctuation	●	●	●	●	●	●	●	●	●
Quotations/Dialogue	●		●	●	●	●	●	●	●
Sentence Patterns		●	●	●	●	●	●	●	●
Sentences: Complex							●	●	●
Sentences: Compound			●			●	●	●	●
Sentences: Fragments			●	●	●	●	●	●	●
Sentences: Run-Ons			●	●	●	●	●	●	●
Subject-Verb Agreement				●	●	●	●	●	●
Verb Forms/Tenses	●			●	●		●	●	●

Teacher Notes

Teacher Notes

Teacher Notes

Teacher Notes

Teacher Notes

Teacher Notes

Teacher Notes

Teacher Notes